Respect the User's Time

Respect the User's Time

Experience Architecture and Design for Efficiency

Helmut Degen

June 21, 2022

Respect the User's Time
Experience Architecture and Design for Efficiency
Version: 1.0
Author: Helmut Degen
Illustrator: Helmut Degen
Editor: Marilyn Burkley (mgburkley@gmail.com)

Website: www.designforefficiency.com
To report errors and provide feedback, please send a note to: info@designforefficiency.com

Typeset
This document was typeset with the help of KOMA-Script and LaTeX using the kaobook class.

ISBN 13 (Paperback): 978-0-9849559-6-1
ISBN 13 (E-book): 978-0-9849559-7-8
ISBN 13 (PDF): 978-0-9849559-8-5

The PDF version can be downloaded for free via www.designforefficiency.com.

First printed in June 2022 by Helmut Degen

To Britta, Jakob, and Julius

and to all who respect people's time.

Contents

List of Figures

List of Tables

Preface

The backstory

The content of this book is something that I have been musing about for quite some time. It was initially motivated by a basic question: *how do customers of the company I work for benefit from user experience?*

The typical answers – "ease of use," "joy of use," "delight," "learnability," "fewer errors," "brand awareness," and "brand recognition" – didn't work too well. It's hard to assign a monetary value to them. And even the classic competitor argument, which often works well, wasn't too convincing either. This is particularly true when the project budget is tight or a product or service is almost ready to be shipped.

The company I work for specializes in technology-heavy products for several industries. You can take the word "heavy" literally: if such a product falls on your foot, it hurts. Although there are many differences between these industries, there are a few commonalities. One of them is the aim to maximize the automation level and reduce the "human-in-the-loop," the operator's involvement. By automating their processes, companies that purchase and use my employer's products can lower their operational costs as well as their total cost of ownership. I realized that this line of thinking resonates with the business acumen of my colleagues.

What is the connection between automation and user experience? Doesn't *more* automation mean *less* user involvement and therefore less user experience? Yes and no. It means that we need to be cognizant of when and how to involve users. We have to do it in a more targeted, meaningful way.

An increased level of automation is not only a topic for industrial applications, it is also a topic for consumers. In our homes, we can program our heating and cooling systems and monitor their performance through a mobile app (reduced involvement: we don't have to turn the heating or cooling system on or off, or we don't have to walk to the controller to change the settings). We receive automatic reminders about doctor appointments (reduced involvement: we don't have to look up the date ourselves or call to confirm our appointment). In online shopping, websites offer easier ways to order products with fewer clicks (reduced involvement); even subscription-based purchases are offered (significantly reduced involvement: we set it up only once without additional involvement in the future). If someone rings the doorbell, we can have the request redirected to our phone and can respond via the phone (reduced involvement: we don't have to open the door). With upcoming Internet of Things (IoT) applications, we can expect even more reductions in user involvement over the next few years.

This is not only applicable to individual applications. Many such applications today are part of larger digital ecosystems.[1] For instance, e-commerce systems include purchases, delivery, returns, and warranties. Home automation systems include maintenance of cooling and heating systems, security, and controlling of lights and appliances. Airline systems include purchasing of tickets, check-in, access to electronic boarding passes and entertainment systems, and redeeming of miles.

1: A digital ecosystem is a *distributed, adaptive, open socio-technical system with properties of self-organisation, scalability and sustainability inspired from natural ecosystems* [1].

A digital ecosystem is designed and developed to produce an outcome of value. A user is involved if a system needs a decision, typically a user input. There are four main factors that affect the efficiency of user involvement: 1) the performance of the technical enablers to reach the point of user involvement, 2) the number of user involvements per outcome, 3) the overall user involvement time per outcome, and 4) the performance of the technical enablers in processing the user input.

When we compare the performance of the technical enablers and the performance of the user, the user is usually the significantly slower contributor. As a consequence, the performance of the digital ecosystem as a whole depends, often significantly, on the user's performance. It determines the *critical efficiency path*[2] of a digital ecosystem.

2: The critical efficiency path is the sequence of user actions or system actions determining the minimum elapsed user involvement time and minimum number of user involvement steps to generate an outcome of value. The term is based on the term *critical path*, as used in project management [2].

Reducing user involvement based purely on technical feasibility (what can be automated) and ignoring the user's acceptance (what shouldn't be automated) will lead to an acceptance issue in many cases. Designing for efficiency means finding the minimum user involvement that is still *acceptable* and *effective*. Only if both criteria, acceptability, and effectiveness, are met, can a higher efficiency be realized, leading to increased productivity of the entire digital ecosystem for *users*. User participation is required during the design and development process. A user-centered design and development approach is essential [3–9].

This thought process seemed reasonable, so I started looking for technique that could be used to "design for efficiency." Surprisingly, while doing research to fill my empty toolbox with design-for-efficiency tools and techniques, I could not find books or articles that explained how to systematically consider efficiency in the design process. Well, in every challenge lies an opportunity. I had to fill the design-for-efficiency toolbox with my own tools, partially re-purposing existing tools and upgrading them to include efficiency. I also developed new tools, and this is still an ongoing process. All the tools in this book have been applied many times in industrial projects and refined over time. A few are published in peer-reviewed publications.

Many of us know that such a discovery or author journey is full of surprises. One positive surprise was gaining the insight to separate the design activities into an experience architecture phase and an experience design phase. The experience architecture phase defines the "higher-level view" which is called here the "user involvement system." The user involvement system consists of its constituting elements, the "user involvement points," and their relationships. The design phase focuses on the design of the user involvement points. Both phases are needed to achieve efficiency. They are connected with involvement goals that include efficiency goals and time savings.

The use of time is not only important for humans in the role of a user. The use of time is relevant for all of us. As the jazz musician Miles Davis succinctly said:

"Time isn't the main thing. It's the only thing."

Designing for efficiency demonstrates that we respect users' time and want to help them make better use of it. If this book raises awareness for the importance of being mindful and respectful of people's time, it will have achieved a lot.

The introduction of a user involvement system and its experience architecture brings an extended scope with new tasks, skills, and responsibilities. A new role is proposed, which is called here *experience architect*. An experience architect needs to have many years of design experience. In addition, an experience architect has a more strategic view of the ecosystem under design. S/he is a partner with other project stakeholders, such as software architect, a test architect, a project manager, or a portfolio and product manager. In order to be a partner with the aforementioned stakeholders, the experience architect needs to be knowledgeable and experienced about the market, the business model, the application domain, technologies, product management, project management, systems thinking, requirements engineering, design thinking, and other areas.

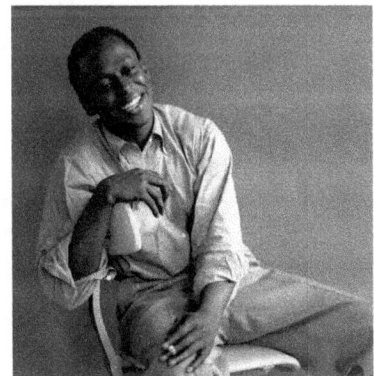

Figure 1: Miles Davis, photographed in his New York City home around 1955-1956; source: Wikimedia; photographer: Tom Palumbo; license: CC BY-SA 2.0

An experience architecture role profile is defined in Chapter 21 (Experience Architect) on page 575

If we build a house like we build software ...

Without an (experience) architect

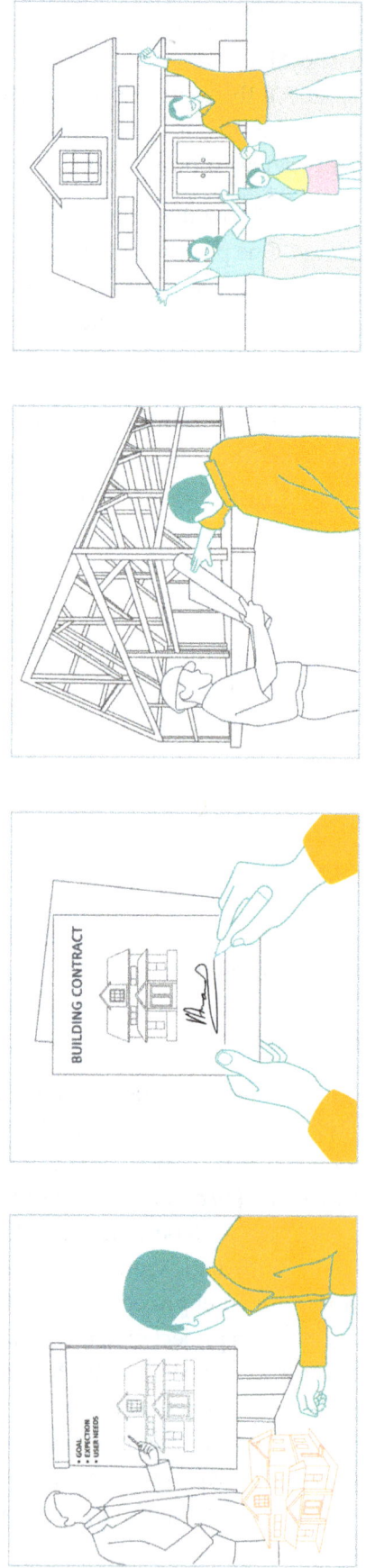

With an (experience) architect

Story: Helmut Degen; artwork: Yao Tong

Figure 2: Contribution of an (experience) architect; courtesy: Siemens Technology

Such a role requires the ability to define a *user involvement system*, informed by the value proposition, the market segments, the business case, technology constraints and other influential factors, and not just the ability to design a single user involvement point. It also requires motivating engineers and developers to look for alternative solutions and to push the technology envelope. Junior design colleagues can grow into the role of an experience architect over time.

An experience architect can be compared to a building architect. A building architect designs a building in its environment. Many of them manage a building project from start to finish, within a given budget. They supervise contributors and manage stakeholders, such as civil engineers and the construction team. They work with regulatory bodies to get the plans and the building approved.

I hope this book inspires the experience community. I would be very appreciative of community feedback. Therefore, you can post comments on the website or send an email. All input will be considered.

Website:
https://www.designforefficiency.com/
Email: info@designforefficiency.com

One last remark: I learned a lot working for my employer, and I am grateful for that experience. However, all opinions expressed in this book are solely my own and do not express opinions of or endorsements by my employer.

Helmut Degen, June 2022

Acknowledgments

Each book project is an investment of time. Not only the author's time, but also the time of many people who offered to help and to sacrifice time they could have spent with their significant others. This is true of the author's family and friends as well as members of the global design, human–computer interaction, and user experience communities who voluntarily contributed to the ongoing writing of this book. I want to express my deep gratitude to all of them, their significant others included! Thank you!

A deep thanks goes to my significant others: Britta, Jakob, and Julius.

These are the colleagues and friends who provided review comments or inspired the book in other ways (in alphabetical order): Ilia Adami (Institute of Computer Science - FORTH; Crete, Greece), Tobias Ahlgrim (Siemens; Princeton, NJ, USA), Pavan Athreya (Siemens; Princeton, NJ, USA), Yunus-Emre Atmaca (Siemens; Nuremberg, Germany), Christoph Brand (Siemens; Princeton, NJ, USA), Christof Budnik (Siemens; Princeton, NJ, USA), Arquimedes Martinez Canedo (Siemens; Princeton, NJ, USA), Erica M. Cardenas (Lausanne, Switzerland), Michael Golm (Roche; Tucson, AZ), Claus Gronau (Siemens; Munich, Germany), Gustavo Guillen (Siemens; Fountain Valley, CA, USA), Thomas Herrmann (Ruhr-Universität Bochum; Bochum, Germany), Dennis Klingebiel (Sacramento, CA, USA), Vassilis Kouroumalis (Institute of Computer Science - FORTH; Crete, Greece), Charif Mahmoudi (Siemens; Princeton, NJ), Georgi Markov (Siemens; Princeton, NJ, USA), Parinitha Nagaraja (Siemens; Princeton, NJ, USA), Stavroula Ntoa (Institute of Computer Science - FORTH; Crete, Greece), Torsten Pannier (Siemens; Berlin, Germany), Kerstin Roese (Siemens; Erlangen, Germany), Holger Schmidt (Siemens; Jacksonville, FL, USA), Yao Tong (EY Design Studio; New York City, NY, USA), Christoph Wienands (Lincoln Financial Group; Portsmouth, NH, USA), Chris Woods (Siemens; Chicago, IL, USA), Siyu Zhao (Siemens; Princeton, NJ, USA), Yunsheng (Inken) Zhou (Yahoo; Sunnyvale, CA, USA).

I also want to thank the participants who attended "Experience Architecture and Design for Efficiency" tutorials and provided valuable feedback.

Tino Procaccini owns the pizza restaurant "Tino's Artisan Pizza Co." with several locations in New Jersey, USA. Tino and his team allowed me to perform context of use analysis and to take photos of the pizza making process which enriched the book and my insights into the pizza business. BTW: Tino's pizza is really great. A big "mille grazie" goes to Tino and his team.

Figure 3: Tino's Artisan Pizza Co.; courtesy: Tino Procaccini; URL: https://www.nojunkpizza.com/

Federico Marotta has kindly created the template I used in this book. The template is based on Edward Tufte's popular books about information visualization [10–12]. Another "mille grazie" goes to Federico.

Last but not least, I want to thank Marilyn Burkley for her excellent editing job.

LET'S GET STARTED ...

Introduction | 1

Time is money.
Benjamin Franklin

Why efficiency?

"Good design is good business," declared IBM's chief executive officer Thomas J. Watson Jr. in a lecture at the University of Pennsylvania in 1973 [13]. The well-known McKinsey study from 2018 supports that statement: companies that invest in design outperform companies that don't, in revenue and total return to shareholders, by almost to two to one [14].

There are a few takeaways from the McKinsey study:

▶ The relevance and priority of design should take into account the interest of shareholders, not only the interest of top companies managers.

▶ It is relevant to discuss design at top management levels. However, the top management does not necessarily know how to manage design, especially which design metrics should be used to manage design activities and outcomes.

This book introduces user involvement metrics (see Chapter 4 (User Involvement Metrics) on page 75) which can assist top management to measure the impact of investments in design when it comes to efficiency.

In some cases, news about design even has a direct impact on a company's valuation. After Jonathan Ive, the former chief design officer at Apple, announced his departure from Apple on June 27, 2019, Apple's stock price plunged by about two percentage points the same day (see Figure 1.1).

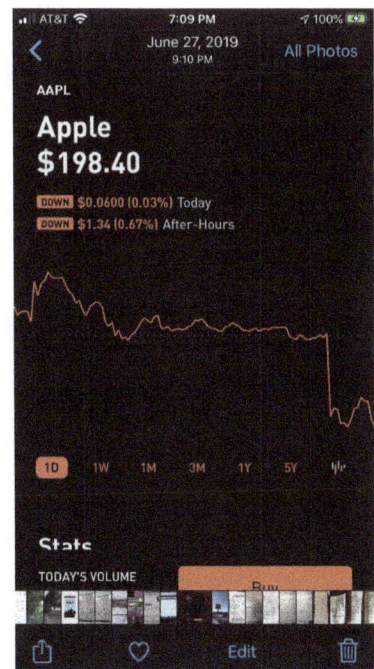

Figure 1.1: Apple's stock price plunged by about two percentage points after Ive's announcement; the snapshot was taken 9:10pm (EDT) on June 27, 2019

In this book, the outcome of a design and development effort is called an *application*. An organization or individual that develops an application is called a *vendor*; an organization or individual that adopts an application is called a *customer*.

From past research about return on investment (ROI) and business value of design, we know that investment in design leads to all kinds of benefits [14–16].

There are key benefits for organizations or individuals (customers) that use the designed application:

▶ Increased productivity
▶ Decreased user errors
▶ Decreased training cost or effort
▶ Decreased cost for ongoing user support
▶ Enhanced reputation for using high-quality applications

There are other benefits for organizations that develop applications and invest in design (vendors):

▶ Early common understanding about what kind of application is under design and development and what the application vision is
▶ Decreased costs by making more changes, and more inexpensive changes, early in the design and development life cycle and making fewer, more expensive changes late in the design and development lifecycle
▶ Decreased time to market
▶ Decreased user support / hotline costs (if the vendor is not compensated for it)
▶ Increased customer loyalty / revenue
▶ Increased brand value
▶ Increased company value
▶ More patents / stronger IP portfolio

The benefits are visualized in an experience flower (see Figure 1.2) that shows experience internal (e.g., efficiency) and experience external (e.g., increased productivity) benefits of experience contributions. The stem of the flower is the application domain for which an application is designed and developed. Understanding the application domain is a pre-requisite for experience professionals to create original, meaningful involvement concepts.

Benefits for customers are beneficial for vendors, too. For instance, in the list above, the benefit "increased productivity" covers the three other cost-related benefits: reduction of errors, training cost, and user support. It probably also influences the reputation benefits.

In 2019, the company InVision conducted a study with 2,229 customers from its customer base [16]. The study was intended to measure the design maturity of its customer. Although "design maturity" was not defined in the study, nor could any definition be found in the literature, it is reasonable to define it as the *degree*

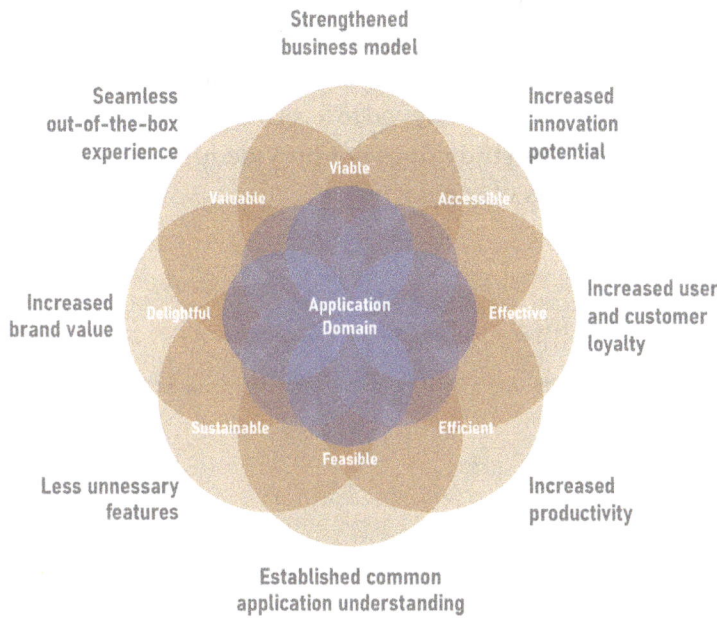

Strengthened
business model

Seamless
out-of-the-box
experience

Increased
innovation
potential

Viable

Valuable   Accessible

Increased
brand value

Delightful   Application   Effective
              Domain

Increased user
and customer
loyalty

Sustainable   Efficient

Feasible

Less unnessary
features

Increased
productivity

Established common
application understanding

Figure 1.2: Experience flower

to which an organization formalizes, integrates, and optimizes design processes continuously to support business strategies and objectives. The InVision study distinguishes between five maturity levels and assigns companies to those levels (see Figure 1.3).

Distribution of companies to design maturity levels

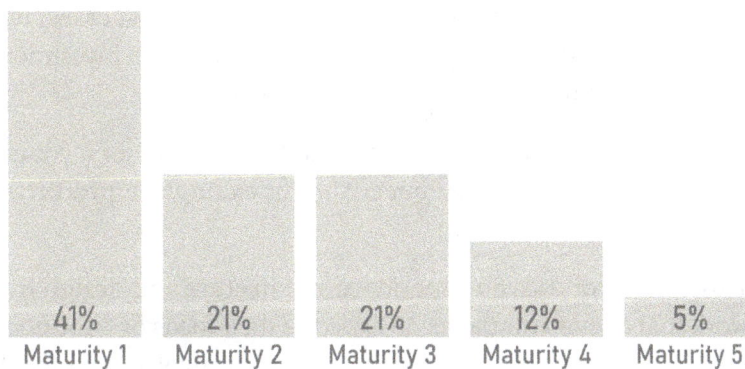

| 41% | 21% | 21% | 12% | 5% |
| Maturity 1 | Maturity 2 | Maturity 3 | Maturity 4 | Maturity 5 |

Source: InVision, The New Design Frontier, 2019; based on 2229 respondents

Figure 1.3: Distribution of companies to maturity levels; source: InVision [16, p. 11]

Among other results, the study reports that cost savings (for customers) are one of the benefits realized by companies investing in their design. The degree of cost savings depends on the design maturity level. Of the companies assigned to maturity level 1, only 16 percentage report cost savings for their customers, whereas 85 percentage of companies assigned to level 5 report that same benefit (see Figure 1.4). The study does not provide further information on specific amounts of cost savings.

Cost Savings

Companies which report Cost Savings as realized benefit

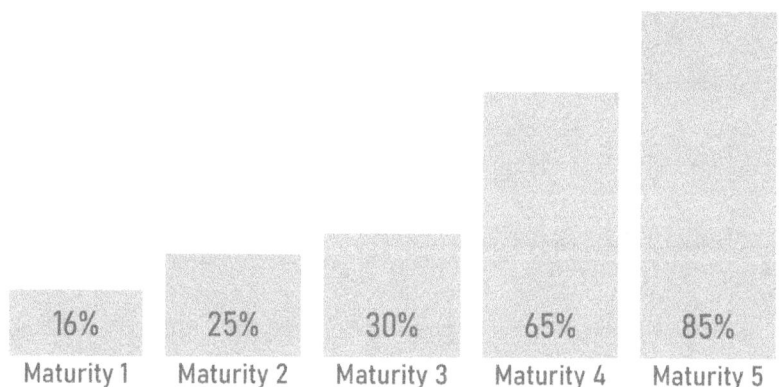

16%	25%	30%	65%	85%
Maturity 1	Maturity 2	Maturity 3	Maturity 4	Maturity 5

Source: InVision, The New Design Frontier, 2019

Figure 1.4: Relationship between maturity level and realized cost savings; source: InVision [16, pp. 17–25]

The take-away from the InVision study is that the magnitude of cost savings, as a result of productivity improvements, depends to a certain extend on the design maturity. "In most cases, it's 20 years"[17, 18] after a company has started systematic investment in design before it reaches the highest maturity level.

The question is, Does it really have to take so long for a company to deliver a key customer benefit — for example, a productivity increase?

This book proposes an experience architecture and design framework that allows companies to expedite their focus on productivity increase by increasing the efficiency of user involvement for their users and customers without the need to increase the organization wide maturity level.

Here are a few case studies, which hint that this is possible and creates benefits for users:

▶ Usability work performed at IBM led to design changes which resulted in an average reduction of 9.6 minutes per task which a projected internal savings of $6.8 million in 1991 alone (see [19], reference found in [15]).

► After implementing usability improvements in Oracle's database manager, database administrators were able to perform their tasks 20 percent faster (see [20], reference found in [15]).

► General Electric invested in user experience with Industrial Internet design experience software which resulted in a 100 percent productivity increase and $30 million in savings in the first year ([21]; I couldn't find a statement from GE regarding the productivity improvements.)

Inferring from these examples, we see that focusing on productivity is beneficial for the customer and that productivity through design is an achievable outcome of the design and development process. Now, how exactly does design support productivity increases?

Let's first clarify what productivity means. Productivity is *the ratio of output to input*. It describes how much input is needed to produce an output [22].

The question remains, How can design can contribute to performance increases? Usability[1] , according to the ISO 9241 standard family, has three quality attributes: effectiveness, efficiency, and satisfaction. Effectiveness is the "accuracy and completeness with which user achieve specified goals" [23, clause 3.1.12]. Efficiency is the "resources used in relation to the results achieved [23, clause 3.1.13]. Satisfaction is the "extent to which the user's physical, cognitive and emotional responses that result from the use of a system, product or service meet the user's needs and expectations [23, clause 3.1.14]. Effectiveness is a prerequisite for efficiency.

1: Usability is defined as "extent to which a system, product or service can be used by specified users to achieve specified goals with effectiveness, efficiency and satisfaction in a specified context of use" [23, clause 3.1.1]

Efficiency and productivity are related. While productivity focuses on outcomes per resource, efficiency focuses on resources per outcome. They are reciprocal. Increased efficiency means the use of fewer resources for the same outcome. It leads to higher productivity for an individual or an organization.

Under the assumption that efficiency includes less time needed for an outcome, higher efficiency leads to more disposable time for users, as private citizens and employees (see Figure 1.5). If the extra disposable time is wisely used, it can lead to a higher quality of life. For an organization, a higher level of efficiency for individuals leads to higher productivity, which can lead to more profit. If the extra profit is shared among the employees, it can lead to a higher quality of life for them. At the end of the day, both individuals and organizations benefit from efficiency improvements.

Benefits of higher efficiency

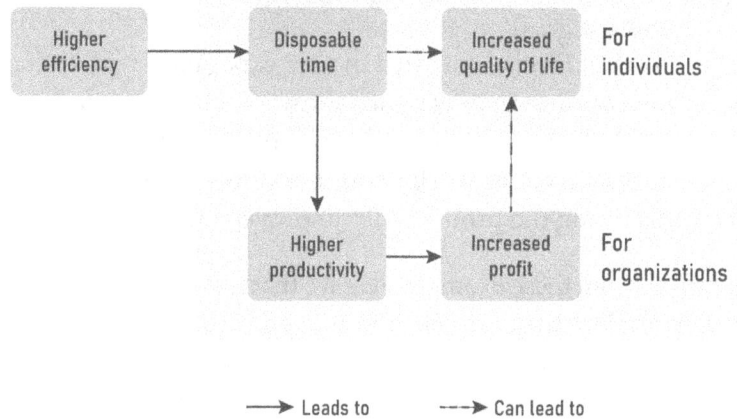

Figure 1.5: Benefits of higher efficiency

What are some examples of efficiency benefits?

As previously mentioned, efficiency is often related to time. In the context of user experience, there are certain known time limits that have different meanings for users in different situations [24, pp. 54–60]. These time limits are depicted in Figure 1.6.

▶ Instantaneous: This category includes response times for low-level actions related to interaction devices, such as responses to mouse clicks, mouse movements, or keystrokes. A user can feel a delay if a response takes longer than 0.2 seconds as a result of their action. For instance, if a user moves the mouse, the position of the mouse pointer should shift in 0.2 seconds or less, so that the user experiences the movement as an instant reaction to their action.

▶ Immediate: this includes response times for changes of dialog elements, such as view changes and page turns. The acceptable range is from half a second to one second. If the response of a dialog element to a user's action takes more than one second, the user recognizes the delay. However, their attention stays focused on the current thought and they feel in control.

▶ Continuous: This category could also be called "flow." It includes an upper response-time limit so as not to interrupt the flow of the user. The acceptable range is from two to five seconds. If a system's response takes more than five seconds, the user's flow is interrupted, and their attention may deviate from the current task.

▶ Captive: This category defines a response-time limit after which a user will likely abort the task. The maximum response time limit is from seven to ten seconds. After this point, users tend to start doing something else.

▶ Completion: A user should be able to complete a simple task in one minute or less.

Time limits

Instantaneous	0.1 - 0.2 sec.
Immediate	0.5 - 1 sec.
Continuous	2 - 5 sec.
Captive	7 - 10 sec.
Completion	≤ 1 min

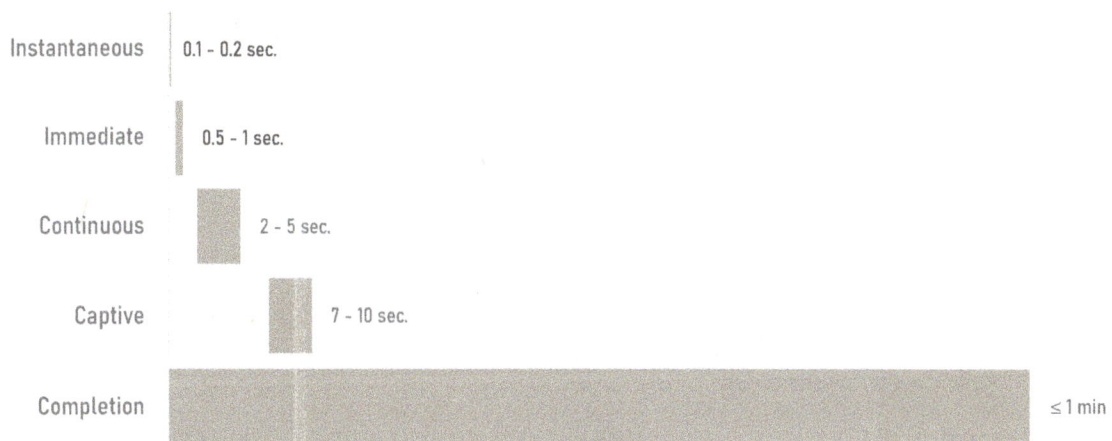

Sources: Seow 2008, Norman Nielsen 2009

Figure 1.6: Time limits

The "continuous" response-time limit is an important one because it has to do with *flow*. Flow is defined as a "fluid state of being productively engaged with a task without being aware of the technology that is driving it" [25, p. 4387]. Flow activities provide "enjoyable experiences" [26, p. 72] and lead to the greatest performance and the fewest number of errors, together with the highest satisfaction [27]. Csikszentmihalyi [26, p. 74] depicted the flow model in a diagram (see Figure 1.7).

A response time of less than five seconds keeps the user in the flow. They enjoy the activity as long as they stay in the "flow channel" [26, p. 74]. When they are in the flow, they are neither bored (because the activity is not too easy) nor anxious (because the activity is not too difficult). Challenges and skills are balanced. The more skills a person has gained, the more challenges they need to stay in that flow channel.

As several studies indicate, a system response times that's too slow affects users' behaviors and performance:

▶ Just noticeable difference: When dragging an object with a finger on a touch screen, users realized a just noticeable

Flow Model

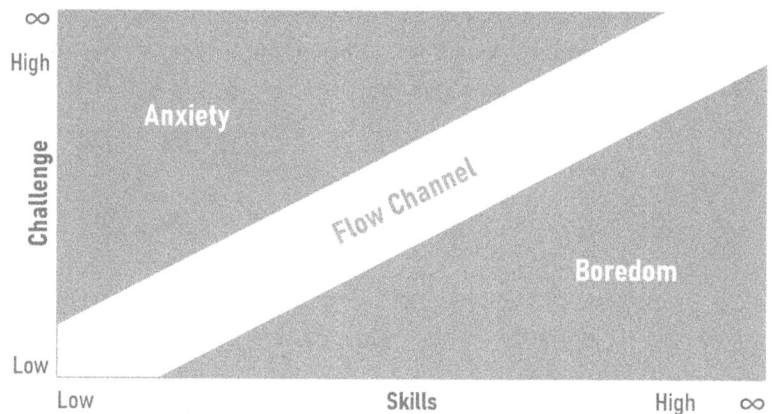

Source: Mihaly Csikszentmihalyi: Flow

Figure 1.7: Flow model [26, p. 74]

difference (JND) of 11 milliseconds of latency. The JND for tapping was 55 milliseconds [28, p. 1831].

▶ Productivity: When the response time increased from 0.5 seconds to 3.0 seconds, the time to complete the tasks increased from 27 to 57 minutes [29]. A system response time of 1.49 seconds degraded performance, measured by problem-solving time, compared to response times of 0.16 seconds and 0.49 seconds [30].

▶ Error rate: When the response time was 12 seconds or more, the error rate went up [31, p. 978].

▶ Anxiety and stress: Long response times cause anxiety [32] and stress [33].

▶ Satisfaction implications: The shorter the system response time, the higher the user satisfaction. In this study, the measured response times for different UI widgets ranged from less than 100 milliseconds to 18 seconds with different satisfaction levels [34].

The aforementioned response time limits indicate that time savings of less than a second can make a significant difference for users. Performance improvement case studies confirm that users response to smaller and larger time savings [35]:

▶ After Pinterest decreased wait time by 40 percent, searching and sign-up increased by 15 percent.

▶ After COOK reduced the average page load by 0.85 seconds, conversations increased by 7 percent, pages per session increased by 10 percent and bounce rates were reduced by 7 percent.

► DoubleClick analyzed the relationship between loading times and user's activities. It "found out that sites loading within 5 seconds had 70 percent longer sessions, 35 percent lower bounce rates, and 25 percent higher ad viewability than sites taking nearly four times longer at 19 seconds." The result is not a big surprise because five seconds is the upper limit for keeping users in their flow.

► "For Mobify, every 100 ms decrease in homepage load speed worked out to a 1.11% increase in session-based conversion, yielding an average annual revenue increase of nearly $380,000. Additionally, a 100 ms decrease in checkout page load speed amounted to a 1.55% increase in session-based conversion, which in turn yielded an average annual revenue increase of nearly $530,000."

Similar examples can be found for industrial applications. Some companies and industries promote their applications with efficiency key performance indicators (KPIs).

► Sam Ratnam et al. [36] analyzed five automated laboratory instruments for the diagnosis of sexually transmitted diseases by measuring and comparing their efficiency for the operator. They measured the *hands-on time* and the *walk-away time* of the instruments for defined test samples. The study found that the most efficient instrument had a total run time of 3:57 (h:mm) and the least efficient instrument a total run time of 6:20 (h:mm). One instrument had a hands-on time of only 38 minutes, while another instrument had a hands-on time of about 144 minutes (almost three times more).

Hands-on time reflects the time an operator spends interacting with the device, i.e., manually performing tasks. In the usability world, this is expressed as *time-on-task*. The walk-away time measures how long the operator can walk away from the automated system without interrupting its operation, in order to be able to perform other tasks. The sum of the hands-on time and the walk-away time is called *total run time*.

► Insook Cho et al. [37] performed a comparative study analyzing the effectiveness and efficiency of six electronic nursing record (ENR) systems. "Efficiency scores were significantly different across ENRs as was the time to complete tasks, ranging from 226.3 to 457.2 s," which means that the least efficient ENR takes twice as much time as using the most efficient.

► Peter Ramsey [38] performed a study to find out whether so-called "challenger" banks are better in terms of customer service than established banks. One part of the study involved finding out how many working days and how many clicks it takes to open a bank account. The number of working days varied from two days to 36 working days. The difference is a factor of 18. The number of clicks for opening a bank account varied from 24 clicks to 120 clicks, a factor of five.

► In a blog post, Erietta Sapounakis [39] emphasizes that some organizations focus on their internal, operational efficiency

Canvas

Overlay canvas

Canvas control

Canvas function

Content

Alert

Content control

Content function

User action

System action

Interaction device

System function

Figure 1.8: Design elements with their color codes; the design elements are introduced in Section 13 (Design elements) on page 345.

rather than on the external, customer's efficiency. She illustrates this point with a case study from Melbourne, Australia. The public transportation system authority replaced tram conductors, who sold tickets, with ticketing machines for operational efficiency and cost reasons. Sapounakis states that the effectiveness *and* efficiency for customers went down because the conductors not only sold tickets, but also played other roles of value for customers, for example, giving advice. "Customers have their own view of efficiency."

▶ Matthew Dixon et al. [40] performed a study about the relationship between customer service quality and customer loyalty. During the study, 75,000 people were asked to share their experience with non-face-to-face interactions (B2B and B2C). One result of the study was that efficiency for customers has a positive influence on their loyalty.

Another good way to increase the efficiency for users is to focus not so much on time, but on the number of user involvement steps. Figure 1.9 shows a wire frame design of a product page with a purchase now order system designed to make the checkout process more efficient for users. Another way to achieve an even higher level of efficiency is a subscription option (see Figure 1.10). Initial user involvement is required to set it up, but no additional user involvement is necessary, as long as the subscription is valid.

This book introduces user involvement metrics (see Chapter 4 (User Involvement Metrics) on page 75) and applies them to defining target user involvement times (see Section 1 (Target involvement time) on page 298) and user involvement steps (see Section 1 (User involvement goals) on page 295). Furthermore, it presents a technique that allows to systematically reduce user involvement steps (see Section 12 (GAIS) on page 319) to increase efficiency for users.

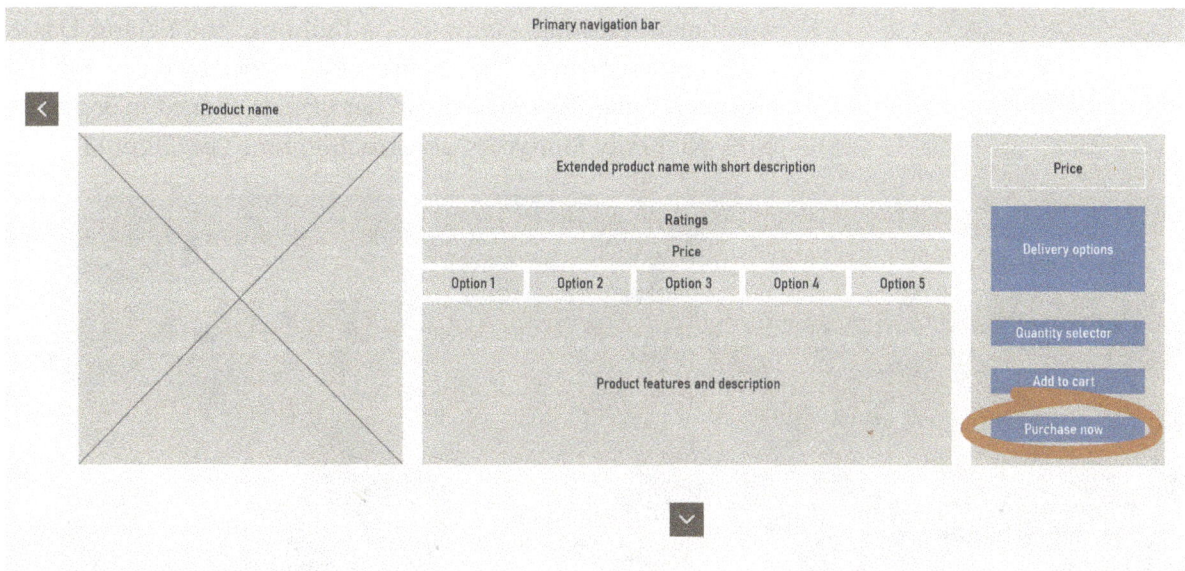

Figure 1.9: Product page; the color codes correspond with the color codes of the design elements (see Figure 1.8).

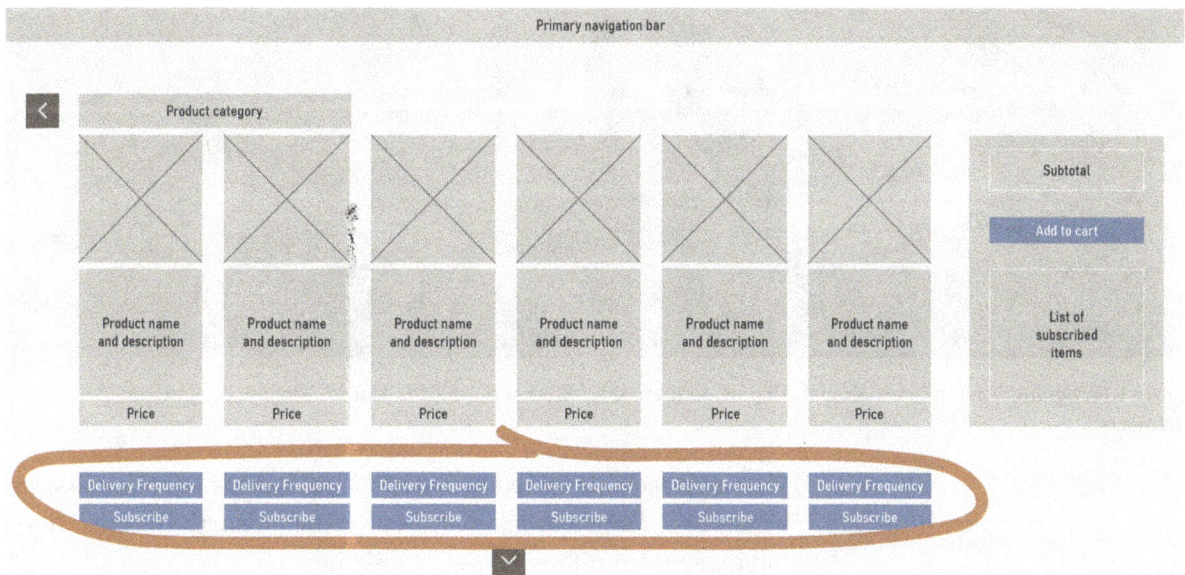

Figure 1.10: Subscription page; the color codes correspond with the color codes of the design elements (see Figure 1.8).

Another interesting example is a building: the Beijing Daxing International Airport. The airport was designed by the British Iraqi architect Dame Zaha Hadid and her firm. It opened in September 2019, after only four years' construction time (see Figure 1.11).

Figure 1.11: Beijing Daxing International Airport; rendering by Methanoia ©Zaha Hadid Architects; courtesy: Zaha Hadid Architects

The airport is designed in a star shape and therefore nicknamed "Starfish." Time was a key driver for the airport's design. Here is an excerpt from the architect's website:

> *Five aircraft piers radiate directly from the terminal's main central court where all passenger services and amenities are located, enabling passengers to walk the comparatively short distances through the airport without the need for automated shuttle trains. As a result, the terminal's compact design minimises distances between check-in and gate, as well as connections between gates for transferring passengers. This radial configuration ensures the farthest boarding gate can be accessed in a walking time of less than 8 minutes.* [41]

The design not only took into consideration minimizing the time for the passengers to reach the gates, but because the services and amenities are centralized, passengers need less time to explore and use the area. The design also allows passengers to better plan their

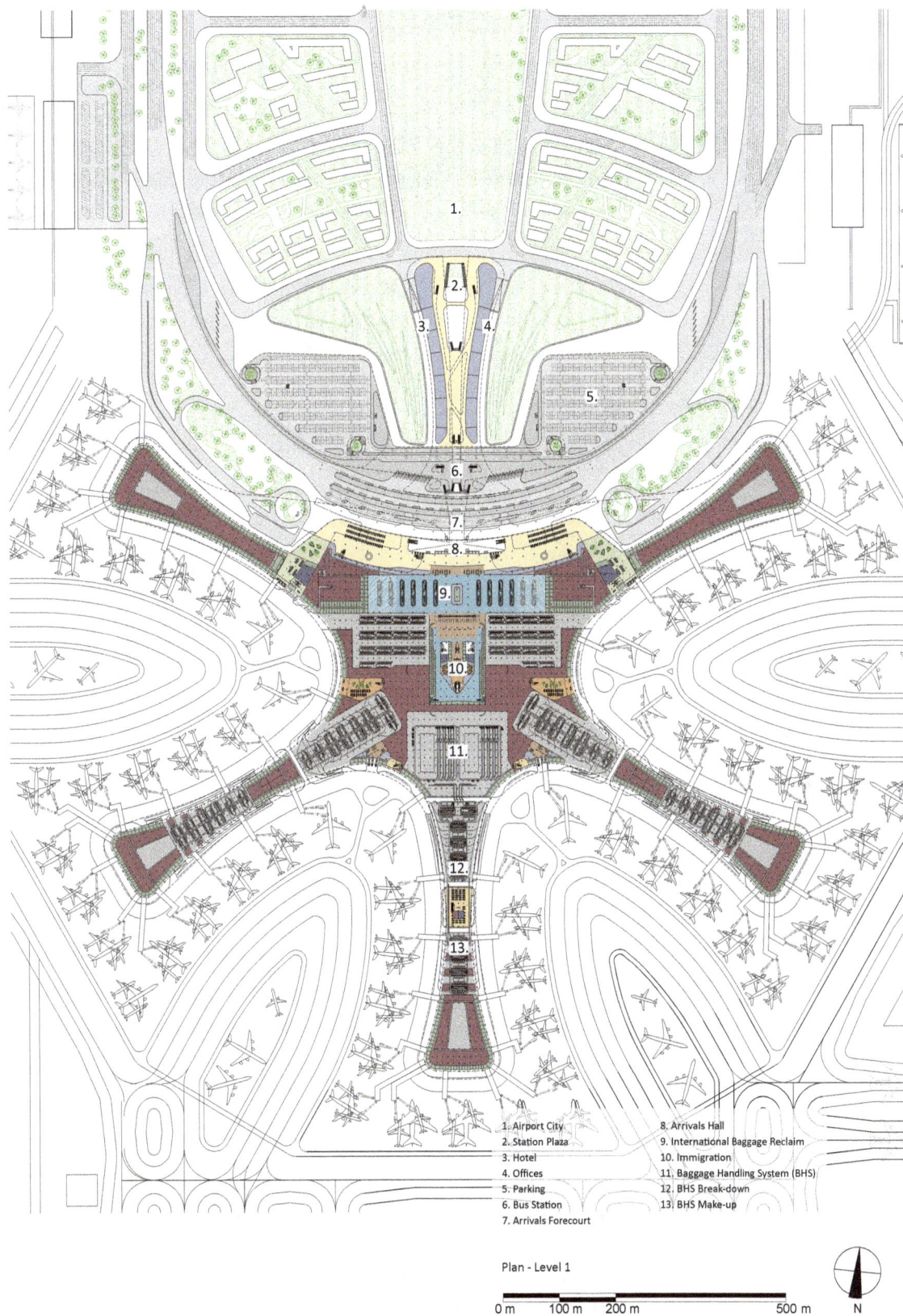

Figure 1.12: Beijing Daxing International Airport floor plan (level 1); courtesy: Zaha Hadid Architects

stay in the airport. A passenger's entire travel experience becomes less stressful (see Figure 1.12).

24

1 *Introduction*

Where are we today with efficiency?

Moore's law says that the number of transistors in a dense integrated circuit (IC) doubles about every two years [43].

During the last fifty years, the number of transistors has increased following Moore's law [42]. Transistors are the atomic building blocks of data processing. In the last ten years (2010 through 2020), the number of transistors on an integrated circuit chip increased by more than factor twenty (see Figure 1.13).

Moore's Law - The number of transistors on integrated circuit chips (1971 - 2020)

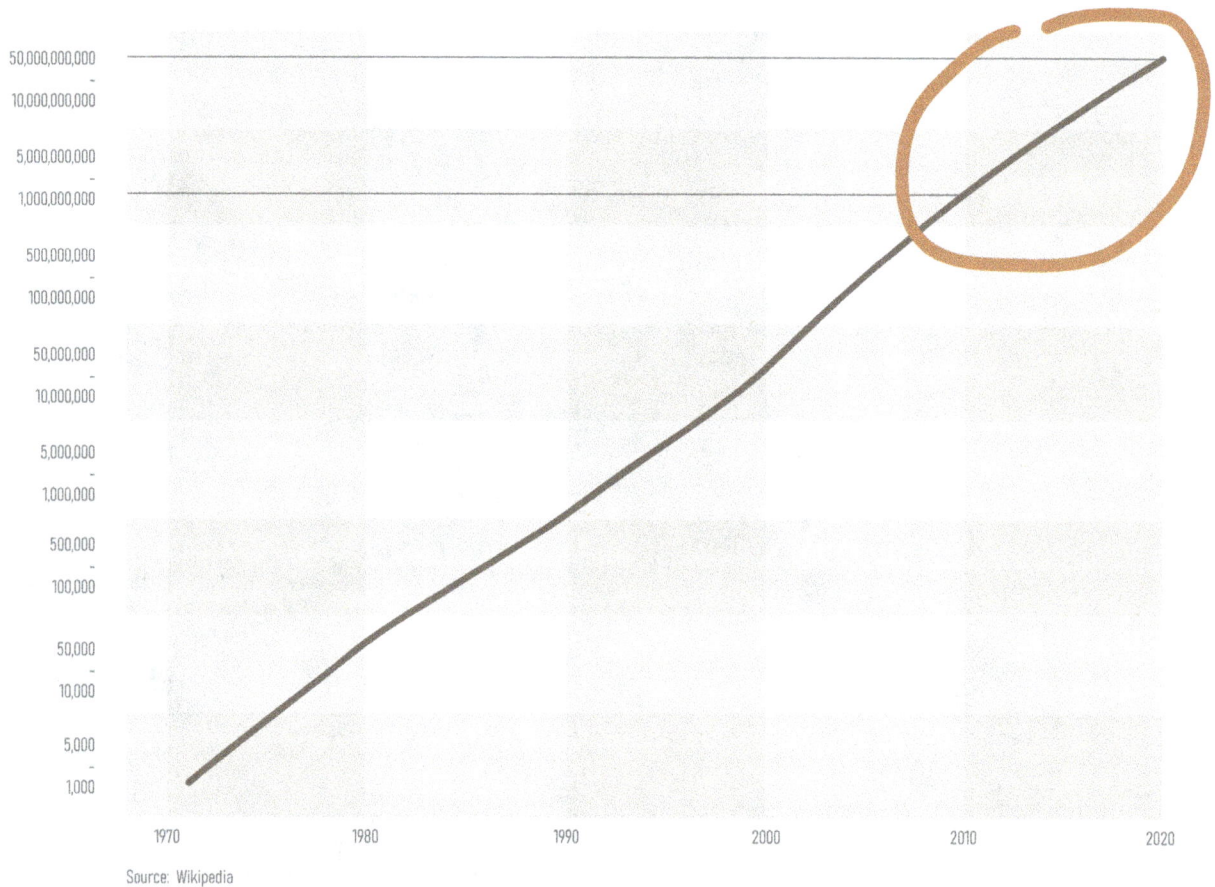

Source: Wikipedia

Figure 1.13: Moore's Law [42, 43]

The average response times did not improve during the same time period. For desktop computers, it stayed more or less the same, around eight seconds. For mobile devices, it more than doubled over the last couple of years and is now around 18 seconds (see Figure 1.14). For desktop computers, the response time is longer than the continuous flow limit of five seconds. For mobile devices, the reported average response time is longer than the captive time limit of ten seconds. Both response times interrupt the user's flow. So far, the system response time has not decreased as a result of the increased silicon power.

We have web analytic tools that measure user actions to optimize websites [44, 45] which measures user actions, but not system response times. Performance testing tools [46–48] measure system response times but not user actions.

Loading time for desktop and mobile

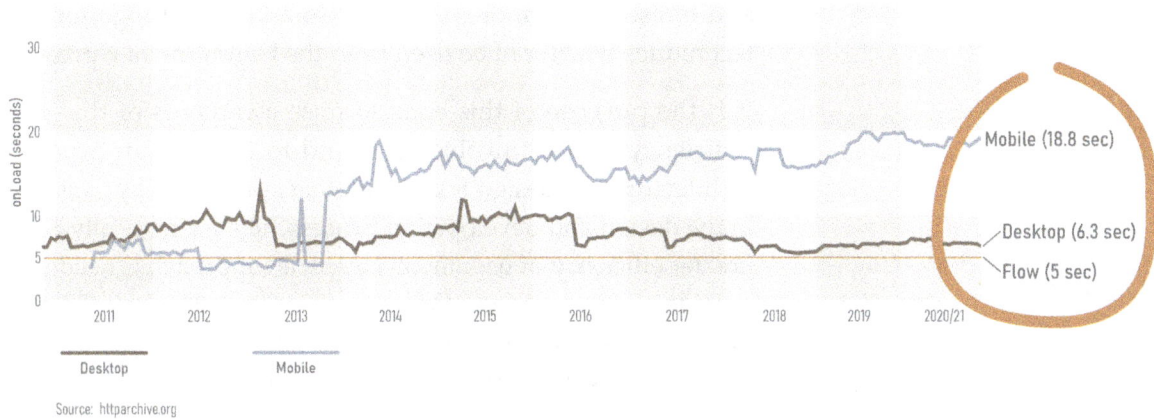

Source: httparchive.org

Figure 1.14: Loading time [49]

Beside techniques and tools for the more technical perspective, there are few techniques that help us to achieve greater efficiency from a design perspective. For instance, summative usability tests can measure time-on-task [50–52]. We can measure fixations and saccades with eye tracking equipment [53], and we can apply the goals, operators, methods, selection rules (GOMS) technique and the keystroke-level model (KLM) that predict execution times for users [54]. What is different in this book and what concepts are worthwhile to write and to read about?

In order to use the abovementioned techniques and tools, we need a relatively detailed design that has already been at least partially implemented. If we wait too long to find out that something is not as efficient as it should be, there won't be enough time or budget left in the project to make the necessary changes. To use a metaphor: If we want to develop a racing bike, we cannot expect a successful outcome if we start designing a cruiser bike and then figure out in tests that it does not perform like a racing bike. The intent of developing a racing bike needs to be considered from day one of the project.

The abovementioned efficiency techniques and tools have their purpose and merit in the design and development process. However, I'd rather call them *test for efficiency* techniques and tools, not *design for efficiency*, because some level of implementation is needed to be able to assess the achieved efficiency.

Efficiency of user involvement is so far not an established and actively pursued design quality, neither in software engineering nor in user experience design. The change of system response times, or their lack of, indicates a systemic problem. The computational resources are not directed toward efficiency for (external) user involvement but to benefit internal system resources. This reminds us of the case study from Melbourne. Probable reasons are insufficient awareness combined with insufficient techniques and tools. Furthermore, there is also a lack of design tools and techniques which can be used from the beginning of a project.

It is the purpose of this book to raise awareness of the quality "efficiency of user involvement" and to propose an experience architecture and design framework that systematically considers it in the design and development process. To systematically achieve greater efficiency of user involvement, an approach is needed that considers efficiency from day one of a project. The techniques and tools in this book are created for *architecture and design for efficiency* from the get-go, not merely to "test for efficiency."

What are strategies to increase efficiency?

With experience architecture and design for efficiency, we should focus not so much on the question "What should the user do for the application?" but on the question "What should the application do for the user?" The idea is to make the lives of users as easy as possible by allocating actions and decisions to the application rather than to the user but doing it in a way that is acceptable to the user.

Interaction and intervention

In the remainder of the book, the term "user involvement" is used to express either a user interaction or user intervention. The terms "user participation" and "stakeholder participation" are used to express the involvement of users or stakeholders in the design and development *process*.

From an user involvement perspective, we talk about two types of user involvements: user interaction and user intervention [55, 56] (see also Figure 1.15).

Interaction in the context of human-computer interaction can be defined as *action that occurs between one or more people and one or more technical systems that have an effect upon one another* (based on [57]). In the context of human-computer interaction, an interaction between a user and a technical system typically takes place for the purpose of achieving the user's goal. Interaction is user controlled. It is supported by system actions that are directly or indirectly triggered by the user's actions and executed by system functions. The system generated outcome for the user becomes the stimulus and trigger for the user to plan and perform the next user's action. From a user's perspective, interaction requires many individual

User involvement types

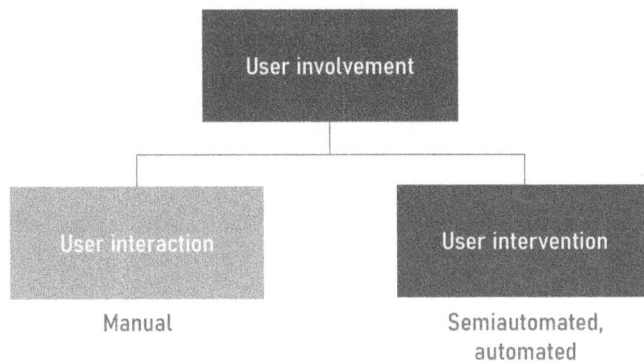

Figure 1.15: User involvement types

user actions and system actions in order to achieve the intended outcome. Interaction feels like a "manual" experience.

Intervention is an "action by the user that takes place during the usage of an automated system and initiates a diversion from the predefined behavior" [55, p. 42]. Intervention is system controlled. It occurs when a user-initiated process deviates from the predefined behavior and the system requests a decision from a user. There are several differences between intervention and interaction.

One difference is the existence of a *predefined behavior*. Both involvement types know a predefined behavior. It is different how it is used. When a user is involved in "interaction," there is often a predefined behavior in the user's mind. Such a predefined behavior is stored in what is often called a *mental model* [58, 59]. It determines which actions the user performs (or would like to perform), and in which sequence to generate a certain outcome and to achieve a certain goal. In the case of "intervention," the predefined behavior is implemented in and executed by the technical system.

One focus of user-centered design is to design and implement a system that is compatible with the mental model of the target user role.

Another difference is *divergence*. This means that the system can run into a situation where it has diverged from the predefined behavior or it is going to diverge from it. In such a situation, the system interrupts the execution and requests a decision from the user. In order to continue the predefined behavior, the user makes a decision where and how the system should continue. When the system follows the predefined behavior, the user does not have to be actively involved to achieve the outcome. Therefore, intervention feels like a "semiautomated" or "automated" experience for the user.

Control and automation

Figure 1.16: Interaction vs Intervention

There is another major difference between interaction and intervention: level of control and automation (see Figure 1.16). Control and automation are trade-offs. The more control a user has, the less the system is automated, and the less efficient user involvement is. The less control a user has, the more the system is automated, and the more efficient user involvement is. In this sense, user interaction is less efficient for the user than user intervention. Independent from the efficiency level, there is always a minimum of automation and a minimum of control.

The same system may have both an interaction and an intervention mode. An airplane is such a system. It has an autopilot mode (intervention) that can be turned on and turned off. When the autopilot mode is turned off, the system is in an interaction mode.

Using control and automation, there are various tactics for making user involvement more efficient (see Figure 1.17):

▶ Tactic 1: Make user interaction more efficient; that is, the user needs to perform fewer actions. User involvement remains in "user interaction" mode.
▶ Tactic 2: Move user involvement from user interaction to user intervention; this is, increase the automation level significantly. A plan with a predefined behavior is implemented. The system takes over decision-making and involves the user only when a divergence occurs.
▶ Tactic 3: Make user intervention more efficient; that is, increase the automation level. User involvement remains in "user intervention" mode and the automation level is further increased.

Higher efficiency is achieved by reducing user control and increasing the automation level. This book proposes two strategies to

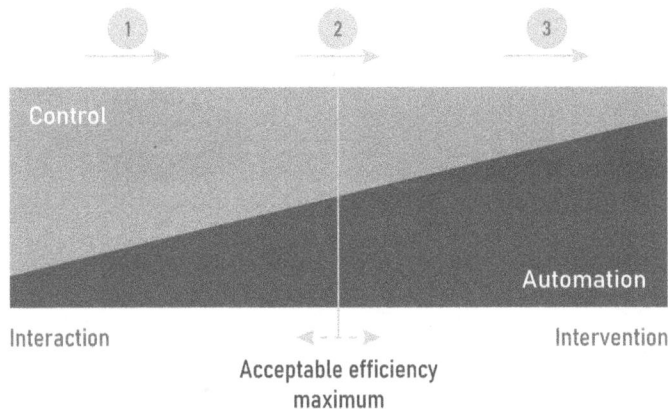

Figure 1.17: Efficiency improvements tactics

systematically increase the efficiency of user involvement:

- ► Reduce user involvement steps
- ► Reduce user involvement time

A reduction in user involvement steps typically leads to a reduction in user involvement time. A reduction in user involvement time may *not* necessarily lead to a reduction in user involvement steps. The reason is that system actions can be made more efficient that leads to a reduced user involvement time while the number of user involvement steps stays the same.

Reduce user involvement steps

One approach to achieving higher efficiency is the systematic reduction of user involvement steps, ideally to one or none. This is, surprisingly, often possible (see Figure 1.18).

The experience architecture and design framework introduces several techniques to systematically reduce the number of user involvement steps:

- ► Experience foundation
  - The discovery of the business plan (see Chapter 3 (Business Model) on page 49) as a foundational result
  - The discovery of the workflow (as is) (see Chapter 5 (Workflow (as is)) on page 117) as a foundational result
  - The discovery of responsibilities per user role (see Chapter 6 (User Roles) on page 149) as a foundational result
- ► Experience architecture

Several involvement steps

Step 1   ...   Step n   →   Outcome

One involvement step*

Step   →   Outcome

No involvement step*

Outcome

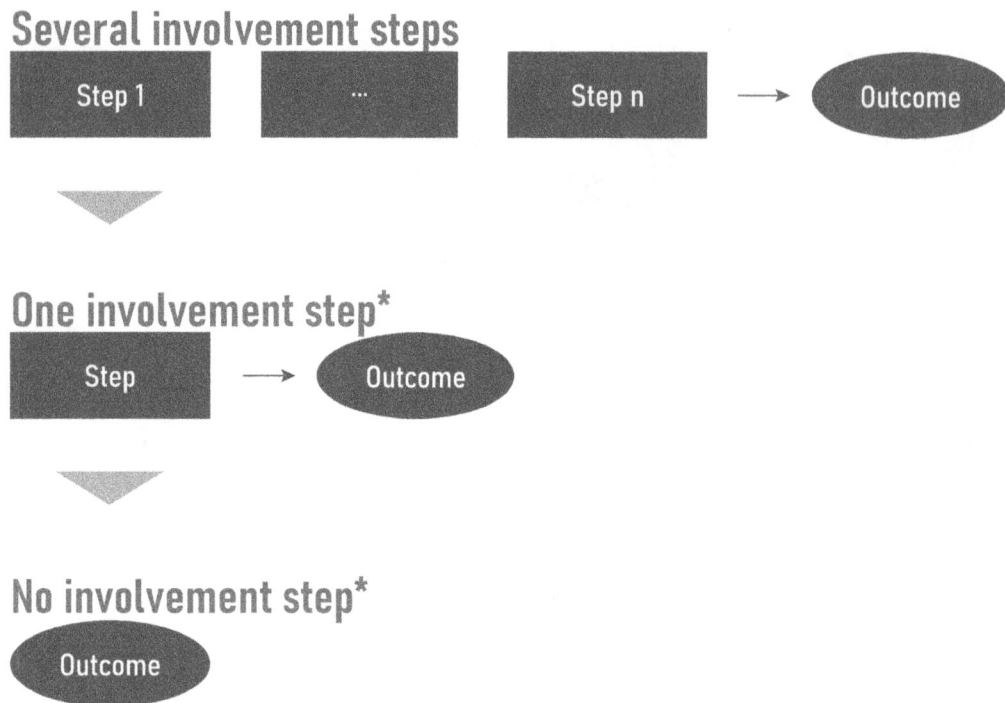

*Works surprisingly often

Figure 1.18: Reduce user involvement steps

- The identification of the primary user task to optimize the involvement concept for the most relevant user task (see Section 1 (Primary user task) on page 290)
- The involvement hypotenuse as a mental tool to reduce user involvement steps per user task (see Section 12 (User involvement hypotenuse) on page 316)
- The systematic reduction of user involvement steps with GAIS (see Section 12 (GAIS) on page 319)
- The documentation of all target user involvement steps as quantitative goals in the involvement goal matrix (see Section 1 (Involvement goal matrix) on page 332).

▶ Experience design

- A system of design elements including a canvas and different types of areas that support the targeted placement of design elements to achieve a minimal number of involvement steps (see Section 13 (Areas) on page 360)
- The systematic creation of an involvement concept with minimal design elements (see Chapter 14 (Explore Con-

cepts) on page 387)

- The systematic refinement of an involvement concept for efficiency with twelve design efficiency techniques (see Chapter 15 (Refine Concept) on page 439)
- The determination of actual user involvement steps (see Chapter 15 (Refine Concept) on page 439)
- The interaction complexity estimation for the seed concepts with the big I notation (see Section 16 (Interaction complexity) on page 497)
- The assessment of the actual user involvement steps against the target user involvement steps (see Chapter 17 (Assess Concepts) on page 531)

Reduce user involvement time

The reduction of user involvement time is another strategy to increase efficiency for users. A simplified diagram shows the intent of reduced user involvement time (see Figure 1.19).

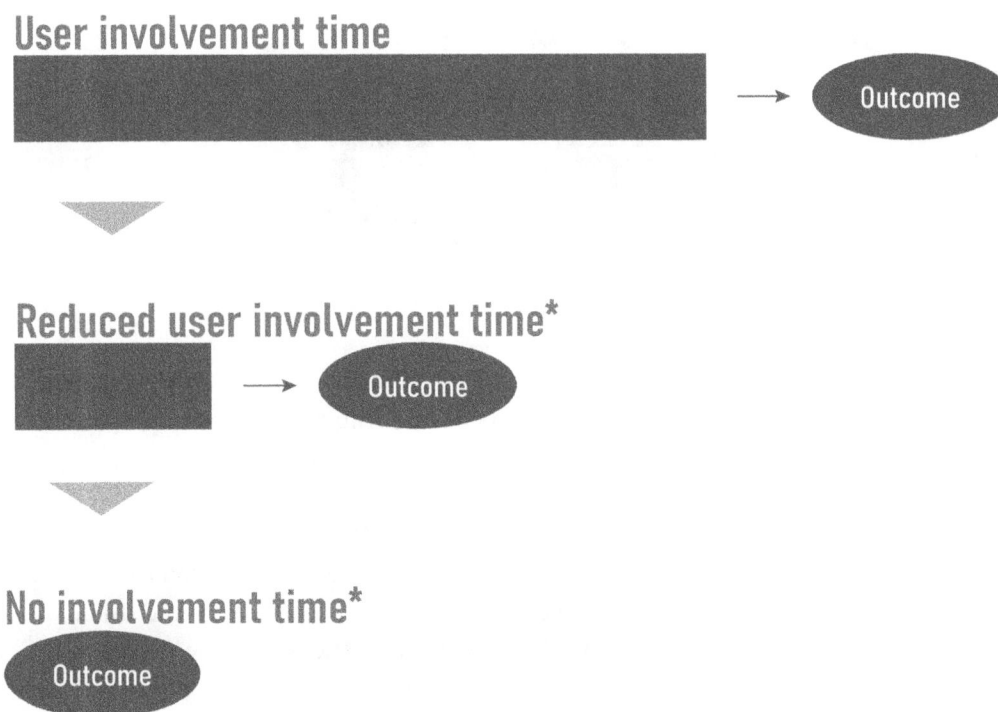

User involvement time

Outcome

Reduced user involvement time*

Outcome

No involvement time*

Outcome

*Works surprisingly often

Figure 1.19: Reduce user involvement time

The reduction of user involvement time requires looking at aspects of user involvement that contribute to involvement time. It considers both user actions and system actions that contribute to the user involvement time. It also considers metrics for user intervention. The proposed approach introduces a user involvement metric taxonomy that can be used to measure user involvement times and frequencies (see Figure 1.20).

User involvement metric taxonomy

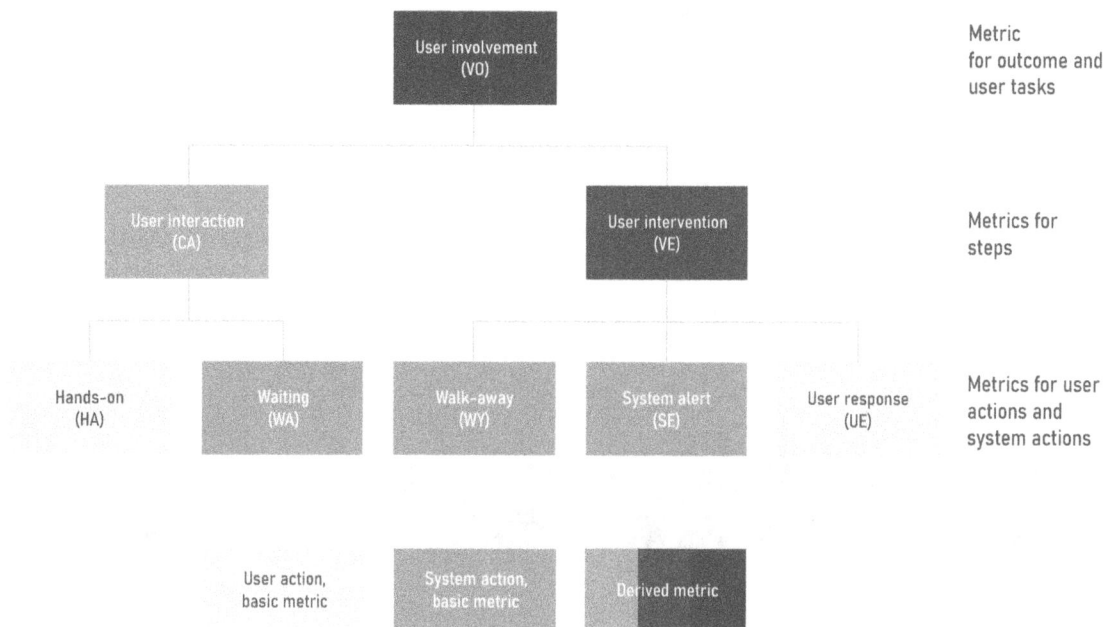

Figure 1.20: User involvement metric taxonomy

The experience architecture and design framework introduces several techniques to systematically determine target user involvement times:

▶ Experience foundation

- The discovery of the business plan (see Chapter 3 (Business Model) on page 49) as a foundational result
- The discovery of the workflow (as is) (see Chapter 5 (Workflow (as is)) on page 117) as a foundational result
- The discovery of responsibilities per user role (see Chapter 6 (User Roles) on page 149) as a foundational result
- The introduction and definition of user involvement metrics for time, frequency, and productivity (see Chapter 4 (User Involvement Metrics) on page 75)

▶ Experience architecture

- The definition of the workflow (to be) with target user involvement times (see Section 9 (Define estimated target times) on page 224)
- The definition of the user involvement system with user involvement points (see Chapter 10 (User Involvement System) on page 241) and its target system alert times (see Section 10 (Scenario views) on page 254)
- The assignment of target user involvement times to user tasks for each user involvement point (see Section 1 (Target involvement time) on page 298)
- The documentation of all target user involvement times as quantitative goals in the involvement goal matrix (Section 1 (Involvement goal matrix) on page 332)

▶ Experience design

- A system of design elements that also includes functions and their non-functional properties to realize the target user involvement times (see Section 13 (Design elements) on page 345).
- The systematic creation of an involvement concept with minimal design elements (see Chapter 14 (Explore Concepts) on page 387)
- The systematic refinement of an involvement concept with twelve design efficiency techniques (see Chapter 15 (Refine Concept) on page 439)
- The systematic determination of the actual user involvement times with the speed test (see Chapter 16 (Evaluate Concepts) on page 493)
- The assessment of actual user involvement times against target user involvement times (see Chapter 17 (Assess Concepts) on page 531)

What are challenges for efficiency?

What can be made more efficient should not necessarily be made more efficient. Efficiency does not automatically equal acceptance and effectiveness. There are limits to how much efficiency is acceptable and useful for users.

Find an acceptable efficiency maximum　When we design for efficiency, we can assign functions to the system to automate certain tasks and to take the user out of the loop. The efficiency may increase, but the acceptance may drop. A design-for-efficiency approach needs to consider that efficiency itself cannot be isolated from other qualities — it always requires the consideration of the qualities *acceptance* and *effectiveness*.

One of the challenges is to find the highest acceptable efficiency, here called the *acceptable efficiency maximum*, abbreviated AEMax (see also Figure 1.17). The acceptable efficiency maximum may vary from user group to user group and from user task to user task.

Keep users engaged   There is extensive research about human performance and human involvement in automated systems [60–67]. Examples are systems that monitor and control plants, like nuclear power plants, or autopilots in airplanes. These are good examples of highly efficient systems, because they are designed and developed for automation, the highest possible efficiency level. The higher the level of automation, the less operators or pilots (as the users are called) are interacting with the system in daily operations. They merely monitor the system's performance, and their interaction is only needed if something extraordinary happens that cannot be managed by the automated system itself.

Research about automated systems with human involvement indicates that a high level of automation works fine, as long as everything goes as planned. Problems occur when a highly automated system does not work as planned, and the operator or pilot has to resolve an exceptional situation. Operators or pilots may have a lack of situational awareness and/or lack of knowledge of how to resolve an exceptional situation, which is counterproductive to overall performance, with and without the user. Researchers conclude that a medium level of automation addresses situational unawareness because at this level operators or pilots are still frequently involved in decision making and therefore stay aware [61, 64–66].

Gain and maintain user's trust   Another challenge is to gain and maintain users' trust. This is especially true for use of complex, opaque, and/or non-deterministic technologies, such as those based on artificial intelligence (AI) and machine learning (ML). With the support of such technologies, the system can detect patterns and make recommendations that are not easily achievable with rule-based, deterministic algorithms. However, in many cases, it is not clear to users how accurate, reliable, and unbiased such recommendations are. The concerns with AI-based technology are about interpretability, transparency, fairness, ethics, and reliability, which all influence user's trust.

A lot of research is being conducted at the moment to better understand what to explain to users and how to explain it to gain the users' trust [68–84]. Companies have defined principles for the use of AI. For instance, Google lists a number of principles for the development and use of AI-based enablers [85]. If tasks are delegated to an AI-enabled technology, it potentially increases the efficiency; however, users need to trust such enablers, otherwise they may not accept them.

Conclusion   Efficiency is not a silver bullet. What can be made more efficient should not necessarily be made more efficient. An efficient design is not automatically acceptable. If it is not acceptable, it is not effective. We need a human-centered design and development approach to find out which level of efficiency is acceptable to users and how to support users' demand for control. Such an approach is described in this book.

What is unique about this book?

Besides the techniques and tools mentioned above, I've looked at many books, articles, and blogs. Based on my research, I consider this book to be unique for the following reasons:

- ► It is focused on "architecture and design for efficiency": The book systematically describes how to design for efficiency from the very beginning of a project. It is, as far as I know, the only book that focuses on experience architecture and design for efficiency in a "how-to" book. It is worthwhile to emphasize that many techniques and tools described in this book are also applicable to designs that do not focus on efficiency.
- ► It is example centered: it uses one non-trivial example ("The World of Pizza") and demonstrates the design process with its techniques, tools, and templates end-to-end.
- ► It is practice proven: the book is written by a practitioner (and researcher). It contains practice-proven techniques, tools, and templates.

Last but not least: Does this book describe the one and only path to architecture and design for efficiency? Absolutely not. The world is big, diverse, and full of ideas, complementary ones and competing ones. This book presents one way to do it. I hope it will inspire colleagues to come up with other, complementary and even better ways to increase efficiency for our users.

What's in, what's out?

At the beginning of the writing process, a decision needed to be made about whether the techniques, tools, and templates should be presented individually and isolated from the architecture and design process. I felt that in that case it might become difficult to understand when to apply them and how, and how the results would inform or influence subsequent steps.

Therefore, I made the decision to use a human-centered design process as a context of use for the presented techniques, tools, and templates. The selected process presented here is based on the human-centered design process described in ISO 9241-210 [86].

The main intent of introducing the human-centered design process is to make it easier for readers to understand when and how to apply the presented techniques, tools, and templates. Introducing the context and its steps does not imply that the presented techniques, tools, and templates can only be applied in those specific process steps. If readers see other process steps as equally or even more appropriate, the techniques and templates can be used there, too. The framework supports reuse of technique, tools, and template since they are modular.

It does not mean, either, that all techniques, tools, and templates must be applied. Each project has its own needs, and the entire framework can be considered a toolbox. Techniques, tools, and templates can be selected and applied, motivated by project needs. A guide is presented later to assist in selecting appropriate techniques, tools, and templates for different project types (see Section 1 (Experience guide) on page 39).

The techniques, tools, and templates presented in this book are applicable to task-based applications that are designed to accomplish a task and to generate an outcome of value. The faster the user can create the outcome of value, the better.

The design for efficiency approach is not intended for applications with a business model built on keeping the user involved for as long as possible, such as games, advertisements financed online content, social media etc.

The book does not cover technical performance optimizations. There are other books that cover that topic in depth.

The described approach can be applied to several interaction modalities, including voice, gesture etc. The examples in the book use graphical user interfaces. The presented approach can be applied to all commercially available screen sizes.

How to read the book?

Experience scope

The experience scope is shown in a circular diagram, called the "experience wheel" (see Figure 1.21). It consists of three parts. The first part (moving clockwise) is "experience foundation." It contains all the basics: business model, workflow (as is), use contexts and user roles. The second part is called "experience architecture" and contains the workflow (to be), the user involvement system, the user involvement points, and the involvement goals. Associated with the architecture are the involvement goals. The third part is called "experience design," consisting of the involvement concepts, user interfaces, requirements, and specifications. It is worthwhile to point out that the context of use and the users are also listed as constraints at the top of the wheel. The user interfaces need to work with the users and within a specific context of use. The elements are styled as a wheel to show that the user interfaces, users, and use context belong together.

The introduced parts of the experience wheel are described in this book, in the part "Experience Foundation," "Experience Architecture," and in the part "Experience Design."

Experience process

The underlying design and development process is depicted in Figure 1.22. It consists of the following phases:

▶ *Discover* experience foundation: The discovery phase focuses on the business, the domain, the use context, and the user. The business model is elicited, together with the involved user roles. The context of use for the identified user roles is analyzed and documented, including the workflow (as is), user involvement metrics (as is), users' activities (as is), constraints, pain points, and wishes, as well as known practices. Strength and weaknesses of the workflow (as is) are identified. A user role profile is created for each identified user role. To gather the information, I often conduct co-creation workshops, observations, interviews, and desk research in my daily work. Access to end users is a necessity.

▶ *Define* experience architecture: Based on the insights from the discovery phase, the user involvement system is defined, with its user involvement points. Each user involvement point can become its own design project. The involvement goals are defined and documented in the involvement goal matrix with quantitative user involvement goals (target times

The term "user" refers to representatives of target user groups. I differentiate between "end user" and "proxy user." End users are users. Proxy users are individuals who have knowledge of or experience with end users but do not belong to the target user groups themselves. Usually, I use the term "users" to refer to end users. If I want to emphasize that end users are meant and not proxy users, I use the term "end users."

Experience Wheel

Users

Contexts of use

Experience
Foundation

Specifications

Requirements

Experience
Design

User
interfaces

Involvement
concept

Business
model

Workflow
(as is)

User roles

Experience
Architecture

User
involvement
points

Workflow
(to be)

User
involvement
system

Involvement goals

Helmut Degen (CC BY-NC-SA 4.0)

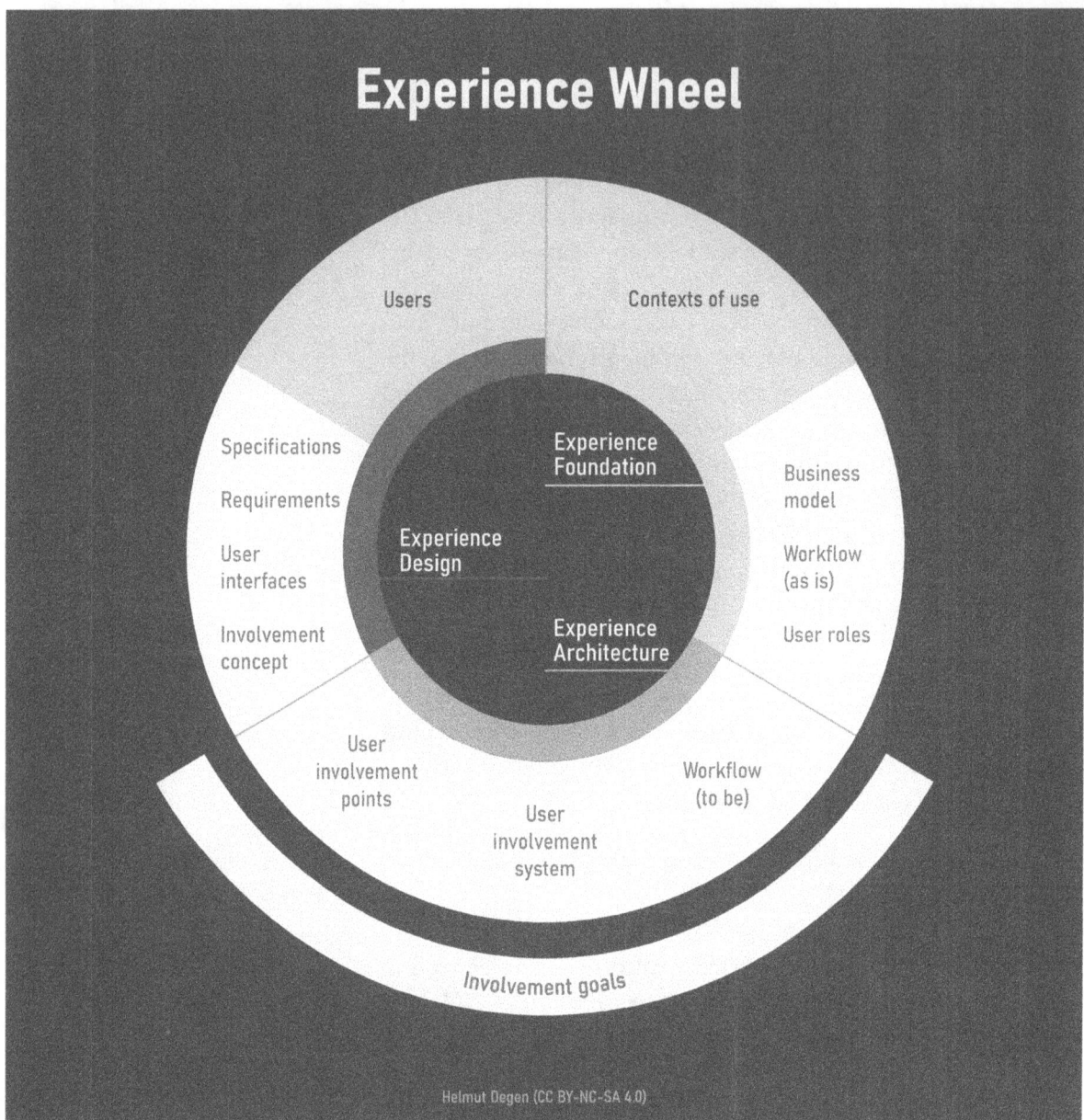

Figure 1.21: Experience wheel

and steps per user task), qualitative user involvement goals, and business goals.

▶ *Design* involvement concepts: For each user involvement point, a user involvement concept is created. The first step is the exploration of user involvement concepts. The initial concepts are called *seed concepts*. The seed concepts are iteratively and systematically explored, refined, assessed, and excluded. The focus here is on breadth and variety. Only one of the refined seed concepts will be selected and called the *sprout concept*. This process is highly iterative with frequent user and stakeholder participation. The involvement goals are used to keep the exploration and exclusion of involvement concepts under control.

▶ *Refine and specify* user interfaces: The selected sprout concept will be refined into user interfaces. The focus here is on completeness and finishing. Many missing design elements are added for the user tasks in scope. This process is still highly iterative, but the design boundaries of the sprout concept should be honored. The result is a fully designed user interface, including mockups and necessary user interface specifications for the implementation team.

▶ *Implementation guidance* for application implementation: The front end will be implemented either in-house or by an external development team. In this phase, it is critical to guide the implementation of the entire application, including the front end and functional elements of the back end. Although several forms of user interface specifications (e.g., concepts, mockups, requirements, user stories etc.) are available, they are always incomplete. It is recommended that the experience professional performs frequent quality assurance for the implementation work.

▶ *Evaluate* application: With a formal evaluation (formative or summative), the implemented application (or parts of it) is evaluated against the evaluation goals.

This book covers the Discovery, Define, and Design phases (see Figure 1.22).

The main flow of the process diagram could be interpreted as a strict waterfall approach, meaning that the phases are executed sequentially. This is a possibility. However, the two main ingredients for achieving high-quality architecture and design are *time* and *iterations*. Therefore, the process can and should be applied iteratively. The iterative nature of the process is indicated by the small arrows that point to the center of the diagram, and by the arrows that point from the center of the diagram toward the phases. Users and stakeholders participate frequently in all phases.

Since the experience architecture provides a comprehensive overview of the application under design, it is recommended that the first two phases (experience foundation and experience architecture) be completed first, before starting the design phase. It is normal for uncertainties to occur during the Define and Explore phase. They are typically clarified by going back to previous phases.

Experience guide

Here is a guide that helps you identify the relevant steps for your project situation (see Figure 1.23): You want to ...

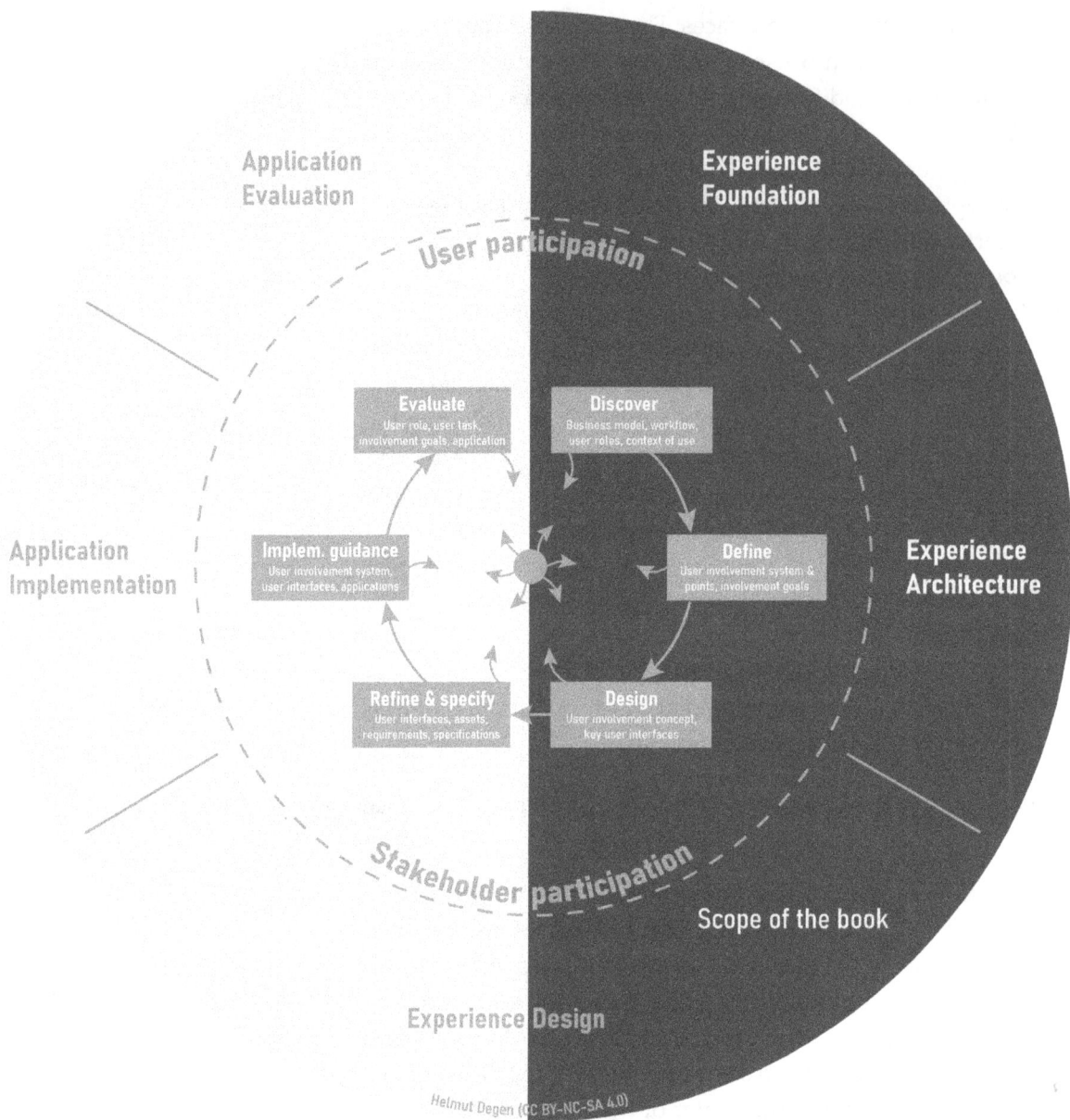

Figure 1.22: Iterative human-centered design and development process

- ▶ improve an existing stand-alone app ("Brownfield / Existing" & "App").
- ▶ improve multiple existing apps that form an ecosystem ("Brownfield / Existing" & "Ecosystem").
- ▶ create a new stand-alone app ("Greenfield / New" & "App").
- ▶ create multiple new apps that form an ecosystem ("Greenfield / New" & "Ecosystem").

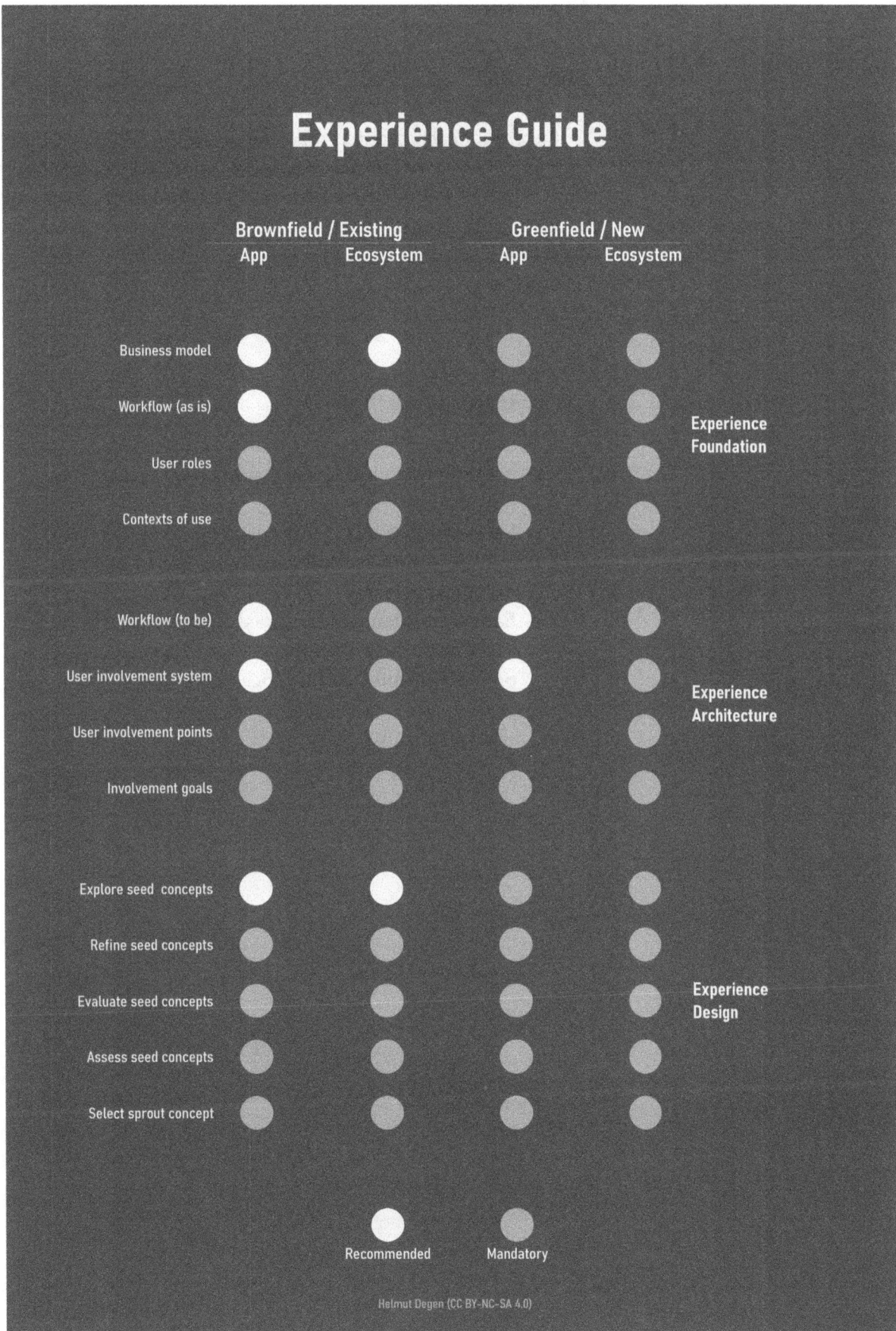

Figure 1.23: Experience guide

Summary

Shortcuts

At the end of each chapter, the content for the "World of Pizza" example is summarized. The boxes are connected through hyperlinks. The links allow the reader to click through the book with a focus on the created examples, step by step. You can try it now, and you'll see within a few minutes how the content evolves, from "zero to hero."

A shortcut through the book

- ▶ A shortcut box is displayed at the end of each chapter.
- ▶ Each shortcut box, or the page beneath the short cut box summarizes the evolving World of Pizza example content.
- ▶ Each box contains hyperlinks that enable navigation to the short cut box in the next or the previous the previous chapter. Just go ahead and try it ...

- ▶ ... to Business Model

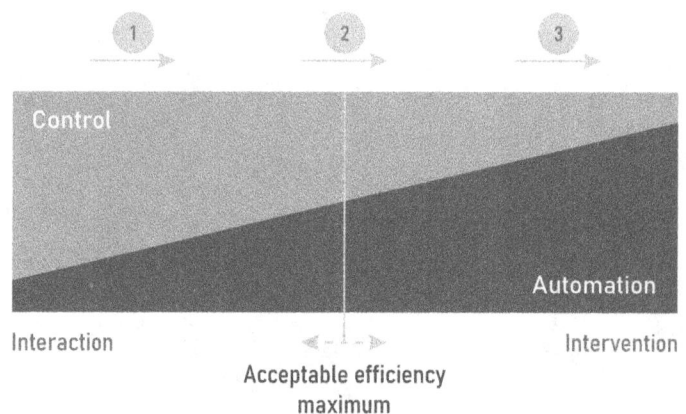

Control

Automation

Interaction   Acceptable efficiency   Intervention
                    maximum

Exercise 1.1

Goal   Select an example domain and application.

Completion criteria:

- ▶ The example domain is foreign to the experience professional.
- ▶ The example includes several user roles (customer and vendor roles).
- ▶ The experience professional has access to at least one person who is knowledgeable about the selected application domain and who is their user representative.

PART 1: EXPERIENCE FOUNDATION

Experience Foundation | 2

Time is what we want most, but what, alas! we use worst
William Penn

Purpose

The purpose of the Experience Foundation part, and the work involved, is to lay a foundation for experience architecture and design. A few important questions are answered here: What value is generated by the application under design? How is the value currently generated? How does experience architecture and design support the value generation? Which user roles are involved? What is the context(s) of use while users are involved?

Answers to these questions establish the foundation for experience architecture and experience design. The workflow (as is) answers the question of how value is currently generated. It becomes a baseline for workflow and efficiency improvements that are introduced when defining the experience architecture. The workflow baseline also helps to determine quantitative efficiency improvements, expressed with the user involvement metrics.

The user role profiles in combination with the context of use profiles are the key ingredients for defining the experience architecture and later for designing the involvement concept.

An overview of the parts of the experience foundation phase is depicted in Figure 2.1.

Experience Foundation Views

Define business model

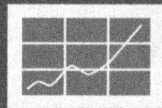

Define workflow (as is)

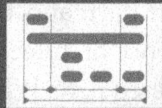

Define user role(s)

Define context(s) of use

Figure 2.1: Experience foundation views

Business Model | 3

It's the only thing you can't buy.
I mean, I can buy anything I want basically but I can't buy time.
Warren Buffett

Purpose

In order to create a design that provides value, it is critical to understand the business model of what is being designed.

> **Definition 1** (Business model) *Rationale of how an organization creates, delivers, and captures value.* [87]

Understanding the business model helps us to understand which parts of the application under design require special attention. The need to understand the business model is independent of whether a vendor organization is a for-profit business or a nonprofit. Creating value does not have to be interchangeable with "making money." Creating value means that the customers or other beneficiaries receive something of value, and the organization that offers the value gets something in return. For instance, if an application is made available for free, a measurable unit of success could be the average user rating or the number of downloads, page visits, or user reviews.

To understand the business model, we use a business model template (see Figure 3.1) that is based on the popular business model canvas [88] and tailored for design relevance (see also [89, 90]).

The template is applied to our World of Pizza example. The result is depicted in Figure 3.2. Each element will be explained in more detail in the remaining part of this section.

Business model

Name
What is the name of the application under design?

General understanding

Segments and roles
What are the market segments? What are the user roles per segment?

User roles

Workflows

Needs
Which need is addressed per segment and role?

User roles

Value proposition
What differentiates the new offering from existing ones?

Involvement goals

Offering
What do you offer for each segment?

General understanding

Business goals
What are business-motivated involvement goals?

Involvement goals

Revenue / cost
How to generate revenue or reduce cost?

Involvement goals

Market size
How many units do you plan to distribute / sell per year?

Involvement goals

Experience value
How does experience add value? How does efficiency add value?

Involvement goals

Figure 3.1: Business model template; the brown labels show where the information is used in the subsequent phases of the design process

Name
What is the name of the application under design?

World of Pizza (WoP)

Segments and roles
What are the market segments? What are the user roles per segment?

- Household: manager, member
- Company: team lead, team member, team assistant
- Restaurant: manager, baker, driver

Needs
Which need is addressed per segment and role?

- Customer: live healthfully and frugally
- Restaurant manager / baker: growth
- Driver: funds

Value proposition

- Customers: compare pizzas across restaurants
- Restaurant manager: increase revenue and reduce costs
- Baker: reduce costs
- Driver: compare delivery jobs

Offerings
What do you offer for each segment?

- Customer: order and receive pizza
- Restaurant manager: monitor and control operation
- Baker: optimization of baking process
- Driver: find delivery jobs

Business goals
What are business-motivated involvement goals?

- Enable comparison of pizzas from different restaurants
- Add new products
- Display at least 9 product items at a glance
- Driver: compare delivery jobs by rate

Revenue / Costs
How to generate revenue or reduce cost?

- Gross revenue: order value plus 10% delivery fee, minimum $7.
- Cost: 70% of order value for restaurant; delivery fee -$1 for driver
- Net revenue: 25% of order value

Market size (SOM)
How many units do you plan to distribute / sell per year?

Orders per year:
- Year 1: 109,500 orders
- Year 2: 1,095,000 orders
- Year 3: 10,950,000 orders
- Year 4: 109,500,000 orders

Experience value
How does experience add value? How does efficiency add value?

- Customers: search pizza efficiently across restaurants
- Restaurant manager: deviation alerts
- Baker: optimization alerts for baking
- Driver: Compare delivery jobs by rate

Figure 3.2: Business model for WoP

Example selection

Let me briefly explain why I have chosen to use the pizza example. From experience and from asking colleagues about qualities of good user experience books, I heard again and again the word "examples." The response that struck me most was this: "When I open a user experience book, I go first to the example." I know from my own reading and teaching experience that examples are an effective way to communicate how techniques work. This thought led to the realization that I needed one or more examples.

The next question was: should I use sporadically several, disconnected examples or should I use one example end-to-end. I learned from being a student and a teacher that using one end-to-end example is more effective than using several, disconnected examples. This is particularly true if the techniques and the content are connected, as they are in our case. It is the reason why I chose one example for the entire book.

The next question was, which example? I could have used an industrial example, like a manufacturing controller. But I was certain that I would lose at least 90 percent of my readers after the first sentence introducing the manufacturing controller example. I was looking for an example that most readers could relate to and understand. So I needed an example from the consumer domain. The example needed to be easy to relate to but complex enough so that different perspectives could be shown. I was looking into food ordering, water irrigation systems, and home automation. The irrigation system lacked the breadth of a more complex ecosystem. When I compared the home automation system with the food order example, I concluded that readers could better relate to online ordering.

As market research shows, food is ordered in all regions worldwide. I am aware that not everyone orders or eats pizza. I am hopeful that readers can replace "pizza" with whatever type of food they prefer to order and eat. The example includes an entire ecosystem, including the ordering part, the management part (managing the store), the back-office part (ordering ingredients, paying employees and suppliers, etc.), the production part (making pizza), and the delivery part. For reasons of brevity, this book focuses on the ordering and delivering part only. The example is completely fictitious. However, it is influenced by market data, insights from observing the pizza making process in Tino's restaurant, and personal experiences.

So, let me introduce you to the World of Pizza ...

Business model

Name

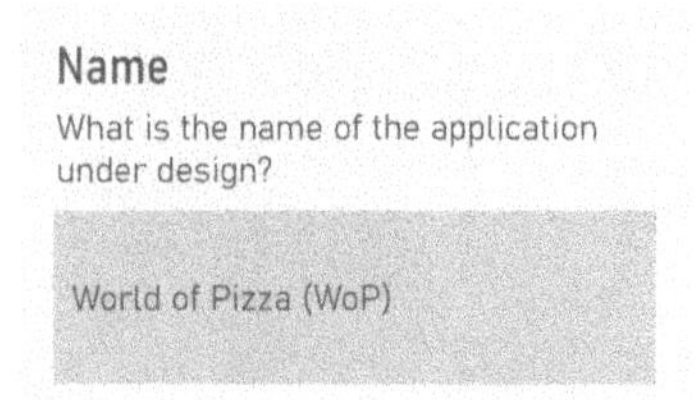

Name

What is the name of the application under design?

World of Pizza (WoP)

Figure 3.3: Business model - Name

It's a good practice to give your application a name, so you can easily refer to it. We call our application

▶ World of Pizza (or WoP)

It's like an Uber for pizza. The name indicates that WoP offers a large variety of pizza types.

Segments and roles

Technique

What are the market segments? What are the user roles per market segment?

A market segment is a group of customers with similarities, such as needs, common interests, life styles, or demographic profiles in an otherwise heterogeneous market.

Since we have a specific interest in design and user experience, our interest is also in user roles. Therefore, we identify initial user roles for each market segment. Each segment has at least one user role, often several. We identify initial user roles per market segments and consolidate them later (see Section 3 (User role consolidation) on page 178).

Segments and roles

What are the market segments?
What are the user roles per segment?

- Household: manager, member
- Company: team lead, team member, team assistant
- Restaurant: manager, baker, driver

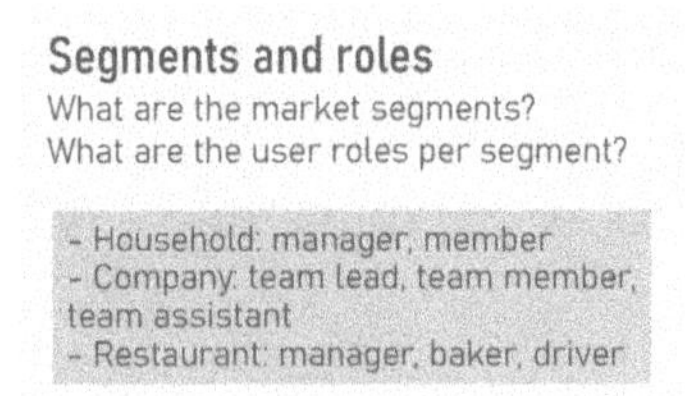

Figure 3.4: Business model - Market segments and user roles

World of Pizza

WoP serves two market segments: private households and enterprises. The private household contains two user roles:

▶ Household manager
▶ Household member

Both can be individuals who make the decision to order pizza and who select and order pizza.

In enterprises, there are three initial user roles:

▶ Team member
▶ Team lead
▶ Team assistant

Team leads or team members select pizzas. Team assistant often order pizzas.

The restaurant itself has user roles that WoP serves:

▶ Restaurant manager
▶ Baker
▶ Driver

The restaurant manager organizes and monitors the restaurant's operations. The baker bakes the pizza as ordered. The driver delivers the ordered pizzas to the customers which can be private households or enterprises.

Needs

Technique

A need is the most abstract design driver.

Definition 2 (Needs) *Drivers of peoples' actions.* [91]

Needs are drivers that influence people's decisions, including the apps they download from the app store, the products they purchase, and the movies they watch. If we, as experience professionals, understand the motivations for decisions, we understand a lot about our users. We can consider such motivations, or drivers, in our design.

There are a variety of influences on experience decisions. A need is the most abstract one. Although it is abstract, it has a strong influence on the direction we take with our design decisions. A need can be compared to Polaris, also known as the North Star (in the Northern Hemisphere) and the Crux, also known as the Southern Cross (in the Southern Hemisphere). For centuries before the compass was invented, sailors used the stars for navigation. They will never be reached, but they guide. A need has a similar guidance function for design decisions.

To better understand what needs are, we need an introduction to four different domains: the life domain, the business domain, the application domain, and the involvement domain. The domain model looks somewhat like a teddy bear's head, which is why it is called here the Teddy Bear Model (see Figure 3.7).

The two outer circles belong to the need domain.

The left-hand overlapping circle expresses *vendor needs*. These are the user needs of shareholders and employees working for the

Figure 3.5: Polaris (North Star); source: Wikimedia; creator: Jim Thomas; license: CC BY-SA 3.0

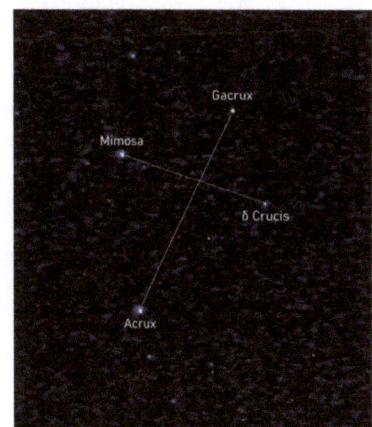

Figure 3.6: Crux (Southern Cross); source: Wikimedia; creator: JoKerozen; license: CC BY-SA 2.5

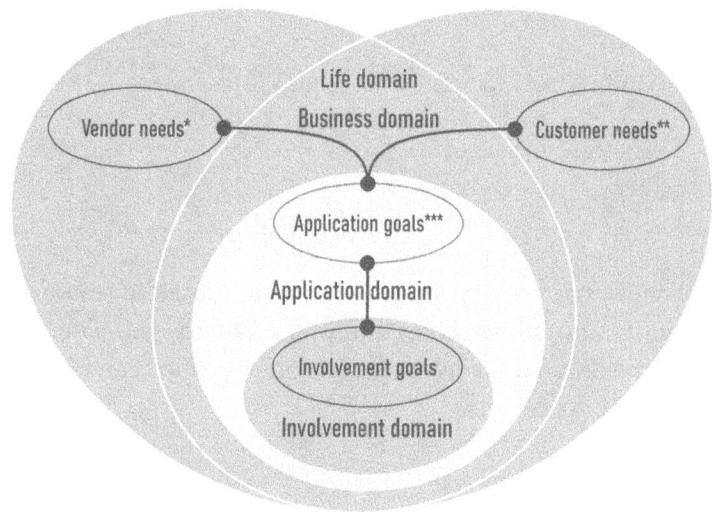

*Users as members of the vendor organization, with their user needs.
**Users as members of the customer organization or as consumers, with their user needs.
***User's goals are a subset of or derived from application goals.

Figure 3.7: Teddy bear model

vendor organization. Because employees help to run a sustainable business, their needs are allocated to the business domain. Since employees are also private human beings with their own lives, the life domain is also assigned to them.

The right-hand overlapping circle expresses *customer needs*. These are the user needs of employees of a customer organization or end customers. If the customer is an enterprise organization (B2B), its needs are allocated to the business domain and the life domain. If customers are end customers, meaning private citizens, their needs are allocated to the life domain. Needs answer the *why* question, that is, why a vendor offers an application and why a customer uses it.

The lighter-colored circle within the overlapping circles is the *application domain*. This area reflects the user tasks and the application-specific user goals. It describes *what* the user can do with the application, for example, selecting a pizza, ordering a pizza, writing a message, reading the news, etc. We design the user involvement system to support the application domain.

The circle within the application domain is the *involvement domain*. This circle reflects the way the user performs tasks with an application — in other words, *how* the user is involved with the application.

The overlapping of the vendor and customer needs indicates that vendor and customer needs must be balanced. The teddy bear

ISO/IEC 25064 defines a user need as a "prerequisite identified as necessary for a user, or a set of users, to achieve an intended outcome, implied or stated within a specific context of use." [92, clause 4.19] Here is an example from the same standard: "An account manager (user) needs to know the number of invoices received and their amounts (prerequisite), in order to complete the daily accounting log (intended outcome) as part of monitoring the cash flow (context of use)." [92, clause 4.19, Example 2] A user need identified in the aforementioned ISO standard is comparable to what is called in this book an application goal.

model behaves like a teeter totter, on purpose. If the vendor and customer needs are not balanced, the model will tilt to one side or the other. A tilted business model means that the business is either not viable enough for vendors or not desirable enough for customers and will most likely fail. A tilting teddy bear can be interpreted as a shaking head that expresses disagreement with the considered business model.

Needs of the life domain   Whether a user is a business customer, a consumer, or an employee, each user is also a private citizen that has needs in the life domain.

Maslow's pyramid of human needs can be used as a model to express the needs of the life domain (see Figure 3.8).

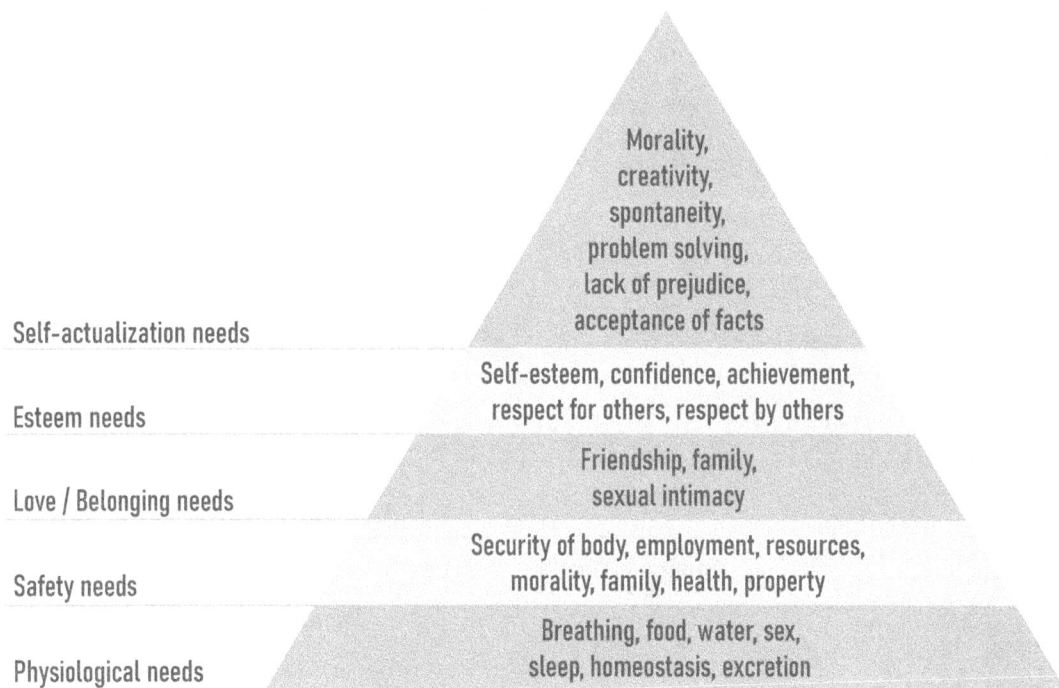

Self-actualization needs — Morality, creativity, spontaneity, problem solving, lack of prejudice, acceptance of facts

Esteem needs — Self-esteem, confidence, achievement, respect for others, respect by others

Love / Belonging needs — Friendship, family, sexual intimacy

Safety needs — Security of body, employment, resources, morality, family, health, property

Physiological needs — Breathing, food, water, sex, sleep, homeostasis, excretion

Source: Abraham Maslow

Figure 3.8: Maslow's pyramid of needs; source: [93, 94]

The pyramid consists of five layers. Maslow constructed it like a ladder. He assumed that humans can reach the second step of the ladder only after they have reached the first one, and so on. This stepwise approach is disputed. However, the need levels provide useful guidance for articulating user needs for our purposes.

Needs of the business domain   A business needs pyramid, which is structured similarly to Maslow's pyramid of needs, identifies levels of business needs (see Figure 3.9).

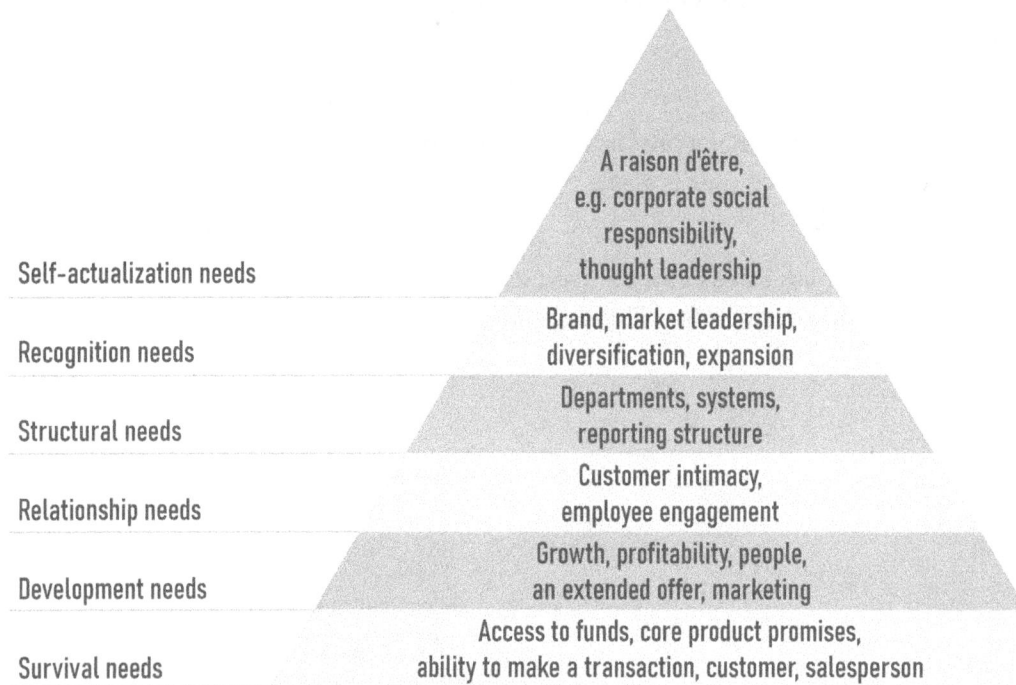

Self-actualization needs	A raison d'être, e.g. corporate social responsibility, thought leadership
Recognition needs	Brand, market leadership, diversification, expansion
Structural needs	Departments, systems, reporting structure
Relationship needs	Customer intimacy, employee engagement
Development needs	Growth, profitability, people, an extended offer, marketing
Survival needs	Access to funds, core product promises, ability to make a transaction, customer, salesperson

Source: https://www.b2binternational.com

Figure 3.9: Pyramid of business needs; source: [95]

We can articulate business needs by selecting one of the listed business needs per layer.

User need   A user need reflects a vendor need (from the business and/or life domain) or a customer need (from the life domain).

> **Definition 3** (User need) *Driver from the life domain or from the business domain.*

A user can have one or more needs. A user as an employee should have needs from the life domain and the business domain.

User goal   A user goal reflects an application goal.

> **Definition 4** (User goal) *User intended state.*

A user goal that is achieved with the application under design is called an *application goal*. A user goal should support a user need. A user goal should not reflect an involvement goal. It would be self-referential and therefore useless.

Below is a table with two examples of how different customer needs can steer the experience architecture and design into very different directions (see Table 3.1).

Table 3.1: User needs and goal examples

Need/goal	Example 1	Example 2
User need: life domain ("Why")	Live healthfully and frugally (safety need)	Have fun with family and friends (love/belonging need)
User goal: application goal ("What")	Find pizza that conforms to my diet and my budget	Ordering and eating pizza is fun for a group of people
Involvement goal ("How")	Filter pizza (e.g., diet, cost, quality, etc.)	Group order wizard, random pizza or slice selector, group game on pizza box

You may want to check your user need statement against the pyramids. A typical mistake is that user needs are articulated as statements reflecting the application or involvement domain and not of the life or business domain. User goals should reflect the application domain and not the involvement domain

In her book "UX Strategy," [90] Jaime Levy describes with real world examples how experience design addresses users' needs and creates an application's value proposition.

Word of Pizza

Let's go back to our pizza example. We have two consumer user roles, the "household manager" and the "household member." They may have a physiological need, meaning their eating habits are about calorie intake. Alternatively, they may have a need to eat healthfully and to be frugal. Both needs correspond to the safety level. Sometimes, it's about having lunch or dinner together with others; this would be at the love/belonging level.

For our World of Pizza example, we have identified the need "live healthfully and frugally" (safety needs level) as applicable.

If we assume that the pizza restaurant has existed for a while, it probably has passed the "survival needs" level. Let's assume that the main interest of the restaurant owner, the manager, and the baker is business growth (development needs level).

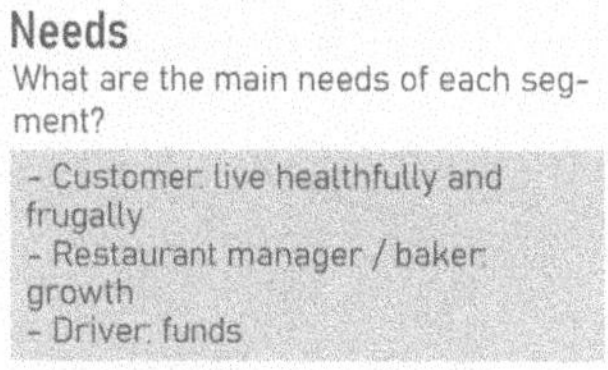

The drivers are responsible for delivering the pizza. If the drivers are not employees of the restaurant but freelancers who are paid per delivery trip, the need will probably be related to the hourly wage, which corresponds to "access to funds" (survival needs level). We articulate it here as "funds."

Needs
What are the main needs of each segment?

– Customer: live healthfully and frugally
– Restaurant manager / baker: growth
– Driver: funds

Figure 3.10: Business model - Needs

The needs of the different roles are:

► Customers: live healthfully and frugally
► Restaurant owner and manager: growth
► Baker: growth
► Driver: funds

Value proposition

Technique

A value proposition is "promise of value to be delivered, communicated, and acknowledged" [96].

A value proposition is allocated in the application domain. It addresses a need (life and/or business domain) and is realized in the involvement domain. An effective value proposition gives customers a reason to select or purchase a given product or service.

Word of Pizza

Market analysis   When the market analysis for this book was performed, three types of offerings for online food ordering were identified [97]:

► Aggregator
► New delivery
► Restaurant chain

An "aggregator" offers restaurants a platform on which to display and sell their products. Customers can explore, compare, and order. The restaurant pays a margin to aggregators for this service and handles the delivery itself. Aggregators have been on the market since 2004. Examples are Foodpanda, Grubhub, and Just Eat.

"New delivery" companies provide a product similar to that of aggregators, but in addition they handle delivery, typically with drivers as independent contractors. Restaurants pay a fixed margin (from 10 to 20 percent of the order value) to the new delivery platform. Customers also pay the platform a margin (around 10 percent) and/or a small flat fee. New delivery platforms are on the market since about 2013. Examples are Deliveroo, Delivery Hero, Uber Eats, and Foodora.

In the third type of offering, restaurant chains, the restaurants themselves offer their products directly to customers. Customer pay for the product and often a delivery fee. All the large pizza chains (Domino's, Pizza Hut, etc.) have their own apps for this purpose.

A weakness of current mobile apps The companies representing these three types of offerings make their services available through mobile applications. The new business idea of our fictitious World of Pizza example is similar to the aggregator and new delivery types.

To understand what World of Pizza intends to improve, we need to look at the navigation pattern of the mobile apps just mentioned. All these apps use the same navigation pattern: they ask the user to choose a restaurant from a list of restaurants *first* before the user can select and order one or more products from that restaurant (see Figure 3.11).

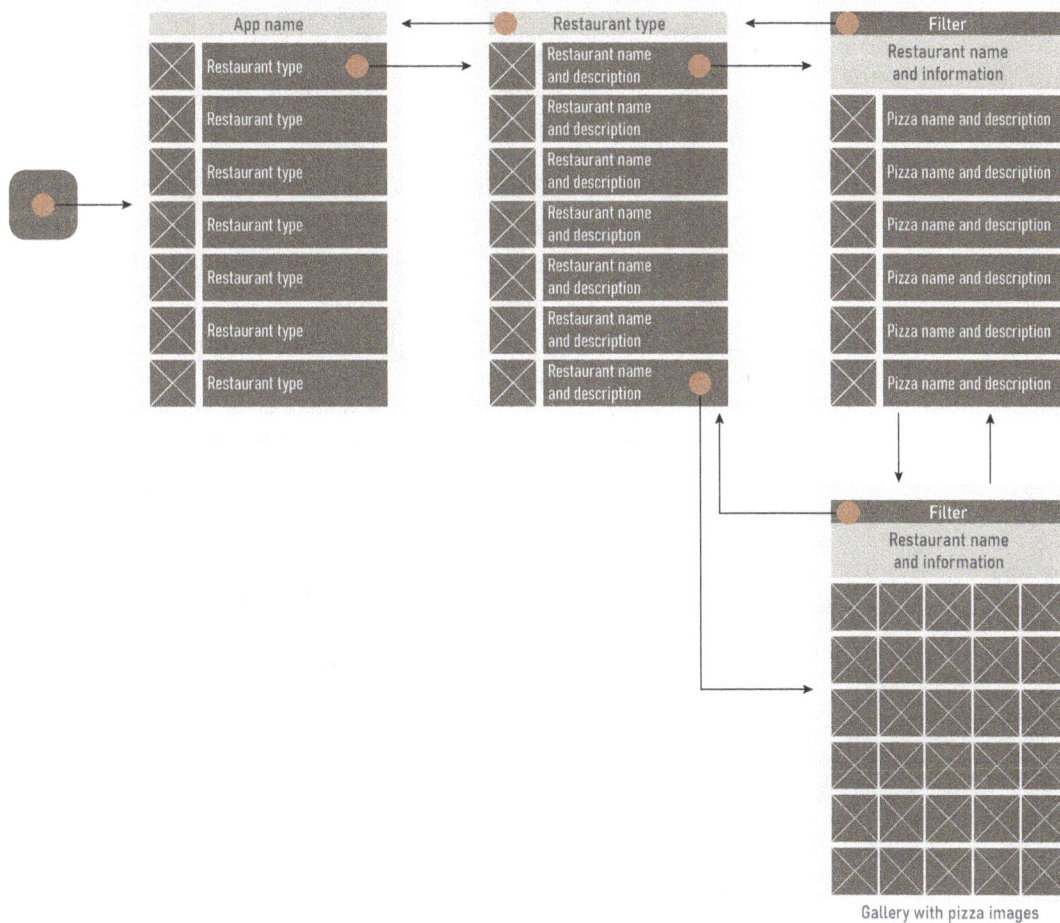

Figure 3.11: Competitor apps - navigation structure

This "restaurant-first, product-second" navigation principle has advantages and disadvantages:

▶ Advantages

• the customer can rely on the quality of a restaurant.

- When a customer orders several products in one order and thus the delivery fee is relatively low.
- The customer may get a discount for an order value that exceeds a certain threshold.
- Well-known restaurants have an advantage because of their brand reputation.

▶ Disadvantages

- Customers have difficulty to find the best pizza Margherita or (fill in the blanc) in town; best can mean "cheapest," "best quality," "best taste," "fastest," "most healthy," or a combination of these.
- Customers have difficulty seeing trends in the popularity of different pizza types (Hawaiian, Chicago style, New York style, thin crust, etc.).
- Lesser known restaurants find it challenging to be recognized, even with their best products.

Business opportunity The disadvantages of the typical navigation pattern create a business opportunity. A customer should be able to filter, find, and select a pizza first, meeting their own selection criteria, independently of which restaurant offers the pizza. The navigation principle "product first" replaces the navigation principle "restaurant first."

In other words, the pizzas should not be organized by restaurant, but by pizza categories.

World of Pizza The value proposition of the World of Pizza app is "product first." It allows customers to compare pizzas from several restaurants. The navigation principle is "product first," not "restaurant first." Pizzas are not organized by restaurant, but by pizza categories. Therefore, users can find the best, cheapest, highest quality, or fastest pizza Margherita in town. This is assumed to be more customer focused than organizing pizza by restaurant and therefore provides a richer and more beneficial experience for customers.

The principle "product first" addresses the user need "Live healthfully and frugal" better than the principle "restaurant first."

The value proposition is:

▶ Compare pizzas across restaurants ("product first")

Value proposition
What differentiates the new offering?

- Customers: compare pizzas across restaurants
- Restaurant manager: increase revenue and reduce costs
- Baker: reduce costs
- Driver: compare delivery jobs

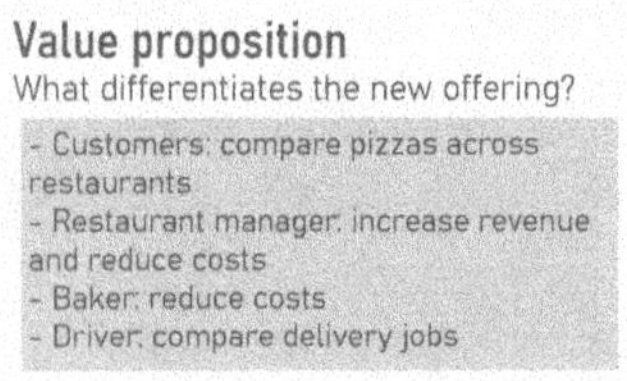

Figure 3.12: Business model - Value proposition

Offering

There is sometimes confusion about what an offering is and what a deliverable is. They are related; the deliverable is the vehicle by which the offering is realized. For instance, a mobile app (the deliverable) is the vehicle that offers pizza (the offering). Often, the offering is a service.

For pizza customers, the offering is a service that allows them to order pizza, get pizza delivered, and pay for the pizza via credit card. For a pizza restaurant, the offering is an alternative sales channel by which to sell pizza. Another offering is an optimization of restaurant processes. For the driver, the offering is to earn money by delivering pizzas.

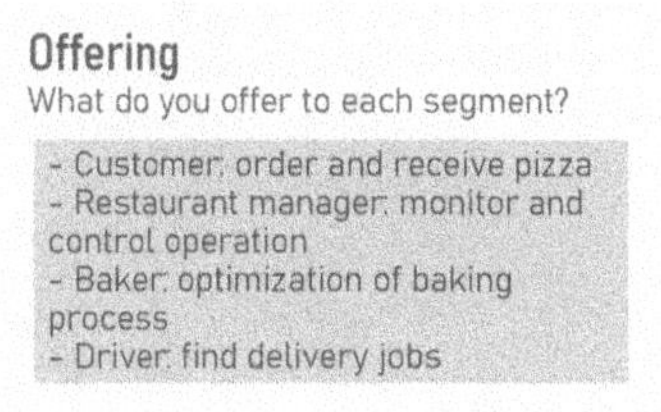

The offerings for the different roles are:

- For customers: order and receive pizza
- For restaurant owner/manager: monitor and control operation
- For baker: optimize baking process
- For driver: find delivery jobs

Offering
What do you offer to each segment?
- Customer: order and receive pizza
- Restaurant manager: monitor and control operation
- Baker: optimization of baking process
- Driver: find delivery jobs

Figure 3.13: Business model - Offering

Business goals

A business has often expectations regarding user involvement right from the start, which can have a direct influence on architecture or design decisions. We call those expectations business-motivated involvement goals, or short business goals. They are partially derived from competitor analysis and are used to strengthen the value proposition.

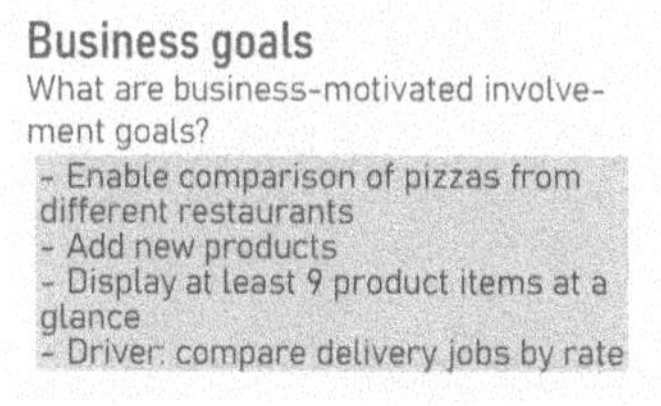

There are the following business-motivated involvement goals for WoP:

- Enable the comparison of pizzas from different restaurants ("product first")
- Enable extension of new products
- Display at least nine products at a glance[1]
- Compare delivery jobs by hourly rate

The business-motivated involvement goals will be reflected in the involvement goal matrix as vendor involvement goals (see Section 1 (Vendor involvement goals) on page 331).

Business goals
What are business-motivated involvement goals?
- Enable comparison of pizzas from different restaurants
- Add new products
- Display at least 9 product items at a glance
- Driver: compare delivery jobs by rate

Figure 3.14: Business model - Business goals; they will be used for deriving involvement goals (see Section 1 (Vendor involvement goals) on page 331.

1: This business goal is derived from Miller's law [98]. It states that humans can hold about seven items (plus or minus two) in their short-term (or working) memory. The business owner's interest is to display a maximum number of products at a glance. Because of Miller's law, the minimum number is set to nine.

Market size

Technique

Market size data provide additional useful insights. They help us understand how many customers are potentially going to use the application under design.

There are established distinctions between three different markets [99]:

▶ The total addressable market (TAM) is the total available market for a product or service. In the case of our pizza example, it's the worldwide food market.
▶ The serviceable available market (SAM) is the portion of the total addressable market that is targeted by the offered product or service. In our pizza example, it's the worldwide pizza market.
▶ The serviceable obtainable market (SOM) is the market that can realistically be reached. In our case, it's the pizza market served by pizza restaurants in a particular region.

We look here at the serviceable obtainable market (SOM).

Understanding market size helps experience professionals to make business-supporting design decisions. Knowing the market size is useful for defining the user involvement system and user involvement metrics such as system alert times and system alert frequencies (see Section 10 (Scenario views) on page 254).

World of Pizza

Market analysis   In 2019, there were 101.2 million people in the United States who ordered food online. A slight majority were female (52.5 percent) (see Figure 3.15).

United States Online Food Delivery

Gender distribution - User population: 101.2 million

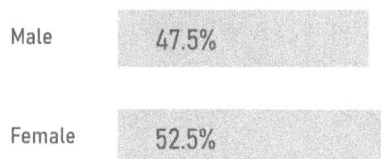

Male   47.5%

Female   52.5%

Source: Statista Global Consumer Service, October 2019

Figure 3.15: Gender distribution in online food ordering; source: Statista 2019

The sample included users from 18 to 64 years of age. About half of them were between 18 and 44 (51.9 percent), and the other half between 45 and 64 (48.1 percent) (see Figure 3.16).

United States Online Food Delivery

Age groups distribution - User population: 101.2 million

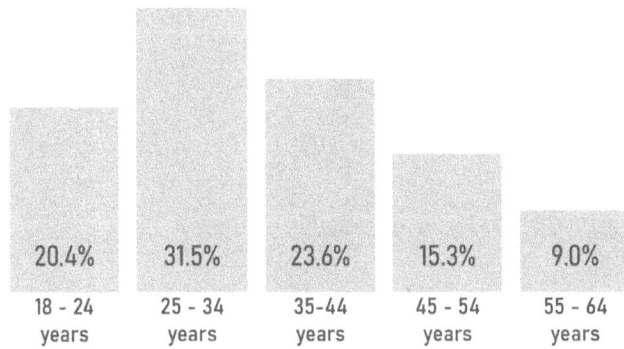

| 20.4% | 31.5% | 23.6% | 15.3% | 9.0% |
| 18 - 24 years | 25 - 34 years | 35-44 years | 45 - 54 years | 55 - 64 years |

Source: Statista Global Consumer Service, October 2019

Figure 3.16: Age distribution in online food ordering; source: Statista 2019

The majority of users were in the low- or middle-income category (75.5 percent), and the rest (24.5 percent) had a high income. The income ranges are not defined in the available data (see Figure 3.17).

United States Online Food Delivery

Income distribution - User Population: 101.2 Million

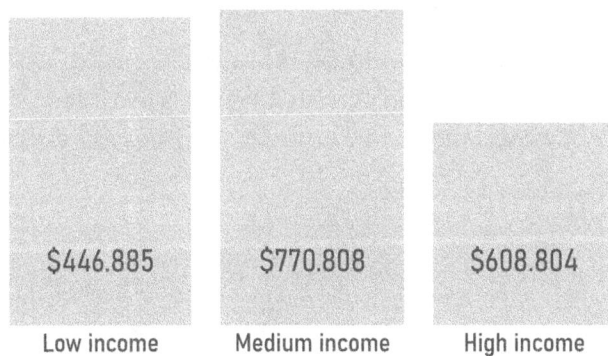

| $446.885 | $770.808 | $608.804 |
| Low income | Medium income | High income |

Source: Statista Global Consumer Service, October 2019

Figure 3.17: Income distribution in online food ordering; source: Statista 2019

The revenue generated through online ordering of food in 2020 was $23.99 billion. The revenue estimated for 2024 is about $29.22

billion, which would be an increase of 5.1 percent (see Figure 3.18).

United States Online Food Delivery

Revenue changes between 2020 and 2024 (in billion $)

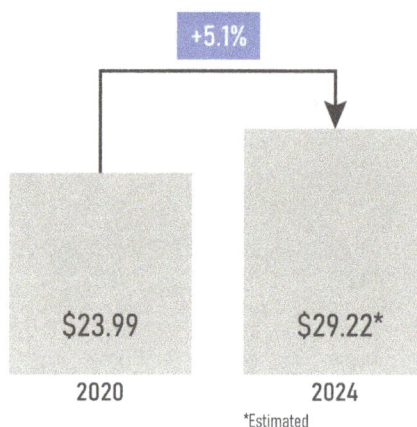

Source: www.statista.com

Figure 3.18: Revenue through online ordering of food; source: Statista 2019

The average revenue per user (ARPU) is divided between applications for platform-to-consumer delivery (aggregators and new delivery) and those for restaurant-to-consumer delivery.

The ARPU for platform-to-consumer delivery in 2017 was $167.06 and is estimated to increase to $183.07 in 2024 (growth rate: 9.6 percent). The ARPU for restaurtant-to-consumers delivery in 2017 was $198.10 and is estimated to grow to $206.27 by 2024 (growth rate: 4.1 percent) (see Figure 3.19).

Grubhub, Uber Eats, and Doordash dominate the field, with 60 percent of the market. With 25 percent, Domino's owns the largest market share as an restaurant-to-consumer app (see Figure 3.20).

United States Online Food Delivery

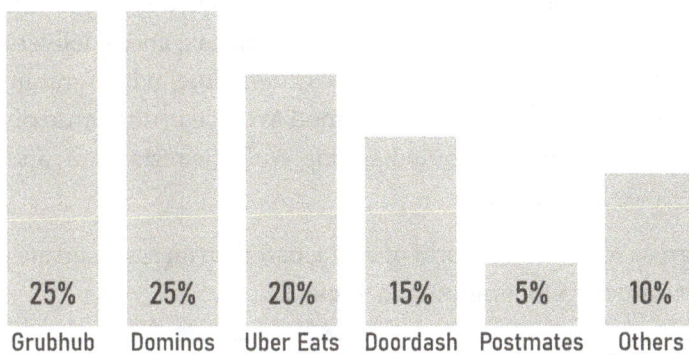

Average Revenue Per User (ARPU) in US$

Platform-to-Consumer Delivery   Restaurant-to-Consumer Delivery

+9.6%   +4.1%

$167.06 $183.07* $198.10 $206.27*

2017   2024   2017   2024

*Estimated

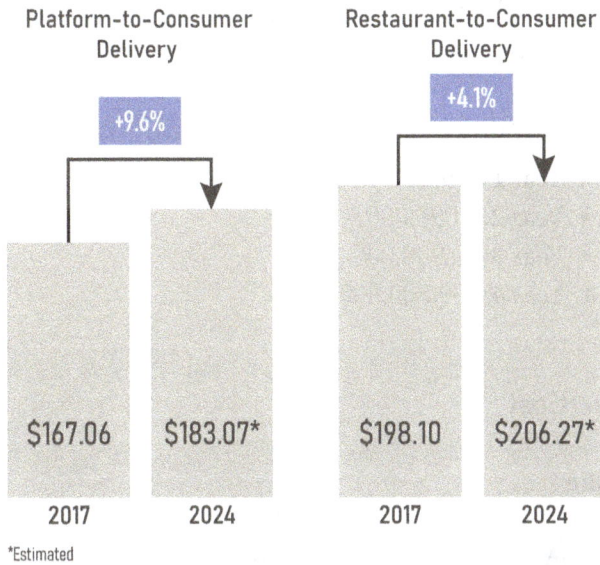

Source: Statista Global Consumer Service, October 2019

Figure 3.19: ARPU of users; source: Statista 2019

United States Online Food Delivery

Usage share

25%   25%   20%   15%   5%   10%

Grubhub   Dominos   Uber Eats   Doordash   Postmates   Others

Source: Statista Global Consumer Service,
based on Beyond Data GmbH and SimilarWeb Ltd., January 2020.

Figure 3.20: Usage share; source: Statista 2019

World of Pizza   The serviceable obtainable market (SOM) for our World of Pizza is estimated as follows:

► Number of restaurants per year that deliver pizza:

- Year 1: 100
- Year 2: 1,000
- Year 3: 10,000
- Year 4: 100,000

► Average number of orders per restaurant per day: three (1,095 per restaurant per year)

► Average number of orders per year:

- Year 1: 109,500
- Year 2: 1,095,000
- Year 3: 10,950,000
- Year 4: 109,500,000

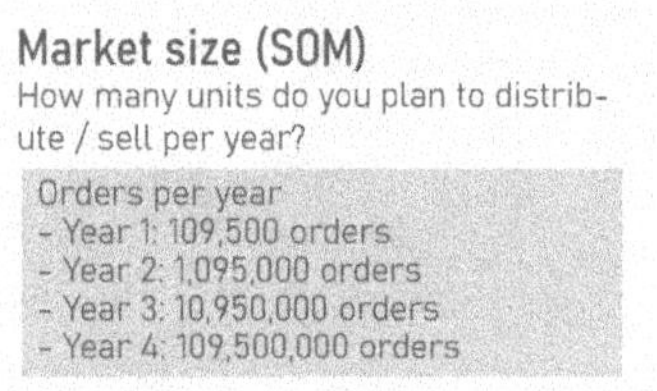

Market size (SOM)
How many units do you plan to distribute / sell per year?

Orders per year
- Year 1: 109,500 orders
- Year 2: 1,095,000 orders
- Year 3: 10,950,000 orders
- Year 4: 109,500,000 orders

Figure 3.21: Business model - Serviceable obtainable market

The University of St. Gallen in Switzerland has developed a business model navigator with more than fifty business model patterns that can assist in exploring, selecting, and configuring an appropriate business model for a business under consideration [100].

Revenue/Cost

Technique

To understand how experience architecture and design can support generated value, we need to know how value is generated. In many cases, value is generated by cost reductions, or by revenue increases, potentially both.

Revenue / cost
How to generate revenue or reduce cost?

- Gross revenue: order value plus 10% delivery fee, minimum $7.
- Cost: 70% of order value for restaurant; delivery fee -$1 for driver
- Net revenue: 25% of order value

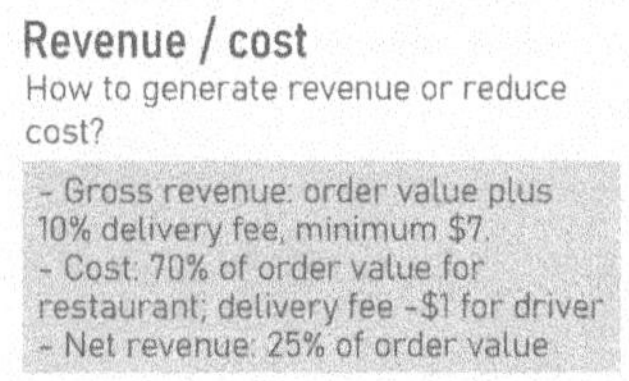

Figure 3.22: Business model - Revenue generation or cost reduction

World of Pizza

The main income for WoP comes from through a commission for each order (30 percent), plus one dollar for each delivery. Per order, the customer pays the price of the pizza, the tax, and a delivery fee. The delivery fee is 10 percent of the order value, with a minimum of seven dollar. Based on an assumed average order value of $25, the money will be distributed among WoP, the restaurant, and the driver (see Figure 3.23).

The gross revenue for World of Pizza, based on an assumed average order value of $18, is shown in Table 3.2.

Revenue item	Amount
Order value	$18.00
Delivery fee per order (10 percent of order value, minimum $7)	$7.00
Tip (18 percent of order value)	$3.24
WoP gross revenue	$28.24

Table 3.2: WoP gross revenue

WoP Gross Revenue   **WoP Cost**   **WoP Net Revenue**

	WoP Gross Revenue	Revenue Restaurant	Revenue Driver	WoP Net Revenue
Order value	$18.00	$12.60		$5.40
Delivery fee	$7.00		$6.00	$1.00
Tip (18% of order value)	$3.24		$3.24	
Total	**$28.24**	**$12.60**	**$9.24**	**$6.40**
	Customer's payment	70% of order value	Delivery fee - $1.00 100% tip	30% of order value $1 per delivery

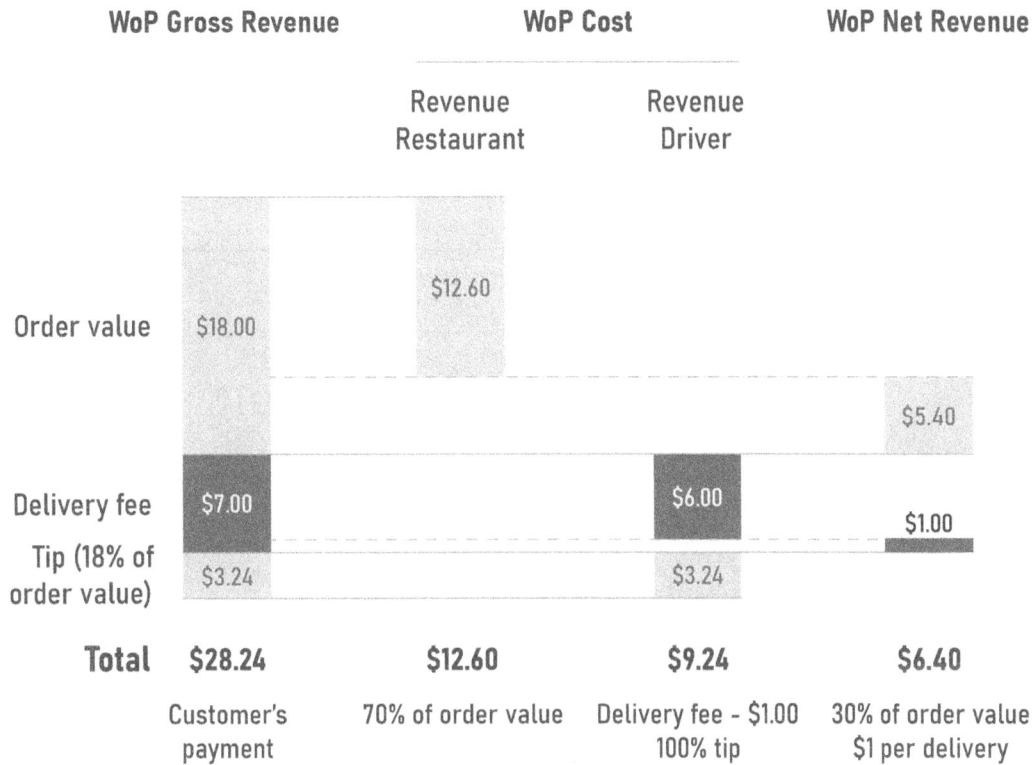

Figure 3.23: Revenue and cost distribution

The cost for World of Pizza, based on an assumed average order value of $18, is shown in Table 3.3.

Cost item	Amount
For restaurant: 70 percent of order value	$12.60
For driver: Delivery fee - $1.00	$6.00
For driver: 100 percent of paid tip	$3.24
WoP cost	$21.84

Table 3.3: WoP cost

The net revenue for World of Pizza, based on an assumed average order value of $18, is shown in Table 3.4.

Revenue item	Amount
WoP gross revenue	$28.24
WoP cost	($21.84)
WoP net revenue	$6.40

Table 3.4: WoP net revenue

WoP will keep about 25% of the gross revenue.

Based on the assumed average number of orders per restaurant and year (1.095), and the determined serviceable obtainable market, the calculated gross revenue, net revenue, and cost projections for the first four years are shown in Table 3.5 and in Figure 3.24.

Table 3.5: Net revenue projection; assumptions: three orders per restaurant per day; $25.00 average order value; 18 percent average tip (of order value).

Year	Restaurants	Orders	Gross revenue	Costs	Net revenue
Year 1	100	109,500	$3,092,280	$2,391,480	$700,800
Year 2	1,000	1,095,000	$30,922,800	$23,914,800	$7,008,000
Year 3	10,000	10,950,000	$309,228,000	$239,148,000	$70,080,000
Year 4	100,000	109,500,000	$3,092,280,000	$2,391,480,000	$700,800,000

Revenue and cost projection (in million $)

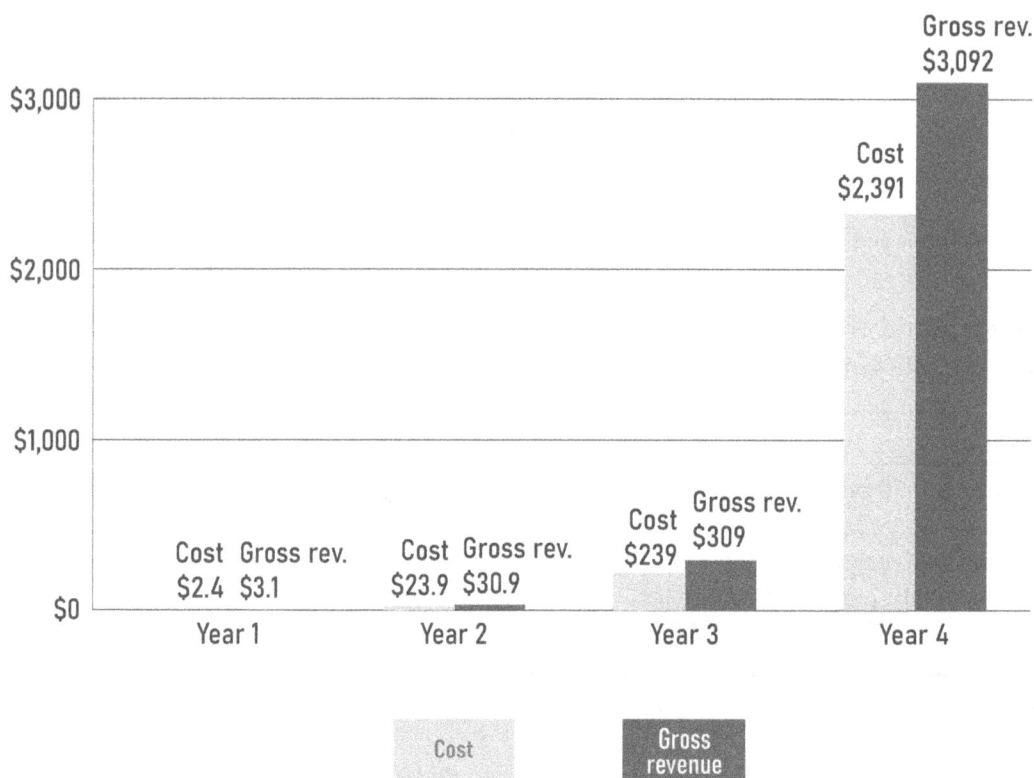

Figure 3.24: Gross revenue, cost and net revenue projection

Experience value

Technique

It is useful to state how experience architecture and design can contribute to the business model, particularly to the value proposition.

It is possible that a value proposition will not provide an opportunity for experience professionals to contribute. When defining the business model, we are still in an early stage of a project. This means that if there is no opportunity for contributions, it is early enough to leave the project without having burned through too much budget and time.

Here, we want to capture how experience architecture and design contribute to the value proposition, and how architecture and design for efficiency can contribute to it.

World of Pizza

We can now outline design directions to support the business model and the value proposition.

- ▶ For customers: Be able to efficiently search for pizzas among restaurants, while meeting the budget and dietary needs (addressed need: live healthfully and frugal)
- ▶ For restaurant manager: Improve operational efficiency; be aware of operational deviations (addressed need: growth)
- ▶ For baker: Improve operational efficiency; be aware of delays; be aware of when to restock (addressed need: growth)
- ▶ For driver: Find pizza delivery jobs with the highest hourly rate (addressed need: funds)

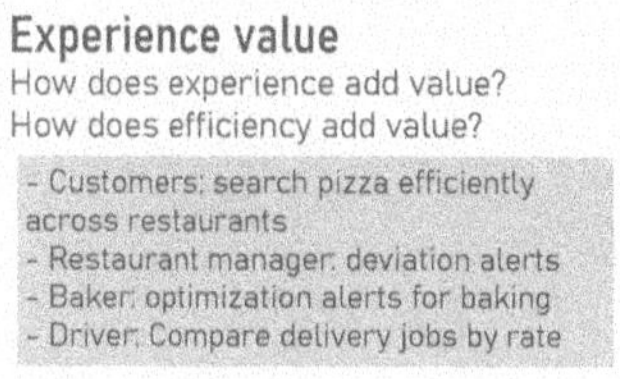

In addition to supporting the value proposition, experience contributions can also support efficiency:

- ▶ For customers: Find pizzas efficiently
- ▶ For restaurant manager: Become aware of operational deviations efficiently
- ▶ For baker: Become aware of delays and restock items efficiently
- ▶ For driver: Find pizza delivery jobs efficiently

In a nutshell, we see that experience contributions can indeed support the business model and the value proposition. We can already see an experience direction without having created any design artifacts yet.

Experience value
How does experience add value?
How does efficiency add value?

- Customers: search pizza efficiently across restaurants
- Restaurant manager: deviation alerts
- Baker: optimization alerts for baking
- Driver: Compare delivery jobs by rate

Figure 3.25: Business model - Experience value

The design principles are referred to throughout the book and summarized in Chapter 22 (Design Principles) on page 577.

The business model consideration concludes with the first design principle:

A value decision is a design decision

Which endeavor an experience architecture and design contributes to – or not – is the first decision: The "what" (application, user roles, user tasks), the "why" (needs and goals), and the "whom" (user roles) all determine the value of the experience contribution. This value decision is the first design decision.

Summary

Business model

► Move on to <u>User Involvement Metrics</u>
◄ Go back to <u>Introduction</u>

Name
What is the name of the application under design?

World of Pizza (WoP)

Segments and roles
What are the market segments?
What are the user roles per segment?

- Household: manager, member
- Company: team lead, team member, team assistant
- Restaurant: manager, baker, driver

Needs
Which need is addressed per segment and role?

- Customer: live healthfully and frugally
- Restaurant manager / baker: growth
- Driver: funds

Value proposition

- Customers: compare pizzas across restaurants
- Restaurant manager: increase revenue and reduce costs
- Baker: reduce costs
- Driver: compare delivery jobs

Offerings
What do you offer for each segment?

- Customer: order and receive pizza
- Restaurant manager: monitor and control operation
- Baker: optimization of baking process
- Driver: find delivery jobs

Business goals
What are business-motivated involvement goals?

- Enable comparison of pizzas from different restaurants
- Add new products
- Display at least 9 product items at a glance
- Driver: compare delivery jobs by rate

Revenue / Costs
How to generate revenue or reduce cost?

- Gross revenue: order value plus 10% delivery fee, minimum $7.
- Cost: 70% of order value for restaurant; delivery fee ~$1 for driver
- Net revenue: 25% of order value

Market size (SOM)
How many units do you plan to distribute / sell per year?

Orders per year:
- Year 1: 109,500 orders
- Year 2: 1,095,000 orders
- Year 3: 10,950,000 orders
- Year 4: 109,500,000 orders

Experience value
How does experience add value?
How does efficiency add value?

- Customers: search pizza efficiently across restaurants
- Restaurant manager: deviation alerts
- Baker: optimization alerts for baking
- Driver: Compare delivery jobs by rate

Key learnings

Understanding the business model helps us to understand the bigger picture. It helps us to ask better questions and recognize dependencies between the life, business, application, and involvement domains. With this knowledge, we can make decide whether we want to contribute and how to support the value proposition.

Understanding the business model is crucial for good design decisions. Otherwise, our contributions may not achieve their full potential. If there is no visible connection between experience contributions and the value proposition, we may just become decorators or beautifiers of an application and should consider passing that opportunity.

Furthermore, if the business model is weak or not well defined, you may want to think twice about whether you want to contribute to that effort. A value decision is a design decision. A weak value proposition and business model can hardly lead to a strong design.

Tips and tricks

To elicit the business model, I suggest running a workshop. People in the following roles should be invited: product manager, technical lead, project manager, experience architect.

I've done this exercise in different documentation formats, in each case mapping the business model with nine squares: (a) I used a 23 x 33-inch posterboard and wrote the content on sticky notes. (b) I used a large white board, which I had prepared with the topics in the grid (in black). The group provided the content, which I filled into the grid (in red) for better readability. (c) I have simply used a large sheet of paper (11 x 17) in a workshop format with different groups. Each group had a booklet with templates for the business model, journey map etc., where they made notes.

I recommend using a whiteboard for the following reasons: First, you can easily make changes (which is also possible with sticky notes, but not so good with the booklet). Second, you can read the notes on the whiteboard from two to five meters, of five and a half yards (which is not possible with the sticky notes or the booklet).

One disadvantage of the booklet is that after you turn a page, you cannot see the content on the previous page anymore. You don't have this problem with posters and the whiteboard. If you offer this exercise as a service, the posters look most professional; however, they are not very practical to transport.

The whiteboard is the most practical and environmentally friendly solution. After the completion, you take a picture of the whiteboard and digitalize the content, for example on a slide. You can do the same, of course, with sticky notes and with the booklet.

I recommend reserving 90 minutes for a business model session. If the business model is already developed, one session is most likely sufficient. If the business model is not fully developed, follow-up sessions may be needed.

Exercise 1.2

Goal Identify the business model for the selected example.

Material Business model template; whiteboard or sticky notes, markers.

Completion criteria:

- ▶ The business model template is filled out.
- ▶ How experience architecture / design contributes to the value proposition is documented.
- ▶ How experience architecture / design contributes to experience value and efficiency is documented.

User Involvement Metrics 4

Jeder Zustand, ja, jeder Augenblick ist von unendlichem Wert.
(Each situation, indeed, each moment is of infinite value.)
Johann Wolfgang von Goethe

Motivation

Professionals tend to speak in their industry's jargon and expect that everyone else understands it. Think about a plumber who talks about the quality of a grease or a solder. You may be smiling right now. Now think about how often you've heard someone explain experience design by talking about user journey maps, wire frames, diary studies, and design systems. The term *user journey map* is like the plumber's grease – it's jargon that doesn't mean much to those who are not experience professionals.

When talking about design, it is beneficial to use a language that is comprehensible for non-experience professionals. One of those languages is numbers. Don't be afraid of them; if you can solve this equation: $5 + 8 = x$, or this one: $\frac{15}{5} = y$, you are capable of following the explanations in this metrics section. Numbers are very useful and applying them properly makes the speaker appear competent – a very advantageous effect in a domain where personal opinions and preferences are still often used to make decisions. Numbers can help us to make decisions more objectively more often.

The lingua franca for quantities is Arabic numerals, also known as the Hindu-Arabic numeral system. It was invented between the first and forth centuries AC, by Indian mathematicians. It is a positional decimal numeral system [101]. Many cultures worldwide have adopted it [102]. Even if you don't speak the language of a country or region, you will most likely be able to negotiate a price on the farmer's market in that country or region. Numbers help to increase confidence in negotiations [103]. Why? Because numbers are well

I was once hired to design an engineering tool. It was the first time the project team had worked with an experience professional. I went through the normal design process, applied many standard tools and techniques, and had weekly user group meetings [104]. I used design goals (see Chapter 12 (Involvement Goals) on page 313) to justify design decisions and the selection of interaction concepts. Senior management started to talk about "usability," as they called it. The interesting point is how they talked about it. They said, "Usability will help to increase the efficiency by *40 percent*." That's it. They always mentioned the 40 percent when they talked about the reason for bringing usability on board. Why? Because it was a language they understood; the 40 percent was business-relevant, and they felt comfortable talking about "usability" with a number. Since then, I call it the *40 percent language*.

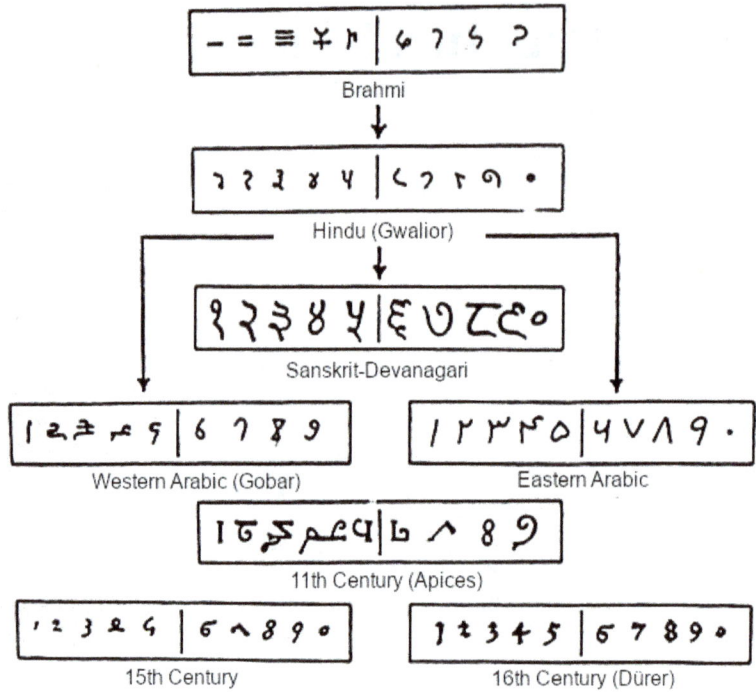

Figure 4.1: History of Arabic numerals; source: Wikimedia; creator: Tobus; license: CC BY-SA 4.0

understood across professions, countries, ages, education levels, genders, religions etc. They express determination, confidence, skill, objectivity, measurability, and predictability. Using numbers reduces the risk of misunderstandings. We can utilize this fact for defining, measuring, and communicating the quantity of some aspects of experience architecture and design.

To be able to talk in numbers, we are going to introduce a set of metrics called *User Involvement Metrics*.

If you think you're not ready for this chapter, don't worry. You may skip it for now and come back to it after you have read other parts of the book.

User involvement metrics

Metric taxonomy

The term *metric* is used for a quantitative measurement that is mathematically specified. Example: The time it takes to order and receive one pizza. The word *measurement* is used to express a measured value for a metric. Example: It took 43 minutes (the measurement) to order and receive one pizza (the metric).

Human-computer interaction metrics are not new. There are known metrics and measurements for keystrokes [54] as well as for "time-on-task," e.g., summative usability tests [50] [52, p. 10]. The established metrics and measurements focus on user steps (keystroke-level model, or KLM) and on user tasks.

The established metrics and measurements have the following limitations:

► They focus on activities, measuring user interaction and user tasks. They do not consider measurements relative to an outcome of value.

► They focus on user interaction. They do not measure different types of user intervention, for example, how often an application requests a decision from a user or how long it takes a user to respond to a decision request.

► They measure time. They do not measure frequencies of user involvement.

To broaden metrics beyond time-on-task, we introduce what is called here *user involvement metrics taxonomy* [105, 106]. The metrics are called *user involvement metrics*, abbreviated *UIMs*. They reflect the two previously introduced user involvement types: user interaction and user intervention (see Figure 4.2 and also Section 1 (Interaction and intervention) on page 26).

The UIMs consists of five *basic* metrics (hands-on, waiting, walk-away, system alert, and user response) and three *derived* metrics (user interaction, user intervention, and user involvement) (see Figure 4.3).

For basic metrics, time and frequencies can be measured. For instance, hands-on time and waiting time expresses "time-on-task" in user interactions. In user interventions, system alert frequency and user response frequency measure how often an application informs the user about a certain state and how often the user responds that alert. User response time expresses how long it takes a user to respond to a system alert. Walk-away time expresses how long a user can be away from an application doing something else while the application is performing a task (semi)automatically. Walk-away frequency expresses how often the user can walk away from an application to do something else.

For derived metrics, time, frequencies, and productivity can be measured. For instance, it can be measured how long it takes for a user to perform one or more user tasks to generate one outcome of value (time metric). Derived metrics can also measure the frequency. For instance, it can be measured how often a user performs an action, step, or user task to generate an outcome of value (frequency). It can also be measured how many outcomes of value are generated within a certain amount of time (productivity metric).

User involvement (VO) consists of interaction, intervention, or both. User involvement is a metric for user tasks and for the generation of an outcome of value consisting of one or more user tasks. It is measured in time, frequency, and productivity. The involvement time begins with the start of the first user task and

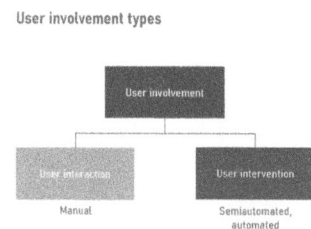

Figure 4.2: User involvement types

User involvement metric taxonomy

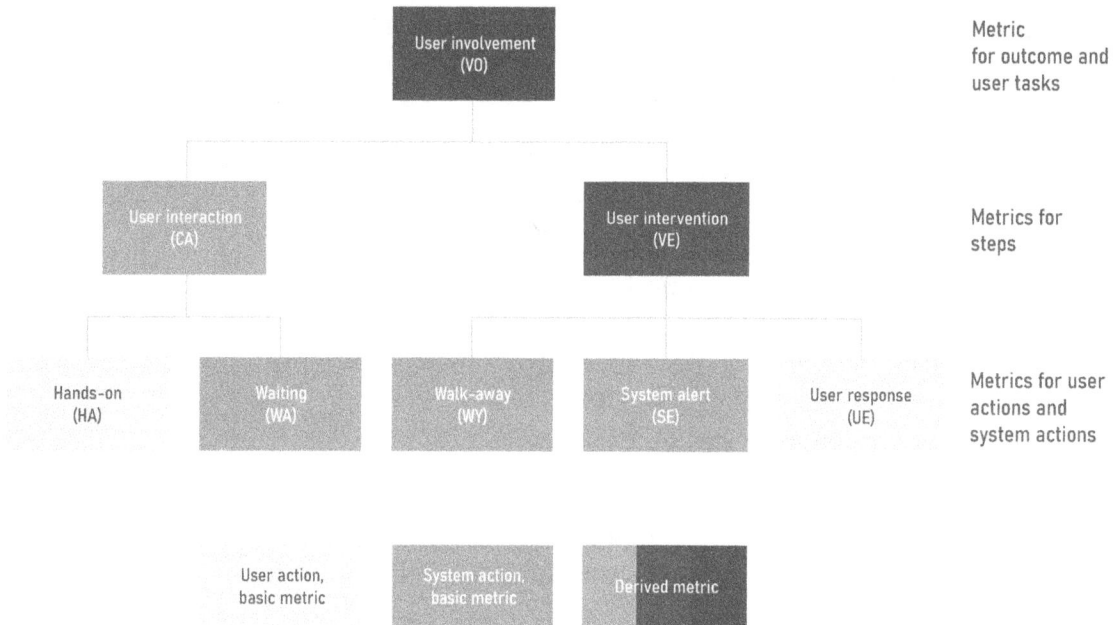

Figure 4.3: User involvement metric taxonomy

ends with the completion of the last user task that generates the outcome of value. The user involvement time is the sum of user interaction times (CAT) and/or user intervention times (VET). It is a metric for user tasks and for the generated outcome of value.

▶ **User interaction (CA)** User interaction is the sequence of hands-on and waiting. It can be measured in time and frequency. The interaction time is the sum of hands-on time (HAT) and waiting time (WAT). User interaction is a metric for steps consisting of user and system actions.

- **Hands-on (HA)** A user interacts with a system and drives the task completion forward. Hands-on can be measured in time and frequency. The time counter typically begins when the user starts perceiving and cognitively processing the presented content and controls. It ends when the user has completed a data entry or has triggered a control. Hands-on is a metric for user actions.

- **Waiting (WA)** A system processes the user's input and updates the system output (which becomes input for the user). Waiting can be measured in time and frequency. The waiting time starts after the user has triggered a control, so that the system can process the entered content, and it ends when the system has completed the process and has completely rendered content and controls perceivable for users. Waiting is a metric for system actions.

▶ **User intervention (VE)** User intervention consists of walk-away, system alert, and user response. It can be measured in time and frequency. The elapsed intervention time is the sum of the elapsed walk-away time (WYT), the elapsed system alert time (SET), and the elapsed user response time (UET). User intervention is a metric for steps, consisting of walk-away, system alert, and user response actions.

- **Walk-away (WY)** Walk-away expresses the idea that a user can walk away from a system while the system performs a task without the need for the user to provide inputs. Walk-away is measured in time and frequency. The walk-away time starts after a user has initiated a system task and ends when the system has finished presenting content and controls for the user. Walk-away is a metric for system actions.

- **System alert (SE)** System alert is the process of providing an alert to the user as a response to an incident. It is measured in time and frequency. The system alert time starts when an incident occurs and ends when the system has presented an alert to the user about that incident. System alert is a metric for system actions.

- **User response (UE)** The user response is the user's process of constructively responding to a system alert. It is measured in time and frequency. The user response time starts when the system alert is perceivable to the user and ends when the user has formulated a constructive response cognitively or when the user has triggered a responsive action. User response is a metric for user actions.

Each single action (user action or system action) is assigned to one of the five basic metrics. A sequence of actions forms a step. Depending on whether the actions are "interaction" actions or "intervention" actions, the step is identified either a user interaction or a user intervention. A sequence of steps forms a user task. Each user task and sequence of user tasks that generate the outcome of value is assigned to the derived metric "user involvement." The user involvement metric can consist of a sequence of user interaction metrics, a sequence of user intervention metrics, or a sequence of mixed user interaction and user intervention metrics (see Figure 4.4).

Today's applications are becoming increasingly complex. They often consist of multiple software elements as well as hardware

Assignments of actions to steps to tasks & outcome of value

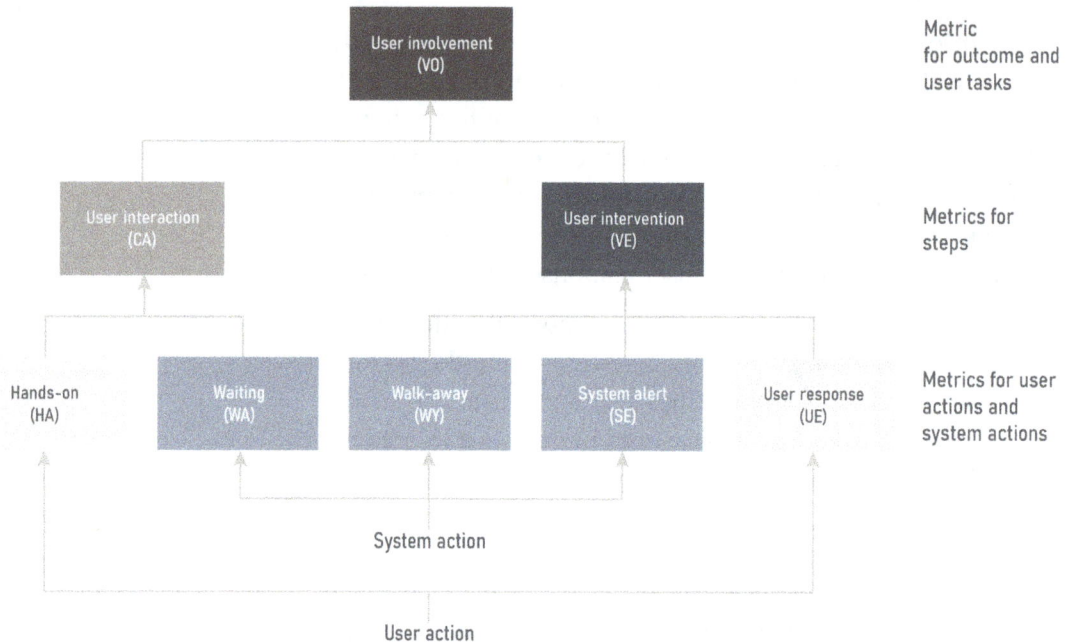

Figure 4.4: Mapping of actions to steps, steps to tasks, and tasks to outcome of value

systems (like IoT devices). Some of their processes are automated, so user involvement is purposely not needed or only partially needed. If a process is automated and takes a while, the user can walk away and do something else. In vitro diagnostic devices are examples of systems that are designed with walk-away time in mind [36]. The walk-away metric was introduced so that we can measure walk-away time and walk-away frequency for (semi)automated processes. Waiting time should always be minimized but walk-away time should sometimes be maximized and sometimes minimized, depending on the scenario. The walk-away metric is very interesting and is elaborated on in Section 1 (Walk-away metrics) on page 97 of this chapter.

Metric samples

The metric is composed of five elements: calculation, user involvement type, unit, index, (activity,scope)":

▶ Calculation: Defines the calculation formula and applies to all metric with the exception of single user or system actions
▶ User involvement type: Defines which user involvement type is being measured

- ▶ Unit: Defines what is measured, typically time or frequency
- ▶ Index: Expresses specific cases of a metric
- ▶ Activity: Defines the user or system activity for which the metric should be calculated
- ▶ Scope: Defines the larger scope for which an activity should be calculated

Sample values for calculations are as follows:

- ▶ (None): There is no parameter for frequency metrics or for basic time metrics for single actions.
- ▶ E: for elapsed time
- ▶ N: for net involvement time
- ▶ T: for total involvement time
- ▶ RE: for the ratio between an elapsed time of choice and the elapsed user involvement time
- ▶ P: for productivity, the outcome of value relative to a time metric or a frequency metric

To specify the type of user involvement, the following letters are used:

- ▶ Hands-on (HA): Identifies a user-initiated hands-on action
- ▶ Waiting (WA): Identifies a waiting period for users, a system-initiated action
- ▶ Walk-away (WY): Identifies a walk-away, a system-initiated action
- ▶ System alert (SE): Identifies a system alert action
- ▶ User response (UE): Identifies a user response action
- ▶ User interaction (CA): Identifies an interaction step consisting of one or more actions
- ▶ User intervention (VE): Identifies an intervention step consisting of one or more actions
- ▶ User involvement (VO): Identifies one or more user tasks or a generated outcome of value
- ▶ User actions (UA): Identifies all user-initiated action (i.e., hands-on, user response)
- ▶ System actions (SA): Identifies all system initiated actions (i.e., waiting, walk-away, system alert)

For units, two letters are used:

- ▶ Time metrics (T), answering the question, How long does it take?
- ▶ Frequency metrics (F), answering the question, How often does it occur?

For indexes, two letters are used:

▶ Dependent user actions or steps (D), influencing the elapsed user involvement time

▶ Independent user actions or user steps (I), not influencing the elapsed user involvement time.

For activities, the following values are used:

▶ Action (A): Measurement for one or more actions
▶ Step (S): Measurement for a one or more steps
▶ User task (U): Measurement for a one or more user tasks

For scope, the following values are used:

▶ Action (A): Measurement for one or more actions
▶ Step (S): Measurement for a one or more steps
▶ User task (U): Measurement for a one or more user tasks
▶ Outcome (O): Measurement for generating one or more outcomes of value

The metric syntax is described in more detail in Section 23 (Metric syntax) on page 580.

Sample metrics are shown in Table 4.1.

Table 4.1: User involvement sample metrics. **Calculation**: N = net time; T = total time; E = elapsed time; P = productivity; R = relative. **Metric**: HA = hands-on; WA = waiting; WY = walk-away; SE = system alert; UE = user response. **Unit**: T = time; F = frequency. **Parameters**: A = action; S = step; U= user task; O = outcome

Metric description	Time metric	Frequency metric
Hands-on actions per outcome O	HAT(A,O)	HAF(A,O)
Waiting action per outcome O	WAT(A,O)	WAF(A,O)
Walk-away action per outcome O	WYT(A,O)	WYF(A,O)
System alert action per outcome O	SET(A,O)	SEF(A,O)
User response action per outcome O	UET(A,O)	UEF(A,O)
Elapsed hands-on time for user task(s) U per outcome O	EHAT(U,O)	-
Elapsed waiting time for user task(s) U per outcome O	EWAT(U,O)	-
Elapsed walk-away time for user task(s) U per outcome O	EWYT(U,O)	-
Elapsed system alert time for user task(s) U per outcome O	ESET(U,O)	-
Elapsed user response time for user task(s) U per outcome O	EUET(U,O)	-
Elapsed user action time for user task(s) U per outcome O	EUAT(U,O)	-
User action frequency for user task(s) U per outcome O	-	UAF(U,O)
Elapsed system action time for user task(s) U per outcome O	ESAT(U,O)	-
System action frequency for user task(s) U per outcome O	-	SAF(U,O)
Elapsed user interaction time for user step S per outcome O	ECAT(S,O)	-
User interaction frequency for user step S per outcome O	-	CAF(S,O)
Elapsed user intervention time for user step S per outcome O	EVET(S,O)	-
User intervention frequency for user step S per outcome O	-	VEF(S,O)
Elapsed user involvement time for user task(s) U per outcome O	EVOT(U,O)	-
Total user involvement time for user task(s) U per outcome O	TVOT(U,O)	-
Net user involvement time for user task(s) U per outcome O	NVOT(U,O)	-
Relative elapsed hands-on time for user task(s) U per outcome O	REHAT(U,O)	-
Relative elapsed waiting time for user task(s) U per outcome O	REWAT(U,O)	-
Relative elapsed walk-away time for user task(s) U per outcome O	REWYT(U,O)	-
Relative elapsed system alert time for user task(s) U per outcome O	RESET(U,O)	-
Relative elapsed user response time for user task(s) U per outcome O	REUET(U,O)	-
Relative elapsed user action time for user task(s) U per outcome O	REUAT(U,O)	-
Relative elapsed system action time for user task(s) U per outcome O	RESAT(U,O)	-
Outcome(s) O per elapsed user involvement time T	PEVOT(T)	-
Outcome(s) O per user task frequency	-	$PVOF_U(F)$
Outcome(s) O per user step frequency	-	$PVOF_S(F)$
Outcome(s) O per user action frequency	-	$PVOF_A(F)$

The most often used metrics are:

▶ $EVOT(UT_{1..n}, O)$, the elapsed user involvement time for all user tasks to generate an outcome of value.
▶ $ECAT(UT_{1..n}, O)$, the elapsed user interaction time for all user tasks to generate an outcome of value.
▶ $EVET(UT_{1..n}, O)$, the elapsed user intervention time for all user tasks to generate an outcome of value.

Time metrics for WoP

To show how the metrics are used, we introduce measurement samples for the World of Pizza example (see Figure 4.5).

User task, consisting of several steps	Step, consisting of several actions	User actions and system actions			
UT 1 Select pizza (VO$_1$)	S 1-1 Open app (CA$_1$)	A 1-U 3 sec Open app (HA$_1$)	A 2-S 5 sec App displays pizza list (WA$_1$)		
	S 1-2 Select filter (CA$_2$)	A 1-U 4 sec Select filter area (HA$_2$)	A 2-S 3 sec Display filter area (WA$_2$)	A 3-U 5 sec Select and ativate filters (HA$_3$)	A 4-S 3 sec Update pizza list (WA$_3$)
	S 1-3 Select pizza (CA$_3$)	A 1-U 25 sec Review pizza list (HA$_4$)	A 2-U 1 sec Select pizza (HA$_5$)	A 3-S 3 sec Display single pizza (WA$_4$)	
	S 1-4 Review pizza (CA$_4$)	A 1-U 15 sec Review pizza (HA$_6$)	A 2-U 1 sec Select pizza (HA$_7$)		
UT 2 Order pizza (VO$_2$)	S 2-1 Check out pizza (CA$_5$)	A 1-U 47 sec Check out pizza (HA$_8$)	A 2-S 5 sec Display order summary (WA$_5$)	A 3-U 17 sec Submit order (HA$_9$)	A 4-S 8 sec Display order confirmation (WA$_6$)
	S 2-2 Review order confirmation (CA$_6$)	A 1-U 4 sec Review order confirmation (HA$_{10}$)			
UT 3 Monitor status (VO$_3$)	S 3-1 Monitor status (VE$_{0,1}$)	A 1-S 2940 sec Bake & deliver pizza (WY$_1$)	A 2-U* 9 sec Request status (HA$_{11,12,13}$)	A 3-S* 15 sec Display status (SE$_{1,2,3}$)	A 4-U* 12 sec Review status (UE$_{1,2,3}$)

*Action is performed three times per order.

User task, consisting of several steps	Step, consisting of several actions	User actions and system actions				
UT 4 Receive pizza (VO$_4$)	S 4-1 Open door (VE$_{0,1}$)	A 1-S 5 sec Ring doorbell (SE$_4$)	A 2-U 20 sec Open door (UE$_4$)			
	S 4-2 Receive pizza (CA$_7$)	A 1-S 14 sec Hand over pizza box (WA$_7$)	A 2-U 5 sec Receive pizza box (HA$_{14}$)			
	S 4-3 Tip driver (CA$_8$)	A 1-S 3 sec Display tip options (WA$_8$)	A 2-U 5 sec Select tip option (HA$_{15}$)	A 3-S 4 sec Display tip summary (WA$_9$)	A 4-U 5 sec Submit tip (HA$_{16}$)	A 5-S 7 sec Display tip confirmation (WA$_{10}$)
	S 4-4 Review tip confirmation (CA$_9$)	A 1-U 4 sec Review tip confirmation (HA$_{17}$)	A 2-U 1 sec Close app (HA$_{18}$)	A 3-S 1 sec App closes (WA$_{11}$)		

Figure 4.5: Decomposition of user tasks, steps, and actions

UT.1
Select pizza (VO₁)

| S.1-1 Open app (CA₁) | | S.1-2 Select filter (CA₂) | | | | S.1-3 Select pizza (CA₃) | | | S.1-4 Review pizza (CA₄) | |

| A.1-U (HA₁) | A.2-S (WA₁) | A.1-U (HA₂) | A.2-S (WA₂) | A.3-U (HA₃) | A.4-S (WA₃) | A.1-U (HA₄) | A.2-U (HA₅) | A.3-S (WA₄) | A.1-U (HA₆) | A.2-U (HA₇) |

3 sec / 5 sec / 4 sec / 3 sec / 5 sec / 3 sec / 25 sec / 1 sec / 3 sec / 15 sec / 1 sec

UT.2
Order pizza (VO₂)

| S.2-1 Check out pizza (CA₅) | | | | S.2-2 Review ... (CA₆) |

| A.1-U (HA₈) | A.2-S (WA₅) | A.3-U (HA₉) | A.4-S (WA₆) | A.1-U (HA₁₀) |

47 sec / 5 sec / 17 sec / 8 sec / 4 sec

UT.3
Monitor status (VO₃)

S.3-1
Monitor status (VE_D.1)

| A.1-S (WY₁ⱼ) | A.2-U (HA₁₁,₁₂,₁₃) | A.3-S* (SE₁,₂,₃) | A.4-U* (UE₁,₂,₃) |

2940 sec / 9 sec / 15 sec / 12 sec

*Action is performed three times per order.

UT.4
Receive pizza(VO₄)

| S.4-1 Open door (VE_D.2) | | S.4-2 Receive pizza (CA₇) | | S.4-3 Tip driver (CA₈) | | | | | S.4-4 Review tip confirmation (CA₉) | | |

| A.1-S (SE₄) | A.2-U (UE₄) | A.1-S (WA₇) | A.2-U (HA₁₄) | A.1-S (WA₈) | A.2-U (HA₁₅) | A.3-S (WA₉) | A.4-U (HA₁₆) | A.5-S (WA₁₀) | A.1-U (HA₁₇) | A.2-U (HA₁₈) | A.3-S (WA₁₁) |

5 sec / 20 sec / 14 sec / 5 sec / 3 sec / 5 sec / 4 sec / 5 sec / 7 sec / 4 sec / 1 sec / 1 sec

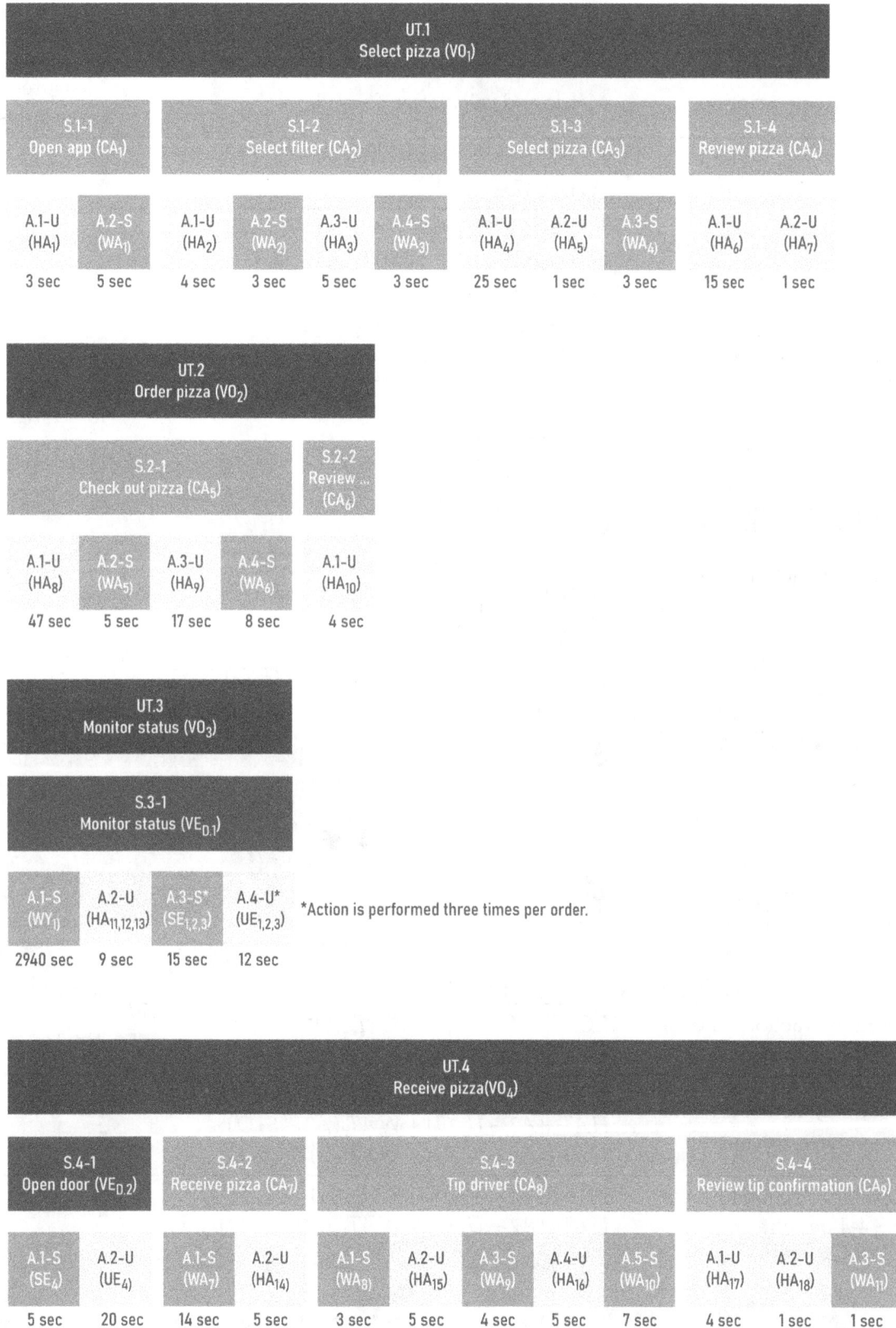

Figure 4.6: Assignment of actions, steps, and user tasks to metrics

Measurements for the user tasks and steps are shown in Table 4.2:

Table 4.2: Time metrics for WoP example

Time metric description	Metric and calculation formula	Measurement (in seconds)
Elapsed interaction time for step S 1-1 per outcome O	$ECAT_1(S1-1,O) = HAT_1(A1-U,O) + WAT_1(A2-S,O)$	$8 = 3 + 5$
Elapsed interaction time for step S 1-2 per outcome O	$ECAT_2(S1-2,O) = HAT_2(A1-U,O) + WAT_3(A2-S,O) + HAT_3(A3-U,O) + WAT_3(A4-S,O)$	$15 = 4+3+5+3$
Elapsed interaction time for step S 1-3 per outcome O	$ECAT_3(S1-3,O) = HAT_4(A1-U,O) + HAT_5(A2-U,O) + WAT_4(A3-S,O)$	$29 = 25+1+3$
Elapsed interaction time for step S 1-4 per outcome O	$ECAT_4(S1-4,O) = HAT_6(A1-U,O) + HAT_7(A2-U,O)$	$16 = 15+1$
Elapsed involvement time for user task UT 1 per outcome O	$EVOT_1(UT1,O) = ECAT_1(S1-1,O) + ECAT_2(S1-2,O) + ECAT_3(S1-3,O) + ECAT_4(S1-4,O)$	$68 = 8+15+29+16$
Elapsed interaction time for step S 2-1 per outcome O	$ECAT_5(S2-1,O) = HAT_8(A1-U,O) + WAT_5(A2-S,O) + HAT_9(A3-U,O) + WAT_6(A4-S,O)$	$77 = 47+5+17+8$
Elapsed interaction time for step S 2-2 per outcome O	$ECAT_6(S2-2,O) = HAT_{10}(A1-U,O)$	4
Elapsed involvement time for user task UT 2 per outcome O	$EVOT_2(UT2,O) = ECAT_5(S2-1,O) + ECAT_6(S2-2,O)$	$81 = 77+4$
Elapsed intervention time for step S 3-1 per outcome O	$EVET_1(S3-1,O) = WYT_1(A1-S,O) + HAT_{11,12,13}(A2-U,O) + SET_{1,2,3}(A3-S,O) + UET_{1,2,3}(A4-U,O)$	$2976 = (49 \times 60) + (3 \times 3) + (3 \times 5) + (3 \times 4)$
Elapsed involvement time for user task UT 3 per outcome O	$EVOT_3(UT3,O) = WYT_1(A1-S,O)$	2940
Elapsed intervention time for step S 4-1 per outcome O	$EVET_2(S4-1,O) = SET_4(A1-S,O) + UET_4(A2-U,O)$	$25 = 5+20$
Elapsed interaction time for step S 4-2 per outcome O	$ECAT_7(S4-2,O) = WAT_7(A1-S,O) + HAT_{14}(A2-U,O)$	$19 = 14+5$
Elapsed interaction time for step S 4-3 per outcome O	$ECAT_8(S4-3,O) = WAT_8(A1-S,O) + HAT_{15}(A2-U,O) + WAT_9(A3-S,O) + HAT_{16}(A4-U,O) + WAT_{10}(A5-S,O)$	$24 = 3+5+4+5+7$
Elapsed interaction time for step S 4-4 per outcome O	$ECAT_9(S4-4,O) = HAT_{17}(A1-U,O) + HAT_{18}(A2-U,O) + WAT_{11}(A3-S,O)$	$6 = 4+1+1$
Elapsed involvement time for user task UT 4 per outcome O	$EVOT_4(UT4,O) = EVET_2(S4-1,O) + ECAT_7(S4-2,O) + ECAT_8(S4-3,O) + ECAT_9(S4-4,O)$	$74 = 25+19+24+6$
Elapsed involvement time for all user tasks per outcome O	$EVOT(UT_{1..4},O) = EVOT_1(UT1,O) + EVOT_2(UT2,O) + EVOT_3(UT3,O) + EVOT_4(UT4,O)$	$3163 = 68+81+2940+74$

Absolute, derived time metrics and measurements for all user tasks
are shown in Table 4.3:

Table 4.3: Absolute, derived time metrics for WoP example

Time metric description	Time metric and calculation formula	Time measurement (in seconds)
Elapsed hands-on time for all user tasks per outcome O	$EHAT(UT_{1..n}, O) = \sum_{i=1}^{4} EHAT(UT_i, O)$	$151 = 54 + 68 + 9 + 20$
Elapsed waiting time for all user tasks per outcome O	$EWAT(UT_{1..n}, O) = \sum_{i=1}^{4} EWAT(UT_i, O)$	$56 = 14 + 13 + 0 + 29$
Elapsed walk-away time for all user tasks per outcome O	$EWYT(UT_{1..n}, O) = \sum_{i=1}^{4} EWYT(UT_i, O)$	$2940 = 0 + 0 + 2940 + 0$
Elapsed system alert time for all user tasks per outcome O	$ESET(UT_{1..n}, O) = \sum_{i=1}^{4} ESET(UT_i, O)$	$20 = 0 + 0 + 15 + 5$
Elapsed user response time for all user tasks per outcome O	$EUET(UT_{1..n}, O) = \sum_{i=1}^{4} EUET(UT_i, O)$	$32 = 0 + 0 + 12 + 20$
Elapsed user action time for all user tasks per outcome O	$EUAT(UT_{1..n}, O) = EHAT(UT_{1..n}, O) + EUET(UT_{1..n}, O)$	$183 = 151 + 32$
Elapsed system action time for all user tasks per outcome O	$ESAT(UT_{1..n}, O) = EWAT(UT_{1..n}, O) + EWYT(UT_{1..n}, O) + ESET(UT_{1..n}, O)$	$3016 = 56 + 2940 + 20$
Elapsed user interaction time for all user tasks per outcome O	$ECAT(UT_{1..n}, O) = \sum_{i=1}^{4} ECAT(UT_i, O)$	$198 = 68 + 81 + 0 + 49$
Elapsed user intervention time for all user tasks per outcome O	$EVET(UT_{1..n}, O) = \sum_{i=1}^{4} EVET(UT_i, O)$	$3001 = 0 + 0 + 2976 + 25$

Relative time metrics are calculated by dividing one metric by
another. The result is a percentage value. Relative time metrics and
measurements for the World of Pizza example are shown in Figure
4.7.

Specific elapsed time metrics

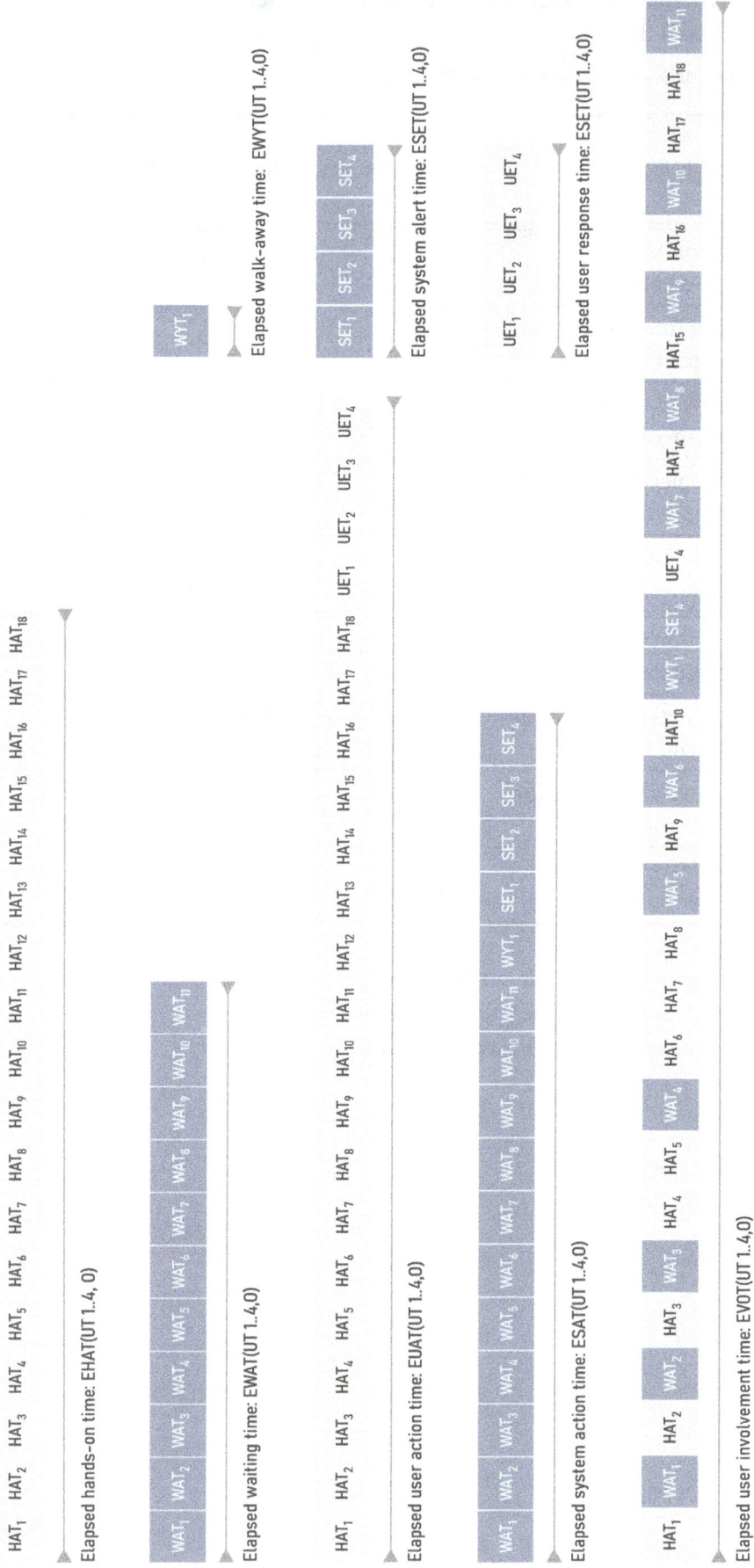

Figure 4.7: Elapsed user involvement time metrics

Relative time metrics and measurements are shown in Table 4.4:

Table 4.4: Relative, derived time metrics for WoP example

Time metric description	Time metric and calculation formula	Relative time measurements (in percentage)
Relative elapsed hands-on time per outcome O	$REHAT(UT_{1..n}, O) = \frac{EHAT(UT_{1..n},O)}{EVOT(UT_{1..n},O)}$	$\frac{151}{3163} = 4.8\%$
Relative elapsed waiting time per outcome O	$REWAT(UT_{1..n}, O) = \frac{EWAT(UT_{1..n},O)}{EVOT(UT_{1..n},O)}$	$\frac{56}{3163} = 1.8\%$
Relative elapsed walk-away time per outcome O	$REWYT(UT_{1..n}, O) = \frac{EWYT(UT_{1..n},O)}{EVOT(UT_{1..n},O)}$	$\frac{2940}{3163} = 92.9\%$
Relative system alert time per outcome O	$RESET(UT_{1..n}, O) = \frac{ESET(UT_{1..n},O)}{EVOT(UT_{1..n},O)}$	$\frac{20}{3163} = 0.6\%$
Relative user response time per outcome O	$REUET(UT_{1..n}, O) = \frac{EUET(UT_{1..n},O)}{EVOT(UT_{1..n},O)}$	$\frac{32}{3163} = 1.0\%$
Relative elapsed user action time per outcome O	$REUAT(UT_{1..n}, O) = \frac{EUAT(UT_{1..n},O)}{EVOT(UT_{1..n},O)}$	$\frac{183}{3163} = 5.8\%$
Relative elapsed system action time per outcome O	$RESAT(UT_{1..n}, O) = \frac{ESAT(UT_{1..n},O)}{EVOT(UT_{1..n},O)}$	$\frac{3016}{3163} = 95.4\%$
Relative user interaction time per outcome O	$RECAT(UT_{1..n}, O) = \frac{ECAT(UT_{1..n},O)}{EVOT(UT_{1..n},O)}$	$\frac{198}{3163} = 6.3\%$
Relative user intervention time per outcome O	$REVET(UT_{1..n}, O) = \frac{EVET(UT_{1..n},O)}{EVOT(UT_{1..n},O)}$	$\frac{3001}{3163} = 94.9\%$

Dependent and independent actions for user intervention

The situation is not always so simple when it comes to user intervention. User intervention means that the system more or less automatically generates an outcome of value, and the user can be involved in monitoring the progress, checking the status, or responding to a system alert.

Some user interventions are necessary to achieve the outcome of value, such as responding to a system alert that requests a decision from the user before proceeding. Other user interventions are not necessary to achieve the outcome of value; one example is checking the system's status. When calculating elapsed user involvement time, we should distinguish between these two cases. We call an intervention that has no influence on achieving the outcome of value *independent*. An example is checking an order status. We call an intervention that *does* have an influence on achieving the outcome of value *dependent*.

▶ Dependent user intervention (abbreviated "D")

▶ Independent user intervention (abbreviated "I")

If a user intervention step is dependent, the metric expression is $EVET_D$. The letter D in the index indicates that the step is dependent. If a user intervention step is independent, the metric expression is $EVET_I$, indicated with the letter I in the index.

Our pizza delivery system, from a user's perspective, operates more or less automatically when it comes to baking and delivering the pizza. The user can request an order status that is marked as "independent action" and "independent step" in Figure 4.8. This means that the intervention has no influence on the generation of the outcome. In our WoP example, monitoring the status (Step S 3-1) is an example of an independent intervention step and is marked in Figure 4.5 with "I.1" (*I* stands for independent).

The other case is that the intervention has an influence on the generation of the outcome of value. In our pizza example, it is the intervention step "ring doorbell" that is a system-generated alert and requests the user to open the door. If the user does not open the door, the pizza won't be delivered.[1] The user needs to respond to the request. This means that the user has to open the door which is an example of a dependent intervention. In our pizza example, opening the door (Step S 4-1) is marked in Figure 4.5 with "D.1" (*D* stands for dependent).

On the action level, the actions "walk-away time," "system alert," and "user response" can be dependent or independent. On the step level, only the user intervention can be dependent or independent (user interaction is always dependent). The elapsed time metrics are expressed as follows:

▶ $EWYT_D$ (dependent waiting time action)
▶ $ESET_D$ (dependent system alert action)
▶ $EUET_D$ (dependent user response action)
▶ $EVET_D$ (dependent user intervention step)
▶ $EWYT_I$ (independent waiting time action)
▶ $ESET_I$ (independent system alert action)
▶ $EUET_I$ (independent user response action)
▶ $EVET_I$ (independent user intervention step)

An independent action or step is not considered in the calculation of the elapsed involvement time. If a step has at least one dependent action assigned, the step is marked as dependent (see example S 3-1 in Figure 4.5 and Figure 4.6 where action A 1-3 Bake and deliver pizza is a dependent action).

1: Let's exclude the possibility that the delivery person simply leaves the pizza on the front porch, where it gets cold.

Dependent and independent user intervention steps and actions

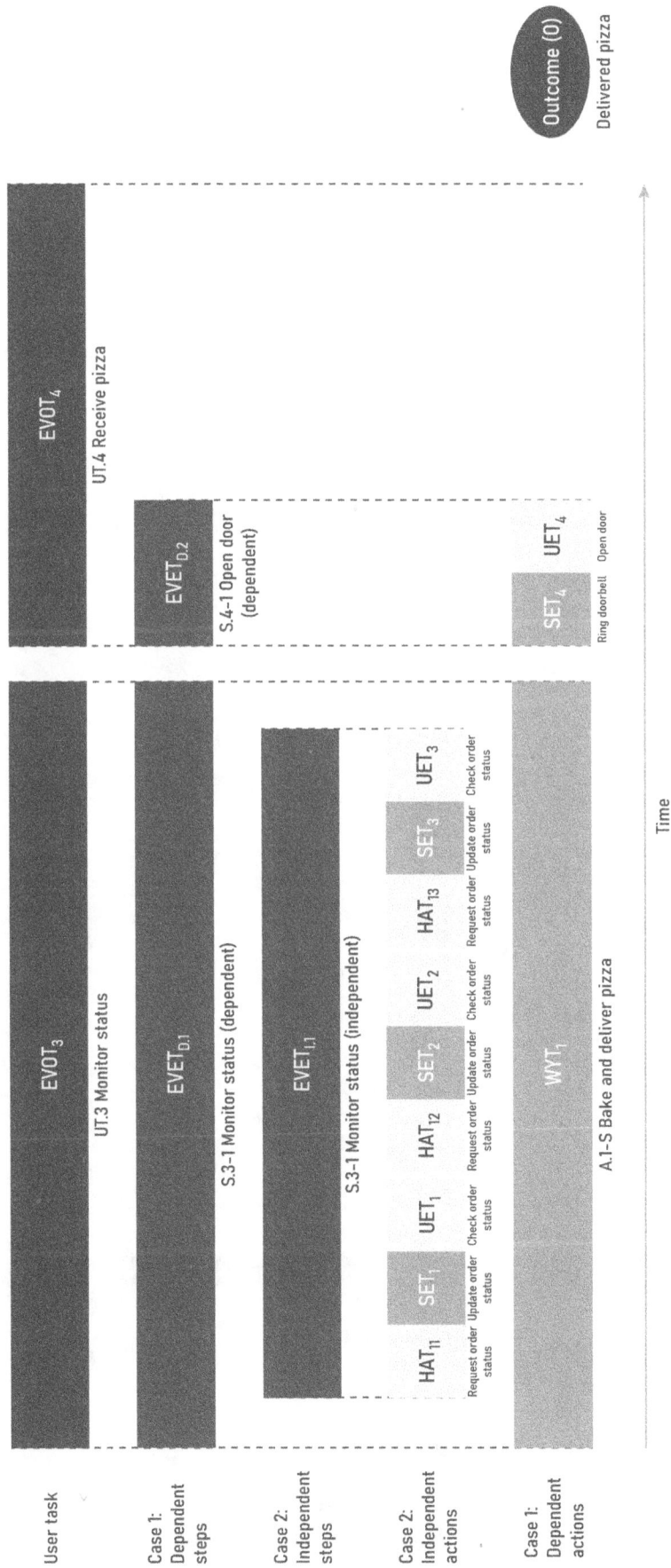

Figure 4.8: User intervention cases

This thought is reflected in the calculation of the elapsed time for the UT 3 "monitor status":

$$\blacktriangleright\ EVOT_3(A, O) = EVET_{D.1}(A, O) = EWYT_1(A, O)$$

$EWYT_1(O)$ expresses the metric for the dependent walk-away action A 1-3 Bake and deliver pizza. The calculation excludes independent steps, which in this case is step S 3-1 Monitor status.

Efficiency sweet spot for time

Using metrics and measurement is necessary for understanding the current situation. However, it would be useful to understand where we want to be, in general, to achieve acceptable efficiency.

Different user involvement scenarios (without walk-away time)

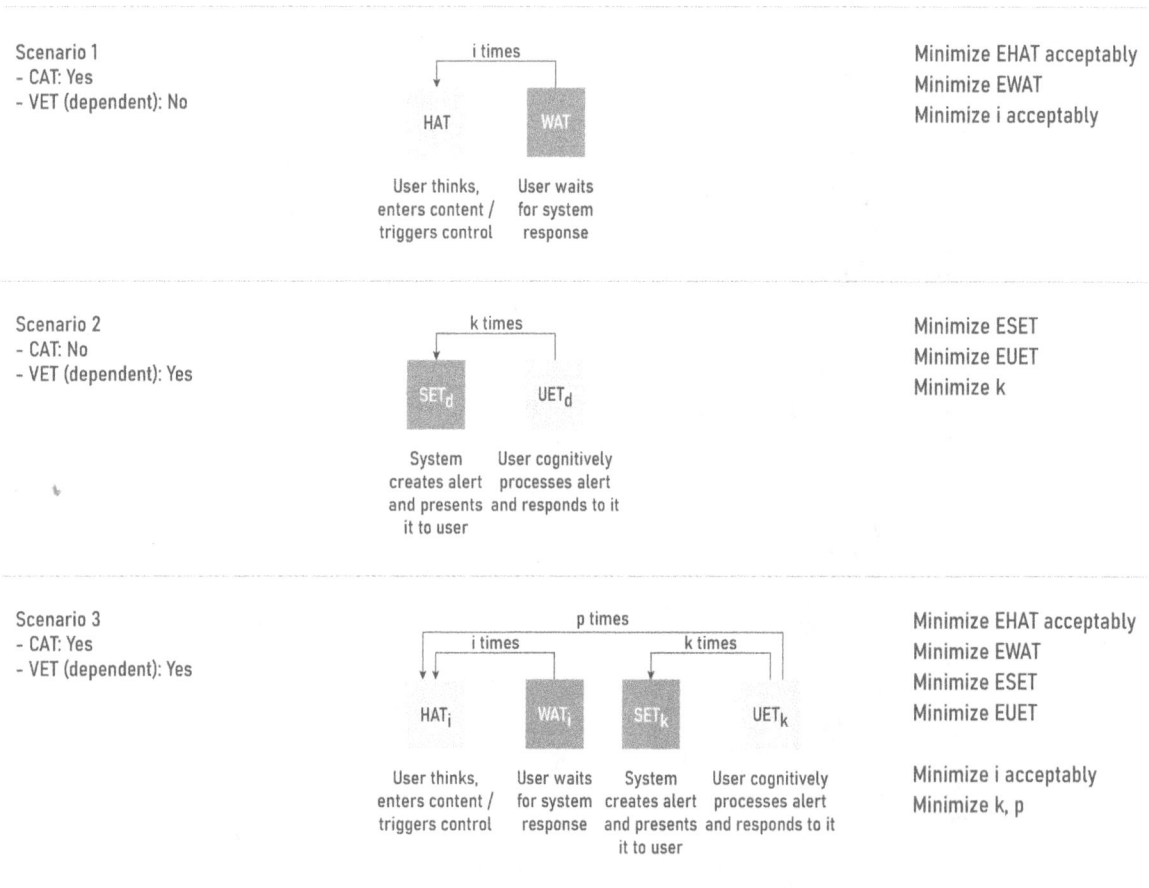

Figure 4.9: User involvement scenarios (without walk-away time)

Walk-away time and frequency will be addressed separately in Section 1 (Walk-away metrics) on page 97.

Different user involvement scenarios (without walk-away) are displayed in Figure 4.9. It is indicated per scenario how to achieve a higher efficiency.

Based on such bottom-up considerations, we can now abstract the thoughts and define a conceptual efficiency sweet spot for user involvement time, not considering walk-away time. It is expressed with two metrics. One is used to express the relative user action time for dependent actions. The relative user action time should be as long as possible, which means that the relative system action is as short as possible. This is what we want.

The relative user action time is defined as follows:

▶ $REUAT_D(UT_{1..n}, O) = \frac{EUAT_D(UT_{1..n},O)}{EVOT(UT_{1..n},O)}$; $UT_{1..n}$: all user tasks; O: outcome of value

If the $REUAT_D(UT_{1..n}, O)$ value is close to 1, we know that the majority of the user involvement time is attributed to dependent user actions and the system actions are relative short. This is what we want, in order to achieve high efficiency.

To avoid having absolute user action times that are too long, we need a second metric: the elapsed user action time which should be as short as possible. The elapsed user action time for dependent actions is defined as follows:

▶ $EUAT_D(UT_{1..n}, O) = EHAT_D(UT_{1..n}, O) + EUET_D(UT_{1..n}, O)$; $UT_{1..n}$: all user tasks; O: outcome of value

With the defined user involvement metrics, we can now express the efficiency sweet spot for user involvement time. It is visualized in Figure 4.10 as an efficiency metric quadrant that allows us to identify the efficiency sweet spot.

User involvement sweet spot for time

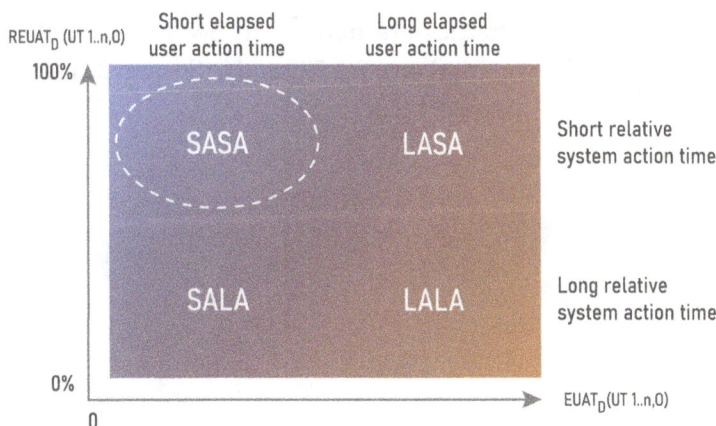

Figure 4.10: User involvement sweetsport for time

Let's look at each quadrant:

▶ SASA (Short elapsed user action time, short relative system action time): This is what efficient user interaction looks like (sweet spot).

▶ LASA (Long elapsed user action time, short relative system action time): It might be reasonable to see whether the hands-on time can be made more efficient, by optimizing the user interface.

▶ SALA (Short elapsed user action time, long relative system action time): The system action is relatively slow. The system's performance should be investigated and optimized to benefit the user.

▶ LALA (Long elapsed action time, long relative system action time): The user interaction time is long and the system's performance is slow. There should be an investigation into how both can be improved.

The threshold between short and long relative system action times is not fixed (for instance 50 percent) and depends on the application and the domain.

Frequency metrics for WoP

Frequency metrics express how often a user, or the system is involved in an action, a step, or a user task for the generation of an outcome of value.

Since we have all the information we need for calculating the frequency in the example shown in Figure 4.5 and Figure 4.6, we can calculate the measurements for selected frequency metrics (see Table 4.5).

Sample frequency metrics are defined in Section 23 (Selected absolute frequency metrics) on page 589 and in Section 23 (Selected relative frequency metrics) on page 591.

Table 4.5: Frequency metrics for WoP example

Frequency metric description	Frequency metric	Frequency measurement
Number of hands-on actions per outcome	$HAF(A, O)$	18 (A 2-U is performed three times per order)
Number of waiting actions per outcome	$WAF(A, O)$	11
Number of walk-away actions per outcome	$WYF(A, O)$	1
Number of system alert actions per outcome	$SEF(A, O)$	4 (A 3-S is performed three times per order)
Number of user response actions per outcome	$UEF(A, O)$	4 (A 4-U is performed three times per order)
Number of all user actions per outcome	$UAF(A, O) = HAF(A, O) + UEF(A, O)$	$22 = 18 + 4$
Number of dependent user actions per outcome	$UAF_D(A, O) = HAF_D(A, O) + UEF_D(A, O)$	$16 = 15 + 1$
Number of independent user actions per outcome	$UAF_I(A, O) = HAF_I(A, O) + UEF_I(A, O)$	$6 = 3 + 3$
Number of all system actions per outcome	$SAF(A, O) = WAF(A, O) + WYF(A, O) + SEF(A, O)$	$16 = 11 + 1 + 4$
Number of dependent system actions per outcome	$SAF_D(A, O) = WAF_D(A, O) + WYF_D(A, O) + SEF_D(A, O)$	$13 = 11 + 1 + 1$
Number of independent system actions per outcome	$SAF_I(A, O) = WAF_I(A, O) + WYF_I(A, O) + SEF_I(A, O)$	$3 = 0 + 0 + 3$
Number of user interaction steps per outcome	$CAF(S, O)$	9 (nine steps are classified as user interactions)
Number of user intervention steps per outcome	$VEF(S, O)$	2 (steps S 3-1 and S 3-2 are classified as user interventions)
Number of all actions per outcome	$VOF(A, O) = HAF(A, O) + WAF(A, O) + WYF(A, O) + SAF(A, O) + UEF(A, O)$	$38 = 18 + 11 + 1 + 4 + 4$
Number of steps per outcome	$VOF(S, O)$	11
Number user actions per user task 4	$UAF(A, UT4)$	6 (one user response action and five hands-on actions of user task UT 4 receive pizza)
Number system actions per user task 4	$SAF(A, UT4)$	6 (one system alert action and five waiting actions of user task UT 4 receive pizza)

Efficiency sweet spot for frequency

Like the efficiency sweet spot for time, we have different factors that influence the efficiency sweet spot for frequency. One factor is a minimal frequency threshold. Because users often like to maintain a certain amount of control, zero involvement (that is, $UAF_D(O) = 0$) is not always acceptable to them. Therefore, we should consider a minimal frequency threshold that can be higher than 0. A frequency threshold is displayed as a dotted vertical line in Figure 4.11.

The second factor is the frequency of user involvement actions per outcome of value. When it comes to efficiency, more efficient user involvement means a minimal acceptable frequency for dependent user actions. This is expressed with the metric $UAF_D(UT_{1..n}, O)$.

► $UAF_D(A, O) = HAF_D(A, O) + UEF_D(A, O)$; A: all actions; O: outcome of value

The third factor is the involvement time itself. Low frequency may lead to high cognitive load and longer times. It means efficiency is not increased. The sweet spot should be in an area with a short elapsed user action time. This is expressed as follows:

► $EUAT_D(A, O) = EHAT_D(A, O) + EUET_D(A, O)$; A: all actions; O: outcome of value

The combination of these three factors are displayed in the frequency sextant (see Figure 4.11). Here is a short description of each area:

► LOSA (Too low, unacceptable frequency, short elapsed system action time): The frequency is too low (unwanted loss of control) and the system action time is short.
► LOLA (Too low, unacceptable frequency, long elapsed system action time): The frequency is too low (unwanted loss of control) and the system action time is (too) long.
► RISA (Low acceptable frequency, short elapsed system action time): The frequency is just right and the system action time is short (sweet spot).
► RILA (Low acceptable frequency, long elapsed system action time): The frequency is just right and the system action time is too long.
► HISA (Too high frequency, short elapsed system action time): The frequency is too high (too many steps) and the system waiting time is short.
► HILA (Too high frequency, long elapsed system action time): The frequency is too high (too many steps) and the system action time is too long.

User involvement sweet spot for frequency

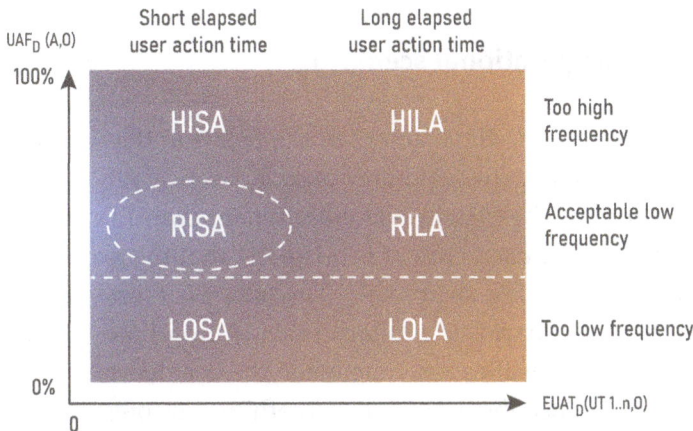

Figure 4.11: User involvement sweetspot for frequency

The frequency threshold needs to be determined per domain and application. The sweet spot for frequency is the RISA area. It gives the user sufficient control (acceptable frequency) and relatively short waiting times.

Walk-away metrics

There are many applications today that are part of complex ecosystems that may consist of software only or software integrated with hardware devices (e.g., IoT devices). Examples of software-only applications are social media apps, time management apps, photo apps, and e-commerce systems. Examples of systems with integrated hardware and software are home security applications (lamps, cameras etc.), manufacturing systems, and building monitoring and control systems.

Users provide inputs to such systems that are then processed by system elements. Due to system complexity or limited system performance, such processes can take a significant amount of time, far beyond the 10 seconds of acceptable waiting time. Waiting time can be minutes, hours, or even days. If the waiting time exceeds 10 seconds, users often direct their attention to something else. In order to be transparent and fair to the user in terms of the user's time, and not to frustrate them, a different "waiting time" concept is needed for such systems, called "walk-away" time.

There are three known scenarios where walk-away time plays a role, with varying optimization targets:

▶ One-time operational scenarios: minimize walk-away time
▶ Continuous operational scenarios: maximize walk-away time
▶ Frequent maintenance scenarios: maximize walk-away time

One-time operational scenarios

The attribute "one-time" refers to the fact that the user-initiated process should be executed only once, not repeatedly. The process is executed by the system and takes longer than 10 seconds to be completed. The user's intent is normally that the process should be completed as fast as possible. The walk-way time for one-time operational scenarios is similar to the waiting time. The waiting time becomes a walk-away time when the user has to wait so long that they can use the time to do something else of value.

Examples of one-time operational scenarios:

▶ Copy machine or printer: Start a print job, walk away, and return when the print job is completed. The walk-away time is typically in the range of half a minute to several minutes.
▶ Automatic coffee machine: Press the start button, walk away, and return when the coffee is made and filled into a cup. The walk-away time for making a coffee is typically in the range of half a minute to one minute.
▶ Online order: Submit an online order, walk away, and get back to it when the delivery can be picked up. The walk-away time is in the range of one day to several days, and sometimes weeks.
▶ Oven: Turn on the oven and walk away; come back when the target temperature is reached, and then put something in. The walk-away time is in the range of several minutes.

Figure 4.12 shows four one-time operational scenarios with walk-away times.

There are two parameters per scenario that distinguish them from each other. One parameter is whether an incident is reported (yes/no). The second parameter is whether the progress of the system process is monitored and reported to the user (yes/no). For all four scenarios, the walk-away time should be as short as possible.

One-time operation scenarios

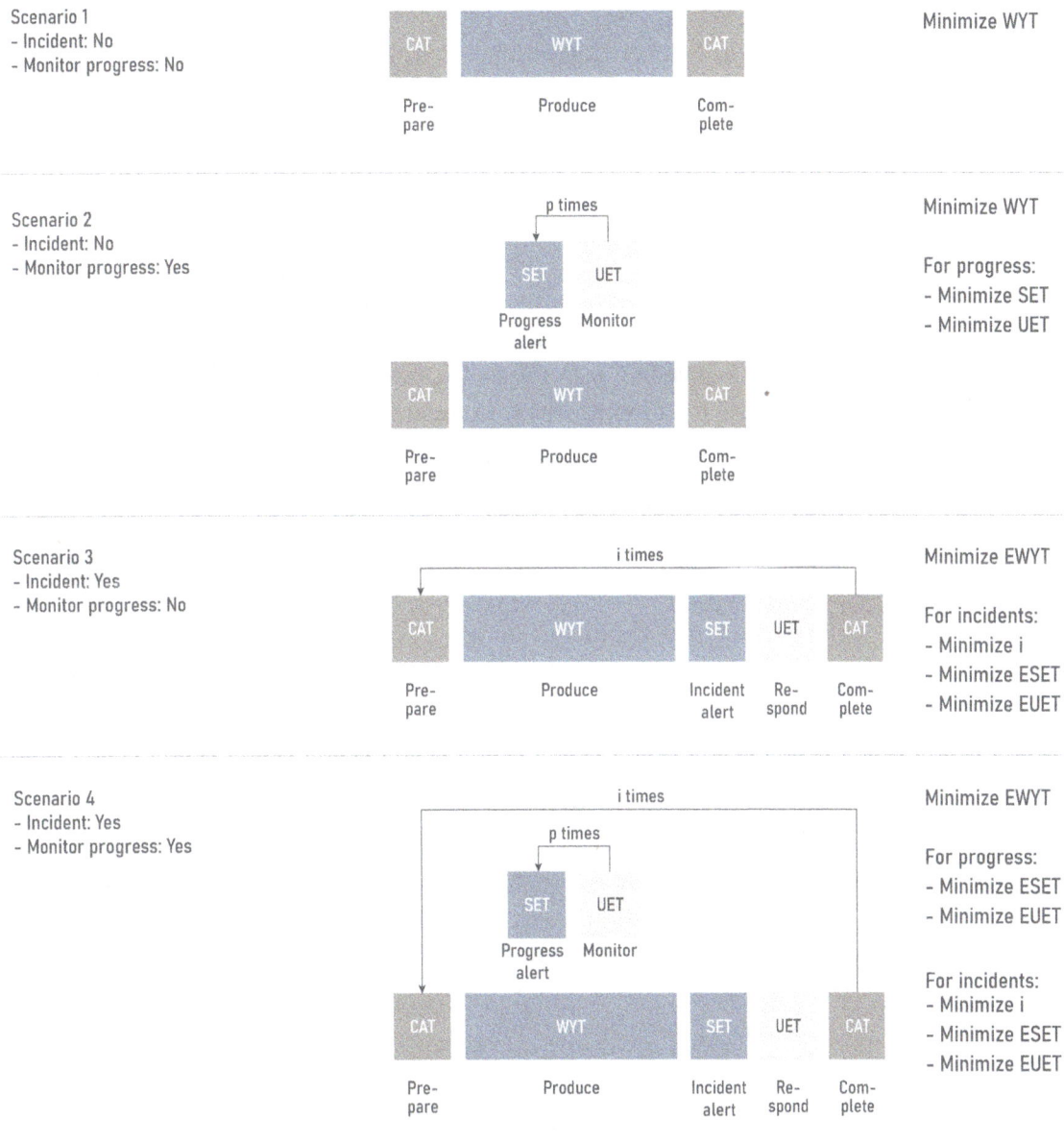

Scenario 1
- Incident: No
- Monitor progress: No

Pre-pare — Produce (WYT) — Com-plete

Minimize WYT

Scenario 2
- Incident: No
- Monitor progress: Yes

p times
SET UET
Progress alert Monitor

Pre-pare — Produce (WYT) — Com-plete

Minimize WYT

For progress:
- Minimize SET
- Minimize UET

Scenario 3
- Incident: Yes
- Monitor progress: No

i times
Pre-pare (CAT) — Produce (WYT) — Incident alert (SET) — Re-spond (UET) — Com-plete (CAT)

Minimize EWYT

For incidents:
- Minimize i
- Minimize ESET
- Minimize EUET

Scenario 4
- Incident: Yes
- Monitor progress: Yes

i times
p times
SET UET
Progress alert Monitor

Pre-pare (CAT) — Produce (WYT) — Incident alert (SET) — Re-spond (UET) — Com-plete (CAT)

Minimize EWYT

For progress:
- Minimize ESET
- Minimize EUET

For incidents:
- Minimize i
- Minimize ESET
- Minimize EUET

Figure 4.12: One-time operational scenarios

Continuous operational scenarios

There is another set of scenarios in which the user sets up a process, starts it, and walks away. The process is executed continuously until the user stops or changes it. This type of scenario is called "Continuous operational scenarios." The intent of the user is to stay away as long as possible, and not be bothered with the execution of the process. Examples of such processes are as follows:

► Heating/Cooling: The house's heating / cooling system is turned on and left to run until the user turns it off or changes a set temperature.

► Subscribing to a newspaper: The subscription is started, and the newspaper is delivered every day until the user changes or cancels the subscription.

► Subscribing to utilities: The user signs up to get electricity, gas, water, and/or internet delivered, and it is delivered until the user changes or cancels the subscription.

► Car: The autopilot is turned on and the car drives autonomously until the driver turns it off.

For enterprises, walk-away times for continuous operational scenarios have direct implications on productivity and total cost of ownership. For instance, the walk-away time is used as a purchase selection criterion for in vitro diagnostic devices [36].

Figure 4.13 shows four continuous operational scenarios with a walk-away time.

The four scenarios have the same parameters as the previous one-time scenarios. In the case of continuous scenarios, the walk-away time should be as long as possible, and at the same time, the number of interventions (that is, interruptions) should be as low as possible.

Frequent maintenance scenarios

Another type of scenarios beside the operational scenarios is the maintenance scenario. The purpose of maintenance is to keep a system operational and in a healthy state.

There are two types of maintenance tasks: scheduled (repeated) and unscheduled (one-time). Using an everyday example like a car is useful for explaining the difference between scheduled and unscheduled maintenance activities. Scheduled activities are frequent and plannable, like service checkpoints (every 10,000 miles/kilometers, 20,000 miles/kilometers, etc.). Refueling is also an example of a scheduled maintenance activity. Other examples are oil changes, brake pad replacement, rotation, or replacements of tires, etc.

Unscheduled maintenance activities are those that are not plannable at all or are difficult to plan for. As the name implies, they typically come as a surprise. Often, they consist of repairs or replacement of broken parts.

Both types of maintenance activities are important. Due to their frequency, the scheduled maintenance activities, with their intervals,

Continuous operation scenarios

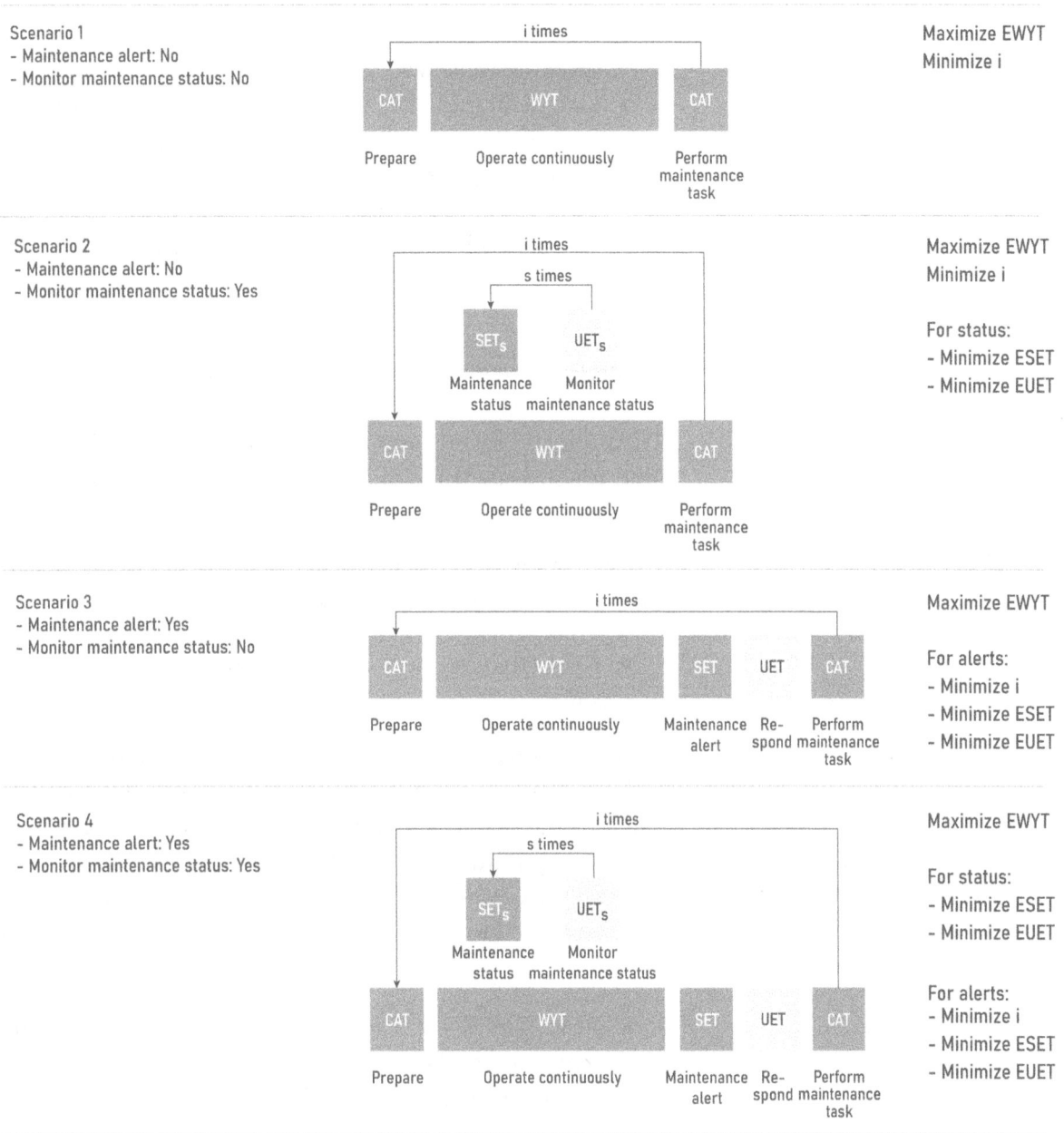

Figure 4.13: Continuous operational scenarios

have a larger impact on the involvement of maintainers. Therefore, we are going to focus on scheduled maintenance activities in the remainder of this chapter.

Scheduled maintenance tasks need to be performed according to a defined maintenance schedule. The time between such maintenance tasks is measured as walk-away time for maintainers. Examples of such maintenance tasks and walk-away times are as follows:

- ▶ Copy machine or printer: Refill toner and paper; walk-away and come back to refill it.
- ▶ Automatic coffee machine: Refill water, beans, and empty grounds; walk-away and come back to refill / empty it again.
- ▶ Car: Refill fuel, check water and air pressure; drive the car for a while; refill fuel, check water and air pressure etc.
- ▶ In vitro diagnostics analyzer: Refill the consumables, empty the bin, calibrate the device; walk-away to do something else; go back to refill the consumables, empty the bin, and calibrate the device again.

Efficiency sweet spot for maintenance walk-away time

There are also several scenarios that are applicable to scheduled (and unscheduled) maintenance tasks, which are visualized in Figure 4.14.

For the maintenance activities, we are interested in *maximizing* the walk-away time. This is expressed with

- ▶ $EWYT_M(UT_{1..n}, O)$; $UT_{1..n}$: all user tasks; O: Outcome of value.

Walk-away time often depends on the consumption of materials and maintenance cycles. Both depend on the use of the application and its productivity. The walk-away time of an application can be extended by reducing its productivity. To make the relationship between walk-away time and productivity of an application transparent, we need to introduce a productivity metric. It is expressed as

- ▶ $PEVOT(UT_{1..n}, O) = \frac{O}{EVOT(UT_{1..n}, O)}$; O is number of outcomes and $EVOT(UT_{1..n}, O)$ is the elapsed time to generate the O outcome of value; $UT_{1..n}$: all user tasks; O: outcome of value.

Frequent maintenance scenarios

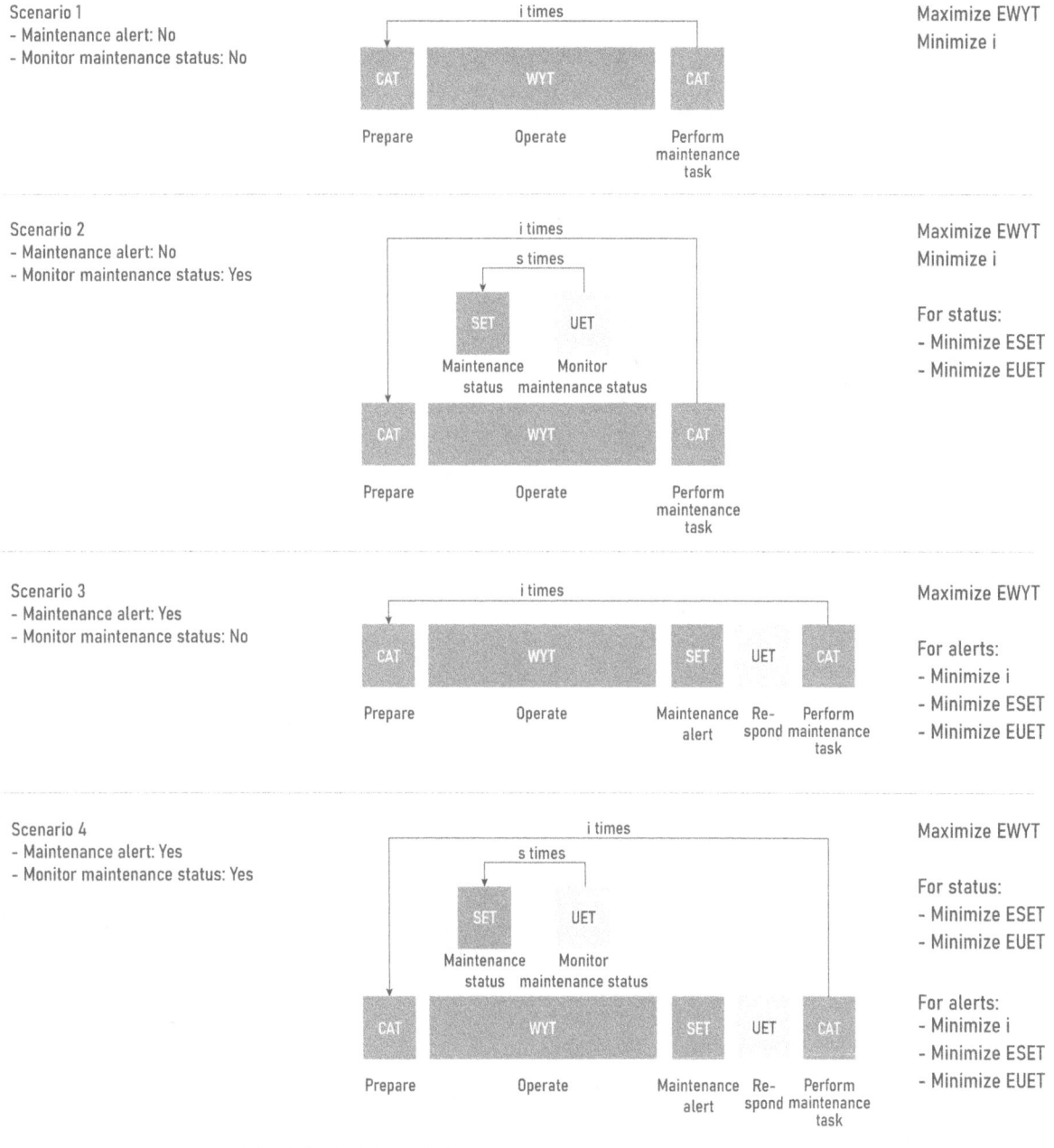

Figure 4.14: Maintenance scenarios

We can now define the sweet spot for maintenance walk-away time. It is visualized in the top right quadrant (sweet spot) of Figure 4.15.

▶ SOHO (Short elapsed maintenance walk-away time, high productivity): The maintenance walk-away time is too short and the productivity of outcomes is sufficiently high.

▶ LOHO (Long elapsed maintenance walk-away time, high productivity): The maintenance walk-away time is sufficiently long and the productivity of outcomes is sufficiently high (sweet spot).

▶ SOLO (Short elapsed maintenance walk-away time, low productivity): The maintenance walk-away time is too short and the productivity of outcomes is too low.

▶ LOLO (Long elapsed maintenance walk-away time, low productivity): The maintenance walk-away time is sufficiently long but the productivity of outcomes is too low.

Sweet spot for maintenance walk-away time

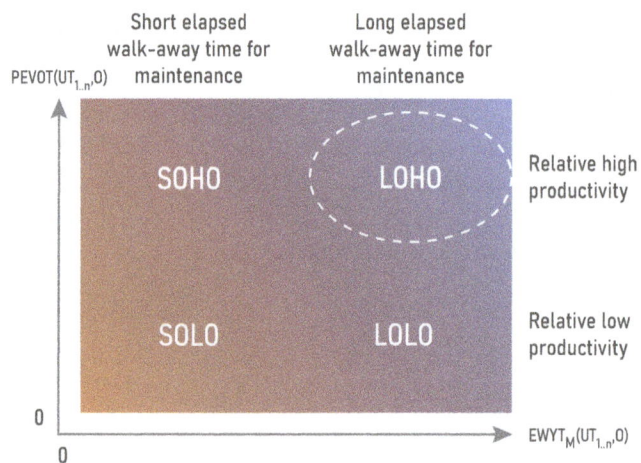

Figure 4.15: Sweetspot for maintenance walk-away time

A threshold for the minimum acceptable elapsed walk-away times relative to the productivity need to be defined per application and domain.

Coffee machine example 1

There are several easy ways to gain efficiency savings when it comes to walk-away times. In this section, we look at how to determine and improve walk-away time. To demonstrate how this works, we need an example. I could use the example of a pizza oven needing to be refilled with wooden logs, but that is a bit too simple. Therefore, I'd like to introduce another device. To stay in the theme of Italian cuisine, I'll use the example of an automated coffee machine.

I switch now from the word applica-tion *to the word* device *because frequent maintenance is often needed when hardware is involved.*

Considerations and calculations for walk-away time are introduced in two steps, with two coffee machine examples. To introduce the main calculations, we'll use a simple coffee machine example. A second, more complex example is used to show optimization potentials for walk-away time.

Let's start with the first, simple coffee machine. It uses coffee pods, which the user adds and removes per cup of coffee. The coffee machine has one *intervention item*: water.

▶ Water tank: 32 oz./0.95 liters

To refill the water tank, there is one user (maintenance) task:

▶ UT 1 refill water tank

Production unit

To calculate walk-away frequencies and times, we first need to define *production unit*. A production unit is the base metric we use to measure and compare the frequencies and the elapsed time of walk-away times. The production unit is abbreviated "PUT." Samples of PUT are time (e.g., operating hours), volumes (e.g., gallons, liters), and items (e.g., tests, printed papers, cups). The production unit in the case of the coffee machine is item-based: cups (of coffee).

▶ PUT: cups

No intervention capacity

To determine how often a maintenance task need to be performed, we must express how many product units can be produced without the need for intervention. We call this amount *no intervention capacity*, abbreviated *NIC*.

With the water tank, the coffee machine can make six cups of coffee without being refilled.

▶ NIC = 6 cups

Production references

To calculate intervention frequency (how often intervention is required), we need a reference number of PUTs. The reference number is the expected number of items produced per hour, per day, per week etc. We call this reference a *reference number for production*, abbreviated as *ROP*.

In our case, the assumption is that the coffee machine is used in an office environment, and we use an assumed number of outcomes produced per day.

► ROP = 30 cups

In addition, it is often reasonable to relate intervention tasks to a time reference called *reference number for time* , which we call here *ROT*. In our case, the ROT is defined as the duration of an office day.

► ROT = 12 hours = 720 minutes

The intervention frequencies for the given NIC and the production reference are displayed in Figure 4.16.

Walk-away frequency per ROT for single intervention item

The walk-away frequency per ROT is defined as:

► $WYF_S(ROP, NIC) = \left\lfloor \frac{ROP}{NIC} \right\rfloor$

We can apply the formula to our coffee machine example:

► $WYF_S(ROP, NIC) = \left\lfloor \frac{30cups}{6cups} \right\rfloor = 5$

It means that the water needs to be refilled five times during the business day of 12 hours.

Mean walk-away time per ROT for single intervention item

We can now calculate the mean walk-away time for a single intervention item. It is defined as

► $MWYT_S(ROT, ROP, NIC) = \frac{ROT}{WYF_S(ROP, NIC)}$

In the case of our coffee machine, the mean walk-away time is

► $MWYT_S(720minutes, 30cups, 6cups) = \frac{720minutes}{5} = 144$ minutes

Based on the defined ROT, ROP, and NIC, the water tank needs to be refilled every 144 minutes.

Intervention frequency for NIC 6 (W)

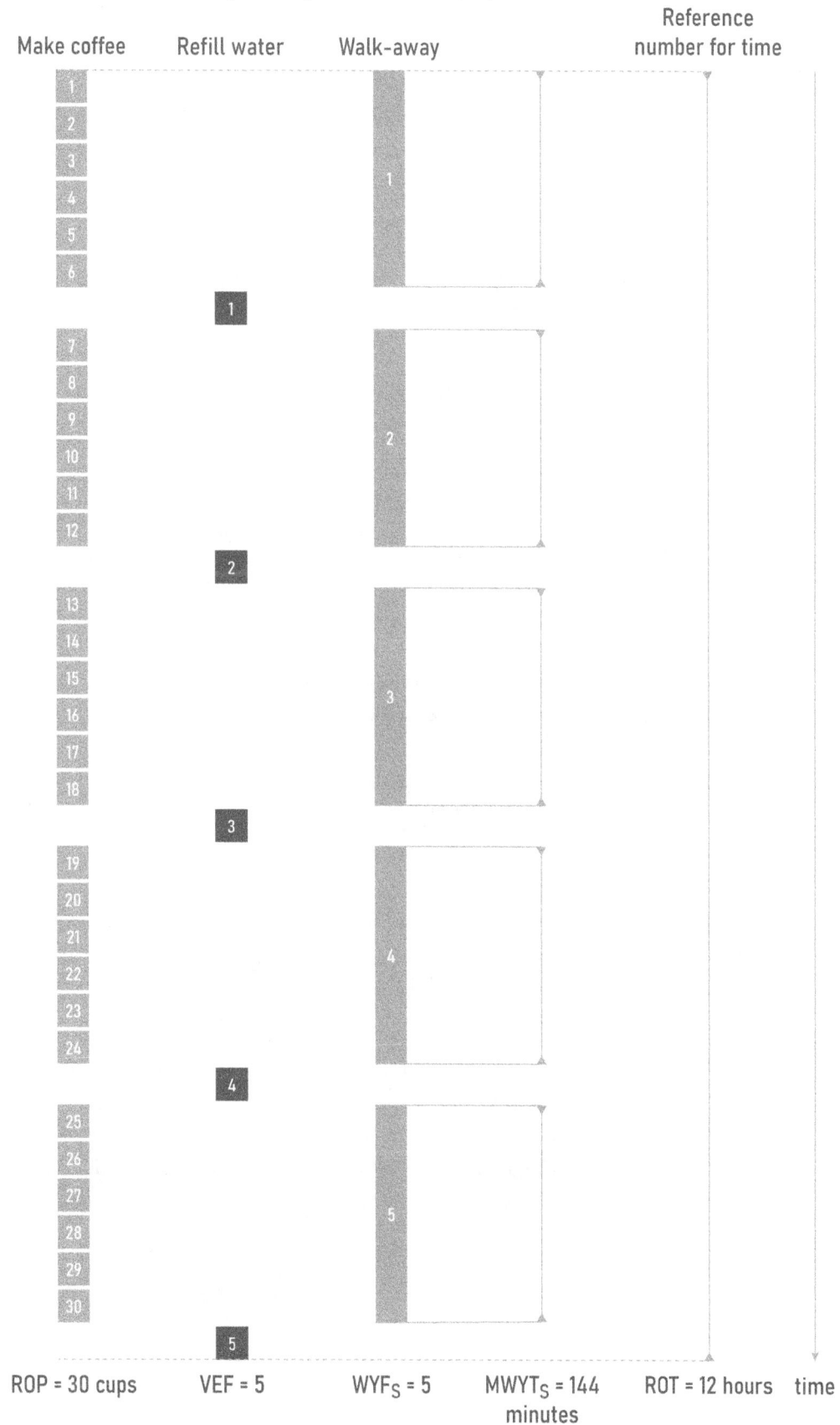

Figure 4.16: Intervention frequencies for NIC 6 (W)

Coffee machine example 2

The first coffee machine example was intentionally simple in order to introduce key metrics for walk-away time. The second example is more realistic. It has three *intervention items*: two types of consumables (water, beans) and one type of waste (grounds).

The volume of the consumables and the grounds will be measured using the following containers, which are integrated into the coffee machine:

- ▶ Water tank
- ▶ Bean container
- ▶ Grounds container

Associated with the three intervention items are the following user (maintenance) tasks:

- ▶ UT 1 refill water tank
- ▶ UT 2 refill bean container
- ▶ UT 3 empty grounds container

No intervention capacity

Because the containers for the three intervention items have different volumes, we have a different NIC for each intervention item:

- ▶ NIC_{Water} = 6 cups
- ▶ NIC_{Bean} = 5 cups
- ▶ $NIC_{Grounds}$ = 4 cups

In the remainder of this section, the NIC representing 6 cups for water, 5 cups for beans, and 4 cups for grounds is abbreviated as "6-5-4" (Water-Beans-Grounds).

We will start this second example by calculating the mean walk-away time and frequency for each intervention item separately (as single intervention item). Afterwards, we will perform the calculations for *multiple* intervention items and see the benefits of doing so. Later, we'll consider how to systematically extend the walk-away times and reduce the frequencies thereof.

Walk-away frequency per intervention item

The ROP and ROT have not changed:

- ROP: 30 cups
- ROT: 12 hours = 720 minutes

Therefore, the walk-away frequencies for a single intervention item for water, beans, and grounds are as follows (see Table 4.6):

Table 4.6: Walk-away frequency for a single item for NIC triple 6-5-4 (W-B-G)

User task	$WYF_S(ROT, ROP, NIC)$
UT 1 refill water tank	$WYF_S(ROT, ROP, NIC_{Water}) = \lfloor \frac{30}{6} \rfloor = 5$
UT 2 refill bean container	$WYF_S(ROT, ROP, NIC_{Bean}) = \lfloor \frac{30}{5} \rfloor = 6$
UT 3 empty grounds container	$WYF_S(ROT, ROP, NIC_{Grounds}) = \lceil \frac{30}{4} \rceil = \lfloor 7.5 \rfloor = 7$

Mean walk-away time per intervention item

There is a total of 18 intervention tasks per ROC. The mean walk-away times for a single intervention item for water, beans, and grounds are (see Table 4.7).

Table 4.7: Mean walk-away time for a single item for NIC 6-5-4 (W-B-G)

User task	$MWYT_S(ROT, ROP, NIC)$
UT 1 refill water tank	$MWYT_S(ROT, ROP, NIC_{Water}) = \frac{720 minutes}{5} = 144$ minutes
UT 2 refill bean container	$MWYT_S(ROT, ROP, NIC_{Bean}) = \frac{720 minutes}{6} = 120$ minutes
UT 3 empty grounds container	$MWYT_S(ROT, ROP, NIC_{Grounds}) = \frac{720 minutes}{7} = 103$ minutes

The walk-away frequency per intervention item is displayed in Figure 4.17.

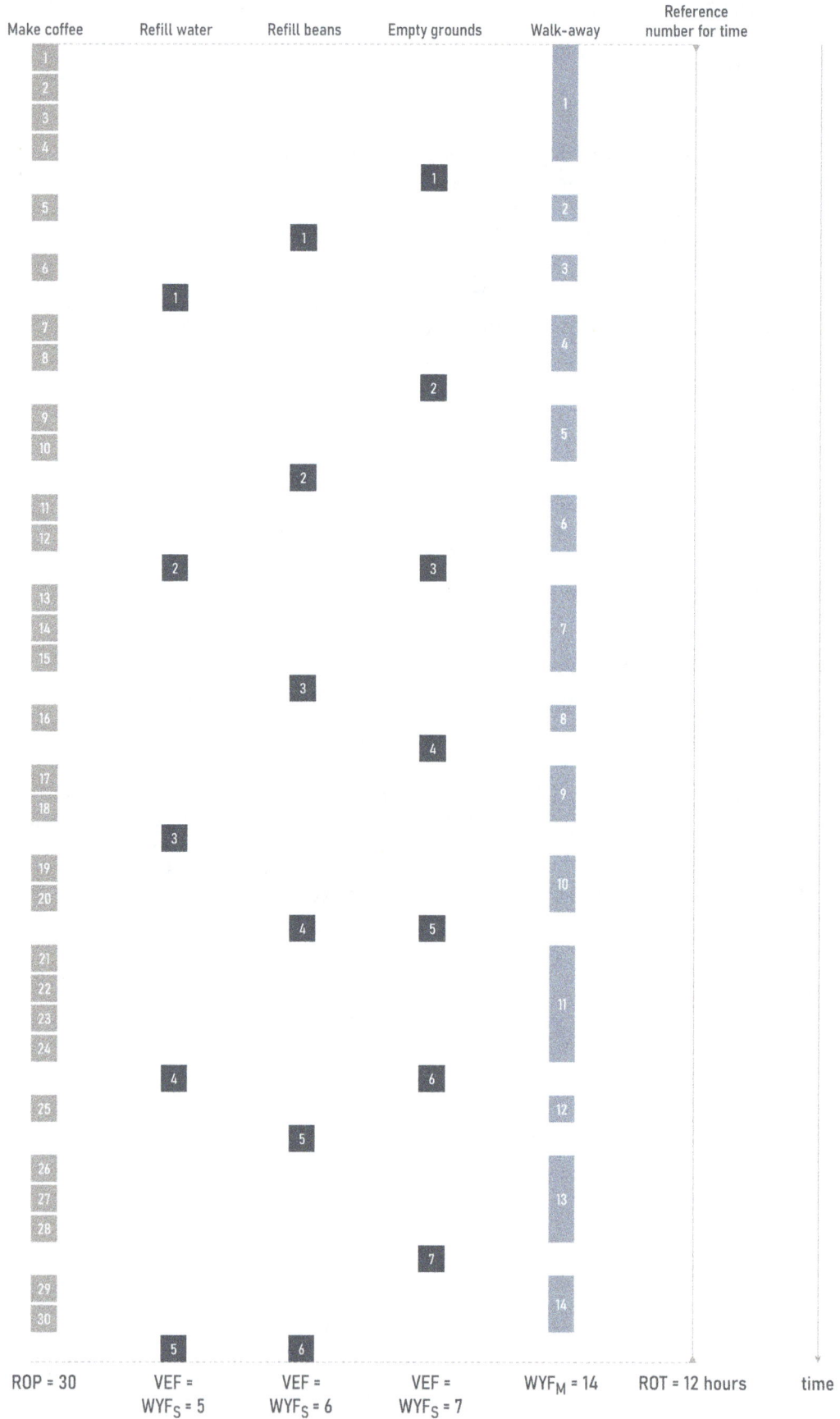

Figure 4.17: Walk-away frequencies for NIC 6-5-4 (W-B-G)

Walk-away frequency for multiple intervention items

The diagram shows that there is a total of 18 (= 5 + 6 + 7) intervention tasks for water, beans, and grounds. However, if we look at the intervention tasks combined, we see that we have only 14 interruptions, expressed as walk-away frequencies, or WYF_M (see Table 4.8 and Figure 4.17).

Table 4.8: Comparison of walk-away frequencies for single and multiple intervention items

Perform one or more user tasks together	Walk-away frequency for single intervention item $WYF_S(ROT, ROP, NIC)$	Walk-away frequency for multiple intervention items $WYF_M(ROT, ROP, \{NIC_W, NIC_B, NIC_G\})$
UT 1 refill water only	5	2
UT 2 refill beans only	6	4
UT 3 empty grounds only	7	4
UT 1 and UT 2 refill water and refill beans together	n/a	1
UT 1 and UT 3 refill water and empty grounds together	n/a	2
UT 2 and UT 3 refill beans and empty grounds together	n/a	1
UT 1, UT 2, and UT 3 refill water, refill beans, and empty grounds together	n/a	0
Total	18	14

This is an important distinction. The reason for the different numbers is that some intervention tasks can be performed at the same time, so they do not increase the walk-away frequency (or the number of interruptions). We can leverage such overlaps to reduce the walk-away frequency in cases where we have multiple intervention items.

Therefore, we need to introduce two new metrics: mean intervention frequency for multiple intervention items ($MWYF$) and mean walk-away time for multiple intervention items ($MWYT$).

The mean walk-away frequency for multiple intervention items is defined as:

▶ $WYF_M(ROT, ROP, \{NIC_1, ..., NIC_n\})$ [cups]; n is the number of intervention items for a defined NIC.

$MWYF_M$ is best determined with a simulation. Figure 4.17 shows how it can be simulated in principle.

In our example, in every 12-hour period we have to perform 18 intervention tasks, refilling water and coffee beans and emptying grounds container. However, we have 14 interruptions where the 18 intervention tasks are performed.

▶ $WYF_M(ROT, ROP, \{NIC_W, NIC_B, NIC_G\}) = 14.$

Mean walk-away time for multiple intervention items

The calculation of the elapsed walk-away time depends on the walk-away frequency. We do not use a single NIC value for the mean walk-away time for multiple intervention items, so we need to adjust the formula accordingly.

The formula is:

▶ $MWYT_M(ROT, ROP, \{NIC_W, NIC_B, NIC_G\}) = \frac{ROT}{WYF_M}$

We can now apply the formula to our coffee example 2.

▶ $MWYT_M(ROT, ROP, \{NIC_W, NIC_B, NIC_G\}) = \frac{720 minutes}{14}$
= 51.4 minutes.

This means that every 51.4 minutes, one or more of the intervention tasks has to be performed to keep the coffee machine operating.

Calculations for other NIC combinations are shown in Table 4.9.

Increase walk-away frequency for multiple intervention items

Reducing the number of user interventions for multiple intervention items reduces the number of interruptions for users which is often beneficial. To achieve that, we need to increase the walk-away frequency for multiple intervention items. How do we do that?

Increasing the walk-away frequency for multiple means to increase the minimum walk-away frequency ($MinWYF_M$). This means we need to modify the NICs in order to increase the greatest common factor. Table 4.9 shows variations of NICs that were modified to systematically increase the WYF_M.

The WYF_M calculations for the different NIC combinations were done in Excel with a simple simulation.

Depending on the NIC, the walk-away frequency will be reduced from 15 (NIC 6-2-2) to 5 (NIC 6-6-6). The mean walk-away time was trippled at the same time from 48.0 minutes (NIC: 6-2-2) to 144 minutes (NIC: 6-6-6).

The relationship between selected NIC values and the mean walk-away time for multiple intervention items is shown in Figure 4.18.

Table 4.9: Variety of NICs and its implication on walk-away frequency and mean walk-away time for multiple intervention items

Intervention tasks	ROP = 30 cups, ROT = 12 hours				
	NIC: 6-2-2	NIC: 6-4-2	NIC: 6-5-4	NIC: 6-3-3	NIC: 6-6-6
UT 1 refill water only	0	0	2	0	0
UT 2 refill beans only	0	0	4	0	0
UT 3 empty grounds only	0	5	4	0	0
UT 1 and UT 2 refill water and refill beans together	0	0	1	0	0
UT 2 and UT 3 refill water and empty grounds together	0	3	2	0	0
UT 1 and UT 3 refill beans and empty grounds together	10	5	1	5	0
UT 1, UT 2, and UT 3 refill water, refill beans, and empty grounds together	5	2	0	5	5
$VEF_S(ROT, ROP, \{NIC_{W,B,G}\})$	35	27	18	25	15
$WYF_M(ROT, ROP, \{NIC_{W,B,G}\})$	15	15	14	10	5
$MWYT_M(ROT, ROP, \{NIC_{W,B,G}\})$	48 min	48 min	51.4 min	72 min	144 min

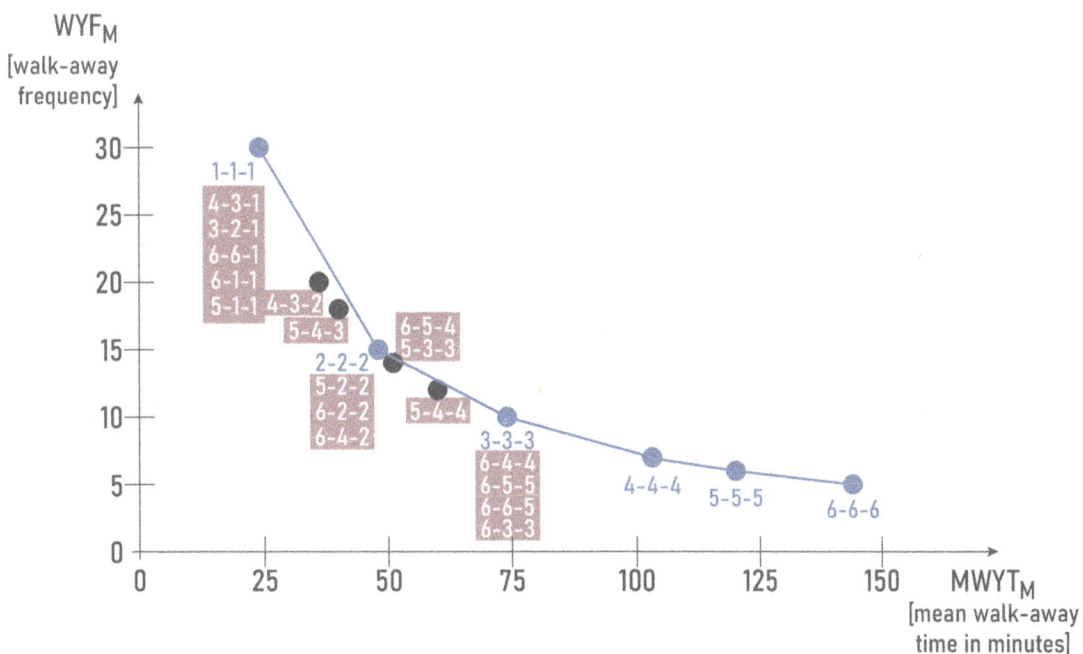

Figure 4.18: Relationship between NIC values, walk-away frequency, and mean walk-away time for multiple intervention items; NIC: Water - Bean - Grounds; as an example how to read the graph: for NIC 5-2-2, the coffee machine requires a mean walk-away time of 48 minutes, which equals a walk-away frequency of 15 cups.

The NICs with a red background provide capacities that do not benefit the mean walk-away time or frequency for multiple intervention items. It would be more beneficial to use an equal number of NICs per intervention item, for example, by reducing them.

Summary

User involvement metrics

► Move on to <u>Workflow (as is)</u>
◄ Go back to <u>Business Model</u>

User involvement metric taxonomy

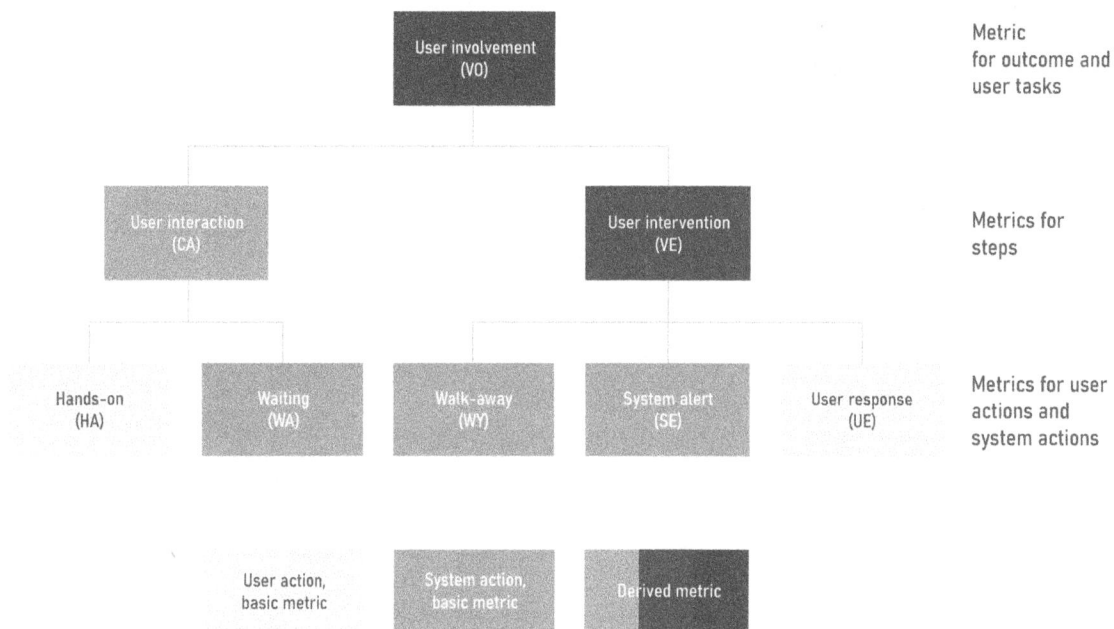

Lessons learned

Key Time Indicators The key time indicators specify types of times that are useful to consider during the discovery phase and the design phase of a design project. The UIMs will be applied to specify the current user involvement times and the target involvement times.

Tips and tricks

User involvement times There is not a lot to say about the UIMs, other than this: use them. Adding time information to workflows and steps increases the relevance of the work in the eyes for management. Time information can be translated into money. In other words, part of the design work is expressed in a "currency" that is understood by management. That's a good thing!

Exercise 1.3

Goal Determine selected user involvement metrics for an application of your choice.

Material User involvement metrics

Completion criteria:

- ▶ The outcomes of value, user tasks, steps, and actions are identified and documented according to Figure 4.5.
- ▶ Each user and system action has an assigned time value.
- ▶ The metrics $REUAT_D(UT_{1..n}, O)$ and $UAF_D(A, O)$ are calculated.

Workflow (as is) | **5**

One thing you can't recycle is wasted time.
Taiichi Ohno

Purpose

To create an experience architecture, we need to understand the bigger picture. The workflow (as is) provides such a useful view as a starting point. It documents which user roles are involved today and when they contribute what to achieve an outcome of value.

The workflow (as is), in combination with user involvement metrics, establishes a baseline that we can use to check that changes do indeed introduce an efficiency improvement, or any other type of improvement. Improvements cannot be demonstrated without a baseline.

In this chapter, we go over the steps for how to create a workflow (as is) and how to identify workflow weaknesses. The user involvement metrics are applied to the workflow (as is). If some of the responsibilities outlined in the workflow (as is) are not well understood, a user journey map (as is) can be useful to clarify certain details. The workflow (to be) will be covered in Chapter 9 (Workflow (to be)) on page 219.

Workflow (as is)

The workflow (as is) is a tool used to explore and document which user role is involved, in which sequence and with which contribution, as of today. It also reveals activities that take place in parallel and may cause inefficiencies.

The workflow template we use is shown in Figure 5.1. It uses a swim lane diagram technique. Each user role has its own swim lane. This visualization makes it easy to see who is involved when, with which contribution, and in which sequence.

Workflow (as is)

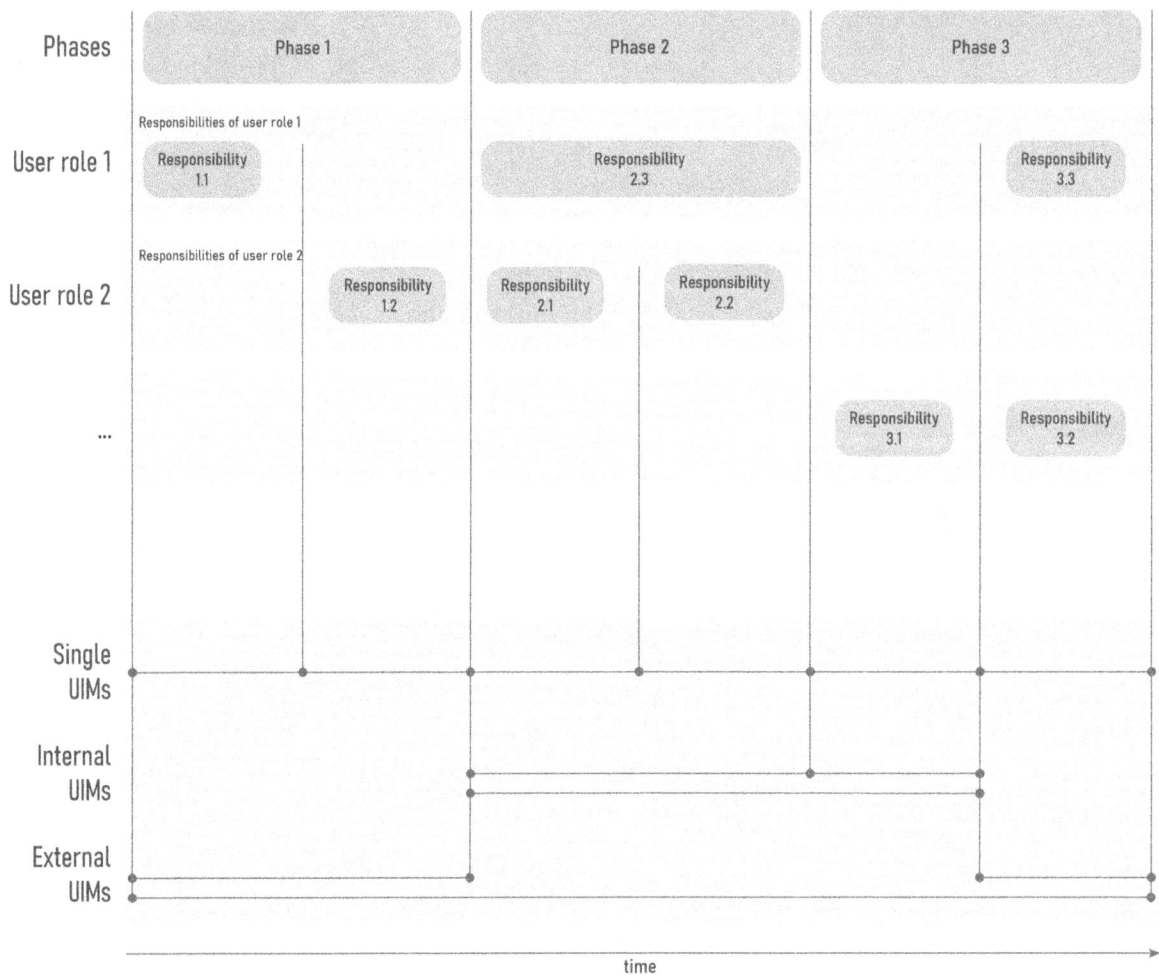

Figure 5.1: Workflow (as is) template

In addition to the user roles and their responsibilities, we capture user involvement metrics in the bottom lane. It is beneficial to distinguish between internal UIMs and external UIMs. "External" means that the time information is measurable and visible to users of the customer organization. "Internal" means that the user involvement metrics are measurable and visible to users of the vendor organization.

There is no strict order for identifying a workflow (as is). However, the following steps have proved to be reasonable:

▶ Step 1: Identify phases

- ► Step 2: Identify user roles and their responsibilities per phase
- ► Step 3: Mark phases that support the business model
- ► Step 4: Map phases or responsibilities to a road map
- ► Step 5: Assign user involvement metrics and determine measurements
- ► Step 6: Identify pain points per responsibility
- ► Step 7: Identify workflow weaknesses

We will create the workflow (as is) for World of Pizza, applying each of the steps. We'll use an empty workflow canvas as a starting point (see Figure 5.2).

Step 1: Identify phases

When it comes to workflows, a typical pitfall is that the identified activities or responsibilities become too detailed too soon. It is therefore useful to outline the top workflow level with phases first.

In our World of Pizza example, we look at three phases: 1) manage inventory, 2) sell pizza, and 3) administer business (see Figure 5.3).

It is beneficial to map all phases of the workflow (as is), even if there were some we do not plan to support with our application under design. Documentation of all phases ensures that we can see the big picture.

Step 2: Identify user roles and responsibilities per phase

After we have identified the phases, we can start identifying the responsibilities per user role that contribute to each phase. Responsibilities consists of a group of activities.

There will be some back-and-forth between the responsibilities and the user roles. It is therefore beneficial to check: Are all user roles identified for one phase? Are all responsibilities for each user role identified?

Each responsibility is mapped on a timeline that goes from left (past) to right (future). If responsibilities take place at the same time, they appear on the swim lane diagram in parallel.

In addition, we can mark phases that are out of scope for our application under design. Such an early determination can save some time. For phase we have marked as "out of scope," we can later reevaluate whether it would be a smart decision to keep that phase out of scope.

Phases

Household manager
Household member
Team assistant
Team member
Team lead

Manager
Assistant manager

Baker
Assistant baker

Driver

Single
UIMs

Internal
UIMs

External
UIMs

time

Figure 5.2: Workflow canvas

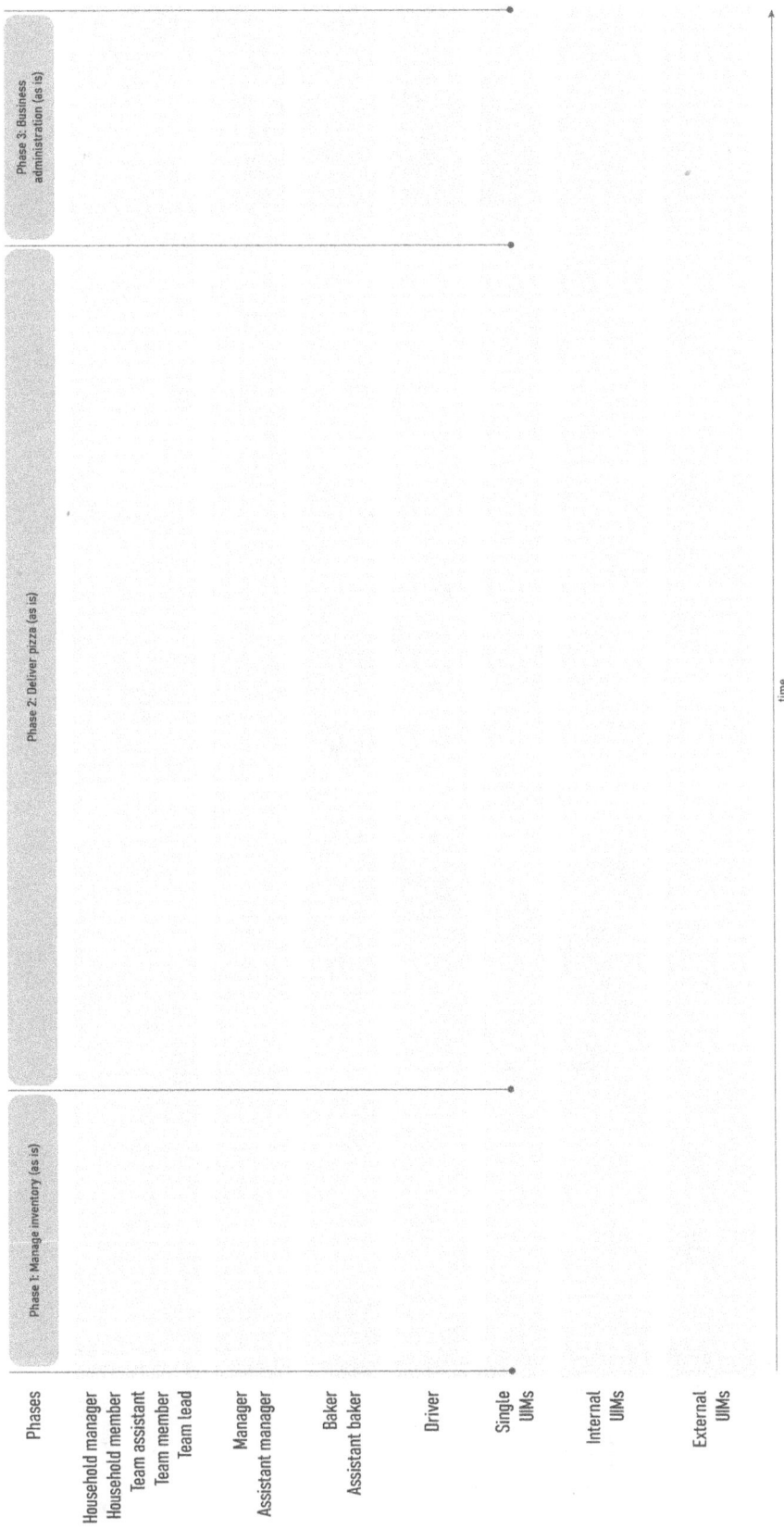

Figure 5.3: Step 1: Identify phases

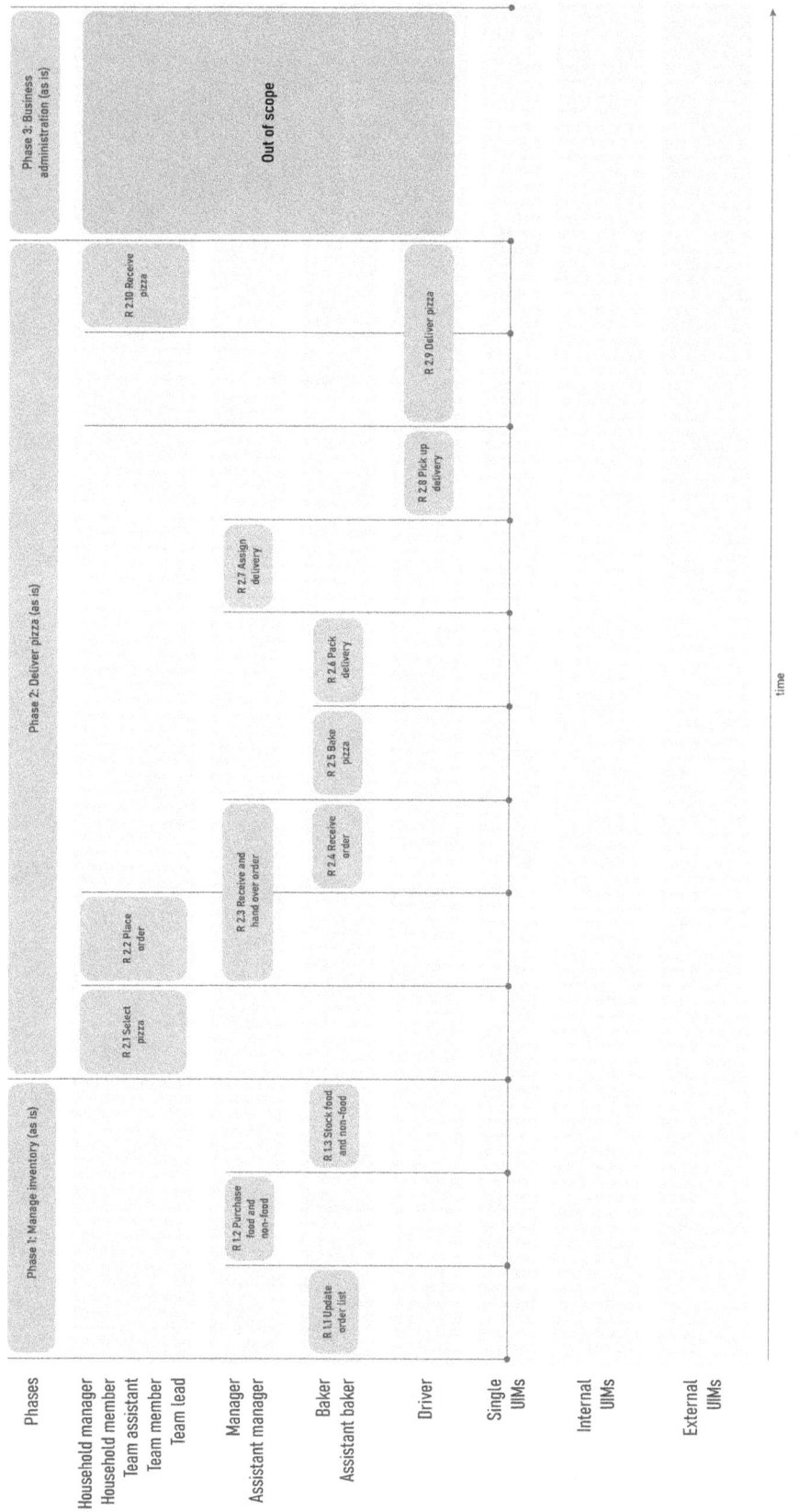

Figure 5.4: Step 2: Identify roles and responsibilities

In our WoP example, we can see that several user roles order and receive a pizza (household manager, household member, team assistant, team member, team lead). We have two roles identified for the manager and the baker positions. It is beneficial to list several initial user roles first (see Figure 5.4).

An extension of the responsibilities is the identification and documentation of the outcome per responsibility (see Figure 5.5).

For each identified user role, we will later create a user role profile. If we see that two or more user roles are similar in terms of needs, goals, and responsibilities, we will consolidate them into fewer user roles. This step is described in Section ?? (??) on page ??.

Step 3: Mark phases that support the business model

The next step is to mark which of the phases support the business model. This step is a sanity check to ensure that the phases really contribute to the outlined business model. Some phases may contribute, and others may not. It also helps to prioritize the phases. All this information helps you to create a road map, for example, by starting with the phase that contributes most to the business model.

In our WoP example, phase 2 supports the business model (see Figure 5.6). There is no business model articulated for phase 1 (manage inventory). Since phase 3 (administer business) is out of scope, a business model is not needed.

Step 4: Map phases or responsibilities to a road map

Now we map the phases or responsibilities to the road map. Nowadays, road maps have a short-term perspective. The mapping typically consists of mapping to different minimal viable products (MVPs) (e.g., MVP 1, MVP 2, etc.).

For our WoP example, phase 2 (sell pizza) is mapped to MVP 1 and phase 1 (manage inventory) to MVP 2 (see Figure 5.7).

The mapping of phases and responsibilities to the road map is an exercise that should be aligned with the entire project team, including the product manager, the technical architect, and the project sponsor. It is possible, and often recommended, to map not only entire phases but also single responsibilities to MVPs.

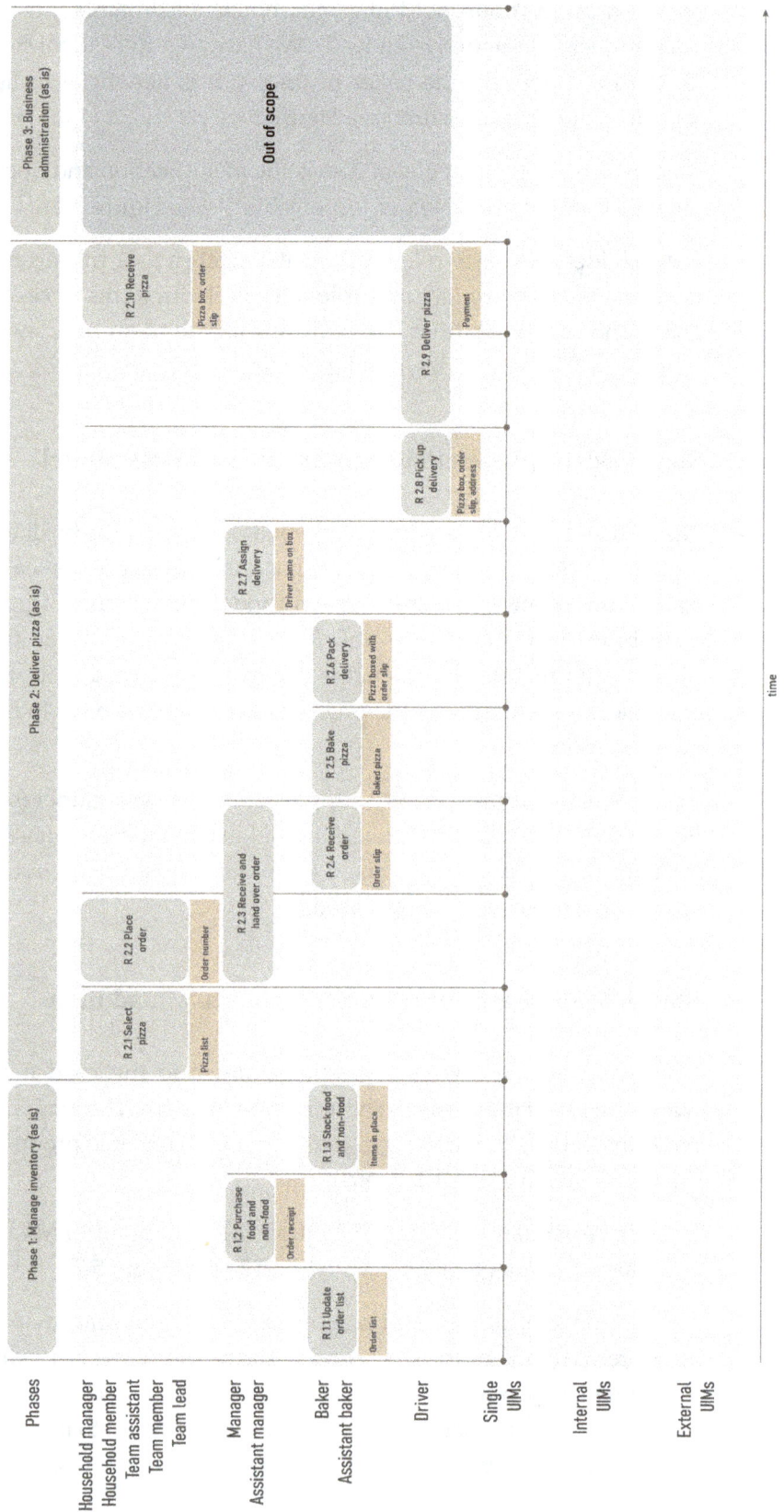

Figure 5.5: Step 2: Documented outcomes per responsibility (useful extension of step 2)

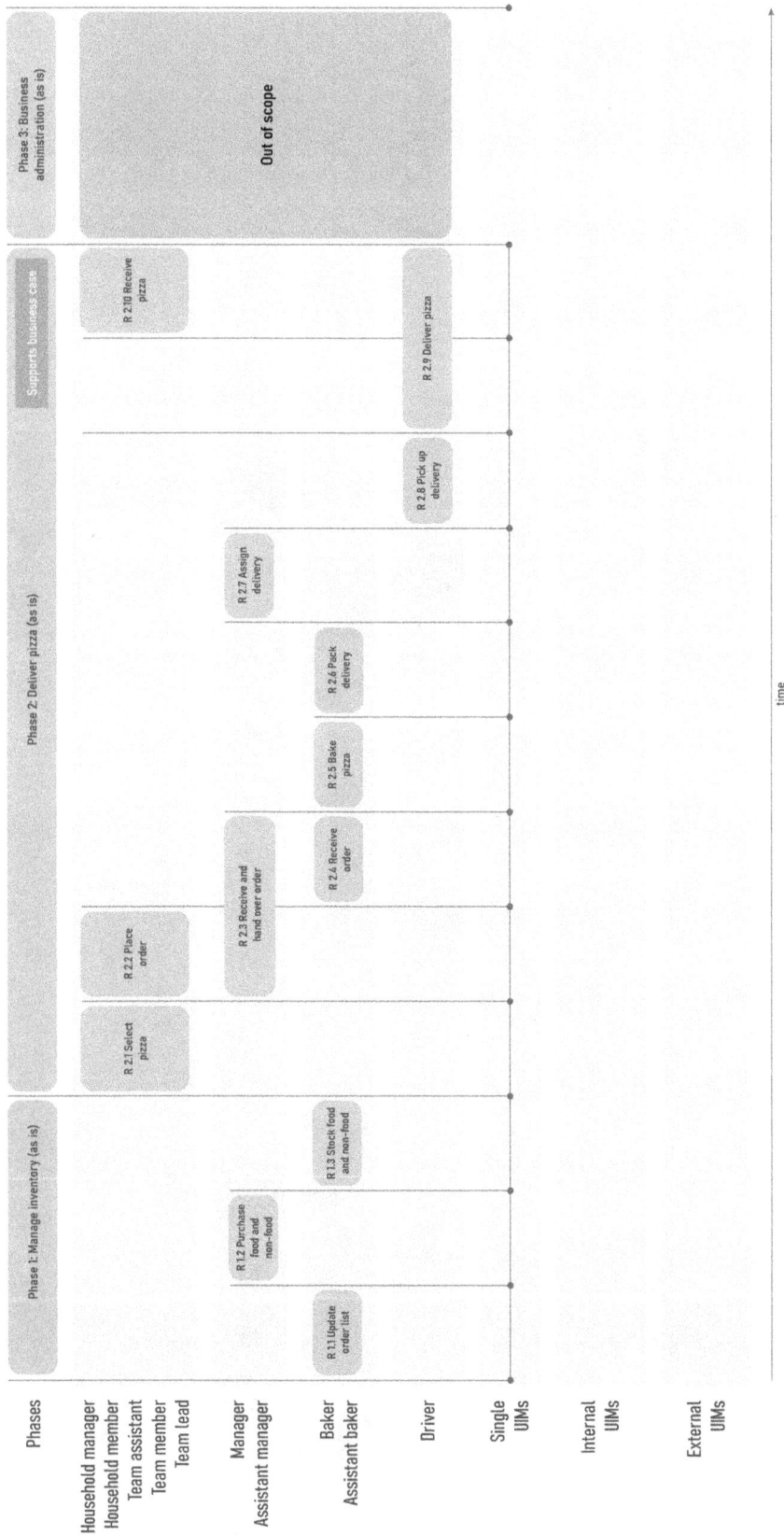

Figure 5.6: Step 3: Mark phases that support the business model

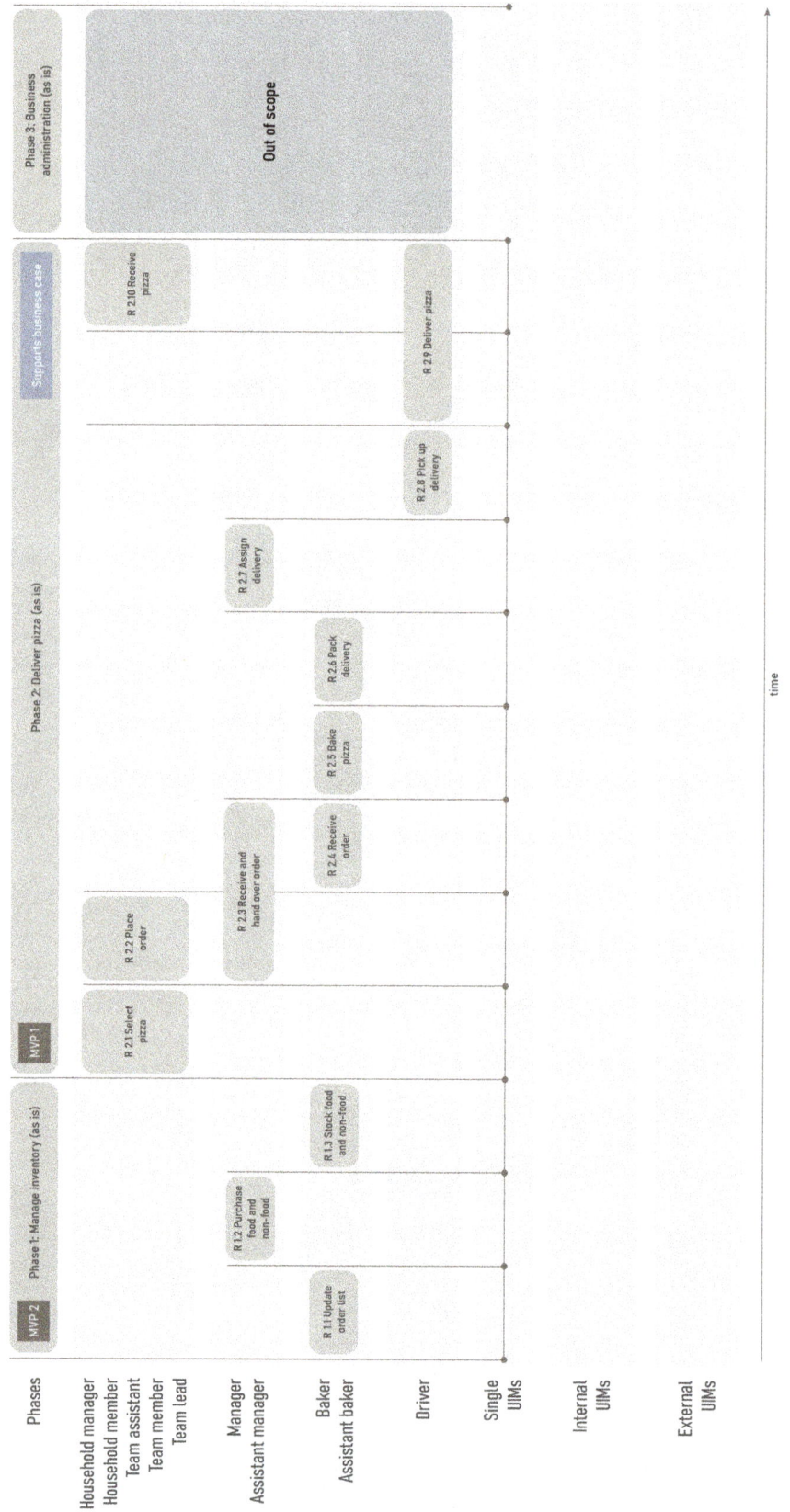

Figure 5.7: Step 4: Map phases or responsibilities to a road map

Step 5: Assign user involvement metrics and determine measurements

After we have identified the responsibilities per phase, we can add the user involvement metrics and measurements to the workflow diagram (see Figure 5.8). Here, we use the metrics as introduced in Chapter 4 (User Involvement Metrics) on page 75.

In the WoP example, the most used metrics are elapsed interaction time (*ECAT*), elapsed intervention time (*EVET*), and elapsed involvement time (*EVOT*). It is beneficial to distinguish between external and internal UIMs. External UIMs are experienced by customers and internal UIMs by employees who deliver services to the customers. The measurements should be actual measurements or reasonable estimates of the current situation. Metrics and actual measurements for our WoP example are documented in Figure 5.8. Key measurements are summarized in Table 5.1.

User involvement metric	Workflow (as is)
Internal UIMs	
EVOT (from receipt to packing)	7 min.
EVOT (from pickup to arrival)	21 - 31 min. (mean: 26 min.)
EVOT (from receipt to arrival)	28 - 38 min. (mean: 33 min.)
External UIMs	
EVOT (from selection to ordering)	7 min.
EVOT (from arrival to tip)	3 min.
ECAT (from selection to tip)	10 min.
EVOT (from selection to tip)	39 - 49 min (mean: 44 min.)

Table 5.1: Actual involvement time measurements

Measurements of the current situation ("as is") enable you to check that a change introduces an improvement. Without a baseline, such an improvement can be claimed, but not demonstrated. This thought is reflected in our next design principle:

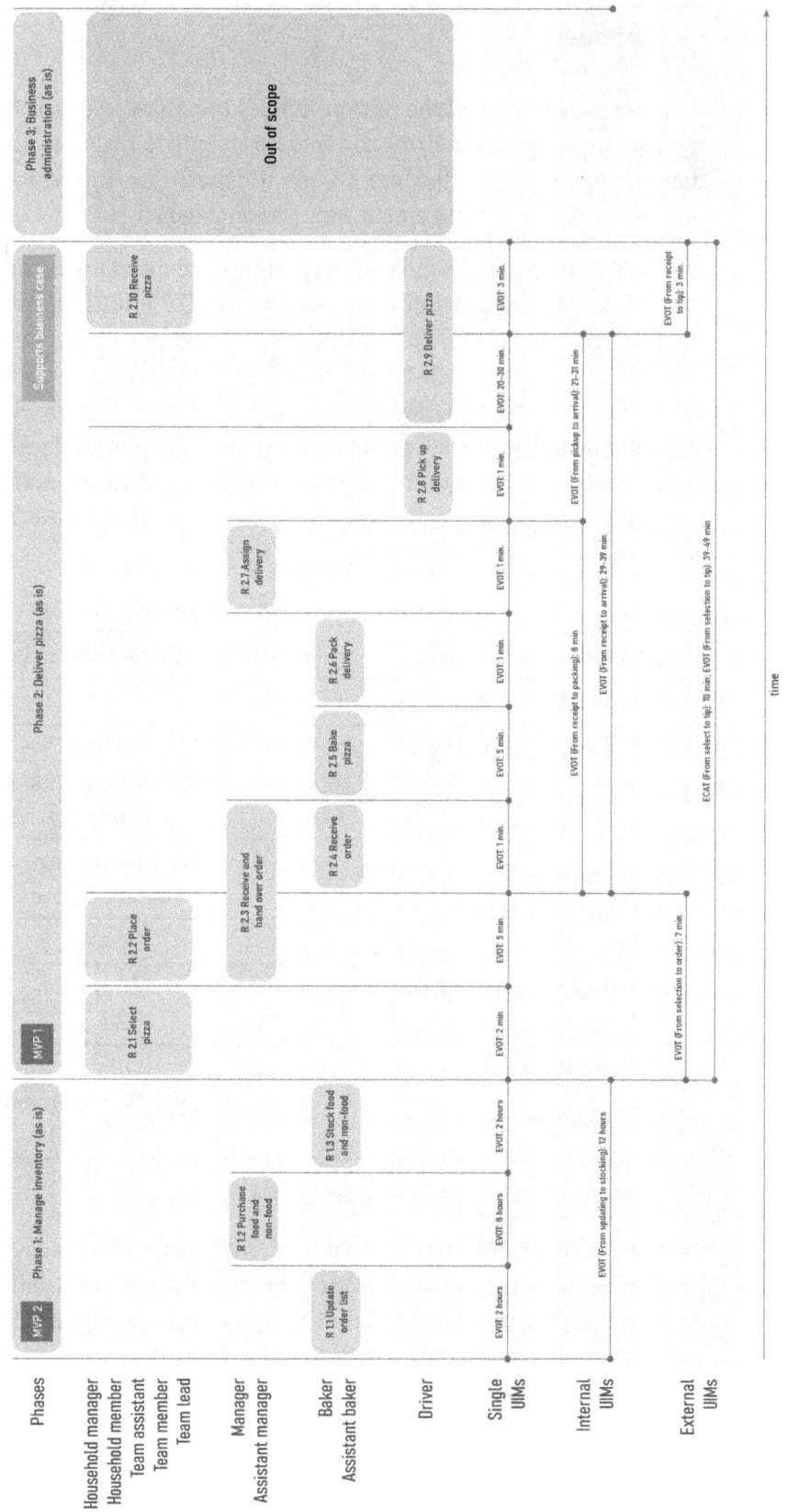

Figure 5.8: Step 5: Assign user involvement metrics and determine measurements

A case needs a base

To demonstrate that a new design introduces improvements, we first need to determine a baseline of the current situation. Otherwise, we have no evidence that the new design will improve anything. For that reason, measuring the baseline is a necessity. Furthermore, the baseline provides useful guidance throughout the design process.

Step 6: Identify pain points per responsibility

The next step is the identification of responsibility-specific pain points. This is an optional step, because there are other steps in the architecture and design process where pain points can be identified.

There are several advantages of identifying pain points for the workflow (as is):

Pain points can be identified as part of a user journey map (as is) (see Section 5 (User Journey Map (as is)) on page 136) and when identifying user roles (see Section 3 (Pain points and wishes) on page 167). A detailed technique for how to elicit pain points and how to differentiate between pain points and wishes is described in Section 3 (Pain points and wishes) on page 167.

- ▶ It gives you an overview (big picture) early in a project about existing pain points across the entire ecosystem.
- ▶ It gives you the ability to rank pain points and to scope and plan the project based on the most important pain points.
- ▶ It gives user representatives or members of the project team the opportunity to share their pain points, which, in many cases, opens an "emotional valve." This can help to smooth an otherwise tensioned-filled project. The identified pain points can be elaborated on later.

The pain points are noted and assigned to the responsibility where they occur (see Figure 5.9). The time measurement can be a useful trigger for identifying pain points, particularly when performance of responsibilities takes much longer than expected.

Representatives of the relevant user roles (end users), as documented on the workflow (as is), should be the ones to identify the pain points, not proxy users.

Ranking technique

After collecting pain points, it is useful to try to understand the importance of the identified pain points from the user's perspective.

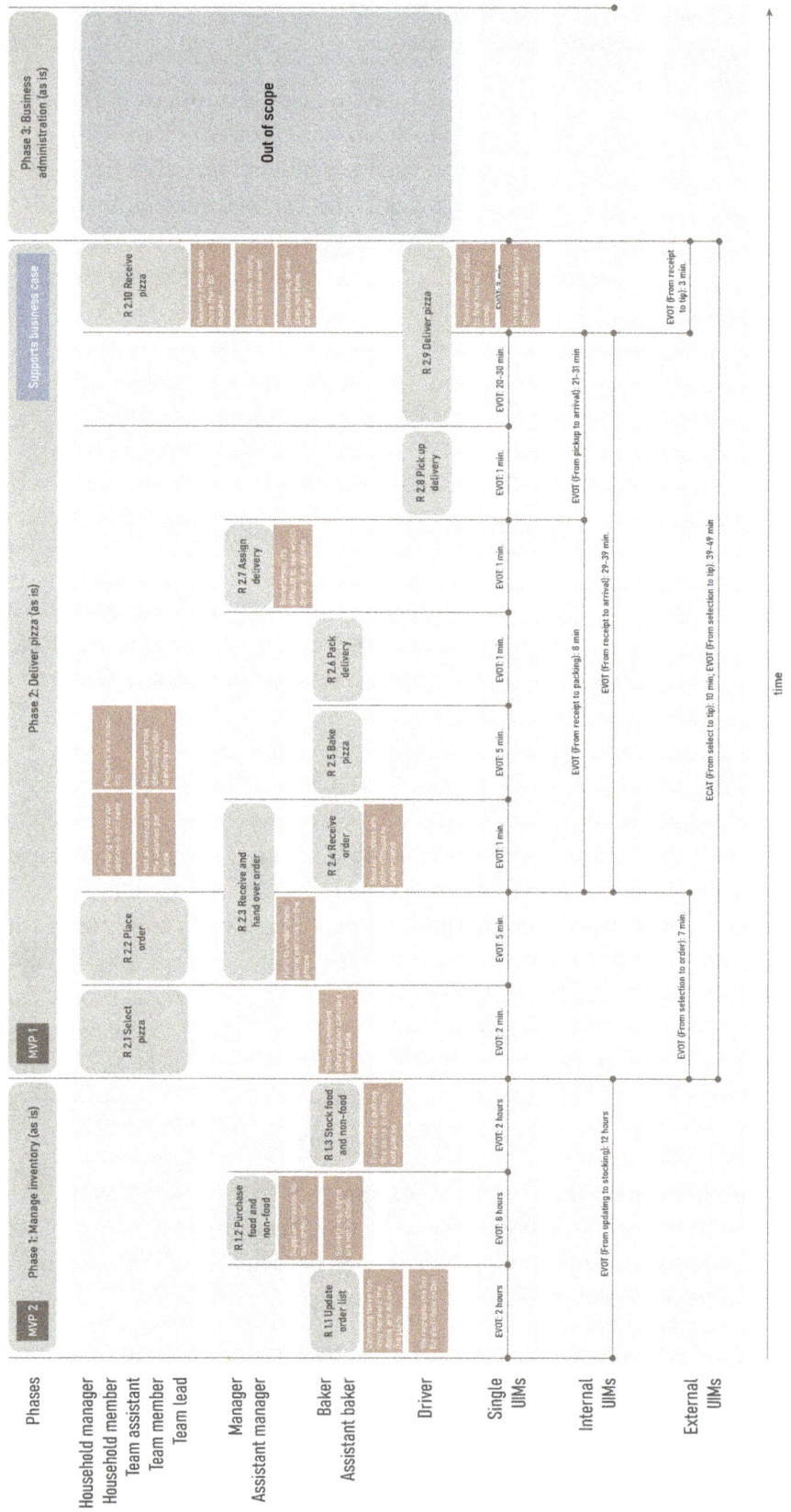

Figure 5.9: Step 6: Identify pain points per responsibility (optional)

Therefore, we like to ask the user to *rank* the pain points or put them in an order of importance. The items are order from 1 (most important) to *n* (least important).

There are a few things that should be considered when ranking pain points:

- ▶ Only end users should rank their pain points. If someone other than an end user needs to be included in the pain point ranking exercise (for instance, for corporate political reasons), it is advisable to keep such ranking results separate from the end users' ranking results.
- ▶ Each ranking needs a ranking criterion. A reasonable ranking criterion is the achievement of the defined goal. Another useful ranking criterion is which pain point should be addressed first.
- ▶ If you interview a group of users, you could ask all users to come up with a group ranking. Ranking as a group has the advantage of collective common sense. On the other hand, group ranking is highly biased. Often, a few opinion leaders in the group influence the other group members. To obtain an unbiased group ranking, it's effective to ask users to keep their ranking decisions hidden from other group members. In a face-to-face setting, they could write their ranking sequence on a sheet of paper or a sticky note (see Figure 5.10). In a remote setting, they could type their ranking into a chat window, without submitting it. The facilitator would wait until everyone had entered their rankings and then asks the users to submit them simultaneously. The facilitator would then collect the individual rankings and calculate the average ranking.

We'll apply the described ranking technique to World of Pizza. Let's assume that four users were asked to rank the identified pain points. The ranking was initiated with, "Please put the pain points in a sequence. The pain point that you want to see addressed first gets the number 1, the pain point that you want to see addressed second gets the number two, etc. Please make sure you rank the pain points, not the ideas for solutions." We received a list of ranked pain points from each user. For each pain points, the rankings were added together and divided by the number of users. The pain point with the lowest average number should be addressed first. The ranking result is shown in Table 5.2 on the following page.

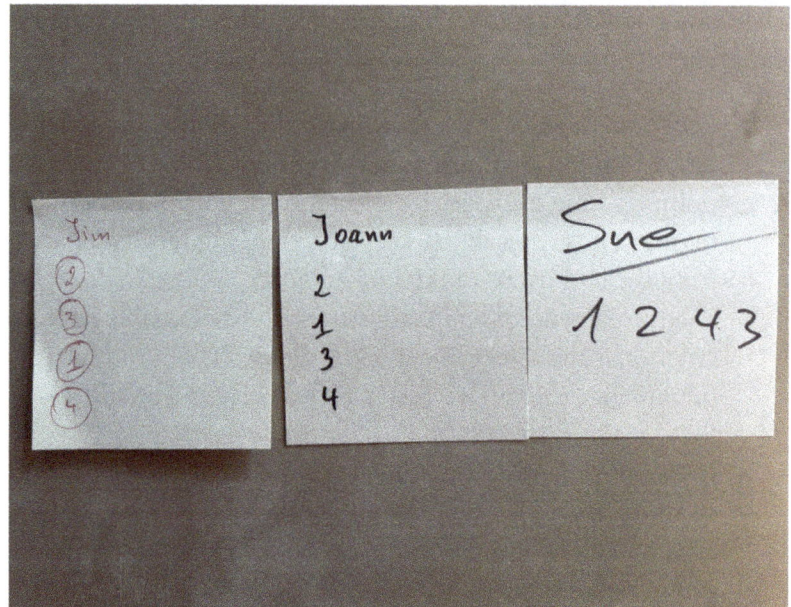

Figure 5.10: Ranking from different participants, documented on sticky notes

Table 5.2: Users' ranking of pain points; the pain point with the lowest mean value becomes number 1 (most important pain point).

| Pain points | Ranking results of four users | | | | | Overall ranking |
	User 1	User 2	User 3	User 4	Mean	
Pizza attributes are missing (e.g., diet, image)	4	2	1	3	$\frac{10}{4} = 2.5$	2
They don't understand me on the phone	1	1	2	1	$\frac{5}{4} = 1.25$	1 (most important)
Delivery takes too long	2	3	3	2	$\frac{10}{4} = 2.5$	2
Driver does not have change	3	4	4	4	$\frac{15}{4} = 3.75$	4 (least important)

Step 7: Identify workflow weaknesses

After the workflow (as is) is completely described, including the pain points, we can identify its weaknesses, including weaknesses related to efficiency. To simplify the process, we can use a weakness checklist:

▶ Middleman: The outcome of one activity is passed through a middleman from one person to another. That middleman may be an inefficiency and can potentially be cut out.

▶ Overlaps: Several individuals perform overlapping tasks that contain redundancies and inefficiencies.

▶ Media friction: The outcome of an activity is in one format, the input for the next activity is in another format, and the data must be transferred. The needed media transfer is a potential inefficiency.

▶ Lack of information: Due to a lack of information, individuals can't plan their work. Lack of information often causes unnecessary waiting time and can contribute to inefficiencies.

▶ Avoidable manual effort: Individuals are using manual effort that is avoidable and could be taken over by the application.

▶ Too many context changes: Individuals are working on too many tasks at the same time, and changing tasks cost avoidable effort.

▶ Insufficient training: Individuals are not trained sufficiently to perform certain tasks, and they must expend extra effort to learn how to do them.

▶ Time-based inefficiency: The amount of time designated for some responsibilities is too long.

▶ Other inefficiencies: There could be other types of inefficiencies, due to such things as old technology or lack of process definition or process training.

The weakness checklist may not be complete, but it provides useful guidance. We can now check to see which of the weaknesses exist in our current workflow:

Middleman   One weakness is the role of the restaurant manager, which becomes a bottleneck for the entire operation. The restaurant manager functions as a middleman. With the introduction of technology, the order can be transferred directly to the kitchen without involving the restaurant manager.

Overlaps   Due to the middleman function of the restaurant manager, there are overlaps between the customer, the manager (when receiving the order), and the kitchen (when handing over the order).

Friction   The telephone-and-paper–based order system has several weaknesses:

- ▶ The use of the telephone to place and receive orders opens the door to misunderstandings. In addition, it takes longer than necessary.
- ▶ Writing the orders on separate order slips makes it hard to keep an overview of the orders.
- ▶ Some of the order slips are difficult to read and can result in the baking of pizza that wasn't ordered.
- ▶ Some customers need to wait to place an order. This waiting time is not only inconvenient for the customers but can lead to a loss of business.
- ▶ The kitchen lacks visibility about which pizza should be done by when. Normally, there is only one pizza baker in the kitchen. Due to the paper-based ordering system, it is difficult to determine whether a second cook is needed to process the pizza orders in a timely manner.

Lack of information   The driver availability board is poorly maintained. Sometimes, orders are created that shouldn't have been, due to lacking overview of driver availability.

Avoidable manual effort   We can identify two weaknesses:

- ▶ Writing the order on paper order slips.
- ▶ Assigning drivers to deliveries.

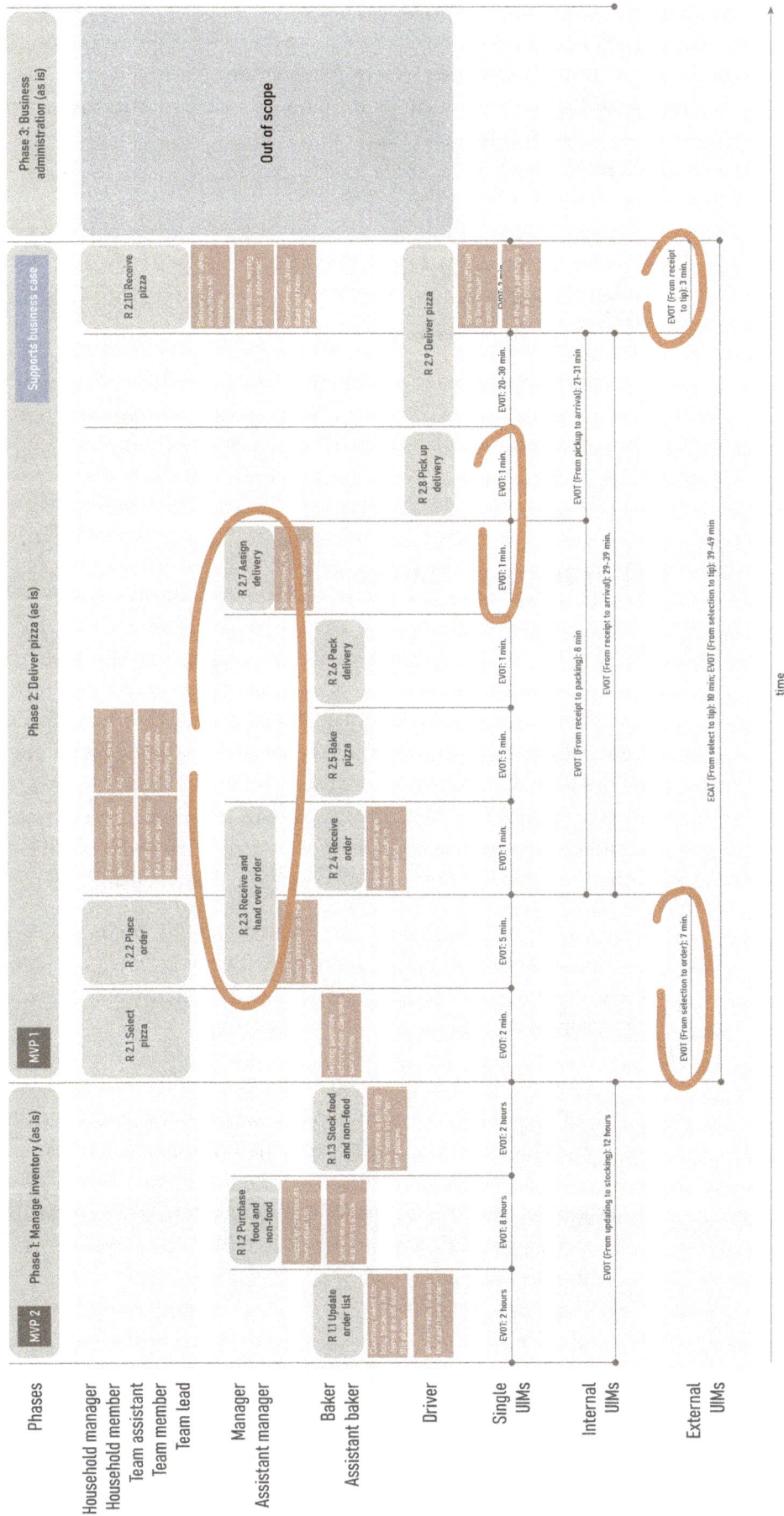

Figure 5.11: Step 7: Identify workflow weaknesses

Time-based inefficiencies These measurements can be improved:

- ▶ It takes five minutes to place an order. This is too long for the customer as well as for the manager.
- ▶ It takes one minutes to hand over an order to the kitchen, which is too long.
- ▶ It takes two minutes to assign a delivery and to pick it up, which is too long.
- ▶ It takes three minutes to hand over a pizza to a customer and to receive a tip, which is too long.
- ▶ The EVOT for placing an order and receiving a pizza is 39–49 minutes, which is too long.

Identified weaknesses are marked in Figure 5.11. They will be addressed in the phase "workflow (to be)," where we'll create a new workflow (to be) (see Chapter 9 (Workflow (to be)) on page 219).

User Journey Map (as is)

Purpose

The workflow (as is) provides a useful overview of the user roles and their involvement, expressed as responsibilities along a timeline. It shows how certain phases are executed today. In many cases, the workflow level is sufficient. However, in some cases, more details about certain responsibilities of a user role are needed. This is a situation where a user journey map (as is) can be useful.

A user journey map needs to be created only if there is a need for information that cannot be identified with a workflow (as is) alone. Here are typical information-related needs that justify the creation of a user journey map:

- ▶ A workflow (as is) was created, but it still looks confusing, inconsistent, or incomplete; a detailed investigation into selected responsibilities may help to clarify the workflow (as is).
- ▶ Certain responsibilities or important details of responsibilities are not known; a deep dive will help to uncover these missing details.
- ▶ User involvement metrics and measurements are not available or are difficult to estimate; a bottom-up approach will help to estimate the time per responsibilities.
- ▶ The project has the need to see an overview about the touch points per user role; touch points are not shown on the workflow level.

▶ It is known that certain user roles have certain pain points that cannot be explained on the workflow level; a more detailed investigation is needed to be able to identify and understand these pain points.

In this regard, the creation of a user journey map (as is) is an optional step in the experience foundation process. It helps to mitigate the risk of working with inaccurate, misleading, or incomplete information.

To include efficiency relevant time information, a customized user journey map template is used (see Figure 5.12). Many user journey map templates use an emotional state indicator (happy face, neutral face, sad face) to identify pain points and their magnitude. Based on my industrial experience, emotional states are often not a reliable indicator for pain points and their magnitude. It is the reason why the emotional journey is not considered in the template. However, time and frequency information combined with ranked pain points has proven to be a strong indicator for pain points and inefficiencies.

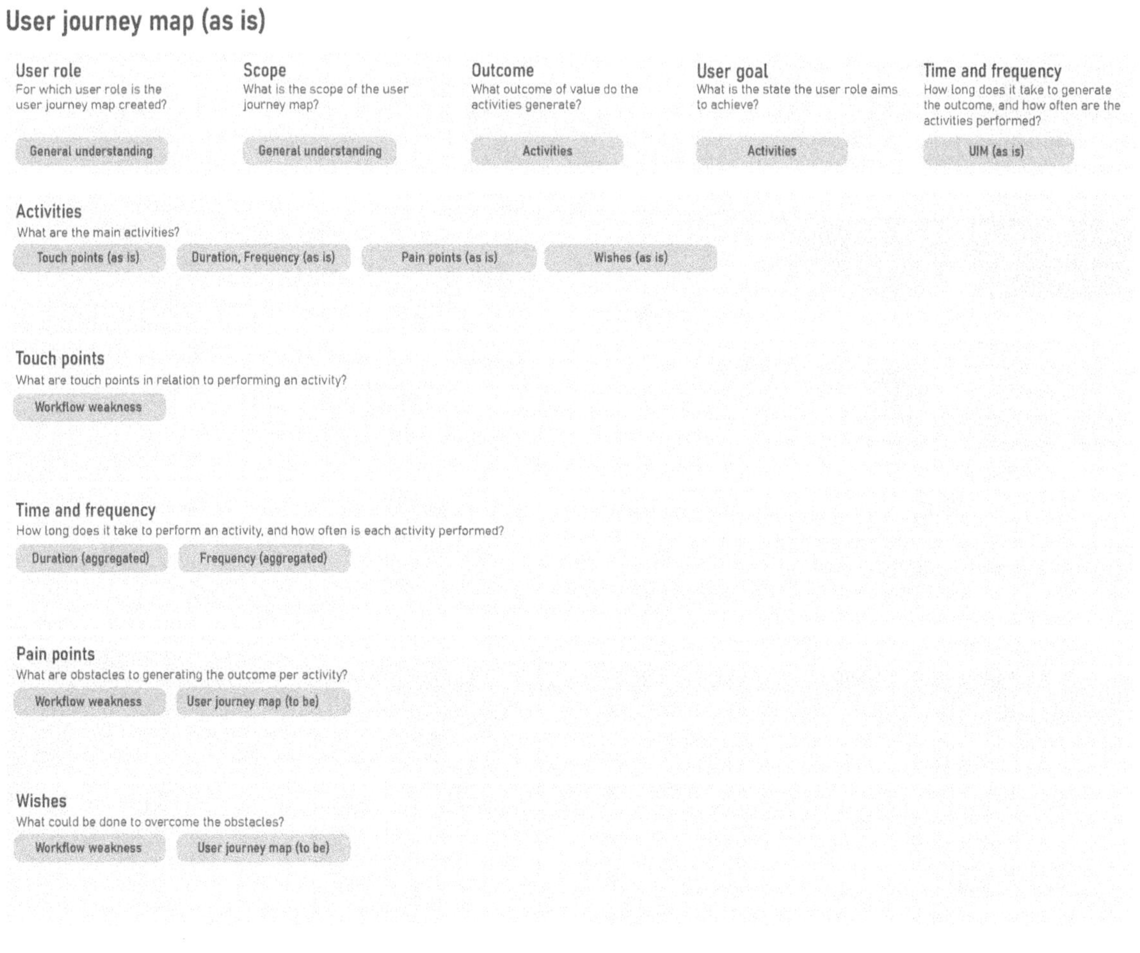

User journey map (as is)

User role
For which user role is the
user journey map created?

General understanding

Scope
What is the scope of the user
journey map?

General understanding

Outcome
What outcome of value do the
activities generate?

Activities

User goal
What is the state the user role aims
to achieve?

Activities

Time and frequency
How long does it take to generate
the outcome, and how often are the
activities performed?

UIM (as is)

Activities
What are the main activities?

Touch points (as is)   Duration, Frequency (as is)   Pain points (as is)   Wishes (as is)

Touch points
What are touch points in relation to performing an activity?

Workflow weakness

Time and frequency
How long does it take to perform an activity, and how often is each activity performed?

Duration (aggregated)   Frequency (aggregated)

Pain points
What are obstacles to generating the outcome per activity?

Workflow weakness   User journey map (to be)

Wishes
What could be done to overcome the obstacles?

Workflow weakness   User journey map (to be)

Figure 5.12: User journey map template (as is)

In the remainder of this user journey map (as is) section, we will discuss a user journey map (as is) for the user role "household manager" for the responsibilities "R 2.1 place order" and "R 2.9 receive pizza," which are also shown in the workflow (as is) (see top lane in Figure 5.11). A user journey map is created for one user role only and can cover on one or more responsibilities.

Details for R 2.1 Place order

The user journey map of the user role "household manager" for the responsibility R 2.1 Place order is shown in Figure 5.13.

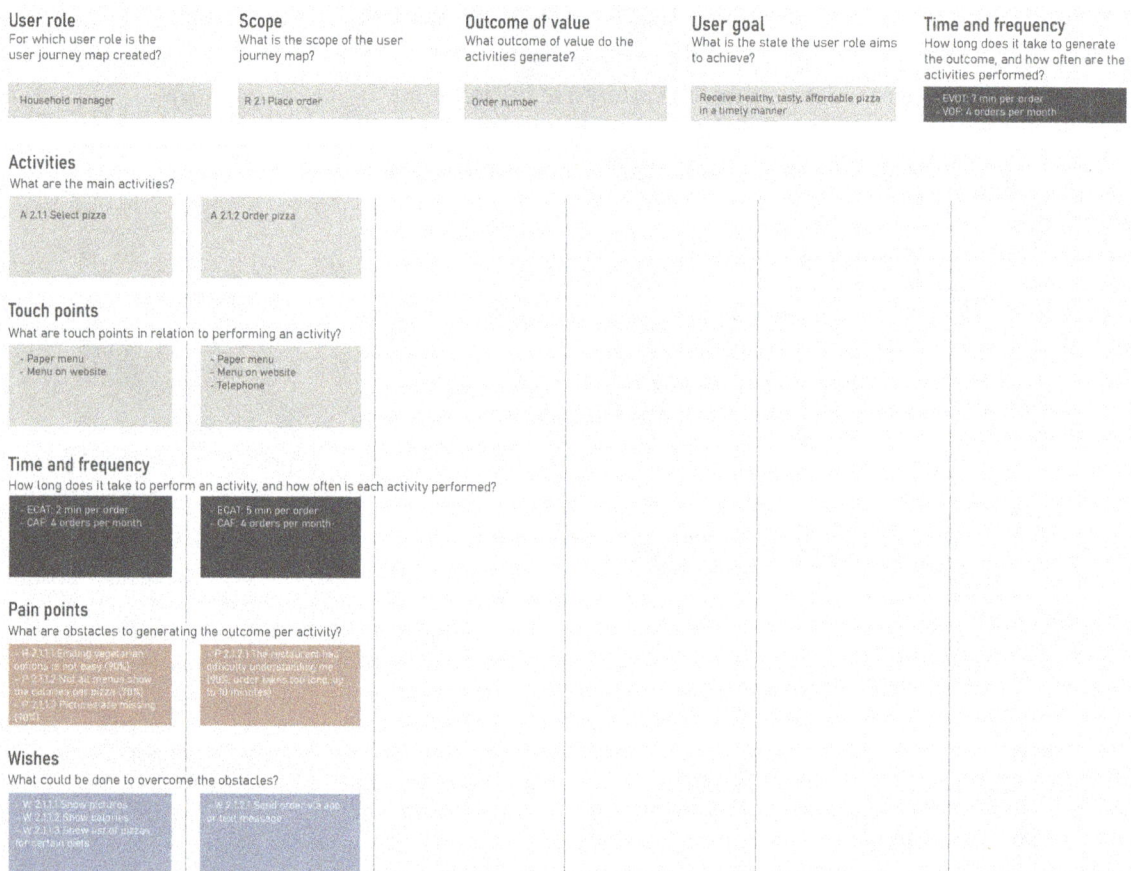

User role	Scope	Outcome of value	User goal	Time and frequency
For which user role is the user journey map created?	What is the scope of the user journey map?	What outcome of value do the activities generate?	What is the state the user role aims to achieve?	How long does it take to generate the outcome, and how often are the activities performed?
Household manager	R 2.1 Place order	Order number	Receive healthy, tasty, affordable pizza in a timely manner	- EVOT: 7 min per order - VOF: 4 orders per month

Activities
What are the main activities?

A 2.1.1 Select pizza	A 2.1.2 Order pizza

Touch points
What are touch points in relation to performing an activity?

- Paper menu - Menu on website	- Paper menu - Menu on website - Telephone

Time and frequency
How long does it take to perform an activity, and how often is each activity performed?

- ECAT: 2 min per order - CAF: 4 orders per month	- ECAT: 5 min per order - CAF: 4 orders per month

Pain points
What are obstacles to generating the outcome per activity?

- P 2.1.1.1 Finding vegetarian options is not easy (90%) - P 2.1.1.2 Not all menus show the calories per pizza (70%) - P 2.1.1.3 Pictures are missing (10%)	- P 2.1.2.1 The restaurant has difficulty understanding me (10%), order takes too long, up to 10 minutes)

Wishes
What could be done to overcome the obstacles?

- W 2.1.1.1 Show pictures - W 2.1.1.2 Show calories - W 2.1.1.3 Show list of pizzas for certain diets	- W 2.1.2.1 Send order via app or text message

Figure 5.13: R 2.1 Place order: User journey map (as is)

User role   *For which user role is the user journey map created?*

A user journey map focuses on one *user role* only.

We focus here on the user role "household manager."

User role

Household manager

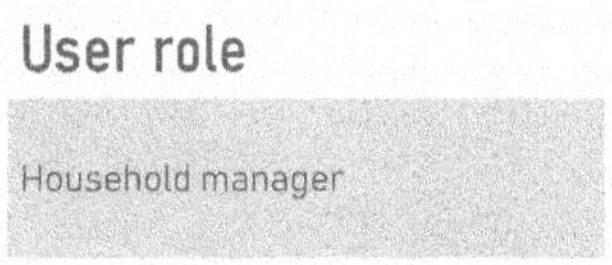

Figure 5.14: R 2.1 Place order: User role

Scope   *What is the scope of the user journey map?*

The *scope* of the user journey map (as is) is one selected responsibility.

In our WoP example, the scope is R 2.1 Place order.

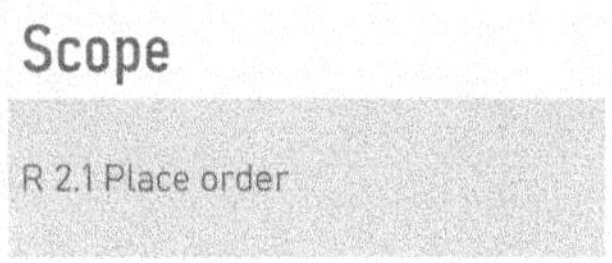

Scope

R 2.1 Place order

Figure 5.15: R 2.1 Place order: Scope

Outcome of value   *What outcome of value do the activities generate?*

An *outcome of value* defines what the activities of the user journey map create. An outcome is tangible and has value for the user role.

In our WoP example, the outcome of the responsibility R 2.1 Place order is an order number.

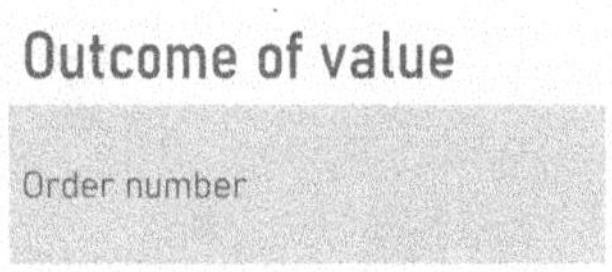

Outcome of value

Order number

Figure 5.16: R 2.1 Place order: Outcome

User goal   *What is the state the user role aims to achieve?*

The *user goal* is an intended state.

For the household manager, the goal is to receive healthy, tasty, affordable pizza in a timely manner.

User goal

Receive healthy, tasty, affordable pizza in a timely manner

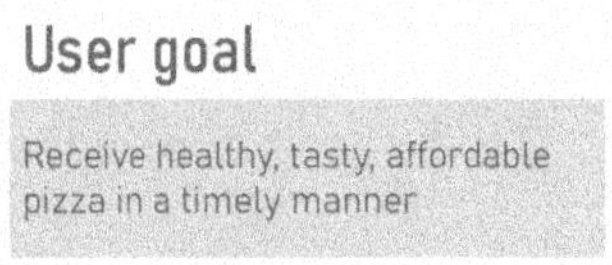

Figure 5.17: R 2.1 Place order: User goal

Time and frequency per outcome   *How long does it take to generate the outcome, and how often are the activities performed?*

The *time* information is an aggregate, a sum of the time information for each activity. The time information can be expressed as an elapsed time or as a working time. Elapsed time refers the difference between the beginning of the first activity and the end of the last activity.

Frequency considers how often the outcome is generated, relative to a reference time window. Typical reference time windows are "per hour," "per day," "per week," "per month," "per quarter," and "per year." We use the user involvement metrics to express the time and frequency information (see Section 4 (Metric taxonomy) on page 76).

Time and frequency

EVOT: 7 min per order
VOF: 4 orders per month

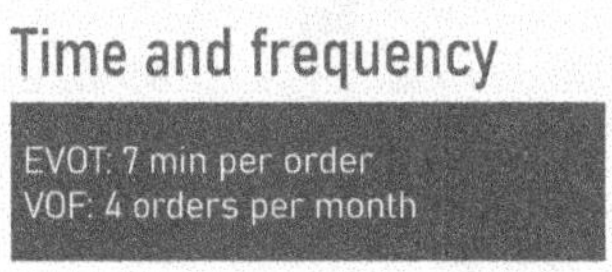

Figure 5.18: R 2.1 Place order: Time and frequency per outcome

In our WoP example, the user role "household manager" needs about seven minutes to select a pizza and place an order. On average, the household manager orders a pizza once per week or about four times per month.

Activities

R 2.1 Place order
- A 2.1.1 Select pizza
- A 2.1.2 Order pizza

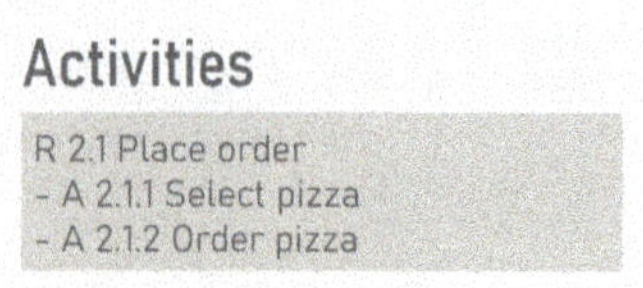

Figure 5.19: R 2.1 Place order: Activities

Touch points

A 2.1.1 Select pizza
- Paper menu
- Menu on website

A 2.1.2 Order pizza
- Paper menu
- Menu on website
- Telephone

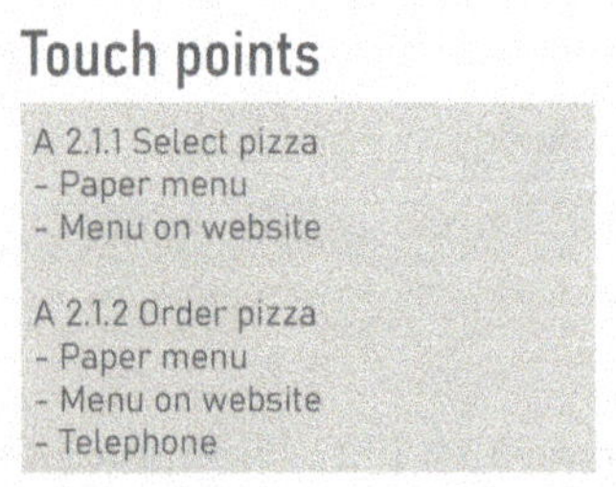

Figure 5.20: R 2.1 Place order: Touch points

Time and frequency

A 2.1.1 Select pizza
- ECAT: 2 min per order
- CAF: 4 orders per month

A 2.1.2 Order pizza
- ECAT: 5 min per order
- CAF: 4 orders per month

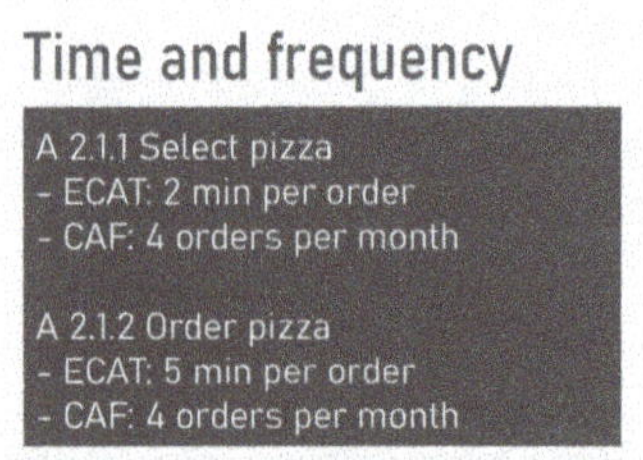

Figure 5.21: R 2.1 Place order: Time and frequency per activity

Pain points

A 2.1.1 Select pizza
- P 2.1.1.1 Finding vegetarian options is not easy (90%)
- P 2.1.1.2 Not all menus show the calories per pizza (70%)
- P 2.1.1.3 Pictures are missing (90%)

A 2.1.2 Order pizza
- P 2.1.2.1 The restaurant has difficulty understanding me (90%)

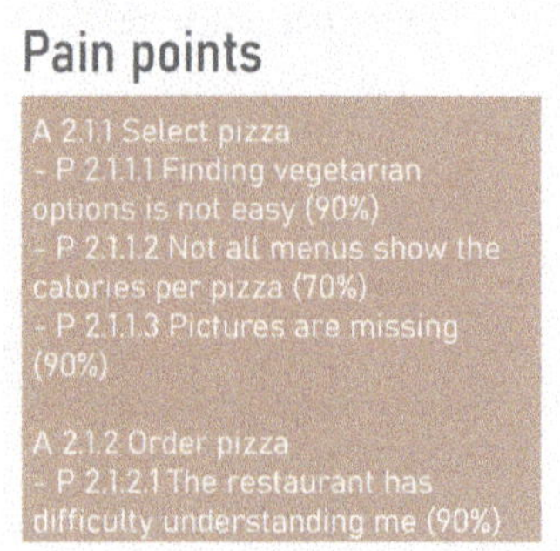

Figure 5.22: R 2.1 Place order: Pain points

Activities   *What are the main activities?*

The *activities* are actions that the user performs to generate the defined outcome and achieve the defined goal.

In our WoP example, the household manager's activities are A 2.1.1 Select pizza and A 2.1.2 Order pizza.

The subsequent information regarding *touch points*, *time*, *pain points*, and *wishes* is elicited for each activity. The dotted lines in the template indicate which touch points, time and frequencies, pain points, and wishes belong to which activity.

Touch points   *What are touch points in relation to performing an activity?*

Touch points describe artifacts or tools the user interacts with or uses when performing an activity.

In our WoP example, the household manager uses either a paper version of the menu or a website to select a pizza, and the same touch points plus a phone to place the order. We can see that the use of different media (paper, website, phone) indicates an inefficiency, because the user has to switch between the different touch points.

Time and frequency per activity   *How long does it take to perform an activity, and how often is each activity performed?*

Time for activities describes the time it takes per activity. *Frequency* describes how often an activity is performed.

In our WoP example, it takes two minutes for the household manager to select a pizza and five minutes to make the phone call and place the order. The household manager orders a pizza about four times per month (about once per week).

Pain points   *What are obstacles to generating the outcome per activity?*

A *pain point* is an obstacle for the user when performing an activity to achieve a goal. Pain points should be identified by the end users. Identifying pain points sounds easier than it is. In my experience, when users are asked to name pain points, they typically mention wishes. A methodology for how to elicit genuine pain points is described in Chapter 6 (User Roles) on page 149.

In our WoP pizza examples, we have identified a few pain points. For the activity "select pizza," one pain point was "Can't find veggie pizza" (90 percent of the time). Another pain point is the lack of calorie information per pizza (70 percent of the time) and missing pictures of pizzas on the website (90 percent of the time). That last item is interesting because traditional pizza menus don't show pictures.

For the activity "order pizza," a pain point is communication issues, misunderstandings between the customer and the restaurant employees when an order is placed via phone (90 percent of the time).

Wishes *What could be done to overcome the obstacles?*

Wishes are expectations of how a pain point can be addressed or overcome. Incorporating wishes is not so much about adopting the user's idea unchallenged, but rather seeing the direction the wish is taking. Wishes should be used to validate the correct understanding of a pain point. The wishes are part of the pain point identification and are described more in detail in Chapter 6 (User Roles) on page 149.

Wishes

A 2.1.1 Select pizza
- W 2.1.1.1 Show pictures
- W 2.1.1.2 Show calories
- W 2.1.1.3 Show list of pizzas for certain diets

A 2.1.2 Order pizza
- W 2.1.2.1 Send order via app or text message

Figure 5.23: R 2.1 Place order: Wishes

In the case of our WoP example, the user mentioned three wishes: show pictures of pizza, show calories contents of pizza, and list pizza by diet type. The wishes are no surprise, which indicates we have a good understanding of the pain points.

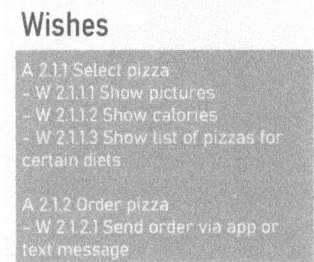

Details for R 2.9 Receive pizza

The user journey map for the second responsibility for customers, R 2.9 Receive pizza, is shown in Figure 5.24.

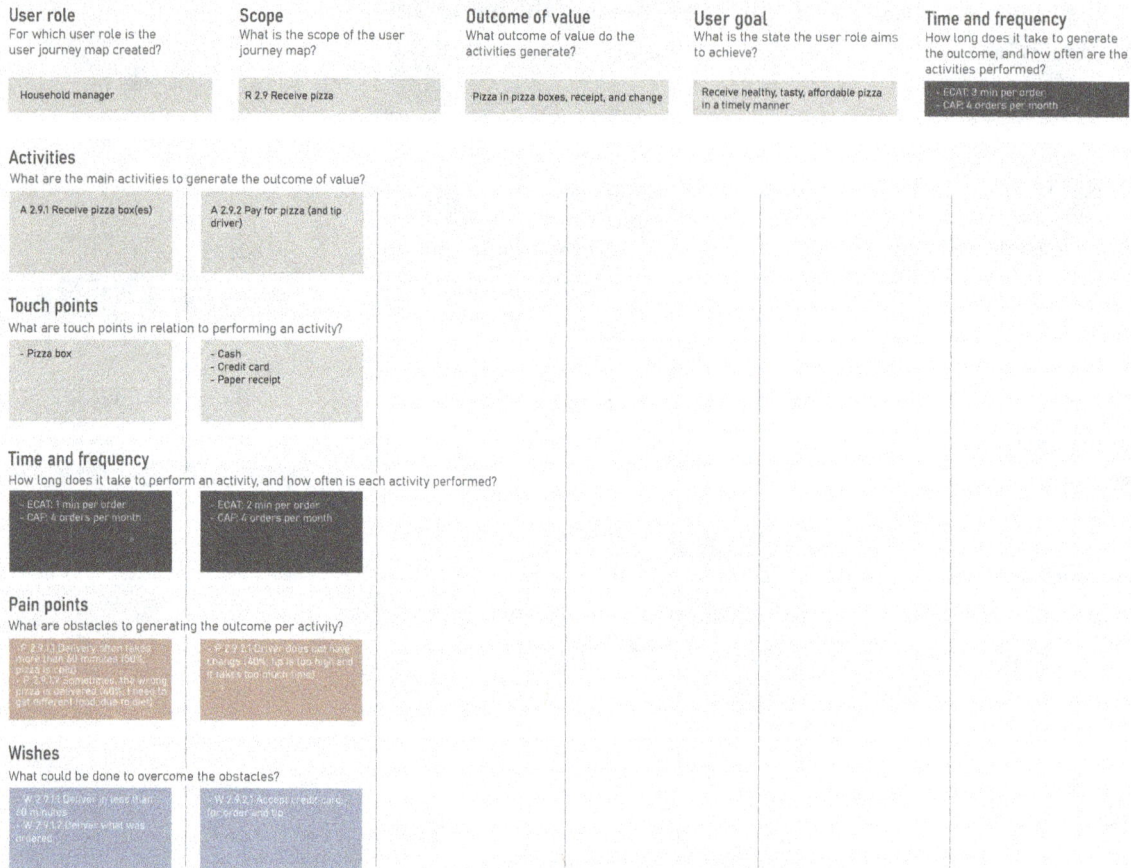

Figure 5.24: R 2.9 Receive pizza: User journey map (as is)

User role   *For which user role is the user journey map created?*

The *user role* is "household manager," the same user role we used for the previous user journey map.

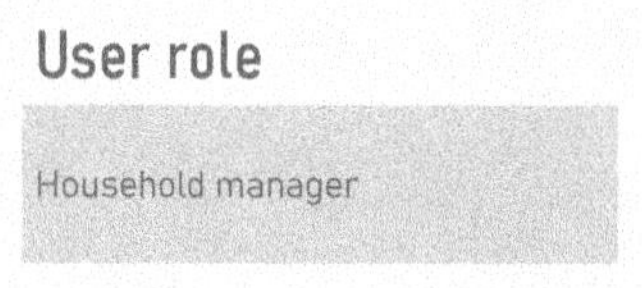

User role

Household manager

Figure 5.25: R 2.9 Receive pizza: User role

Scope   *What is the scope of the user journey map?*

The *scope* is the second responsibility of the household manager, called R 2.9 Receive pizza. This scope covers the receival of the pizza and the payment, including the tip for the driver.

Scope

R 2.9 Receive pizza

Figure 5.26: R 2.9 Receive pizza: Scope

Outcome of value   *What outcome of value do the activities generate?*

The *outcome* of this responsibility is the pizza received in a pizza box, a receipt, and any change given to the customer.

Outcome of value

Pizza in pizza boxes, receipt, and change

Figure 5.27: R 2.9 Receive pizza: Outcome

User goal   *What is the state that the user role aims to achieve?*

The *user goal* is the same goal as in the previous responsibility: to receive healthy, tasty, affordable pizza in a timely manner.

User goal

Receive healthy, tasty, affordable pizza in a timely manner

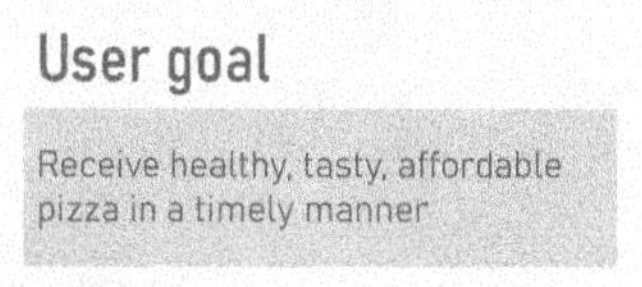

Figure 5.28: R 2.9 Receive pizza: User goal

Time and frequency per outcome   *How long does it take to generate the outcome, and how often are the activities performed?*

The elapsed time is three minutes per order for receiving a pizza. The frequency is four times per month.

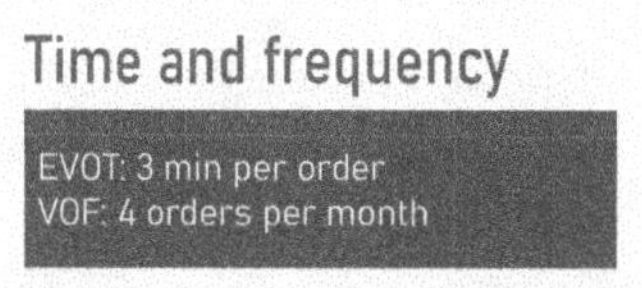

Time and frequency

EVOT: 3 min per order
VOF: 4 orders per month

Figure 5.29: R 2.9 Receive pizza: Time and frequency per outcome

Activities   *What are the main activities?*

In our WoP example, the household manager's activities are A 2.9.1 Receive pizza and A 2.9.2 Pay for pizza (including the tip for the driver).

Activities

R 2.9 Receive pizza
- A 2.9.1 Receive pizza box(es)
- A 2.9.2 Pay for pizza (and tip driver)

Figure 5.30: R 2.9 Receive pizza: Activities

Touch points   *What are touch points in relation to performing an activity?*

In our WoP example, the household manager uses a website or paper version of the menu to select a pizza, and the same touch points plus a phone to place the order.

Time and frequency per activity   *How long does it take to perform an activity, and how often is each activity performed?*

In our WoP example, it takes one minute for the household manager to receive a pizza and another two minutes to pay for it, including tipping the driver. The household manager does it about once per week, or about four times per month.

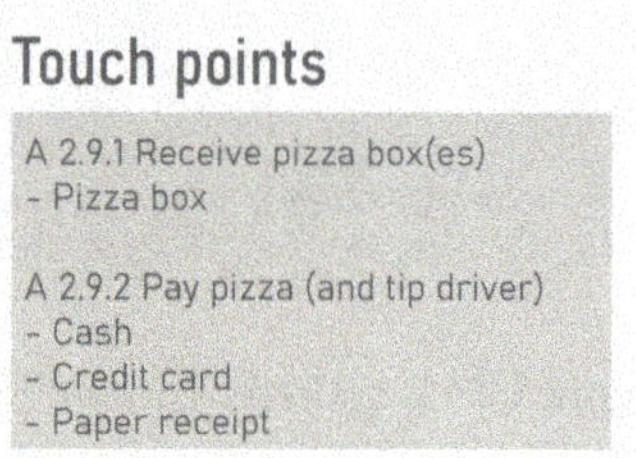

Touch points

A 2.9.1 Receive pizza box(es)
- Pizza box

A 2.9.2 Pay pizza (and tip driver)
- Cash
- Credit card
- Paper receipt

Figure 5.31: R 2.9 Receive pizza: Touch points

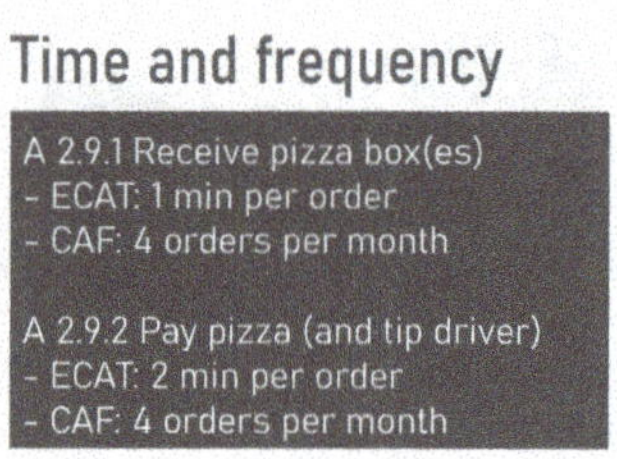

Time and frequency

A 2.9.1 Receive pizza box(es)
- ECAT: 1 min per order
- CAF: 4 orders per month

A 2.9.2 Pay pizza (and tip driver)
- ECAT: 2 min per order
- CAF: 4 orders per month

Figure 5.32: R 2.9 Receive pizza: Time and frequency per activity

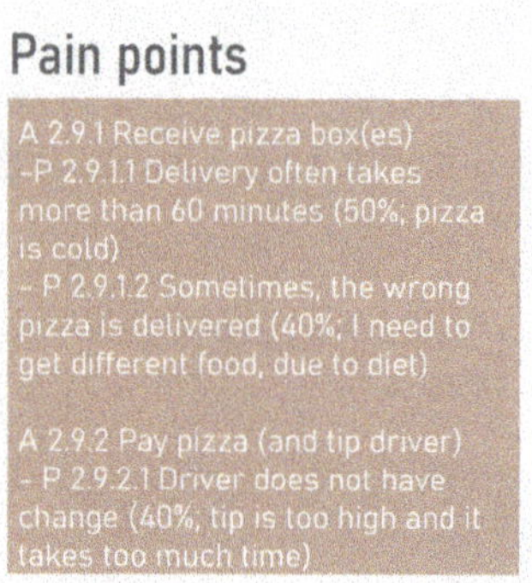

Pain points

A 2.9.1 Receive pizza box(es)
- P 2.9.1.1 Delivery often takes more than 60 minutes (50%; pizza is cold)
- P 2.9.1.2 Sometimes, the wrong pizza is delivered (40%; I need to get different food, due to diet)

A 2.9.2 Pay pizza (and tip driver)
- P 2.9.2.1 Driver does not have change (40%; tip is too high and it takes too much time)

Figure 5.33: R 2.9 Receive pizza: Pain points

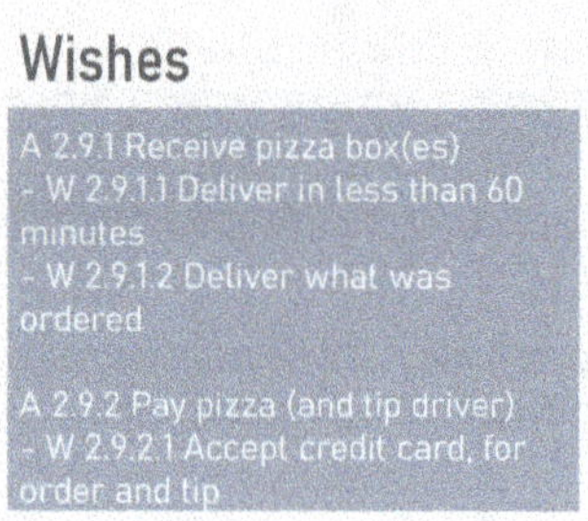

Wishes

A 2.9.1 Receive pizza box(es)
- W 2.9.1.1 Deliver in less than 60 minutes
- W 2.9.1.2 Deliver what was ordered

A 2.9.2 Pay pizza (and tip driver)
- W 2.9.2.1 Accept credit card, for order and tip

Figure 5.34: R 2.9 Receive pizza: Wishes

Pain points *What are obstacles to generating the outcome per activity?*

We have identified two pain points for the activity "receive pizza box(es)." One is that the delivery often takes more than 60 minutes (50 percent of the time) which leads to a cold pizza. Another pain point is that the wrong pizza is being delivered (50 percent of the time).

For the activity "pay for pizza (and tip driver)," we found one pain point: the driver does not have change (40 percent of time) which can lead be an embarrassing situation for all involved. A negative result of this could be that the driver ends up with a larger tip than intended.

Wishes *What could be done to overcome the obstacles?*

One wish for the first pain point (delivery takes too long) is to have the pizza delivered in less than 60 minutes, and, for the second pain point, what is delivered should be what was ordered. As for tipping the driver, it should be possible to pay for both the pizza and the tip with a credit card, to avoid the issue with change.

Summary

Workflow (as is)

▶ The time between ordering a pizza and receiving it is 39 to 49 minutes (EVOT), which is too long.

▶ The manager is too involved in every order. The manager should intervene only when necessary.

▶ Move on to <u>User role</u>

◀ Go back to <u>User Involvement Metrics</u>

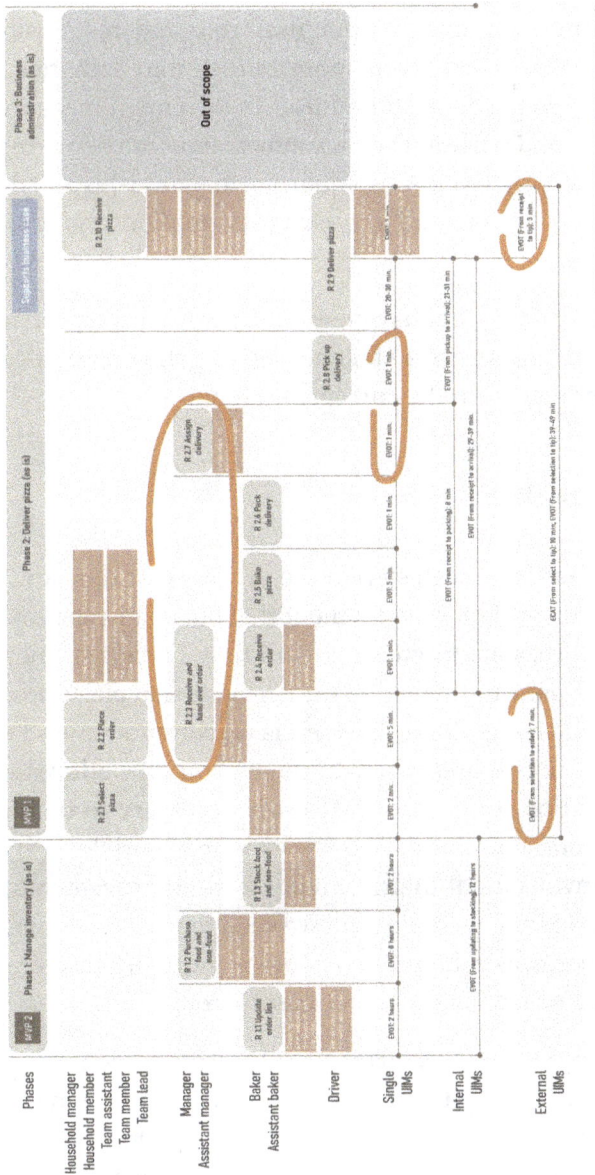

Lessons learned

Workflow (as is)   The workflow (as is) is visualized with a swim lane diagram. It shows phases, user roles, and responsibilities per user role. Furthermore, it is marked with phases that support the stated business model. Phases or responsibilities are mapped to road maps that can be expressed as MVPs (minimal viable products) or MUPs (minimal usable products). In addition, the workflow (as is) shows user involvement metrics and identified workflow weaknesses. A workflow (as is) is an effective tool to get an overview of the current responsibilities and can be used as a baseline. The baseline allows you to provide evidence that a future workflow has introduced improvements.

User journey map (as is)   The user journey map (as is) allows you to gain more insights per user role and responsibility. It helps to break down the responsibilities into activities, and to identify touch points, detailed user involvement measurements, pain points, and wishes. The time information can be aggregated to the responsibility level. A user journey map (as is) is an additional tool used to understand the current situation and to identify weaknesses.

Both the workflow (as is) view and the user journey map (as is) help to bring various stakeholders together with a common understanding about the current situation.

Tips and tricks

Workflow (as is)   Each step in the process cost time and money. Therefore, there should be a benefit that outweighs the cost. There are several reasons to create a workflow (as is): 1) There is no common understanding, or no understanding at all, of how things are currently being done. 2) There is no common understanding about weaknesses and which of them should be addressed with the application under design. 3) It is necessary to demonstrate that the proposed solution, expressed with a workflow (to be) and the user involvement metrics, will create improvements and increases the efficiency. To do that, we need to have user involvement measurements as a baseline. If one or more of these reasons is applicable, a workflow (as is) is a useful tool.

Based on my experience, many workflows can be defined in four to eight hours. This is often perceived as a reasonable and affordable effort. Since it is often difficult to get people into a (virtual) room for eight hours, the session can be sliced into two-hour segments. A domain expert for the workflow (as is) should be present, a user representative, and maybe another person. Three people are ideal for workflow sessions. If more people are interested, they can be brought in later as reviewers.

We all love details! One of the biggest challenges is to keep the workflow on a high level that is informative, affordable to create and affordable to maintain. As a rule of thumb, a workflow (as is) should not contain more than five phases. Each phase should have several contributing user roles. A phase should not have more than five responsibilities per user role. If it is difficult to stay on a high level, an outside moderator may be able to keep the exercise on track.

User journey map (as is) Getting trapped in too much detail is also a risk when developing user journey maps. Try to keep the map at as high a level as possible. The intent is not to design the application here. It should provide meaningful data for understanding the activities, identifying pain points, wishes, and time information. That's really all. For the user journey map, I suggest using a white board rather than sticky notes. Sticky notes are hard to read from two meters/yards or more, and they are not environmentally friendly.

Exercise 1.4

Goal Describe the current workflow (as is) with UIMs for your selected example that include all user roles. Identify the weaknesses of the workflow (as is).

Material Workflow (as is) template; user journey map template; UIMs; checklist of workflow weaknesses

Completion criteria:

- ▶ The workflow (as is) shows internal and external UIMs.
- ▶ The workflow (as is) shows several phases (not more than five); for each phase, it shows several user roles with several responsibilities (not more than five per user role).
- ▶ External and internal user involvement metrics and measurements are assigned to the workflow (as is).
- ▶ For at least one responsibility, a user journey map (as is) is created and documented.
- ▶ The pain points are ranked by at least three users. The final rank is calculated.
- ▶ For each weakness item in the workflow, there is a note about whether it applies or does not apply, with a reason.

User Roles | 6

Time isn't the main thing. It's the only thing.
Miles Davis

Purpose

Why are users important?

At a glance, this book appears to be about designing and developing a technical application. So why is there a chapter about users? Well, designing and developing a technical application successfully requires more than just technical considerations. There are at least three good reasons why the user is important and plays a key role in the success of an application.

We design a human-technical system

For an application to be successful, the user needs to be able to generate an outcome of value. The user cannot generate the outcome without the technical application, and the technical application cannot generate the outcome without the user. The user and the technical application need to work together.

This is relatively easy to demonstrate. Let's assume a user wants to send a message to someone (outcome of value) via a text message application (technical application) on a mobile phone. Let's move the mobile phone one meter (or one yard) away from the user, so they cannot reach it (and the mind and speech recognition are turned off ☺). What is the phone doing right now? It's "waiting" for the user's input. What is the user doing? Maybe the user is staring at the phone and thinking about the person who is supposed to receive the message. Maybe the user is considering switching to

Figure 6.1: Rocky Balboa Statue in Philadelphia, PA, USA; artist: A. Thomas Schomberg

other types of technology (sheet of paper, paper envelope, pen, and stamp; carrier pigeon; smoke signs) to write and send the message. Maybe the user will solve the problem like Rocky did when he yelled through the window alerting the neighborhood that Adrian, the sister of his best friend Paulie, was with him: *"Yo, Paulie – Ya sister's with me! I'll call ya later."* [107, p. 48]

Generation of an outcome of value requires the user and the technical application to work together. The application cannot do it without the user, and the user cannot do it without the application. This is even true to some extent if the technical application is automated; the user still needs to configure it and to start it initially.

Such dependency between different entities to achieve something together has a name: it is called a system. A *system* is a "combination of interacting elements organized to achieve one or more stated purposes" [108, clause 4.1.46]. The user is one system element and the technical application (or technical system) is another system element. They interact within a context of use. The stated purpose is the generation of the outcome of value (see Figure 6.2). In this book, the user together with the technical application is considered a system, more specifically a human-technical system, abbreviated HTS.

Definition 5 (Human-technical system) *System consisting of one or more users and a technical application working together to achieve one or more stated purpose.*

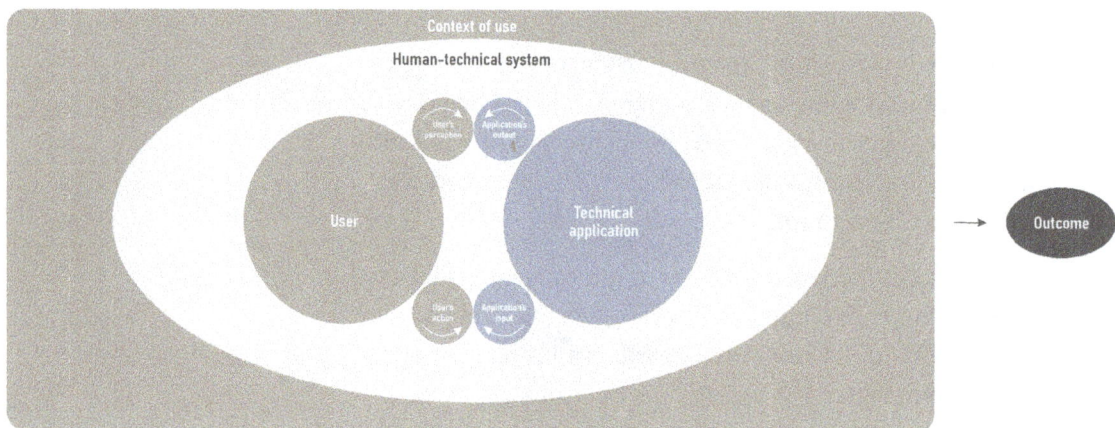

Figure 6.2: Human-technical system

A human-technical system has all the characteristics of a human-made system. It has a system environment with environmental conditions (called the context of use). It has interfaces or interactions with system external entities (including other human-technical systems, other technical applications, and/or other humans). It consists of system elements that interact with each other (users and technical application). It has a stated purpose (the generation of an outcome of value) [109, 110]. A human-technical system is considered in this book a system category in its own right.

The ability to generate an outcome of value is a property of the human-technical system that none of its system elements (i.e., the user or the technical application) has. Remember, the technical application cannot send a text message without the user, and the user cannot send a text message without the technical application (unless the user is Rocky, of course). This kind of property has a name, too. It's called an "emergent" property [111]. Emergence is the "principle that whole entities exhibit properties which are meaningful only when attributed to the whole, not to its parts" [110, p. 314]. The definition means that the "whole," the system, can do something that none of its parts can do.

For instance, a car with its driver can move something or someone from point A to point B, but none of its parts can do that. An airplane with a pilot can fly in a controlled way, but none of its parts can fly in a controlled way. A bicycle with a rider can ride, but none of its parts can do it. The emergent property is the reason the system was invented in the first place. The system elements were added because they contribute something that helps to realize the emergent property.

For a human-technical system, the emergent property is to "generate the outcome of value." A key enabler of that emergent property is the interaction between the technical application and the user. In this book, we call this interaction "user involvement." Because we cannot generate the outcome of value without the user, we determine the success of our architecture and design decisions based on the qualities of the human-technical system, not just on the qualities of the technical application. When it comes to architecture and design for efficiency, we focus on efficiency for the user and not on the efficiency of the technical application. We can say that we design a human-technical system that generates the outcome of value in the most effective and efficient way *for the user*.

Here is the first answer to the question of why users are important: the user is an element of the human-technical system necessary for realizing the emergent behavior "generate the outcome of value." Ignoring the user adds a significant risk, possibly leading to a

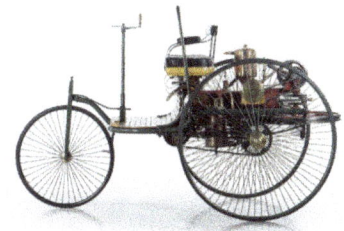

Figure 6.3: Patent-Motorwagen Nummer 1 (patent motor vehicle no. 1), invented by Carl Benz in Mannheim, Germany, 1885; source: Wikimedia & Daimler AG; licenses: GNU Free Documentation License, CC BY-SA 3.0

Figure 6.4: Wright Flyer, invented by Orville and Wilburt Wright in Dayton, Ohio, USA, 1903; source: Wikimedia; photographer: John T. Daniels; license: public domain

Figure 6.5: Laufrad (run bike), invented by Baron Karl von Drais in Mannheim, Germany, 1817; source: Wikimedia; photographer: Daderot; license: public domain.

You may remember the cited case study from Melbourne (see Section 1 (What are some examples of efficiency benefits?) on page 16) where the public transportation system authority replaced tram conductors, who sold tickets, with ticketing machines for operational efficiency and cost reasons [39]. The authorities focused on the internal operational efficiency (the efficiency of the technical application) and not on the efficiency for customers (the efficiency of the human-technical system).

A broader system scope than human-technical system is known as a "socio-technical system" that includes social organizations and more complex and diverse systems [112–114].

1: There are exceptions: safety-critical systems like airplanes, cars, locomotives, nuclear power plants, and others require the user to be trained and certified. User training changes users. However, the idea of changing the user is rare in the landscape of human-technical systems and in most cases is not wanted.

situation in which the outcome of value cannot be generated at all, or not as efficiently as intended.

Context of use and the user constitute user-centered constraints

There is another reason why users are important. Let's discuss what is being designed and what is not. The architecture and design decisions are made for the technical application. The user is not subject to any architecture and design decisions. We do not change the user. The user is a given, a constraint for the technical application.[1]

Sometimes, the context of use is subject to architecture and design decisions, for instance when the workflow or the environment is modified for the application under design. Sometimes the context of use is a constraint.

There are many known human factors that can be considered as constraints [6, 54, 115–121]. Let's look at one factor that can be compared between humans and computers: clock speed. The clock speed expresses how many cycles per second a processor can execute instructions [122]. Today (2022), processors have a clock speed that is measured in gigahertz. A processor with a clock speed of 1 gigahertz can execute up to 1 billion (10^9) instructions per second. It is expected that this number will go up over the next few years.

The clock speed of a human can be determined by measuring the minimum reaction time. A human has a minimum reaction time of about 200 milliseconds. This means that a human can perceive a simple informational stimulus, cognitively process it, and execute a motor action in about 200 milliseconds, as a minimum [123, Figure 1]. Thus, a human has a maximum clock speed of about 5 Hz (five executions per second). This number is fixed. It is a constraint for the human-technical system. From a clock speed perspective, the human user is a bottleneck. This is a relevant insight for efficiency; it indicates that architecture and design decisions should attempt to minimize the frequency of user involvements to avoid or at least minimize the user's clock speed bottleneck.

There is another relevant human factor called the "mental model" [6, 58, 124, 125]. A mental models is a cognitive representation of an external reality [124]. Users have mental models of all aspects of life: how to perform certain job-related tasks, how to shop, how to cook, how to drive a car, etc. If something doesn't work according to a user's mental model, the user has a problem and gets stuck. Getting stuck is the opposite of what we want to achieve with efficient user involvement. It is therefore essential to understand a user's mental models. They are a constraint too.

Here we call applicable insights about the user and the context of use *user-centered constraints*. These are constraints that should be reflected on when decisions are being made for the technical applications, in order to optimize the human-technical system (see Figure 6.6). To ensure the intended quality of the human-technical system, it should be tested frequently as it evolves. The test results will influence the architecture and design of the technical application.

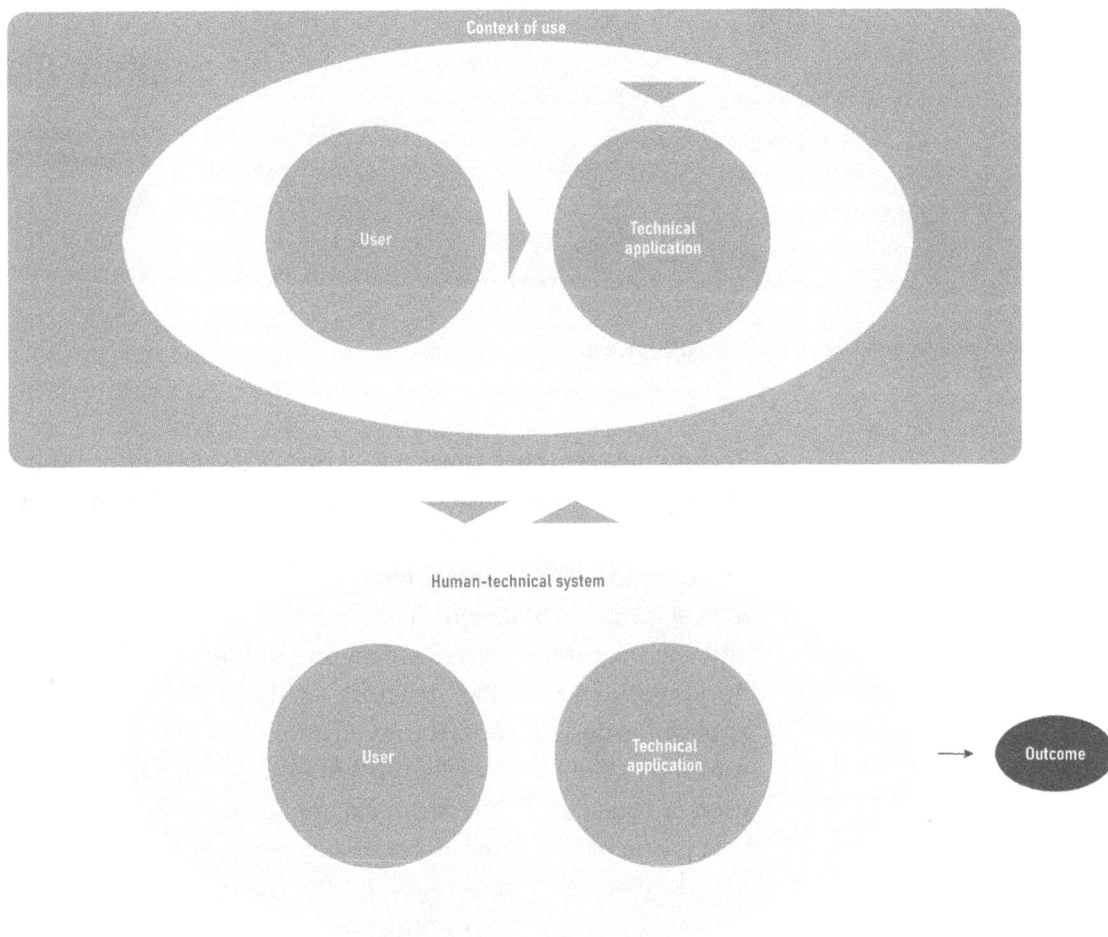

Figure 6.6: Dependencies to optimize a human-technical system

Now we have the second answer to the question of why users are important: users and their contexts of use constitute user-centered constraints and inputs for the architecture and design of the technical application to optimize the human-technical system.

Starting with user-centered constraints is cost-effective and leads to high quality

The third reason the user is mentioned in this book is because, when you're in the design and development process, user-centered constraints should be considered. There are two basic approaches to that issue (see Figure 6.7).

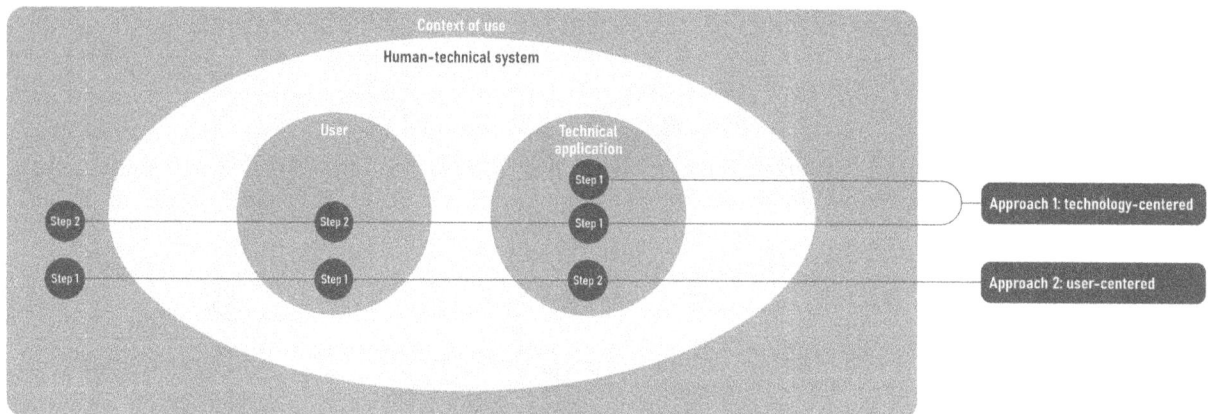

Figure 6.7: Technology-centered vs. user-centered approach

Technology-centered approach Approach 1 (see upper approach in Figure 6.7) starts with designing and developing the technical application. User-centered constraints do not play a role at all. The user interface is considered a technical task that leads to a *technology-centered design*. It means that the function allocation and the user interface reflect the mental model of engineers or developers and/or the structure of the used technology. The application design is often centered around a technical architecture, functions, or objects (see Figure 6.8). A user's mental model is not used or considered. The technical application is released without user participation. User involvement obstacles are a certainty and are addressed as change requests after the application is launched. At least for industrial applications, many users have to attend training to learn how to use them; such trainings are time- and cost-intensive and would not be necessary if a user-centered approach had been applied.

Design and development approaches

Technology-centric approaches

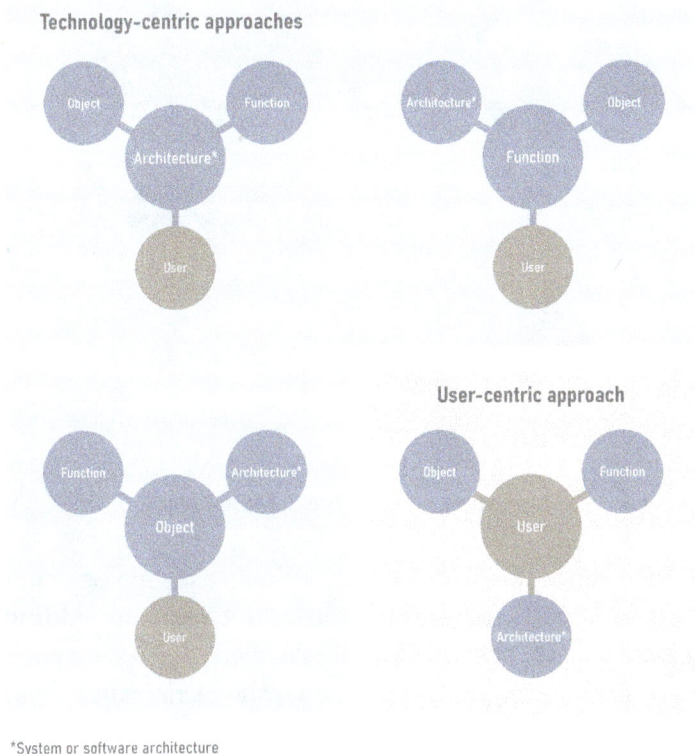

User-centric approach

*System or software architecture

Figure 6.8: Design and development approaches

A variation of this approach is to involve users at the end of the design and development process. Many obstacles for user involvement will be detected, and only some of them can be addressed (the design and development project is almost over, the budget is mostly spent, and the launch date is around the corner). Other obstacles might be addressed with new entries in the user manual and in the online help. Fundamental problems like function allocation and workflow obstacles won't be addressed at all.

The technology-centered approach results in a working technical application (a system element of the human-technical system). It usually does not lead to an optimized human-technical system. The technical application can reach a local quality optimum, at best. When applying approach 1, the project manager should allocate budget and time to address the user involvement obstacles late in the project. Such obstacles are not even a risk–they are a certainty.

User-centered approach Approach 2 (see lower approach in Figure 6.7) starts with the discovery of the user role profile and the context of use (i.e., the user-centered constraints). Architecture and design decisions are made for the technical application based on the knowledge of user-centered constraints. This approach leads to an optimized human-technical system with a *user-centered design* as a result.

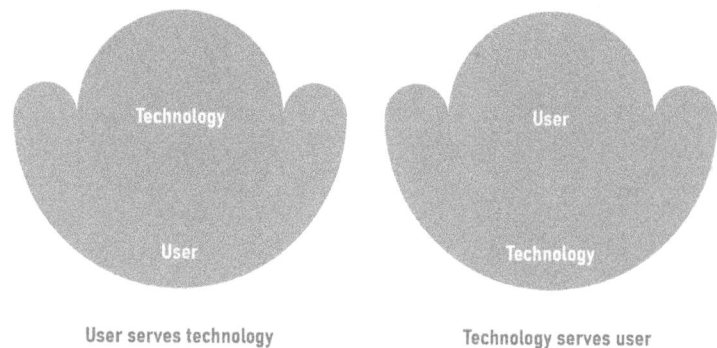

Figure 6.9: Technology-centered and user-centered approaches

Since the user-centered constraints influence technology choices, and the user participates from the very beginning, additional budgeting for late obstacle fixes is not needed. Any mismatches between user's expectations and what the technical application offers for the user are detected and addressed along the way. Furthermore, the realized quality of the human-technical system is typically higher.

If the project budget and the resulting quality are important considerations in a design and development project, approach 2, the user-centered approach, should be chosen. It allows to create an architecture and design of a human-technical system that generates the outcome of value with *the smallest amount of resources and time* to achieve the *global quality optimum for the user* (see [104] for additional benefits of applying a user-centered design approach). A user-centered approach is needed to create a first class user experience quality.

An visualization of both approaches is depicted in Figure 6.9. The technology-centered approach (approach 1) puts technology front and center. The technical application is designed and developed without (or with insufficient) consideration of user-centered constraints. To put it bluntly: the user serves technology.

The user-centered approach (approach 2) puts the user front and center. The user-centered constraints are discovered and defined first. Based on those insights, the technology and technical application are invented, developed, selected, and/or customized to support the user. To put it bluntly: technology serves the user.

To achieve high efficiency for the user, we have to fine tune the user involvement, like the inner workings of a clock, a race car,

Such a user-centered approach should not be confused with "agile development." Agile development is a way to allocate work packages to people on a frequent basis. Agile development does not ensure a user-centered approach. Unfortunately, it is rather the opposite. Agile development (the word "development" says it) is often applied as "implement first–maybe design later" which reflects a technology-centered approach.

or a precision instrument. The optimization requires an *excellent* understanding of the user-centered constraints from the beginning. To apply architecture and design for efficiency successfully, a user-centered approach is a necessity.

Understanding users

Defining a user role is not purely a documentation activity. The definition is the result of talking to users, observing them and studying artifacts and tools they use to achieve their goals [126, 127]. What cannot be directly observed is the user's motivation, beliefs, and the mental models. Understanding those things is the result of empathetic engagement with users.

Empathy can be defined as "the capacity to understand what another person is experiencing from within the other person's frame of reference, i.e., the capacity to place oneself in another's shoes" [128]. The expression "from within the other person's frame of reference" is important. It expresses that empathy is not just an attitude or knowing something about another person. It is the ability to experience the world from the perspective of that other person in a certain role. If done well, empathy even allows one to derive the user's preferences, based on a gained understanding of their motivations and mental models. In this sense, empathy enables us to *predict* users' preferences to some extent, which is very helpful during a project. For that reason, just "being empathetic" is insufficient. As experience professionals, we need to "act empathically."

Acting empathically is needed throughout the entire design project, not only at the beginning–for instance in a co-creation workshop where sticky notes are collected and glued on a wall (and then posted on social media). Therefore, I prefer calling it an "empathy journey." It is relevant in all project phases, including the discovery, definition, design, implementation, and evaluation phases. Throughout that journey, curiosity and humility should guide us to ask questions and to learn something new about our users along the way that shapes our image of them.

Just as Michelangelo chiseled David out of the marble block, we need to chisel an image of our users. This process requires time and many interactions with our users. Just as Michelangelo removed everything from the marble block "that was not David," we need to remove everything from our mental marble block that is not our user. We need to overcome our bias by defining user profiles based on facts and evidence, not assumptions or templates. It is much better to say "I don't know" than to claim to know something derived from our own experience of the world, which can be biased.

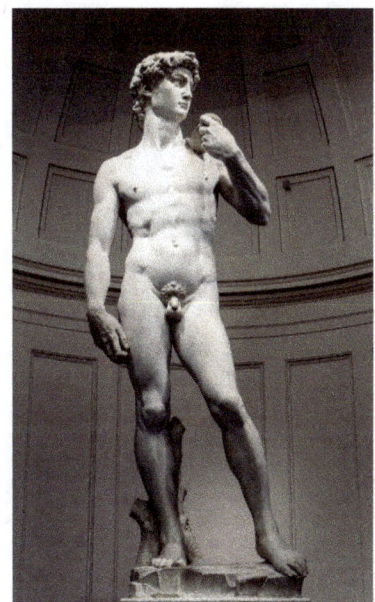

Figure 6.10: David (1501 - 1504); artist: Michelangelo di Lodovico Buonarroti Simoni; photographer: Livioandronico2013; source: Wikimedia; photographer: Livioandronico2013; license: CC BY-SA 4.0

2: Research shows that unconscious bias can influence persona definitions [129, 130]. There are several blog posts that discuss the risk of unconsciously biased persona definitions, and how to avoid them.

Such bias can add a significant risk to our projects. This includes the use of personas with insufficient evidence.[2] To avoid wrong or unvetted assumptions and to know what we need to chisel away, we need to talk *to* our users, not to talk (or write) *about* them.

This book describes several tools to elicit the user-centered constraints. All tools assume that at least one representative of the user groups (more is better) participates in the discovery sessions and provides the information. Ideally, the user reps are end users, not proxy users.

The workflow (as is) and the user journey map (as is) were presented in the previous chapter. A user role profile template will be introduced in the next section. It defines the type of information we need to know about a user role. Another tool is the nuggets board (see Section 3 (Nuggets board) on page 175) which summarizes specific insights from users ("nuggets"). The use context profile defines an applicable context of use (see Chapter 7 (Contexts of use) on page 189).

User role profile

A user is an "individual or group that interacts with a system or benefits from a system during its utilization" [131, clause 4.1.52]. We are going to create a user role profile for each user role in the scope of the project.

> **Definition 6** (User role) *A function or part performed by a user, or end user, with its own set of connected needs, goals, responsibilities, tasks, behaviors, preferences, and abilities.*

A user role profile is a description documenting the attributes of a user role. User role profiles are effective in documenting the learnings from an empathy journey. They benefit us in the following way:

- ▶ User role profiles are helpful outlining what users' motivations are, relative to the project and the application domain. The proposed user role profile contains the applicable variety of socio-demographic information (characteristics) and behavioral information (needs, goals, responsibilities, pain points).
- ▶ The needs and goals of each user role will influence design decisions.
- ▶ Responsibilities are part of the user role profile. Responsibilities relevant for the design project are marked "in scope." The

other responsibilities are marked "out of scope." All in-scope responsibilities can be elaborated on with user journey maps.

► The pain points help us to understand early in the project which parts of the responsibilities require special attention. Identifying pain points helps us to scope the design project and to set a focus that benefits the users and the business.

► Some user characteristics directly influence design decisions such as font size (influenced by age range), use of language, canvas flow (influenced by education, training, or experience), interaction device types (influenced by involvement context), and interaction modalities (influenced by work tools/equipment).

User role profiles should be considered in the context of additional insights like workflows and context-of-use definitions. The user role profile template guides us to elicit relevant information from users. It is advisable to observe and interview several individuals for the same user role. Inputs from multiple individuals help us to understand which information is rather role specific and which information expresses an individual interpretation, preference, or experience. Based on several interviews, a single profile per user role can be derived. If a project or organization requires it, personas or archetypes can be derived from such a user role profile.

The user role profile shown in Figure 6.11 is a template that has proved to be useful in industrial projects. Like all templates, it can be adjusted to address the needs of a design project.

In the remainder of this section, the user profile of the user role "household manager" is described.

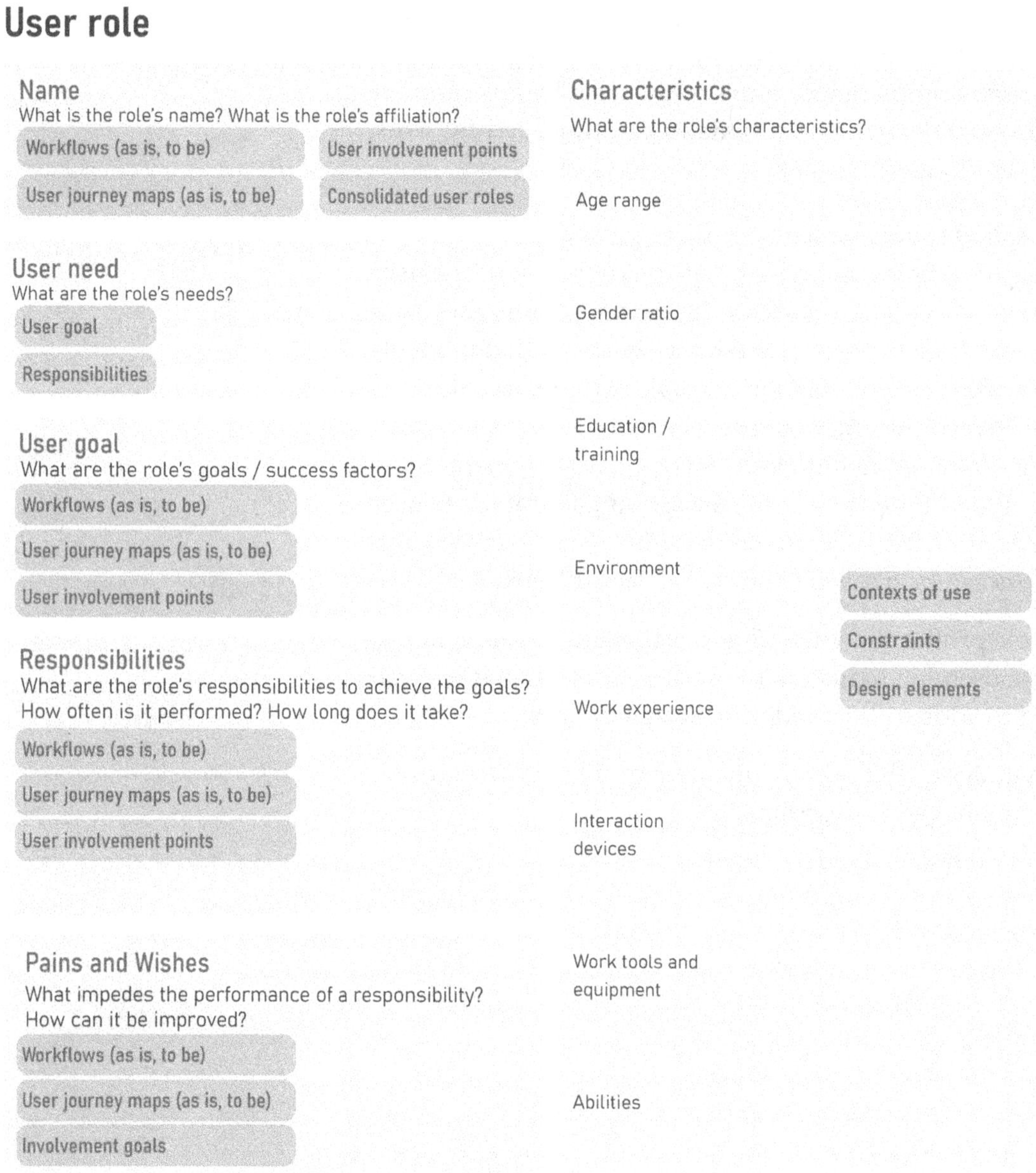

User role

Name
What is the role's name? What is the role's affiliation?

Workflows (as is, to be)   User involvement points

User journey maps (as is, to be)   Consolidated user roles

User need
What are the role's needs?

User goal

Responsibilities

User goal
What are the role's goals / success factors?

Workflows (as is, to be)

User journey maps (as is, to be)

User involvement points

Responsibilities
What are the role's responsibilities to achieve the goals? How often is it performed? How long does it take?

Workflows (as is, to be)

User journey maps (as is, to be)

User involvement points

Pains and Wishes
What impedes the performance of a responsibility? How can it be improved?

Workflows (as is, to be)

User journey maps (as is, to be)

Involvement goals

Characteristics
What are the role's characteristics?

Age range

Gender ratio

Education / training

Environment

Contexts of use

Constraints

Design elements

Work experience

Interaction devices

Work tools and equipment

Abilities

Figure 6.11: User role profile template

User role: Household manager

Name
What is the user role's name? What is affiliation?

Household manager (affiliation: household)

User need
What are the user role's needs?

UN 1 Live healthfully and frugally

User goal
What are the user role's application related goals?

UG 1 Eat healthy, tasty, affordable food in a timely manner

Responsibilities
What are the role's responsibilities to achieve the goals?
How often is it performed? How long does it take?

R 1 Ask everyone for pizza preferences (1 per week, about 5 minutes)
R 2 Select and order pizza (UG 1) (1 per week, about 10 minutes)
R 3 Prepare table (1 per week, about 10 minutes)
R 4 Receive pizza (UG 1) (1 per week, about 45 to 60 minutes)
R 5 Prepare to eat (1 per week, about 2 minutes)

Pains and Wishes
What impedes the performance of a responsibility?
How can it be improved?

Pains	Wishes
Difficult to understand me (R 1) (50% wrong pizza delivered)	Order online
A large order gets messed up (R 1, R 2) (75% wrong pizza delivered)	
Delivery often takes 60 minutes (R 2) (50% pizza is cold)	Track order status
The driver does not have change (R 2) (40% embarrassment, overpayment)	Pay tip online

Characteristics
What are the user role's characteristics?

Age range	18 to 88 years old
Gender ratio	Balanced
Education and training	From high school drop out to postgraduate degree holder
Work experience	Not applicable
Environment	Home, office, on the road
Work tools and equipment	Credit card for payment
Interaction devices	Desktop PC, tablet, mobile phone, smart speaker, mouse, keyboard, touch screen
Abilities	Read, write, hear, use fingers

Figure 6.12: Household manager - user role profile

Name *What is the user role's name? What is the affiliation?*

Each user role is identified by its name and an affiliation such as a company. The name will be used throughout the project. It should be obvious, simple, and easy to understand. If a workflow (as is) has been defined, the user roles should be listed there and can be carried over. If such a workflow has not yet been defined, the business model should list initial user roles that can serve as a starting point.

A user role with the same name can have different needs, responsibilities, and tasks in different companies. The difference often depends on the company's size. For instance, in small enterprises, employees often cover more than one job role, so their needs are blended. In large enterprises, job roles are usually more specialized and separated. To be able to distinguish between user roles with the same name but different responsibilities, we assign an affiliation to each user role.

For the affiliation "enterprise organization," we consider three user roles for our pizza application:

▶ Team member
▶ Team manager
▶ Team assistant

For affiliation "private households," we distinguish between

▶ Household member
▶ Household manager

Characteristics *What are the user role's characteristics?*

User characteristics introduce constraints for the design. It is important to understand and consider them, otherwise we risk that our experience solution won't be effective, efficient, and satisfactory for our target user groups.

Here are the characteristics that should be captured for each user role:

▶ Age range
▶ Gender ratio
▶ Education and training
▶ Work experience
▶ Environment
▶ Work tools and equipment
▶ Interaction devices
▶ Abilities

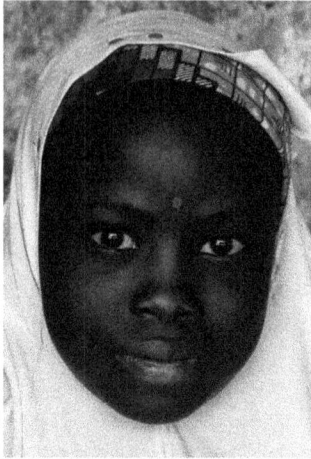

Figure 6.13: Girl (user group "household member"); source: Pexels; photographer: Muhammadtaha Ibrahim Ma'aji; license: Pexels License

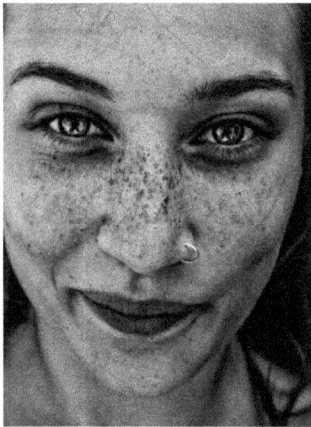

Figure 6.14: Adult (user group "household member/manager"); source: Pexels; photographer: Francesca Zama; license: Pexels License

Figure 6.15: Senior (user group "household member/manager"); source: Pixabay; photographer: pisauikan; license: Pixabay License

Based on project needs, the list can be modified.

Age range is needed because different ages have different conditions. The human body and its abilities and limitations change with age [132–134]. One of the age-influenced capabilities relevant to architecture and design decisions is vision. Our eyesight becomes worse with age. Therefore, the applicable age range has a direct influence on font size. If you design for a younger audience, smaller font sizes are acceptable. If you design for an audience 50 or older, larger font sizes should be considered [135–138]. A font size calculator is a useful tool [139]. The selected font sizes can be evaluated by the target users on the target device with reading tests.

In our pizza example, we assume an age range for the household manager from

▶ 18 to 88 years old

Gender ratio The gender ratio defines the gender mix for a certain user role. Gender ratio does not encourage gender discrimination, but the fact is that there are still professions where one gender is dominant. When we select individuals as user role representatives, we want to make sure that the gender ratio of the selected individuals reflects the gender ratio of the user group.

In our pizza example, the gender ratio is

▶ Balanced

Education and training One of the contributions of a formal education is to unify, to some extent, our understanding of certain parts of the world (e.g. the human body (medicine), the laws of nature (physics, chemistry), how to make computers and software work (computer science) etc.). For a given topic, people with the same formal education speak the same language and use the same theories, models, methods, and tools. These things become part of their mental model and we can use them when creating an involvement concept. Therefore, we need to be aware of which formal education our user group shares.

For the user role "household manager," the education range is

▶ From high school drop out to those with post-graduate degrees

Environment defines the physical, social, and/or situational setting in which the user interacts with the application. Very often, this is the home, the office, the school, or the road (e.g., in public transportation or in a car). For industrial applications, it can be a specific industrial environment, such as a manufacturing floor, a gas

Characteristics
What are the user role's characteristics?

Age range	18 to 88 years old
Gender ratio	Balanced
Education and training	From high school drop out to post-graduate degree
Work experience	Not applicable
Environment	Home, office, on the road
Work tools and equipment	Credit card for payment
Interaction devices	Desktop PC, tablet, mobile phone, smart speaker, mouse, keyboard, touch screen
Abilities	Read, write, hear, use fingers

Figure 6.16: Household manager - characteristics

Figure 6.17: Kitchen of Tino's Artisan Pizza Company in Kingston, New Jersey, USA (2021); courtesy: Tino Procaccini

Figure 6.18: Chef hat; source: Wikimedia; photographer: Çin qırğını; license: CC BY-SA 3.0

Figure 6.19: Fire gear; source: Wikimedia; creator: Seattle City Council from Seattle; license: Public domain

turbine, railway tracks, or a restaurant kitchen. All environments can introduce constraints, such as limited light conditions, noise, dirt, privacy, and security concerns, and limited or no access to the internet.

For our user role patron, the environments are

▶ Home
▶ Office
▶ On the road

The internet is assumed to be available all the time and with a decent bandwidth. The environment will be elaborated on further in Chapter 7 (Contexts of use) on page 189.

Work experience Different levels of work experience can influence how an application is used. For complex industrial applications, it is possible that a user with limited work experience would require more guidance than employees with many years under their belt. Therefore, the design would be different for different levels of work experience.

The work experience for the household manager are

▶ No work experience is assumed for the household manager

Interaction device This characteristic addresses the question of which kind of interaction device is used with the application. Example of devices are desktop computers, laptops, tablets, mobile phones, smart watches, mouses, joysticks, and smart speakers.

The "household manager" user role uses

▶ Desktop PC
▶ Tablets
▶ Mobile phone
▶ Smart speakers
▶ Mouse
▶ Keyboard
▶ Touch screen

Work tools and equipment can add additional constraints, for example safety gear (e.g., hard hat, safety glasses, safety gloves, mask, steel toes) and other professional equipment. The work tools and equipment category can also include rules and processes, like safety rules or a procedure for ensuring that all tools are in working order.

Work equipment for our "household manager" user role is

▶ Credit card

Abilities are conditions that can impose additional constraints on the design. Besides things that a person *can* do, this category includes activity limitations, impairments, and participation restrictions [140]. The design for limited abilities is addressed by *accessibility* [141, 142]. For instance, if a job requires the recognition of certain colors, candidates will be screened for color blindness. Therefore, it can be assumed that the user group does not have a certain type of color blindness.

In our pizza example, we do not assume a particular disability in our users. However, we assume that users are able to

- ▶ See
- ▶ Read
- ▶ Hear
- ▶ Write
- ▶ Use fingers (e.g., for touch screens, mouses, and keyboards).

User need   *What are the needs of the user role?*

Needs are drivers of people's actions (see Definition 3 on page 53). The identified user need for all household members, including the household manager, is

- ▶ UN 1 Live healthfully and frugally

The user need statement is refined with the user goal statement.

User goal   *What is the user role's application related goals?*

While needs are agnostic of the application domain, the user goal expresses an intended state within the application domain. The application goal should *not* express information from the involvement domain. It is used to inform and guide the involvement domain, including design decisions, without over-constraining it.

The user goal is

- ▶ UG 1 Eat healthy, tasty, affordable food in a timely manner

The user goal addresses the user need "live healthfully and frugally."

Let's analyze the term of the user goal. The word "healthy" refers to ingredients that are in line with the user's diet constraints and health ambitions. It means that the application should provide filters for nutrition information and calories. It may also imply the need for making transparent which restaurants use food from local

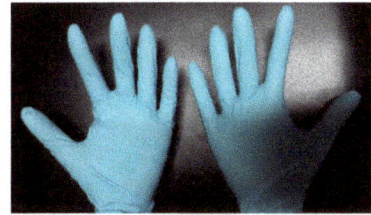

Figure 6.20: Nitrile powder free gloves; source: Wikimedia; photographer: Praewnaaaaaam; license: CC BY-SA 4.0

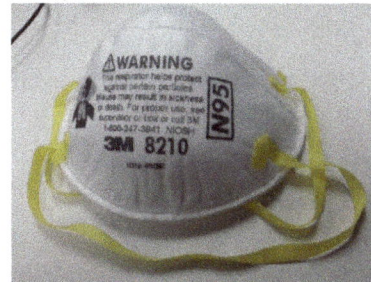

Figure 6.21: N95 particulate respirator; source: Wikimedia; photographer: Banej; license: CC BY-SA 3.0

User need
What are the user role's needs?

UN 1 Live healthfully and frugally

Figure 6.22: Household manager - needs

User goal
What are the user role's application related goals?

UG 1 Eat healthy, tasty, affordable food in a timely manner

Figure 6.23: Household manager - user goal

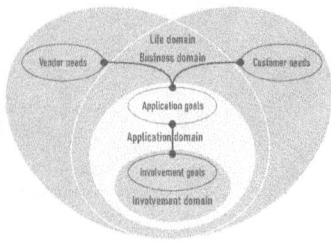

Figure 6.24: User needs are assigned to "customer needs" from the life domain; user goals are assigned to the "application domain."

3: GMO: Genetically modified organism

farmers. Marking a pizza with labels such as "green," "GMO"/"non-GMO"[3] could benefit the user.

The word "tasty" refers to a user's preferences for certain ingredients, as well as to a rating system. The user should be able to filter and sort pizzas by ingredients. It also means that the pizza needs to be hot when it arrives.

The word "affordable" implies the user's ability to find pizzas in certain price ranges. It can mean finding a pizza at a specific price, finding a pizza worth its price, or simply finding the cheapest pizza in town. Affordability influences filtering and sorting functions.

The expression "in a timely manner" expresses that the user does not want too long for an ordered pizza.

A user role can have more than one user goal. If this is the case, the user goals can be listed and identified as "UG 1," "UG 2," etc.

User goals are sometimes confused with an outcome. They are not the same. Table 6.1 shows examples of application-related outcomes and goals.

Table 6.1: Goal and outcome examples

Application	Outcome	User goal	Comment
Food ordering system	Pizza in pizza box	Eat healthy, tasty, affordable food in a timely manner	The pizza is what is being delivered (outcome), and the goal expresses an intent related to food. Pizza is one type of food that can help someone to achieve that goal.
Transportation ticket purchasing system	Ticket	Permission to use transportation vehicle	The ticket is what the ticket machine produces (outcome), and the goal for the passenger is permission to use one or more transportation vehicles (e.g., train, bus, airplane, taxi).
Irrigation system	Water	Healthy plants	The water is what an irrigation system delivers (outcome). To achieve that goal, nutrients might be needed in addition to water.
Home security system	Alarm	Timely response to security incidents	The alarm is what the home security system produces (outcome). The ability to respond to a security incident in a timely manner can be a reasonable goal.

Responsibilities *What are the main responsibilities of the user role? How often is a responsibility performed? How long does it take to perform?*

Each user role has certain responsibilities. This applies to customer roles (e.g., household manager) as well as employee roles (e.g., baker, restaurant manager, driver). Responsibilities summarize the activities of a role. For instance, one of the restaurant manager's responsibilities is to run a smooth operation. This could be measured with performance indicators, such as "the time from order entry to ready for delivery should not be more than 15 minutes." A baker can have responsibilities like baking pizza, ordering, and restocking ingredients, and/or training new employees.

A role-specific responsibility may or may not be supported by the application under design.

Each responsibility summarizes a variety of activities. The focus on responsibilities helps to give an overview of the user role's main activities without going into detail.

Applicable responsibilities can be fleshed out on the nuggets board and the user journey maps (as is).

The identified responsibilities of the user role "household manager" are as follows:

► R 1 Ask everyone for pizza preferences (once per week, about 5 minutes)

► R 2 Select and order pizza (UG 1) (once per week, about 10 minutes)

► R 3 Prepare table (once per week, about 10 minutes)

► R 4 Receive pizza (UG 1) (once per week, about 45-60 minutes)

► R 5 Prepare for eating the pizza (once per week, about 2 minutes)

The information "UG 1" notation behind a responsibility indicates that the responsibility addresses the user goal and can be selected as being in scope. Responsibilities that are not marked with a user goal are most likely out of scope for the application under design.

Besides a list of responsibilities, it is beneficial for efficiency considerations to understand how often a responsibility is performed (frequency), and how long it takes, on average, to perform it (duration). Responsibilities that are performed often and take a long time are excellent candidates for efficiency considerations.

Pain points and wishes   *What hinders the user from achieving a user goal? How can the situation be improved?*

A pain point is a gap or an unwanted situation that should be changed. A wish is an idea that may or may not address a pain point. We should be aware that identified pain points and wishes are probably candidates for significant investment when designing and developing an application. Therefore, we need to understand the pain points and wishes pretty well. The technique I am going

Responsibilities
What are the role's responsibilities to achieve the goals?
How often is it performed?
How long does it take?

R 1 Ask everyone for pizza preferences (1 per week, about 5 minutes)
R 2 Select and order pizza (UG 1) (1 per week, about 10 minutes)
R 3 Prepare table (1 per week, about 10 minutes)
R 4 Receive pizza (UG 1) (1 per week, about 45 to 60 minutes)
R 5 Prepare to eat (1 per week, about 2 minutes)

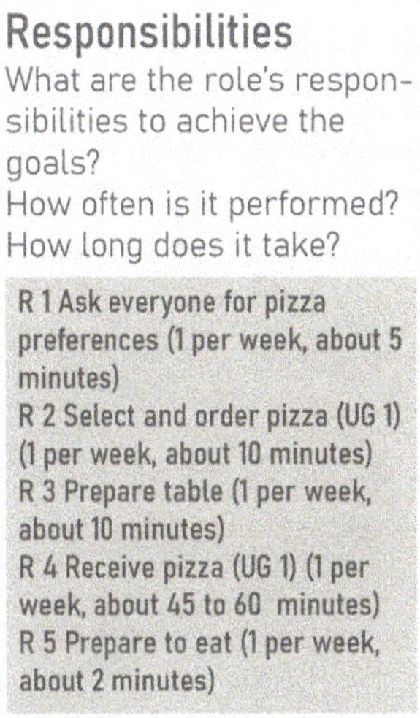

Figure 6.25: Household manager - responsibilities

Pains & wishes
What impedes a user role to achieve an application goal?
How can it be improved?

P 1.1 Difficult to understand me (R.1) (50%, wrong pizza delivered)

W 1.1 Order online

P 1.2 A large order gets messed up (R.1, R.2) (75%, wrong pizza)

P 1.3 Delivery often takes 60 minutes (R.2) (50%, pizza is cold)

W 1.2 Track order status

P 1.4 The driver does not have change (R.2) (40%, embarrassment, overpayment)

W 1.3 Pay tip online

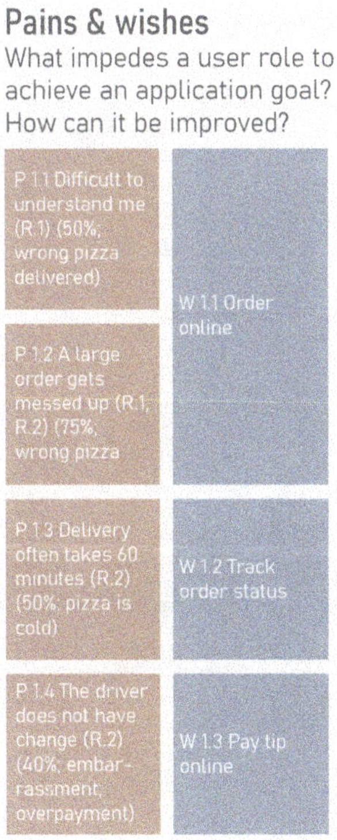

Figure 6.26: Household manager - pain points

Pain point items

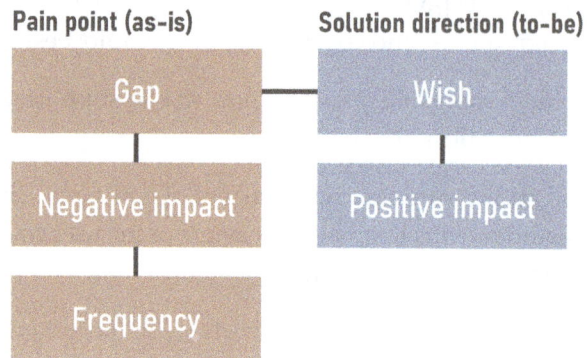

Figure 6.27: Pain point items

to describe is what I use in my projects. It sets the groundwork for efficiency considerations.

The assumptions of the technique are as follows: (1) users are experts in pain points but not in solutions; (2) many people do not think in terms of pain points or gaps but of ideas for possible solutions; and (3) user proposed solutions are in many cases not viable.

The technique described here works if a user starts talking about a possible solution (which is normal) as well as an actual pain point (which does not happen very often). The elements of the technique are visualized in Figure 6.27 and described below. If the user starts talking about a possible solution, we need to work our way back to the pain point. If the user starts with a pain point, we work our way forward to the solution. Let's go through the items one by one.

▶ Pain point (as is): The pain point expresses a situation as of today. It should be an actual experience of the interviewee and include the following three items:

- Gap: The gap is an unwanted situation that should be changed. The gap should be articulated as a deviation, as something that is missing, or as something that does not work very well. A gap should not be articulated as a goal or as a possible solution.
- Negative impact: The negative impact is the consequence of the gap. It helps us to understand the significance of the pain point. This is a bit abstract to formulate as a question. You should initiate the conversation about

the negative impact with a general question such as, What does <pain point> mean for you? or How do you feel about <pain point>? Many negative impacts can mapped to the concepts of time, quality, money and/or personal feeling. If a given negative impact cannot be mapped to quality, money, or time, you should elicit more information from the user about the impact. Maybe there is more to it. The last resort is to ask directly, "What impact does the pain point have on time, quality, or money?"

- Frequency: The frequency expresses how often the pain point occurs, which gives a clue about its significance. If the user struggles to express the frequency, it is good practice to offer categories, or thresholds, for how often the pain point occurs while the activity is being performed—for example, does it occur 10, 25, 50, 75, or 90 percent of the time?

▶ Solution direction (to be): The possible solution is a wish about how to address a gap in the future. It is not available yet, at least not for the person who has experienced the gap. It is possible that the solution is available somewhere else, or for someone else.

- Wish: The wish is the user's idea for how to address a pain point. The wish can be used to validate the given pain point. If the pain point and the wish do not seem to fit together, the interviewer needs to clarify how they fit together.
- Positive impact: The positive impact is the benefit of having a solution in place that overcomes or at least reduces the pain point. The positive impact also helps to validate the pain point. The comparison between the negative and the positive impacts outlines the envisioned benefit of realizing a possible solution.

Sometimes a user switches between the past and the future. The pain point should be described based on *experience* (the past). Furthermore, it should be based on *personal* experience and not hearsay (a good friend of the best friend of my brother's brother-in-law ...). The possible solution should describe a *future idea* that effectively addresses the pain point and not something else.

We need to be careful with the wish itself. Some users do not have the best ideas for how to address a pain point. For our purposes, the wish has a different function: it helps to validate that we understand the pain point correctly. I call this *round-trip elicitation*.

Common techniques with which to elicit pain points and wishes are interviews and co-creation sessions. In both cases, it is better for

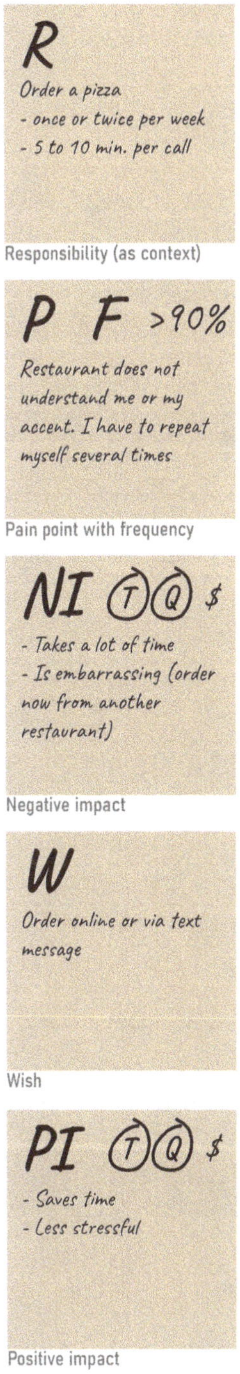

R
Order a pizza
- once or twice per week
- 5 to 10 min. per call

Responsibility (as context)

P F >90%
Restaurant does not understand me or my accent. I have to repeat myself several times

Pain point with frequency

NI (T)(Q) $
- Takes a lot of time
- Is embarrassing (order now from another restaurant)

Negative impact

W
Order online or via text message

Wish

PI (T)(Q) $
- Saves time
- Less stressful

Positive impact

Figure 6.28: User role: Handwritten notes; one set of sticky notes per pain point users (or interviewees) if the dialog is conducted as a conversation and not as an interrogation. The user should not get the impression that they're filling out a questionnaire or survey.

The user should be encouraged to talk freely, and the interviewer should listen and direct the user only when necessary, ideally without interrupting the user's flow too much. Guiding the user is an art, and it takes some talent and many years of experience to manage it in such a way that the interviewee does not feel manipulated. It requires sensitivity, tact, and a lot of discipline.

Due to the depth of the pain point exercise, it is best not to have too many people in the room. Typically, only one or two people will talk, and the others will be bored.

Here is a fictitious but realistic example of a dialogue between an interviewer and a single user trying to identify one pain point. It shows the questions and answers as well as the interviewer's thoughts (see Table 6.2 on the next page). In reality, the answers are often several sentences long.

Table 6.2: Sample dialogue

Role	Spoken sentence	Interviewer's thought
Interviewer	What bothers you when you order a pizza, if anything?	Let's get a pain point
Interviewee	I'd rather order via app or text message.	Great, a wish. Let's work backward.
Interviewer	Very interesting. How do you order now?	Empathy. Let's move to today
Interviewee	I call the pizza place.	Responsibility
Interviewer	Great. How does that go?	Give me a pain point.
Interviewee	Well, it's a pain ...	Ah, good, tell me more.
Interviewer	Tell me more about it. Why is it a pain?	Keep going ...
Interviewee	It takes too long ...	That's a good start ...
Interviewer	I see. Tell me, why does it take so long?	Empathy and beyond ...
Interviewee	Well, you know, I have to repeat myself ...	OK, I've got a hunch ...
Interviewer	You have to repeat yourself? Oh, really. Why is that?	Keep going ...
Interviewee	They don't understand me ...	Stronger hunch ...
Interviewer	What do you mean, they don't understand you?	We're almost there ...
Interviewee	They don't understand me, I mean my accent.	Pain point. Bingo!
Interviewer	I feel for you. How long does it take to place an order?	Empathy. Duration of activity
Interviewee	Hmm, I'd say five to ten minutes. Closer to ten than five.	Responsibility duration
Interviewer	Oh, wow. By the way, how often does it happen that they don't understand you?	Frequency
Interviewee	(Laughs) Well, pretty much all the time.	Frequency confirmed
Interviewer	Really, always? What about the last four weeks?	Let's check ...
Interviewee	Let me think...during the last month? Always, I guess.	Frequency of pain
Interviewer	Wow. Just a question: How often do you order a pizza via phone?	Frequency of responsibility
Interviewee	I guess once or twice per week	Thank you!
Interviewer	It seems it bothers you to call them. Why is that?	Negative impact, please ...
Interviewee	Well, it's embarrassing. And in my opinion it takes too long.	Great, got it.
Interviewer	What would you change?	Wish
Interviewee	I'd order online, or by text. I don't want to speak to them.	Wish is confirmed and addresses the pain point; round trip complete
Interviewer	So that I understand, what difference would it make for you?	Positive impact
Interviewee	No stress, less time, and I'd get the right pizza every time–I hope (laughs)	Great, got the positive impact.
Interviewer	Thank you so much, that was very insightful!	I am happy with this pain point.

While the interviewee is talking, the interviewer (or a separate note taker) takes notes. It is recommended that the interviewee is able to see the notes. This has two advantages. One is that the interviewee can see what is being documented, which builds a trusting relationship between them. The second advantage is that the interviewee can validate the correctness and completeness of the notes. The interviewer should even encourage the interviewee to validate the notes. In a remote setting, it is recommended that the screen be shared so the interviewee can watch as notes are documented. In a face-to-face setting, the notes can be written on sticky notes and placed where the interviewee can see them (see Figure 6.30 and Figure 6.29)

It is a lot of work for interviewees to talk about pain points. It's usually a new situation for them. Because of this, and because of the amount of information that's needed, it's reasonable to identify three to six pain points per one-hour session.

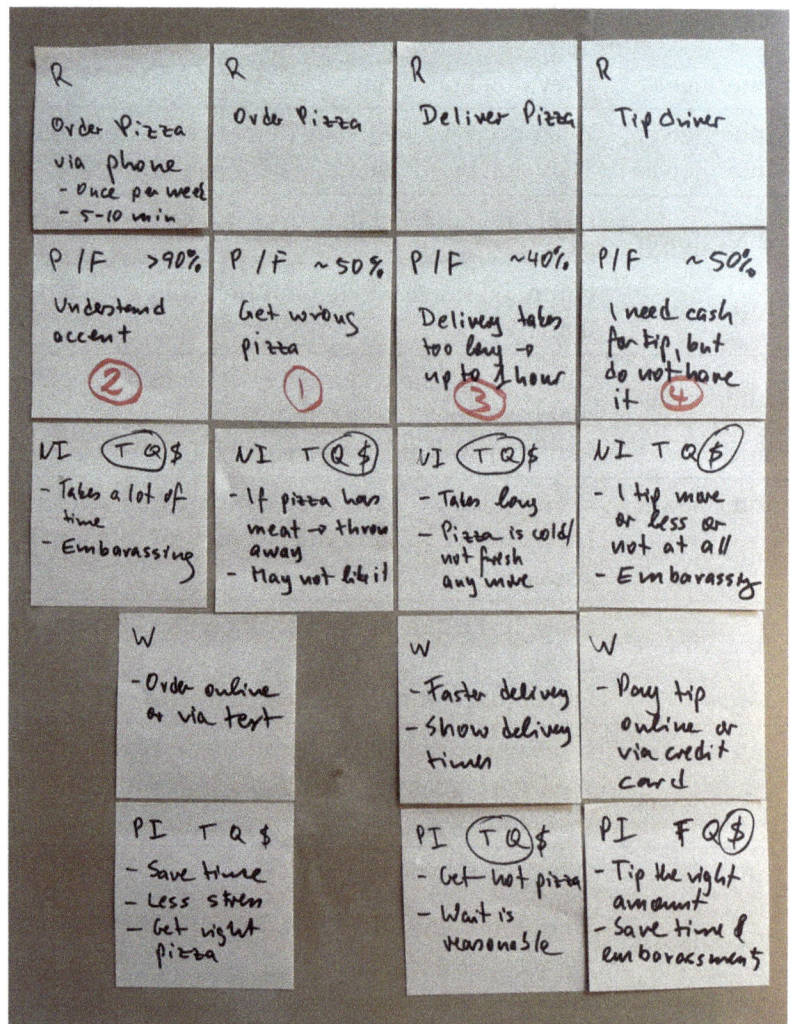

Figure 6.29: Sticky note samples; the numbers is red circle reflect the ranking of the pain points

If an interview is performed with a small group that's sitting close together, around a table for example, the use of sticky notes has several advantages:

▶ They can be placed on a table or a wall so everyone can see them (and, hopefully, read them).

▶ It is beneficial to organize the sticky notes in a grid pattern (see Figure 6.30). Each row is reserved for one type of information (e.g., responsibility, pain point, negative impact). Each column is reserved for one pain point. When a participant brings up a point, the facilitator makes a note and assigns it to correct element in the grid. The grid can be prepared beforehand, meaning all the sticky notes are already on the table or the wall. The facilitator can also create the grid while taking notes. The grid allows the participants to see which information is going to be elicited. It sets expectations and makes the facilitator appear prepared and knowledgeable.

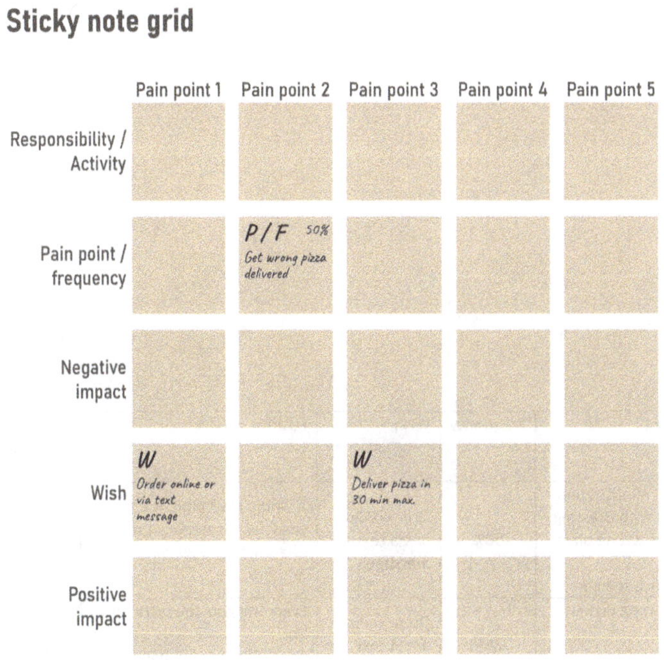

Sticky note grid

	Pain point 1	Pain point 2	Pain point 3	Pain point 4	Pain point 5
Responsibility / Activity					
Pain point / frequency		P/F 50% Get wrong pizza delivered			
Negative impact					
Wish	W Order online or via text message		W Deliver pizza in 30 min max.		
Positive impact					

Figure 6.30: Sticky note grid

▶ The sticky notes can be easily reorganized and replaced.

▶ Sticky notes can be conveniently stacked and transported (see Figure 6.31)

▶ Sticky notes can be used with a defined color code (e.g., pain point in red, wish in green, etc.). I personally refrain from using a dedicated color code. There is always a color that's missing, and then the sticky note grid starts looking messy. It leaves the impression of the facilitator being unprepared. Instead, I use one color and mark each note with a letter

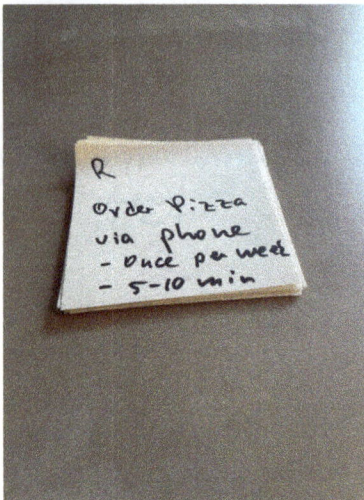

Figure 6.31: Sticky note stack

designating the intended content of that note (see the letters in the upper left corner of each sticky note in Figure 6.29).

Before concluding the pain point exercise, the participants should *rank* the *pain points*. If there are several people involved in the ranking, you need to take care of the ranking bias. Two ranking techniques are described in Section 5 (Ranking technique) on page 129.

After completion of the interview, you want to take a picture of the notes. They can be stacked for handy transport and are easy to reassemble for additional documentation and analysis (see Figure 6.31).

During the COVID-19 pandemic, all interviews were conducted remotely. Interview results such as gaps, responsibilities, and wishes were captured online and in text documents and were shared through a remote meeting application. An example of a text document with user role, goals, responsibilities, and gaps is shown in Figure 6.32.

User role: Household manager

User goal

- UG 1 Eat healthy, tasty, affordable food

Responsibilities

- R 1 Ask everyone for pizza preferences
- R 2 Select and order pizza (UG 1)
- R 3 Prepare table
- R 4 Receive pizza (UG 1)
- R 5 Prepare eating the pizza

Pain points

Ranking to support goal UG 1	Gap	Negative impact	Frequency	Wish	Positive impact	Impacted responsibility
1	PP 1 When ordering pizza via phone, the restaurant has difficulties to understand me.	It takes 5 to 10 minutes per order, and it is embarrassing. Sometimes, the wrong pizza is delivered. → Time, negative feeling	90%	Order online or via text message.	It would save time; it is less stressful. I'd receive more often the right pizza. → Time	R 2
4	PP 2 A larger order (> 4 pizza) gets messed up.	Partially, the wrong pizzas are delivered. → Quality, customer satisfaction	75%	Order online or via text message.	Everyone gets the pizza they like. → Quality, health, happy faces	R 2, R 4
2	PP 3 The delivery takes too long, up to 60 min. I could do something else, but don't know when the pizza arrives.	I am starving and can't do anything else. → Time, customer satisfaction	50%	Track delivery status; deliver faster.	Pizza is still hot; I can manage my time better until the pizza arrives. → Quality, happy faces	R 4
3	PP 4 The driver does not have change.	It is embarrassing. Sometimes the driver gets more tip than I planned to pay. → Money, Time	40%	Pay tip online or via credit card.	Tipping does not depend on the change. → Money, Time	R 4

Figure 6.32: Pain point documentation in a text document

Nuggets board

Technique

The user role profile is a useful template for documenting information and insights about the user roles that can be used as design inputs. However, it is necessary to gather insights that cannot be acquired with an interview-style approach but must be gained by observation. Observation involves watching how a user representative performs certain activities and making notes about interesting things they do or use.

A nuggets board is a technique used to document observations. It holds in one place the key insights ("nuggets") per user role.

A nuggets board is different from a workflow diagram. A workflow diagram shows the responsibilities of all involved user roles along a timeline. A nuggets board shows insights for only one user role.

A nuggets board is also different from a user journey map. A user journey map is an analysis tool. It documents the activities per responsibility, including touch points, pain points, and wishes as articulated by users; a nuggets board documents relevant insights based on observations. The observed users might not be aware of the relevance of such observations to the experience professional.

A nuggets board template is visualized in Figure 6.33. A separate nugget board should be created for each user role. To understand them in their context, each insight is assigned to an activity. The gained insights, or nuggets, are used to influence the workflow (to be), the user involvement points, and the involvement goals.

The template consists of two main areas: 1) activities and 2) observations and reasons. Activities are useful contexts for the individual insights. The activity bar should contain activities that may not be supported by the application under design. Extending activities beyond what is supported by the application is useful to show the bigger activity picture per user role.

Beneath the activity bar is the observation area. Each observation that was considered an insight of interest is shown here and assigned to an activity. Each observation is annotated with a reason. The reason should explain why the user was doing what was observed. An observation can be augmented with a photo or an artifact sample.

Nuggets board

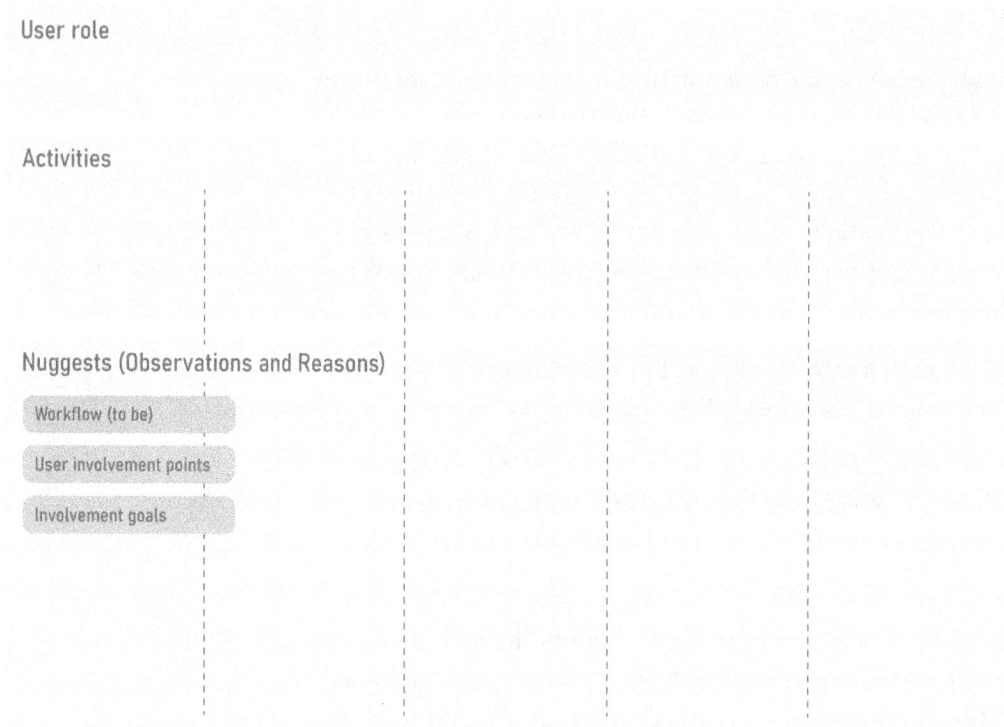

User role

Activities

Nuggets (Observations and Reasons)

Workflow (to be)

User involvement points

Involvement goals

Figure 6.33: Nuggets board template

World of Pizza

Here we'll show two sample nugget boards. The first board is for the user role "baker" (see Figure 6.34).

The nugget board for the baker lists five activities, three of which are extended with nuggets. The focus here is on the order slip. The manager is considering replacing paper order slips with an electronic version, so it is of interest how the order slip is currently being handled. The first observation, assigned to the activity "prepare pizza," is augmented with a photo that shows the location of the paper order slip during the pizza preparation process.

The nuggets board for the household manager (see Figure 6.35) also happens to show five activities. The first insight is about writing down the requested pizzas (with a sample of a note showing each person's name next to their requested pizza).

User role

Baker

Activities

Read order	Prepare pizza	Bake pizza	Cut pizza; add toppings	Box pizza; prepare deliver-able for driver

Nuggets (Observations and Reasons)

	Prepare pizza	Bake pizza		Box pizza
	O: Baker puts order slip above the baking area.	O: Baker puts order slip above the area where pizza is cut and boxed.		O: After pizza is boxed, baker inserts order slip into box.
		R: Order slip works as a reminder of which pizza is in the oven		
	R: For special orders, every item is mentally checked			R: Driver uses the order number on the order slip to identify the pizza delivery.

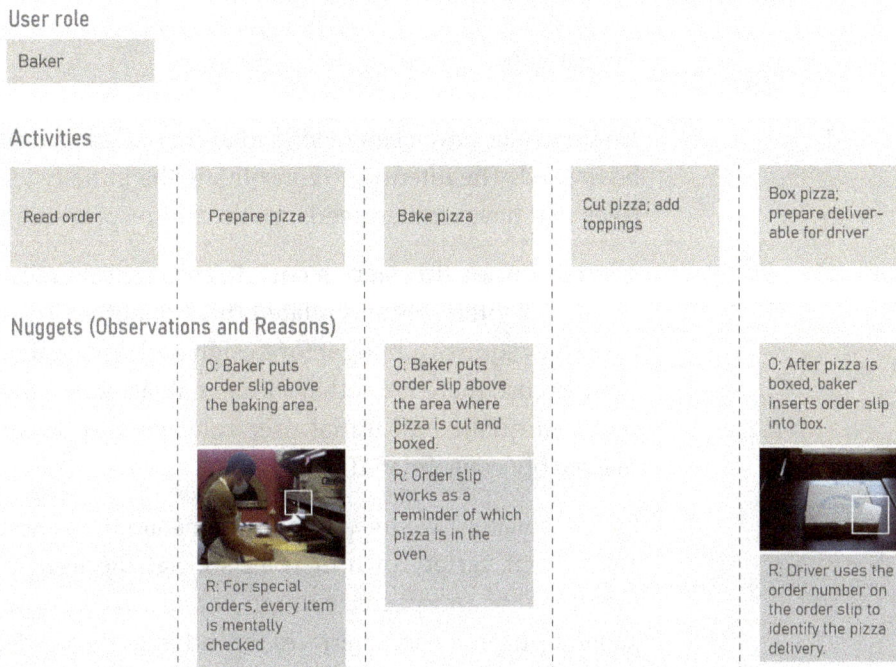

Figure 6.34: Nuggets board for baker

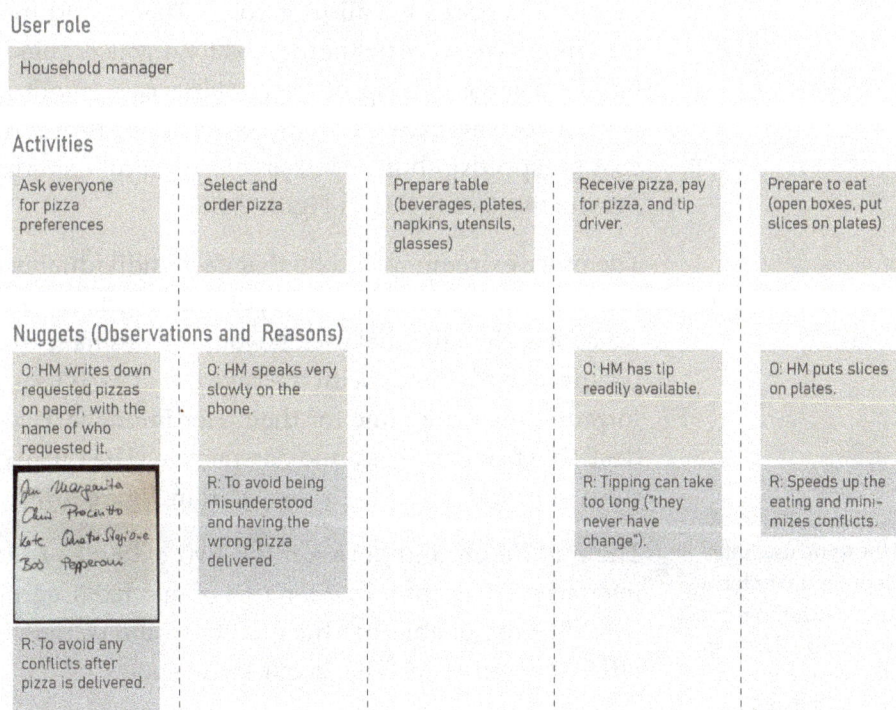

User role

Household manager

Activities

Ask everyone for pizza preferences	Select and order pizza	Prepare table (beverages, plates, napkins, utensils, glasses)	Receive pizza, pay for pizza, and tip driver.	Prepare to eat (open boxes, put slices on plates)

Nuggets (Observations and Reasons)

Ask everyone	Select and order		Receive pizza	Prepare to eat
O: HM writes down requested pizzas on paper, with the name of who requested it.	O: HM speaks very slowly on the phone.		O: HM has tip readily available.	O: HM puts slices on plates.
	R: To avoid being misunderstood and having the wrong pizza delivered.		R: Tipping can take too long ("they never have change").	R: Speeds up the eating and mini-mizes conflicts.
R: To avoid any conflicts after pizza is delivered.				

Figure 6.35: Nuggets board for household manager

User role consolidation

Technique

All user roles have been identified and profiled, and now they will be revised. The intent is to consolidate the initially identified user roles that have similar needs, goals, and responsibilities.

The reason for this step is cost. Each user role receives its own set of user interfaces and related functionalities. This means each user role requires a budget for design and development activities. Besides cost, there is another influential factor: quality. To balance cost and quality, all initial user roles should be reviewed and reasonably consolidated.

By "reasonable" we mean that the consolidation should maintain a sufficient variety of user roles so that the user interface and functionality are specific enough per user role. We want to avoid general-purpose user interfaces that address the needs of too many user roles and are therefore too complicated to use. On the other hand, we want to avoid user roles that are too specialized and user interfaces that increase the budget but do not create value for the users.

Let's look at two extremes. Imagine if there was be only one set of user interfaces for all user roles. This would mean that the user interfaces were not optimized for any user role. They would be like a large catalog of user interfaces without role specific workflows. This extreme would be desirable from a development cost perspective, but not desirable from an experience quality perspective (see LOLO in Figure 6.36).

The other extreme would be that each individual user (not user role!) received an individual set of user interfaces– like a tailored suite for each individual user. It would be desirable from the user's perspective of course, with the caveat that each user would have to wait quite some time for their user interface. It would not be desirable from an economic perspective. The quality of use and the cost would be too high (see HIHI in Figure 6.36).

For now, we'll use the term "user interface sets." This is a preliminary term and will be replaced with the term "user involvement point" (UIP) in Chapter 11 (User Involvement Point) on page 283. Each consolidated user role has its own user involvement point with its own set of user interfaces, potentially with different modalities.

The middle ground between the two extremes is a set of user interfaces that is optimized for a set of selected user roles. The cost would be reasonable and the quality would be high enough (see HILO in Figure 6.36. This is our sweet spot.

Now, the question is, How many user roles should we have? The proposed approach here is to consolidate the initial user roles into so-called *consolidated user roles*. We can consolidate initial user roles that have similar needs, goals, and responsibilities.

Sweetspot for cost per user and quality of use

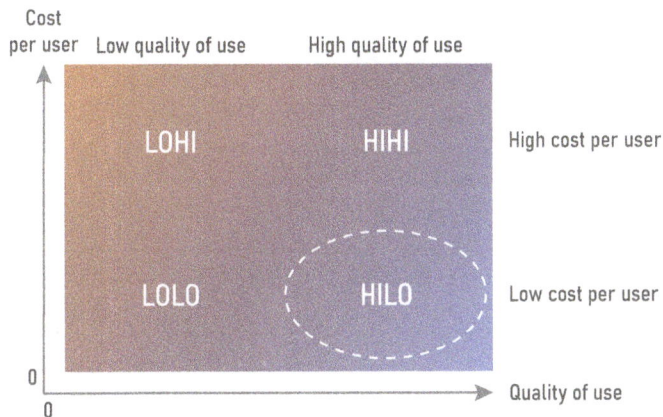

Figure 6.36: Sweet spot of cost per user and quality of use

World of Pizza

In World of Pizza, we have identified ten initial user roles. These roles and their responsibilities are shown in the two left columns of Table 6.3 on the following page.

The five initial user roles that represent customers have overlapping responsibilities. This includes the customers with private household affiliation and those with enterprise affiliation. Therefore, we are going to consolidate all initial customer user roles into one consolidated user role called "patron," but we'll keep them separate from the other initial user roles.

The two initial manager user roles have the same responsibilities. These are different from the responsibilities of the baker and the driver. Therefore, the two manager roles are consolidated into one user role called "manager."

The two bakers have the same responsibilities, which are different from the driver's responsibilities. Therefore, the two baker roles are consolidated into one user role called "baker."

The driver's role is different from all the others. Therefore, we'll keep the role separate and call it "driver."

The consolidated user roles with their responsibilities are shown in the two right columns of Table 6.3 on the next page.

For the remainder of the book, when we say "patron" we'll be referring to the user profile shown in Figure 6.37.

Table 6.3: Consolidation of initial user roles

Initial user role	Initial responsibilities	Consolidated user role	Consolidated responsibilities
Household member	Select pizza, eat pizza	Patron	Place order, receive pizza
Household manager	Ask for order requests, select pizza, order pizza, receive pizza, tip driver		
Team member	Select pizza, eat pizza		
Team assistant	Ask for order requests, select pizza, order pizza, receive pizza, tip driver		
Team lead	Ask for order request, select pizza, order pizza, receive pizza, tip driver		
Manager	Monitor operations, take customer orders, address deviations	Manager	Monitor operation, address deviations
Associate manager	Monitor operations, take customer orders, address deviations		
Chef baker	Accept order, bake pizza, box pizza	Baker	Accept order, bake pizza, box pizza
Associate baker	Accept order, bake pizza, box pizza		
Driver	Pick up pizza, deliver pizza	Driver	Accept delivery order, pick up pizza, deliver order

Name
What is the user role's name? What is the affiliation?

UR 1 Patron (affiliation: household and enterprise)

User need
What are the user role's needs?

UN 1 Live healthfully and frugally

User goal
What is the user role's goal?

UG 1 Eat healthy, tasty, affordable food

Responsibilities
What are the responsibilities performed to achieve the goals? How often are they performed? How long do they take?

R 1 Ask everyone for pizza preferences (1 per week, about 5 minutes)
R 2 Select and order pizza (UG 1) (1 per week, about 10 minutes)
R 3 Prepare table (1 per week, about 10 minutes)
R 4 Receive pizza (UG 1) (1 per week, about 45 to 60 minutes)
R 5 Prepare to eat (1 per week, about 2 minutes)

Pains and wishes
What impedes the performance of a responsibility? How can it be improved?

P 1.1 Difficult to understand me during (R 1) (50% wrong pizza delivered)
P 1.2 A large order gets messed up (R 1, R 2) (75% wrong pizza delivered)
P 1.3 Delivery often takes 60 minutes (R 2) (50% pizza is cold)
P 1.4 The driver does not have change (R 2) (40% embarrassment, overpayment)

W 1.1 Order online
W 1.2 Track order status
W 1.3 Pay tip online

Characteristics
What are the user role's characteristics?

Age range	8 to 88 years old
Gender ratio	Balanced
Education and training	From 3rd grade to postgraduate degree holder
Work experience	Not applicable
Environment	Home, office, on the road
Work tools and equipment	Credit card for payment
Interaction devices	Desktop PC, tablet, mobile phone, smart speaker, mouse, keyboard, touch screen
Abilities	Read, write, hear, use fingers

Figure 6.37: User role profile: patron

User role map

Technique

Sometimes there are many user roles, and their relationship is not always obvious. Therefore, it would be beneficial to understand their relationships and how each role or group of user roles contributes to the ecosystem.

The relationships between user roles and how they contribute to value generation can be visualized with a user role map. Figure 6.38 shows the elements of a simple user role map, which consists of one or more user role groups. It shows how each user role group contributes to the ecosystem. Furthermore, it shows the goal of each user group. And for each user role group, the relationships between the individual user role are visualized.

User role map

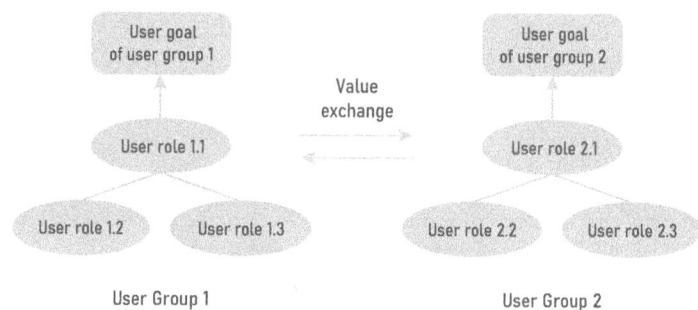

Figure 6.38: User role map - template

World of Pizza

A user role map for World of Pizza is depicted in Figure 6.39. It consists of three groups: supplier, restaurant, and patron.

In the supplier group, we have three different roles: a manager or owner, a packer, and a driver. The manager or owner has a coordination role. This role is supported by a packer and a driver. The goal is to grow the business. The second group is the restaurant with a similar structure. The supplier and the restaurant are connected through a value chain consisting of orders, delivery of supplies, and payment.

A third user role group are the patrons. They also may have a coordinating role if more than one pizza is ordered. An example of a coordinator in the family is one family manager collecting and

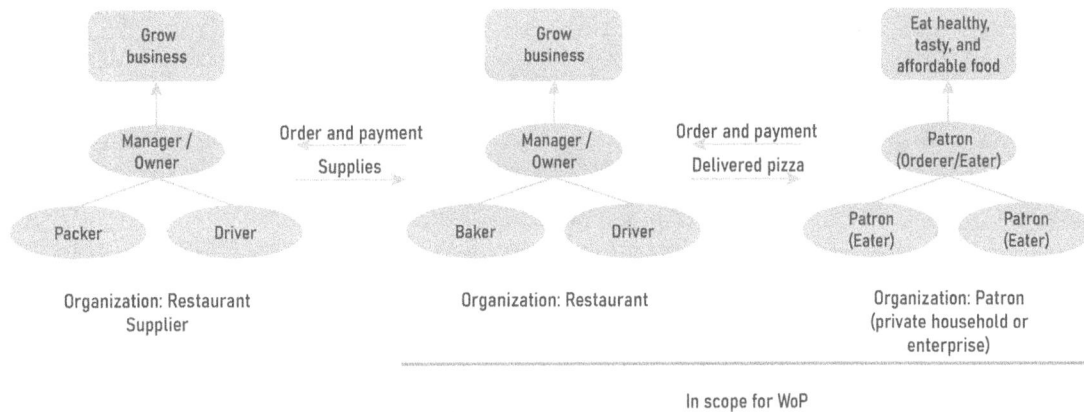

Figure 6.39: User role map - World of Pizza

placing the order for the whole family. An enterprise example is a team assistant, collecting individual orders from all team members and then placing the order. The patron group is connected to the restaurant group through the value chain elements of orders, payment, and delivery.

The user role map may include user roles and groups that are beyond the scope of the project. This can make sense if you want to show more context. It is good practice to mark the user groups and user roles that are in scope of the project.

Summary

User Roles

▶ Move on to <u>Context of use</u>
◀ Go back to <u>Workflow (as is)</u>

Name
What is the user role's name? What is the affiliation?

UR 1 Patron (affiliation: household and enterprise)

User need
What are the user role's needs?

UN 1 Live healthfully and frugally

User goal
What is the user role's goal?

UG 1 Eat healthy, tasty, affordable food

Responsibilities
What are the responsibilities performed to achieve the goals? How often are they performed? How long do they take?

R 1 Ask everyone for pizza preferences (1 per week, about 5 minutes)
R 2 Select and order pizza (UG 1) (1 per week, about 10 minutes)
R 3 Prepare table (1 per week, about 10 minutes)
R 4 Receive pizza (UG 1) (1 per week, about 45 to 60 minutes)
R 5 Prepare to eat (1 per week, about 2 minutes)

Pains and wishes
What impedes the performance of a responsibility? How can it be improved?

P 1.1 Difficult to understand me during (R 1) (66%, wrong pizza delivered)	W 1.1 Order online
P 1.2 A large order gets messed up (R 1, R 2) (75%, wrong pizza delivered)	
P 1.3 Delivery often takes 60 minutes (R 2) (50%, pizza is cold)	W 1.2 Track order status
P 1.4 The driver does not have change (R 2) (40%, embarrassment, overpayment)	W 1.3 Pay for online

Characteristics
What are the user role's characteristics?

Age range	8 to 88 years old
Gender ratio	Balanced
Education and training	From 3rd grade to postgraduate degree holder
Work experience	Not applicable
Environment	Home, office, on the road
Work tools and equipment	Credit card for payment
Interaction devices	Desktop PC, tablet, mobile phone, smart speaker, mouse, keyboard, touch screen
Abilities	Read, write, hear, use fingers

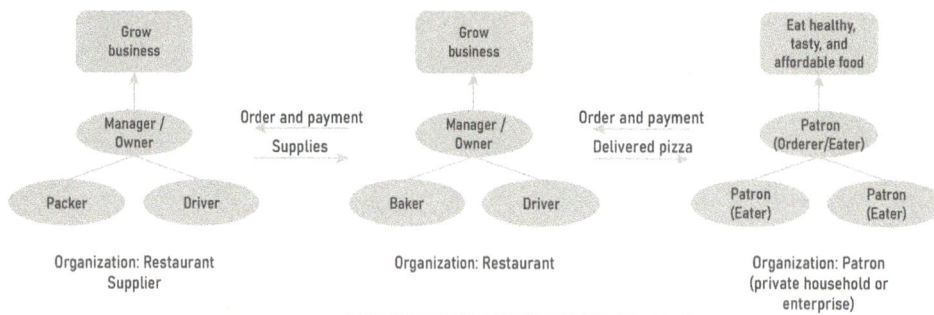

Organization: Restaurant Supplier — Grow business — Manager / Owner — Packer, Driver

Order and payment / Supplies

Organization: Restaurant — Grow business — Manager / Owner — Baker, Driver

Order and payment / Delivered pizza

Organization: Patron (private household or enterprise) — Eat healthy, tasty, and affordable food — Patron (Orderer/Eater) — Patron (Eater), Patron (Eater)

In scope for WoP

Key learnings

The user and the technical application are system elements of a human-technical system. The emerging property is the generation of the outcome of value. A key enabler for the human-technical system is user involvement. The user and sometimes the context of use are constraints. The technical application is subject to experience architecture and design decisions. The goal of making such decisions is to optimize the human-technical system (not the technical application) by considering the user-centered constraints. To optimize the human-technical system, a user-centered design and development approach should be applied. It reflects a "technology serves user" philosophy.

The user role profile is structured in several parts that build on each other. The content of a user role profile is used in later phases and steps. For instance, for each applicable responsibility, a user journey map (as is) can be created. Each activity per responsibility will become an activity in the journey map (as is). It is expected that the pain points will appear again in the user journey map.

The elicitation of pain points requires a structured approach to include all relevant parts: the gap, the frequency, the negative impact, the wish, and the positive impact. The elicitation approach should ideally take place as a conversation between the interviewee and the interviewer. This is a more comfortable experience for the user, and the results are probably better.

The number of user roles is a cost multiplier for architecture and design projects. Therefore, it can be beneficial to consolidate the initial user roles. The number of user roles should be large enough that the use quality is acceptable for each role, but not so large that it's unaffordable (HILO is the sweet spot; HILO stands for "high quality" and "low cost").

The user role map outlines which user roles belong together and what goals they have. The organization of user roles into groups helps to reveal what their relationship is.

Tips and tricks

Access to end users   One foundational element of a solid experience architecture and design is an excellent understanding of the user-centered constraints, which include the users and their user profiles. The user role profiles, including the pain points, should be created with end users, not with proxy users. Interviewing proxy users adds a risk to the project. However, using proxy users is better than not using any at all. It is worthwhile to invest time and money to gain access to end users. Insights about them are the most important foundation for the experience architecture.

Detailed responsibilities If you face the issue of getting too detailed regarding responsibilities, just write down what you have, then group and summarize them. Several activities can be summarized into one responsibility.

Pain points and wishes The elicitation of pain points is often not straightforward. It requires time, patience, and active navigation between what the interviewee says and what the interview is attempting to elicit. The flow of the user's speech should not be interrupted; rather, it should be directed. The direction, or redirection, takes place through encouragement and questions. Here are some sample questions per information item:

- ▶ Wish (as a starting question): If you could make a change, what would it be? If you could, what would you improve? If you could decide to make a change to the <application name>, or add something to <application name>, what would it be? If you had three wishes to make about improvements to <application name>, what would you wish for?
- ▶ Wish (to address an already revealed problem): How would you solve that problem? What would you like the <application name> to do for you?
- ▶ Gap (as a continuation of the wish): Why is that? Why do you want that? Why are you so interested in the <wish>?
- ▶ Frequency (as a continuation of the gap): How often does it happen? How often does it happen per <hour/day/week/month/year>?
- ▶ Negative impact: How does it affect you? How does it influence you? What does it mean for you?

Here are a few encouraging sentences to keep the user engaged and talking:

- ▶ To express relevance: That sounds very important. That sounds significant. I haven't heard that before, really interesting. Great, I've learned something today.
- ▶ You want to know more: Could you please elaborate? Could you please give me an example? I'd like to know more about this. Could you explain exactly how do you do this?
- ▶ You didn't understand the explanation: That sounded very important. I'm not sure I got the full picture. Could you rephrase what you said?
- ▶ You don't know what to say: That sounds really interesting. Thank you for sharing.

- ▶ To move on to the next topic: These are very useful insights. Thank you so much for sharing. I've learned a lot today. Considering the time, I'd like to move on to the next topic; there is probably a lot more to learn.

If you see that the pain points are expressing too many possible solutions, apply the Why-Why technique. It will help you to step back and understand why the solution was presented. You can stop asking why once you've found your negative statement.

If the interviewer and the interviewee are in the same room and the room is small or only a table is available, sticky notes are a good way to document and share the interview results with the interviewee. Sticky notes can also be stuck on a white board, or a wall. After the interview, the sticky notes have to be digitalized.

If the interview takes place remotely, a table is a reasonable format for documentation. It allows the interviewer to capture entire sentences per element (e.g., gap, possible solution, positive impact, negative impact). The table also has the advantage that additional documentation is not needed after the interview.

Exercise 1.5

Goal Identify several initial user roles; consolidate them and have at least two consolidated user role profiles: one customer user role and one vendor user role.

Material User role template; nuggets board; user role consolidation criteria; user role map

Completion criteria:

- ▶ The user role is defined for at least one customer and one vendor.
- ▶ The role name is distinguishable from other role names.
- ▶ The identified needs are mapped to an item on one of the two needs pyramids.
- ▶ About three to four responsibilities are identified per user role.
- ▶ At least three pain points are documented.
- ▶ For at least one user role, a nuggets board is created.
- ▶ The identified user roles are consolidated.
- ▶ A user role map, including all user roles, is documented.

Contexts of use | 7

Time is the most valuable thing a man can spend.
Theophrastus

Purpose

Users use applications in different contexts. For instance, some applications are used in an office environment, some in public areas, some at home, and some in a car. Certain factors of these environments have an influence on how well an application can be used and whether it can be used at all. For instance, it can be challenging to listen to voice messages in a noisy public square or to try to use a touch screen in a hospital where gloves are necessary.

These environments are referred to as "contexts of use." In this chapter, we'll focus on "contextual conditions," which are the factors that can have an influence on the user performing user tasks with a given application. The context of use includes both the current and the intended environments [126, 127, 143, 144].

Formally, the workflows (as is and to be) are part of the context of use. In this book, the workflow (as is) was discussed earlier (see Chapter 5 (Workflow (as is)) on page 117), mainly because the workflow (as is) is a discovery tool, helping us to identify the contributing user roles. This context of use chapter was positioned after the user role chapter because the user role profile helps us to identify the different contexts of use per user role. The discovery of the contextual conditions per context of use takes place after a context of use is identified as relevant for a user role.

Contextual conditions

ISO 9241-11 defines the context of use as the "combination of users, goals and tasks, resources, and environment." "The 'environment' in a context of use includes the technical, physical, social, cultural and organizational environments." [23, clause 3.1.15]

Twenty or thirty years ago, computers were available mostly as desktop computers and were used for a specific purpose in a specific environment (e.g., an office). Since there were no mobile devices, the environment of computers did not change. This, of course, is not the case today.

Now computers are available as different form factors, from small devices (watches, phones) to larger, less mobile devices (desktops). Users perform the same user tasks in different environments (car, home, office, public transportation). The same devices are used for both work and private purposes. With the increasing prevalence of home offices, work tasks and personal tasks are being intermingled and performed in the same environment. Several devices are used at the same time. Often, a user starts a user task in one context of use (e.g., a car) and continues the same user task in another context of use (e.g., an office). Sometimes users start one task on one device in one environment (e.g., a remote meeting on a mobile phone in a car) and continue the same user task on a different device in another environment (e.g., on a laptop computer in an office environment). Because of this increasing variability, an understanding of the situational context of use is essential.

The context of use can be pictured as an environment. However, not all aspects of the environment have an influence on the user when performing user tasks to achieve certain goals. The approach in this book is therefore to extract the contextual factors that potentially influence the user when performing a user task, so they can be addressed with architecture and design decisions. We call such factors "contextual conditions."

> **Definition 7** (Contextual conditions) *Situation-specific ambient, social, organizational, technical, and involvement factors that potentially impact users in performing their user tasks to achieve their goals.*

ISO/IEC 25063 lists technical/technological, social/organization, and physical environment. The standard does not mentioned conditions, just instances of the mentioned environments. [145, clause 5.6]

Contextual conditions are often situational. Each identified condition requires at least a consideration during the architecture and design phase of an experience project. Many conditions need an architecture and design mitigation, which in turn requires project budget and time.

Here are examples of environments, contextual conditions, and corresponding architecture or design mitigations:

▶ A voice-controlled application for a manufacturing facility (environment) is under design. The application will be used on the shop floor with significant background noise (ambient condition) in certain areas. To address the environmental factor "noise," it is decided to add a second modality, "GUI/-text" (architecture mitigation), in which system outputs are not only spoken to the user but also displayed on a graphical user interface. The user is able to provide inputs via voice and by entering texts or selecting options via graphical controls (design mitigation).

▶ An airport facility (environment) intends to inform passengers about planned and actual departure and arrival times of flights. The lighting is assumed to be "good" (ambient condition). The flight status data is displayed on a large wall. The distance of passengers from the display is, on average, about 10.9 yards, or 10 meters (involvement condition). To enable passengers to read the text, the selected font size is 506 pixels (design mitigation). Due to the text size, a significant amount of space is needed; therefore, the information will be displayed on several boards, organized as a grid (design mitigation).

▶ A chef works in a pizza restaurant kitchen (environment) making pizza. An application is under design to make orders available through a touch screen. The chef's hands are often wet (involvement condition), so s/he is not able to use a touch screen all the time. To address the factor "wet hands," hardware controls like a water-resistant mouse (design mitigation) are installed to allow the chef to accept orders with wet hands.

▶ An existing software application (technical condition) requires a feature extension. The new canvases, or extensions of existing canvases, should be consistent with the design style and integrated into the existing canvas flows (involvement condition). To achieve consistency, the applicable design system is applied to the extension, and existing canvas flows are extended to integrate the extension (design mitigation).

▶ The project for a new handheld blood analyzer has started. The main target user group is nurses. When treating patients and drawing blood, nurses wear medical gloves (involvement condition), so they should be able to use the handheld analyzer with gloves. The analyzer should be easy to clean. The design team explores different types of touch-enabling interfaces (design mitigation) that enable nurses to interact safely, effectively, and efficiently with the analyzer while

Figure 7.1: Manufacturing facility; source: Wikimedia; photographer: Mixabest; license: CC BY-SA 3.0

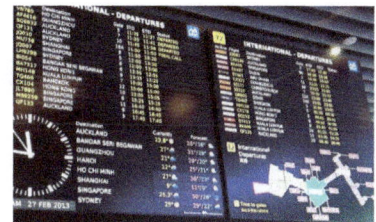
Figure 7.2: Large displays; source: Wikimedia; photographer: Richarnet; license: CC BY-SA 4.0

The font size was determined with the following parameters: distance: 1000 cm; visual acuity: 0.7; ratio of x-height to font size: 0.47; virtual resolution ppi: 160; text type: reading; lighting: good. [139]

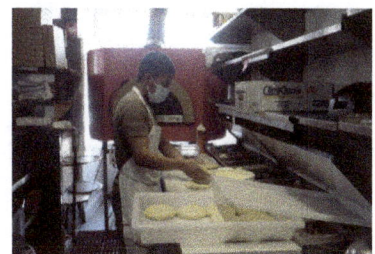
Figure 7.3: Baker in Tino's pizzeria; courtesy: Tino Procaccini

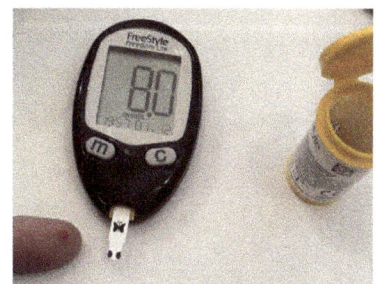
Figure 7.4: Blood glucose meter; source: Wikimedia; photographer: Omstaal; license: CC BY-SA 4.0

wearing gloves.

▶ A company develops an enterprise resource management application. User research shows that different companies apply different numbers of approval steps for different roles (organizational condition). The development team decides to offer an approval workflow that is customizable (architecture and design mitigation).

We can see from the examples above that some of the contextual factors (e.g., distance to displays, workflow variances, wet hands) lead directly to architecture and design mitigation. Other contextual factors require the introduction of special equipment that becomes a contextual factor (e.g., gloves).

Context of use profile

To document the environment and the contextual conditions, a context of use template is used (see Figure 7.5).

Context of Use

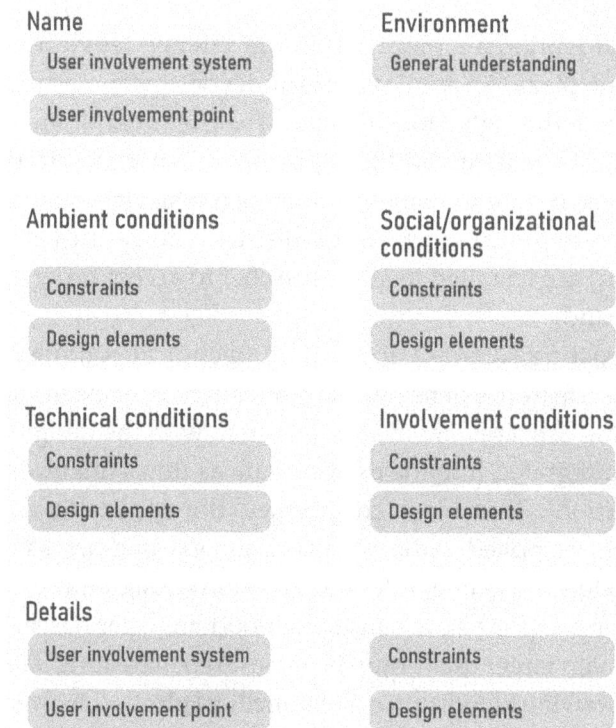

Name	Environment
User involvement system	General understanding
User involvement point	

Ambient conditions	Social/organizational conditions
Constraints	Constraints
Design elements	Design elements

Technical conditions	Involvement conditions
Constraints	Constraints
Design elements	Design elements

Details	
User involvement system	Constraints
User involvement point	Design elements

Figure 7.5: Context of use profile template

Context of use profile: Restaurant kitchen

The context of use profile is shown for the restaurant kitchen in the World of Pizza example (see Figure 7.6).

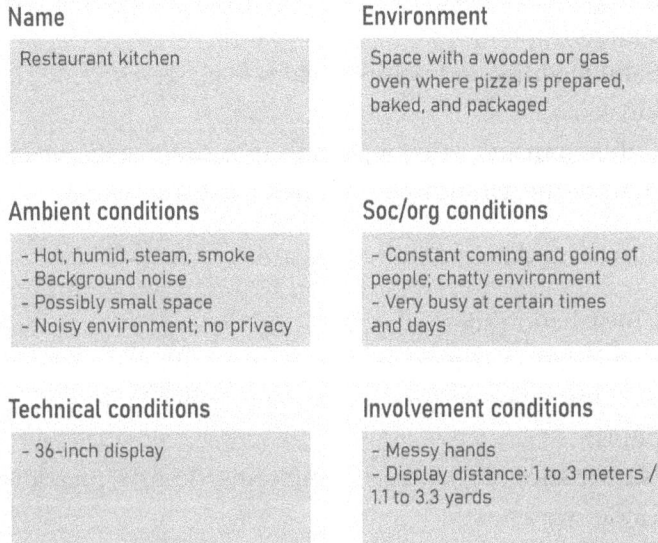

Name

Restaurant kitchen

Environment

Space with a wooden or gas oven where pizza is prepared, baked, and packaged

Ambient conditions

- Hot, humid, steam, smoke
- Background noise
- Possibly small space
- Noisy environment; no privacy

Soc/org conditions

- Constant coming and going of people; chatty environment
- Very busy at certain times and days

Technical conditions

- 36-inch display

Involvement conditions

- Messy hands
- Display distance: 1 to 3 meters / 1.1 to 3.3 yards

Details

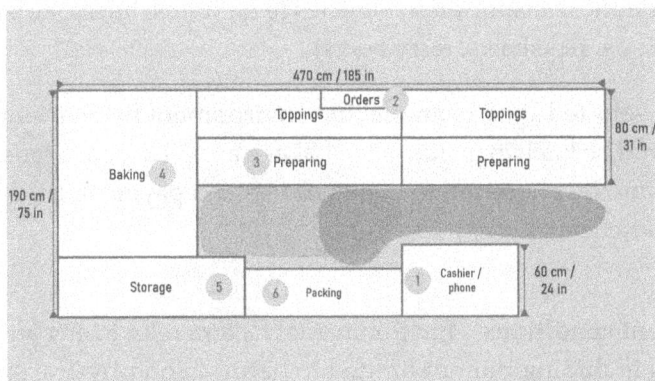

Figure 7.6: Context of use profile for restaurant kitchen

Name The name should identify a context of use and distinguish it from other contexts of use.

If a context of use has a temporary aspect to it, the name should include the temporary aspect. Some examples: "Garden – in the morning," "Garden – in the afternoon," "Garden – at night," "Kitchen – down times," "Kitchen – busy," etc.

For our WoP example, the name of the environment is "restaurant kitchen." This sufficiently identifies the context of use and distinguishes it from other contexts of use.

Name

Restaurant kitchen

Figure 7.7: Kitchen - Name

Environment

Space with a wooden or gas oven where pizza is prepared, baked, and packaged

Figure 7.8: Kitchen - Environment

Environment   We identify the physical environment with a few key characteristics. Examples of indoor environments are:

- ▶ Office (open space or closed space)
- ▶ Accommodations (e.g., hotel, guest rooms, guest apartments)
- ▶ Manufacturing facilities (e.g., shop floors)
- ▶ Maintenance and repair facilities (e.g., car repair, service centers)
- ▶ Sales facilities and points of sales (e.g., stores, malls, indoor kiosks)
- ▶ Public transportation terminals (e.g., train stations, bus stations, airports, subway stations, cruise terminals)

Examples of outdoor environments are:

- ▶ Construction sites
- ▶ Public spaces (e.g., streets, walk-ways, plazas, parks, zoo)
- ▶ Accommodations (e.g., restaurant terrace, hotel swimming pools)
- ▶ Nature sites (e.g., forests, mountains, deserts, meadows)
- ▶ Under water
- ▶ Transportation vehicles (e.g., bicycles, scooters, motor bikes, cars, trucks, ships)
- ▶ Public transportation vehicles (e.g., trains, buses, airplanes, taxis, rickshaws, ferry boats)

In our selected WoP example, the environment is the restaurant kitchen. The kitchen includes the baker's area. The manager's area, including the phone for accepting orders and payment, is adjacent to the kitchen.

Ambient conditions

- Hot, humid, steam, smoke
- Background noise
- Possibly small space
- Noisy environment; no privacy

Figure 7.9: Kitchen - Ambient conditions

Ambient conditions   Environmental factors refer to any ambient factors including but not limited to natural and physical spaces, outdoors and indoors. Ambient factors include the following:

- ▶ Temperature ranges
- ▶ Humidity ranges
- ▶ Air pressure ranges
- ▶ Oxygen levels
- ▶ Dust or fog
- ▶ Illumination ranges
- ▶ Vibrations
- ▶ Noise
- ▶ Privacy

Ambient factors exist in every environment. Many ambient conditions may motivate users to use additional equipment.

For instance, low temperature can motivate a user to wear gloves or mittens, making the use of touch screens difficult or impossible. Humidity, heat, dust, or fog can cause steam or haze, which may inhibit the visual field. Very dark environments can make it difficult to use input devices like keyboards and mouses. Very bright environments can make it difficult to see content on a screen. The use of public transportation or public space has an influence on privacy. Being in certain outdoor spaces may have an influence on the temperature, humidity, air pressure, and oxygen levels.

In our WoP example, the ambient condition of the kitchen is warmth. The oven can reach 900 degrees Fahrenheit (about 480 degrees Celsius). The space is rather small. Because it is an open kitchen, it is noisy and there is no privacy for the chef.

Social / organizational conditions   Social and organizational factors include rules, policies, or habits of human organization. They can occur in a crowd (e.g., an urban area or an event location), or with a specific set of people (e.g., in an office). We are interested here in social and organizational factors that can influence the user when performing a task.

The sequence of activities performed by a group of people is an example of social or organizational conditions. Such a sequence of activities is often called a workflow or a process. Another social or organizational condition is whether and how individuals are directed or interrupted in certain activities. Having the authority to interrupt or to give directions is an indication of one's status.

Communication networks are another example of social or organizational conditions. Informal communication networks often have opinion leaders, people that others look to for opinions and news. Formal communication networks have reporting lines.

Habits are another type of social and organizational condition. People get into the habit of performing certain tasks. For instance, one person always orders the pizza. Another person opens the door and receives the ordered pizza.

In our WoP example, the order, baking, and packaging process consists of the following steps, with time information.

During busy times, two pizza chefs work in the kitchen. One prepares the pizzas and places them in the oven. The other chef checks the pizzas, changes positions in the oven, takes them out, and puts them into the boxes or onto plates.

Social/org conditions

- Constant coming and going of people; chatty environment
- Very busy at certain times and days

Figure 7.10: Kitchen - Social/organizational conditions

Figure 7.11: Manager takes an order on the phone; courtesy: Tino Procaccini

Figure 7.12: Manager places order for baker; courtesy: Tino Procaccini

Figure 7.13: Baker prepares dough; courtesy: Tino Procaccini

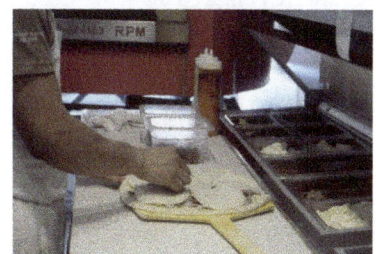

Figure 7.14: Baker covers pizza with toppings; courtesy: Tino Procaccini

Time studies, motion studies, and time/motion studies help to give insight into the current situation of workflows and how to improve them. [119, 146–148]

User role and activity	Duration per activity	Elapsed time (m:ss)
Manager receives order, prints order slip, and hands it over to kitchen	42 sec.	0:42
Baker reads order slip	3 sec.	0:45
Baker prepares pizza	72 sec.	1:57
Baker bakes pizza	93 sec.	3:30
Baker places pizza on table	5 sec.	3:35
Baker cuts pizza	8 sec.	3:43
Baker adds final toppings	14 sec.	3:57
Baker puts pizza in box and inserts order slip	5 sec.	4:02

Table 7.1: Goal and outcome examples

Technical conditions

- 36-inch display

Figure 7.15: Kitchen - Technical conditions

Figure 7.16: Baker pushes pizza into oven; courtesy: Tino Procaccini

Figure 7.17: Pizza bakes in oven; courtesy: Tino Procaccini

Technical conditions   Technical factors include software and other technologies that can have an impact on user involvement. It includes technologies like these:

▶ Devices
▶ Operating systems
▶ Software and cloud environments
▶ Availability and bandwidth of internet or intranet

Technical conditions need to be considered because the application under design needs to interface with or be integrated into such a condition.

In our WoP example, the only technical condition is a 36-inch display monitor, which will be placed in the kitchen to replace the paper order slips.

Involvement conditions   Involvement conditions have a direct impact on how a user perceives or interacts with the application under design. Examples of involvement conditions are

▶ Anything perception-related (audio, vision, and tactile)
▶ Anything affecting how inputs are provided, e.g., dirty fingers, gloves, limited space

Some involvement conditions may force a user to use certain equipment, which can make it harder for them to perceive information from the application under design or can prevent them from providing inputs into it.

In our WoP example, there are several involvement conditions. Because the chef bakes the pizza with his hands, without gloves, the hands are messy. Therefore, it's not feasible for the baker to use touch screens.

Another involvement condition is the distance of the display from the baker. The distance is about 1 to 3 meters (1.1 to 3.3 yards).

Details The detail section allows to enter more details of a condition of interest. A map can be added, a photo, or any other background material which provides useful additional information about one of the described conditions.

Details

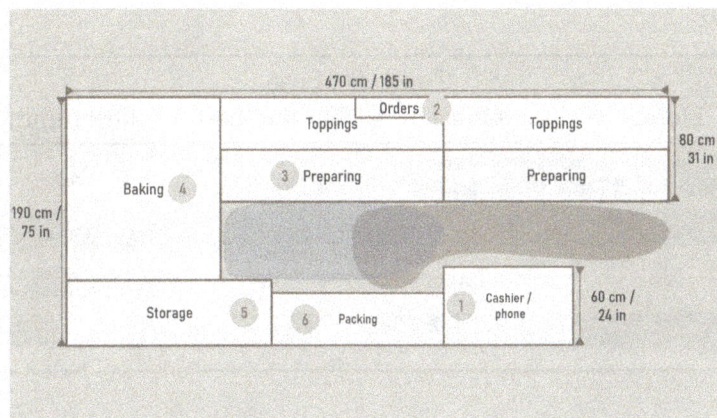

Figure 7.24: Kitchen - Details

The Detail section (see Figure 7.24) of the context of use template allows you to enter more details of a condition of interest. A map can be added, or a photo, or any other background material that provides useful additional information about one of the described conditions.

Other material could be placed here too, like photos of the kitchen and the manager's station.

Figure 7.18: Baker takes pizza out of oven; courtesy: Tino Procaccini

Figure 7.19: Baker cuts pizza; courtesy: Tino Procaccini

Figure 7.20: Baker refines pizza; courtesy: Tino Procaccini

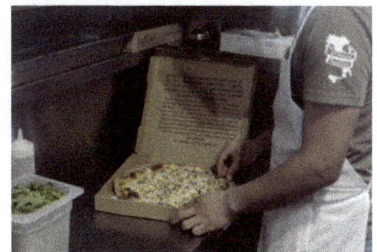

Figure 7.21: Baker puts pizza into box; courtesy: Tino Procaccini

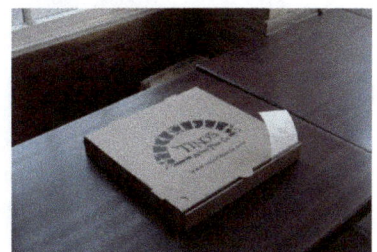

Figure 7.22: Pizza is boxed; courtesy: Tino Procaccini

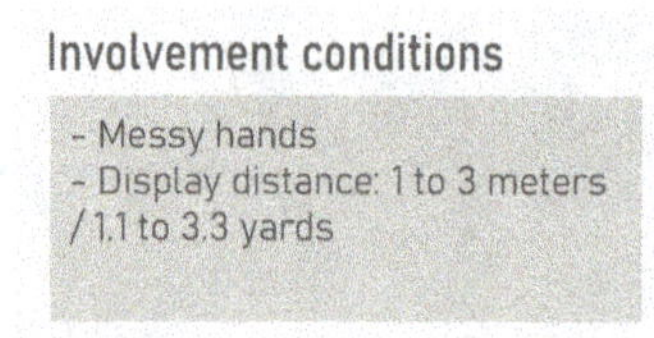

Involvement conditions

- Messy hands
- Display distance: 1 to 3 meters / 1.1 to 3.3 yards

Figure 7.23: Kitchen - Involvement conditions

Mapping to user groups

It happens frequently that different user groups share some of the identified contexts of use. To understand the applicability of the contexts of use for different user groups, a mapping of contexts of use to user roles is documented in a mapping table (see Table 7.2).

The mapping does not contain user tasks per use context yet, because they are not defined yet. This will be done later as part of the user involvement point specification (see Chapter 11 (User Involvement Point) on page 283).

Table 7.2: Mapping of user roles to contexts of use

(Consolidated) user roles	Contexts of use			
	Home	Office	On the road	Restaurant
Patron	Yes	Yes	Yes	No
Manager	Yes	Yes	Yes	Yes
Baker	No	No	No	Yes
Driver	Yes	Yes	Yes	Yes

If one user role is assigned to several use contexts, it can mean that the same user task can be performed in different use contexts. Here is an example: a customer selects a pizza in one use context (e.g., a car) and continues ordering the pizza in another use context (e.g., the office). Architecture and design decisions should consider use context switches. This is of particular interest if the interaction modality or device changes in different contexts of use (for instance from a mobile device to a desktop computer).

Summary

Context of Use

▶ Move on to Workflow (to be)
◀ Go back to User role

Name

Restaurant kitchen

Environment

Space with a wooden or gas oven where pizza is prepared, baked, and packaged

Ambient conditions

- Hot, humid, steam, smoke
- Background noise
- Possibly small space
- Noisy environment; no privacy

Soc/org conditions

- Constant coming and going of people; chatty environment
- Very busy at certain times and days

Technical conditions

- 36-inch display

Involvement conditions

- Messy hands
- Display distance: 1 to 3 meters / 1.1 to 3.3 yards

Details

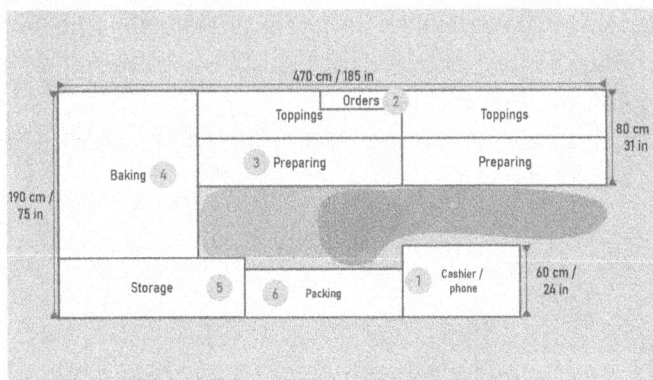

Figure 7.25: Context of use for restaurant kitchen

Key learnings

The context of use identifies the environments in which the application under design will be used. Furthermore, the context of use identifies conditions that may influence how the user performs tasks and achieves the goal.

The conditions consist of ambient conditions, social/organizational conditions, technical conditions, and involvement conditions.

Tips and tricks

It is helpful to visit the users' environment and observe how they perform their tasks. This will reveal unconscious habits and preferences and can help to identify nuggets that cannot be identified in an interview-style elicitation session.

Exercise 1.6

Goal Identify at least two contexts of use and document them.

Material Context of use profile template; user role to context of use mapping table

Completion criteria:

- ▶ For all user roles, all applicable contexts of use are identified.
- ▶ At least two contexts of use are profiled, using the template.
- ▶ For one context of use, a time study was performed and the results are documented.
- ▶ Each user role is mapped to the applicable contexts of use.

PART 2: EXPERIENCE ARCHITECTURE

Experience Architecture | 8

It's really clear that the most precious resource we all have is time.

Steve Jobs

Motivation

Major technology changes

From a device and involvement perspective, many things have changed since the Apple Macintosh became the first mass market personal computer with a graphical user interface in 1984 [149]. With the user interaction principle of direct manipulation, based on a graphical user interface, the Macintosh expanded computer use beyond computer scientists and interested individuals to the general population. The invention of the World Wide Web (WWW) at the beginning of the 1990s enhanced the use of computer- and software-based services beyond locally installed applications [150]. The WWW enables worldwide sharing and consumption of information by consumers and enterprises. The introduction of cloud services established the use of scalable data storage and computing power [151]. The invention of commercially available mobile phones in the 1980s introduced the concept of devices that anyone could use on the go [152].

xG cellular networks (we use 5G in 2022 [153]) will significantly increase the performance, reliability, and safety of cellular network-based mobile services. xG is expected to expedite the adoption of mobile services for applications that are not available as mobile services today. Internet of Things (IoT) devices, together with applications hosted in cloud services and connected to local wireless networks or xG, make it possible to monitor and control everyday devices from any location with internet access.

Major process changes

Besides product evolutions and revolutions, there have been changes to the way products are developed. The waterfall-style development process was established in the 1970s and 1980s as a response to the "software crisis" of the 1960s [154, 155]. In the 1980s, user-centered design was introduced [5]. It was formalized in ISO 13407 [156] and later incorporated into the ISO 9241 standard family [86]. In the 1970s, agile development was first used in manufacturing and found its way into the software development world in the 2000s[157]. Today it is the prevalent software development approach. A fully user-centered design and development approach, as we know it from building architecture [158] or from industrial design [159], is not established as of today—not yet.

While design tasks in the past often applied to single applications, many applications are part of a multi-user ecosystem. Due to the abovementioned technology advances and changes in the design and development process, the way users participate in the process and the way they use applications have evolved, too. Some of these changes are listed and explained later in this section.

Major user involvement changes

Contexts and situations of use

From single devices with a single context of use to multiple devices and multiple contexts of use

Figure 8.1: Change of contexts and situations of use

In the past, users performed their tasks on a specific device in one context of use. This was true for work as well as for leisure. Devices were used for special purposes, for example, a desktop computer or a laptop for work tasks and a mobile device for communication. Personal time and work time were more or less separate.

Today, the lines between devices, applications, and contexts and situations of use are blurring. Devices sometimes have a shared use for both work and personal tasks ("bring your own device," or BYOD). Both work tasks and personal tasks are performed during work time and personal time. Professional tasks are performed in personal environments (e.g., car, home office) and personal tasks are performed in professional environments (office and private environment for use as home office). Tasks (e.g., attending a virtual meeting) are started on one device (e.g., a mobile phone) in one environment (e.g., a car) and are continued on another device (e.g., a laptop) in another environment (e.g., at home). The same task is even performed on several devices at the same time [160, 161].

One challenge is to identify and define applications that support the various individual and blended uses in different contexts and that can switch between devices. Another challenge is deciding how to identify and define the fact that the same application is used on different devices at the same time.

> ► Strategic view: What are the various relevant contexts and situations of use? Which applications are needed by a single user to support the different contexts and situations of use? How can we support the use of several devices in parallel? How can we support device switching while a task is being performed?
> ► Tactical view: How can we design for user tasks in a specific context and situation and for one device? How can we design for context switching?

User involvement

From single tasks with user interaction to multiple tasks with a mix of user interaction and user intervention

In the past, users worked with one device, often a desktop or laptop computer, to perform certain tasks. The user "interacted" with an application (see Section 1 (Interaction and intervention)).

Today, many users employ several devices in parallel. While they focus on one main task, other tasks are running in the background. For instance, someone has submitted an online order for a product and receives notifications about delivery updates. Sometimes they are asked to make a decision (e.g., "The product you ordered, ABC, is out of stock, but we can offer an equivalent product, DEF. Do you want that?"). When users receive such a notification or request, it is usually when they are not actively working on that task. An

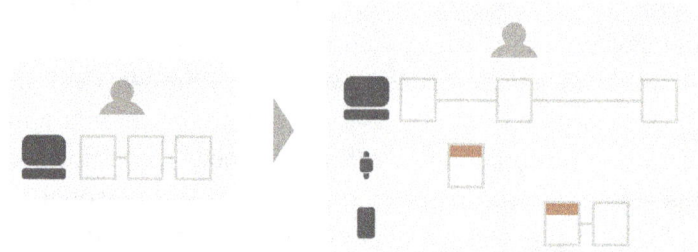

Figure 8.2: Changes in user involvement

external entity pulls them into it by triggering the request. This type of user involvement is called here "intervention" [55, 56]. A user intervenes in an otherwise semiautomated process. Alerts and status updates keep users informed about status changes in background-running semiautomated tasks. Therefore, users must switch their attention between the task being performed and the alerts appearing for other tasks. They have to find a way to get back to the main task with minimal impact and effort during this context switching. In the future, the use of augmented and mixed reality will play a major role in this process.

An application under design can be either the interrupting application or the application that is being interrupted. In the former case, the challenge is to design the application so that a user easily finds their way back into task performance mode after an interruption (where did I leave off?) to easy context switching. In the latter case, the challenge is to define how often a user should be alerted/interrupted and how quickly they should be informed. To be actionable for users, an alert will either require an immediate response or will serve as a reminder to the user to later initiate a needed action.

▶ Strategic view: How do we guide the user back into the interrupted task? About which changes or deviations should a user be informed? How frequently and how quickly should the user be informed? What type of content and controls are needed to make alerts immediately actionable for users?

▶ Tactical view: How should we design guidance content? How should we design alerts? How should we design proposed actions for users? How should we design alert settings?

Application scope

From single-device application scope to multiple-user, multiple connected device specific application scope

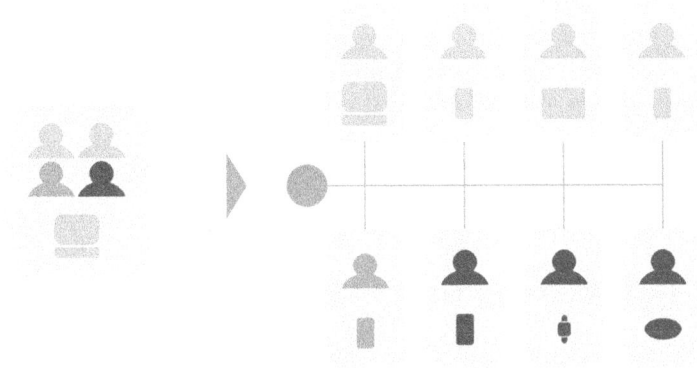

Figure 8.3: Change in application scope

Applications were developed as multipurpose individual applications. Often several user roles were assigned to one application. Applications were designed and developed for one device (e.g., desktop computer) with one modality. They were developed as stand-alone or client/server applications.

Today, several applications can be used to support one ecosystem. Applications support a limited number of user tasks, often just one or two. One user role often uses several applications, each with a limited set of user tasks. Several applications may be created for the same user role and specialized for different device types and modalities (e.g., desktop computer, laptop, cell phone, smart speaker), often optimized for a certain context of use. A limited application scope supports efficiency of use. The variety of applications for the ecosystem uses the same data set and integrates with some of the same services, hosted in the cloud. The variety of applications for different user roles works together as a network, keeping each other up to date about changes.

One challenge is to identify and define one or more applications assigned to a user role, a context of use, and limited user tasks and modalities. Another challenge is to ensure that all the diverse applications work together and that alerts and status updates are shared with the necessary frequency and in a timely manner.

▶ Strategic view: How do we identify and define the different applications and their modalities per user role? How do we ensure that the applications work properly together, including the frequency and timeliness of alerts and status updates?

▶ Tactical view: How can we design a single application for one device type, modality, and user role?

Explainability

From certainty to uncertainties

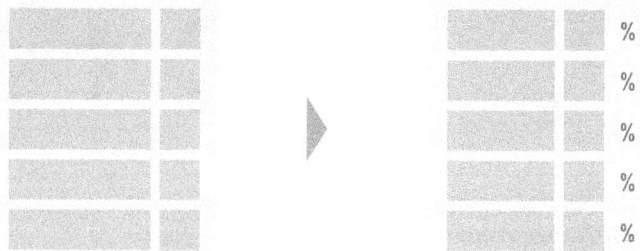

Figure 8.4: Changes to certainty

With the mass introduction of the desktop metaphor (graphical user interface, direct manipulation) in the 1980s with the Apple Macintosh, the road to mass adoption of computers was paved. The typical user had little or no understanding of how computers worked. But many people started to use them, and many understood the general principle of computers and software: instructions are executed one after another, in an algorithm implemented by a human. Programs with the same inputs will produce the same results. People trusted software and the results it generated.

With advanced technology, the use and adoption of artificial intelligence–based algorithms took off—particularly those with capabilities based on machine learning (ML). The use of ML introduced a paradigm shift in two ways. The first was that the ML-based capabilities were no longer implemented by humans, but by software that was "trained" to have certain capabilities. The second shift was that the capabilities could produce different outputs with the same inputs, depending on the training data. Certainty had been replaced with uncertainty. Because of uncertainties, ML-based capabilities and their calculated results require a new transparency, so that users can gain trust in the results and in the capabilities themselves. The transparency should consist of the provision of additional information that explains the uncertainties [70–84]. ML-based capabilities are particularly relevant for improving efficiency for users.

▶ Strategic view: What kind of explanations are needed to gain the user's trust?
▶ Tactical view:How should we design the explanations?

Definition, design, and development process

From feature-centered development to user-centered design and development

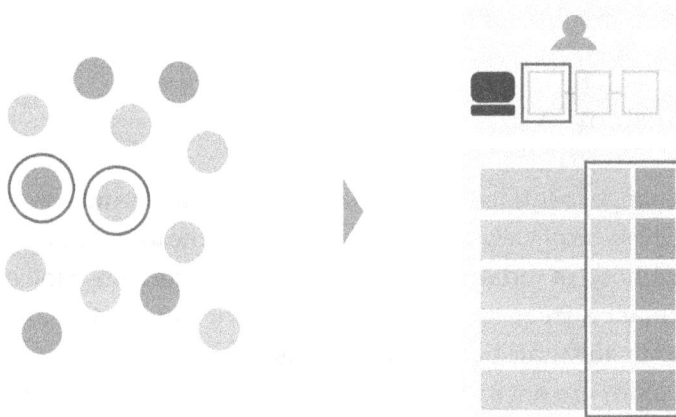

Figure 8.5: Changes in the design and development process

In the past, experience architecture and design contributions were an afterthought in many development projects. An application was defined with user stories, or development was steered by requirements, sometimes enhanced with use cases. After the technical concept was defined and approved, experience professionals could design screens whose functionality was already defined by a technical concept. An experience contribution was in reality a user interface design contribution.

Today, experience contributions are more often taking place in parallel with technical decisions. In more and more cases, experience contributions are leading design and development projects. User roles, contexts of use, user tasks, and task flows are defined. Function identification and allocation are part of the experience contribution. Concepts and interactive mockups are created and establish a common understanding among all project stakeholders, including the sponsor and user representatives. Users participate frequently and provide feedback. Interactive mockups are used to discuss the value proposition with the product manager and technical requirements with the development team.

One challenge is knowing how to define and design the ecosystem scope, aligned with product management, while staying user-focused. Another challenge is providing inputs into technical feasibility studies and process feasibility results and still delivering the intended top-tier experience.

> ► Strategic view: How do we define and organize the ecosystem scope, including all applications, driven by user goals and needs? How can we collaborate with product management and the technical team to realize the intended top-tier experience?
> ► Tactical view: How do we collaborate with product management and with the technical requirements to get the concepts and mockups implemented for an individual application (e.g., a subset of the ecosystem scope)?

Conclusions

Each change mentioned above has both a strategic and a tactical view. The tactical view can be addressed with the tools, techniques, and methods of today's user-centered design toolbox. However, performance, frequency, certainty, and other properties are addressed by the strategic view. Today's user-centered design process and toolbox are not capable of addressing the strategic view systematically.

It is the author's experience that addressing the strategic view requires a new approach. The proposal made here is to add a new phase to the user-centered design process for ecosystems. To master the complexity of user involvement for ecosystems, an *experience architecture* for the ecosystem under design needs to be identified, defined, and specified. It consists of several views, including a workflow (to be), a user involvement system, user involvement points, user involvement properties, and involvement goals as the main views and deliverables. Ecosystem-wide user involvement properties are emergent properties.

Examples of user involvement properties are functions, performance characteristics, and frequencies. When ML-based technology is used, equality properties to avoid data bias and certainty properties to establish trust and fairness are relevant too. Today, such properties are often specified by technical experts, for instance, software architects. Sometimes they are not specified at all and are a coincidental by-product of a developed application.

In order to ensure that the specified user involvement properties are the right ones and effectively address user needs and goals, a new role is needed. Here, this role is called *experience architect*. The work and decisions of an experience architect are driven by the users' needs and goals.

Experienced user-experience designers with sufficient expertise and experience in design, business, technology, domains, projects, and people can be effective experience architects. An experience architect is best skilled to define and specify them. Each ecosystem project or program should have an experience architect with the same voice as the product manager, the project manager, and the system/software architect

Experience architecture

The word "architecture" stems from the Greek word ἀρχιτέχτων (architekton), which is a composite of the words ἀρχι (archi), meaning "chief," and the word τέχτων (tekton), meaning "structure." An architect is a chief, or master, of a structure [162]. User involvement is determined by the structure of the user involvement system and the user involvement points.

> **Definition 8** (Experience architecture) *Organization principle of a user involvement system.*

An experience architecture is needed for complex user involvement in ecosystems. An experience architecture introduces an organizational principle that defines and specifies user involvement to address the needs of the involved users.

An experience architecture ...

- ▶ organizes the user involvement of an ecosystem.
- ▶ defines and specifies user involvement-related-behaviors and properties.
- ▶ allows mapping user involvement element to a road map, so that the value proposition can be realized step by step.
- ▶ allows the systematic integration of new user involvement elements into a well-defined structure.

The experience architecture defines and specifies the user involvement organizational principle with its properties and goals. It is the proposed ecosystem concept whereby the product manager realizes the value proposition. It also provides inputs for technology exploration and selection, so that the proposed ecosystem concept can be realized within project, market, and business constraints. For experience designers, it contains individual but connected

Terry Winograd used the concept of an "interaction architecture" and "interaction design" to emphasize the importance of an outside-in perspective of interactive systems [163, 164]. Winograd understood "architecture" as an environmental, physical concept, not so much a concept to define and organize a user-centered network of application as part of an ecosystem.

design work packages with their properties and goals. The above-mentioned relationship between the stakeholders is visualized in Figure 8.6.

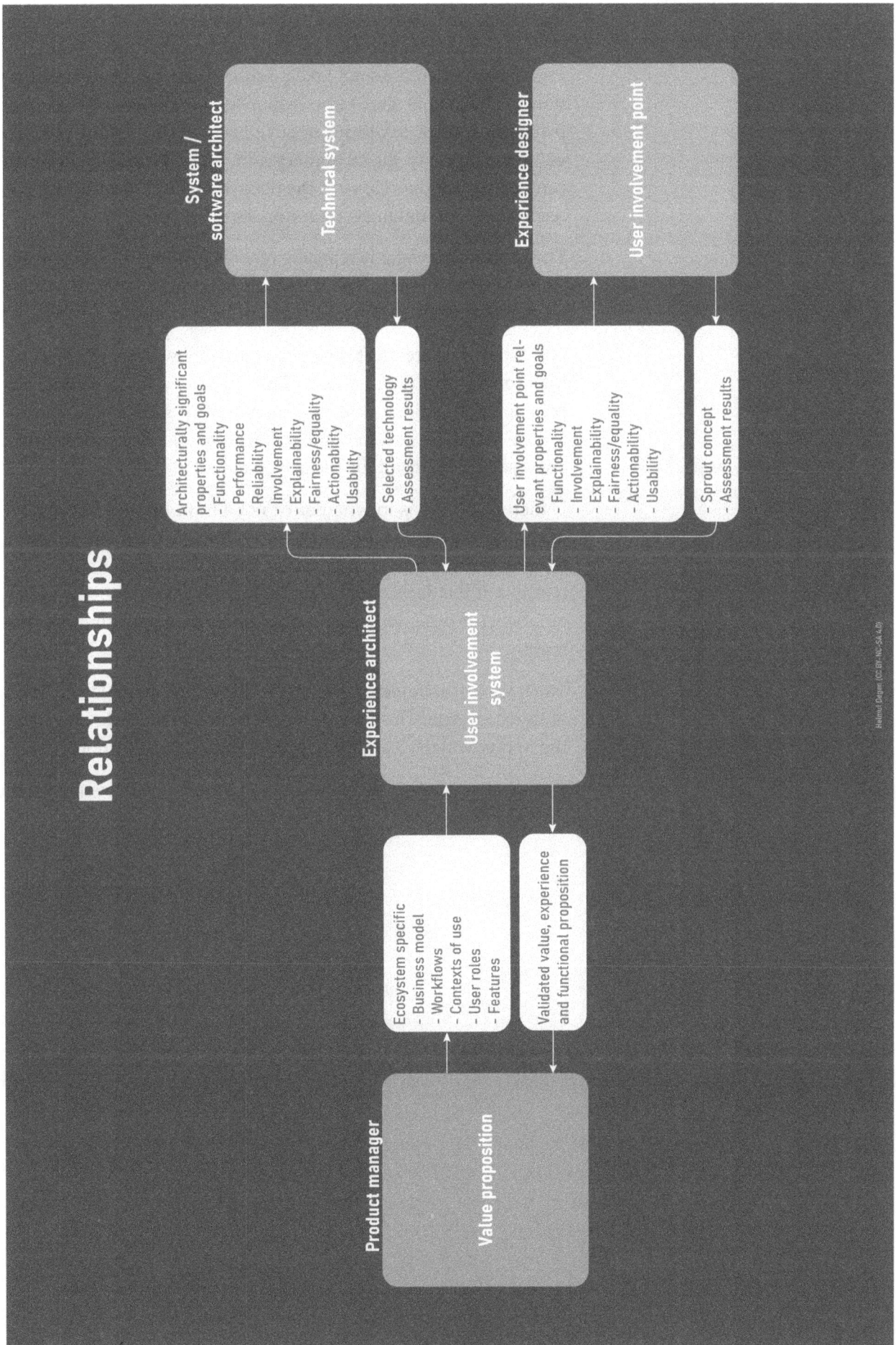

Figure 8.6: Relationship between product manager, experience architect, system/software architect, and experience designer

Introducing a new role means partially shifting existing responsibilities to that new role and partially adding new responsibilities. Such a shift often does not take place without conflicts. The question is which role should be responsible for what. The general principle applies, as always in business: aim for highest possible value and quality for customers and users. From this aim, we can derive that the role with the needed skill set should have the responsible for making certain decisions.

The product manager is typically responsible for the value proposition of an ecosystem. This translates into the selection of market, market segments, regions, features, pricing model, and cost.

The experience architect is responsible for how users interact and intervene with the ecosystem. This translates into involvement principles, functions, and nonfunctional properties like performance, reliability, explainability, fairness/equality, actionability, and usability relevant for user involvement.

If there is doubt as to whether or not a topic should be decided on by an experience architect, the following question can help to clarify: if the topic can be better decided on with inputs from users, or if the decision impacts user involvement, the experience architect (or designer) should most likely be responsible for that topic.

The technical architect is responsible for technical implementation of the ecosystem. This includes the selection of the technology and the implementation of the ecosystem with its applications.

The various views of the experience architecture are visualized in Figure 8.7.

Experience Architecture Views

Define workflow (to be)

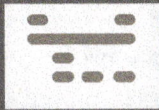

**Establish
user involvement system**

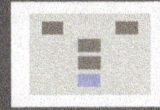

**Define user involvement
target times**

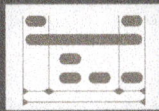

**Define user involvement scenarios
(white-box views)**

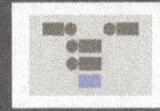

Define user journey map (to be)

Define user involvement points

Identify user involvement points

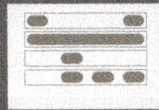

Minimize user involvement steps

**Define user involvement system
(black-box view)**

Define involvement goals

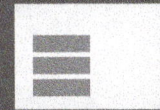

Figure 8.7: Experience architecture views

Summary

Lessons learned

Defining and specifying an experience architecture is proposed as a new project phase to enable mastery of user involvement in complex ecosystems. An experience architecture introduces an organizational principle that defines and specifies user involvement to address the needs and goals of the involved users. An experience architecture defines several views, contributing to the definition of the user involvement system, which will be described in the remainder of part 2.

An experience architecture and its various views are used for focused discussions with important project stakeholders. It is used to discuss with product managers how well the value proposition is supported. The specified user involvement properties and goals should be used as technology selection criteria. Elements of the experience architecture are design work packages, which are then executed by experience designers.

Tips and tricks

Stakeholder involvement   Product management and technology experts should be actively involved in the definition and specification of the experience architecture for several reasons. One important reason is that the stakeholders have knowledge that the experience architect may not have. This knowledge will find its way into one of the experience architecture views. Another important reason is that involvement of stakeholders creates co-ownership and increases the likelihood of their acceptance of the different views.

When involving product managers, technology leads, developers, and project managers in defining and specifying the different views, the author has not experienced hostile behavior. Rather, it was the other way around: the various views (user involvement system, scenarios, user involvement points, target) were immediately understood as adding value to the project. Everyone tried to help define them.

User focused with evidence   The different views are similar to what the technical experts define. It is essential to always look at the specifications and the decision from a user perspective, ideally backed up with evidence. For instance, if performance is discussed, it is useful to study what is perceived in that industry as "high performance" and as "low performance," with examples and measurements. Based on that, a reasonable performance number can be derived that is able to address users' needs and goals and is also feasible.

Workflow (to be) | 9

Don't waste my time!
Unknown

Purpose

This chapter describes the first two steps in creating the experience architecture. It defines the workflow (to be) as the starting point for the user involvement system and the estimated target user involvement times.

If a project team has decided to create a workflow (as is), the workflow (to be) should be derived from the workflow (as is) and the identified workflow weaknesses (see Section 5 on page 133).

If a project team has decided not to create a workflow (as is), the workflow (to be) needs to be created from scratch. Ideally, this should take place in a workshop with a few subject matter experts.

Define workflow (to be)

Create workflow (to be)

For reading convenience, the workflow (as is) with identified weaknesses is displayed in Figure 9.1. The workflow (to be) and the user involvement system will focus only on Phase 2: Deliver pizza.

The workflow (to be) is shown in Figure 9.2.

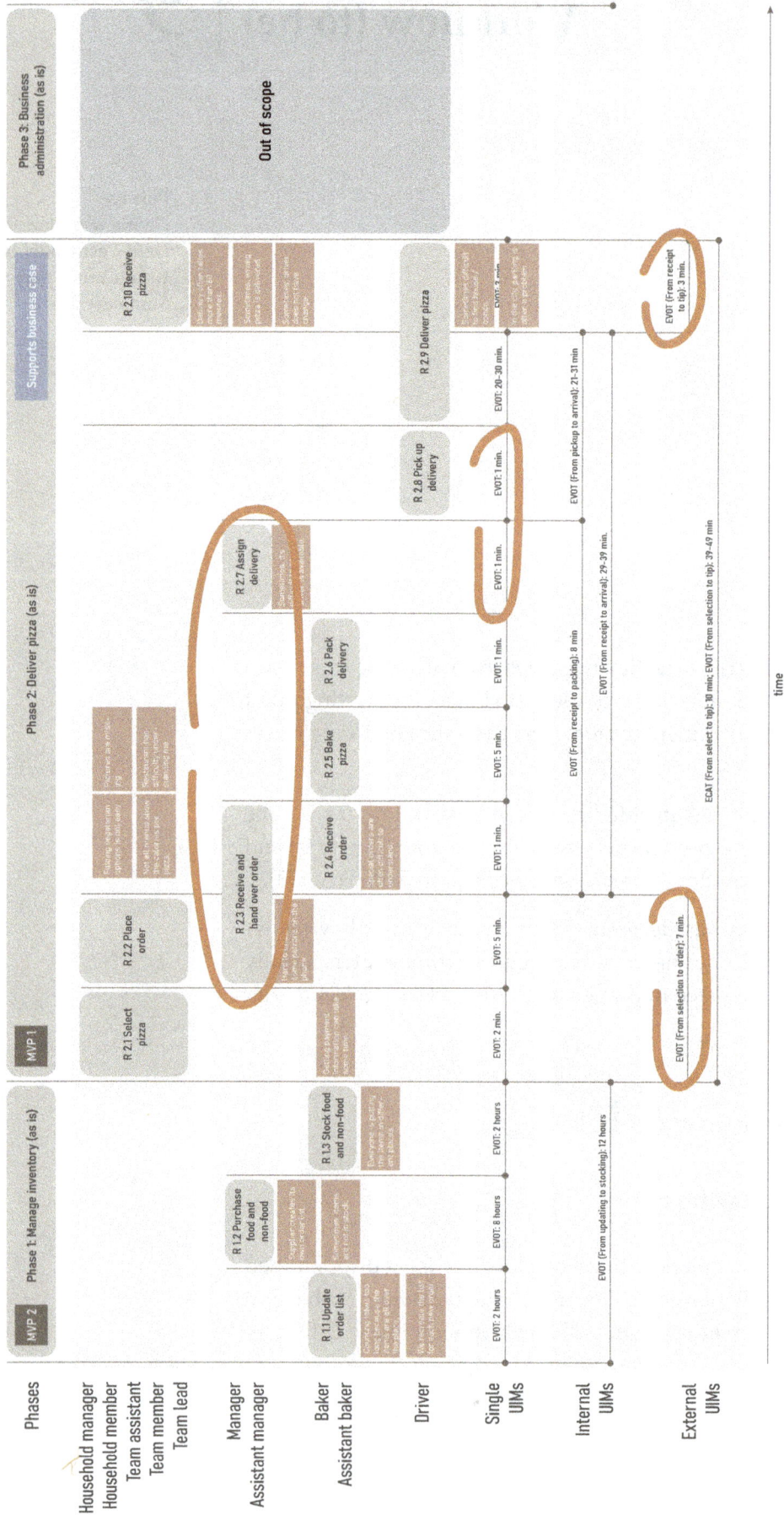

Figure 9.1: Step 7: Identify workflow weaknesses

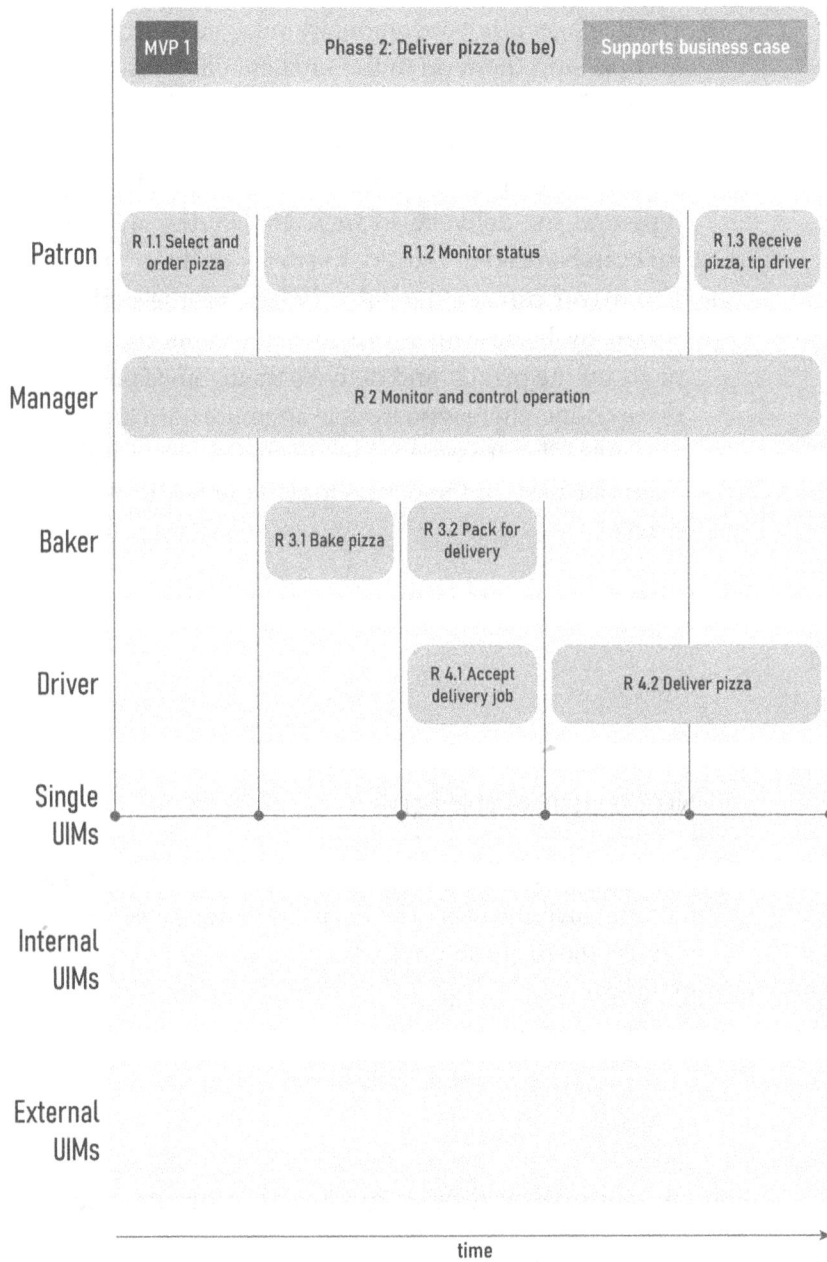

Figure 9.2: WoP Workflow (to be)

The new workflow has significantly fewer activities in total and per user role. Specifically, the following improvements have been applied:

▶ The patron will select and order a pizza online. S/he can monitor the order status and request that the pizza be delivered. Payment, including the driver's tip, takes place online.

▶ The manager is not operationally involved in accepting orders and passing them on to the kitchen, etc. This will be done online. The manager is only monitoring the operation and making decisions when necessary.

▶ The baker can print a label for each box that shows the order type and the delivery address. It also displays a bar code that can be used to retrieve the order online.

▶ The driver can see the delivery jobs on the mobile phone, sorted by hourly rate. The driver accepts the jobs online, picks up the pizzas, and delivers them. Since payment takes place online, there is no trouble anymore with having change available. The driver can close a delivery order online, which opens an alert for the patron to provide feedback and tip the driver.

The insights lead us to the next design principle:

No design *is* design

The decision to involve the user also entails the decision not to involve the user. The decision to design something includes the decision not to design something. There isn't no design.

Assign user goal and outcome of value per user role

After the workflow (to be) is defined, the outcome of value and the user goal per user role can be assigned. This information was already defined in the user role profile (see Section 2 (User role: Household manager) on page 161).

The user goal will keep us informed throughout the architecture phase and into the design of the seed concept. It will give us steady guidance for our decisions. The outcome of value is also important;

however, it is a more tactical result. Per user role, the outcome of value and the user goal are added (see Figure 9.3).

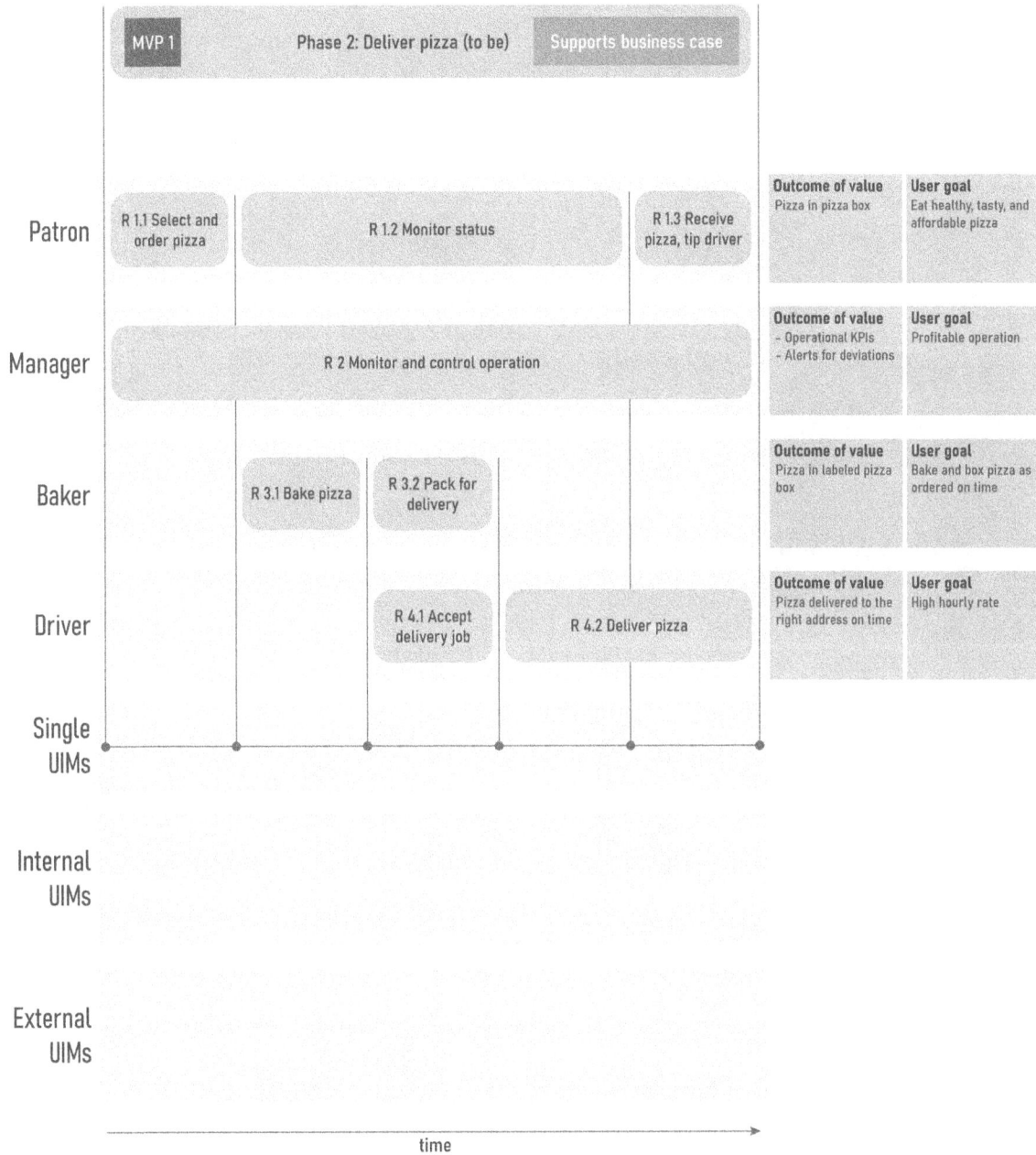

Figure 9.3: WoP Workflow (to be) with the outcome of value and user goal

While the outcome of value is the main deliverable per user role, the user goal is a main success factor per user role. It answers the question of how to make a user happy.

Define estimated target times

The swim lane of the to-be version already looks simplified compared to the as-is version. However, the truth lies in the numbers. The estimated target user involvement times should be defined with knowledge about current and possible practices, technology, and some optimism. The updated workflow diagram with target user involvement times is depicted in Figure 9.4.

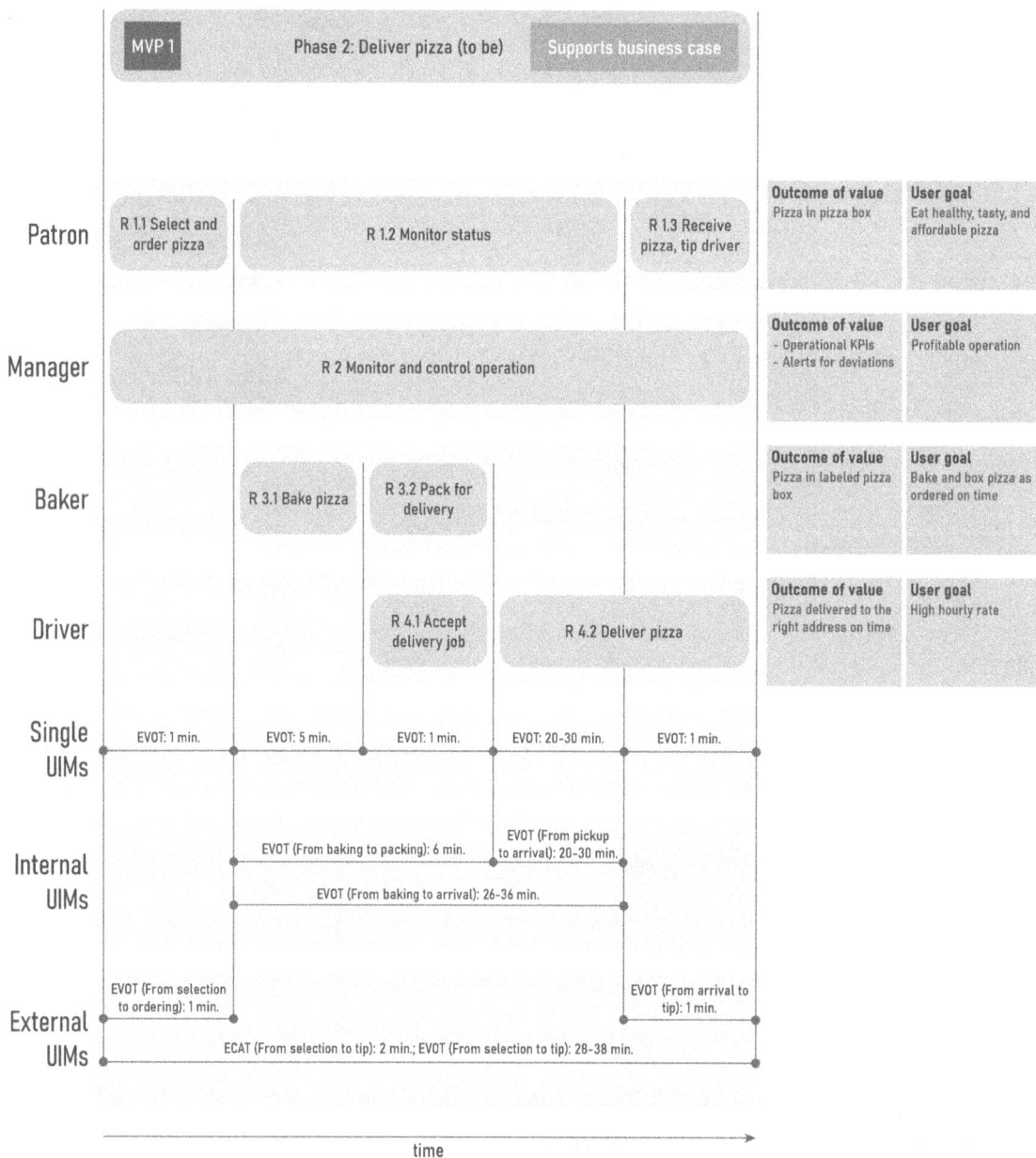

Figure 9.4: WoP Workflow (to be)

Based on the actual user involvement times (see Table 5.1 on page 127 or Figure 9.1), and with the estimated target user involvement time, we can calculate the estimated target involvement time savings (see Table 9.1). An absolute estimated times saving is calculated with $EATS = AAT - TAT$; a relative estimated time saving is calculated with $ERTS = \frac{AAT-TAT}{AAT}$ (see Section 23 (Selected savings metrics) on page 595).

Table 9.1: Estimated user involvement time savings

User involvement metrics	Workflow (as is) Actual user involvement times (AAT)	Workflow (to be) Target user involvement times (TAT)	Estimated user involvement time savings (EATS and ERTS)
Internal UIMs			
EVOT (From receipt to packing)	8 min.	5 min.	3 min. (38%)
EVOT (From pickup to arrival)	21-31 min. (mean: 26 min.)	20-30 min. (mean: 25 min.)	1 min. (4%)
EVOT (From pickup to tip)	24-34 min. (mean: 29 min.)	21-31 min. (mean: 26 min.)	3 min. (10%)
External UIMs			
EVOT (From selection to ordering)	7 min.	1 min.	6 min. (86%)
EVOT (From arrival to tip)	3 min.	1 min.	2 min. (67%)
ECAT (From selection to tip)	10 min.	2 min.	8 min. (80%)
EVET (From selection to tip)	29-39 min. (mean:34 min.)	26-36 min. (mean: 31 min.)	3 min. (9%)
EVOT (From selection to tip)	39-49 min. (mean: 44 min.)	28-38 min. (mean: 33 min.)	11 min. (25%)

The estimated time savings can be used as a decision gate in the project. If the estimated savings look promising and meet the minimum savings expectations, the project can go ahead and define the user involvement system. If the estimated savings do not look promising or do not meet the minimum savings expectations, the workflow (to be) can be revised. It is also possible to abort the project, due to insufficient estimated savings that may not support the business model.

Estimated user involvement time savings up to 33% are highlighted in orange; savings from 34% to 66% in purple, and above 66% are in blue, here and later in this book.

User journey map (to be)

Sometimes project stakeholders do not have a good understanding of the domain. In other cases, project stakeholders may disagree on how to improve a situation. In both cases, there is probably an insufficient common understanding of important details.

To overcome this knowledge gap, a deep dive into user roles can be helpful. A user journey map (to be) per user role can provide the needed details and insights and help to create a common understanding among project stakeholders and users. A user journey map (to be) can be used to derive a workflow (to be), but also to validate an outlined workflow (to be).

The template for a user journey map (to be) is shown in Figure 9.5.

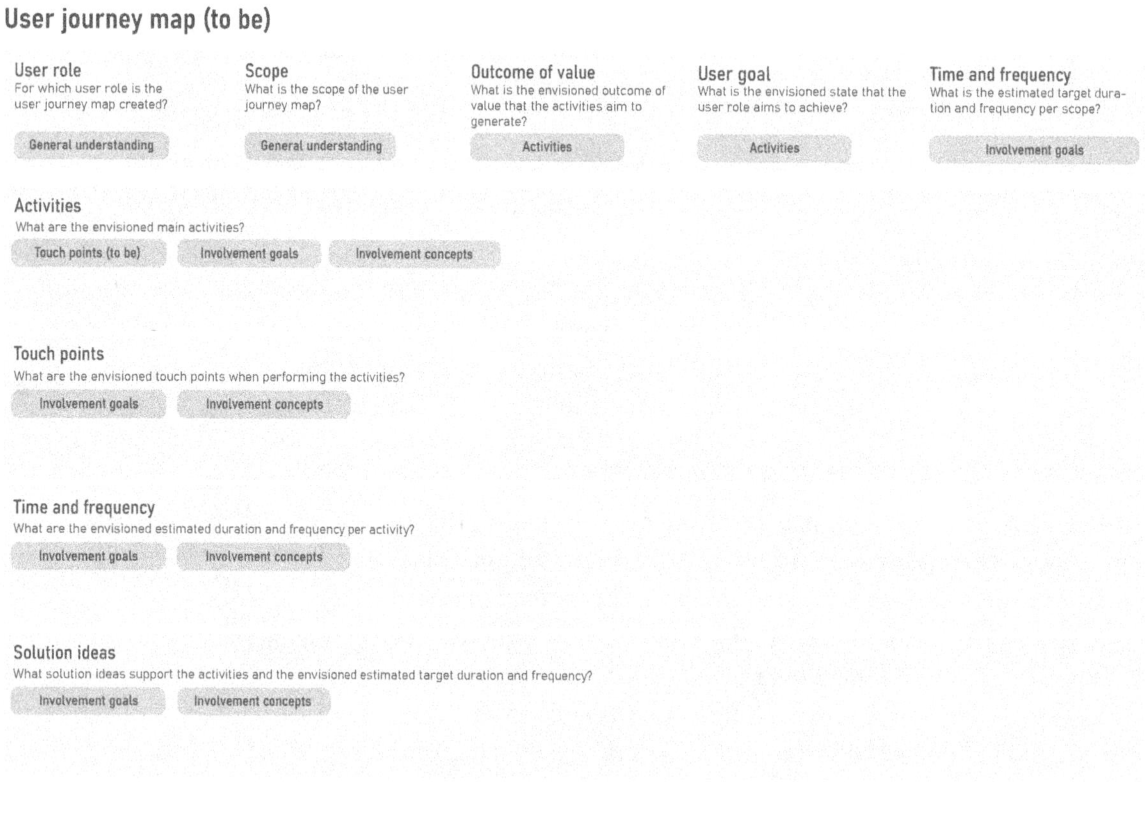

User journey map (to be)

User role	Scope	Outcome of value	User goal	Time and frequency
For which user role is the user journey map created?	What is the scope of the user journey map?	What is the envisioned outcome of value that the activities aim to generate?	What is the envisioned state that the user role aims to achieve?	What is the estimated target duration and frequency per scope?
General understanding	General understanding	Activities	Activities	Involvement goals

Activities
What are the envisioned main activities?

Touch points (to be)   Involvement goals   Involvement concepts

Touch points
What are the envisioned touch points when performing the activities?

Involvement goals   Involvement concepts

Time and frequency
What are the envisioned estimated duration and frequency per activity?

Involvement goals   Involvement concepts

Solution ideas
What solution ideas support the activities and the envisioned estimated target duration and frequency?

Involvement goals   Involvement concepts

Figure 9.5: User journey map (to be) template

There are a few differences between this template and the user journey map (as is) template:

- ▶ The user journey map expresses the "to be," that is, the future state.
- ▶ The elapsed time and duration expresses the estimated target involvement time and frequency

▶ The part called "wishes" was replaced by "solution ideas." These are useful to validate that what the contributor has in mind is in line with the facilitator's thoughts. Furthermore, some of the solution ideas might actually be useful and can be incorporated into the new involvement concepts.

The user journey map (to be) template will be applied for the user role "Patron" in our World of Pizza example for the three responsibilities R 1.1 "Select and order pizza," R 1.2 "Monitor status," and R 1.3 "Receive pizza and tip driver."

Details for R 1.1 Select and order pizza

The user journey map (to be) for the user role Patron and for the responsibility R 1.1 Select and order pizza is displayed in Figure 9.6.

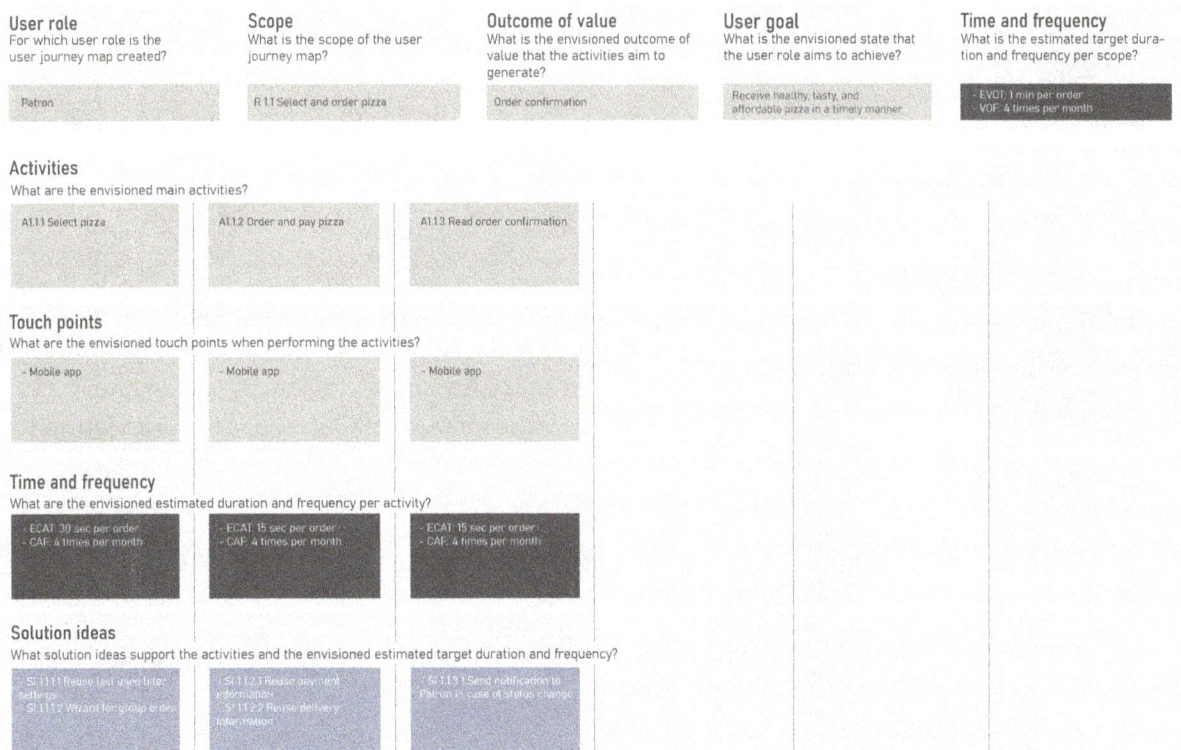

Figure 9.6: User Journey Map (to be): Patron: R 1.1 Select and order pizza

Each content item of the user journey map (to be) will now be briefly discussed.

User role   *For which user role is the user journey map created?*

The *user role* identifies for which user this user journey map (to be) is created.

The user role is the Patron.

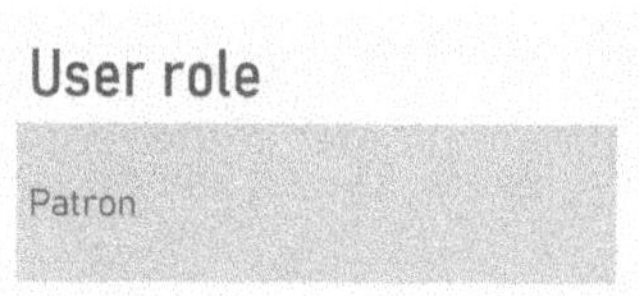

User role

Patron

Figure 9.7: R 1.1 Select and order pizza: User role

Scope   *What is the scope of the user journey map?*

The *scope* makes a reference to the selected responsibility from the workflow (to be) for which the user journey map (to be) was created.

The scope of this user journey map is the responsibility R 1.1 Select and order pizza.

Scope

R 1.1 Select and order pizza

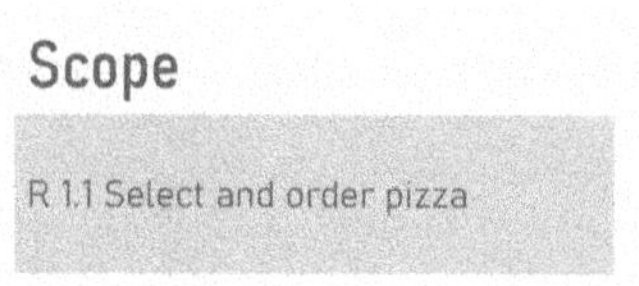

Figure 9.8: R 1.1 Select and order pizza: Scope

Outcome of value   *What is the envisioned outcome of value that the activities aim to generate?*

The *outcome of value* is the tangible deliverable for the user as a result of performing the activities.

The outcome for the identified activities is an order confirmation.

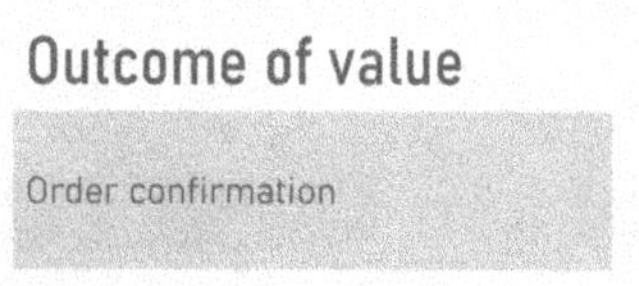

Outcome of value

Order confirmation

Figure 9.9: R 1.1 Select and order pizza: Outcome

User goal   *What is the envisioned state that the user role aims to achieve?*

The *user goal* is the user benefiting target state as a result of the entire workflow for the selected user role, not only as a result of the user journey map. Articulating a larger goal ensure to provide appropriate guidance for the (smaller) scope of a user journey map (to be).

The user goal for the patron is to receive a healthy, tasty, and affordable pizza in a timely manner.

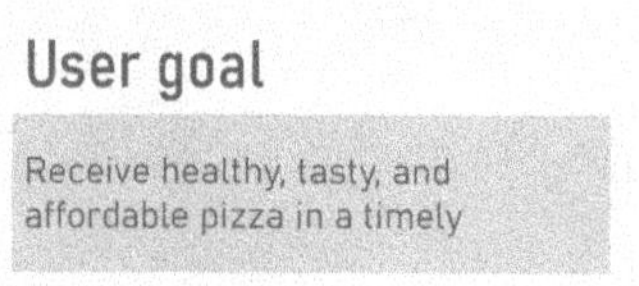

User goal

Receive healthy, tasty, and affordable pizza in a timely

Figure 9.10: R 1.1 Select and order pizza: Goal

Time and frequency per scope   *What is the estimated target duration and frequency per scope?*

The *target duration and frequency* expresses the estimated user involvement time and frequency. The duration and frequency should be broken down for each activity and then aggregated to a time and frequency number for the entire user journey map.

In total, the target elapsed user involvement time is one minute. This time is meant for frequent users, not for first-time users. The estimated target user involvement frequency is four times per month. This means it is assumed that one user orders at least one pizza per week, or about four pizzas per month.

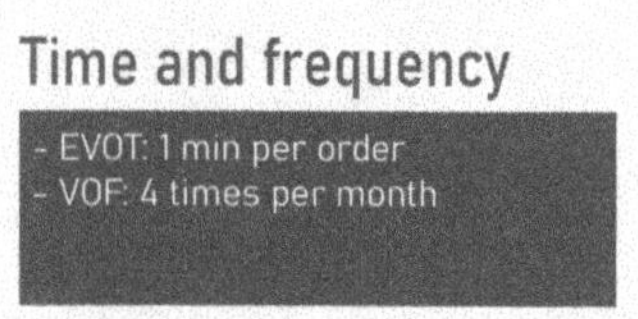

Time and frequency

- EVOT: 1 min per order
- VOF: 4 times per month

Figure 9.11: R 1.1 Select and order pizza: Time and frequency (to be) per scope

Activities *What are the envisioned main activities?*

The main focus is on those *activities* that are relevant for the user journey map and for the application under design. Each activity is identified in a column on the user journey map. For each activity, attributes like touch points, time, and solution ideas are generated.

The main activities for the user journey map R 1.1. Select and order pizza are as follows:

- ► Select pizza
- ► Order and pay pizza
- ► Read order confirmation

Touch points *What are the envisioned touch points when performing the activities?*

Touch points

The only touch point we have here is a mobile phone app for the Patron

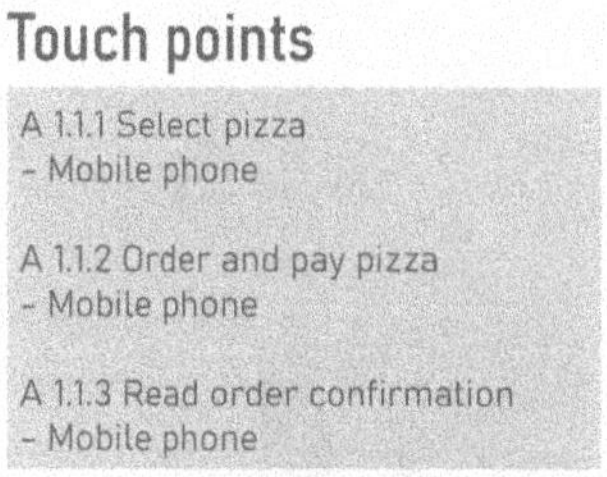

Time and frequency per activity *What are the envisioned estimated duration and frequency per activity?*

It is envisioned that the first activity will take a bit longer than the others, but not longer than three minutes (elapsed and working time). It is envisioned that the other two activities will not take longer than 30 seconds (elapsed and working time) each. This short amount of time is expected to be achievable and to contribute to increases in efficiency.

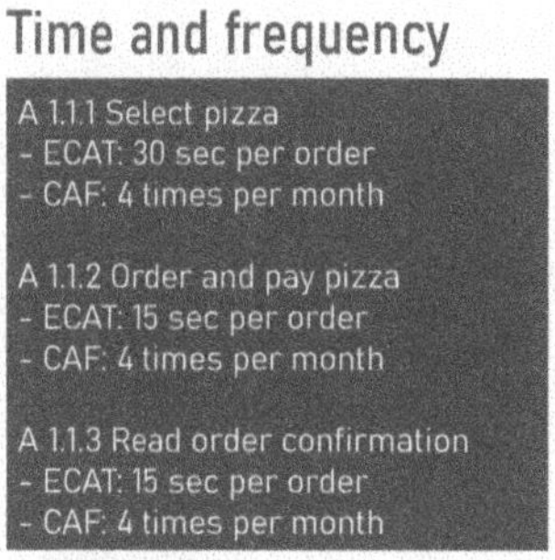

Solution ideas *What solution ideas support the activities and the envisioned estimated target duration and frequency?*

To prepare for upcoming design decisions, it makes sense to elicit wishes, or solution ideas, for each envisioned activity.

We can assume that the patron would benefit from being able to automatically use the last-used filter settings. For group orders, a wizard could help to speed things up. To expedite the ordering and payment steps, the automatic reuse of order and payment information would be beneficial. After the order was submitted, the patron would benefit from notifications of changes in delivery status, including whether the delivery was delayed.

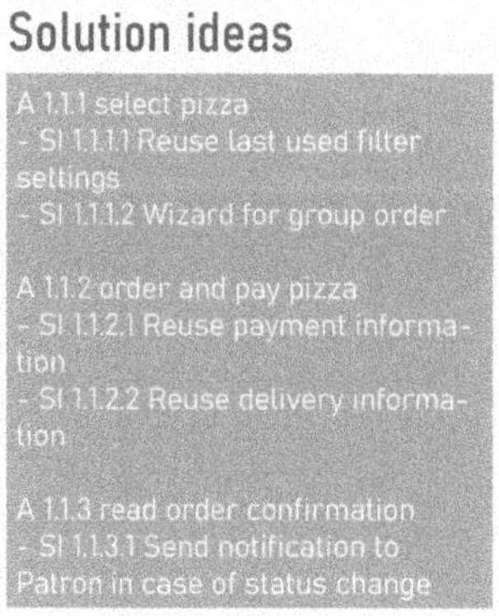

Activities (to-be)

R 1.1 Select and order pizza
- A 1.1.1 Select pizza
- A 1.1.2 Order and pay pizza
- A 1.1.3 Read order confirmation

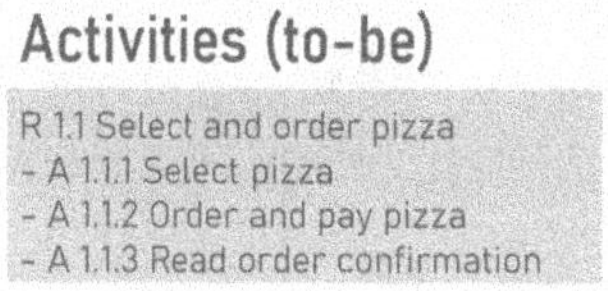

Figure 9.12: R 1.1 Select and order pizza: Activities

Touch points

A 1.1.1 Select pizza
- Mobile phone

A 1.1.2 Order and pay pizza
- Mobile phone

A 1.1.3 Read order confirmation
- Mobile phone

Figure 9.13: R 1.1 Select and order pizza: Touch points

Time and frequency

A 1.1.1 Select pizza
- ECAT: 30 sec per order
- CAF: 4 times per month

A 1.1.2 Order and pay pizza
- ECAT: 15 sec per order
- CAF: 4 times per month

A 1.1.3 Read order confirmation
- ECAT: 15 sec per order
- CAF: 4 times per month

Figure 9.14: R 1.1 Select and order pizza: Time and frequency (to be) per activity

Solution ideas

A 1.1.1 select pizza
- SI 1.1.1.1 Reuse last used filter settings
- SI 1.1.1.2 Wizard for group order

A 1.1.2 order and pay pizza
- SI 1.1.2.1 Reuse payment information
- SI 1.1.2.2 Reuse delivery information

A 1.1.3 read order confirmation
- SI 1.1.3.1 Send notification to Patron in case of status change

Figure 9.15: R 1.1 Select and order pizza: Solution ideas

Details for R 1.2 Monitor status

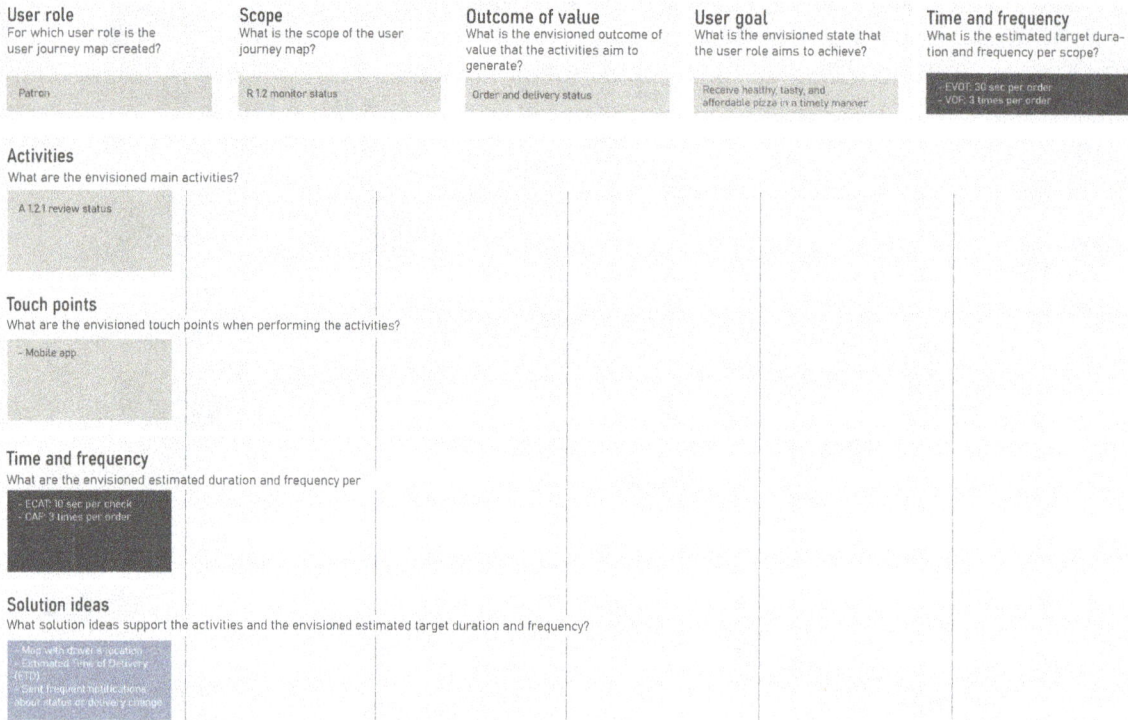

User role
For which user role is the
user journey map created?

Patron

Scope
What is the scope of the user
journey map?

R 1.2 monitor status

Outcome of value
What is the envisioned outcome of
value that the activities aim to
generate?

Order and delivery status

User goal
What is the envisioned state that
the user role aims to achieve?

Receive healthy, tasty, and
affordable pizza in a timely manner

Time and frequency
What is the estimated target duration and frequency per scope?

- EVOT: 30 sec per order
- VOF: 3 times per order

Activities
What are the envisioned main activities?

A 1.2.1 review status

Touch points
What are the envisioned touch points when performing the activities?

- Mobile app

Time and frequency
What are the envisioned estimated duration and frequency per

- ECAT: 10 sec per check
- CAP: 3 times per order

Solution ideas
What solution ideas support the activities and the envisioned estimated target duration and frequency?

- Map with driver's location
- Estimated Time of Delivery
(ETD)
- Sent frequent notifications
about status or delivery change

Figure 9.16: User Journey Map: Patron: R 1.2 Monitor status

User role *For which user role is the user journey map created?*

The user role is the same, a user journey map for the user role Patron.

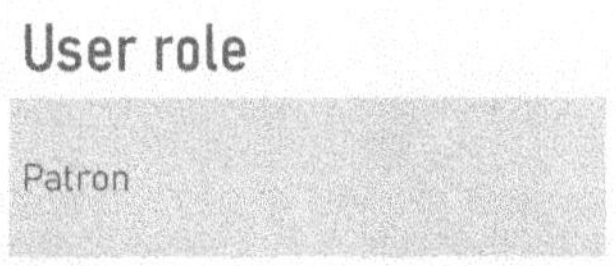

Scope *What is the scope of the user journey map?*

The scope this time is the second interaction point for the patron, after submitting the order: review order and delivery status.

Outcome of value *What is the envisioned outcome of value that the activities aim to generate?*

The outcome of value for the identified activities is the order and delivery status.

User goal *What is the envisioned state that the user role aims to achieve?*

The user goal is to receive healthy, tasty, and affordable pizza in a timely manner.

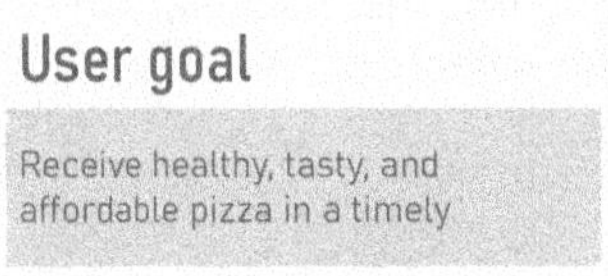

Time and frequency per scope *What is the estimated target duration and frequency per scope?*

The envisioned time per check is about 10 seconds (elapsed time and working time). It is expected to be performed three times per order, so the total hands-on time is 30 seconds, and the total time for completion is about 20 to 30 minutes.

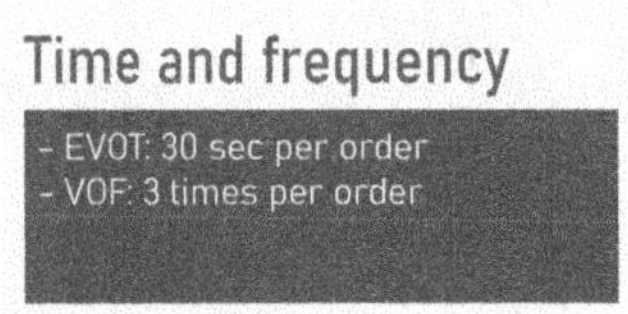

Activities *What are the envisioned main activities?*

There is only one main activity, i.e., to monitor the status. This activity will give the current status of the order or the delivery.

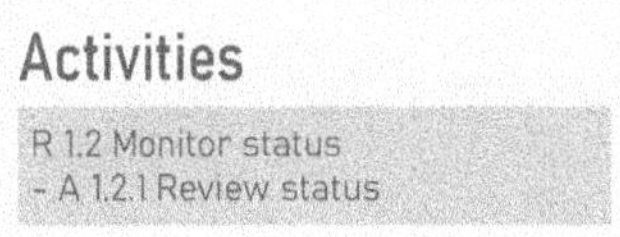

Touch points *What are the envisioned touch points when performing the activities?*

The only touch point we have here is a mobile phone app for the Patron.

User role

Patron

Figure 9.17: R 1.2 Monitor status: User role

Scope

R 1.2 Monitor status

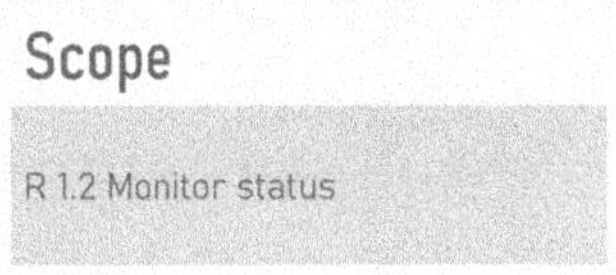

Figure 9.18: R 1.2 Monitor status: Scope

Outcome of value

Order and delivery status

Figure 9.19: R 1.2 Monitor status: Outcome

User goal

Receive healthy, tasty, and affordable pizza in a timely

Figure 9.20: R 1.2 Monitor status: User goal

Time and frequency

- EVOT: 30 sec per order
- VOF: 3 times per order

Figure 9.21: R 1.2 Monitor status: Time and frequency (to be) per scope

Activities

R 1.2 Monitor status
- A 1.2.1 Review status

Figure 9.22: R 1.2 Monitor status: Activities

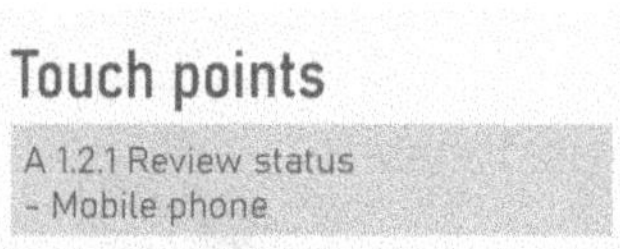

Touch points

A 1.2.1 Review status
- Mobile phone

Figure 9.23: R 1.2 Monitor status: Touchpoints

Time and frequency

A 1.2.1 Review status
- ECAT: 10 sec per check
- CAF: 3 times per order

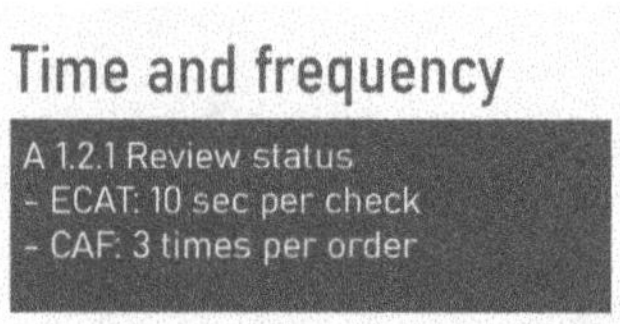

Figure 9.24: R 1.2 Monitor status: Time and frequency (to be) per activity

Solution ideas

A 1.2.1 Review status
- SI 1.2.1.1 Map with driver's location
- SI 1.2.1.2 Estimated Time of Delivery (ETD)
- SI 1.2.1.3 Sent frequent notifications about status or delivery change

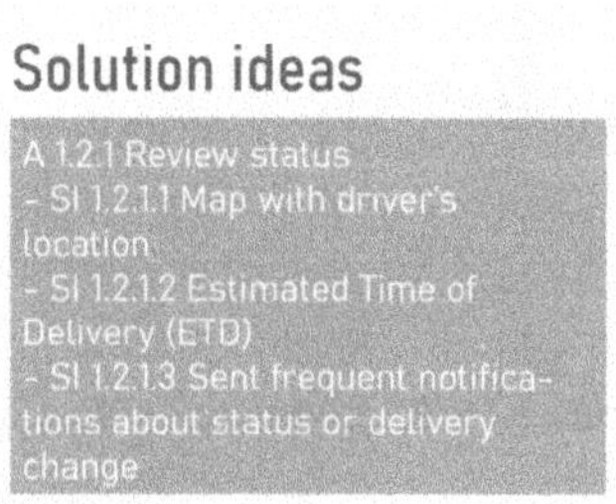

Figure 9.25: R 1.2 Monitor status: Solution ideas

Time and frequency per activity *What are the envisioned estimated duration and frequency per activity?*

Each check is expected to take about 10 seconds. It is assumed that the patron will check the status three times per order. This means that the hands-on time is 30 seconds, and the total time for completion is 20 to 30 minutes, depending on how long it takes the restaurant to deliver the pizza.

Solution ideas *What solution ideas support the activities and the envisioned estimated target duration and frequency?*

A solution idea to support the patron is to provide a map with the driver's location and the updated estimated time of delivery. It would also be useful for the patron to receive a notification update about the status after each status change or as a time countdown (e.g., delivery in 15 minutes, in 10 minutes, in 5 minutes).

Details for R 1.3 Receive pizza and tip driver

In Figure 9.26, we see the third user journey map (to be) for the patron.

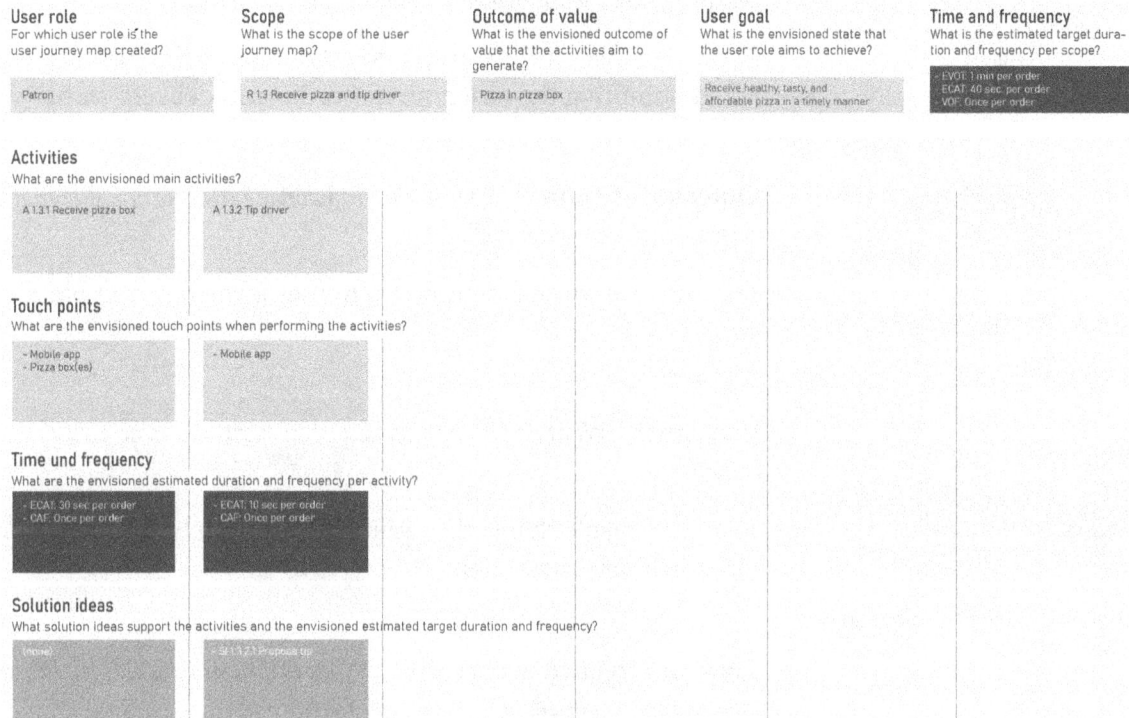

Figure 9.26: User Journey Map: R 1.3 Receive pizza and tip driver

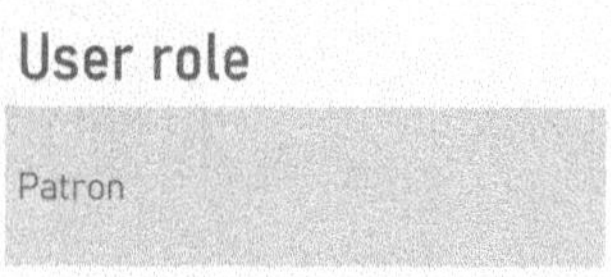

User role *For which user role is the user journey map created?*

The user role is the same, a user journey map for the user role patron.

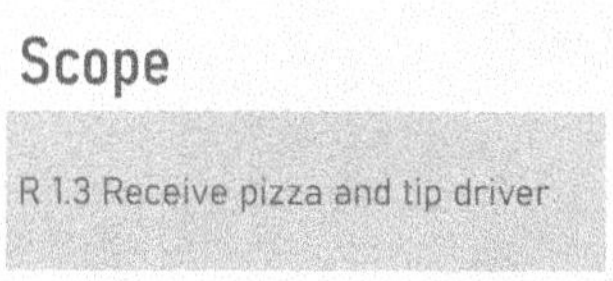

Scope *What is the scope of the user journey map?*

The scope this time is the second interaction point for the patron, after submitting the order: review order and delivery status.

Outcome of value *What is the envisioned outcome of value that the activities aim to generate?*

The outcome for the identified activities is the received pizza in a pizza box.

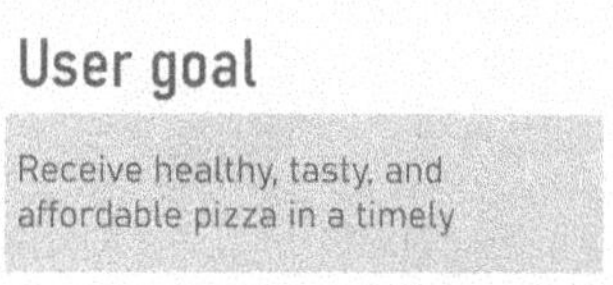

User goal *What is the envisioned state that the user role aims to achieve?*

The goal hasn't changed: Receive healthy, tasty, and affordable pizza in a timely manner.

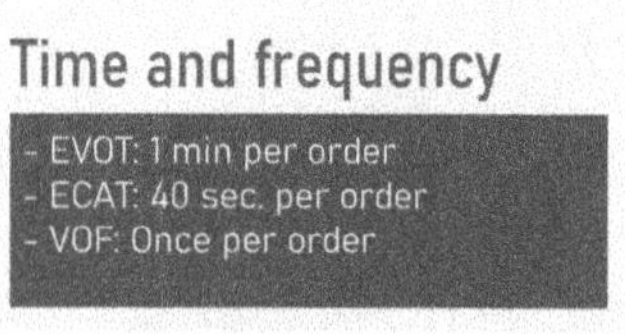

Time and frequency per scope *What is the estimated target duration and frequency per scope?*

In total, the envisioned time per check is about 10 seconds (elapsed time and working time). It is expected to be performed three times per order, so hands-on time is 30 seconds, and total time for completion is 20 to 30 minutes.

Activities *What are the envisioned main activities?*

There are two main activities: receiving the pizza and tipping the driver. Remember, the payment was done online when the order was submitted, so we don't have a payment step here.

Touch points *What are the envisioned touch points when performing the activities?*

The touch point for receiving the pizza is the pizza box. The patron may use the mobile app to check the order and make sure the delivered pizza is what they ordered.

The only touch point for paying the tip is the mobile phone app.

User role

Patron

Figure 9.27: R 1.3 Receive pizza and tip driver: User role

Scope

R 1.3 Receive pizza and tip driver

Figure 9.28: R 1.3 Receive pizza and tip driver: Scope

Outcome of value

Pizza in pizza box

Figure 9.29: R 1.3 Receive pizza and tip driver: Outcome

User goal

Receive healthy, tasty, and affordable pizza in a timely

Figure 9.30: R 1.3 Receive pizza and tip driver: User goal

Time and frequency

- EVOT: 1 min per order
- ECAT: 40 sec. per order
- VOF: Once per order

Figure 9.31: R 1.3 Receive pizza and tip driver: Time and frequency (to be) per scope

Activities

R 1.3 Tip driver
- A 1.3.1 Receive pizza box
- A 1.3.2 Tip driver

Figure 9.32: R 1.3 Receive pizza and tip driver: Activities

Time and frequency per activity   *What are the envisioned estimated duration and frequency per activity?*

For each activity, we estimate a hands-on time of 30 seconds and a total completion time of 30 seconds. They are performed once per order.

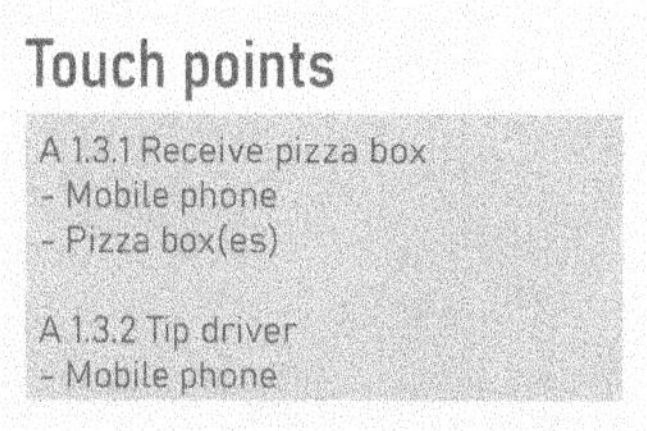

Solution ideas   *What solution ideas support the activities and the envisioned estimated target duration and frequency?*

To speed up the process of tipping the driver, precalculated or suggested tip amounts could be proposed for selection by the patron.

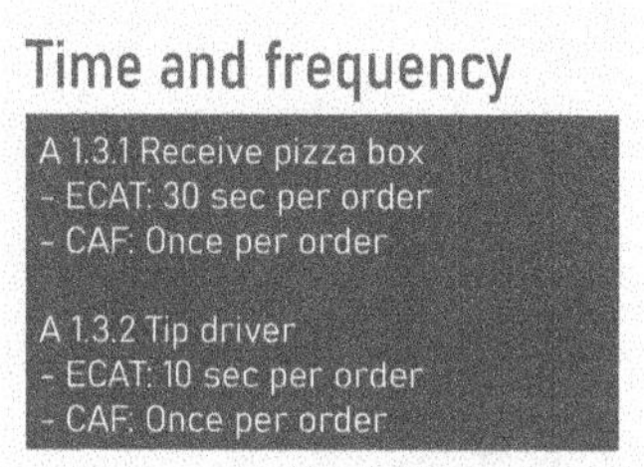

Alternative views

Each template and tool has a purpose and contributes to reducing uncertainties and/or increasing clarity. The benefits of using a tool and creating clarity should outweigh the effort of using it.

Sometimes it is possible that a bit more clarity for the outlined workflow (to be) is needed, but that the path to create user journey maps (to be) would be too much of an effort. In this case, it would be sufficient to simply extend the workflow (to be) with additional information. An example with added solution ideas per responsibility is shown in Figure 9.36. Other information could be added too, of course.

Touch points

A 1.3.1 Receive pizza box
- Mobile phone
- Pizza box(es)

A 1.3.2 Tip driver
- Mobile phone

Figure 9.33: R 1.3 Receive pizza and tip driver: Touchpoints

Time and frequency

A 1.3.1 Receive pizza box
- ECAT: 30 sec per order
- CAF: Once per order

A 1.3.2 Tip driver
- ECAT: 10 sec per order
- CAF: Once per order

Figure 9.34: R 1.3 Receive pizza and tip driver: Time and frequency (to be) per activity

Solution ideas

A 1.3.1 Receive pizza box
(none)

A 1.3.2 Tip driver
- SI 1.3.2.1 Propose tip

Figure 9.35: R 1.3 Receive pizza and tip driver: Solution ideas

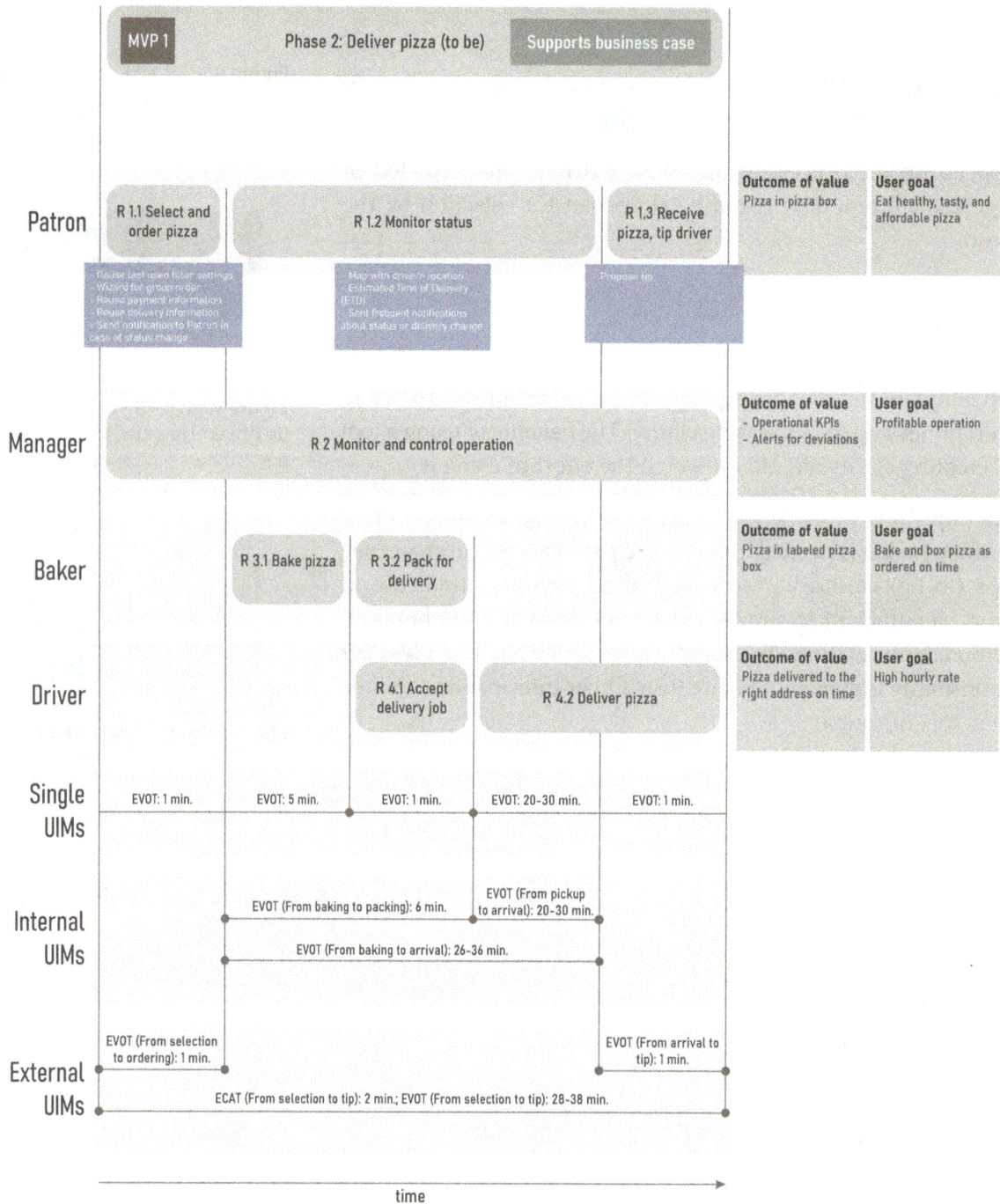

Figure 9.36: WoP Workflow (to be) with additional information

Summary

Workflow (to be)

► Move on to User Involvement System
◄ Go back to Context of use

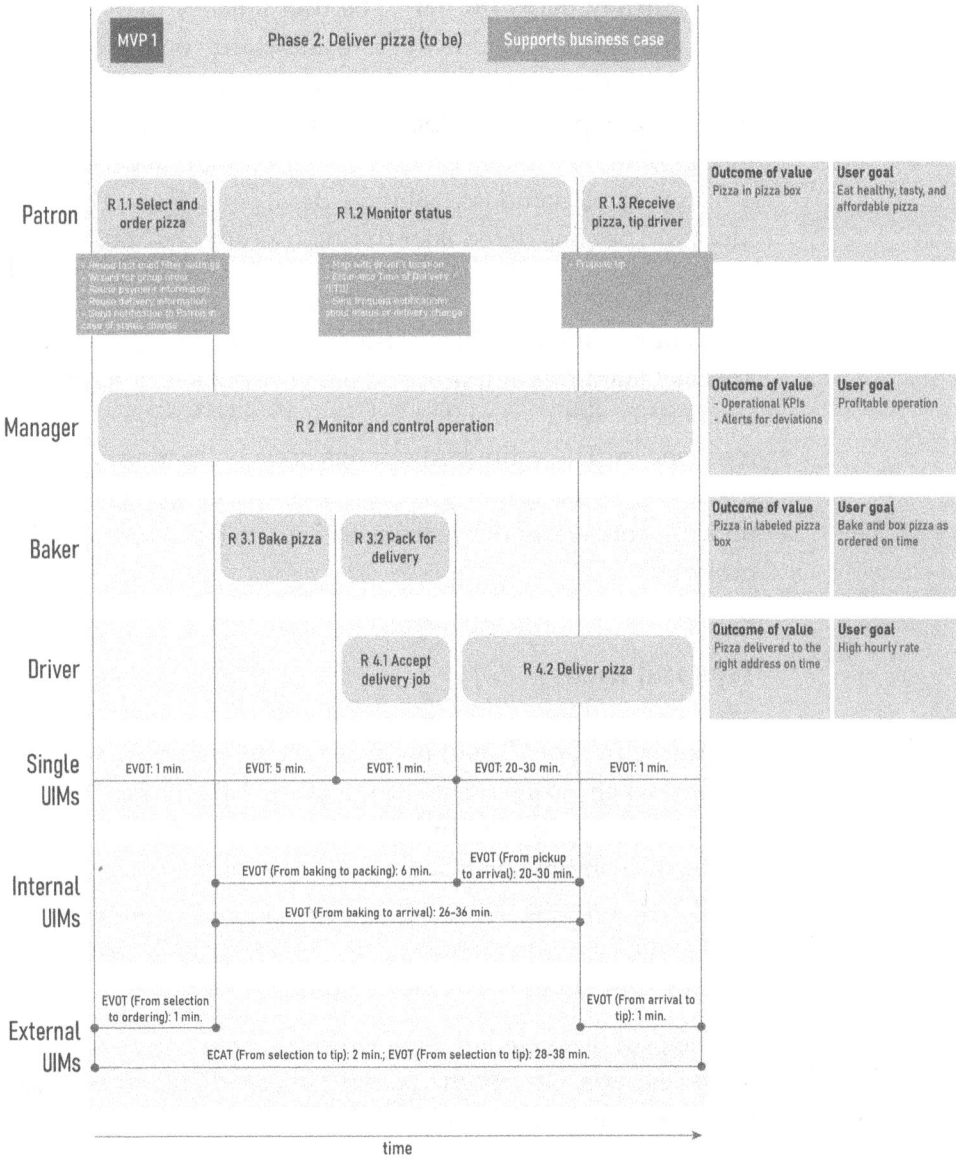

Lessons learned

Workflow (to be)   The workflow (to be) is created in three steps. First, it is outlined and addresses the identified weaknesses from the workflow (as is). Then the outcome of value and the user goal per user role are added. This information can be carried over from the user role profile. The last step is the definition of the estimated target user involvement times and frequencies for internal and external user involvement metrics.

User journey maps (to be)   The user journey map (to be) is a tool to reduce uncertainties and to add clarity on top of what the workflow (to be) contains. A user journey map (to be) is created per user role and per responsibility. It allows one to explore activities, touch points, and time and frequency information per activity, as well as possible solutions (solution ideas) per activity. The solution ideas will be considered later during concept exploration.

Envisioned savings   The envisioned time and frequency savings are calculated by comparing actual user involvement times and frequencies with estimated target user involvement times and frequencies. The estimated savings are a ballpark number—not exact, only an indication. They help you to decide whether to move on with a project, to revise the workflow (to be), or even to abort a project.

Tips and tricks

Workflow (to be)   There is always the tendency to become too detailed when it comes to the workflow (to be). The responsibilities should be based on the time and frequency information. In the proposed workflow (to be), the workflow for the patron is broken down into only three responsibilities. This is because time information for those three responsibilities is sufficient. More detailed information is not needed on a workflow level.

It is helpful to create a workflow (to be) with one or two subject matter experts. User participation can be useful, if users oversee the entire workflow.

User journey maps (to be)   The user journey map (to be) is a useful tool if there is a lack of detail or the subject matter experts do not agree on certain responsibilities of the workflow. If one or a few responsibilities are not clear enough, it can be beneficial to create a user journey map (to be) just for those. A user journey map (to be) is a tool to address uncertainties and to add clarity. It is a means, not an end.

Envisioned savings   It is important to understand that envisioned savings express a ballpark figure and are not an exact one. When you estimate the target user involvement time and target user involvement frequency for "to be," try to involve several people in the estimation exercise. If you need a more structured method for estimating, you may want to look into Planning Poker®[165]. It is a method from the Agile world, which is applicable here. It is fun and makes the assumptions behind estimates transparent.

Exercise 2.1

Goal   Describe the future workflow (to be) and calculate the estimated savings.

Material   Workflow (to be) template, user journey map (to be) template, user involvement metrics.

Completion criteria:

- ► The workflow (to be) is created and documented.
- ► The workflow (to be) shows the outcome of value and the user goal per user role
- ► The workflow (to be) shows internal and external estimated target involvement times.
- ► For one user role, the user journey map (to be) is created and documented.
- ► The estimated time savings are calculated.
- ► Based on the estimated savings, a recommendation with a rationale is made and documented how to proceed with the project.

User Involvement System | **10**

There's no good way to waste your time.
Wasting time is just wasting time.
Helen Mirren

Purpose

So far, we have designed the new workflow with the responsibilities and the target user involvement times and frequencies. This chapter describes how a user involvement system (UIS) is derived from the workflow (to be) and specified.

> **Definition 9** (User involvement system) *Instance of a human-technical system consisting of one or more users and an interactive system working together to achieve one or more stated purpose.*

There are several reasons for the introduction of a user involvement system:

▶ **Multiple user roles, multiple devices, multiple contexts of use**: A user involvement system is capable of defining and specifying the involvement of multiple user roles using potentially multiple devices in potentially multiple contexts of use in one ecosystem.

▶ **Modular**: A user involvement system consists of constituting elements called user involvement points (UIPs). It is a modular approach that allows us to consider each user involvement point as a more or less independent design project. It also allows us to add new user involvement points and integrate them into a well-defined user involvement system.

▶ **System wide functions and properties**: A user involvement system allows us to define and specify user involvement–related functions and performance properties across multiple user involvement points, so-called emergent properties. It is input for the exploration and selection of technology and the experience design phase.

The process of defining and specifying a user involvement system with its constituent elements, the user involvement points, is performed with the following steps:

- ▶ Step 1: Define black box view
- ▶ Step 2: Establish user involvement system
- ▶ Step 3: Specify scenario (white box) views

Black box view

Template

The first step is the definition of an outside-in view, the so-called "black box view" of the user involvement system under design. A template to specify the black box view is shown in Figure 10.1.

Blackbox view of user involvement system

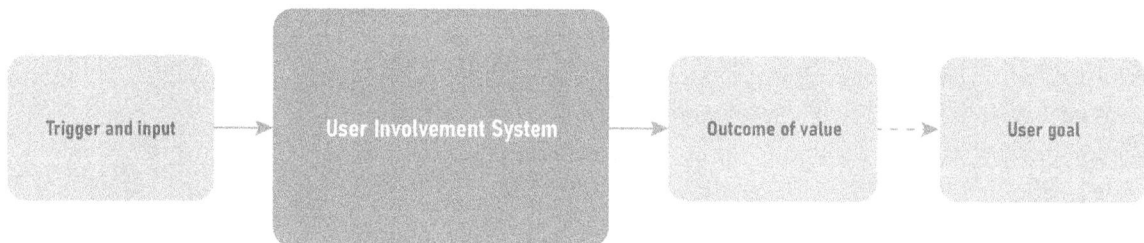

Figure 10.1: Black box view of a user involvement system

As shown in Figure 10.1, the elements of a black box view are trigger and input, the UIS itself, the outcome of value, and the user goal.

Trigger and input

A trigger is defined here as a "motivation that prompts a user to perform a task." There can be internal and external motivations. Table 10.1 shows examples of internal motivations and related external motivations that can be triggers of user actions.

Table 10.1: Examples of internal and related external motivations

Internal motivation	Related external motivation	Main outcome
Hunger	Being asked to order a pizza	Pizza delivered
Needing to be somewhere	Being asked to call a taxi	Taxi arrives
Desiring to say something to someone	Receiving a message from someone	Message sent
Wanting to know what is going on in the world	Receiving a news notification	News checked
Wanting to write down an idea	Being asked to take notes	Notes taken

An input is the initially needed content to perform the first user involvement point.

User involvement system

The user involvement system is identified with the general scope. The scope should be able to process the trigger and the input and generate the outcome of value. In step 1, the user involvement system remains a black box. Its elements will be established in step 2 and their behaviors specified in step 3.

Outcome of value and user goal

The black box view also specifies the outcome of value of the user involvement system. The outcome of value is the stated purpose of the user involvement system. A UIS typically produces many outcomes. To keep an eye on the most relevant outcome, we focus on the outcome of value for the key beneficiary of the UIS.

The user goal is a user-desired application goal. It reflects the stated purpose. The outcome of value supports achievement of the user goal.

Validation

After the user involvement system has been identified from an outside-in perspective, it is worthwhile to validate it. Good validation questions to ask are as follows:

- ▶ VQ 1: Does the outcome of value address the motivation?
- ▶ VQ 2: Is the intended scope of the identified user involvement system able to deliver the outcome of value?
- ▶ VQ 3: Does the outcome of value support the user goal?
- ▶ VQ 4: Does the user goal address the user need?

World of Pizza

Let's define the black box view for our WoP example. We have a trigger, an input, a user involvement system scope, an outcome of value, and a user goal (see Figure 10.2).

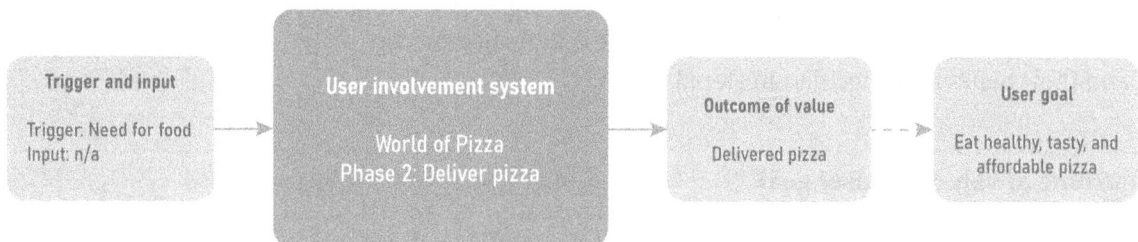

Figure 10.2: Black box view of WoP

Trigger and input

The trigger for ordering a pizza is the need for food. The hungry person either orders a pizza for him/herself (internal motivation) or asks another person to order a pizza for him/her (external motivation for the person who orders the pizza).

In our case, there is no input needed or available.

User involvement system

In our WoP example, the user involvement system focuses on phase 2, "deliver pizza." Phase 1, "manage inventory," and phase 3, "business administration," are currently out of scope.

Outcome of value and user goal

For the WoP example, the outcome of value is a delivered pizza. Although a user involvement system produces many outcomes, the black box view focuses on key aspects of the system. Therefore, it specifies only the outcome of value, which is the delivered pizza.

The user goal is to eat healthy, tasty, and affordable food. This has not changed since we created and consolidated the user role profile in the "User Role" section (see Section 2 (User role profile) on page 158).

Validation

Let's validate the identified user involvement system with the proposed validation questions:

- ► VQ 1: Does the outcome of value address the motivation? The outcome of value is a delivered pizza. A pizza addresses a need for food. The answer is yes.
- ► VQ 2: Is the intended scope of the identified user involvement system able to deliver the outcome of value? The intended scope is to deliver a pizza per order request. The identified user involvement system indicates that a pizza will be delivered. The answer is yes.
- ► VQ 3: Does the outcome of value support the user goal? The outcome of value is a delivered pizza. The user goal is eating a healthy, tasty, and affordable pizza. We need to assume that the user has selected a healthy, tasty, and affordable pizza. The answer is "possibly" (it depends on the pizza that's ordered).
- ► VQ 4: Does the user goal address the user need? The user goal is to eat healthy, tasty, and affordable pizza. The user need is to live healthily and frugally. The goal attribute 'healthy' addresses the need attribute 'healthily.' It can be debated whether pizza is healthy food at all. The second attribute pair is affordable (goal) and frugal (need). Being frugal may not be consistent with getting a pizza delivered to a home in a pizza box. If we see "frugal" as an ecological goal, ordering a pizza is probably not addressing that need. If the focus is only on the payment, it may.

In our case, the outlined user involvement system looks reasonable so far. We can go ahead and identify the user involvement points.

It sometimes seems silly to ask the validation questions. But based on the author's experience, many projects fail because they do not successfully support the user's goals and needs with their outcome.

In these cases, the delivered outcome is just an outcome, not an outcome of value.

Establish UIS

Identify user involvement points

Template

The workflow (to be) with its responsibilities provides the foundation for defining and specifying a user involvement system. A grouped set of responsibilities becomes a *user involvement point*. Later, a user involvement point becomes a design project and is typically implemented with one application, for example, a mobile application. All applications together form the user involvement system that is able to generate the outcome of value.

Let's define what a user involvement point is.

> **Definition 10** (User involvement point) *A constituting element of a user involvement system.*

There are different ways to group responsibilities:

- ▶ Vertical grouping: Group responsibilities of several user roles (see Figure 10.3).
- ▶ Horizontal grouping: Group several responsibilities of one user role (see Figure 10.4).
- ▶ Hybrid grouping: Group several responsibilities of several user roles (see Figure 10.5).

The result of the grouped responsibilities is called a user involvement map, abbreviated UIM.

The result of the grouped responsibilities is called a *user involvement map*, abbreviated *UIM*.

A vertical grouping has the advantage of grouping the responsibilities of several user roles. It is therefore resourceful (complying with the cost criterion). However, if too many user roles are assigned to one UIP, the user involvement may become too complex for the assigned user roles, not fully supporting the experience criterion. A vertical grouping also requires several vertical groups to cover the entire workflow so that the outcome of value can be created (addressing the value criterion).

In theory, all responsibilities could be assigned to one UIP, which would most likely lead to a difficult and inefficient experience.

User Involvement Map - Vertical Grouping

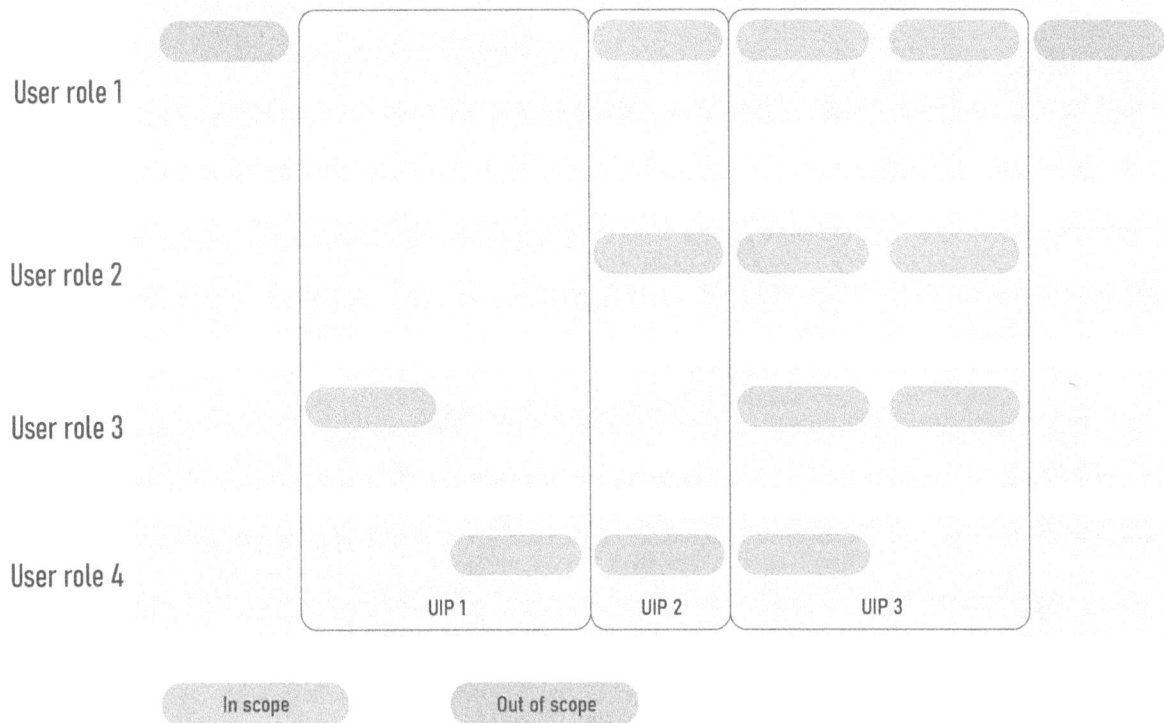

Figure 10.3: User involvement map with vertical grouping

A horizontal grouping often covers an entire workflow for one user role. Therefore, it creates an outcome of value early on (complying with the value criterion). It often achieves an acceptable experience quality (complying with the experience criterion). It is often acceptable from a budget perspective (complying with the cost criterion).

A hybrid grouping offers the opportunity to combine the advantages of the vertical and the horizontal groupings for selected responsibilities.

It is worthwhile to mention that responsibilities that are out of scope for the application under development should not be removed from the user involvement map but rather marked as "out of scope." Making such decisions transparent to the project team often saves a lot of time and headaches.

The grouping of responsibilities should consider the following grouping quality criteria:

▶ Experience criterion: How can we make users feel comfortable with the involvement experience? This question addresses *experience quality*. We should avoid grouping too

User Involvement Map - Horizontal Grouping

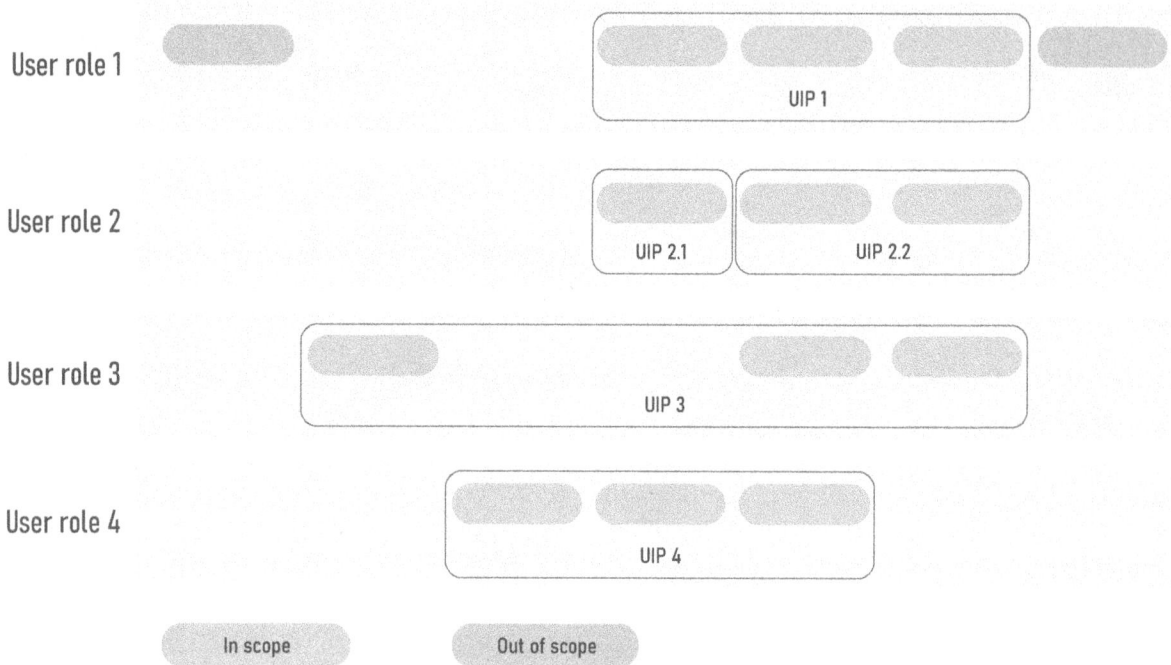

Figure 10.4: User involvement map with horizontal grouping

many responsibilities, particularly from different user roles, so that the experience becomes too complicated. We should also avoid splitting the responsibilities of one user role into different groups, so that a single user requires different applications to perform tasks that belong together from a user's perspective. This is another way to make the experience too complicated.

▶ Cost criterion: How can we keep the number of groups small? This question addresses *design and development cost*. Each group may receive its own application. Each application has its own design and development overhead. This means that having too many groups (and applications per group) will increase design and development costs.

▶ Completeness criterion: How do we ensure that all responsibilities are grouped? This question addresses the *complete coverage* of responsibilities. It should help to avoid responsibilities being missed so that the outcome of value cannot be generated.

The quality and cost questions need to be balanced, with the result that a maximum experience quality is delivered within an acceptable budget.

User Involvement Map - Hybrid Grouping

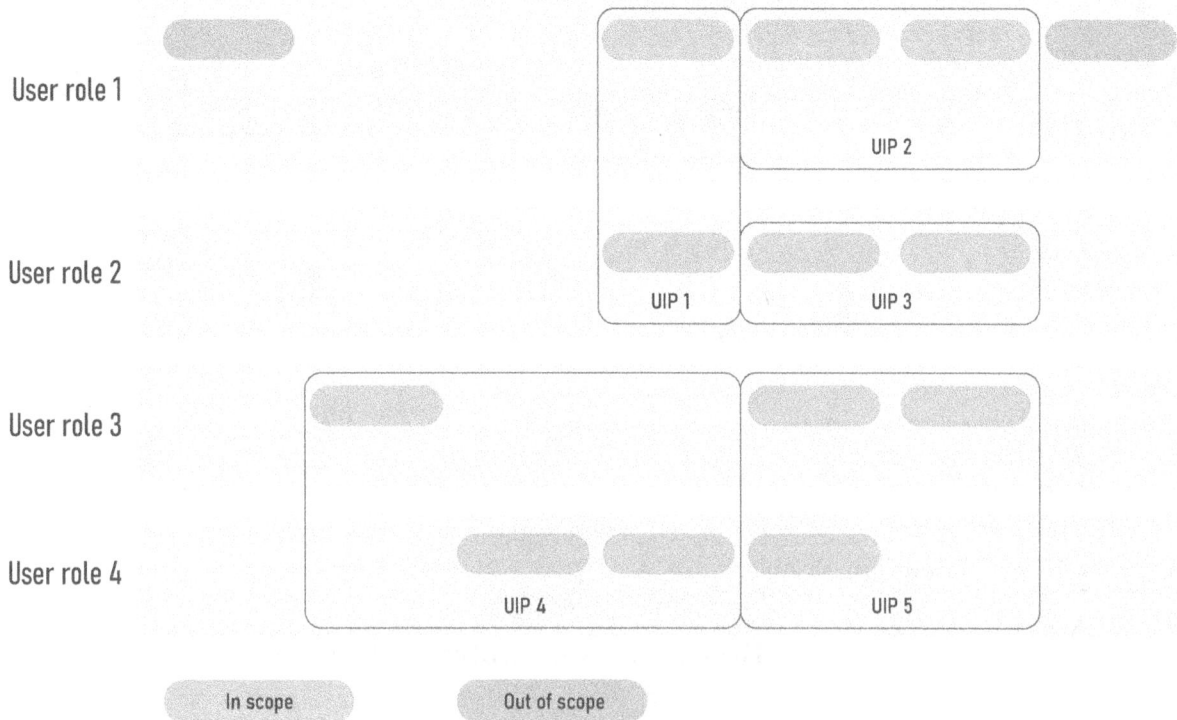

Figure 10.5: User involvement map with hybrid grouping

World of Pizza

We will now apply the technique to our World of Pizza example. First, the user involvement points are identified. Since the user roles have different user tasks and user goals, the user involvement points become role specific (horizontal assignment, see Figure 10.6).

All user roles have their own UIP. This means that all user roles will have one application through which they can use the World of Pizza ecosystem.

To be able to validate that each UIP contributes effectively to the user involvement system, the outcomes of value and the user goals per user role are shown in Figure 10.6.

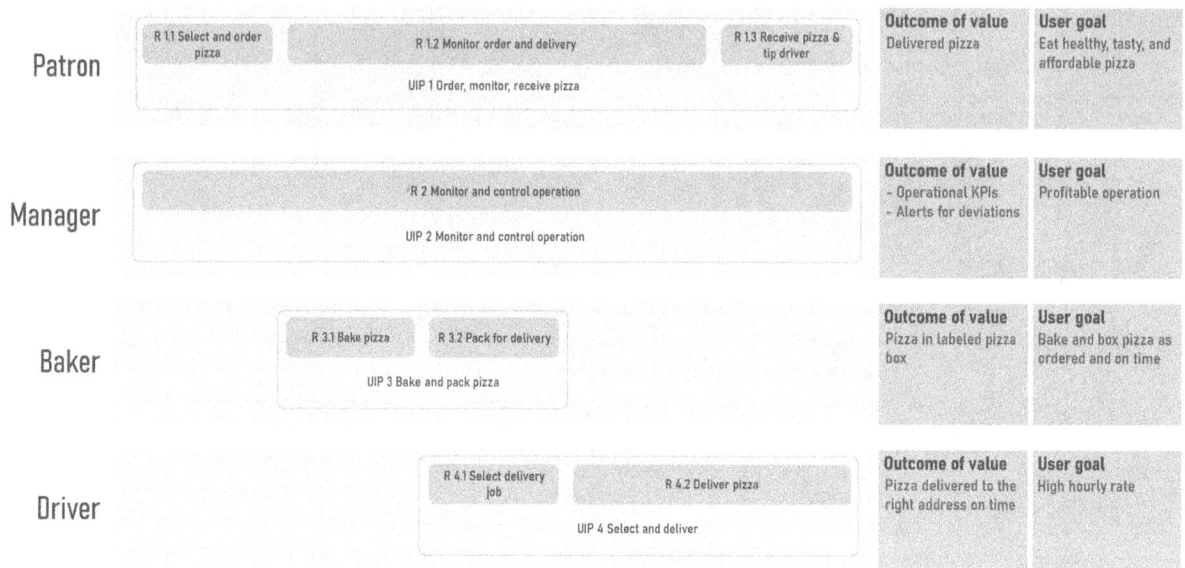

Figure 10.6: User involvement map for WoP

Design the user involvement system

Template

We can now take each user involvement point and declare it an element of the user involvement system. In addition, there is normally one technical involvement point (TIP). It represents a technical system element that triggers actions or content transitions to user involvement points without user involvement.

Definition 11 (Technical involvement point) *(Technical) system element of a user involvement system.*

We use a simple template to visualize the user involvement system with its elements (see Figure 10.7).

The user involvement system consists of one element per user involvement point and one element in total representing the technical involvement point.

World of Pizza

We take each identified user involvement point from the user involvement map (see Figure 10.6) and map it into a box representing the user involvement system. In addition, one technical involvement point is added. This mapping results in the first-level

Elements of a user involvement system

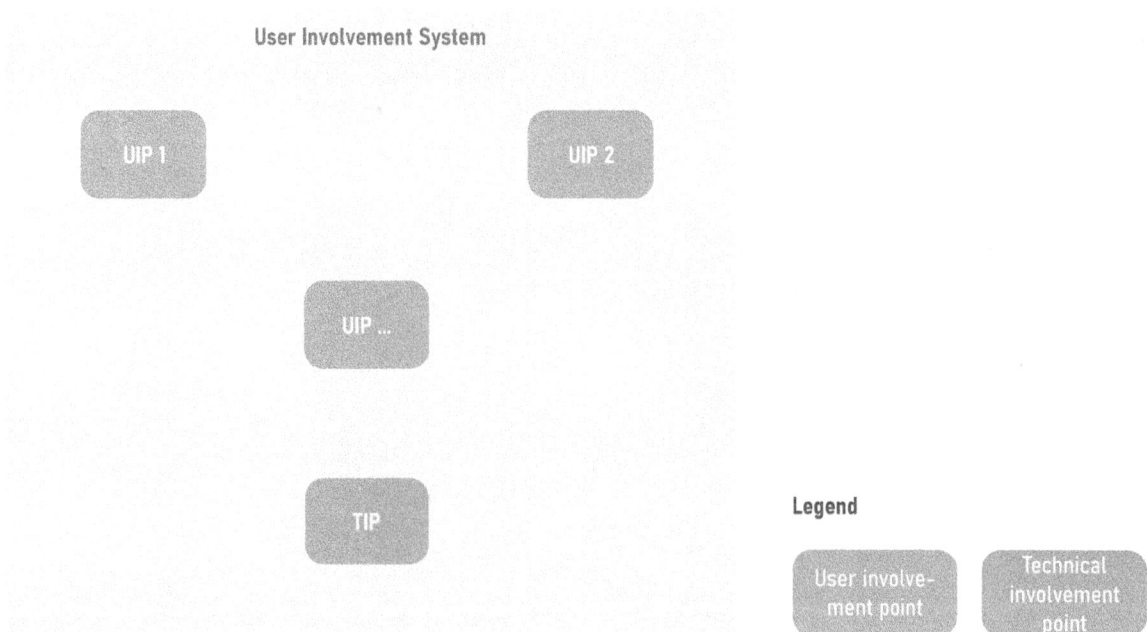

User Involvement System

UIP 1

UIP 2

UIP ...

TIP

Legend

User involve-
ment point

Technical
involvement
point

Figure 10.7: Elements of user involvement system template

decomposition of the user involvement system for World of Pizza (see Figure 10.8).

The user involvement system is now established. In the next chapter, we are going to specify the user involvement system for specific behaviors that are relevant to the success of the user involvement system.

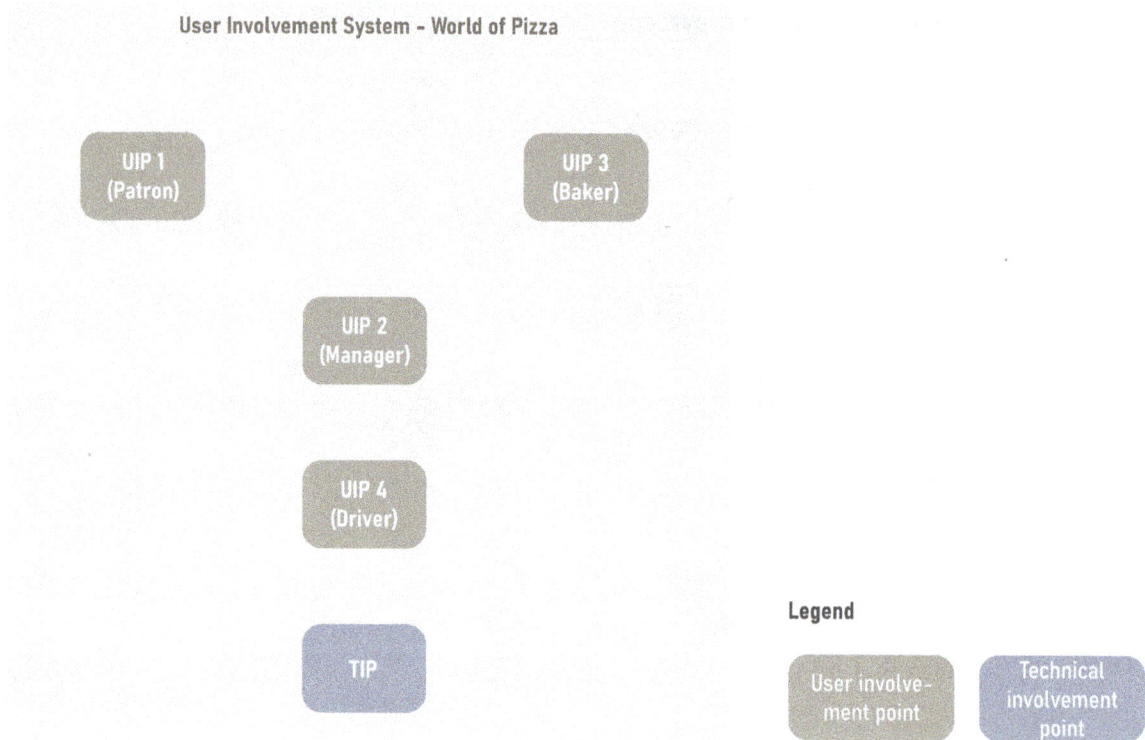

Figure 10.8: User involvement points for WoP

Use context view

Templates

Every user-centered design needs to consider the context of use. Therefore, we use a view that shows which UIP is used in which context of use (see Figure 10.9).

Each UIP can be assigned to one or more contexts of use. One context of use can include one or more UIPs.

World of Pizza

In the foundation part of the process, we identified the contexts of use (see Chapter 7 (Contexts of use) on page 189). In our World of Pizza example, we have four contexts of use:

- ► Home
- ► Office
- ► On the road
- ► Restaurant

Context of use view template

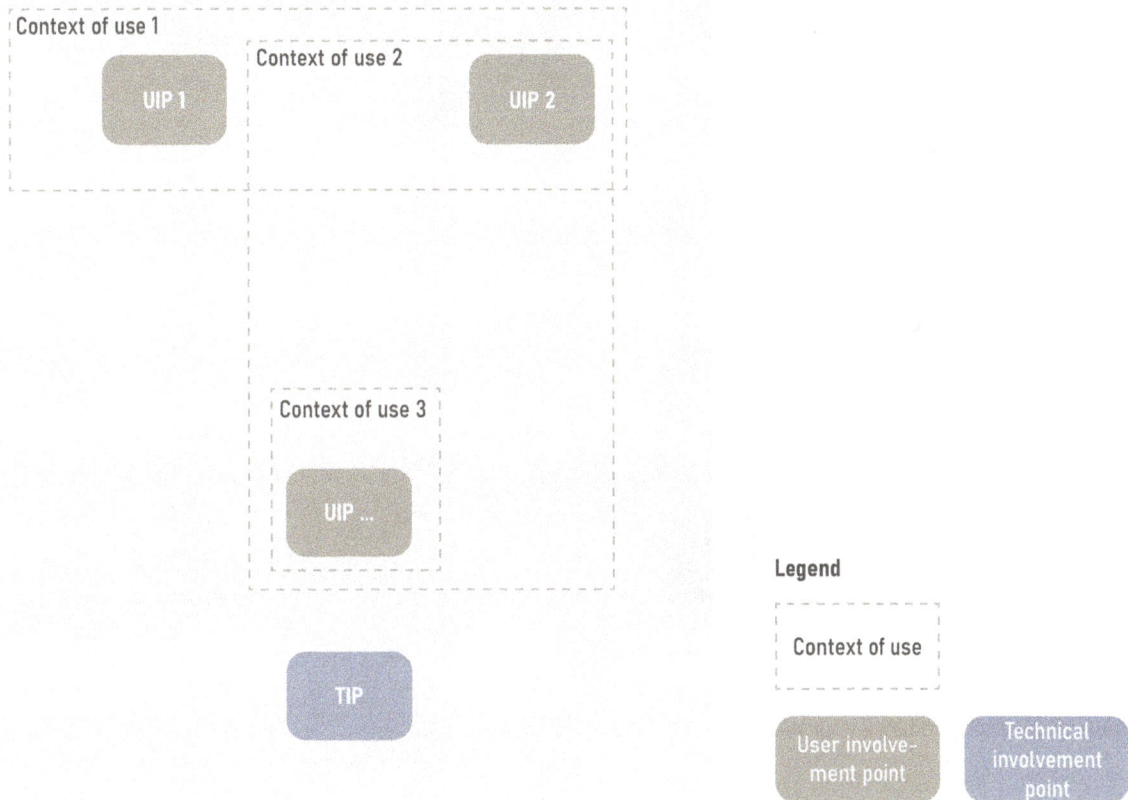

Figure 10.9: User context view template

The question is, which UIP is used in which context of use? The mapping of the UIPs to the different contexts of use is shown in Figure 10.10.

The information encoded in Figure 10.10 can also be shown in a table (see Table 10.2).

UIP	Home	Office	On the road	Restaurant
UIP 1 (Patron)	Yes	Yes	Yes	No
UIP 2 (Manager)	Yes	Yes	Yes	Yes
UIP 3 (Baker)	No	No	No	Yes
UIP 4 (Driver)	Yes	Yes	Yes	Yes

Table 10.2: Mapping of UIPs to contexts of use

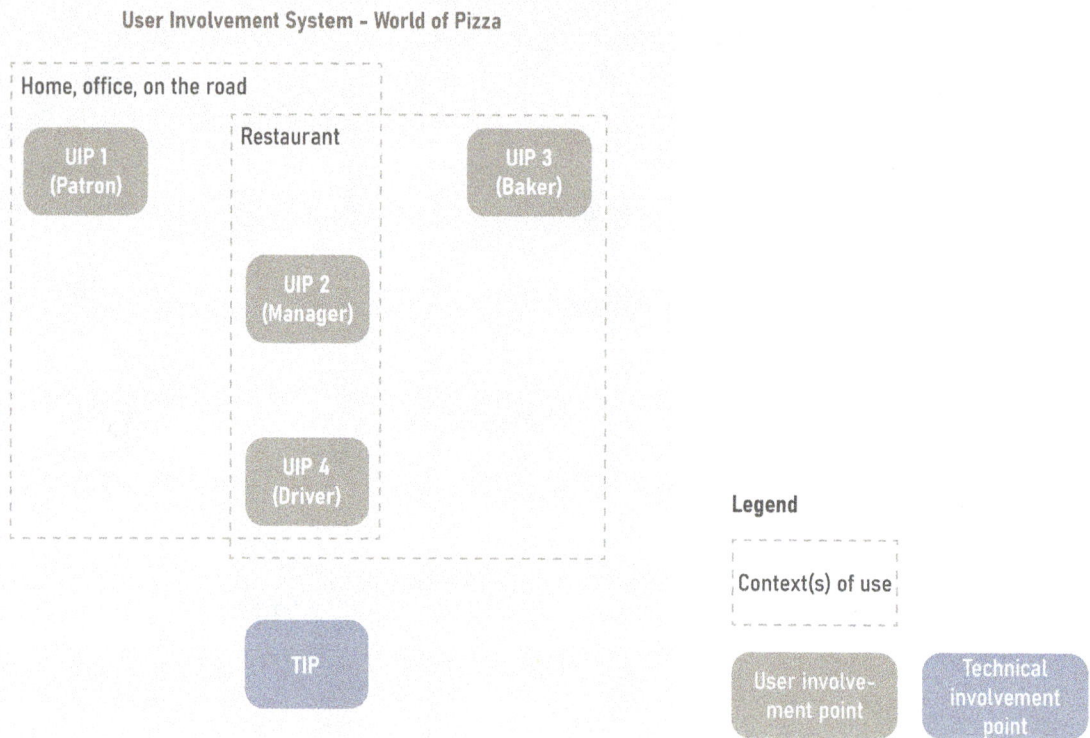

Figure 10.10: Use context view of WoP

Scenario views

There are several scenario views of the user involvement system that specify certain system behaviors. Such behaviors are critical to the success of the user involvement system and are prerequisites for the experience design.

The scenario views proposed below have been used in industrial projects where they demonstrated their usefulness. However, they are most likely incomplete; fellow colleagues are invited to add other useful views.

Value flow view

Template

The value flow view defines how an outcome of value is generated as a happy path with the elements of the UIS. It includes the trigger and the input as well as the contributing user involvement points and the outcome of value with the user goal.

The value flow view shows all UIPs of the user involvement system and connects the contributing UIPs with arrows. The numbers indicate the sequence of UIP contributions (see Figure 10.11).

Value flow view template

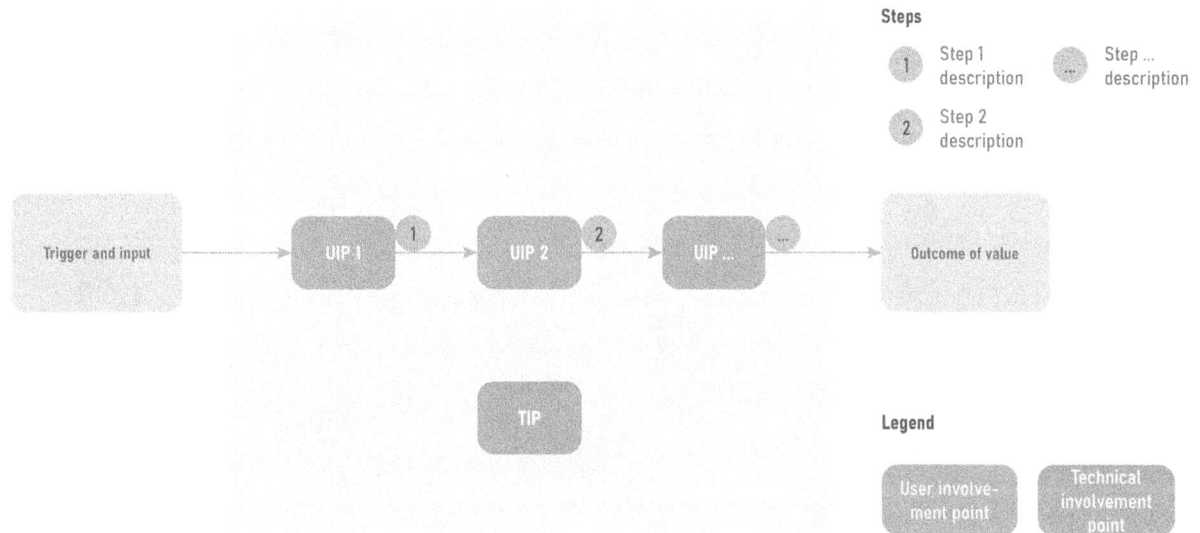

Figure 10.11: Value flow view template

World of Pizza

The value flow for ordering and receiving a pizza consists of four steps:

- ▶ Step 1: Patron selects and orders pizza
- ▶ Step 2: Baker bakes and packages pizza
- ▶ Step 3: Driver accepts delivery job, picks up pizza, and delivers pizza to patron
- ▶ Step 4: Patron receives delivered pizza and tips driver

The steps and their sequence, mapped to the UIPs, are shown in Figure 10.12.

We can see here that UIP 1 (patron) contributes twice to the value flow. UIP 2 (manager) does not contribute at all in the happy path scenario. This reflects the intent to remove the manager from the daily operations and only involve them in cases of deviation.

The value flow view communicates most concisely the purpose of the user involvement system with its functional properties. Because time is an essential property for efficiency, the value flow view will be extended with a value flow specification table (see Table

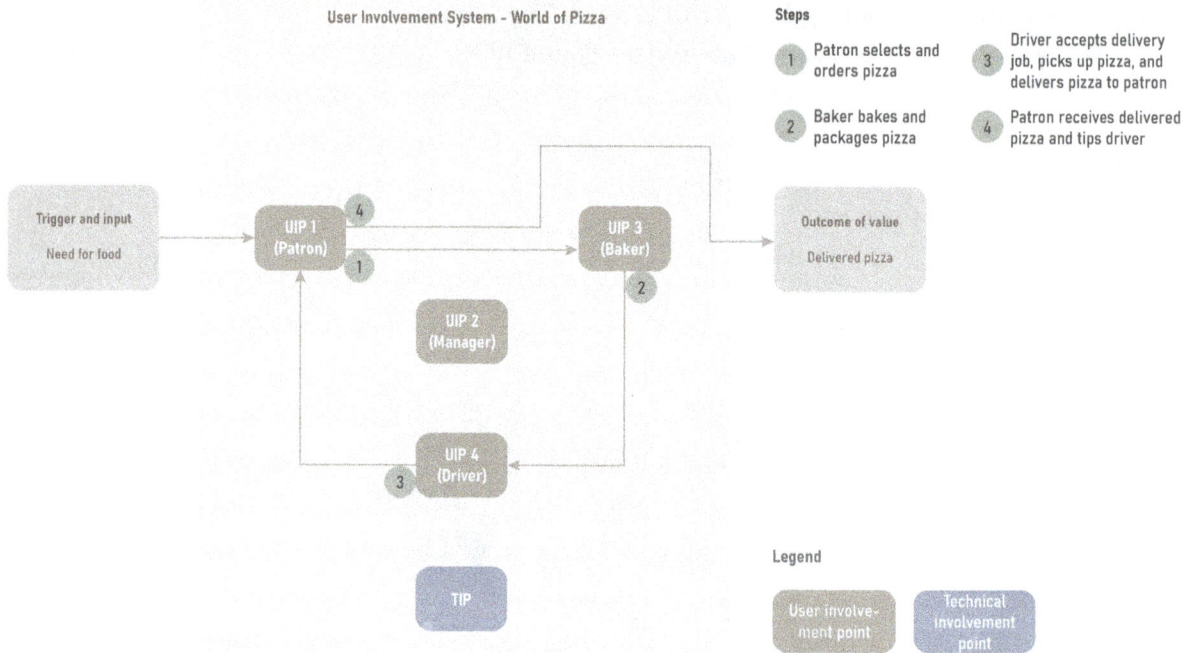

Figure 10.12: Value flow view of WoP

10.3). The estimated target involvement times are taken from the workflow (to be) (see Figure 9.4).

Trigger & input	Outcome of value	Estimated target involvement time
Need for food	Pizza delivered	ECAT ≤ 2 min.
Need for food	Pizza delivered	EVOT ≤ 33 min.

Table 10.3: Order status specification table for WoP

Object states flow view

Introduction

Now that we have established the user involvement system with its user involvement points, we can define and specify the data flow between the UIPs.

To support the emergent property of generating the outcome of value for an ecosystem, there are many data exchanges between UIPs. This means that a user action triggered in one UIP causes a data flow to another UIP. A typical example is the status change of an object, as when a pizza is ordered, which will be discussed in this section. Ordering a pizza in UIP 1 (patron) causes a status change in UIP 2 (baker).

It is important to understand that the data flow focuses only on the flow *between* user involvement points, not within a user involvement point. This will be covered in part 3, "Experience Design."

Another type of data flow is the flow from a technical involvement point (TIP) to one or more user involvement points. Some data flows are initiated by the technical involvement points, which cause an update in one or more UIPs. An example is a reminder. The technical user involvement point may have a reminder set to provide feedback, and this reminder triggers a status change in UIP 1 (patron).

There is no data flow modeled here from a user involvement point to a technical involvement point. The reason is that such a modeling aspect would spill over into the area of technical design, which is done by the software architects. Therefore, to avoid overlapping or conflicting work results, the technical system is represented by only one technical involvement point.

It is the responsibility of the experience architect to define and design the user involvement system with its different views. It is the responsibility of the software or system architect to define and design the technical system with its different views. The user involvement system's various views are inputs for the software/system architecture.

Template

Any kind of data flow can be modeled. Here we show examples of objects with discrete states (e.g., order object) and with continuous states (e.g., driver's location). The example and template here shows an object that has several states over its lifetime. In World of Pizza, this would be an order. It is essential to know which states an order can have, which UIPs trigger which state, and which states are triggered by the TIP.

Therefore, we use a view that shows the different states and the flows between UIPs and the TIP and between different UIPs. The template is shown in Figure 10.13.

A diagram form is used here that allows the expression of connections between UIPs on one hand and between the TIP and UIPs on the other hand, through dots. The dots displayed on the right-hand side of a UIP (or of the TIP) mean that the UIP (or the TIP) causes that state. It means that the state is an output of the UIP or the TIP. The dots on the left-hand side of a UIP mean that a UIP receives that state as an input from another UIP or the TIP. Each output state requires a corresponding input state and vice versa.

Object states flow view template

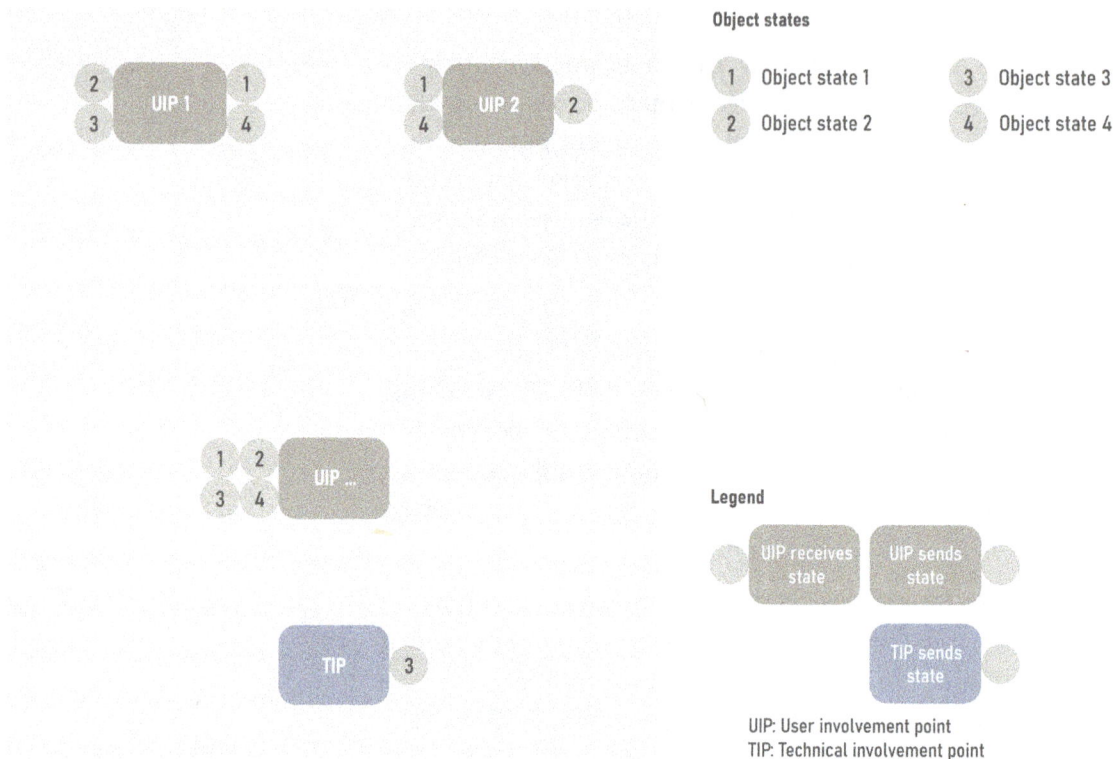

Figure 10.13: Object states flow view template

The dots were chosen over arrows to reduce information overload, which can easily happen with many arrows in a diagram. The kind of diagram used here is called a dot-connection diagram, or DC diagram.

For technical involvement points in the user involvement system, we focus only on the outputs (i.e., one or more dots on the right-hand side). In reality, the technical system is "aware" of all status changes. The focus of the user involvement system is to focus on user involvement, not how the technical system is defined, designed, and implemented. Technical experts have their own methods of modeling such behaviors and properties.

The template shows three types of information: It defines the different states. It defines which UIPs produce which states (or which states are produced by the TIP). And it defines which UIPs receive which states as an input.

World of Pizza

Order object In our WoP example, an order is an object with different states. A patron has submitted an order (state 1), the baker has accepted the order and started baking (state 2), and the baker has baked and boxed a pizza (state 3). A driver has started the delivery (state 4), the delivery is completed (state 5), and the patron has tipped the driver (state 6).

Figure 10.14 shows which UIP can set the states (these states are displayed on the right-hand side of a UIP) and which UIP has received an object with a certain state (these states are displayed on the left-hand side of a UIP).

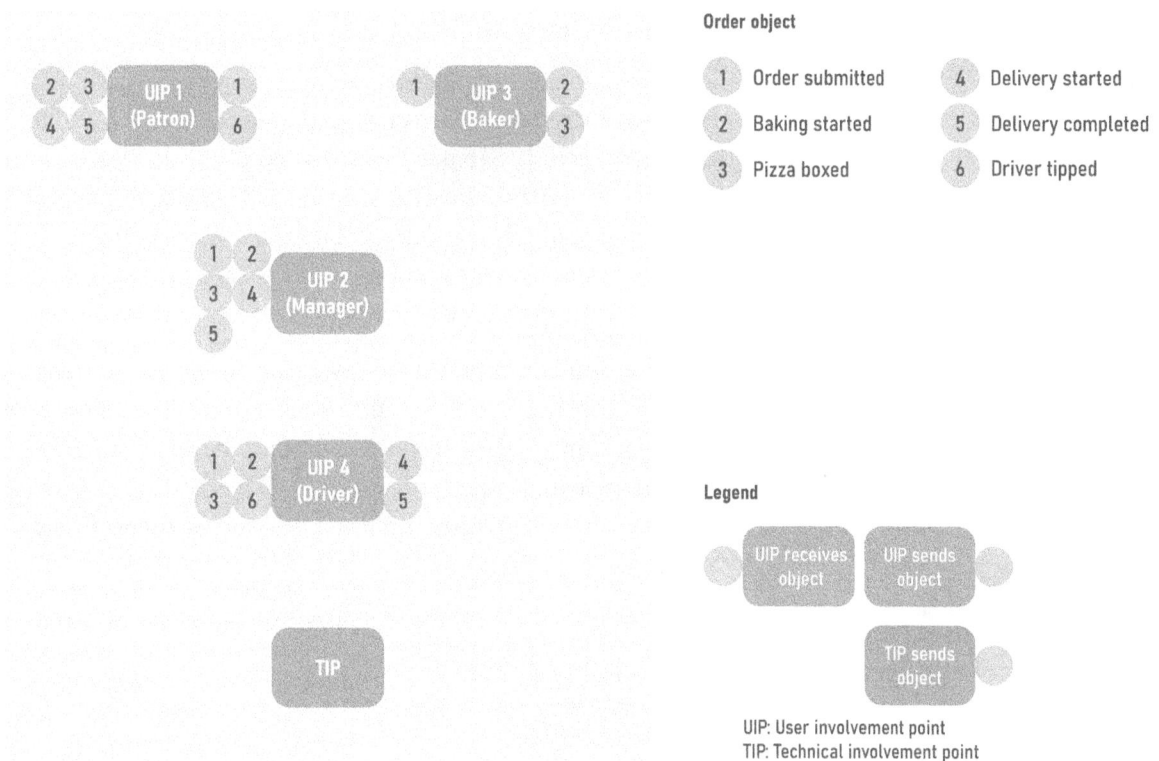

Figure 10.14: Order state flow view for WoP

For the order object, all state transitions are initiated by a user and represented by a UIP. The TIP is not involved. UIP 2 (manager) does not initiate any state changes but is informed about all state changes except the change to state 6 (driver tipped). The experience architect could have decided to inform the manager about the driver being tipped, but the decision was made not to, because this is a matter between the patron and the driver and is not of concern to the manager.

For similar reasons, the baker is only informed about the change to state 1 (order submitted). The baker then initiates two state changes: state 2 (baking started) and state 3 (pizza boxed). The baker is not informed about state changes beyond state 3.

Before we go further, I'd like to pause and reflect on what was done here and for what reason. The state flow view is a way to define the changes in state and the transitions between UIPs or between the TIP and UIPs. The important point is that the experience architect defines them, anticipating what states will need to be included in the experience design phase. If a state does not exist, it cannot be designed later on. If a UIP is not able to change a state, a function won't be available, and therefore there is no reason to later add a control to the user interface. If a UIP is not able to receive a state, such content will not be available later for the user interface. Thus it is clear that the definition and transition of states is a prerequisite to achieving user experience quality.

Going back to our order status example: Say there was a discussion about whether state 6, "driver tipped," should be reported to UIP 2 (manager) and UIP 3 (baker), and that the decision was made not to inform these UIPs about state 6, because it is none of their business. This means that UIP 2 (manager) and UIP 3 (baker) will not have access to such information later, and therefore that information does not need to be considered for the design.

With this information, the software architect can now define a model to consider the intended states. These days, the definition and specification of such states is usually done by software architects, not by experience professionals. Taking over this task as part of the experience architecture is essential to achieve efficiency, as we can see in the specification table.

The object states are specified in an order status specification table (see Table 10.4 on the next page).

Besides showing the state flows between UIPs, the table contains more detailed information about the trigger condition and the design elements associated with each state. Such a specification table defines in detail what content and controls should be available per state. That information is a prerequisite for the design phase and is input for the system/software architecture.

Table 10.4: Order states flow specification table for WoP

Sender	Object ID	Trigger condition(s)	Design elements	Receiver	System alert time	System alert frequency
UIP 1	O.1 Order submitted	Order submitted (state 1)	Content: Order number; pizza ID; delivery address; pickup time;	UIP 2, UIP 3, UIP 4	≤ 10 sec	Once
UIP 3	O.2 Baking started	Baking started (state 2)	Content: Order number; pizza ID; baker name; delivery address; pickup time;	UIP 1, UIP 4	≤ 10 sec	Once
UIP 3	O.3 Pizza boxed	Pizza boxed (state 3)	Content: Order number; pizza ID; baker name; delivery address; pickup time;	UIP 1, UIP 4	≤ 10 sec	Once
UIP 4	O.4 Delivery started	Delivery started (state 4)	Content: Order number; pizza ID; driver name; delivery address; ETA time;	UIP 1, UIP 2	≤ 10 sec	Once
UIP 4	O.5 Delivery completed	Delivery completed (state 5)	Content: Order number; pizza ID; driver name; delivery address; ETA time;	UIP 1, UIP 2	≤ 10 sec	Once
UIP 1	O.6 Driver tipped	Driver tipped (state 6)	Content: Order number; pizza ID; driver name; tip amount (absolute and percentage of order value)	UIP 4	≤ 10 sec	Once

Customer feedback object   Another example of an object state view is the customer feedback object (see Figure 10.15). It follows the same principle.

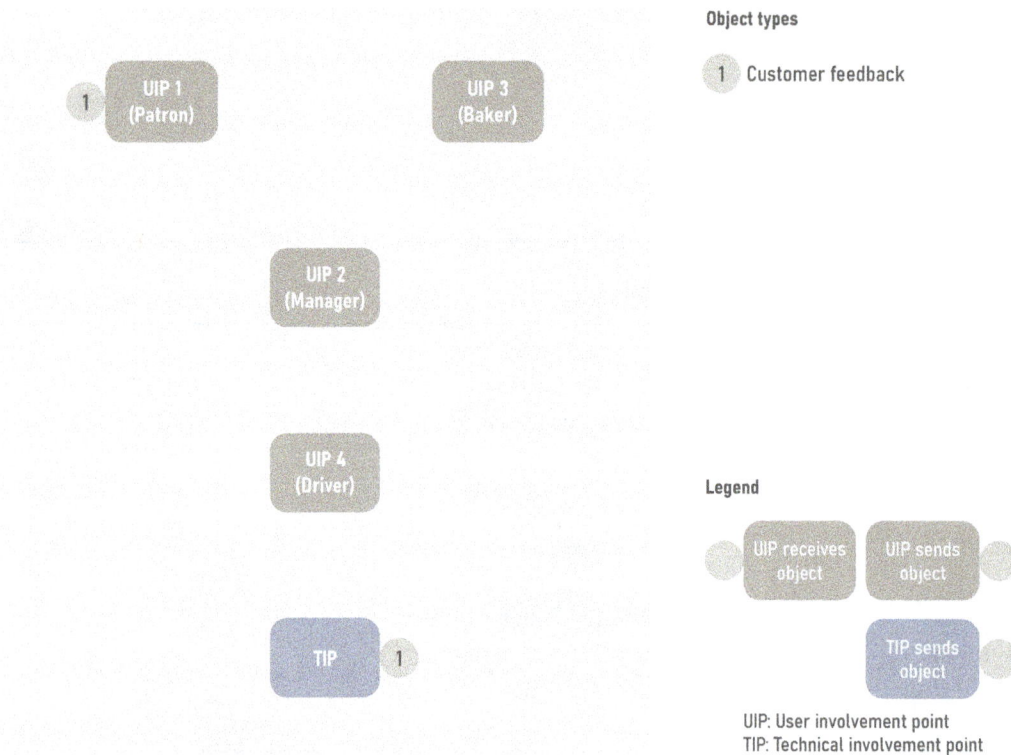

Object types

1 Customer feedback

UIP 1
(Patron)

1

UIP 3
(Baker)

UIP 2
(Manager)

UIP 4
(Driver)

Legend

UIP receives
object

UIP sends
object

TIP sends
object

TIP

1

UIP: User involvement point
TIP: Technical involvement point

Figure 10.15: Customer feedback flow for WoP

The customer feedback request object is triggered by the TIP 15 minutes after the order changes to state 5 (delivery completed) or 6 (driver tipped). The UIP 1 (patron) receives the customer feedback request. If the patron does not submit feedback, a reminder is sent 24 hours later. Two more reminders are sent, each 24 hours after the previous one.

After the patron has submitted feedback, UIP 2 (manager), UIP 3 (baker), and UIP 4 (driver) are informed of it.

The repetition is specified in the specification table under "system alert frequency." The time is specified under "system alert time" (see Table 10.5 on the facing page).

If the system alert frequency and system alert time are not known at this point of the project, they can be specified as customer configurable with a value range. For instance, the system alert time can have a value range from 1 second to 20 seconds. The system alert frequency can have a value range from 0 to 64.

Table 10.5: Customer feedback specification table for WoP

Sender	Object ID	Trigger condition(s)	Design elements	Receiver	System alert time	System alert frequency
TIP	F.1 Feed-back request	State 5 or State 6; Feedback not submitted	Content: Order number, driver name;	UIP 1	≤ 10 sec	First time: after 15 min; second and third time: every 24 hours
UIP 1	F.2 Feed-back sent	User submitted feedback	Content: Order number, driver name, delivery address, feedback rating, feedback comments	UIP 2, UIP 3, UIP 4	≤ 10 sec	once

Driver's location   It is also possible that an object has a continuous state, meaning that the permissible values are defined with a range. The values of a continuous state can change permanently, or they can stay the same. An example of an object with a continuous state is the driver's location (see Figure 10.16 and Table 10.6 on the next page).

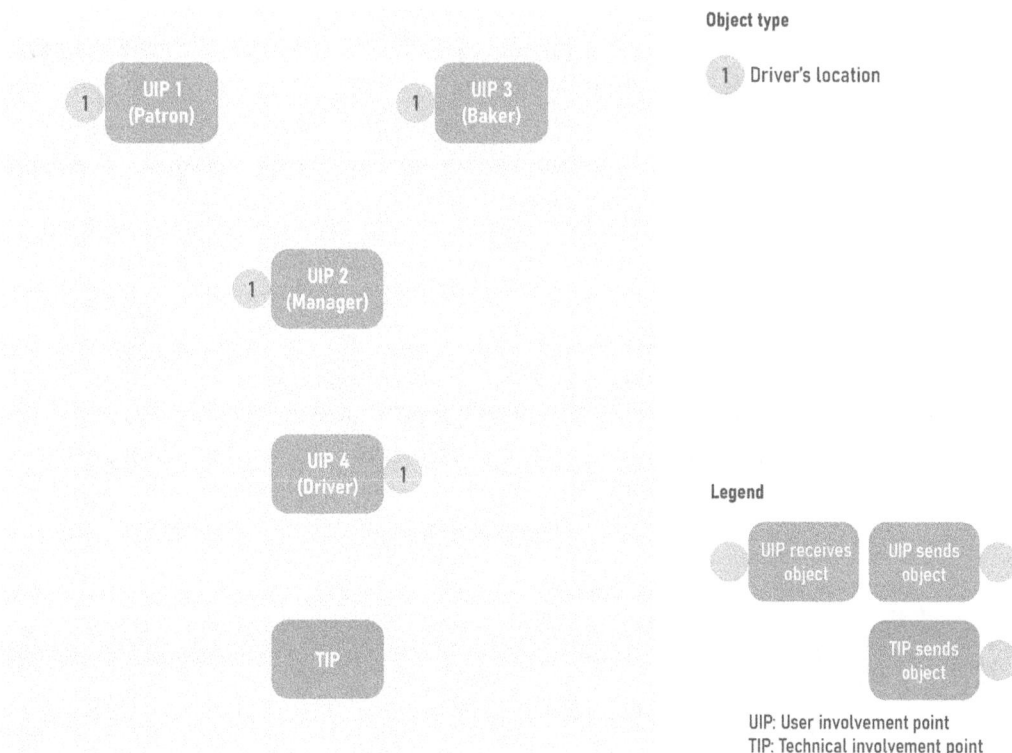

Figure 10.16: Driver's location for WoP

"Continuous" needs to be specified as a system alert frequency value. It is often a value below 10 seconds. In the case of a driver's location, the frequency can range from 1 second to 60 seconds as a configurable value (see Table 10.6).

Table 10.6: Driver's location specification table for WoP

Sender	Object ID	Trigger condition(s)	Design elements	Receiver	System alert time	System alert frequency
UIP 4	D.1 Driver location	State 4 (Delivery started)	Content: GPS coordinates of driver's phone; driver name; order number; ETA	UIP 1, UIP 2, UIP 3	≤ 1 sec	1 sec ≤ n ≤ 60 sec; n is configurable with intervals of 1 second

Monitor object flow view

Monitor objects are important elements for user involvement. They support user intervention and keep users in the loop about the progress and status of (semi)automated processes. If a monitored object value deviates from certain boundaries, an alert might be initiated. Such alerts are described in Section 10 (Alert flow view) on page 266.

For World of Pizza, two objects are monitored as examples. One is the oven temperature as an example of monitoring a property of a system element. The other is monitoring how long it takes a driver to pick up a pizza and deliver it to a patron. The examples are depicted in Figure 10.17.

The monitored data are also specified. 0.1 oven temperature (TIP) is measured every 10 seconds and reported to the baker (UIP 3) every 10 seconds. The completion time from pickup to delivery is measured every time the order object is changed to state 5 (delivery completed). The system alert time is up to 10 seconds. The system alert frequency is once (see Table 10.7 on the facing page).

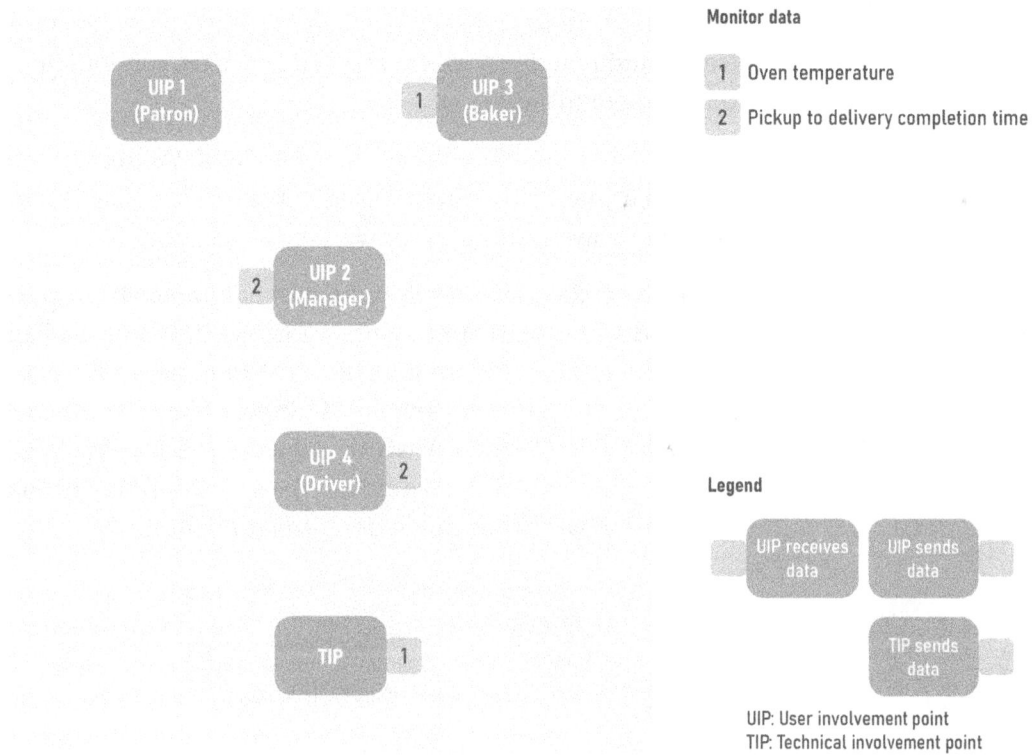

Figure 10.17: Monitor data for WoP

Table 10.7: Monitor object specification table for WoP

Sender	Object ID	Trigger condition	Design elements	Receiver	System alert time	System alert frequency
TIP (Oven)	O.1 Oven temperature	Time trigger	Content: Oven ID, oven temperature	UIP 3 (Baker)	≤ 10 sec	Every 10 sec.
UIP 4 (Driver)	O.2 Pick-up to delivery completion time	Order object, state 5 (delivery completed)	Content: Order number, driver name, delivery address, calculated distance, actual distance, completion time, feedback rating	UIP 2 (Manager)	≤ 10 sec	Once

Alert flow view

Alerts are an important element of user involvement. They support user intervention and keep users in the loop about deviations of (semi)automated processes. The TIP and UIPs can initiate alerts that are sent to UIPs.

In our WoP example, we have several alerts. We recommended creating an alert flow view for each alert to avoid visual clutter. An alert for delayed baking is shown here as an example.

In this case, the baker has forgotten to bake an ordered pizza. If baking does not start after a certain threshold, a "delayed baking" alert is sent. The TIP sends this alert automatically to UIP 2 (manager), UIP 3 (baker), and UIP 4 (driver). The manager can also initiate an alert (reminder), which is then sent to UIP 3 (baker) and to UIP 4 (driver). An alert could also be sent to UIP 1 (patron), but the decision was made not to do this (see Figure 10.18).

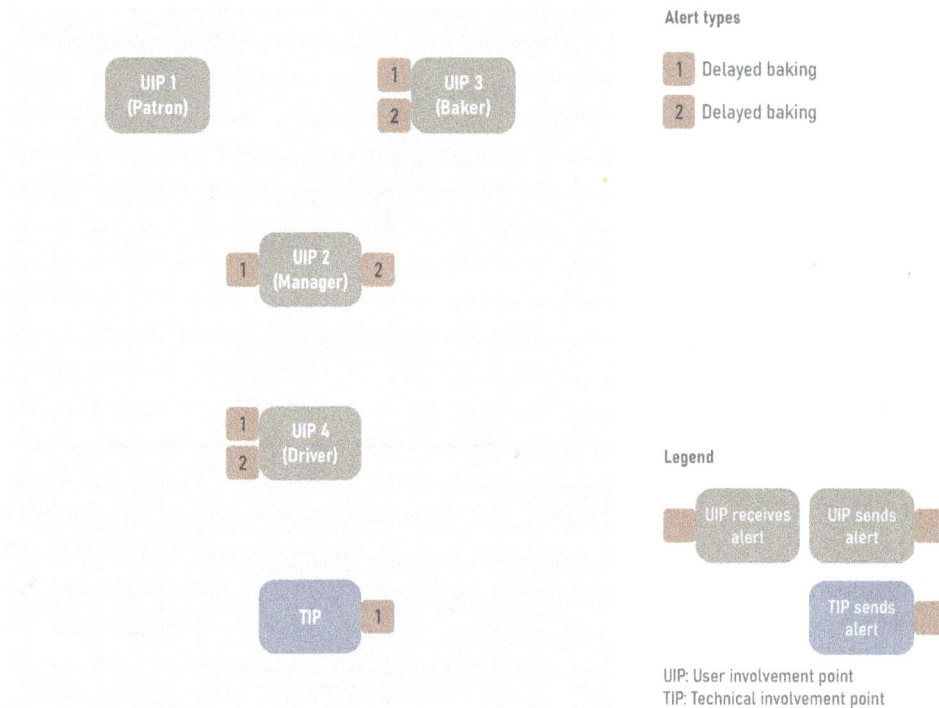

Figure 10.18: Alert for delayed baking for WoP

An alert flow specification table for delayed baking specifies the details (see Table 10.8 on the next page).

The table shows an example where the time and frequency are not hard-coded but contain user-configurable values. Users can select a value that is suitable for their organization.

Table 10.8: Alert specification table for delayed baking

Sender	Alert ID	Trigger condition(s)	Design elements	Receiver	System alert time	System alert frequency
TIP	A.1 Delayed baking	Order submitted (state 1); delay threshold in minutes exceeded (configurable)	Content: Delay length, recommendation; controls: acknowledge	UIP 2, UIP 3, UIP 4	n seconds after change to status 1; n is configurable from 1 sec to 10 min, with a 10-sec interval	n times; n is configurable; $0 \leq n \leq 64$ with interval of 1 sec
UIP 2	A.2 Delayed baking	User submitted alert	Content: Delay length, recommendation; controls: acknowledge	UIP 3, UIP 4	≤ 10 sec	Once

Communication flow view

Many ecosystems allow participants to directly communicate with each other. Often, such communications are supported by direct messages, text messages, or phone calls. The communication services themselves are not part of the application under design; however, the application under design interfaces with such services and launches them with the set address information.

Here is an example: Let's say the pizza driver cannot find the building; the app should support texting or calling the patron. The driver does not need to know the patron's phone number. When the driver initiates sending a text message to the patron, the phone number is automatically retrieved, and the text message app is launched with the phone number.

For several reasons, the TIP and certain UIPs should not be able to have contact with other UIPs. A communication flow diagram for each communication service will clarify which UIPs can communicate with which other UIPs, and through which communication service. For instance, the TIP should not make phone calls to UIPs but send text messages; the TIP should not receive text messages or phone calls. Examples of a text message communication flow (see Figure 10.19) and a phone call communication flow (see Figure 10.20) are visualized.

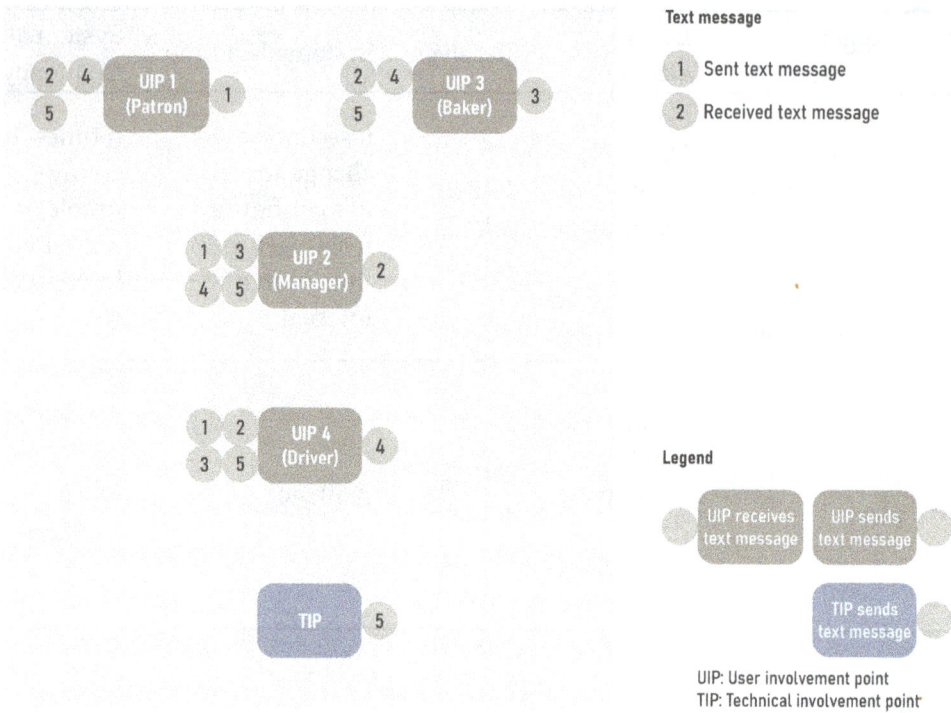

Figure 10.19: Sending and receiving text messages

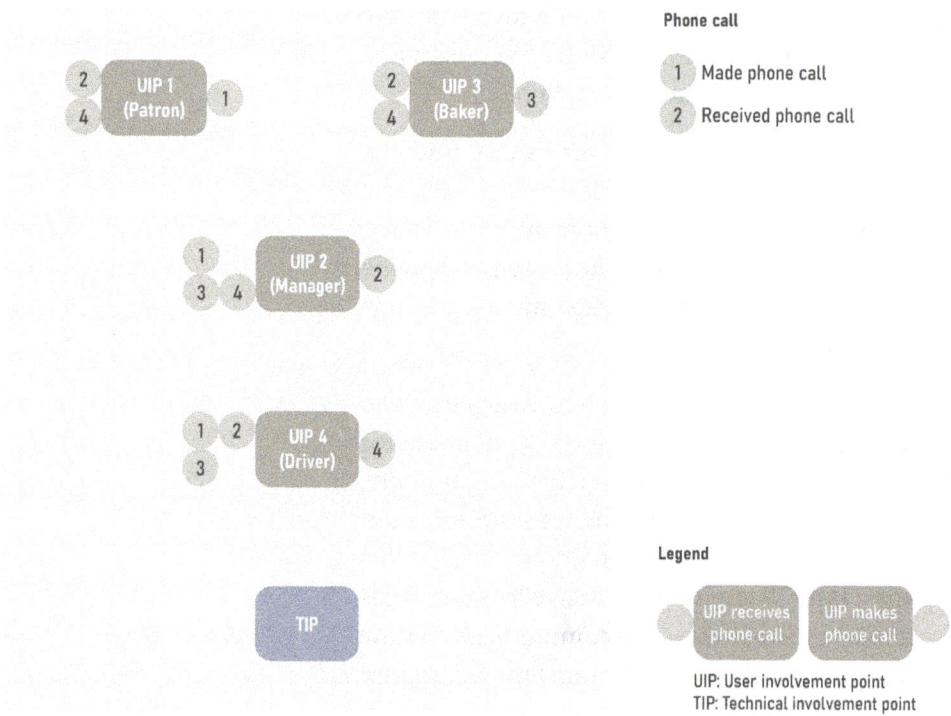

Figure 10.20: Making and receiving phone calls

Alert delivery channel view

There are several types of "events," such as object changes, monitored data, and deviations. Sometimes it might be necessary for the user to be informed about the occurrence of such events. We call a notification about these events an "alert."

Before the user can be alerted about an event, the delivery channels for such alerts need to be defined. There are several potential alert delivery channels: app notifications (desktop app or mobile), text message, email, or even social media posts. In specific environments, such as in cars, alerts can be tactile [166, 167].

The alert delivery channels should be defined and specified per event type, not per user involvement point. A key rationale for selecting an alert delivery channel is the alert type and how timely a response is needed. This rationale applies to the event type, not to the user involvement point.

In our World of Pizza example, we consider three alert delivery channels:

► Notification
► Text message
► Email

In some cases, a user simply needs to be informed, and in other cases a user has to respond to an alert in a timely manner in order to successfully generate the outcome of value. For each event type and delivery channel, it needs to be defined whether the user involvement is for information only (content) or whether the user should be able to respond to (control) the alert. This information is specified in the delivery channels specification table (see Table 10.9).

> The term "alert" is consistent with the user involvement metrics "system alert," "system alert time," and "system alert frequency" for user intervention.

> The design and evaluation of alerts and notifications is an ongoing HCI research topic [168–173].

Table 10.9: Alert delivery channel specification table

Event type	Alert delivery channels			
	App notification	Text message	Email	Phone call
Object state change	Content	Content	Content	n/a
Customer feedback alert	Content	Control	Control	n/a
Driver's location	Content	Content	n/a	Control
Oven temperature	Control	Control	n/a	n/a
Delayed baking alert	Control	Control	n/a	Control

The selection of the delivery channel per event is driven by the channel's effectiveness in making the user aware of the alert and able to respond to it in a timely and proficient manner. The channel selection is therefore driven primarily by how effectively it involves a user. This is why the delivery channels should be specified in the experience architecture.

Device switching

Device synchronization view

The last experience architecture view is cross-device usage, which was mentioned as a current usage pattern (see Section 8 on page 203).

The design and development scope may include several devices and modalities per user involvement point. This means that a user can use several devices in parallel, or they can switch from one device to another while still performing the same user task. Device switching adds additional design inputs to the application under design.

One requirement for device switching is the synchronization of the applications running on different devices. Synchronization means synchronizing the currently selected view (or screen) and updating the content in that view. A device synchronization table specifies how fast syncing takes place on each device and which type of applications should be synchronized.

Table 10.10: Device synchronization specification table

UIP	Desktop		Tablet		Mobile phone		Smart Watch	Smart speaker	Synch time
	Native	Web	Native	Web	Native	Web	Native	Native	
UIP 1 (Patron)	No	No	No	Yes	No	Yes	No	Yes	≤ 1 sec
UIP 2 (Manager)	No	Yes	No	Yes	No	Yes	Yes	No	≤ 1 sec
UIP 3 (Baker)	No	Yes	No	Yes	No	No	No	No	≤ 1 sec
UIP 4 (Driver)	No	No	No	No	No	Yes	No	No	≤ 1 sec

Because the switching concerns the user, the switching synch time should be defined by the experience architect, in collaboration with the system or software architect.

Application access point view

When a user performs a user task in an application on one device ("current device") and intends to switch to another device to continue the task ("target device"), it would be beneficial if the application on the target device actively supported the user in accessing the right view. After accessing the application on the target device, the user may decide to close the application on the current device or to use both devices in parallel.

To support such direct access to the same view and content, application 2 (on the target device) should provide an "application access point" (AAP) that takes the user of application 2 to the same view and content as that displayed in application 1. You can define which pairs of applications need to have such an application access point made available. The application access points are specified in Table 10.11.

Table 10.11: Application access point specification table

Application 1	Application 2 (providing application access point)					
(initially used)	Desktop - Web	Tablet - Web	Mobile - Web	Watch - Native	Speaker - Native	Synch time
Desktop - Web	Yes	Yes	Yes	No	No	≤ 1 sec
Tablet - Web	Yes	Yes	Yes	No	No	≤ 1 sec
Mobile phone - Web	Yes	Yes	Yes	No	No	≤ 1 sec
Smart watch - Native	No	No	No	No	No	n/a
Smart speaker - Native	No	No	No	No	No	n/a

Additionally, a time can be specified that expresses how timely an application 2 keeps an application access point in sync with the view and content changes made in application 1.

Device and application synchronization and switching might be considered more of a technical topic than an experience topic. But successfully switching devices and applications is, first of all, a user involvement topic and should be addressed by an experience architect. The realization of device and application switching requires technical support and implementation by technical experts (which is true of all other architecture and design decisions as well).

UIS levels

Our World of Pizza example is specified as a user involvement system consisting of two levels: level 1, the system level, and level 2, the UIP level. If an ecosystem is more complex, it may make sense to add one or two more levels to manage its complexity.

A user involvement system can consist of one level with one user involvement point only. Formally, such a system is still considered a user involvement system, but the lack of complexity does not warrant the experience architecture methodology. The standard user-centered design tools can be applied to the user involvement point.

For practical purposes, the minimum number of levels for a user involvement system is two. This means the user involvement system consists of a user involvement system level and a user involvement point level. An example is a pizza delivery ecosystem, as shown in this book. There are ecosystems that have a higher complexity; examples are airports, aircraft carriers, and railway stations. They may require three or even four levels, as indicated in Figure 10.21.

Multilevel User Involvement Systems

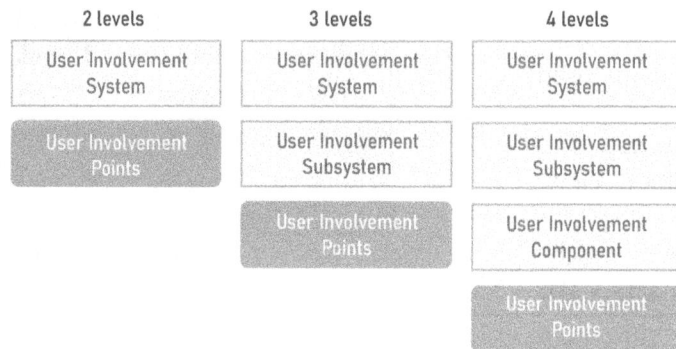

Figure 10.21: Level variations for user involvement systems

We can extend the World of Pizza example with an inventory management level (see Figure 5.7). Adding inventory management increases the complexity of the ecosystem, so it is reasonable to add another level to the user involvement system. The result is a UIS with a user involvement subsystem level and a user involvement point level. The three levels are as follows:

► Level 1: User involvement system "World of Pizza"
► Level 2: User involvement subsystems "1–Manage inventory" and "2–Deliver pizza"
► Level 3: User involvement points per user involvement subsystems

The enhanced user involvement system for WoP, consisting of two user involvement subsystems, is visualized in Figure 10.22.

The decomposition of a system into subsystems or components is a divide-and-conquer technique we know from systems and software engineering [108, 109, 174]. When dependencies exist between user involvement subsystems or user involvement components, they will be specified in the same way as the dependencies between user involvement points, as shown in this chapter.

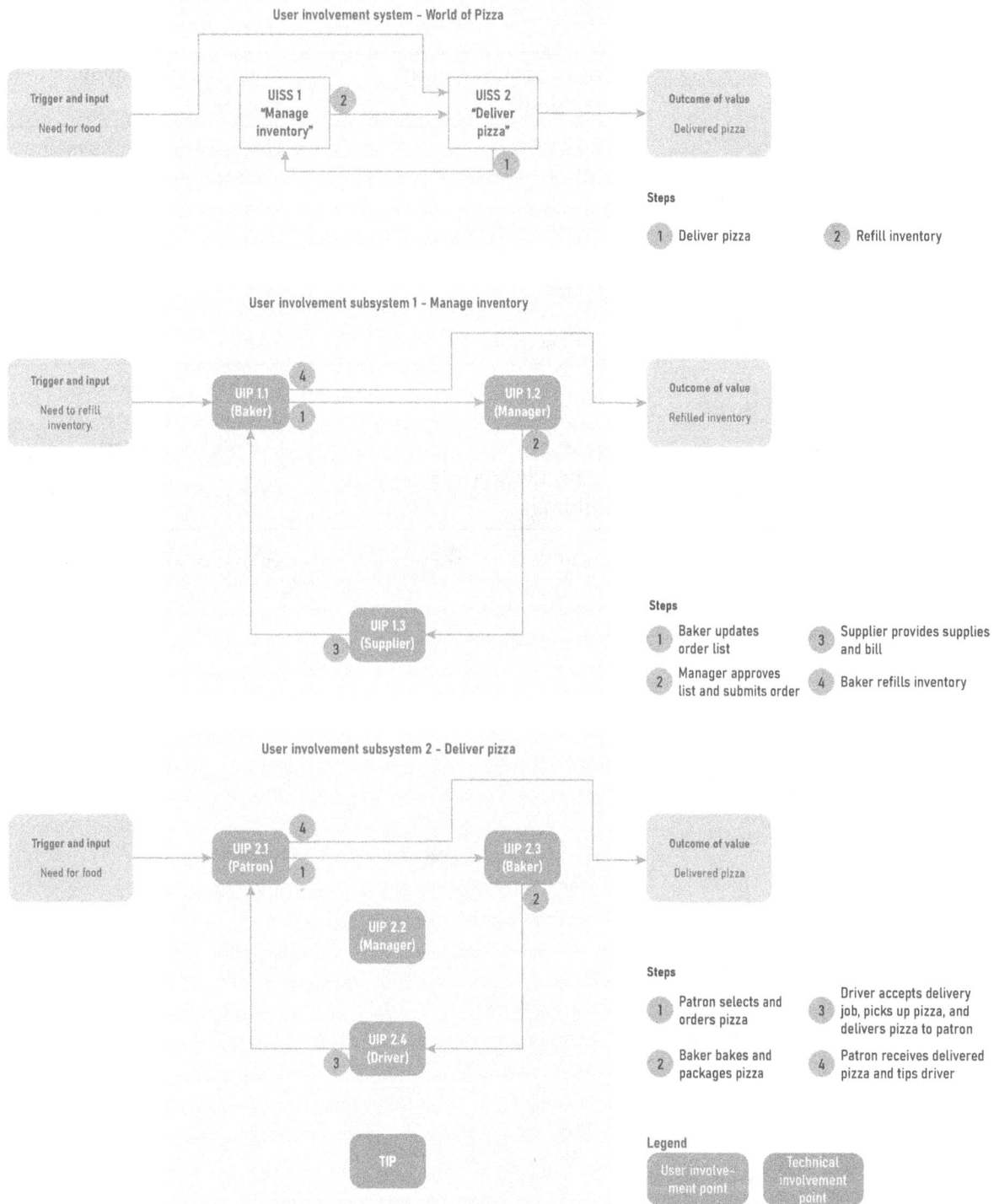

Figure 10.22: User involvement system "World of Pizza" with three levels

User involvement system as a campus metaphor

The user involvement system is still a rather abstract concept. Using the mental model of a campus may help to make the abstract user involvement system more concrete and understandable. Table 10.12

compares components of a campus with components of a user involvement system.

Entity of the campus metaphor	Entity of user involvement system
Campus	User involvement system
Building block	User involvement subsystem
Building	User involvement point
Room	Canvas
Entrance area	Entry canvas
Back room (not entrance area)	Back canvases
Work stations / shelves	Zones
Tools	Controls, functions, interaction devices
Materials	Content and alerts
Communication between buildings	Cross UIP/TIP flows

Table 10.12: Comparison of user involvement system with a campus metaphor

Figure 10.23 shows a visualization of the campus metaphor, applied to the WoP example.

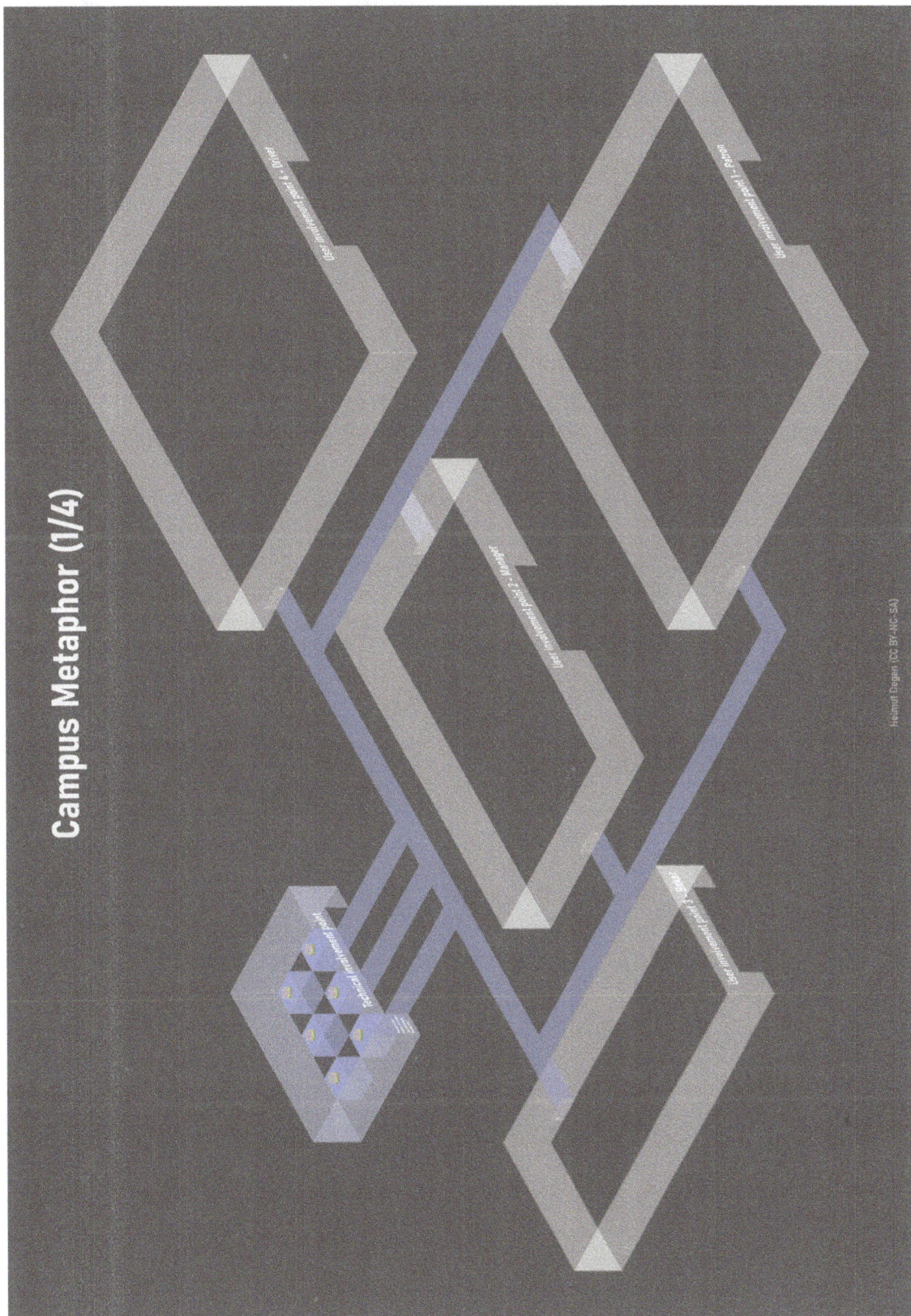

Figure 10.23: UIS and UIPs identified

The campus visualization will be refined at the end of part 2, experience architecture (see Figure 11.26), after step 2 of part 3 (Figure 15.53) and after step 6 of part 3 (see Figure 19.6).

Summary

User involvement system

- ▶ The user involvement system consists of four UIPs
- ▶ The UIPs are horizontally grouped

- ▶ Move on to <u>User Involvement Point</u>
- ◀ Go back to <u>Workflow (to be)</u>

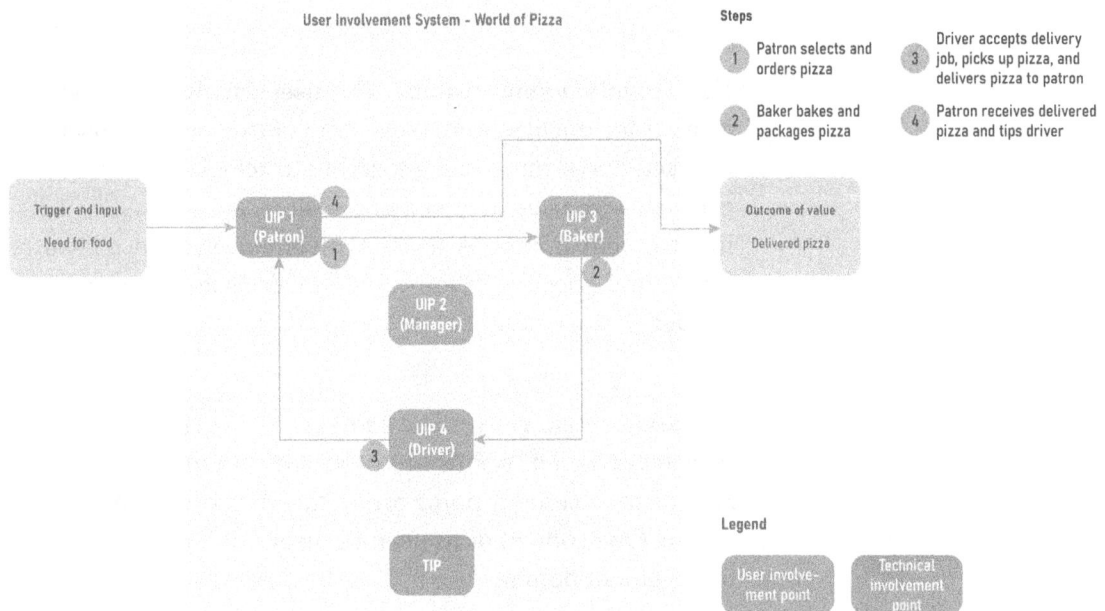

User Involvement System - World of Pizza

Steps

1. Patron selects and orders pizza

2. Baker bakes and packages pizza

3. Driver accepts delivery job, picks up pizza, and delivers pizza to patron

4. Patron receives delivered pizza and tips driver

Trigger and input

Need for food

UIP 1 (Patron)

UIP 2 (Manager)

UIP 3 (Baker)

UIP 4 (Driver)

TIP

Outcome of value

Delivered pizza

Legend

User involvement point

Technical involvement point

Lessons learned

User involvement map   The workflow (to be) is used as a starting point for grouping responsibilities into user involvement points. The resulting new view is called a user involvement map (UIM). The UIM is the working tool used to identify the user involvement points that are the constituting elements of a user involvement system.

There are three grouping styles: A horizontal grouping assembles the responsibilities per user role. A vertical grouping categorizes responsibilities that take place at the same time across multiple user roles. The third grouping type is a hybrid style in which one or more responsibilities per user role and across multiple user roles are grouped together.

User involvement system   The user involvement system is a human-technical system consisting of one or more users and an interactive system working together to achieve one or more stated purposes. A user involvement system is composed of its user involvement points. A user involvement system allows one to define and specify system-wide functions and user involvement properties that could not be specified otherwise.

Contexts of use view   The contexts of use view specifies which user involvement points are used within which contexts of use. A user involvement point can be used in one or more contexts of use. One context of use can be applicable to one or more user involvement points.

Black box view   The black box view specifies the main input and trigger of a user involvement system as well as the outcome of value and the user goal. The black box view identifies the scope of the user involvement system needed to transform the input and trigger into the outcome of value.

Scenario views   There are several scenario views that specify certain behaviors of the user involvement system.

One scenario view is the "value flow view." It defines and specifies in what sequence the user involvement points contribute to transform the input and the trigger into the outcome of value. It is possible that one user involvement point can contribute several times to the value flow.

Another scenario view is the "object states flow view." Certain objects have different states, which are set and changed by different user involvement points. The object states flow view defines and specifies which object state is set and changed by which user involvement point across the life cycle of an object.

Another scenario view is the "monitor object flow view." This view defines and specifies which user involvement point(s) are able to monitor the status of a selected object.

Another important scenario view is the "alert flow view." It defines and specifies which user involvement point(s) are informed about deviations, so they can respond to such deviations.

Each scenario view has a supporting specification table that contains information about that view. Important attributes of a specification table are the frequency (called system alert frequency) and the processing time (called system alert time).

To support the communication of alerts, alert delivery channels need to be defined. An alert delivery channel specification table specifies which event types are communicated to users using which alert delivery channel. Furthermore, it is defined whether an alert delivery channel should support only the presentation of content to users (labeled as "content" in the table) or whether users should also be able to respond to the alert (marked as "control" in the table). Examples of alert delivery channels are app notifications, text messages, emails, social media posts, and others.

To support the use of multiple devices at the same time, or to support device switching, a device synchronization specification table specifies which device switches are supported and how fast the synchronization time should be.

User involvement system levels A user involvement system typically has at least two levels: the system level and the user involvement point level. Our pizza example employs a two-level user involvement system architecture. If an ecosystem becomes more complex, the user involvement system can have one or two more levels. Additional levels help to manage the complexity of complex user involvement systems.

Last but not least, the user involvement system can be compared to a campus. Elements of a campus (e.g., building block, building, room, etc.) are compared to elements of a user involvement system. An infographic has been introduced that shows elements of a campus mapped to the user involvement system. This infographic will evolve over the course of the book.

Tips and tricks

User involvement map   If a project requires the delivery of an application that is able to generate an outcome of value very early, a horizontal grouping is recommended, ideally for one user role from end to end.

If several user groups perform the same user tasks with a similar user goal, a vertical grouping is recommended. It will save design and development time and effort without compromising the quality.

Design and development quality goes up as the number of user involvement points increases. On the other hand, the quality per user involvement point goes down if the number of responsibilities increases, particularly if several user roles are involved. It is critical to find the right balance. A rule of thumb is that each user role has its own user involvement point.

User involvement system   The user involvement system is an abstract concept and partially consists of specification of user involvement for the ecosystem under design. It is critical to have a draft user involvement system early in the project, ideally with the different views. Such views help when having discussions with product management, to check whether the value proposition can be realized. Similar discussions are needed with the system or software architect, so they can start technology explorations.

Another important point is that system-wide functions and properties should be defined early. Only the user involvement system is able to define and specify such functions and properties. They should also be discussed with product management (to ensure the realization of the value proposition) and with technical experts (to determine feasibility).

Black box view   The black box view with the user trigger and outcome of value is the most abstract view of the user involvement system. Even though it does not contain a lot of information, it shows the value the user involvement system creates for users and customers. This view is very useful because it can help to reset architecture or design discussions that are too much into the weeds. The black box view can be used as a compass for the application under design and development.

Scenario views   The scenario views define and specify scenarios important for the ecosystem under design. It is recommended that system alert time and frequency numbers be backed up with evidence, e.g., findings from academic or industrial research.

The scenario views presented here have been used in industrial projects. It can be assumed that they are useful and not necessarily complete. So if you see needed modifications to a scenario view, or the need for additional scenario views, my advice is to go ahead and make the views work for you and publish them, so experience professionals and the research community can benefit from it.

Exercise 2.2

Goal   Define a user involvement system with its user involvement points and different views for your example application.

Material   User involvement map, user involvement system, black box view, context of use view, several scenario views, and specification tables per view.

Completion criteria are:

- ▶ The user involvement map is defined. The grouping type (horizontal, vertical, hybrid) is documented. The reason for the selected grouping type is documented.
- ▶ The value view is documented.
- ▶ At least one object and state view with several states is documented, with a specification table.
- ▶ At least one alert view is documented, with a specification table.
- ▶ The device switch and synchronization tables are documented.

User Involvement Point $\Big|$ **11**

岁月既往，一去不回
(Lost time is never found again)
Chinese proverb

Purpose

So far, we have defined and specified the user involvement system and identified its user involvement points (UIPs). The next step is to specify each user involvement point. A user involvement point is defined as a constituting element of a user involvement system (see Section 10 (Establish UIS) on page 246).

A user involvement point is one of the key outcomes of the experience architecture phase and an input into the experience design phase. A specified UIP communicates the design scope and involvement goals for an experience designer.

In this chapter, we introduce how to define and specify a user involvement point. The steps are as follows:

- ▶ Define user involvement point
- ▶ Determine the primary user task
- ▶ Determine number of target involvement steps (TAS) per user task
- ▶ Determine target involvement time (TAT) per user task

User involvement point

Template

Each UIP outlines the scope of a design project. A template to define and specify a UIP is visualized in Figure 11.1.

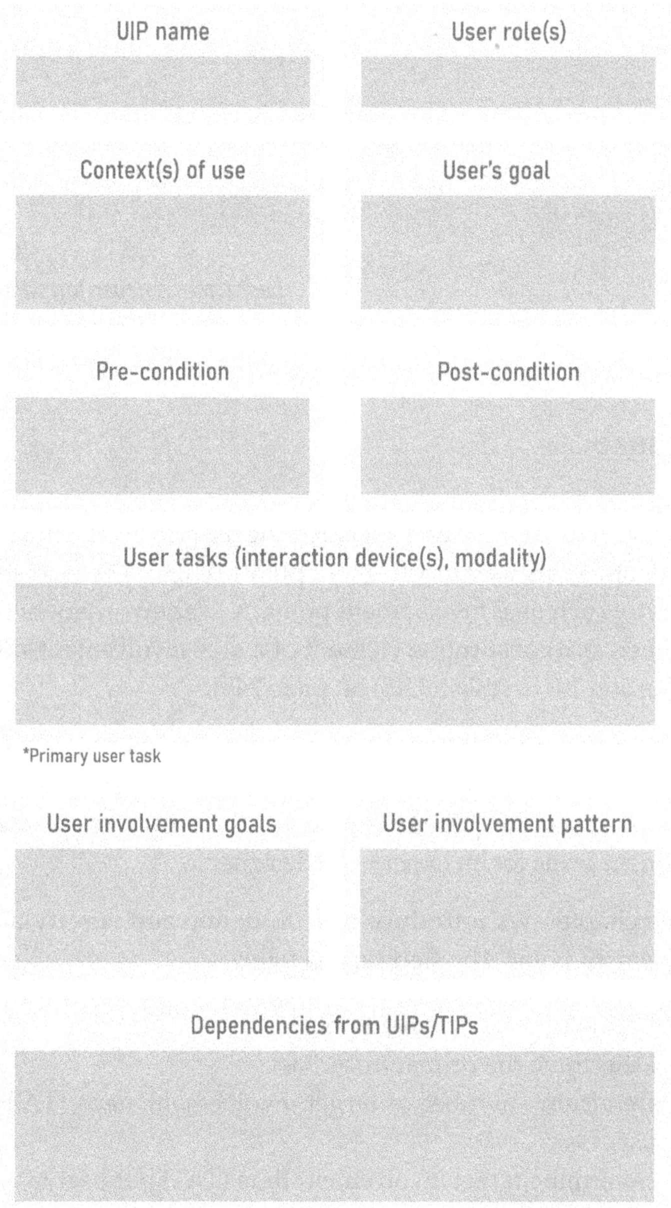

UIP name	User role(s)

Context(s) of use	User's goal

Pre-condition	Post-condition

User tasks (interaction device(s), modality)

*Primary user task

User involvement goals	User involvement pattern

Dependencies from UIPs/TIPs

Figure 11.1: User involvement point template

A user involvement point should not be confused with a "use case." A use case "describes the system's behavior under various conditions as the system responds to a request from one of the stakeholders, called the *primary actor*" [175, p. 1] (italics in original).

A user involvement point does not describe such a system behavior but rather groups user tasks assigned to one or more user roles that pursue the post-condition and the user's goal. The listed user tasks may not be sufficient to achieve the post-condition and the user's goal. Other user involvement points with their assigned user tasks may contribute to the goal too. We can see this in the example below. A single user task could be elaborated on with a use case format. Furthermore, a user involvement point does not express system behaviors.

A user involvement point is different from an "essential use case." An essential use case is a modified use case format. "*An* essential use case *is a structured narrative, expressed in the language of the application domain and of users, comprising a simplified, generalized, abstract, technology-free and implementation-independent description of one task or interaction that is complete, meaningful, and well-defined from the point of view of users in some role or roles in relation to a system and that embodies the purpose or intentions underlying the interaction.*" [3](italics in original)[1] An essential use case was introduced as a new form of task model, building on the format of use cases, and was created for experience professionals, who should avoid assumptions about what the technical system contributes to tasks or interactions. Each user task of a user involvement point could be described with an essential use case format.

1: Constantine and Lockwood revised their initial definition of an essential use case to "a single, discrete, complete, meaningful, and well-defined task of interest to an external user in some specific role or roles in relationship to a system, comprising the user intentions and system responsibilities in the course of accomplishing that task, described in abstract, technology-free, implementation independent terms using the language of the application domain and of external users in role." [176, p. 248]

World of Pizza

The user involvement point UIP 1 for our WoP example is displayed in Figure 11.2. We will explain each box of the UIP.

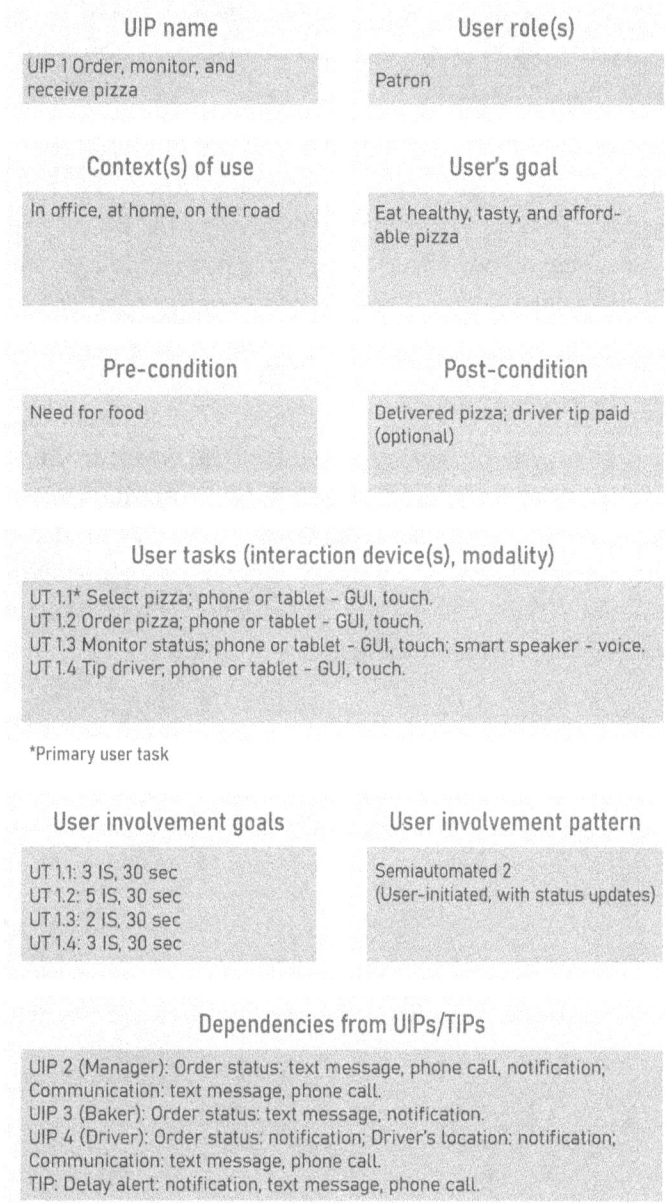

UIP name	User role(s)
UIP 1 Order, monitor, and receive pizza	Patron

Context(s) of use	User's goal
In office, at home, on the road	Eat healthy, tasty, and afford-able pizza

Pre-condition	Post-condition
Need for food	Delivered pizza; driver tip paid (optional)

User tasks (interaction device(s), modality)

UT 1.1* Select pizza; phone or tablet - GUI, touch.
UT 1.2 Order pizza; phone or tablet - GUI, touch.
UT 1.3 Monitor status; phone or tablet - GUI, touch; smart speaker - voice.
UT 1.4 Tip driver; phone or tablet - GUI, touch.

*Primary user task

User involvement goals	User involvement pattern
UT 1.1: 3 IS, 30 sec UT 1.2: 5 IS, 30 sec UT 1.3: 2 IS, 30 sec UT 1.4: 3 IS, 30 sec	Semiautomated 2 (User-initiated, with status updates)

Dependencies from UIPs/TIPs

UIP 2 (Manager): Order status: text message, phone call, notification; Communication: text message, phone call.
UIP 3 (Baker): Order status: text message, notification.
UIP 4 (Driver): Order status: notification; Driver's location: notification; Communication: text message, phone call.
TIP: Delay alert: notification, text message, phone call.

Figure 11.2: User involvement point UIP 1

UIP name

Each UIP has a number and a name. The number and name should be copied from the user involvement map (see Figure 10.3).

The name of our UIP is "UIP 1: Order, monitor and receive pizza."

UIP name

UIP 1 Order, monitor, and receive pizza

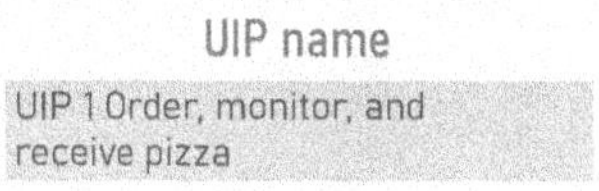

Figure 11.3: UIP 1: Name

User role(s)

One or more user roles are assigned to a UIP. The assignment can be derived from the user involvement map (see Figure 10.3).

The assigned user role to UIP 1 is "Patron."

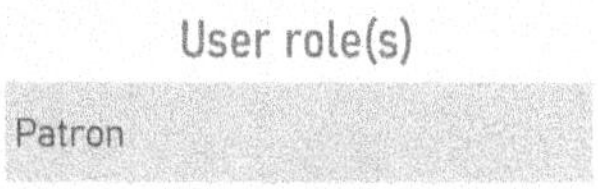

User role(s)

Patron

Figure 11.4: UIP 1: User role(s)

Context(s) of use

Each UIP is assigned to one or multiple contexts of use. The context of use is defined and specified in the context of use view of the user involvement system (see Figure 10.10).

The assigned contexts of use for UIP 1 are the "office, home, and on the road."

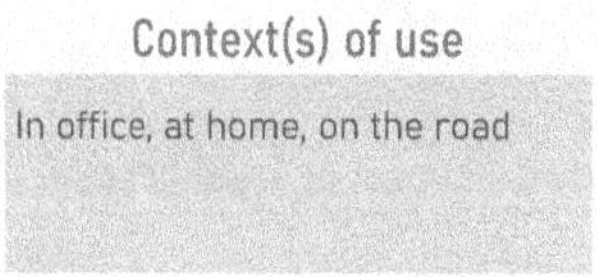

Context(s) of use

In office, at home, on the road

Figure 11.5: UIP 1: Context(s) of use

User's goal

The user's goal expresses the goals of the users, involved in the UIP.

UIP 1 includes one user role only, the Patron. The goal of the Patron is to "eat healthy, tasty, and affordable pizza."

User's goal

Eat healthy, tasty, and affordable pizza

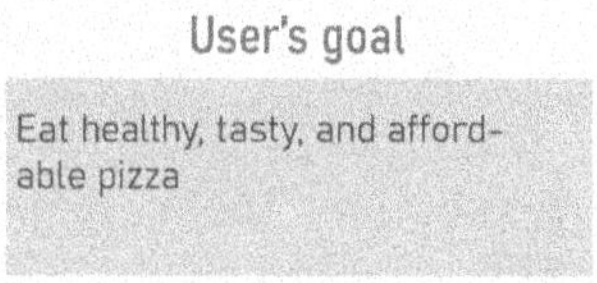

Figure 11.6: UIP 1: User's goal

Pre-condition

The pre-condition and the post-condition mark the boundaries of a UIP. The pre-condition defines the conditions that are true at the beginning of the UIP from a time perspective.

The pre-condition for our UIP is the "need for food."

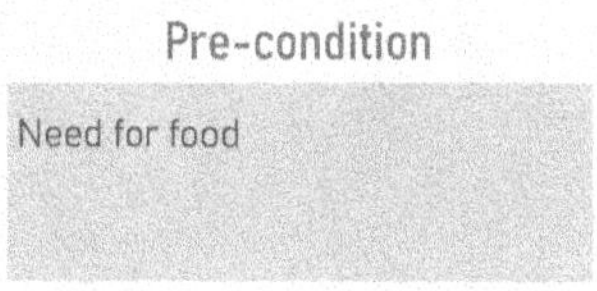

Pre-condition

Need for food

Figure 11.7: UIP 1: Pre-condition

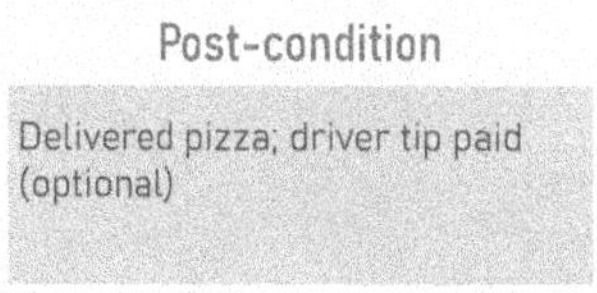

Post-condition

Delivered pizza; driver tip paid (optional)

Figure 11.8: UIP 1: Post-condition

Post-condition

The post-condition defines the second boundary of the user involvement point. It defines the conditions that are true after the user involvement point has been successfully performed. The post-condition focuses on an outcome, not a goal.

In our case, the post-condition is the "delivered pizza." Optionally, it is the "driver tip paid."

User tasks (interaction device(s), modality)

The *user tasks* are core content of a user involvement point. Let's start by defining them:

> **Definition 12** (User task) *User initiated "set of activities undertaken in order to achieve a specific goal" [23, 3.1.11].*

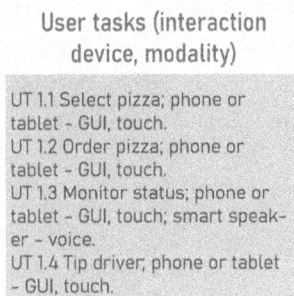

User tasks (interaction
device, modality)

UT 1.1 Select pizza; phone or
tablet - GUI, touch.
UT 1.2 Order pizza; phone or
tablet - GUI, touch.
UT 1.3 Monitor status; phone or
tablet - GUI, touch; smart speaker - voice.
UT 1.4 Tip driver; phone or tablet
- GUI, touch.

Figure 11.9: UIP 1: User tasks (interaction device(s), modality)

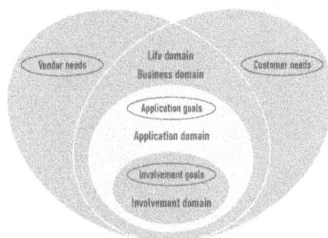

To generate the outcome of value, one or more user tasks might be needed. The user tasks describe what the assigned users per UIP (in their user roles) are supposed to do when the UIP has been implemented. Furthermore, the user tasks of a UIP should be able to transform the pre-condition into the post-condition.

The user tasks are derived from the responsibilities on the user involvement map (see Figure 10.6). The user tasks are from the application domain and should be articulated accordingly (see Figure 11.10).

Figure 11.10: Teddy bear model

One might ask how to derive user tasks from the responsibilities defined on the user involvement map. The general answer is that the list of user tasks should support the scoping and planning of the design work package for the next and future releases. When identifying specific user tasks, it is a reasonable starting point to map each single responsibility on the user involvement map to a single user task. In our case, we make an initial list of user tasks:

▶ UT 1.1 Select and order pizza
▶ UT 1.2 Monitor order and delivery
▶ UT 1.3 Receive pizza and tip driver

It is now worthwhile to refine the initially identified user tasks with the following considerations:

▶ Assignment of involvement goal
▶ Use of different devices and/or modalities
▶ Remove activities that are out of scope
▶ Simplify the language

If one responsibility and the mapped user task needs to be broken down for involvement goal measurements, it can make sense to break an initially mapped user task into parts. Let's take an example from our World of Pizza scenario. The user involvement map has a responsibility called "R 1.1 Select and order pizza." This could become one user task: "UT 1.1 Select and order pizza." But if we wanted to assign a dedicated involvement goal to "select pizza," or one to "order pizza," or to both, it would make sense to separate the responsibility into two user tasks: "UT 1.1 Select pizza" and "UT 1.2 Order pizza."

This idea can be also used to define one user task, by merging multiple responsibilities of one user involvement point.

The second consideration is separating a responsibility into different user tasks if one of the user tasks employs a different device or modality. In our WoP example, we plan to support the user task "monitor status" with a smart speaker. Therefore, it makes sense to keep this user task separate, so it can be planned and executed accordingly.

In the WoP case, we have split the responsibilities "R 1.1 Select & order pizza" into the two user tasks "UT 1.1 Select pizza" and "UT 1.2 Order pizza," because involvement goals are planned for each of them.

The responsibility "R 1.2 Monitor order and delivery" is assigned to the user task "UT 1.3 Monitor status." The name of the task was simplified.

In a second step, the devices and modalities are assigned to each user task. The devices and application types have already been identified and mapped to the user involvement points (see Table 10.10 on page 270). We now need to assign these devices and modalities to the single user tasks.

The third consideration is to remove activities that are out of scope. The responsibility "R 1.4 Receive pizza and tip driver" is assigned to the user task "UT 1.4 Tip driver." The "receive pizza" activity is removed because there is no plan for an application that will support the patron receiving the pizza (e.g., scanning the box with a barcode scanner).

Below is the resulting list of user tasks for UIP 1. The numbering system for the tasks reflects the number of the UIP (to the left of the decimal point) and a number for each user task (to the right of the decimal point).

- ▶ UT 1.1 Select pizza
- ▶ UT 1.2 Order pizza
- ▶ UT 1.3 Monitor order

► UT 1.4 Tip driver

The number to the left of the decimal point refers to the user involvement point number. Reflecting the UIP number in the user tasks makes each user task identifiable across UIPs.

Primary user task

The user interface design we are going to create in a few chapters enables the patron to perform the identified user tasks to achieve the goal. In order to achieve efficiency for users, we need to optimize the user interface design for the most relevant user task. Here the most relevant user task is called the *primary user task*.

> **Definition 13** (Primary user task) *User task for which the involvement concept will be optimized.*

To demonstrate how much the primary user task influences the involvement concept, we'll select two different user tasks as primary user tasks and see which user involvement concept would be created for each of them.

For our WoP app, let's assume that one experience architect has picked UT 1.1 Select pizza as the primary user task, and another experience architect has selected UT 1.4 Tip driver as the primary user task. Different primary user tasks can lead to very different user involvement concepts, as shown in Figure 11.12.

Canvas 1 shows an involvement concept optimized for the primary user task UT 1.1 Select pizza. The focus is on displaying pizza options. Canvas 2 shows an involvement concept optimized for the primary user task UT 1.4 Tip driver. Here the focus is on tipping drivers.

How do we identify the primary user task? The steps are shown in Figure 11.16.

A 0 Create user task pattern We first need to create a user task pattern for the user tasks of the UIP, which should look like one of the patterns in Figure 11.13.

We distinguish between user tasks that are independent from each other and those that are dependent on each other. If certain user tasks depend on each other, they are shown as a horizontal chain (see user task patterns 2 and 3). User task 2 is dependent on user task 1 if user task 2 can only be performed after user task 1 has been completed. In other words, user task B depends on user task A if the performance of user task B requires the successful completion

Canvas

Overlay canvas

Canvas control

Canvas function

Content

Alert

Content control

Content function

● User action

● System action

Interaction device

System function

Figure 11.11: Design elements with their color code

Primary user task
UT 1.1 Select pizza

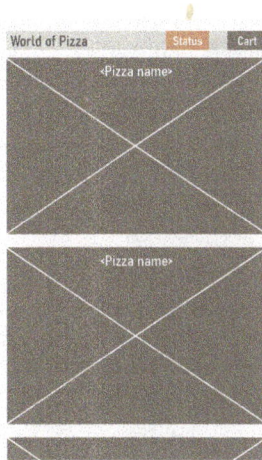

Primary user task
UT 1.4 Tip driver

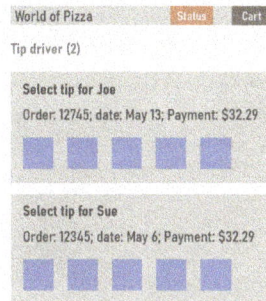

Figure 11.12: Primary user tasks influence the user involvement concept

of user task A. Here are two examples from World of Pizza: The user task "order pizza" requires completion of the user task "select pizza." The user task "monitor status" requires a submitted order that is the completed user task "order pizza."

If user tasks are independent from each other, they are shown vertically (see user task patterns 4, 5, and 6 in Figure 11.13).

User task patterns

User task pattern 1
Single user task

(UT 1)

User task pattern 4
Several independent
single user tasks

(UT 1)
(UT 2)
(UT 3)

User task pattern 2
Sequence of dependent user
tasks

(UT 1)—(UT 2)—(UT 3)

User task pattern 5
Several independent user tasks,
some with a sequence of dependent user tasks

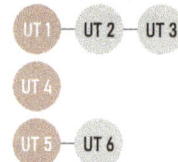

(UT 1)—(UT 2)—(UT 3)
(UT 4)
(UT 5)—(UT 6)

User task pattern 3
Sequence of dependent user
tasks, starting with a one-time
user task

(UT 0)—(UT 1)—(UT 2)—(UT 3)

User task pattern 6
Several independent user
tasks, some with a sequence of
dependent user tasks, starting
with a one-time user task

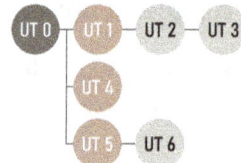

(UT 0)—(UT 1)—(UT 2)—(UT 3)
(UT 4)
(UT 5)—(UT 6)

Legend

● First independent user
task; primary user task

● One-time task;
no candidate for primary
user task

● Independent user task;
candidate for primary
user task

● Dependent user task;
no candidate for primary
user task

Figure 11.13: User task patterns to determine the primary user task

Decision D 1 (yes): Each user task dependents on another (except the first one) The first case considers dependent user tasks only (see user task patterns 1, 2, and 3 in Figure 11.13). We distinguish between two situations: one in which one of the tasks is a one-time user task (see user task pattern 3) and one where there is not a one-time user task (see user task patterns 1 and 2).

Examples of one-time user tasks are setting up a user account, onboarding an IoT device, or entering payment and delivery information. After such a task is performed once, the user does not return to it very often, if at all. In these cases, the first task after the one-time user task is the primary user task (see user task pattern 3 in Figure 11.13). For dependent user task chains that do not contain a one-time user task, the first user task is selected as the primary user task (see user task pattern 1 and 2 in Figure 11.13).

User task pattern 2
Sequence of dependent user tasks

UT 1.1 — UT 1.2 — UT 1.3 — UT 1.4

UT 1.1 Select pizza (primary user task)
UT 1.2 Order pizza
UT 1.3 Monitor status
UT 1.4 Tip driver

Legend

- First independent user task; primary user task
- One-time task; no candidate for primary user task
- Independent user task; candidate for primary user task
- Dependent user task; no candidate for primary user task

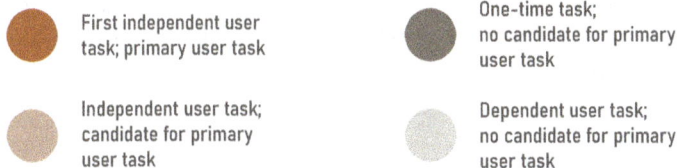

Figure 11.14: User task pattern for WoP

The four user tasks of UIP 1 are an example of user task pattern 2, where we have four user tasks that are dependent on each other. None of them is a one-time user task (see Figure 11.14).

For that reason, the first user task "UT 1.1 Select pizza" is the primary user task (see Figure 11.15).

Decision D 2 (yes): There is one highest ranked independent user task There are applications with user tasks that are not dependent on each other. The user may start with any of them (see user task patterns 4, 5, and 6 in Figure 11.13). How do we determine a primary user task if there are a number of independent user tasks and the user can start with any of them? We rank the user tasks according to their contribution to the user goal. The user task with the strongest contribution to the user goal is selected as the primary user task.

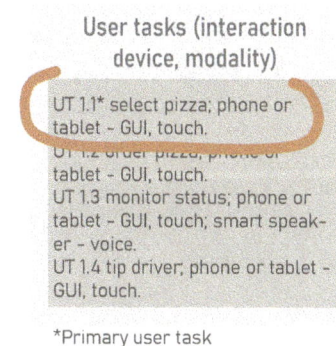

User tasks (interaction device, modality)

UT 1.1* select pizza; phone or tablet – GUI, touch.
UT 1.2 order pizza; phone or tablet – GUI, touch.
UT 1.3 monitor status; phone or tablet – GUI, touch; smart speaker – voice.
UT 1.4 tip driver; phone or tablet – GUI, touch.

*Primary user task

Figure 11.15: UIP 1: Primary user task

Decision D 2 (no): There is are several highest ranked independent user task   If, for some reason, several independent user tasks are considered to contribute equally to the user goal, additional ranking criteria are applied to select one of them as the primary user task:

▶ *Frequency of use*: This criterion is applicable if the application is used frequently. The user task with the highest frequency of use is selected as the primary user task.

▶ *Urgency of use*: This criterion is applicable if the application is something like an alarm or alert that is used to respond to extraordinary events. The user task with the highest urgency or the biggest impact is selected as the primary user task.

▶ *Risk of use*: This criterion is applicable if certain user tasks can impose a high risk or if there are safety concerns. The concept can be optimized to address such high-risk user tasks.

If the application domain is risk-sensitive or needs to comply with safety requirements (for instance, the medical device domain [177]), risk of use may become the most relevant ranking criterion for independent user tasks.

If the result is that there are several highest-ranked user tasks, several of them may become the primary user tasks. For the involvement concept, this means having more design elements, increasing the complexity, and providing less guidance for the user. The decision to allow more than one primary user task often makes the involvement concept more complex, less usable, and less efficient.

Select primary user task

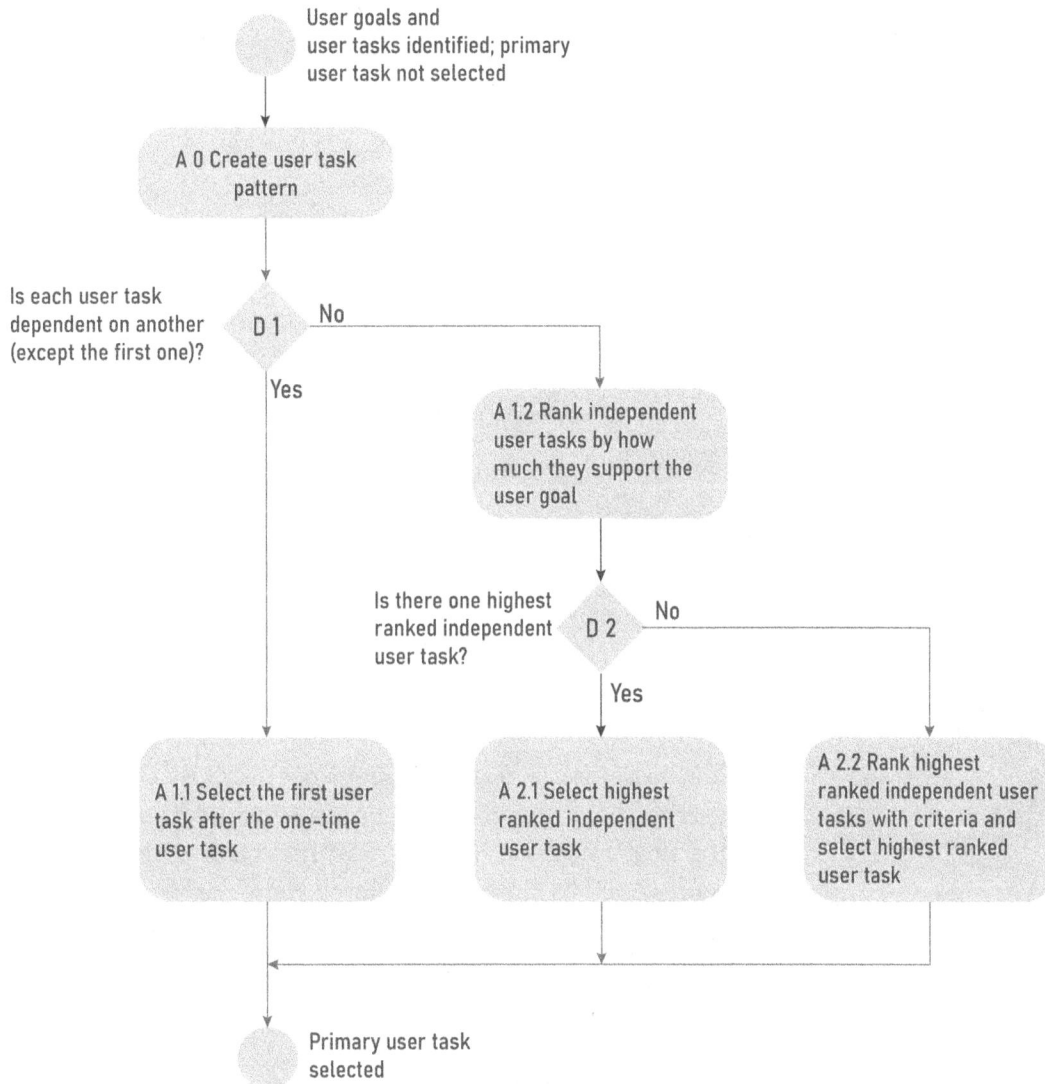

User goals and user tasks identified; primary user task not selected

A 0 Create user task pattern

Is each user task dependent on another (except the first one)? D 1 — No

Yes

A 1.2 Rank independent user tasks by how much they support the user goal

Is there one highest ranked independent user task? D 2 — No

Yes

A 1.1 Select the first user task after the one-time user task

A 2.1 Select highest ranked independent user task

A 2.2 Rank highest ranked independent user tasks with criteria and select highest ranked user task

Primary user task selected

Figure 11.16: Steps to select a user task as a primary user task

User involvement goals

Target involvement steps and target involvement time will be specified and assigned to each user task.

Target involvement steps   We will now define the initial *target involvement steps*, our first quantitative involvement goal. Target involvement steps are abbreviated *TAS*. To determine the target involvement steps, we need to identify the user involvement steps

The initial target involvement steps will be systematically reduced with the GAIS technique, shown in Section 12 on page 314.

per user task. The technique is visualized in Figure 11.17.

User task flow

Figure 11.17: User task flow template

The basic idea is to identify steps per user task that transform the user task specific pre-condition (shown on the left-hand side) into the post-condition (on the right-hand side). The user steps are represented by the brown-colored elements.

The technique can be applied in three variations. In variation 1, the experience architect places only user step elements per user task. This is the simplest and most efficient way to use the technique.

Sometimes it makes sense to show the system response as well, represented by the blue elements (variation 2). If some of the step names are not self-explanatory, an additional description per step can be added (variation 3).

The number of user steps (i.e., the user step elements) are counted and displayed as the target involvement steps per user task on the left-hand side of the diagram. The user involvement steps are abbreviated *IS*.

For each of the four user tasks, we determine the number of user involvement steps. The steps and the step counter are shown in Figure 11.18 on the left-hand side.

For user task 1.1 Select pizza, two variations are shown. Variation 1 only shows the user steps (UT 1.1 Select pizza, case 1). The second variation shows the system steps as well, represented with blue

UT 1.1 Select pizza
Case 1: Via pizza categories (show user involvement steps only)

Case 2: Via filter (shows user and technical involvement steps)

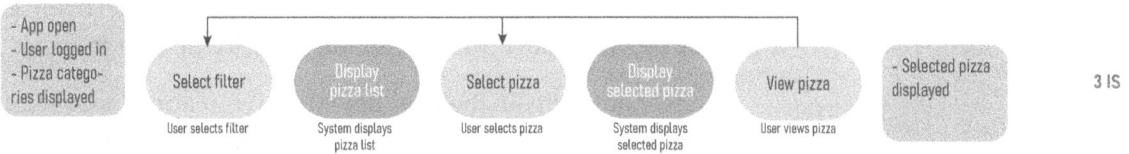

UT 1.2 Order pizza

UT 1.3 Monitor status

UT 1.4 Tip driver

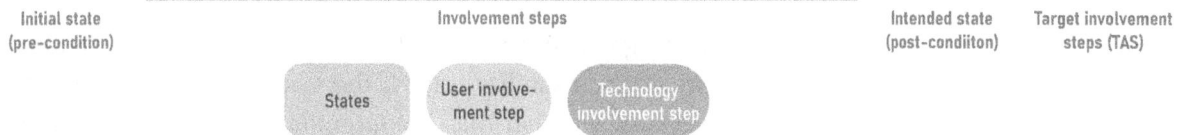

Figure 11.18: User task flows for UIP 1

elements. They are not counted as target involvement steps (UT 1.1 Select pizza, case 2).

For the other three user tasks, variation 1 is used. The counted number of target user involvement steps for the four user tasks are as follows:

- ▶ UT.1 Select pizza: 3 IS
- ▶ UT.2 Order pizza: 5 IS
- ▶ UT.3 Monitor status: 2 IS
- ▶ UT.4 Tip driver: 3 IS

We will capture the target involvement steps per user task in the user involvement point (see Figure 11.19).

For UT 1.1 Select pizza, the target involvement step number means that a user interface concept (here also called user involvement concept or involvement concept) should allow a user to select a

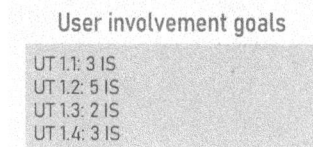

User involvement goals

UT 1.1: 3 IS
UT 1.2: 5 IS
UT 1.3: 2 IS
UT 1.4: 3 IS

Figure 11.19: UIP 1: Target involvement steps

pizza in three steps or less. If a user interface concept does not achieve that target number, the concept won't be accepted.

Target involvement time   The next step is to determine the *target involvement time* per user task, abbreviated *TAT*. We have already defined the target involvement time, when we defined the workflow (to be) (see Figure 9.4). We now map the defined target involvement time per workflow (to be) responsibility to the user tasks.

If a responsibility in the workflow (to be) is mapped to several user tasks, the assigned involvement time per responsibility needs to be distributed to the user tasks.

Based on the workflow (to be), we can map the EVOT numbers to the four user tasks. For each user task, we'll get a target involvement time (TAT) as follows:

User involvement goals

UT 1.1: 3 IS, 30 sec
UT 1.2: 5 IS, 30 sec
UT 1.3: 2 IS, 30 sec
UT 1.4: 3 IS, 30 sec

▶ UT.1 Select pizza: 30 sec.
▶ UT.2 Order pizza: 30 sec.
▶ UT.3 Monitor status: 30 sec.
▶ UT.4 Tip driver: 30 sec.

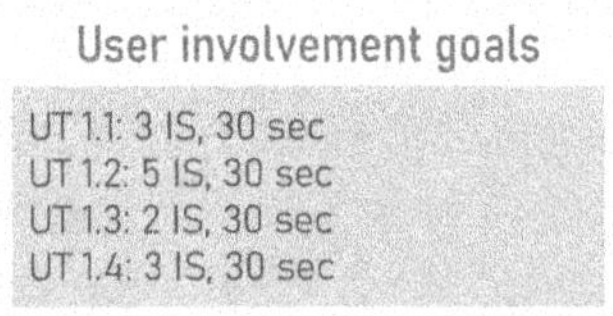

Figure 11.20: UIP 1: Target involvement time

The target involvement time is assigned to each user task (see Figure 11.20).

The target involvement times are used as time-on-task targets for summative usability tests. If the mean time-on-task number per user task is higher than the target involvement time number, the concept won't be accepted.

UIP pattern

From an experience architecture perspective, it is useful to classify the user involvement points based on their different user involvement types. Such types are called here *user involvement pattern*. A user involvement pattern is defined here as an "abstraction of a reusable form of user involvement." The user involvement patterns are closer to architecture patterns [178, 179] than to user interface design patterns [180, 181]. user involvement pattern

The patterns are used to guide the design work and provide a broader concept without over-constraining design decisions. They also help to communicate a rather complex user involvement concept to technical experts and experience design professionals.

The user involvement patterns are separated into three groups: manual, semi-manual, and automated. Each group shows a different pattern and indicates for that pattern how to optimize the user involvement metrics to achieve high efficiency.

Manual user involvement patterns   The manual user involvement pattern assumes that the user is interacting with the application at all times. If the user walks away from the application, the system won't continue producing an outcome.

There are four manual user patterns that can be identified with two parameters:

- ▶ Who initiates the user interaction? (user or system)
- ▶ Does the application provide a status update? (yes or no)

The four manual user interaction patterns are displayed in Figure 11.22.

In MA.1, the user initiates the user interaction and performs it at every step.

In MA.2, the user initiates the user interaction and performs it at every step. In addition, the system monitors progress and captures the status. The user can access the status and monitor the progress.

In MA.3, the system initiates the user interaction. Afterward, the user takes over and performs it at every step.

MA.4 is a combination of MA.2 and MA.3. The system initiates the user interaction. Afterward, the user takes over. While the user interacts with the application, the system monitors the progress. The user can access the status and monitor the progress.

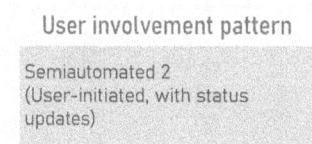

User involvement pattern

Semiautomated 2
(User-initiated, with status updates)

Figure 11.21: UIP 1: User involvement pattern

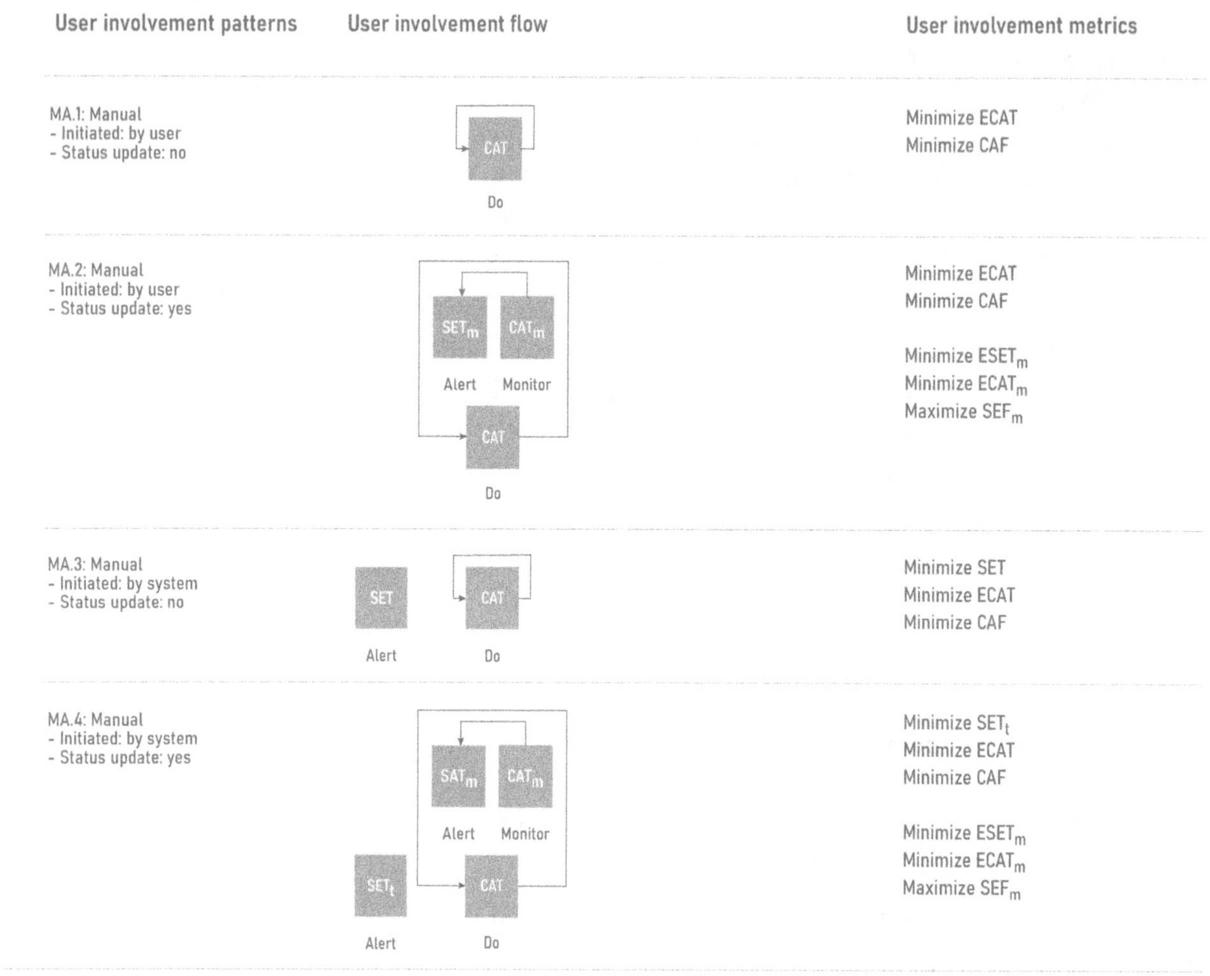

User involvement patterns	User involvement flow	User involvement metrics
MA.1: Manual - Initiated: by user - Status update: no	CAT Do	Minimize ECAT Minimize CAF
MA.2: Manual - Initiated: by user - Status update: yes	SET_m CAT_m Alert Monitor CAT Do	Minimize ECAT Minimize CAF Minimize $ESET_m$ Minimize $ECAT_m$ Maximize SEF_m
MA.3: Manual - Initiated: by system - Status update: no	SET CAT Alert Do	Minimize SET Minimize ECAT Minimize CAF
MA.4: Manual - Initiated: by system - Status update: yes	SAT_m CAT_m Alert Monitor SET_t CAT Alert Do	Minimize SET_t Minimize ECAT Minimize CAF Minimize $ESET_m$ Minimize $ECAT_m$ Maximize SEF_m

Figure 11.22: Manual user involvement patterns

Semiautomated user involvement patterns   There are four semi-automated user involvement patterns (see Figure 11.23) that can be identified with two parameters:

▶ Who initiates the user interaction? (user or system)
▶ Does the application provide a status update? (yes or no)

For SA.1, the user initiates the user involvement. The user interacts with the application for a preparation step. After the user has completed the preparation, the system takes over and produces an outcome of value according to the user's preparation task. The system may alert the user and request a user intervention. After the user has provided a response, the system goes back to production mode. After the system has finished its part of the production, the user takes over and completes it.

SA.2 builds on SA.1. In addition to the steps in SA.1, the system tracks the progress and provides progress information to the user.

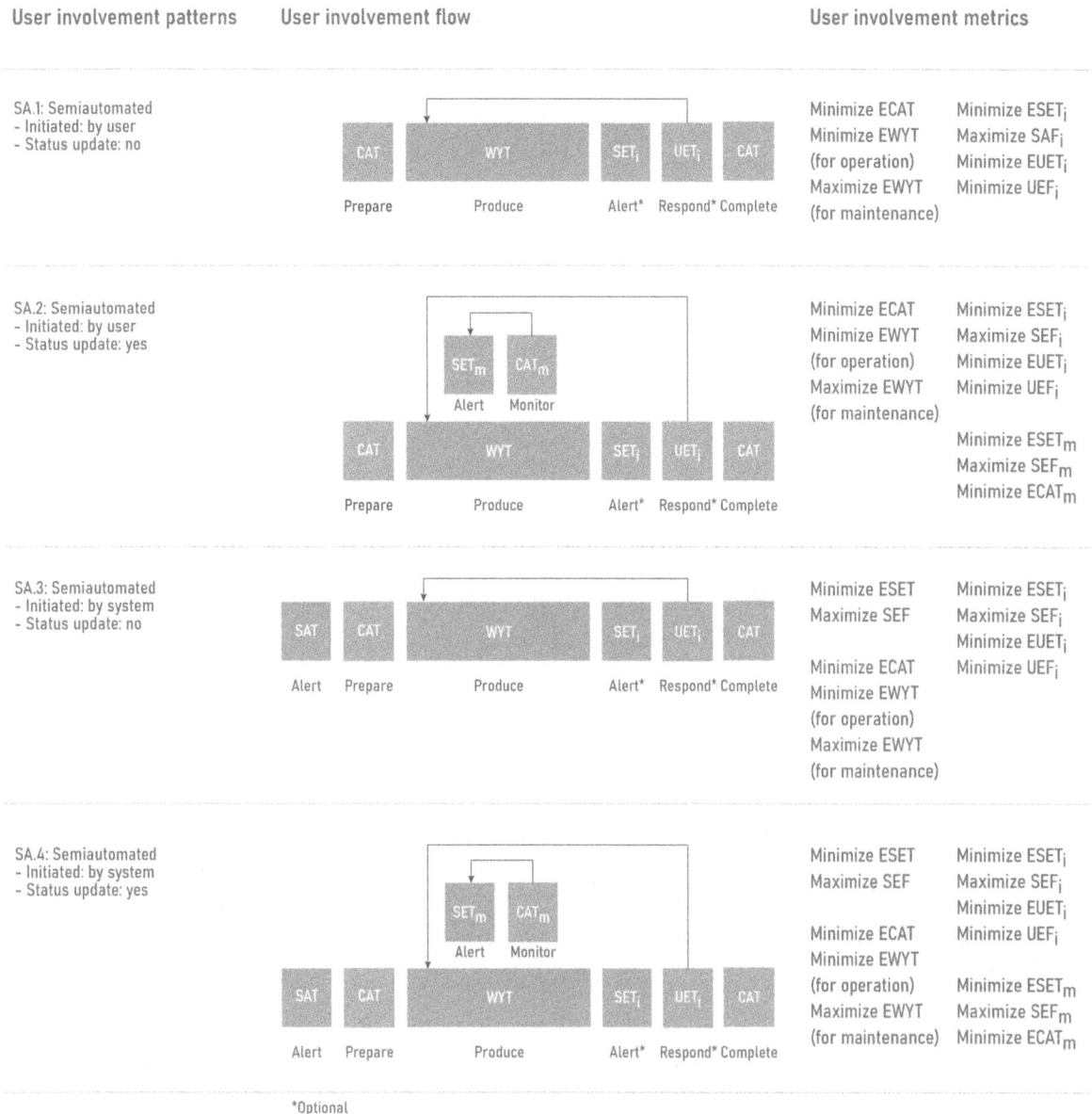

Figure 11.23: Semiautomated user involvement patterns

The user can monitor the progress.

SA.3 builds on SA.1. In this case, the system has initiated the process and alerts the user. The user takes over and performs a preparation. Afterward, the application behaves as in SA.1.

SA.4 is a combination of SA.2 and SA.3. The system initiates the user involvement. Afterward, the user takes over. The system tracks the progress and provides progress information to the user. The user can monitor the progress.

Figure 11.23 shows which user involvement metrics should be optimized for efficiency..

Automated user involvement patterns There are also four automated user involvement patterns (see Figure 11.24) that can be identified with two parameters:

▶ Does the application provide a status update? (yes or no)
▶ Does the application terminate the process? (yes or no)

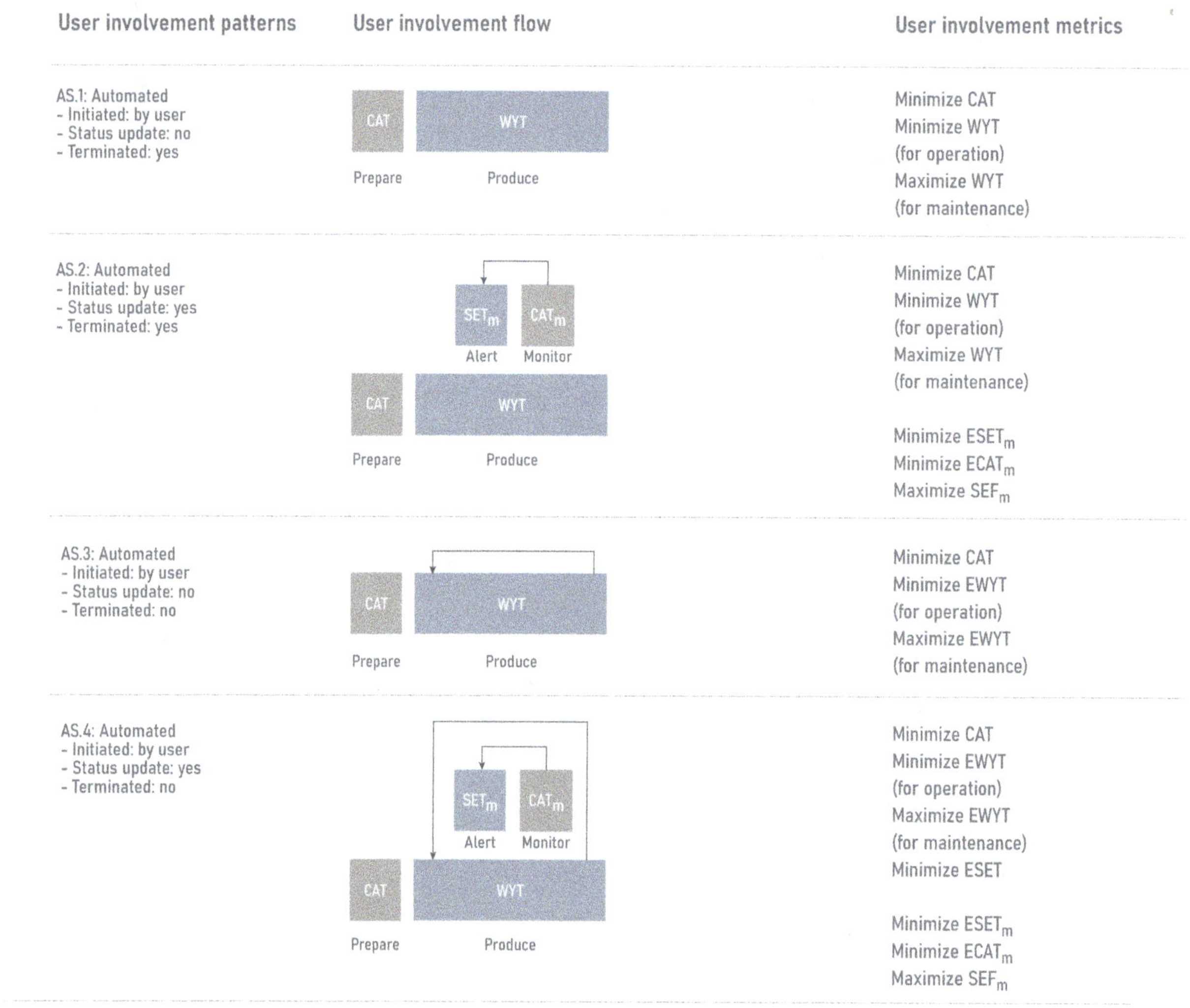

User involvement patterns	User involvement flow	User involvement metrics
AS.1: Automated - Initiated: by user - Status update: no - Terminated: yes	CAT WYT Prepare Produce	Minimize CAT Minimize WYT (for operation) Maximize WYT (for maintenance)
AS.2: Automated - Initiated: by user - Status update: yes - Terminated: yes	SET_m CAT_m Alert Monitor CAT WYT Prepare Produce	Minimize CAT Minimize WYT (for operation) Maximize WYT (for maintenance) Minimize $ESET_m$ Minimize $ECAT_m$ Maximize SEF_m
AS.3: Automated - Initiated: by user - Status update: no - Terminated: no	CAT WYT Prepare Produce	Minimize CAT Minimize EWYT (for operation) Maximize EWYT (for maintenance)
AS.4: Automated - Initiated: by user - Status update: yes - Terminated: no	SET_m CAT_m Alert Monitor CAT WYT Prepare Produce	Minimize CAT Minimize EWYT (for operation) Maximize EWYT (for maintenance) Minimize ESET Minimize $ESET_m$ Minimize $ECAT_m$ Maximize SEF_m

Figure 11.24: Automated user involvement patterns

In AS.1, the user initiates the user involvement. The user interacts with the application for a preparation step. After the user has completed the preparation, the system takes over. It starts producing an outcome of value according to the user preparation information. After the system has completed the production, it stops automatically.

AS.2 builds on SA.1. In addition to the steps in SA.1, the system tracks the progress and provides progress information to the user. The user can monitor the progress. The progress information has no influence on the production.

AS.3 builds on SA.1. In this case, the system does not stop the production. It continues to produce an outcome of value.

AS.4 is a combination of SA.2 and SA.3. The system continues producing an outcome of value. The user is able to monitor the progress. Monitoring of the progress has no influence on the production.

Figure 11.24 shows which user involvement metrics should be optimized for efficiency.

World of Pizza   After the user has ordered the pizza, it is delivered without user involvement. The user has to receive the pizza and may tip the driver. Therefore, the assigned user involvement pattern is SA.2 for UIP 1.1 and for UIP 1.2.

The baker and the driver are continuously involved in moving the activity forward (therefore they have manual user interaction). Their work is triggered by a system alert. They do not need to monitor the status of their own work. Therefore, the user involvement pattern MA.3 is assigned to them.

The manager is not actively involved in the operation; it moves forward regardless. However, the operation is not in automation mode (therefore, there is semiautomated user involvement). The manager may monitor the operation from time to time and receives alerts if something does not work as expected. Therefore, the manager's involvement type is SA.4.

Dependencies from UIPs / TIP

Another element of the user involvement point is its dependencies to other UIPs and the technical involvement point (TIP). The dependencies only describe content coming from other UIPs and the TIP into the UIP under definition.

The specified user involvement system provides the input for defining dependencies for the UIP under design. The following scenario views should be checked for applicable dependencies for UIP 1:

- ► Object state flows
- ► Monitor object flows
- ► Alert flows
- ► Communication flows

Dependencies from UIPs/TIPs

- UIP 2 (Manager): Order status: text message, phone call, notification; Communication: text message, phone call.
- UIP 3 (Baker): Order status: text message, notification.
- UIP 4 (Driver): Order status: notification; Driver's location: notification; Communication: text message, phone call.
- TIP: Delay alert: notification, text message, phone call.

Figure 11.25: UIP 1: Dependent user involvement points and technical involvement point

Reuse and planning

Reuse

After defining and specifying all UIPs, we have a list of user tasks per UIP. It is possible that similar user tasks are covered in different UIPs. This means there are opportunities for reuse of design artifacts.

It is therefore beneficial to have an overview of the mapping of user tasks to the UIPs, for the following reasons:

► Ability to reuse design artifacts
► Input for planning

There are many ways to structure user tasks. One useful approach is by object view and object transition. An object view provides access to objects—pizzas, orders, etc. Transactions enable users to create or modify objects. For example, "add pizza to shopping cart," "remove pizza from shopping cart," etc.

The technique of mapping the identified user tasks to the user involvement points is applied to the World of Pizza example (see Table 11.1 on the next page). The table is incomplete; however, it shows how the mapping works and its benefits.

We can see from the table that reuse is limited. Only order transactions seem to be used by both patrons and managers.

Table 11.1: Mapping of user tasks to UIPs for WoP; x: applicable

Object	User task	UIP 1 (Patron)	UIP 2 (Manager)	UIP 3 (Baker)	UIP 4 (Driver)
Pizza - views					
	View pizza list	x			
	Sort pizza list	x			
	Filter pizza list	x			
	View single pizza	x			
Pizza - transactions					
	Add pizza to shopping cart	x			
	Remove pizza from shopping cart	x			
	Mark pizza as favorite	x			
Order - views					
	View pizza order summary	x			
	View pizza order confirmation	x			
	View tip order summary	x			
	View tip order confirmation	x			
	View new order list		x	x	
	View all order list		x	x	
	Filter order list		x	x	
	View order details		x	x	
Order - transactions					
	Submit order	x	x		
	Cancel order	x	x		
	Change order status		x		
	Schedule order	x			
	Submit tip	x			
Delivery ticket - views					
	View ticket list		x		x
	Sort ticket list		x		x
	Filter ticket list		x		x
	View single ticket		x		x
Delivery ticket - transactions					
	Accept ticket				x
	Cancel accepted ticket		x		x
	Close ticket		x		x

Release planning

We can reuse the mapping of user tasks to user involvement points for release planning purposes. Table 11.2 on the facing page shows the mapping of user tasks to releases. In our case, we planned only to release R1. We intend to implement UIP 1 first. Therefore, user tasks not supporting UIP 1 haven't been selected. Some of the UIP 1 user tasks are not selected for release R1 because they are considered "nice to have" but not crucial (e.g., "mark pizza as favorite" and "schedule order").

The table could have mapped all user tasks to a future release, such as R2, R3, etc.

Table 11.2: Release planning, based on user tasks for WoP; x: applicable

Object	User task	UIP 1 (Patron)	UIP 2 (Manager)	UIP 3 (Baker)	UIP 4 (Driver)	Release
Pizzas - views						
	View pizza list	x				R1
	Sort pizza list	x				R1
	Filter pizza list	x				R1
	View single pizza	x				R1
Pizzas - transactions						
	Add pizza to shopping cart	x				R1
	Remove pizza from shopping cart	x				R1
	Mark pizza as favorite	x				
Order - views						
	View pizza order summary	x				R1
	View pizza order confirmation	x				R1
	View tip order summary	x				R1
	View tip order confirmation	x				R1
	View new order list		x	x		
	View all order list		x	x		
	Filter order list		x	x		
	View order details		x	x		
Order - transactions						
	Submit order	x	x			R1
	Cancel order	x	x			R1
	Change order status		x			
	Schedule order	x				
	Submit tip	x				R1
Delivery tickets - views						
	View ticket list		x		x	
	Sort ticket list		x		x	
	Filter ticket list		x		x	
	View single ticket		x		x	
Delivery tickets - transactions						
	Accept ticket				x	
	Cancel accepted ticket		x		x	
	Close ticket		x		x	

User involvement system as a campus metaphor

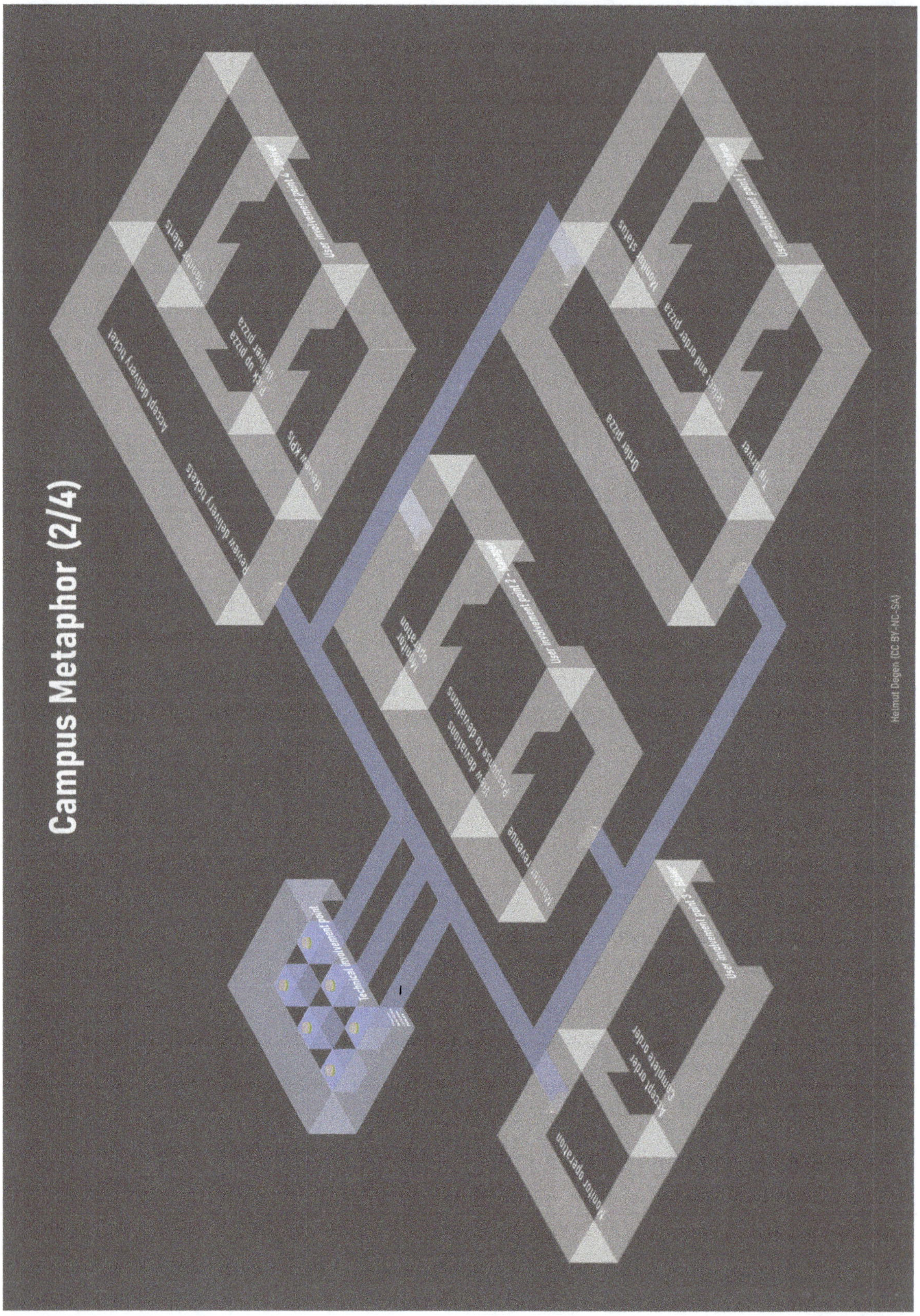

Figure 11.26: UIPs specified

Summary

User involvement points

> ▶ Move on to <u>Involvement Goals</u>
> ◀ Go back to <u>User Involvement System</u>

UIP name	User role(s)
UIP 1 Order, monitor, and receive pizza	Patron

Context(s) of use	User's goal
In office, at home, on the road	Eat healthy, tasty, and affordable pizza

Pre-condition	Post-condition
Need for food	Delivered pizza; driver tip paid (optional)

User tasks (interaction device(s), modality)

UT 1.1* Select pizza; phone or tablet – GUI, touch.
UT 1.2 Order pizza; phone or tablet – GUI, touch.
UT 1.3 Monitor status; phone or tablet – GUI, touch; smart speaker – voice.
UT 1.4 Tip driver; phone or tablet – GUI, touch.

*Primary user task

User involvement goals	User involvement pattern
UT 1.1: 3 IS, 30 sec UT 1.2: 5 IS, 30 sec UT 1.3: 2 IS, 30 sec UT 1.4: 3 IS, 30 sec	Semiautomated 2 (User-initiated, with status updates)

Dependencies from UIPs/TIPs

UIP 2 (Manager): Order status: text message, phone call, notification; Communication: text message, phone call.
UIP 3 (Baker): Order status: text message, notification.
UIP 4 (Driver): Order status: notification; Driver's location: notification; Communication: text message, phone call.
TIP: Delay alert: notification, text message, phone call.

Lessons learned

User involvement points   A user involvement point (UIP) is a constituting element of a user involvement system. It is created by grouping responsibilities of the workflow (to be). User involvement points are often considered one design work package, realized in one project.

Pre-conditions and post-conditions   Pre-conditions and post-conditions bound a user involvement point. Pre-conditions specify conditions that are true when the UIP is being performed by the assigned user roles. The post-condition specifies conditions that are true after the user tasks of the UIP have been successfully executed.

User tasks   A key element of a user involvement point are the user tasks. They are derived from the responsibilities on the user involvement map. The number of user tasks derived from the responsibilities depends on the tracking of involvement goals, how many devices or modalities are used, and scope clarifications.

Dependencies on other UIPs and the TIP   Another important element of the user involvement point is the dependencies from other UIPs and the TIP. They are defined and specified in the user involvement system and carried over, relevant for the UIP under specification.

User involvement goals   The user involvement goals specify target numbers for steps and time. To determine the number of target involvement steps, the user steps are identified per user task and counted. To determine the target user involvement time, the user involvement time from the workflow (to be) is reused and mapped to each user task.

User involvement pattern   A user involvement pattern is an abstraction of a reusable form of user involvement. The patterns are organized into three groups: manual, semiautomated, and automated. Per group, different user involvement patterns are defined and associated with user involvement metrics to achieve high efficiency. The purpose of the user involvement patterns is to simplify user involvement complexity and the communication with technical professionals and experience professionals.

Reuse and planning   Mapping of user tasks to all user involvement points reveals which user tasks can be reused for different UIPs. Mapping of user tasks to releases enables one to focus on the most critical ones first.

Tips and tricks

The user involvement points consolidate the results of the user involvement system. Not every UIP needs to be defined immediately. For instance, if the UIP for the patron should be implemented first, it can be selected, defined, and specified, based on the UIS and with additional user tasks and goals. If the UIP for the baker will be implemented later, it does not have to be defined right now.

The user involvement points are the results of the experience architecture phase, which are inputs for the experience design phase (part 3 of this book). Experience design professionals should therefore be involved in the definition and specification of the user involvement points.

Exercise 2.3

Goal   Define and specify at least three UIPs, and map the user tasks to UIPs and releases for your selected example.

Material   UIP template, workflow (to be), user involvement map, different views of the user involvement system, user involvement patterns

Completion criteria:

- ▶ At least three UIPs are completely defined and specified and documented.
- ▶ For each UIP, the user task pattern for the identified user tasks is created.
- ▶ A release map for user tasks and UIPs is defined and documented.

Involvement Goals | 12

一寸光阴一寸金，寸金难买寸光阴
*(An inch of time is an inch of gold,
but you can't buy that inch of time with an inch of gold)*
Chinese proverb

Purpose

In the previous two chapters, we identified expectations and some goals for the user involvement system and for user involvement points. In this chapter, we will reduce the number of user involvement steps and consolidate all other involvement goals.

Let's briefly define what we mean by "involvement goal."

> **Definition 14** (Involvement goal) *A desired property of a user involvement concept.*

involvement goal

We distinguish between different types of involvement goals:

▶ Quantitative user involvement goals (derived from the workflow (to be) and from the UIP user involvement goals)
▶ Qualitative user involvement goals (derived from insights documented in the user role profile and the user journey maps)
▶ Vendor goals (from the business model; see Section 3 on page 61)

All the goals will be used to articulate expectations for the involvement system and individual applications of that system. The goals help us to assess how good the involvement concepts of such applications are, compared to the articulated goals. They help to identify weaknesses and to select an explored and refined user involvement concept systematically.

The involvement goals should be articulated from the perspective of the application domain. They should express activities, tasks, or steps. They should not contain design elements. The involvement goals can be thought of as a question, and the proposed design can be thought of as an answer to that question. An involvement goal that contains design elements is a self-referential question that already contains the answer. Such goals are useless and should be avoided.

All the different types of involvement goals will be consolidated into an involvement goal matrix. So let's get started ...

Quantitative involvement goals

Reduce user involvement steps

In the last chapter, we identified the primary user task and the user involvement goals for the UIP. In this step, we will attempt to systematically reduce the number of involvement steps per user task. This number will become an acceptance criterion for the involvement concept.

A bit more background information is needed to understand how the reduction works. I'd like to show you a map of one of New York City's boroughs: Manhattan (see Figure 12.1). The section of interest is the street called Broadway that cuts diagonally through the grid and is marked in red. Let's assume we are at point 1 and we want to go to point 3.

Point 1 is at the corner of West 17th Street and Union Square. Point 2 is at the corner of West 34th Street and 7th Avenue, and point 3 is at the corner of West 44th Street and 7th Avenue, also known as Times Square. There are several routes from point 1 to point 3 (Times Square). One is to go from point 1 to point 2 (labeled "a" in Figure 12.1) and then walk up 7th Avenue to West 44th Street (labeled "b" in Figure 12.1). The shortest way is to take Broadway and go straight from point 1 to point 3 (labeled "c" in Figure 12.1).

Figure 12.1: Manhattan Map from 1879, with streetcar lines; author added the blue lines, the blue circles with "1" and "2" and the letters "a," "b," and "c" on the map; source: Wikimedia; authors: SPUI and Paul Sinnett; license: public domain

Why is Broadway the shortest way to get from point 1 to point 3? Pythagoras discovered the reason and articulated a theorem. Pythagoras of Samos (about 570–490 BC) was an Ionian Greek philosopher. He is known for many things, but one of them is his famous theorem that applies to right-angled triangles: $a^2 + b^2 = c^2$. It means that the sum of the areas of the two squares on the legs (a and b) equals the area of the square on the hypotenuse (c) (see Figure 12.3). It also means that the hypotenuse, c, is always shorter than a + b. The hypotenuse is a shortcut.

Why is Broadway the shortest way to get from point 1 to point 3? Because, as our example shows, it is a hypotenuse and therefore

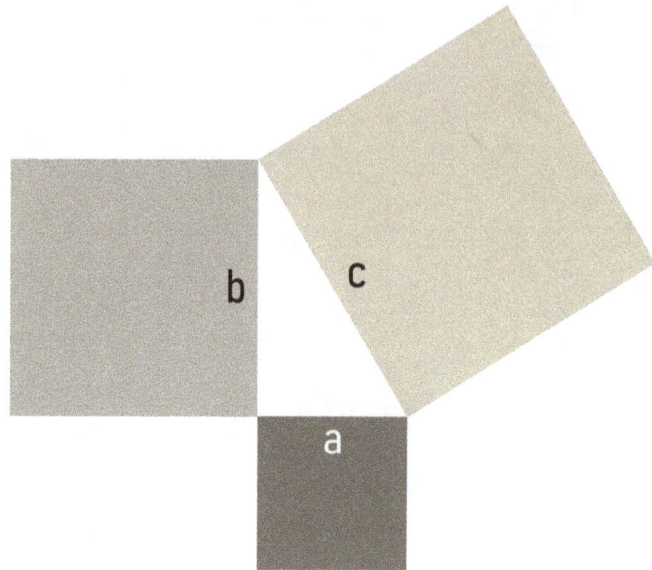

Figure 12.3: Right-angled triangle

Figure 12.2: Bust of Pythagoras; location: Musei Capitolini, Roma; source: Wikimedia; author: Galilea; license: public domain

a shortcut. Wouldn't it be nice if we could find shortcuts for user involvement that would increase efficiency?

User involvement hypotenuse

There is, unfortunately, no right-angled triangle in user involvement. So Pythagoras's theorem does not strictly apply here. However, we can adapt the idea by using a half circle instead. We call this half circle a *user involvement arc*.

Definition 15 (User involvement arc) *Sequence of states representing the beginning and end of potential user involvement.*

The first state of an arc is called the "initial state" and the last state is called the "intended state." A user involvement arc has $n + 1$ states, from state 0 (the initial state) to state n (the intended state). To find a shortcut, the idea is to transfer the initial state from state 0 to another state that moves the starting point of user involvement closer to the intended state. This transfer is realized with a *user involvement hypotenuse* and is comparable to the hypotenuse of a right-angled triangle.

Definition 16 (Involvement hypotenuse) *Transfer of the initial state on the user involvement arc from state 0 to another state.*

Figure 12.4 shows how a user involvement hypotenuse can be mapped to a user involvement arc.

User involvement arc and hypotenuse

**State transitions
without user involvement hypotenuse**

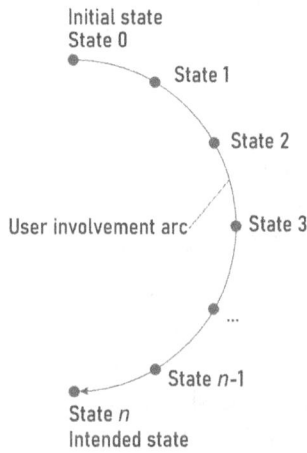

**Transferred initial state
with user involvement hypotenuse**

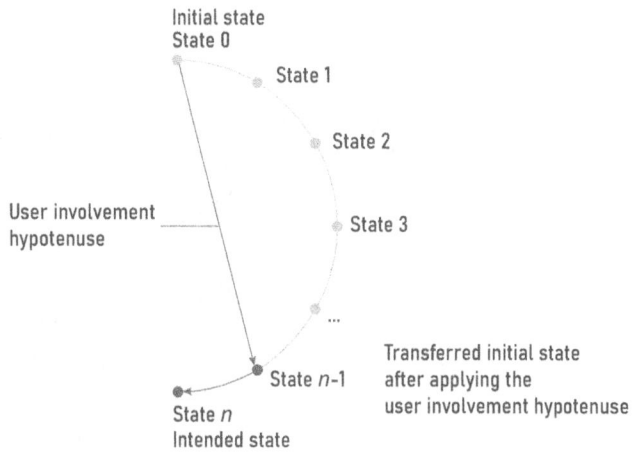

Initial state
State 0
State 1
State 2
User involvement arc
State 3
...
State n-1
State n
Intended state

n user involvement steps needed
to achieve the intended state from the initial state

Initial state
State 0
State 1
State 2
User involvement hypotenuse
State 3
...
Transferred initial state after applying the user involvement hypotenuse
State n-1
State n
Intended state

One user involvement step needed
to achieve the intended state from the new initial state

Figure 12.4: User involvement arc with user involvement hypotenuse

Let's apply the user involvement arc and hypotenuse to the WoP example. Different states for the user task "select and order pizza" are displayed in Figure 12.5

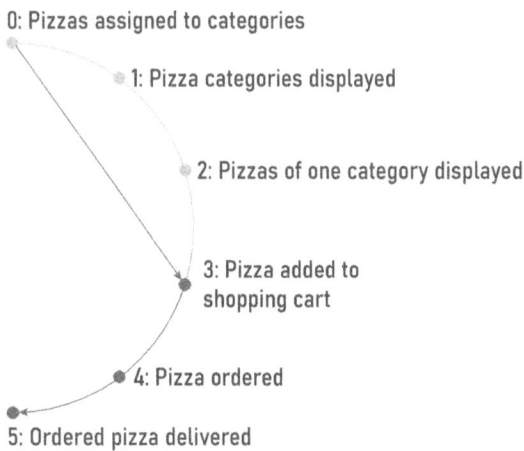

0: Pizzas assigned to categories
1: Pizza categories displayed
2: Pizzas of one category displayed
3: Pizza added to shopping cart
4: Pizza ordered
5: Ordered pizza delivered

Figure 12.5: User involvement arc and the involvement hypotenuse for WoP

An application may present an initial state where pizza categories are displayed (initial state, state 0). The menu shows categories (e.g., meat pizzas, vegetarian pizzas, thin-crust pizzas) without showing the individual pizza products in each category. From here, the user needs to select one of the pizza categories, and the system displays the pizzas assigned to the selected category (taking the user to state 1). From there, the user selects one of the pizzas, which is displayed with its details (state 2). Next, the user adds the pizza to the shopping cart (advancing to state 3). From the shopping cart, the user submits the order (state 4). Finally, the restaurant delivers the ordered pizza to the delivery address (state 5, the intended state).

Each transition to a new state requires a user involvement step. To save the user some steps and to make user involvement more efficient, we can apply the user involvement hypotenuse (see the arrow from state 0 to state 3 in Figure 12.5). Instead of using state 0 (pizzas assigned to categories) as the initial application state, the user involvement hypotenuse changes the initial state to state 3 (pizza added to shopping cart). This means that the application's initial state is a pizza that is already in the shopping cart, or at least in a state from where the user can directly order a pizza in one step. Initially this may not sound realistic, but because many people order the same pizza again and again, this hypothetical case can be seriously considered. If done this way, the user does not have to perform five involvement steps, but only two out of five, which is an efficiency improvement of 60 percent.

The user involvement hypotenuse is a mindset by which to systematically reduce user involvement steps per user task, in order to increase user efficiency. To do this, we apply the GAIS method.

GAIS

Technique

The involvement hypotenuse is a mindset or thinking tool that can help us determine where user involvement should start for a certain user task. Rather than adopting the first option that comes to mind, we should think about it a bit longer and more systematically. And we should keep in mind that where the user journey begins determines the duration of the process and how much of the user's precious time we are taking up by requiring them to stay with the application.

Besides the user involvement hypotenuse's role as a mindset, it can be used in a practical way to help us systematically reduce user involvement steps. The technique presented here is called GAIS [182]. GAIS stands for "Goals, Assumptions, Interaction Steps" and is a cognitive task analysis technique that allows the experience professional to systematically reduce involvement steps for users. It exploits the idea of the involvement hypotenuse.

GAIS was developed and named before the efficiency focus also included user intervention. This is why it uses the word "interaction." However, it is also applicable to intervention. If I was naming it today, I would call it "Goals, Assumptions, Involvement Steps," with involvement including interaction and intervention.

The elements of the GAIS technique are shown in Figure 12.6.

Figure 12.6: Elements of the GAIS technique

The elements are:

▶ Goal (intended state)
▶ Assumptions (initial state)
▶ Involvement steps (to transition from the assumptions to the goal)
▶ Involvement step counter that displays the actual user involvement step per GAIS scenario; the actual involvement steps of the selected GAIS scenario become the involvement steps target

GAIS is applied to each user task or to a sequence of user tasks. We recommend applying GAIS in the following order per user task:

1. Identify the goal (look at the goal [intended state] from the user journey map (to be)).
2. Identify the assumptions (initial state).

3. Identify involvement steps to transition from the assumptions to the goal; start with the scenario that requires the greatest number of involvement steps.
4. Explore scenarios by systematically removing involvement steps to increase the user's efficiency.
5. Select the GAIS scenario with the lowest number of involvement steps that is still acceptable for users.

If the user involvement steps have been identified for the UIP tasks, the steps used in that exercise can be reused for GAIS. The intended state is comparable to the post-condition, and the assumptions are comparable to the pre-conditions.

Each alternative is called a "GAIS scenario." Each GAIS scenario is annotated with several user involvement steps (see Figure 12.7).

GAIS provides a systematic approach for what is also known as "task allocation" or "function allocation" [60, 63, 183–187]. Function or task allocation means deciding which functions or tasks are performed by a human and which are performed by a machine/system with the intent "to maximise operational effectiveness; and to reduce potentially the number of operators required" [187, p. 1027].

Every time an involvement step is removed, the function of that step is moved to the assumption. For instance, if one involvement step covers the entering of payment information, the assumption makes a note that payment information is already known and available for an order, so a user does not have to enter it manually.

The GAIS involvement step counter is used as a "target involvement steps" (TAS) measure.

We can now compare how many involvement steps are required for a user to complete a task with the selected option. We call this the "actual involvement steps" (AAS). There is also some language that describes the relationship between the TAS and the AAS:

▶ If AAS > TAS: The involvement concept is *GAIS inefficient*, also called *inefficient*.
▶ If AAS = TAS: The involvement concept is *GAIS efficient*, also called *efficient*.
▶ If AAS < TAS: The involvement concept is *GAIS super-efficient*, also called *super-efficient*.

GAIS applied to a sequence of initial user involvement steps

Figure 12.7: Systematic reduction of user involvement steps with GAIS

World of Pizza

Here the GAIS technique is systematically applied to the user task "select and order pizza." The results are shown in Figure 12.8.

GAIS scenario 5 is selected. It gives users control over orders and provides a useful starting point. The quantitative involvement step target is derived from the chosen GAIS scenario. With GAIS, the number of involvement steps could be reduced from eight (GAIS scenario 1) to three (GAIS scenario 5).

From GAIS scenario 5, we can derive the following involvement step targets for the individual user tasks for UIP 1:

- ▶ UT 1.1 Select pizza: 0 involvement steps
- ▶ UT 1.2 Order pizza: 1 involvement step
- ▶ UT 1.3 Monitor pizza: 1 involvement step
- ▶ UT 1.4 Tip driver: 1 involvement step

Next, the involvement steps must be added to the involvement goal matrix.

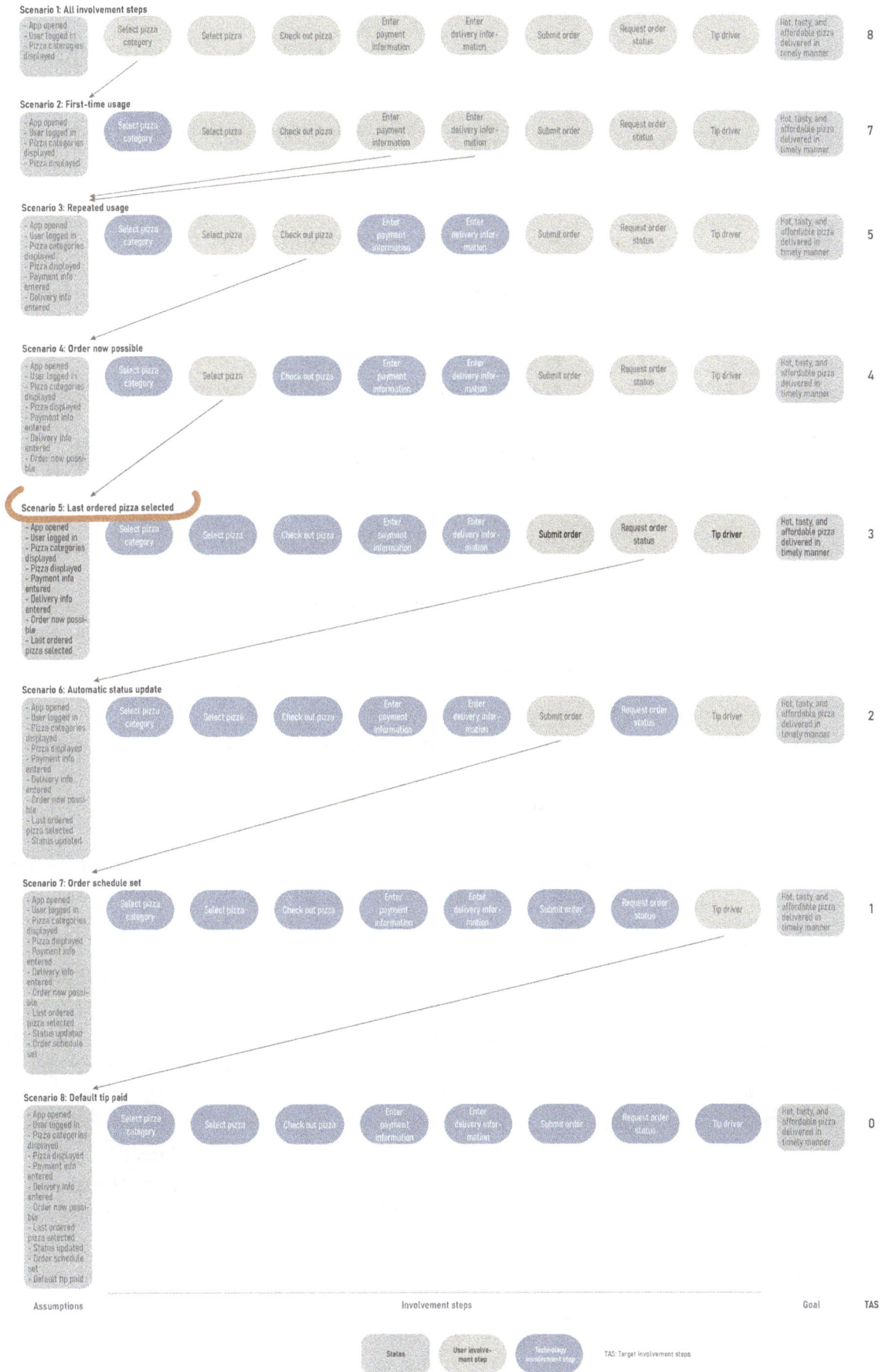

Figure 12.8: GAIS scenarios for UIP 1 "Order, monitor, and receive pizza"

Summary of quantitative involvement goals

The target involvement steps are derived from the GAIS exploration and the selected GAIS scenario.

The user involvement time is reused from the UIP (see Section 1 on page 298). The quantitative goals are as follows:

► QnG 1 Select pizza: 0 involvement steps
► QnG 2 Order pizza: 1 involvement step
► QnG 3 Monitor status: 1 involvement step
► QnG 4 Tip driver: 1 involvement step
► QnG 5 Select pizza: 30 seconds (EVOT)
► QnG 6 Order pizza: 30 seconds (EVOT)
► QnG 7 Monitor status: 30 seconds (EVOT)
► QnG 8 Tip driver: 30 seconds (EVOT)
► QnG 9 Select, order, and receive pizza: 33 minutes (EVOT)

Qualitative involvement goals

Qualitative user involvement goals are derived from all sources that provide qualitative insights. These are, potentially, the user role profiles, the workflows, and the user journey maps.

Derive involvement goals from user journey map (as is)

Responsibility R 2.1 Place order (as is)

We take the pain points and wishes (see figures in the margin) from the user journey map (as is) R 2.1 Place order and derive generalized involvement goals from them.

Pain points

A 2.1.1 Select pizza
- P 2.1.1.1 Finding vegetarian options is not easy (90%)
- P 2.1.1.2 Not all menus show the calories per pizza (70%)
- P 2.1.1.3 Pictures are missing (90%)

A 2.1.2 Order pizza
- P 2.1.2.1 The restaurant has difficulty understanding me (90%)

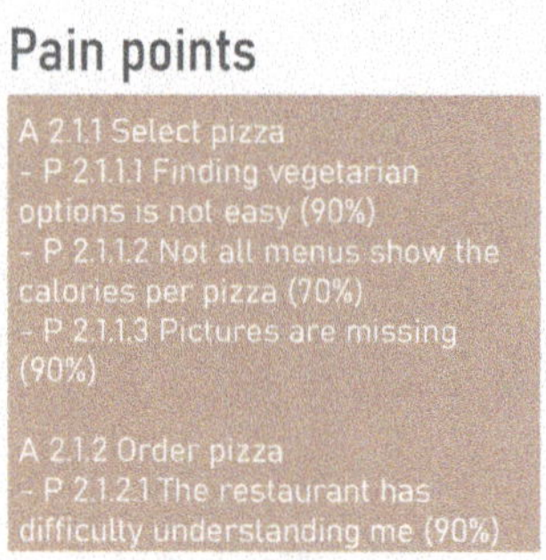

Figure 12.9: Patron - Responsibility; Place order - Pain points

► *P 2.1.1.1 Finding vegetarian options is not easy (90%).* This pain point articulates that it's hard to find a certain type of pizza. We can abstract this to finding pizzas with certain attributes and include diet preferences as attributes. The derived involvement goal is *QIG 1 Enable finding pizzas by attribute (incl. diets).*
► *P 2.1.1.2 Not all menus show the calories per pizza (70%).* This pain point articulates a concern about calories. The underlying intent is most likely health motivated, so we can abstract this a bit more to "calories and ingredients." In a subsequent pain point, a missing picture is mentioned. So we combine the two pain points into one involvement goal. The derived involvement goal is *QIG 2 Display pizza attributes (incl. calories, ingredients, image).*

▶ *P 2.1.1.3 Pictures are missing (90%)*. This is covered by involvement goal QlG 2.

▶ *P 2.1.2.1 The restaurant has difficulty understanding me (90%)*. The underlying need is to avoid voice communication. The WoP project addresses this need by developing an app. Therefore, it won't be captured as a new qualitative involvement goal.

▶ *W 2.1.1.1 Show pictures*. The underlying need is to see how the pizza looks. In some cases, a user recognizes a pizza not by the name but by the picture. QlG 2 already addresses this wish.

▶ *W 2.1.1.2 Show calories*. The underlying need is health. A pizza might be selected because of the number of calories it contains. QlG 2 also addresses this wish.

▶ *W 2.1.1.3 Show list of pizzas for certain diets*. This wish is a generalization of pain point 1.1 and is covered by involvement goal QlG 1.

▶ *W 2.1.2.1 Send order via app or text message*. This goal reflects the idea of the WoP application under design. Because our WoP project addresses it already, it won't be captured as a new qualitative involvement goal.

New derived qualitative involvement goals:

▶ QlG 1 Enable finding pizzas by attribute (incl. diets)
▶ QlG 2 Display pizza attributes (incl. calories, ingredients, image)

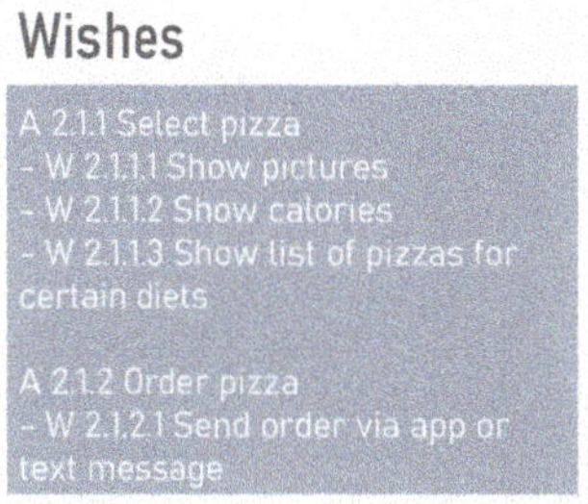

Figure 12.10: Patron - Responsibility; Place order - Wishes

Derive involvement goals from user role profile patron

We repeat the exercise by analyzing the pain points and wishes from the user role profile for the user role patron.

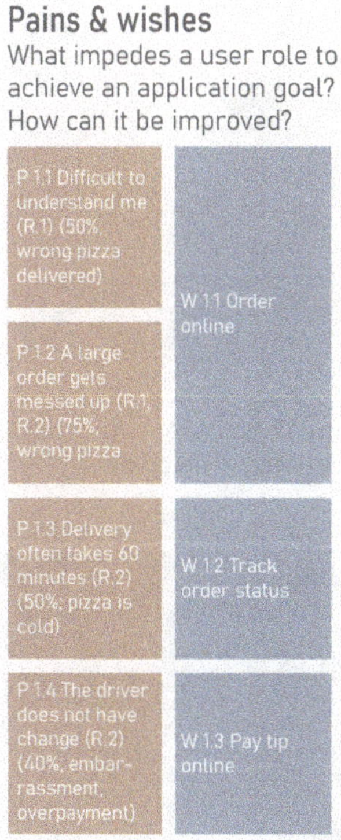

▶ *P 1.1 Difficult to understand me (50%; wrong pizza delivered)*. The underlying need is to avoid voice communication. The WoP project addresses this need by developing an app. Therefore, it won't be captured as a new qualitative involvement goal.

▶ *P 1.2 A large order gets messed up (75%; wrong pizza)*. The underlying need is caused by confusing when taking an order. This pain point articulates that what has been delivered is not what has been ordered. We need to start addressing this pain point in the restaurant. The person packaging the pizza needs to be able to check that the pizza in the box is what has been ordered. We can derive the following involvement goal: *QlG 3 Enable checking of delivered pizza vs ordered pizza*.

▶ *P 1.3 Delivery often takes 60 minutes (50%; pizza is cold)*. The underlying need is caused by cumbersome processes. The

Figure 12.11: Household manager - pain points

perception of how fast time passes by is subjective. To address the issue of perceiving waiting time as too long, we want to allow the user to monitor and track the delivery. The derived involvement goal is *QlG 4 Enable track order and delivery.*

▶ *P 1.4 The driver does not have change (40%; embarrassment; overpayment).* This pain point describes an obstacle when paying the driver with cash. In the future, payment should be made through the mobile app. The derived involvement goal is *QlG 5 Accept payment through app.*

▶ *W 1.1 Order online* This solution idea is addressed by the WoP project. Therefore, it does not lead to a new qualitative involvement goal.

▶ *W 1.2 Track order status* This solution idea is addressed by QlG 4 Enable track order and delivery.

▶ *W 1.3 Pay tip online* This solution idea is addressed by QlG 5 Accept payment through app.

New derived qualitative involvement goals are:

▶ QlG 3 Enable checking of delivered pizza vs ordered pizza
▶ QlG 4 Enable tracking of order and delivery
▶ QlG 5 Accept payment through app

Responsibility R 2.9 Receive pizza (as is)

Pain points

A 2.9.1 Receive pizza box(es)
-P 2.9.1.1 Delivery often takes more than 60 minutes (50%; pizza is cold)
- P 2.9.1.2 Sometimes, the wrong pizza is delivered (40%; I need to get different food, due to diet)

A 2.9.2 Pay pizza (and tip driver)
- P 2.9.2.1 Driver does not have change (40%; tip is too high and it takes too much time)

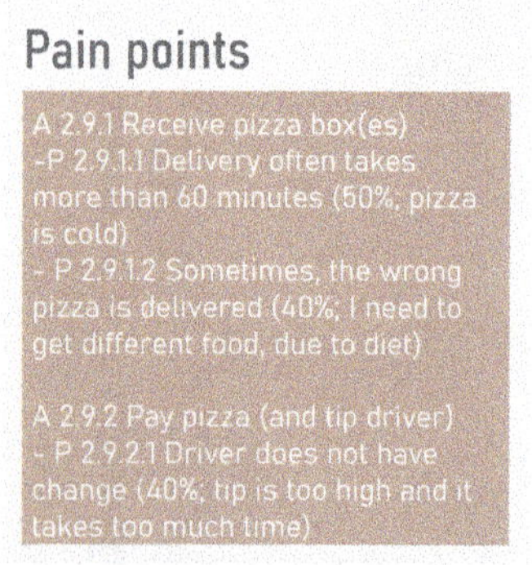

Figure 12.12: Patron - Responsibility; Place order - Pain points

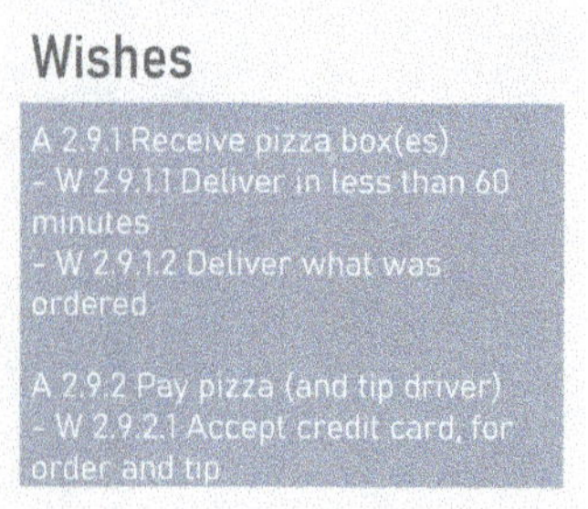

Wishes

A 2.9.1 Receive pizza box(es)
- W 2.9.1.1 Deliver in less than 60 minutes
- W 2.9.1.2 Deliver what was ordered

A 2.9.2 Pay pizza (and tip driver)
- W 2.9.2.1 Accept credit card, for order and tip

Figure 12.13: Patron - Responsibility; Place order - Wishes

We repeat the exercise with the second user journey map for Responsibility 2 "Receive pizza." Let's have a look at the pain points and wishes (see figures in the margin).

▶ *P 2.9.1.1 Delivery takes often more than 60 minutes (60%).* This pain point is already addressed by QlG 4 Enable track order and delivery.

▶ *P 2.9.1.2 Sometimes the wrong pizza is delivered (20%).* This pain point is already addressed by QlG 3 Enable checking of delivered pizza vs ordered pizza.

▶ *P 2.9.2.1 Driver does not have change (40%).* This pain point is already addressed by QlG 5 Accept payment through app.

▶ *W 2.9.1.1 Delivery in less than 60 minutes.* This wish is covered by the new workflow and by QlG 3.

▶ *W 2.9.1.2 Deliver what was ordered.* This is the response to the pain point that the wrong pizza was delivered. The wish is already addressed by involvement goal QlG 4.

▶ *W 2.9.2.1 Accept credit card, for order and tip.* This wish is addressed by QlG 5.

We could not derive new qualitative involvement goals from R 2.9 Receive pizza (as is).

Derive involvement goals from user journey map (to be)

Responsibility R 1.1 Select and order pizza (to be)

We also look at the user journey maps (to be) to identify additional involvement goals. We go through the solution ideas (SI) step by step (see the margin figures also):

▶ *SI 1.1.1.1 Reuse last-used filter settings.* This is an expectation that entered or selected content and filters can be reused for the same user on the next order. :The solution idea leads to a new involvement goal: *QIG 6 Support reuse of user-entered content and settings.* This solution idea can be expanded to include not only settings, filters, and views, but also previously ordered pizzas. The next derived involvement goal is *QIG 7 Provide access to previously ordered pizzas.*

▶ *SI 1.1.1.2 Wizard for group order.* This is an expectation that group orders should be supported. The idea of the "wizard" is a design element. The derived involvement goal will be abstracted as: *QIG 8 Support group orders.*

▶ *SI 1.1.2.1 Reuse payment information.* This is an idea that directly influences the efficiency of the workflow. We covered it already with involvement goal QIG 6.

▶ *SI 1.1.2.2 Reuse delivery information.* This solution idea also addresses efficiency improvements and is covered by involvement goal QIG 6.

▶ *SI 1.1.3.1 Send notification to patron in case of status change.* The patron wants to be updated if something regarding the order or the delivery is changing. This justifies a new involvement goal: *QIG 9 Keep the patron up to date about the order and delivery status.*

The new derived qualitative involvement goals are:

▶ QIG 6 Support reuse of user-entered content and settings
▶ QIG 7 Provide access to previously ordered pizzas
▶ QIG 8 Support group orders
▶ QIG 9 Keep the patron up to date about the order and delivery status

Responsibility R 1.2 Monitor status (to be)

▶ *SI 1.2.1.1 Map with driver's location.* A similar solution idea was already mentioned and is addressed by user involvement goal QIG 4.

▶ *SI 1.2.1.2 Estimated time of delivery.* This solution idea addresses a point similar to that in SI 2.1 and is addressed by QIG 4.

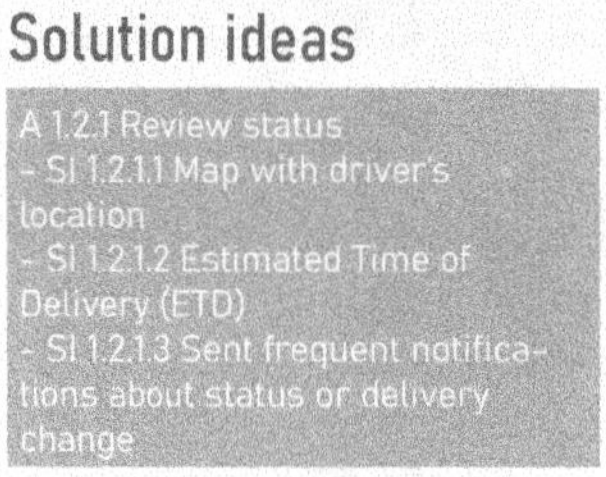

Solution ideas

A 1.1.1 select pizza
- SI 1.1.1.1 Reuse last used filter settings
- SI 1.1.1.2 Wizard for group order

A 1.1.2 order and pay pizza
- SI 1.1.2.1 Reuse payment information
- SI 1.1.2.2 Reuse delivery information

A 1.1.3 read order confirmation
- SI 1.1.3.1 Send notification to Patron in case of status change

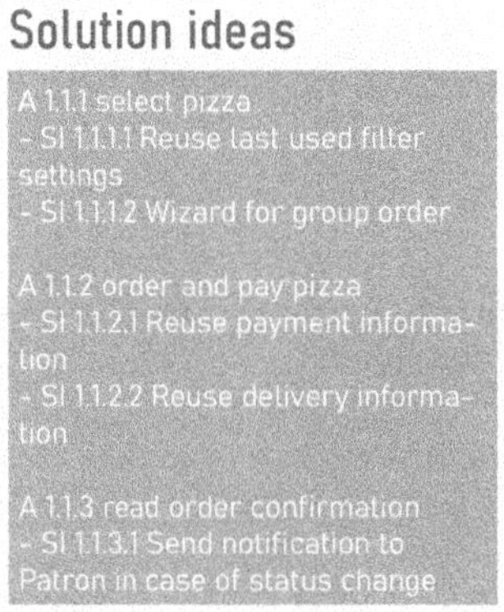

Figure 12.14: Patron - Receive pizza - Solution ideas

Solution ideas

A 1.2.1 Review status
- SI 1.2.1.1 Map with driver's location
- SI 1.2.1.2 Estimated Time of Delivery (ETD)
- SI 1.2.1.3 Sent frequent notifications about status or delivery change

Figure 12.15: Patron - Receive pizza - Solution ideas

Solution ideas

A 1.3.1 Receive pizza box
(none)

A 1.3.2 Tip driver
- SI 1.3.2.1 Propose tip

Figure 12.16: Patron - Receive pizza - Solution ideas

► *SI 1.2.1.3 sent frequent notification about status or delivery change.* A similar solution was mentioned and is addressed by involvement goal QIG 9.

Responsibility 1.3 Receive pizza (to be)

► *SI 1.3.2.1 Propose tip* This is an efficiency-driven need. Patrons have asked that tip amounts be suggested so that they do not have to do the calculations themselves. There is no existing involvement goal that would cover this one. A new user involvement goal is *QIG 10 Propose tip options.*

A new derived qualitative involvement goal is:

► QIG 10 Propose tip options

Selection of qualitative involvement goals

The derived qualitative involvement goals are:

► QIG 1 Enable finding pizzas by attribute (incl. diets)
► QIG 2 Display pizza attributes (incl. calories, ingredients, image)
► QIG 3 Enable checking of delivered pizza vs ordered pizza
► QIG 4 Enable tracking of order and delivery
► QIG 5 Accept payment through app
► QIG 6 Support reuse of user-entered content and settings
► QIG 7 Provide access to previously ordered pizzas
► QIG 8 Support group orders
► QIG 9 Keep the patron up to date about the order and delivery status
► QIG 10 Propose tip options

The list of qualitative involvement goals can be very long. It is usually beneficial to use a short working list. A reasonable way to cut the list is by looking only at the goals that have a major impact on the concept. This means that if we do not consider such goals early in the concept exploration and exclusion process, it is expensive to consider them later because they can cause a substantial change in the concept. In fact, if not considered early, they will most likely require the creation of a new concept. We call user involvement goals with such relevance *significant*[1] .

There are two criteria by which to identify involvement goals that are significant:

► An involvement goal contributes to the primary user task
► An involvement goal contributes to more than one user task

1: The concept of "significance" is based on a technique used in software architecture [188]. *Architectural significant requirements* (ASR) belong to a subset of requirements that "actually determine and shape a software architecture" [189, p. 38].

Since the primary user task substantially influences the design of the involvement concept, it needs to be reflected from the beginning. If it is not considered, the involvement concept will most likely have to be redone, which is costly.

The reason for the second criterion (involvement goal contributes to more than one user task) is that the support of more than one user task has a cross-cutting effect on the involvement concept. Several canvases and design decisions might be impacted if these types of goals haven't been considered from the beginning. Such a change would be costly too.

To identify which involvement goals are supporting either the primary user task or more than one user task, we create a table in which the involvement goals are mapped accordingly.

We will now apply this idea to our WoP example. The mapping of the qualitative involvement goals to the primary user tasks and to the cross-cutting category is shown in Table 12.1 on the next page.

If a goal has a "yes" in column 2 (primary user task) or column 3 (cross-cutting), it is considered "significant" and will be used for assessing involvement concepts.

The excluded involvement goals are still relevant for the application under design and development but not for the exploration and exclusion of the concept. They will be reflected as requirements, user stories, and whatever vehicle is used in a project to communicate desired properties to the design and implementation team. Requirements and user stories are not covered in this book.

Table 12.1: Identification of significant user involvement qualitative goals

Qualitative involvement goal	Primary user task (UT 1.1 Select pizza)	Cross-cutting (supports more than one user task)	Goal is significant
QIG 1 Enable finding pizzas by attribute (incl. diets)	Yes (UT 1.1)	No (UT 1.1 only)	Yes
QIG 2 Display pizza attributes (incl. calories, ingredients, image)	Yes (UT 1.1)	No (UT 1.1 only)	Yes
QIG 3 Enable checking of delivered pizza vs ordered pizza	No (UT 1.4)	No (UT 1.4 only)	No
QIG 4 Enable tracking of order and delivery	No (UT 1.3)	No (UT 1.3 only)	No
QIG 5 Accept payment through app	No (UT 1.2)	No (UT 1.2 only)	No
QIG 6 Support reuse of user-entered content and settings	Yes (UT 1.1, UT 1.2, UT 1.3, UT 1.4)	Yes (UT 1.1, UT 1.2, UT 1.3, UT 1.4)	Yes
QIG 7 Provide access to previously ordered pizzas	Yes (UT 1.1)	No (UT 1.1 only)	Yes
QIG 8 Support group orders	Yes (UT 1.1)	No (UT 1.1 only)	Yes
QIG 9 Keep the patron up to date about the order and delivery status	No (UT 1.3)	No (UT 1.3 only)	No
QIG 10 Propose tip options	No (UT 1.4)	No (UT 1.4 only)	No

Summary of qualitative involvement goals

In conclusion, we will consider the qualitative involvement goals 1, 2, 6, 7, and 8 as significant. They are added as qualitative involvement goals to the involvement goal matrix.

- ▶ QIG 1 Enable finding pizzas by attribute (incl. diets)
- ▶ QIG 2 Display pizza attributes (incl. calories, ingredients, image)
- ▶ QIG 6 Support reuse of user-entered content and settings
- ▶ QIG 7 Provide access to previously ordered pizzas
- ▶ QIG 8 Support group orders

Vendor involvement goals

Besides the customer-driven goals derived from the different users, there are usually vendor involvement goals. They typically aim to drive revenue increases, cost reductions, and/or profit increases. The vendor involvement goals are derived from the business goals that are part of the business model.

Frequently, such business goals are expressed with design elements. It should be determined in which cases the design element is really intended and in which cases the design element is just an example and can be abstracted. If feasible, the vendor involvement goals should avoid mentioning design elements.

We have already defined vendor goals (see Section 3 on page 61). We will now select those that qualify as vendor involvement goals for UIP 1.

Business goals
What are business-motivated involvement goals?
- Enable comparison of pizzas from different restaurants
- Add new products
- Display at least 9 product items at a glance
- Driver: compare delivery jobs by rate

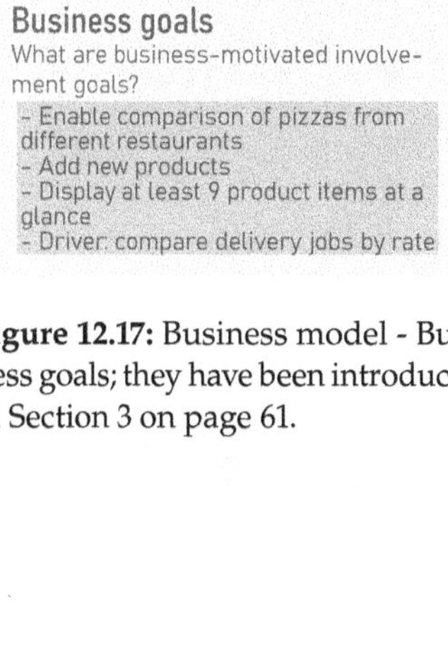

Figure 12.17: Business model - Business goals; they have been introduced in Section 3 on page 61.

- *Enable the comparison of pizzas from different restaurants ("product first")* This business goal is critical to realizing the unique value proposition. It also applies to UIP 1 and will be selected for the involvement goal matrix *VG 1 Enable comparison of pizzas from different restaurants*.
- *Enable extension of new products* The second vendor goal is relevant, so the product portfolio can be enhanced without being constrained by the design. It is relevant for UIP 1 and will be selected as a vendor involvement goal for the user involvement goal matrix *VG 2 Enable extension of the product list*.
- *Display at least nine products at a glance* The third business goal addresses the ability to give the customer sufficient choices after they open the application. It applies to UIP 1 and will be selected as a vendor involvement goal for the involvement goal matrix *VG 3 Enable the display of at least nine products at a glance*.
- *Compare delivery jobs by hourly rate* The last vendor goal addresses the driver's need to maximize their hourly rate. Since this goal belongs to UIP 4, it will not be considered for the involvement goal matrix for UIP 1.

The selected vendor involvement goals are:

- VG 1 Enable comparison of pizzas from different restaurants
- VG 2 Enable extension of the product list
- VG 3 Enable the display of at least nine products at a glance

Involvement goal matrix

We summarize the involvement goals in the *involvement goal matrix* (see Table 12.3 on page 334).

Definition 17 (Involvement goal matrix) *List of all significant involvement goals, used to explore and exclude involvement concepts.*

We will use the involvement goal matrix for the remainder of this book to explore and exclude involvement concepts.

Quantitative user involvement goal
QnG 1 Select pizza: 0 involvement step
QnG 2 Order pizza: 1 involvement step
QnG 3 Monitor status: 1 involvement step
QnG 4 Tip driver: 1 involvement step
QnG 5 Select pizza: 30 seconds (EVOT)
QnG 6 Order pizza: 30 seconds (EVOT)
QnG 7 Monitor status: 30 seconds (EVOT)
QnG 8 Tip driver: 30 seconds (EVOT)
QnG 9 Select, order, and receive pizza: 33 minutes (EVOT)
Qualitative user involvement goal
QlG 1 Enable finding pizzas by attribute (incl. diets)
QlG 2 Display pizza attributes (incl. calories, ingredients, image)
QlG 6 Support reuse of user-entered content and settings
QlG 7 Provide access to previously ordered pizzas
QlG 8 Support group orders
Vendor involvement goal
VG 1 Enable comparison of pizzas from different restaurants
VG 2 Enable extension of the product list
VG 3 Enable the display of at least nine products at a glance

Table 12.2: Involvement goal matrix for WoP

The use of involvement goals to guide the design process and keep it focused and efficient is reflected in the next design principle:

Goals impact the design act

Involvement goals inform the designer about desired properties of the envisioned involvement concept. They outline the border of the design space and keep the design act focused. The involvement goals make the design process itself efficient, they make design decisions explainable and defensible, and they support the creation of an efficient involvement concept.

Summary

Involvement goal matrix

▶ Move on to Involvement Concept: Step 1
◀ Go back to User Involvement Point

Quantitative user involvement goal
QnG 1 Select pizza: 0 involvement step
QnG 2 Order pizza: 1 involvement step
QnG 3 Monitor status: 1 involvement step
QnG 4 Tip driver: 1 involvement step
QnG 5 Select pizza: 30 seconds (EVOT)
QnG 6 Order pizza: 30 seconds (EVOT)
QnG 7 Monitor status: 30 seconds (EVOT)
QnG 8 Tip driver: 30 seconds (EVOT)
QnG 9 Select, order, and receive pizza: 33 minutes (EVOT)

Qualitative user involvement goal
QlG 1 Enable finding pizzas by attribute (incl. diets)
QlG 2 Display pizza attributes (incl. calories, ingredients, image)
QlG 6 Support reuse of user-entered content and settings
QlG 7 Provide access to previously ordered pizzas
QlG 8 Support group orders

Vendor involvement goal
VG 1 Enable comparison of pizzas from different restaurants
VG 2 Enable extension of the product list
VG 3 Enable the display of at least nine products at a glance

Table 12.3: Involvement goal matrix for WoP

Lessons learned

Quantitative goals   The quantitative involvement goals are collected from the updated workflow (to be) with added target involvement times. By applying the GAIS method, we can reduce the number of user involvement steps. Both the target involvement time and the target involvement steps are listed as user-task-specific quantitative involvement goals.

Qualitative goals   The qualitative involvement goals are derived from the pain points, wishes, and solution ideas from the user role profiles and the user journey maps. After its initial identification, we consolidate and select the subset that has influence on the involvement concept. We select the qualitative involvement goals that are significant–those that support the primary user task and/or support more than one user task (i.e., cross-cutting).

Vendor involvement goals   The vendor goals are additional goals that reflect the needs of the business. Only those vendor goals that influence the involvement design for the selected user involvement point should be chosen. Vendor-motivated involvement goals are documented in the business model and are copied and pasted from there into the involvement goal matrix.

Involvement goal matrix   The involvement goal matrix is a list of all significant involvement goals and is used to inform and assess involvement concepts. The involvement goal matrix makes design decisions explainable and defendable.

Tips and tricks

Quantitative goals   Selecting a specific GAIS scenario does not mean that other user involvement flows are excluded. In our case, we selected a GAIS scenario that allows the user to order a pizza with one interaction step after launching the WoP application. Other GAIS scenarios, like entering payment and delivery information, should be supported too. Selecting a specific GAIS scenario means that the app should be able to realize that scenario and the associated number of involvement steps. However, it does not exclude other GAIS scenarios, particularly those with a greater number of involvement steps.

The abstraction level for involvement steps may vary, depending on the abstraction level of the user task. Whatever level you pick, try to keep the involvement steps on the same level, so that the involvement steps measure the same level of user involvement.

If you pick one or more GAIS scenarios to determine the target involvement steps, I'd recommend not being too cautious. Just take an optimistic quantitative target involvement step number (e.g., 1 or even 0 involvement steps) and consider the low number as a design challenge. It's fun. If you work in a corporate environment, I'd suggest reporting a higher number, so you have some wiggle room and are able to exceed your step target, potentially even making the selected involvement concept "GAIS super-efficient" (and you may get a pat on the back).

Qualitative goals   The qualitative involvement goals should be formulated from the application domain perspective, as tasks or activities and without design elements. If such a goal includes design elements, it becomes a design decision. A goal should guide, not over-constrain, the design space.

Here are two examples that show the difference between a statement as a goal and a statement with a design decision. The involvement goal "QlG 1 Enable finding pizza by attribute (incl. diet)" is a goal statement. It provides guidance without mentioning specific design elements. The goal could have been formulated as "QlG 1 Enable filtering pizza by attribute (incl. diet)." This formulation includes a design element and implies a solution that turns the goal into a design decision. This is not what we want. How to achieve "finding pizzas" is up to the design phase.

Another aspect of qualitative involvement goals is the level of abstraction. As you could see during the interpretation of pain points, wishes, and solution ideas, some of the goals have been abstracted. Finding the right level of abstraction is important. Abstraction helps to keep the number of involvement goals short and manageable. Abstraction also opens new opportunities. Here is an example: Instead of saying "Reuse user-entered payment information," we said "Reuse user-entered content and settings." Such a goal goes beyond just payment information. The question is, how far should you go? That is hard to say. If you have achieved the level of world peace, you know you went too far. The best advice I can give: Try to abstract individual wishes, pain points, and solution ideas and keep the goal in the application domain.

Vendor goals   You should only select vendor goals that have a direct influence on user involvement and that are relevant for the user involvement point under definition. All other vendor goals should be ignored for the user involvement goal matrix.

Some vendor goals contain design elements. Try to find out whether the design element is really intentional or whether the intent is broader and the goal can be abstracted and articulated as an activity, without mentioning a design element.

Exercise 2.4

Goal Create an involvement goal matrix.

Material Target involvement time; GAIS; systematic derivation of qualitative involvement goals from user role profile and user journey maps; identification of significant qualitative user involvement goals; vendor goals.

Completion criteria:

- ▶ Target involvement time is derived from the workflow (to be).
- ▶ GAIS scenarios have been explored and documented. One GAIS scenario has been selected.
- ▶ Target involvement steps per user task are updated and documented.
- ▶ Qualitative involvement goals are derived from user journey maps and user role profiles and documented.
- ▶ Significant qualitative involvement goals are identified and documented.
- ▶ Vendor goals are selected and documented.
- ▶ All significant involvement goals are documented in an involvement goal matrix.

Part 3: Experience Design

时光流逝，不可复得。
(Time lost cannot be won again.)
Chinese proverb

Purpose

So far, we have learned about the experience foundation and the experience architecture. In this part of the book, we will learn about experience design. For many readers, it might be the most interesting part. Please don't forget that an experience design is built on the experience foundation. For ecosystems, it is derived from the experience architecture, particularly the user involvement points

In this chapter, we are going to introduce and establish key terms, concepts, and a process. So let's get started ...

Experience design

Design is the process "to define the architecture, system elements, interfaces, and other characteristics of a system or system element" [108, clause 4.1.15]. Our system is the user involvement system with its user involvement points as system elements relevant to the experience design.

> **Definition 18** (Experience design) *A creative act specifying user involvement, aiming to achieve stated goals within given constraints*

A creative act that is not guided by goals and constraints is not considered a design act. Some people might call it play; others might call it art. The point is, a creative act qualifies as a design act, if it is possible to objectively verify and validate that the result of a creative act achieves stated needs, goals, and constraints. If they are not stated, we act in Wonderland. Alice [190, p. 76] seemed to face a similar situation – goal or no goal:

Figure 13.1: Cat; source: Pixabay; author: Natalia Koroshchenko; license: Pixabay license

"Would you tell me, please, which way I ought to go from here?"

"That depends a good deal on where you want to get to," said the Cat.

"I don't much care where –" said Alice.

"Then it doesn't matter which way you go," said the Cat.

"– so long as I get somewhere," Alice added as an explanation.

"Oh, you're sure to do that," said the Cat, "if you only walk long enough."

The design input contains results from the experience foundation phase and from the experience architecture phase, including workflows, user role profiles, context of use, user needs, user goals, pain points, wishes, solution ideas, involvement goals, user tasks, and constraints. We can consider the design inputs as questions, with the design act creating a design output that hopefully answers the questions. In summary, the design act transforms design inputs into design outputs (see Figure 13.2).

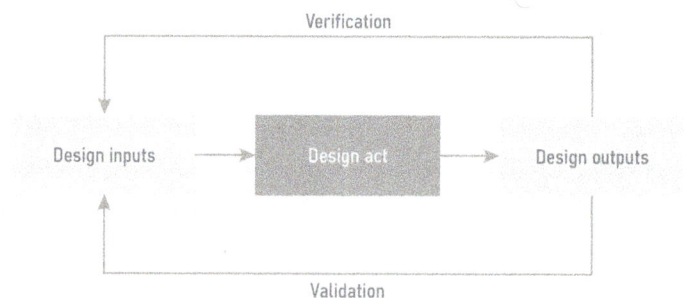

Figure 13.2: Design act

Design outputs include one or more involvement concepts, such as multiple seed concepts and a sprout concept (they will be introduced later in this chapter). It often includes refined user interfaces and requirements. The most mature design output is a specification that describes how to involve users. The specification includes a user interface specification and associated assets (e.g., icons and audio files). The specification is used as a blueprint for the implementation. The design input should contain content that can be used to verify the design output.

Verification of design output means answering the question, Did we design the application right? "Right" here means the design output complies with the involvement goals (involvement domain). Therefore, the design input needs to include involvement goals. The design input should also contain content that can be used to validate the design output. Validation of design output means answering the question, Did we design the right application? "Right" here means the users' needs (life and business domain) and the application and user's goals (application domain) are addressed. It also includes the selection of the right user tasks.

To answer both the validation and the verification questions with yes, the involvement goals must be derived from the user's needs and the user's goals (see Figure 13.3). That's the reason why the experience foundation and the experience architecture are essential for a successful experience design.

ISO 15288-2015 defines verification as "confirmation, through the provision of objective evidence, that specified requirements have been fulfilled" [108, clause 4.1.54] (for the concept verification, involvements goals are used as requirements). Validation is defined as "confirmation, through the provision of objective evidence, that the requirements for a specific intended use or application have been fulfilled" [108, clauses 4.1.53] (for concept validation, user needs and user goals are used as requirements). The verification can be performed as outlined in step 3: test concept (Chapter 16 (Evaluate Concepts) on page 493) and step 4: assess concept (see Chapter 17 (Assess Concepts) on page 531). The validation requires users' participation and is often performed with a usability test.

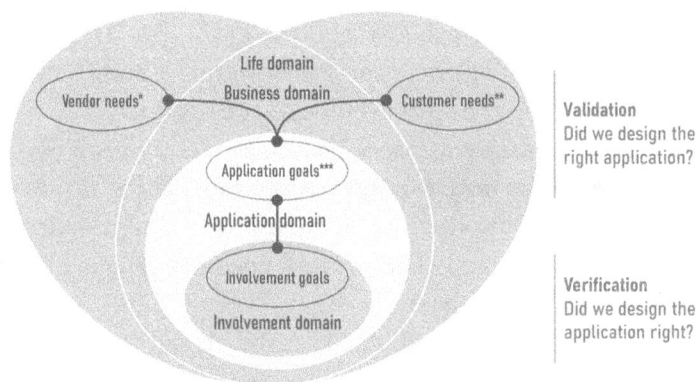

*Users as members of the vendor organization, with their user needs.
**Users as members of the customer organization or as consumers, with their user needs.
***User's goals are a subset of or derived from application goals.

Figure 13.3: Teddy bear model with validation and verification annotation

A design output can have different combinations of answers to the verification and the validation questions. They are shown in the validation–verification quadrant in Figure 13.4.

The four combinations are shown below:

► NoNo (The wrong application was designed wrong): This is a hopeless case. The design should start from the beginning with establishing the experience foundation.
► YoNo (The wrong application was designed right): This case is a trap, because someone could get the impression that

Sweet spot for verification and validation

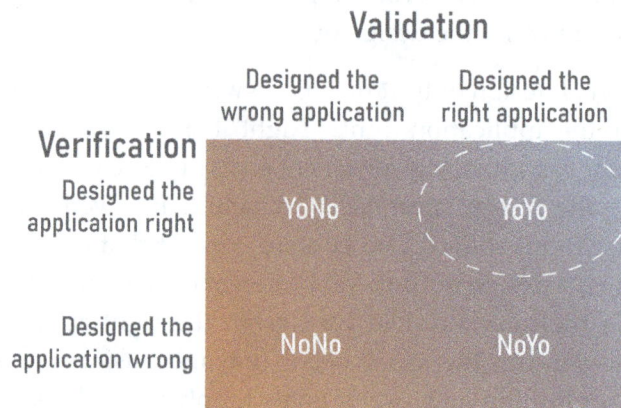

Validation

	Designed the wrong application	Designed the right application
Verification		
Designed the application right	YoNo	YoYo
Designed the application wrong	NoNo	NoYo

Figure 13.4: Validation–Verification Quadrant

the design has created some value. But since the wrong application was designed, the design has no value, and the process should be started over from the beginning with establishing the experience foundation.

▶ NoYo (The right application was designed wrong): This is a case with hope. At least the right application (i.e., needs, goals, user tasks) was identified. It seems that the experience foundation and the experience architecture are strong enough, including the involvement goals. Only the design needs to be changed. The process needs to go back to the experience design phase.

▶ YoYo (The right application was designed right): A solid experience foundation was established with a solid experience architecture and an effective, efficient, satisfactory design (sweet spot).

From the different cases in Figure 13.4, we can see that it is much better to design the right application wrong than to design the wrong application right. It is, of course, best to design the right application right.

Design elements

> **Definition 19** (Design element) *A building block enabling user involvement.*

We have several design elements at our disposal that are displayed in Figure 13.5.

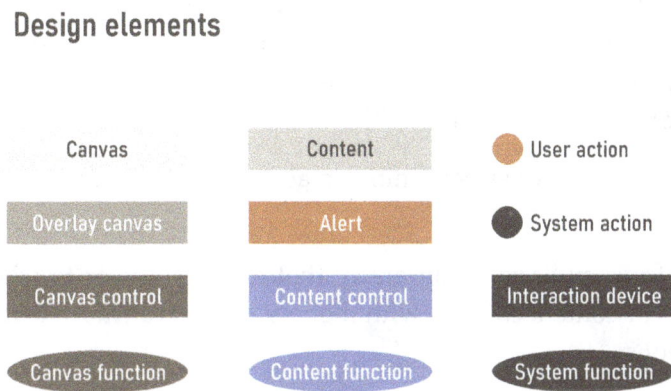

Design elements

Canvas	Content	● User action
Overlay canvas	Alert	● System action
Canvas control	Content control	Interaction device
Canvas function	Content function	System function

Figure 13.5: Design elements

Here is a short overview of the design elements. Some more detailed explanations follow in subsequent sections of this chapter.

A *canvas* is a virtual region for placing and organizing design elements. An example of a canvas is an individual screen on a desktop application.

An *overlay canvas* is a canvas layer on top of another canvas. It often contains content controls. Examples of overlay canvases are toolbars, drop-down or fly-out menus.

A *canvas control* is an element that enables the user to change canvases (e.g., a hyperlink) or to change the focus of a canvas (e.g., a scroll bar). A canvas control does not change content itself.

A *canvas function* is an element that changes the focus area of a canvas. An example is a zoom function. A canvas function does not change content itself, only the way content is presented to users.

A *content* is an element that carries meaning for users and supports the user in performing their tasks and achieving their goal.

An *alert* is a specific type of content that informs the user about a system's status (change) or that requests a user's attention or decision.

A *content control* is an element that enables a user to create, modify, or delete content. An example is a button that enables a user to submit an order (the control "order now" creates the object "order").

A *content function* is a function, associated with the content control that is executed when the user triggers the content control. An example is the function "Submit order" that is associated with the control "Order now."

A *user action* is a user-initiated activity. Typical user actions are perceiving content and cognitively processing content. Another user action is to move body parts (e.g., fingers) to initiate a content control (e.g., click a mouse).

A *system action* is a system-initiated activity that triggers a system function.

An *interaction device* is an entity that enables a user to trigger canvas or content controls with their associated canvas or content functions.

A *system function* is defined as transformation of a defined input into a defined output. A system function is initiated by a system.

In this book, all design elements are visualized with certain colors and shapes. For instance, a canvas is visualized as light brown and as a rectangle. A user action is displayed as a orange circle. These specific colors and shapes are used consistently for the remainder of the book to indicate the type of design element.

Canvas

The canvas is a region for placing and organizing user-perceivable design elements. For mobile applications, a single canvas is often a relatively small area and usually supports one user task. For desktop applications, a canvas is larger and may support several user tasks.

> **Definition 20** (Canvas) *Virtual region for placing and organizing design elements.*

One may presume that a canvas is a design element for a graphical user interface only. However, a canvas can also be applied to other modalities. For instance, a canvas in voice user interface solutions might be a list of available intents that the user can activate. In a gesture modality, a canvas can be defined by the number of gestures that the system can recognize and respond to at a certain point in time.

Canvas size

Depending on the interaction device, a canvas can be of different sizes. We call the size of a canvas the *canvas footage*. The canvas footage can be specified quantitatively, for instance in pixels or other virtual metrics. It can also be expressed qualitatively, such as by the terms "small," "medium," or "large." Canvas A can have a larger canvas footage than canvas B.

Canvas views

There are a couple of different canvas views that provide useful overviews of the canvases used in an application:

Canvas cast   The canvas cast (see Figure 13.6) provides an overview of all used canvases, independent of their context of use. What is meant by "canvas" here is a template with specific design elements for a specific user's intent. In our pizza example, a canvas can be a pizza list view, a single pizza view (agnostic of the specific pizza type), a shopping cart view, etc.

Canvas flow   Another useful view is the canvas flow (see Figure 13.7). The canvas flow is user-task specific. It lists the canvases in their sequence of use when a specific user task is performed. This view helps to determine the number of involvement steps per user task.

The terms "entry canvas" and "back canvas" are assigned based on the position of a canvas in the canvas flow. The canvas that is made available first to a user after opening an application is called here the *entry canvas*. An entry canvas is sometimes known as a "landing page," and there are other names for the entry canvas [191]. Here, each of the other canvases is called a *back canvas*. The back canvases can be enumerated, depending on their position in the canvas flow (see the two canvas flows in Figure 13.7 where canvas 1 is the entry canvas and canvases 2, 3, and 4 are the back canvases). All applications have one entry canvas and often several back canvases to support the flow of steps according to the user's mental model.

The length of a canvas flow per user task, i.e., the number of canvases needed to perform a user task is called here *canvas flow length*, or short "flow length."

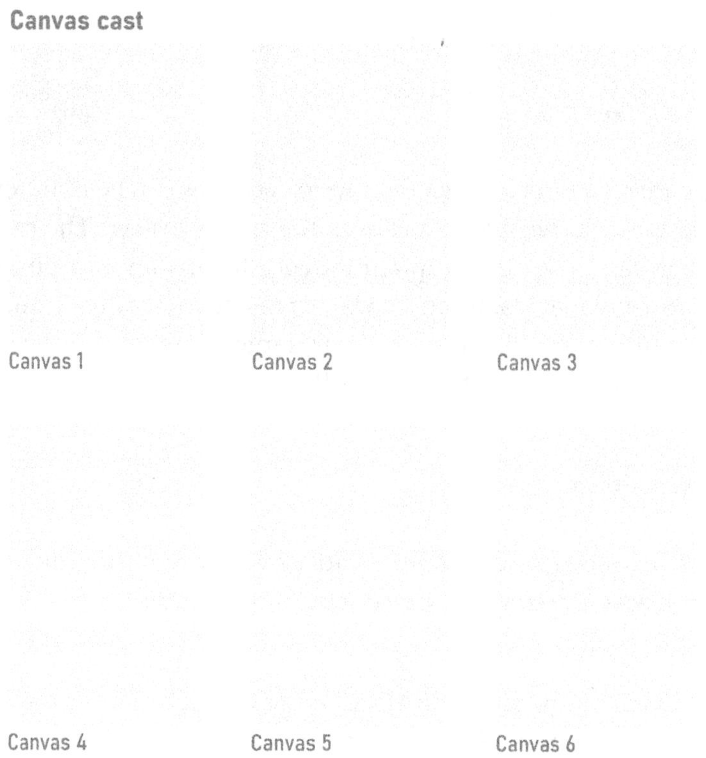

Canvas cast

Canvas 1   Canvas 2   Canvas 3

Canvas 4   Canvas 5   Canvas 6

Figure 13.6: Canvas cast

From an efficiency perspective, we are interested to allow the users to perform user tasks as soon as possible. When we look at a canvas flow, we can separate it into two sub flows. To distinguish and discuss the two flows, we'll call them (Figure 13.8):

The word "path" is borrowed from a building campus. It refers to a foot-path between buildings.

▶ Path flow: Canvas flow from the entry canvas to the last canvas prior to the "start canvas" (per user task). This flow includes the canvases before reaching a task flow.

▶ Task flow: Canvas flow from the "start canvas" to the "end canvas" (per user task). This flow describes the steps to perform a user task.

Canvas flow

User task 1

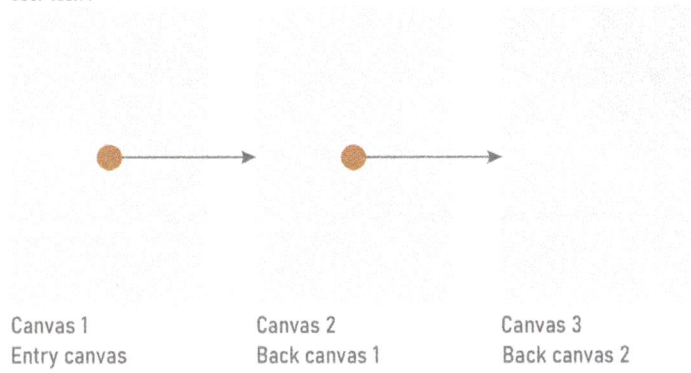

Canvas 1
Entry canvas

Canvas 2
Back canvas 1

Canvas 3
Back canvas 2

User task 2

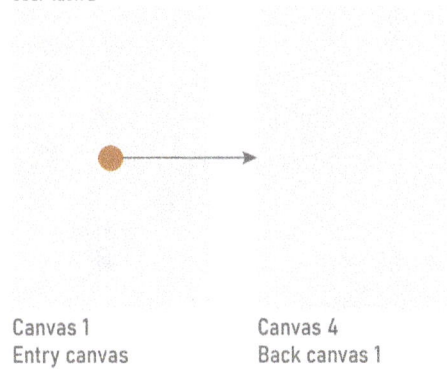

Canvas 1
Entry canvas

Canvas 4
Back canvas 1

Figure 13.7: Canvas flow

Path and task flow

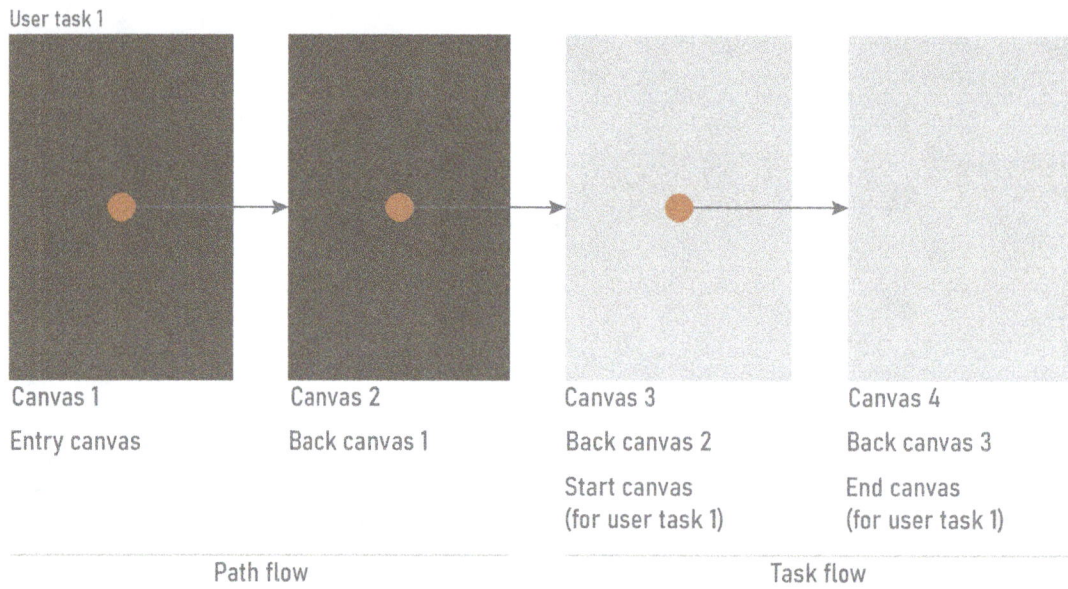

User task 1

Canvas 1

Entry canvas

Canvas 2

Back canvas 1

Canvas 3

Back canvas 2

Start canvas
(for user task 1)

Canvas 4

Back canvas 3

End canvas
(for user task 1)

Path flow

Task flow

Primary user task
(ideal from an efficiency perspective)

Canvas 1

Entry canvas

Start and end canvas
(for primary user task)

Task flow

Figure 13.8: Path flow and task flow

The "entry canvas" marks the beginning of each canvas flow. The "start canvas" marks the beginning of start performing a user task and the "end canvas" the end of a user task flow. Sometimes, the boundaries between a path flow and a task flow can be blurry. To identify the start and end of a task flow, just imagine an application that only supports that one user task. All canvases that are essential to support that user task most likely belong to the task flow.

From an efficiency perspective, the length of the path flow should be zero and the length of the task flow should be as short as possible. This particularly applies to the primary user task (Figure 13.8).

Many legacy engineering applications have a rather long path flow per user task. The reason is that they are organized around objects, functions, or data, but not around user tasks and user goals. Long path flows are an indication of a technology-centered design approach.

Path flows

Canvas types   We stay with the topic of canvas flows a bit longer. From an efficiency perspective, it is reasonable that a user task, at least the primary user task, should start on the entry canvas. It would be useful to express path flow types because it makes it easier to discuss them. That's the reason why we introduce them here.

We start with defining three canvas types here (see also Figure 13.9):

> ▶ "Instant" canvas type (abbreviated I)
> ▶ "Hybrid" canvas type (abbreviated H)
> ▶ "Delayed" canvas type (abbreviated D)

The canvas type "instant" enables the user to start performing a user task, indicated with two design elements: a "content element" (in light brown) and a "control element" (in blue). It is possible that one canvas enables to perform one user tasks (variation 1) or even several user tasks (variation 2).

The canvas type "hybrid" (abbreviated H) contains design elements from canvas type "instant" and from canvas type "delayed." It means that it enables the user to perform a user task instantly and it enables the user to navigate to other canvases.

The canvas type "delayed" (abbreviated D) contains only the design element "canvas control" (e.g., hyperlinks, menus). It does not contain design elements that enable the user to perform a user task instantly. A canvas type D delays the performance of a user task

Canvas type: Instant (I)   Canvas type: Hybrid (H)   Canvas type: Delayed (D)

Start
user task
here

Variation 1

Canvas
elements
(navigation)

Start
user task
here

Variation 2

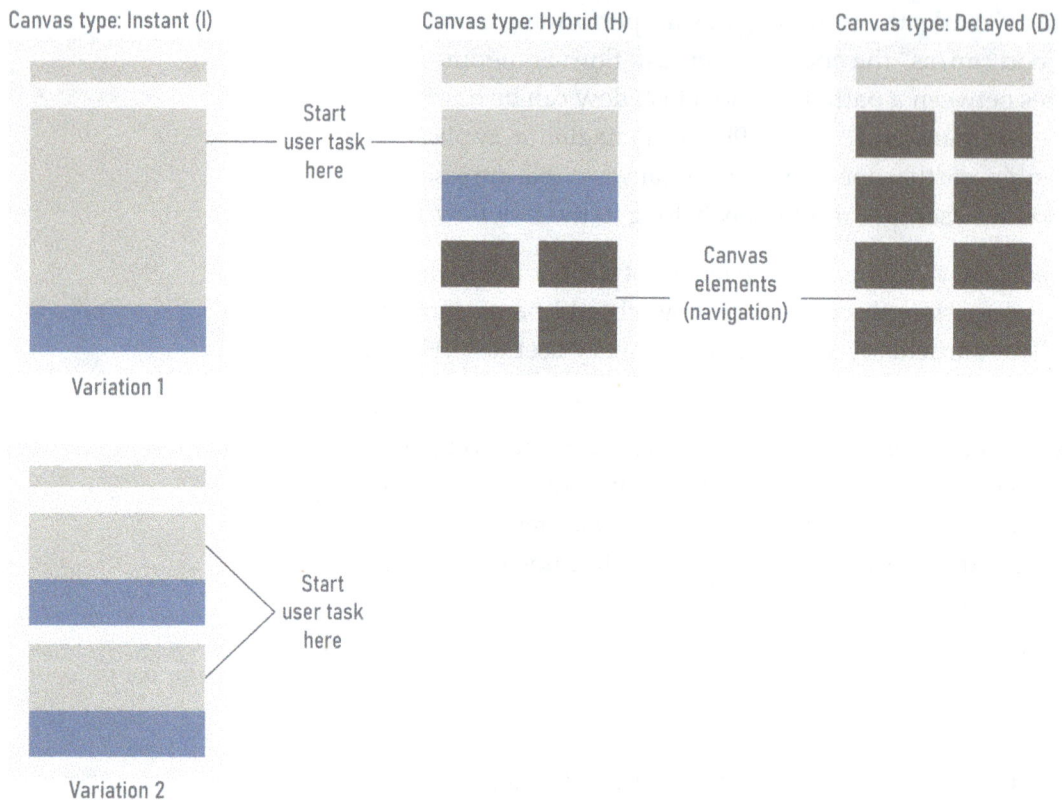

Figure 13.9: Canvas types

because the user has to navigate to a canvas of canvas type I or H first.

We are now equipped to formulate path flow types.

Path flow types   Based on the canvas types, used for the entry canvas, we can identify the following path flow types:

- ► Path flow type "Instant" (abbreviated I)
- ► Path flow type "Hybrid" (abbreviated H)
- ► Path flow type "Delayed" (abbreviated D)

That differentiation is critical because it determines the length of the path flow. The length has an influence on the user's efficiency.

In case of the instant path flow type (see Figure 13.10), the entry canvas is from canvas type "instant." It enables the user to start performing at least the primary user task (see variation 1). If there is sufficient footage, other user task can also be supported (see variation 2).

The hybrid path flow type (see Figure 13.11) uses a hybrid canvas types as an entry canvas. That canvas enables the user to perform

Path flow type: instant

Variation 1: I

User task 1

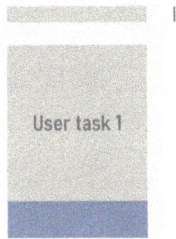

Entry canvas
(Start canvas of
user task 1)

Variation 2: I

User task 1

User task 2

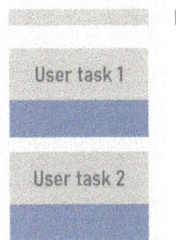

Entry canvas
(Start canvas of
user task 1 and
user task 2)

Figure 13.10: Variations for instant path flow type

at least the primary user tasks, and it allows the user to navigate to other user tasks.

The delayed path flow type (see Figure 13.12) starts with a delayed canvas type as an entry canvas. In this flow type, the user has to navigate to a start canvas first, before being able to start performing a user tasks. As the name indicates, it delays the user's performance and therefore reduces the efficiency.

From an efficiency perspective, the instant and the hybrid flow paths are preferred because they enable users to perform a user task immediately. Ideally, the entry canvas enables to start performing the primary user task.

Path flow type: hybrid

Variation 1: H-I

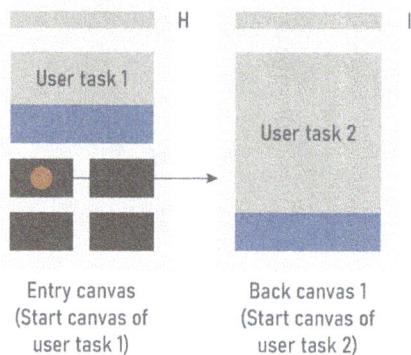

Variation 2: H-H-I

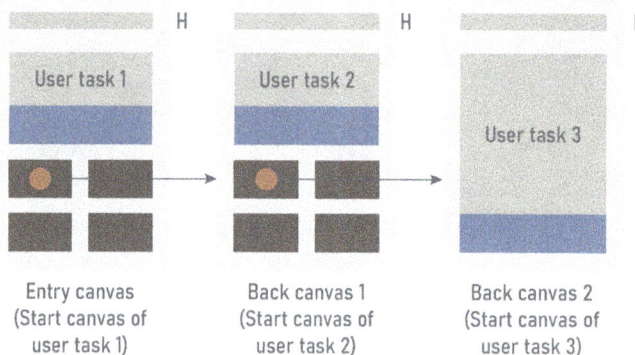

Variation 3: H-D-I

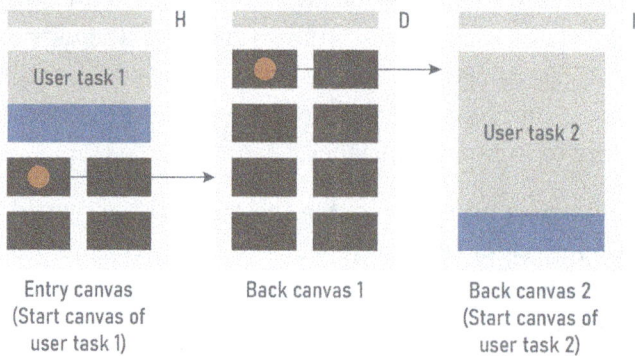

Figure 13.11: Variations for hybrid path flow type

Path flow type: delayed

Variation 1: D-I

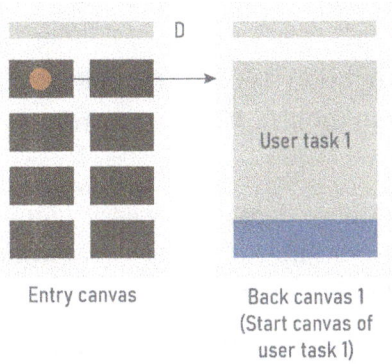

Entry canvas

Back canvas 1
(Start canvas of
user task 1)

Variation 2: D-H-I

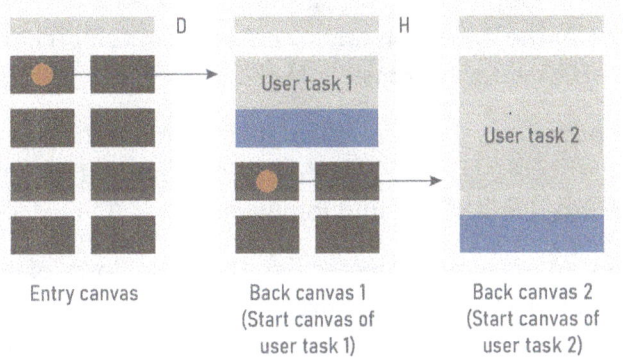

Entry canvas

Back canvas 1
(Start canvas of
user task 1)

Back canvas 2
(Start canvas of
user task 2)

Variation 3: D-D-I

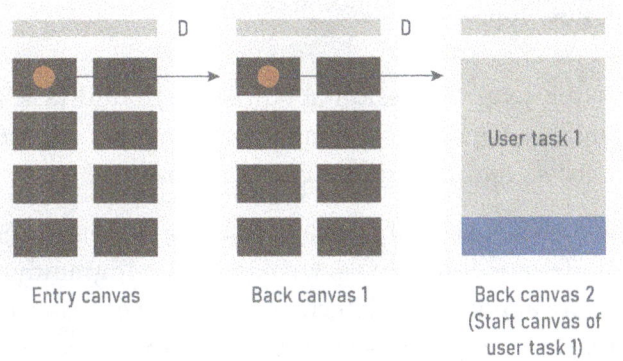

Entry canvas

Back canvas 1

Back canvas 2
(Start canvas of
user task 1)

Variation 4: D-D-H-I

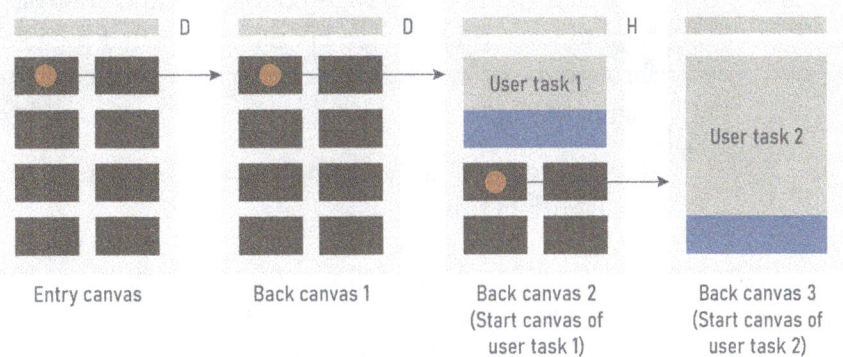

Entry canvas

Back canvas 1

Back canvas 2
(Start canvas of
user task 1)

Back canvas 3
(Start canvas of
user task 2)

Figure 13.12: Variations for delayed path flow type

To summarize the nature of the path flows, the flow can be expressed with the abbreviations of the used canvas types.

The two variations of the instant path flow (see Figure 13.10) are both expressed as "I."

The variations of the hybrid path flow (see Figure 13.11) are abbreviated with H-I (variation 1), H-H-I (variation 2), and H-D-I (variation 3).

The variations of the delayed path flow (see Figure 13.12) are abbreviated with D-I (variation 1), D-H-I (variation 2), D-D-I (variation 3), and D-D-H-I (variation 4).

Using this nomenclature, the path to the start of user tasks can be expressed, too. For the hybrid path flow and variation 1, the path flow for user task 1 is "H" and for user task 2 is "H-I." The path flows for the hybrid variation 2 are for user task 1 "H," for user task 2 "H-H" and for user task 3 "H-H-I."

The path flows for delayed variation 2 for user task 1 is "D-H" and for user task 2 is "D-H-I." For delayed variation 4, the path flow for user task 1 is "D-D-H" and for user task 2 is "D-D-H-I."

From an efficiency perspective, the path flows of Figure 13.10 are preferred. They are short and the primary user task is easily accessible.

Task flow types

After the long discussion about the path and task flows, here is a rather short section about task flow types. Task flows types describe significant variations of task flows.

In many cases, tasks are performed using the same ground canvas. Examples are design tools, writing tools, programming tools etc. There are applications that changes ground canvases to perform a user task. Examples of such user tasks are "check out a product," "onboard a device," "file tax return" etc. These are often user tasks with steps that require different content and controls, or that are hard to learn (like filing a tax return), so that the user is guided through the process step by step using several canvases to reduce cognitive load.

It seems reasonable to distinguish the following task flow types (see Figure 13.13):

Overlays are part of canvas layers and introduced in the upcoming subsection

▶ Spot flow (with and without overlays)
▶ One-way flow (with and without overlays)
▶ Round-trip flow (with and without overlays)

Task flow types

Spot flow

Start canvas
of a user task

Spot overlay flow

Start canvas
of a user task

One-way flow

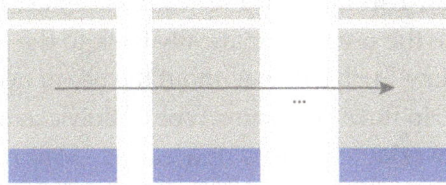

Start canvas	Back canvas 1	Back canvas *n*
of a user task	of a user task	of a user task

One-way overlay flow

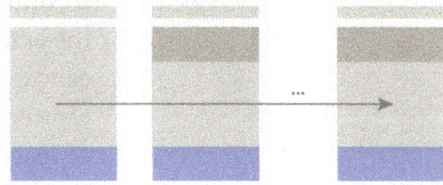

Start canvas	Back canvas 1	Back canvas *n*
of a user task	of a user task	of a user task

Round-trip flow

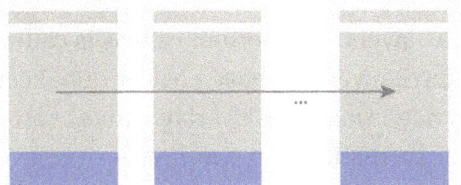

Start canvas	Back canvas 1	Back canvas *n*
of a user task	of a user task	of a user task

Round-trip overlay flow

Start canvas	Back canvas 1	Back canvas *n*
of a user task	of a user task	of a user task

Figure 13.13: Canvas flow types

Spot flow   The "spot flow" takes place on the entry canvas and does not change the canvas focus. An example of this flow is a messaging app. A spot flow allows normally the most efficient flow. A spot flow can exist with a entry canvas only (spot flow), or with an overlay canvas on top of the entry canvas (spot flow with overlay).

An "spot overlay flow" means that the entry canvas stays in the focus area. However, an overlay canvas is placed on top of the entry canvas that partially or fully covers the entry canvas. An example of an spot overlay flow is the responds to notifications on a mobile phone.

One-way flow   One-way flows means that the user is moved away from the entry canvas, and the flow does not take the user automatically back to the entry canvas. A typical example of a one-way flow is ordering a product online. The flow often stops with an order confirmation.

We have two types of one-way flow. One is using plain canvases, without overlays. This flow type is called "one-way flow." The second type uses at least one overlay. This flow type is called "one-way overlay flow."

Round-trip flow   Round-trip flows are flows that depart from the entry canvas and take the user automatically back to the entry canvas at the end of the flow. Such a flow without the use of overlay canvas is called "Round-trip flow." The same type of flow can occur at least partially with overlay canvases and called "round-trip overlay flow."

Canvas layers

We already mentioned canvas overlays when introducing the user task flows. In this subsection, we introduce them all together.

There are different canvas layers. The bottom canvas is called the *ground canvas*. The ground canvas can have an additional canvas on top that is called *overlay canvas*. An overlay canvas can have another overlay canvas. To distinguish the layers over overlay canvases, we call the first overlay canvas (overlay canvas relative to ground canvas) *overlay 1 canvas*, or simply *1st overlay canvas*, the second overlay canvas (overlay canvas relative to of overlay 1 canvas) *overlay canvas 2*, or simply *2nd overlay canvas* etc. Samples of overlay canvases are shown in Figure 13.14 and in Figure 13.15.

We can compare the canvases layers with floors of a building. The "ground canvas" can be compared to the ground floor of a building. The "overlay 1 canvas" can be compared to the second floor of a building in the US (where the ground floor is floor no. 1) that is the first upper floor of a building in Europe (where the ground floor is floor no. 0).

An overlay canvas can be permanent or temporal. Permanent means it stays on top of the ground canvas. Tool bars are examples of permanent overlay canvases. A temporal overlay canvas is often

We can relate the temporal and permanent overlay canvases to technology specific terminology for graphical user interface. A temporal overlay canvas is often implemented as a *modal* dialog, enforcing the user to respond before going back to the ground canvas. A permanent overlay canvas is typically implemented as an *non-modal* dialog. The user can either interact with design elements placed on the ground canvas or design elements placed on the overlay canvas.

Canvas layers - desktop

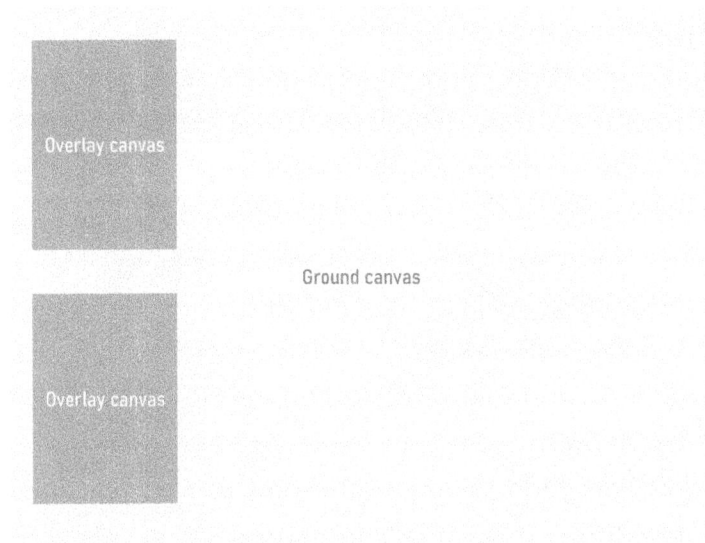

Overlay canvas

Ground canvas

Overlay canvas

Figure 13.14: Ground and overlay canvas for desktop

Canvas layers - mobile device and watch

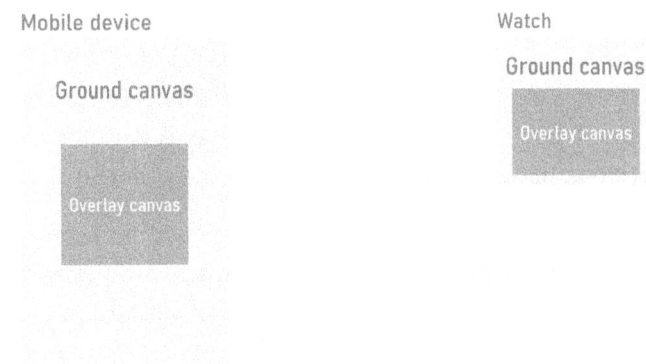

Mobile device

Ground canvas

Overlay canvas

Watch

Ground canvas

Overlay canvas

Figure 13.15: Ground and overlay canvas for mobile device and watch

used to request the user's attention and a confirmation by the user.

A ground canvas can have one or more overlay canvases at the same time. For instance, many design tools use several tool bars that are available as permanent overlay 1 canvases at the same time.

Areas

To design for efficiency, it is useful to identify certain regions of a canvas called *areas*.

Definition 21 (Area) *Canvas regions with relevance for efficiency.*

We can differentiate between different areas of a canvas:

► Entry area
  • Prime area
  • Secondary area
► Back area
► Focus area
► Control area

Entry and back area

The term "entry area" is borrowed from buildings that often have an entrance area. The remaining part of the canvas is called the "back area." This term is also borrowed from buildings.

Eye-tracking based research illustrates how users scan a screen (see Figure 13.16, and [192–194]

A canvas consists of an *entry area* and a *back area*. The entry area is immediately visible to the user, and all design elements placed on the entry area are immediately usable. Design elements placed in the back area can only be reached with at least one navigation step. The entry area is further divided into a *prime area* and a *secondary area*. The prime area is where the eye goes first. To design for efficiency, we aim to place content and controls needed to perform the primary user task on the entry canvas in the prime area of the entry area.

The position of the prime area within the entry area depends on cultural habits. In cultures where people typically read from top to bottom and left to right, the position of the prime area should be in the upper left part of the entry area. In cultures where people read from right to left and top to bottom, the prime area should be positioned in the upper right part of the entry area.

Sample canvases with entry area (incl. prime and secondary area) and back area for desktop and mobile devices are shown in Figure 13.17 and Figure 13.18.

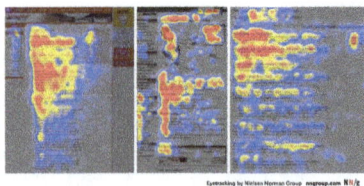

Figure 13.16: F-Shape heat maps; source: Norman Nielsen [192]; license: Copyright and reprint

Focus area

The *focus area* is the area of a canvas that is perceivable and/or usable for a user. After a canvas is launched, the focus area is identical with the entry area. However, the user can navigation to the back area, by moving the focus area to the back area. The focus area is like a window through that a user perceives a canvas.

Canvas and its areas for desktop

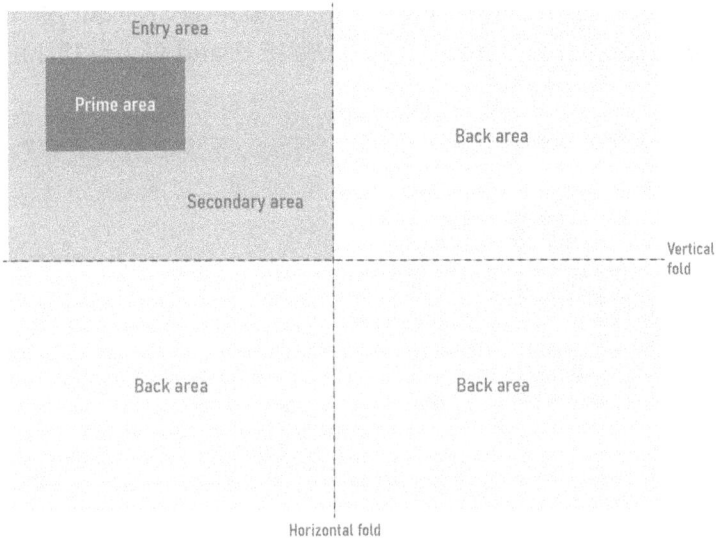

Figure 13.17: Canvas areas for desktop

Canvas areas for mobile devices

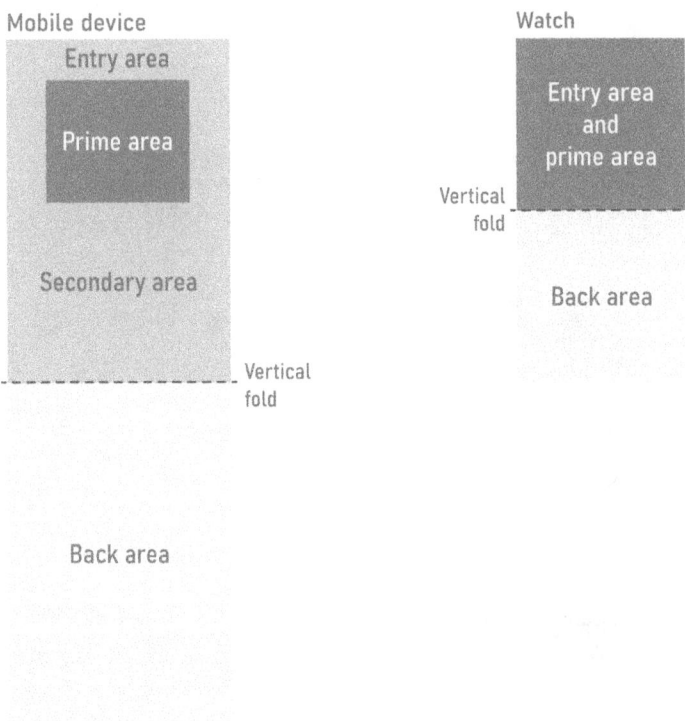

Figure 13.18: Canvas areas for mobile device and watch

The user has two ways to change the focus area. One possibility is a *continuous* navigation. For graphical user interface, a scroll bar is an example for a control for continuous navigation. The second possibility is a *discrete* navigation. A hyperlink to a different webpage or displaying an entry in a menu is an example of a discrete navigation control (see Figure 13.19 and Figure 13.20).

Focus area - desktop

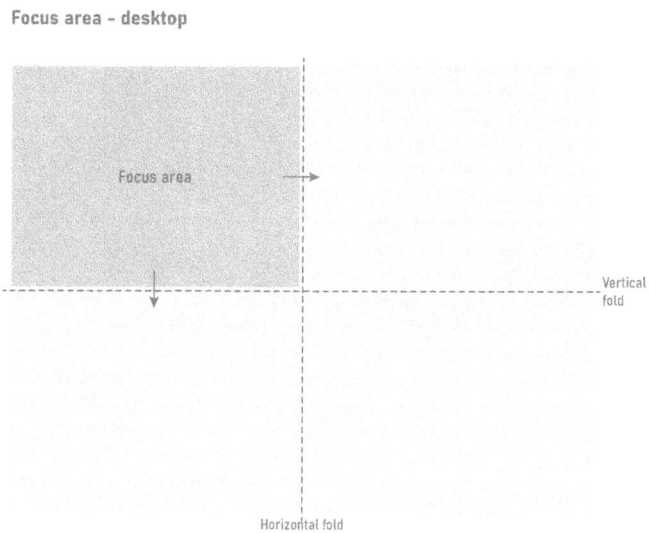

Figure 13.19: Canvas with focus area for desktop

Focus areas - mobile devices

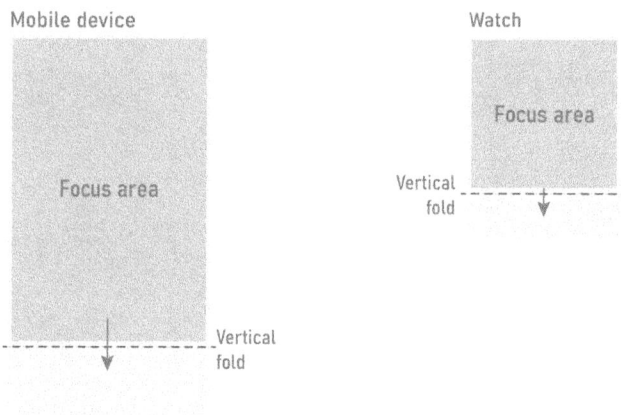

Figure 13.20: Canvas with focus area for mobile device and watch

Control area

After we discussed virtual areas, we are now looking into an area that has relevance for user input actions. To enable a user to provide content inputs and to trigger functions, control elements are needed. Example of control elements are buttons, selection elements (e.g., radio buttons, check boxes, pull down menus), and scroll bars. Not every canvas area is optimal for the placement of control elements. There are canvas areas that support a higher performance for human inputs and canvas area that don't.

The World of Pizza uses a mobile phone with a touch screen as the main interaction device. Therefore, we will focus on a mobile phone with a touch screen here. The basic idea is applicable to other interaction devices and modalities, too.

Figure 13.21 on the left-hand side shows an overview about typical screen sizes for mobile phones (year 2022). For the subsequent considerations, we use the 6 inch / 15.2 cm screen size.

The location of control elements has an influence on the user's performance and therefore the user's efficiency. [195–198] Figure 13.21 on the right-hand side shows the performance values for the different grid tiles.

For our consideration, the results of Zhang et al (2015) [198] was used. The study was performed with right-handed users only. During the study, the phone had to be held with the right hand and users triggered controls with their right thumb. The study determined that it took users on average between 961 and 1090 milliseconds to trigger a control in the upper right and lower right corner of the screen.

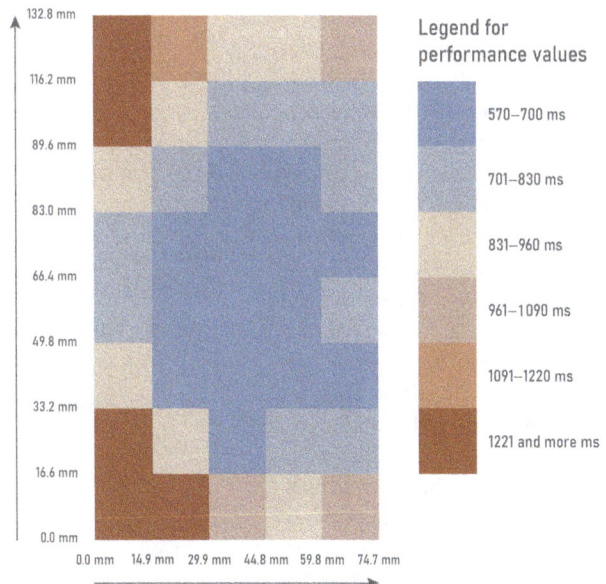

Figure 13.21: Mobile phone screen sizes; the highlighted size is used for the WoP example; source for performance values: [198]

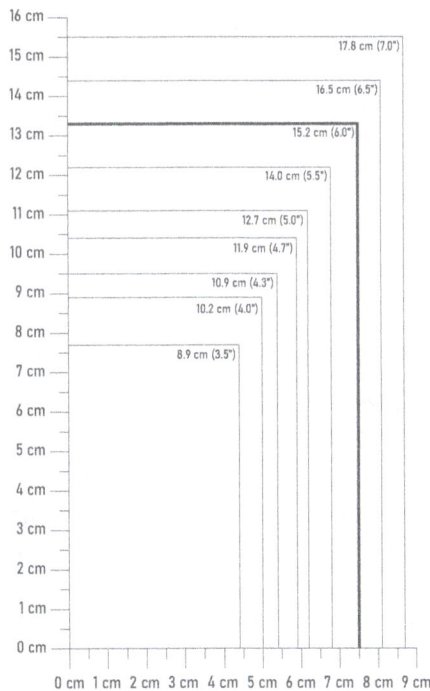

Modified performance grid   Canvas template with control area

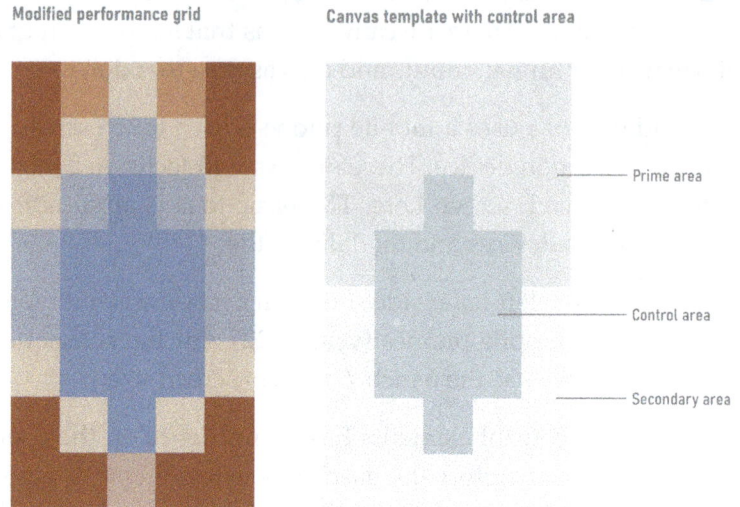

Figure 13.22: Grid with performance tiles and with control area

1: The modification was applied with the following method: The performance values of tiles in column 1 (first column on the left-hand side) were compared with the performance values of the corresponding tiles in column 5. The same procedures was applied to the performance values of tiles from column 2 corresponding tiles in column 4. After comparing the performance values of two tiles, tile with the worse performance value per comparison was kept and replaced the tile with the better performance value. Effectively, the performance tiles of the left two columns replaced the performance tiles of the right two columns. This modification should be considered as a hypothesis and requires validation with a scientific, behavior-based study, involving left-handed and right-handed users.

Since we should design user involvement for lefties and righties, we need to modify the performance tiles to consider the human factors of lefties, too.[1] The result is shown in Figure 13.22 (on the left-hand side). From there, we derived the canvas template with the marked control area in the center (see right-hand side of Figure 13.22).

Area for primary user task

From an efficiency perspective, the preferred area for supporting the primary user task is the prime area of the entry canvas. It enables the user to perform the primary user tasks immediately and in the most prominent area. If the primary user tasks requires controls, the controls should be ideally positioned in the control area.

Preferred area for primary user task on desktop

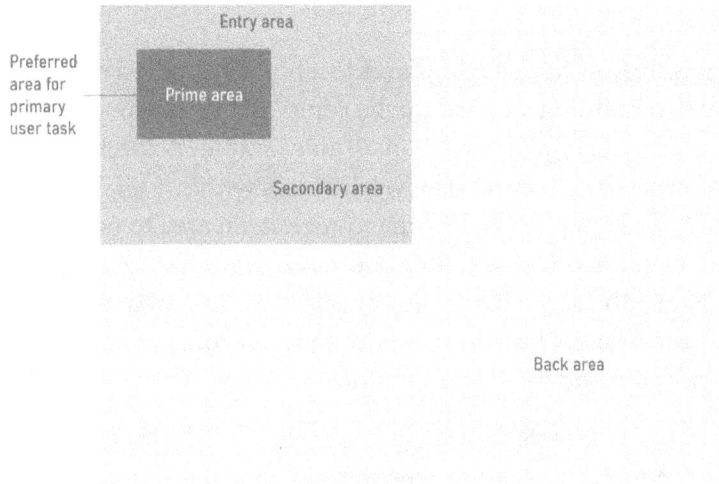

Entry area

Preferred area for primary user task

Prime area

Secondary area

Back area

Figure 13.23: Preferred area for primary user task

Preferred area for primary user task on mobile devices

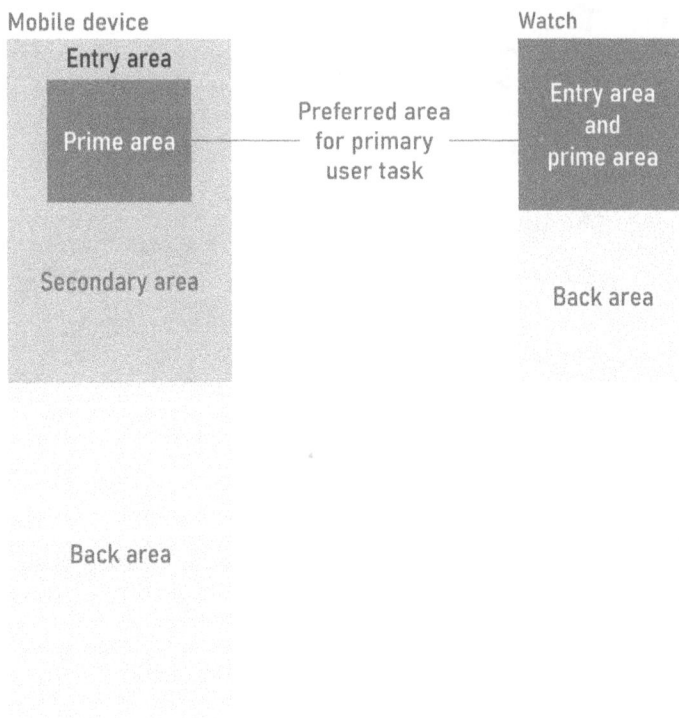

Mobile device

Entry area

Prime area

Preferred area for primary user task

Watch

Entry area and prime area

Secondary area

Back area

Back area

Figure 13.24: Preferred area for primary user task

Zones

> **Definition 22** (Zone) *Canvas area that groups design elements needed to perform one or multiple user steps.*

An application can be compared to a building, and a canvas to a room in a building. A zone can be compared to a workspace place in a room. Let's take a kitchen as an example. A kitchen can be represented by a canvas. The work places within a kitchen can be an area to prepare food, an area to cook it, an area to eat it etc. As much as the work places in a room are organized around tasks and goals, the same principles applies to zones of a canvas. The zones themselves, but also the flow between zones should support the user step and task flow for efficiency.

Figure 13.25 depicts how a canvas is separated into zones. Each zone support one or more user steps.

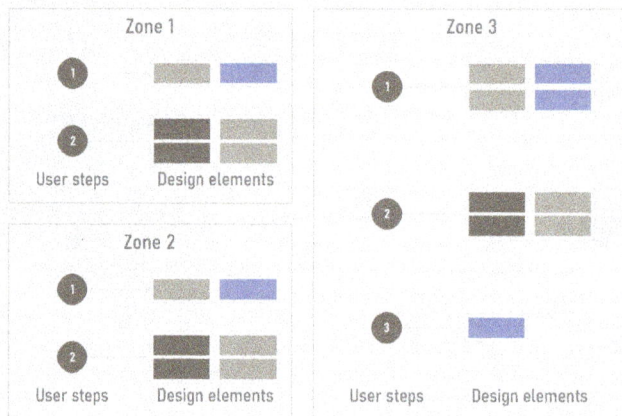

More guidance how to identify zones and how to map design elements to zones is provided later in Section 14 (Identify step flow per canvas) on page 412 and in Section 14 (Mark zones) on page 413.

Figure 13.25: Zones group design elements per user step

The trick is to identify zones according to user steps and their sequence. The flow within a zone (inner zone flow) and the flow across zones (outer zone flow) should support the user's mental model and our ambition for efficiency.

Content and alerts

There are two design elements, representing content for the user. One design element is called *content*.

A content element is a meaning carrying element for users and supports the user to perform their tasks and to achieve their goal. A content element directly or indirectly contributes to the user's goal. Each application has at least one content element that the user is interest in and that either represents the outcome of value, or that is transformed into the outcome of value. A content element can be a text, an image, a video, a line of code, but also a simple or complex engineering or design artifact. An outcome of value can be also a content element in a certain state (e.g., a text sent to someone or an design artifacts, stored somewhere or shared with someone).

There is a special content element that keeps the user informed about what a system is doing while performing a task. This content element is called *alert*.

An alert is a temporary content element which informs the user about a situation or state. It keeps the "human-in-the-loop." It can be a status that informs the user about a system's status, without requesting a user intervention. We call this type of alert "independent" because it does not create a dependency on the generation of the outcome of value (see example on the left-hand side in Figure 13.26).

An alert can also communicate a status or deviation to the user that requires the user to intervene before the application can complete the generation of the outcome of value. We call this type of alert "dependent" because the generation of the outcome of value depends on the user's response (see example on the right-hand side in Figure 13.26).

We aim to express an alert messages in a way it is immediately comprehensible and actionable for our target users. Ideally, a dependent alert makes effective suggestions how to resolve a deviation (see both examples in Figure 13.26). The intent is to minimize the user response time, one of the introduced user involvement metrics (see also Section 4 (Metric taxonomy) on page 76). Content are often placed on the ground canvas, and alerts are often placed on an overlay canvas.

Alerts

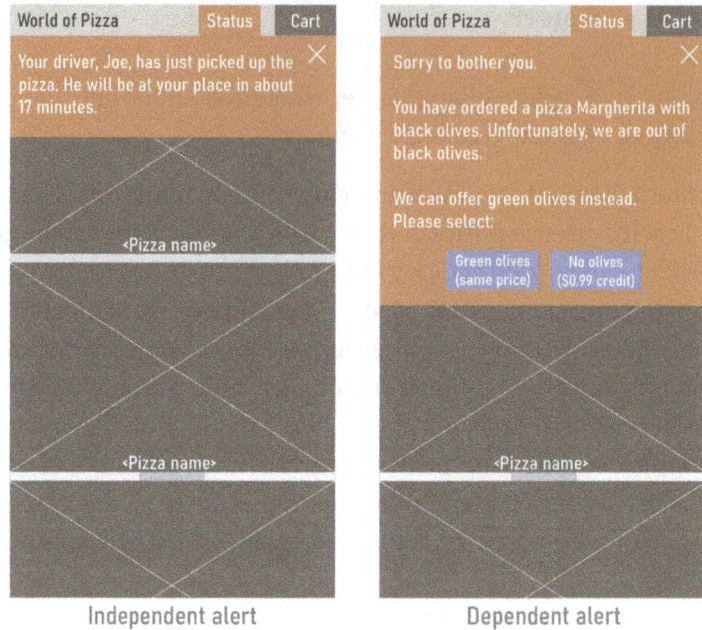

Independent alert   Dependent alert

Figure 13.26: Independent and dependent alerts; the chosen color of the design elements indicates its type (see also Figure 13.5).

Functions and controls

Functions are a non-perceivable design element. Functions transform objects, including canvases and content, from an input state into an output state.

We differentiate here three types of functions:

▶ Content function, associated with content control
▶ Canvas function, associated with canvas control
▶ System function

A *content function* is associated with a *content control*. A content control is often a "submit" button that initiate the execution of the function, associated with the button. A content function is intended to be initiated by a user by triggering a content control. A content function transforms a content from an input state into an output state. An example of content control is "Submit order." When the user triggers the content control "Submit order," the associated content function transforms a pizza in a shopping cart into a submitted order and initiates a payment transaction.

If at least one interaction step is needed to generate the outcome of value, a content function with its content control is a key design element for a user to achieve such outcome of value.

A *canvas function* is associated with a *canvas control*. Examples of canvas controls are scroll bars, zoom functions, and hyperlinks without a content function. A canvas control does not change a content object. It only changes the focus area. When we design for efficiency, we try to avoid the necessity of using canvas controls and functions to perform the primary user task.

A *system function* is a function that transforms content. It is not directly initiated by a user. However, a content function may trigger the execution of a system function in the background. A system function might be essential for generating an outcome of value that is the reason why it is listed here. A system function might be a frequent status update to the user to inform the user about the current status of the pizza order. A system function is realized through a technical involvement point (see Section 10 (Design the user involvement system) on page 250).

If no interaction step is needed to achieve the outcome of value, the generation of the outcome of value is realized by a system function. This is the reason why a system function is an essential design element to achieve efficiency.

Controls are placed on a canvas. Functions are not placed on a canvas, but associated with the placed controls.

Actions and interaction devices

Actions are either performed by users or by the technical system. *User actions* means that users set body parts into motion. The motion is applied to one or more interaction devices (e.g., a mouse or a keyboard) that then triggers a selected control that initiates a function, associated with the selected control.

System actions are initiated by the technical system. After a user has initiated a user action (e.g., start an application), the system responses with several system actions to transform an application and content. If an application is highly automated, system actions execute the automation mode. If the system detects a (unwanted) deviation, a system action is report the deviation by creating a system alert and present it to the user.

User actions and their related controls and functions are often assigned to the "front-end" of a system. System actions are often assigned the "back-end" of a system. However, both are needed to generate an outcome of value.

Constraints

> **Definition 23** (Constraint) *A non-negotiable condition that limits the design space.*

We have four different types of constraints:

- ▶ Business constraints
- ▶ Technology constraints
- ▶ Regulatory constraints
- ▶ Design constraints

It is highly recommended to elicit such constraints as early as possible in the design process. Some of the constraints can already be identified during the scoping of the project, and latest during the discovery phase of a project.

Business constraints   Business constraints are business related decisions that impose a constraint on the design space. Examples for business constraints are: Business processes, business practices, business terminology and wording. An existing business model can be a constraint, too, that influences the business model of the application under design.

An organization may decide to apply a certain process that will constrain the workflow that becomes a constraint for the design and how a user is guided through the user tasks. If this process is not negotiable, it is a business constraint for the design.

Technology constraints   Technical constraints are decisions regarding the use or not use of certain technologies, such as technical platforms, a deployment system such as app stores, development environments, technical interfaces, and programming languages. A very relevant technology constraint is the selection of the front-end technology. This question can probably be clarified already during the scoping of the project.

If such technology decisions are not negotiable, they form a technology constraint.

Regulatory constraints   Regulatory constraints are introduced by applicable regulatory or statutory codes. Applicable regulatory and statutory codes depend on the country or region in which an application will be deployed and the domain.

Many regulatory and statutory codes are common in regulated industries, often for safety reasons. Examples of such industries are medical devices and automotive. Example of such regulatory codes for medical devices are 21CFR820 from the Federal Food and Drug Administration in the United States. [177, 199–201] for medical devices, or several safety standards for railroads [202–205].

If an application is governed by a regulatory or statutory code for the region in which it is planned to be launched, the project team must provide objective evidence that it meets the applicable clauses of applicable codes. Some of such standards impose constraints on the design process or on the application itself. To avoid unnecessary rework, it is highly advisable to identify applicable codes early in the project.

Design constraints   The last group of constraints impose design constraints. A typical candidate is a company style guide or design system with which the design result has to comply with. Other design constraints are imposed by the selected interaction devices, including their interaction modalities such as direct manipulation / vision, gesture, voice / sound etc.

Design universe

We switch gears now. So far, we have looked at design elements and types of elements as building blocks for involvement concepts. Now, we starting looking into the design process. The design process proposed in this book considers the involvement goals (see Chapter 12 (Involvement Goals) on page 313) as exploration and exclusion criteria. Before we look into how the goals are used, we want to zoom out even more and introduce a model that helps to categorize different design options. Let's define first what a design option is.

> **Definition 24** (Design option) *Result of a design act.*

A design option can a first, rough sketch, an early involvement concept, or an option for a final user interface design. It can also be an application under design, or it can be completely unrelated to it.

In order to understand the quality of a design option, we introduce a categorization model, called the design universe.

> **Definition 25** (Design universe) *Model to categorize design options according to their compliance level with involvement goals.*

Outer space

Gray space

Design
space

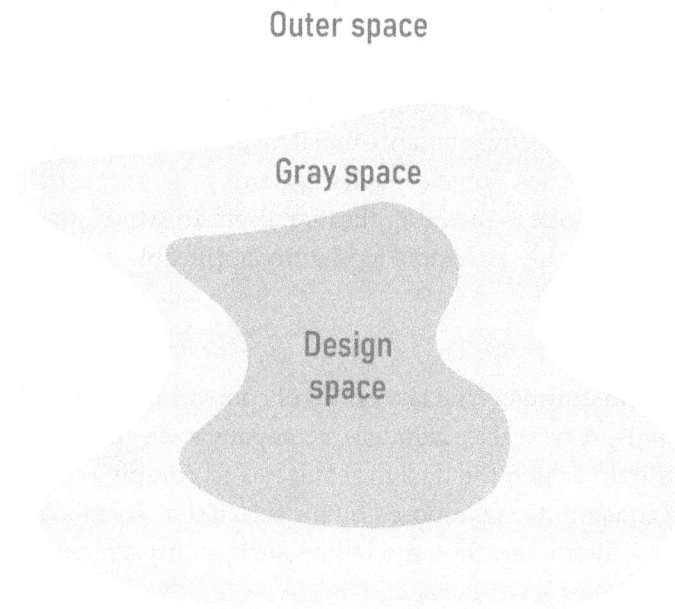

Figure 13.27: Design universe

The design universe consists of three spaces: design space, grey space, and outer space (see Figure 13.27).

The design space is limited to those design options that comply with all involvement goals and with all applicable constraints ("compliant"). The intent of the exploration phase is to find as many design options as possible that belong to the design space. In Figure 13.27, the design space is drawn as an asymmetric shape, on purpose. Each involvement goal and constraints limits the design space and makes it smaller. The involvement goals and constraints can be considered as the boundaries of the design space.

For pragmatic reason, we consider an extension of the design space, called *grey space*. It is the space that contains design options that comply with at least one involvement goal, but not all ("partially compliant"). The grey space is our working space for initial and refined design options that are not fully compliant with the involvement goals.

Furthermore, we also define a space outside the grey space, called the *outer space*. It is the space that contains design options that do not comply with any of the involvement goals ("non-compliant"). There are as many design options in the outer space as stars in the universe - possibly even more.

It is possible that the design space exist and is *empty*. This happens if at least one design option exists, at least in theory, that complies with all involvement goals, but it hasn't been found yet. This situation occurs often at the beginning of the concept exploration phase.

It is also possible that the design space is *non-existent*. It means that no design option exists that complies with all involvement goals. One typical reason for a nonexistent design space is that at least two involvement goals conflict with each other. In such a case, at least one involvement goal should be modified or removed to turn a nonexistent design space into an existent design space. Another typical reason is that at least one of the goals is not achievable. Achievable here does not necessarily refer to project feasibility, but to the user and the user's capabilities. An design space that is not not-existent is called an "existent design space." An existent design space can be empty or can contain at least one design option.

Involvement concept

For the remainder of this book, we only look at involvement concepts as a specific design option type. Insights of the discovery phase (experience foundation) and results of the definition phase (experience architecture) inspire and inform them. Particularly, the involvement goals are a key driver for the formation of involvement concepts.

> **Definition 26** (Involvement concept) *A preliminary design artifact that aims to comply with the stated involvement goals and considers the given constraints.*

To emphasize the exploratory and selection characteristics of the involvement concept process, we call initial involvement concepts, prior to any iterations, *seed concepts*. The eventually selected involvement concept is called a *sprout concept*. The word choices underlying metaphor indicates that the seeds are nurtured to grow. It also indicates that design process in its nature is iterative. Exploration, refinement, evaluate, and assessments steps facilitates that growth. The process also includes that some of the seeds won't make it (i.e., insufficient compliance with involvement goals) and are excluded.

A sprout concept should be in the design space. It means it should meet all involvement goals and constraints. Depending on the coverage of the involvement goals, it should be viable (from a business perspective), create value (from a domain perspective), and should be usable (from a user experience perspective). It may not be feasible yet from a technical perspective.

Since the involvement concept is incomplete, compared to a fully specified user interface or application, it is useful to understand which design decisions are made with an involvement concept and which are not. In general, the explored and refined involvement concepts should be rich enough, so they can be assessed against the stated involvement goals.

Here is a list of design decisions that are typically made with an involvement concept:

- Per user role and user task, a *canvas flow* is identified.
- For the previously mentioned canvas flow, the canvas specific *zones* including their content, controls, and related functions are identified.
- For the previously mentioned canvas flows, the design elements are organized in a canvas layout
- Involvement concepts for the different *modalities* as stated in the user involvement points have been created.

Another way to look at an involvement concept is feasibility. An involvement concept contains most necessary decisions to perform a technical feasibility study. A sprout concept is the basis to derive functional, non-functional, and interface requirements [206].

Here is a (most likely incomplete) list of design decisions that are often not made with an involvement concept:

- Canvases, their zones and design elements that do not address one of the involvement goals.
- Typeface, font size, and font weight
- Wording for labels and text copy
- Visual assets
- Color schemes, color values
- Branding elements and styles (visual, audio, haptic etc.)
- Specific content instances
- (Pixel-exact) measures

An involvement concept is meant to be a *preliminary* design artifact and not meant to be a final design or a user interface specification (i.e. blueprint for implementation). However, the design decisions made in the sprout concept are the basis for additional refinements. Hence, we were interested in compliance with *significant* involvement goals, so that major, costly changes are not expected after an involvement concept was selected as a sprout concept (see also Section 12 (Selection of qualitative involvement goals) on page 328).

Iterative design process

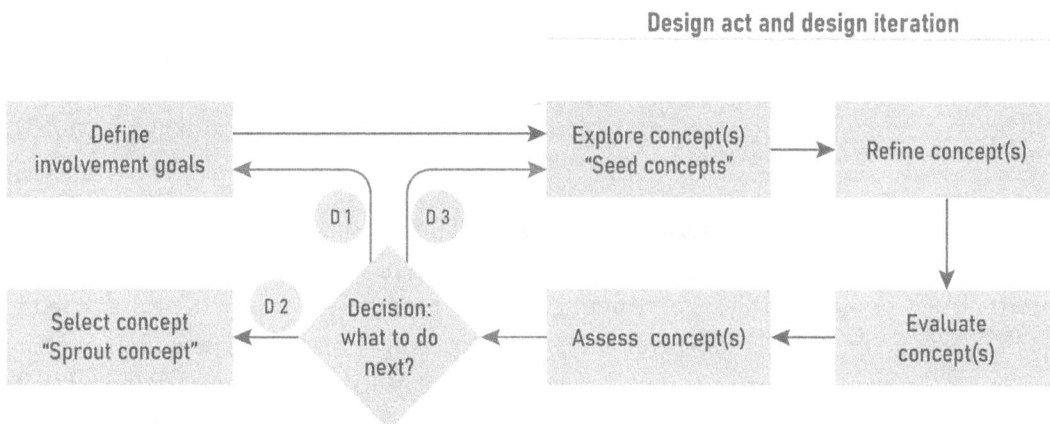

Process steps

The iterative design process supports the creation of a user involvement concept systematically and predictably. The process consists of six steps: explore, refine, evaluate, assess, decide, and select. The expected outcome is a user involvement concept that complies with all involvement goals (see Figure 13.28).

The iterative design process with the involvement goal matrix is based on Pugh's *controlled convergence method* [207, pp. 74–100] [208]. Pugh uses the expression "divergence" for exploration and "convergence" for exclusion.

Iterative design process

Design act and design iteration

Define involvement goals → Explore concept(s) "Seed concepts" → Refine concept(s)

D 1   D 3

Select concept "Sprout concept" ← D 2 ← Decision: what to do next? ← Assess concept(s) ← Evaluate concept(s)

Figure 13.28: Iterative design process

It is assumed that the involvement goals are defined and organized in a involvement goal matrix (see Section 1 (Involvement goal matrix) on page 332). Afterwards, the process starts with exploring concepts.

Explore concept The intent of this step is to create a certain number of involvement concepts, the so called seed concepts. At this stage, it is not important how well the seed concepts comply with the involvement goals. It is more important to go for quantity, meaning to create as many concepts as possible. A certain number of seed concepts can be set as a minimum target for the exploration ("Don't stop the exploration until you have created at least x seed concepts"). Chapter 14 (Explore Concepts) on page 387 lists techniques how to design seed concepts and how to explore more options.

In engineering, such an exploration step is often called "design space exploration" [209–212]. It is the "process of finding a design solution, or solutions, that best meet the desired design requirements, from a space of tentative design points" [213, Section 8.2, first paragraph]. The term "design solution" in the definition is equivalent to what we call "seed concept." The term "design requirement" is equivalent to "involvement goal," and the term "design point" is equivalent to what we called "design option." The definition does not use a term comparable to what we call "sprout concept."

Refine concept   After the seed concepts are explored, they will be refined. The book introduces twelve efficiency techniques that will streamline the seed concepts and make them more efficient. They are described in Chapter 15 (Refine Concept) on page 439.

Evaluate concept   The refined concepts are evaluated with multiple techniques. One techniques is just using it excessively. A speed test is another technique to check that the target involvement time can be met. The third technique is an analytical evaluation technique to estimate the interaction complexity of the refined seed concepts, called big I notation. Both techniques are described in Chapter 16 (Evaluate Concepts) on page 493.

Assess concept   Based on the refined concepts and the evaluation results, the concepts are now assessed against the involvement goals. It will be checked and noted which involvement goal is met and which is not. The result is documented in the involvement goal matrix (see Chapter 17 (Assess Concepts) on page 531).

Iteration decision   The last step of an iteration is a decision what to do next. Three types of next steps are possible: modify involvement goals and reassess the concepts against the modified involvement goals (decision D 1), explore new and/or refine existing involvement concepts (decision D 2), or terminate the iteration and select one of the involvement concepts as the sprout concept (decision D 3). The decision process is described in Chapter 18 (Decide about Iteration) on page 541.

Select concept   After the iterations were terminated, one of the compliant involvement concepts is selected. Considerations and criteria for selecting one of the compliant involvement concepts is described in Chapter 19 (Select Concept) on page 557.

The steps are also shown on a poster (see Figure 13.29).

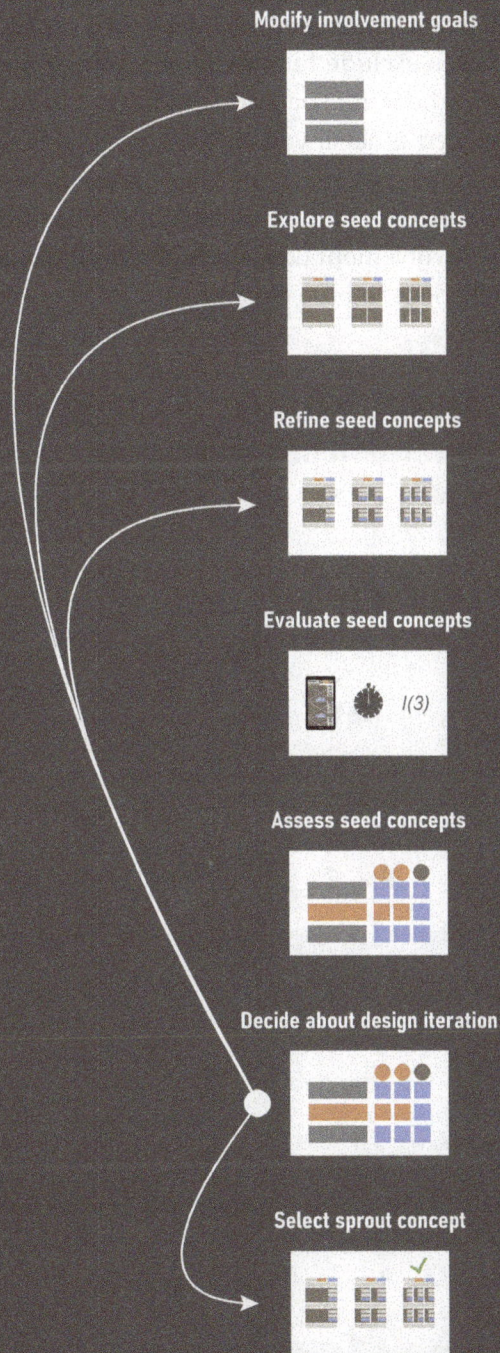

Iterative Design Process

Modify involvement goals

Explore seed concepts

Refine seed concepts

Evaluate seed concepts

Assess seed concepts

Decide about design iteration

Select sprout concept

Helmut Degen (CC BY-NC-SA 4.0)

Figure 13.29: Iterative design process

Map evolving involvement concepts to design universe

The explored, refined, evaluated, and assessed involvement concepts can be mapped to the three spaces of the design universe (see Figure 13.30). The illustration visualizes how refinements and iterations (visualized with dotted arrows) can move involvement concept (represented as a circle) from the outer space (white background) to the grey space, and from the grey space to the design space (brown background). Many seed concepts in the outer space have been excluded immediately (orange circles). Some seed concepts in the outer space are excluded, but ideas or elements have influenced other involvement concepts. Some involvement concepts in the grey space have been refined and eventually excluded. Others made it to the design space. After some refinements, one of the involvement concept in the design space is selected as the sprout concept (blue circle).

Design universe with categorized involvement concepts

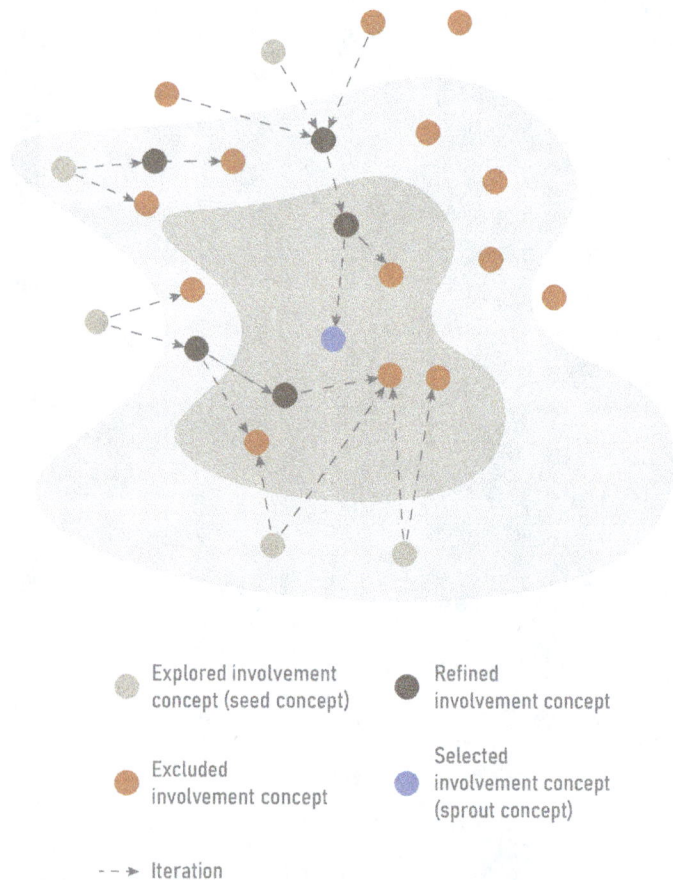

Figure 13.30: Involvement concepts, mapped to the design universe

Exploration and exclusion principle

Figure 13.31 visualizes the exploration and exclusion of the involvement concepts across several iterations. In iteration 1, seven involvement concepts are explored (first row of seven brown circles). After the assessment, four involvement have been excluded (orange circles), so that three are remaining. In iteration two, two additional involvement concepts have been explored (five vertical brown dots). During the assessment, two out of five involvement concepts have been excluded (orange circles), and three are still remaining (brown circles). Out of the three, one involvement concept was selected as the sprout concept (blue circle). The process may require more than two iterations.

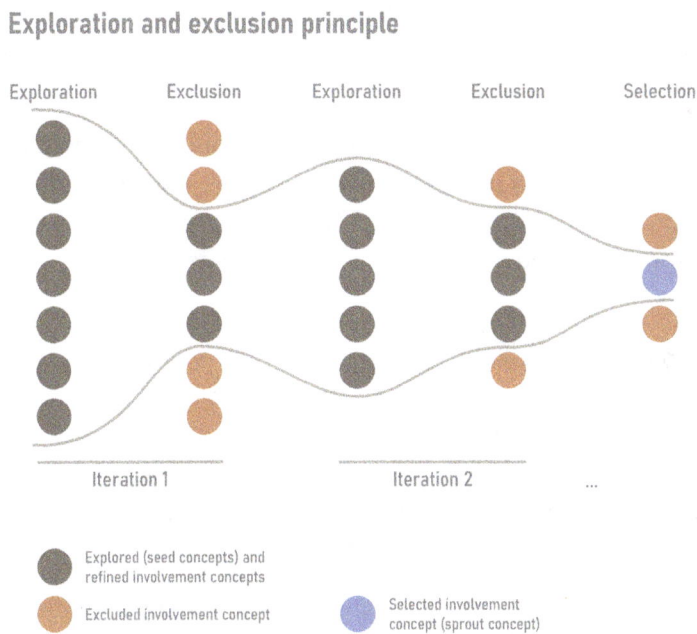

Figure 13.31: Exploration and exclusion principle

Evolving involvement concepts mapped to involvement goal matrix

Figure 13.32 visualizes the iterative design process, mapped to a simplified involvement goal matrix. To distinguish each involvement goal matrix in that diagram, each matrix has its own identifier, indicated beneath each matrix. Each matrix has six involvement goals, assigned to the horizontal rows. The involvement concepts (abbreviated "IC") are listed per column. The involvement goals are used to determine the compliance of an involvement concept against each involvement goal.

Chapter 12 (Involvement Goals) on page 313 describes how to define involvement goals and particularly. Section 1 (Involvement goal matrix) on page 332 in the same chapter provides additional information about the creation of a involvement goal matrix.

Matrix I-1.A ("I-1" stands for iteration 1 and "A" stands for first matrix of that iteration) shows that seven involvement concepts have been explored (IC 1, ..., IC 7). All concepts are refined (matrix I-1.B) and assessed against the involvement goals (I-1.C). The assessment results is reflected by the color of the squares, per involvement concept and per involvement goal. If an involvement concept complies with an involvement goal, the square is colored in blue, otherwise in orange. Based on the assessment result, the involvement concepts one, three, four, and seven have been excluded due to their low compliance rating (matrix I-1.D).

A question is when to exclude an involvement concept. There are cases when involvement concepts in their current form do not comply with all involvement goals. If they can be made compliant, they should be kept. If they cannot be made compliant, they should be excluded. In our sandbox example here, we exclude involvement concepts with four or more orange squares for simplicity reasons (i.e., involvement concepts one, three, four, and seven).

Since no involvement concept complies with all involvement goals, another iteration is needed. The decision was made to refine all kept involvement concepts (i.e., IC 2, IC 5, and IC 6). Another decision was made to add two new seed concepts.

In iteration two, involvement concepts eight and nine have been explored (matrix I-2.A). Afterwards, involvement concepts two, five and six, eight, and nine are refined (matrix I-2.B). All refined involvement concepts are assessed against the involvement goal (matrix I-2.C). The assessment shows that involvement concepts five, six, and nine are fully compliant. The involvement concepts two and eight are excluded (matrix I-2.D).

Since we have three compliant involvement concepts, there won't be any other iteration. One of the three compliant involvement concepts will be selected. For no specific reason, involvement concept six was selected and becomes the sprout concept. Involvement concept five and nine have are excluded (matrix S).

In the subsequent chapters in this part of the book, the steps of the iterative design process are demonstrated with the World of Pizza example.

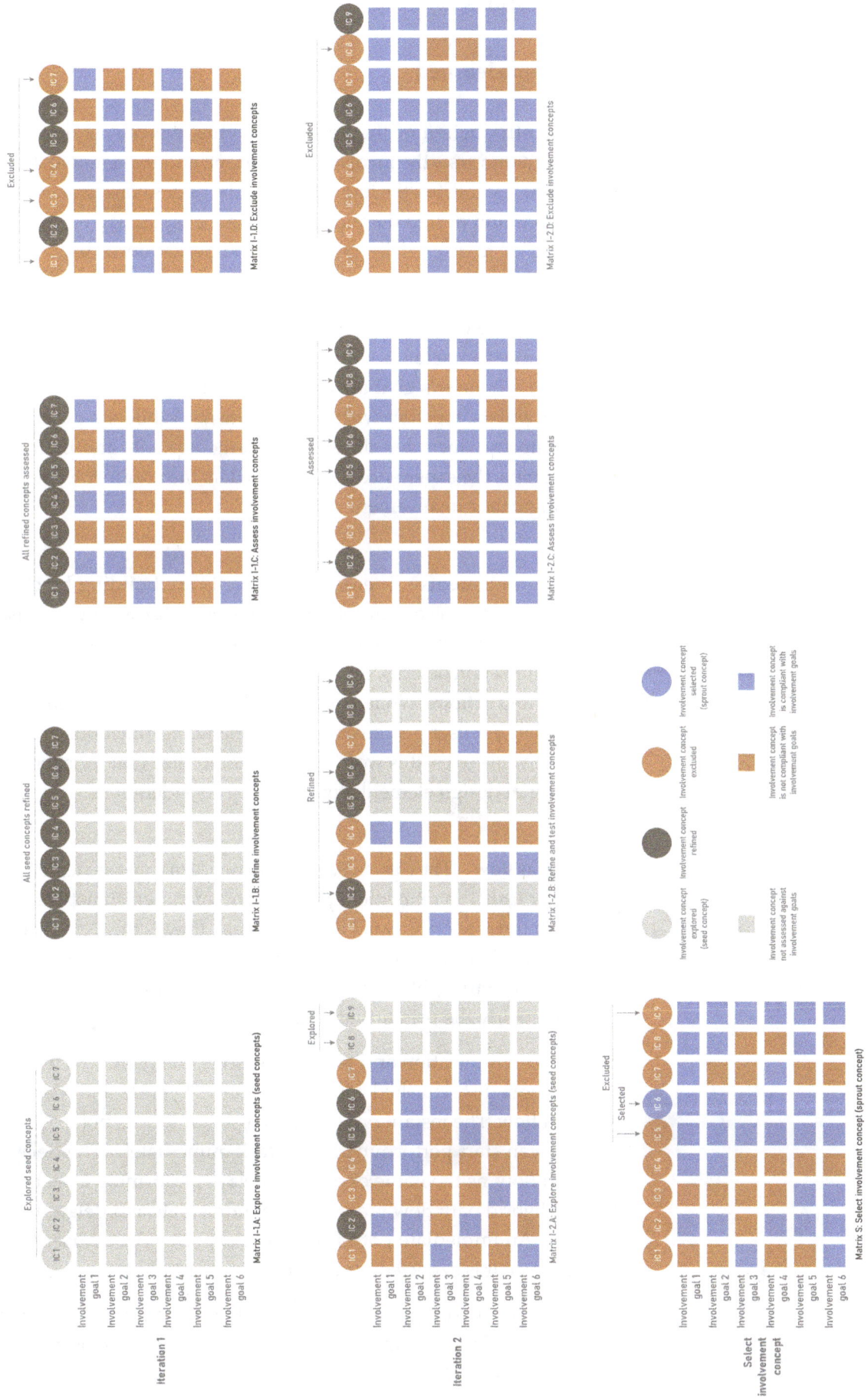

Figure 13.32: Iterative concept exploration and exclusion process

Summary

Lessons learned

The introduction of the design elements, the canvas flows, the design universe, the involvement concept, and the iterative design process establishes the foundation for the discussions about design options and design decisions in the next chapter. We have now a language to discuss design options and design decisions.

Experience design   Experience design is the design of user involvement to achieve stated goals and to address stated users' needs. The user's goal are expressed as part of the user involvement points, together with the user's tasks. While the experience architecture includes all user involvement points and their relationships, the experience design considers the user involvement of a single user involvement point.

Design elements   The design elements are building blocks to enable user involvement. One design element is a canvas that is used to place and organize other design elements. Other design elements are interaction devices, overlay canvas, controls, functions, content, alert, and actions. While interaction devices, canvas, contents, and controls are user perceivable design elements, functions are non-perceivable ones. It is worthwhile to emphasize that functions are essential design elements for efficiency considerations.

Canvas flow   The canvas flow is a sequence of canvases to perform a user task. For refinement purposes, we distinguish between the "path flow" and the "task flow." The task flow is the flow that the user needs to pass to start performing a user task. Ideally, the user can start right from the entry canvas performing user tasks, particularly the primary user tasks.

For communication and analysis reasons, the path flow was furthermore distinguished between "instant," "hybrid," and "delayed" path flow. The instant path flow means that is does not exist. The user can start performing a user task immediately. The delayed path flow, as the name expresses, delays performing a user task. The hybrid path flow is a mixture of immediate and delayed path flow. An immediate path flow is not expected for all user tasks, however, it is expected for the primary user task.

There are also different types of task flows: "spot flow," "one way flow," and "round trip flow." The spot flow keeps the user on the same canvas. The one way flow requires a canvas flow to perform and complete a user task. After the user has reached the last canvas, the user has to find the way back to the entry canvas (therefore, this flow is named "one way flow"). Another multi-canvas flow is the round trip flow. It also requires several canvases to perform and complete a task flow. When the user has reached the last canvas of the flow, the user is taken back to the entry canvas (hence the name round trip flow). Each of the three mentioned task flow types exists also with and without an overlay.

Canvas layers Sometimes, temporary overlays are used to present content to users. These type of overlays are called here "canvas layers." The overlays can be permanent or temporarily. The be able to distinguish between the different canvas types, we call the base canvas "ground canvas," "overlay canvas 1," "overlay canvas 2" etc.

Areas Another important design concept are areas. These are specific canvas regions with relevant for efficiency. Areas are useful for decisions where to place design elements.

We distinguish between entry areas, back areas, focus areas, and control areas. The entry area is the area that is usable to users without any interaction, including changing the focus area. The entry area has more and less prominent areas. The most prominent area is the "prime area." The area outside the prime area is called the "secondary area." The back area is the area that is only reachable when the user changes the focus area. The focus area is what is usable to users. The user can change the focus area with canvas controls and canvas functions that include scrolling, zooming, and hyperlinks. Canvas functions to not change content, just the perspective on content.

The control area is the preferred area to place controls. For mobile devices, it is a center area of the focus area.

For efficiency reasons, the primary user task should be placed in the prime area of the entry canvas.

Zones Zones are canvas areas that group design elements needed to perform one or multiple user steps. Zones are organized by user steps. Design elements are selected based on the effectiveness to support user steps.

Content and alert   A content element is a meaning carrying element for users and supports the user to perform their tasks and to achieve their goal. An alert is a temporary content element that makes the user aware of a certain situation of state. Alerts are essential design elements for user intervention. They often initiate user intervention.

Constraints   Constraints are non-negotiable conditions that limit the design space. There are four known constraint types: Business, technology, regulatory, and design. It is recommended to identify applicable constraints as early in a design project, ideally during the scoping phase. Constraints, as well as involvement goals, define the boundary of the design space.

Design universe   The design universe is a model to categorize design options like involvement concepts according to their compliance with involvement goals and constraints. The design universe consists of three spaces: the design space that contains design options which comply with all involvement goals and constraints. The grey space that contains design options which comply with at least one involvement goal or constraint, but not all. The outer space that contains design options which comply with no involvement goal and constraint.

Design option   A design option is an artifact composed of design elements. A design option can be an option for an early involvement concept, or an option for a refined and specified user interface. For the purpose of this book, we look at involvement concepts as design options.

Involvement concept   The involvement concept is a preliminary design artifact that aims to comply with stated involvement goals and to address the users' needs. An involvement concept is explored, refined, evaluated, assessed, and eventually selected through an iterative design process. The initially explored involvement concepts are called "seed concept," the finally selected involvement concept is called "sprout concept."

Iterative design process   The iterative design process is created to systematically and predictably explore, refine, evaluate, assess, and eventually select an involvement concept. To facilitate such a process, an involvement goal matrix is used to guide the process and to assess the involvement concepts against involvement goals.

If the design space exists, the iterative design process will most likely lead to compliant involvement concepts.

Tips and tricks

Design elements   Probably the most important tip I can give is to think in *flows* when designing for user involvement. Involvement design is a time-based design (like a movie), not a static design (like a picture). Every selected and placed design element needs to support the user's flow to generate the outcome of value. That's why the different flow types have been introduced and discussed here, so that we have a language to conceptualize and discuss different flow types. We will look into this more in detail in the next chapter. Unfortunately, the "design thinking" today is more about design systems. A design system can be understood as a set of interconnected components with a consistent form factor (e.g., colors, typeface, dimensions, texture, material, style) establishing a coherent visual, interaction, and/or involvement language for one or more modalities and channels. However, the value of our work for the user lies in flows. The decision sequence is: user role → user goal → user task → canvas flow → user steps → zones per canvas → design elements per zones. The static individual design elements are the last decisions in that change. We will discuss this more in detail in the next chapter.

The second tip is to use *involvement goals*. This may not be standard design practice, and not everyone may like the idea of goals. They look obligatory and binding, and they are. Their use requires a rationalization of the intended outcome, derived from the discovery and definition phase. The good news is: it is not easy, but not *that* hard. There are harder problems to solve than using articulated goals for design decisions. For instance, the design problem you attempt to solve is probably harder than articulating goals. The goals make the design process transparent, understandable, and explainable. Explainability is an important attribute of experience professionalism that leads to a higher acceptance of the design work and the result. It probably also leads to an improved reputation of the design discipline that is often perceived as using an opinion-driven design approach, and not so much a goal-driven design approach. "opinion-driven" refers to the opinion of the designer, not such much to the opinion of the sponsor or user.

The third tip is to actively use *functions* as design elements. When it comes to efficiency, functions are the way to go. Functions allow to delegate actions to the systems, not to the user. Thinking in functions means to think in what happens between the user interfaces, not so much what happens on the user interfaces. At the end of the day, what experience professionals do is designing a tool to enable a human to acquire an outcome of value. If this can be achieved without user involvement, it is often an even better solution. A user interface is just a means, not a purpose. We sometimes for get that. Using a user interface to acquire an outcome of value means that we request the user's time, attention, and inputs. That's a lot we ask for. To respect the user's time and attention, it should always be considered to use functions to delegate an action from the user to the system. We will also look more into functions in the refinement chapter.

Iterative design process The iterative design process looks rigid, due to the defined steps and the involvement goals. Let me assure that it provides guidance and at the same time sufficient freedom to explore as much as a wanted. The exploration phase should actually ignore the goals and just brainstorm ideas. The assessment later will check the quality of each concept against the involvement goals. In that sense, the process allows creative freedom at the beginning, and keeps the design act on track with the assessment. It is a good balance between creativity and goal orientation.

Exercise 3.1

Goal Map elements of an application of your choice to the introduced design elements and canvas flows. Understand iterative design process better.

Material Application of choice, design elements, iterative design process

Completion criteria:

- ▸ An application of your choice is selected.
- ▸ For the selected application: an example of each design element is identified and documented.
- ▸ For the selected application: at least three different path flows are identified and documented.
- ▸ For the selected application: at least three different task flows are identified and documented.
- ▸ Select one of your past projects: Document the actual applied design process. Map the actual process to the iterative design process. Identify and describe the differences. Which steps from the iterative design process could have benefited your past project and why?

Explore Concepts | 14

A man who dares to waste an hour of time
has not discovered the value of life
Charles Darwin

Purpose

The first step in creating an involvement concept is to explore seed concepts (see Figure 14.1).

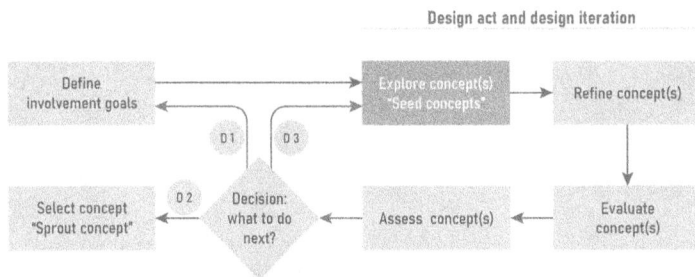

Figure 14.1: Explore concepts

A seed concept is the first experience design artifact. It is informed by the involvement goals and created based on the results of the experience foundation and the experience architecture.

Aiming for efficiency requires that the seed concept meet certain efficiency quality criteria. Such criteria areas follows:

▶ Select only design elements that effectively support the user tasks and the user's goal
▶ Select a minimum number of design elements to avoid unnecessary user involvement

▶ Organize design elements in a way that enables users to process the content and to initiate actions efficiently

To ensure such quality criteria, this chapter introduces a structured design approach. It consists of the following steps, which are described in detail in this chapter and summarized in Figure 14.2.

▶ Refine user tasks
▶ Ask task questions
▶ Identify content
▶ Select design elements
▶ Map canvases to user tasks
▶ Map steps to canvas
▶ Mark zones
▶ Map design elements to zones
▶ Create the baseline concept
▶ Explore seed concepts

The proposed steps and sequence will be applied to the user tasks per user involvement point. They have been proven to work effectively in many industrial projects, particularly in projects with "foreign" and complex application domains. As always in this book, the proposed design approach is a suggestion and can be modified to accommodate preferences of the experience professional and project characteristics.

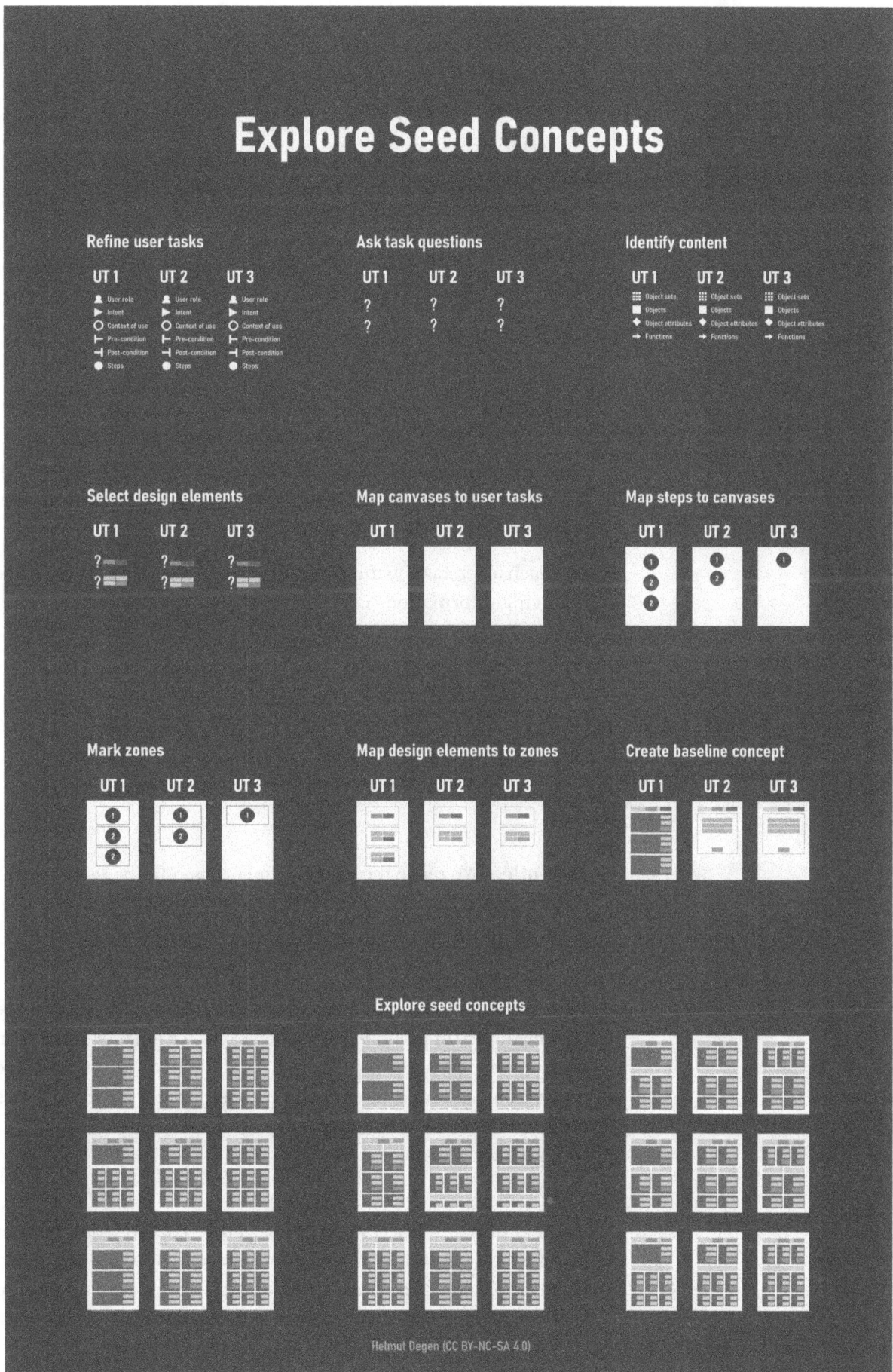

Figure 14.2: Explore seed concepts

Refine user tasks

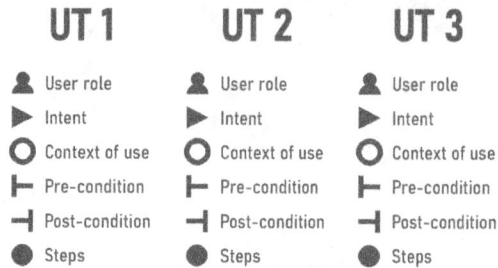

UT 1

- 👤 User role
- ▶ Intent
- ◯ Context of use
- ├ Pre-condition
- ┤ Post-condition
- ⬤ Steps

UT 2

- 👤 User role
- ▶ Intent
- ◯ Context of use
- ├ Pre-condition
- ┤ Post-condition
- ⬤ Steps

UT 3

- 👤 User role
- ▶ Intent
- ◯ Context of use
- ├ Pre-condition
- ┤ Post-condition
- ⬤ Steps

Technique

First, we refine the user tasks that are defined in the user involvement point. By refinement, we mean defining task-specific design assumptions and design targets.

For each user task, we eventually have a description with the following information:

- ▶ User role
- ▶ User's intent
- ▶ Context of use
- ▶ Pre-conditions
- ▶ Post-conditions
- ▶ Steps

User role   We reuse the user role mentioned in the user involvement point. If the user involvement point identified several user roles, we list those that perform the user task under refinement.

User's intent   The user's intent is derived from the goal of the user involvement point. Since user tasks have a smaller scope than user involvement points, the user's intent is contributing to the user's goal. A user's intent can be considered a subgoal and is often *not* identical with a user's goal. The user's intent is a smaller user goal for the selected user task.

Context of use   The context of use can be copied from the user involvement point. It is possible for the user involvement point to list multiple contexts of use. If the user task applies to a subset of such contexts of use, then only the subset will be listed here.

Pre-condition   The pre-condition articulates conditions and states that are true before a user performs the user task under refinement. If the user task is the first user task, the pre-condition of the user involvement point can be reused. Otherwise, a new pre-condition needs to be specified.

Post-condition   The post-condition articulates conditions and states that are true after a user has performed a user task. The post-condition of the last user task is identical with the post-condition of the user involvement point, so it can be reused for the last user task. For all other user tasks, the post-condition needs to be specified.

Steps   If the user task is rather complex, it can be broken down into different steps. If the steps were already identified during the UIP definition (see Section 1 (User involvement goals) on page 295), those steps can be repeated here. If the GAIS technique (see Section 12 (GAIS) on page 319) was applied, the steps from the selected GAIS scenario can be listed here.

World of Pizza

Now we'll apply the task refinement to the WoP example. We'll pick user involvement point UIP 1 "Order, Monitor, and Receive Pizza." UIP 1 has four user tasks:

- ► UT 1.1 Select pizza (primary user task)
- ► UT 1.2 Order pizza
- ► UT 1.3 Monitor status
- ► UT 1.4 Tip driver

We refine each of the four user tasks. The results are shown below.

UT 1.1 Select pizza (primary user task)

- ► User role: Patron
- ► User's intent: Select tasty, healthy, and affordable pizza in a timely manner
- ► Context of use: Office, home, on the road
- ► Pre-conditions
    - Wish to eat something (soon)
    - App is open
    - User is logged in
- ► Post-conditions
    - Pizza is selected (cognitively in a list or displayed in a pizza-specific view)

▶ Steps

- Select filter
- Review pizza

The refinement of user task UT 1.1 repeats the content from the UIP. The user's goal was reduced to "select." The pre- and post-conditions need to be revised. The pre-condition of a UIP applies to the first user task (UT 1.1) and the post-condition of a UIP applies to the last user task (i.e., UT 1.4). However, more pre- and post-conditions may be added per user task.

The steps were copied from the GAIS scenarios.

Here are the user task refinements for user tasks UT 1.2, UT 1.3, and UT 1.4:

UT 1.2 Order pizza

- ▶ User role: Patron
- ▶ User's intent: Order selected pizza
- ▶ Context of use: Office, home, on the road
- ▶ Pre-conditions

  - Pizza is selected (cognitively in a list or displayed in a pizza specific view)
  - Payment information is stored
  - Delivery information is stored

- ▶ Post-conditions

  - Order confirmation is displayed

- ▶ Steps

  - Initiate order
  - Review order summary
  - Submit order
  - Review order confirmation

UT 1.3 Monitor status

- ▶ User role: Patron
- ▶ User's intent: Understand current status and when the ordered pizza will be delivered
- ▶ Context of use: Office, home, on the road
- ▶ Pre-conditions

  - Pizza is ordered

- ▶ Post-conditions

  - Updated order status and estimated time of delivery (ETD) are displayed

▶ Steps

- Request order status (update)
- Review order status

UT 1.4 Tip driver

▶ User role: Patron
▶ User's intent: Reward driver
▶ Context of use: Office, home, on the road
▶ Pre-conditions

- Ordered pizza is delivered

▶ Post-conditions

- Tip order confirmation is displayed

▶ Steps

- Select tip option
- Submit tip order
- Review order confirmation

Ask task questions

UT 1	UT 2	UT 3
?	?	?
?	?	?

Technique

A frequent challenge in the design process is the selection of the right design elements. Sometimes wrong or unnecessary design elements are selected. The challenge often has one root cause: the design professional has an insufficient understanding of the user and the user's activities. Task questions help to provide important information per user task.

Task questions are questions that occur to a user when they are performing a user task. The question help to identify needed design elements.

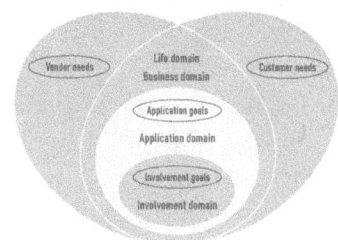

Figure 14.3: Teddy bear model

Task questions should be identified and formulated with the help of user representatives. Based on my experience, user reps have, in most cases, no difficulty formulating task questions or helping to formulate them.

Metaphorically speaking, task questions are like a bridge, serving as a structural foundation between the application domain and the involvement domain (see Figure 14.4).

It is important that task questions be formulated from the application domain (see Figure 14.3) and not from the involvement domain. In other words, the task questions should not mention design elements. In this book, questions that contain their answer are called *self-answering questions*. As it pertains to our bridge metaphor, a self-answering task question is not a bridge but a balcony or platform on the side of the involvement domain.

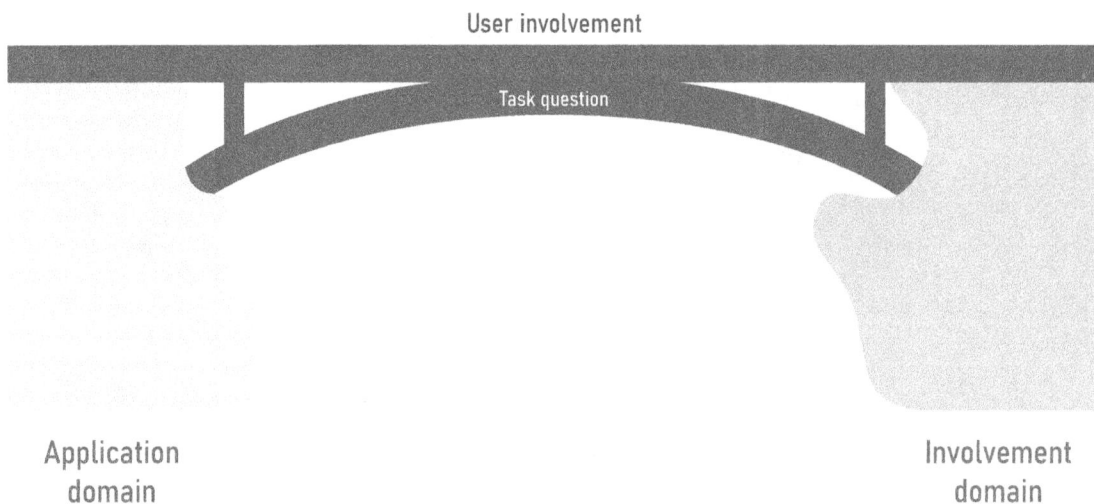

User involvement

Task question

Application
domain

Involvement
domain

Figure 14.4: Application - Involvement bridge

To illustrate the difference between "good" and "bad" task questions, some examples are shown in Table 14.1 on the facing page.

Task questions are formulated per user task. If the user task is too broad, or the user is not familiar enough with the application domain, task questions can also be formulated per step. It is a good idea to capture a reason for each task question; articulating the reason deepens your understanding of the user and their mental model.

World of Pizza

Let's go back to our WoP example. Here is a list of task questions that users try to answer for "UT 1.1 select pizza":

Table 14.1: Good and bad examples of task questions

Intent	Good task question example (application domain oriented)	Bad task question example (involvement domain oriented)
Pizza meets my diet requirements	Which pizzas support my diet? Which pizzas are vegetarian? Which pizzas are vegan?	Where is the filter element to select vegan pizzas? Is there a drop-down menu for diets?
Pizza quality is high (enough)	How good is the pizza?	For the rating, do we use stars or dots?
Pizza costs less than $15	How much is a pizza?	Which colors are used for the price tag?
Pizza arrives within 30 minutes	What is the estimated delivery time?	How is the ETD label designed?
Pizza is "tasty"	What are the selection criteria for a pizza?	Are tags used?

- ▶ TQ 1.1 What is the price of the pizza? Reason: I typically don't purchase pizza that costs more than $15.
- ▶ TQ 1.2 How does the pizza look? Reason: I like to see what I eat before I eat it.
- ▶ TQ 1.3 Does the pizza conform to my diet constraints? Reason: I only eat vegetarian foods.
- ▶ TQ 1.4 How long does delivery take? Reason: I typically do not want to wait more than 45 minutes.
- ▶ TQ 1.5 How good is the service? Reason: I want to buy from a reliable restaurant.

All listed task questions are located in the application and not in the involvement domain. Adding a reason helps us understand the user's motivation for asking the questions, which is not always obvious. It is fine if an interviewed user does not have a reason.

To complete this exercise, let's list task questions for the other three user tasks.

Task questions for user task "UT 1.2 order pizza"

- ▶ TQ 2.1 What was ordered? Reason: I want to confirm that my order was fulfilled as I intended.
- ▶ TQ 2.2 What is the order value? Reason: I want to see that I wasn't overcharged.
- ▶ TQ 2.3 When will it be delivered? Reason: I want to be ready when the pizza is delivered, and I want to check that it won't delivered too late.
- ▶ TQ 2.4 What amount was actually charged? Reason: I want to know exactly how much I'm paying.

Task questions for user task "UT 1.3 monitor status"

► TQ 3.1 What is the order status? Reason: I want to understand where the order is and whether it is delayed.

► TQ 3.2 Where is the driver? Reason: I want to know whether the driver will be here at the ETD.

► TQ 3.3 What is the most recent ETD? Reason: I want to know when the driver will be here so I can plan my time until then.

Task questions for user task "UT 1.4 tip driver"

► TQ 4.1 What is the order value? Reason: I want a reference point for the tip.

► TQ 4.2 What tip amounts are reasonable? Reason: I do not want to calculate the tip myself.

► TQ 4.3 What amount was actually charged? Reason: I want a reference point for the tip.

Identify content

UT 1	UT 2	UT 3
Object lists	Object lists	Object lists
Objects	Objects	Objects
Object attributes	Object attributes	Object attributes
Functions	Functions	Functions

Motivation

Content consists of information that carries meaning for users. It is typically the content that enables a user to perform a user task and that represents the outcome of value. Content drives involvement. It is therefore necessary to identify the content that a user needs to perform user tasks.

Earlier, I mentioned different design methodologies (see Section 6 (Why are users important?) on page 149). These methodologies can be technology-centered or function-centered. They can also be content-centered. Notice that all these methodologies focus on a specific artifact type, but not on the user. Being too content-centered can create problems for users, too. There are plenty of poorly designed dashboards, with data being visualized simply because they exist, not because they help the user to make a decision and initiate a preventive or corrective action.

When creating an involvement concept, we need to use real content. The often-applied "Lorem ipsum" design technique is insufficient and not very useful. Most users don't see things in terms of forms or layouts, they only see the task- and goal-relevant content.

Therefore, an important question for the experience professionals to answer is, Which content (or aggregated content) is needed to enable the user to perform a user task and to answer the task questions? For the user to provide a sufficient answer, representative sample content is needed, not "Lorem Ipsum" content. This section elaborates on how to identify and document sample content.

Technique

There are several types of content that typically needs to be identified.

Object lists and objects   One set of content is object lists and objects. Often, individual objects are organized in lists from which a user can select them. An example is a pizza menu (object list). Each pizza is an object on that list. Here, we identify the object lists we need to support and the objects themselves.

Not every object needs to be organized and accessible through a list. For instance, payment information and delivery information are often organized as one object each but are included in a list of payment objects.

Object attributes   Each object has attributes that specify it. We need to list the attribute name (e.g., pizza name) and an instance of that attribute, e.g., "Margherita."

Functions   A function is applied to an object or to an object list. For instance, a pizza list can be filtered, sorted, or displayed in different views (e.g., list view, tile view, image view).

All content types and functions are identified per user task to ensure that they are reasonable for supporting that task. Follow the principle "select for probability, not for possibility." This means, we should consider objects, object lists, and functions that have an 80% or greater likelihood of being used, and ignore the rest.

World of Pizza

Object lists and objects

- ▶ UT 1.1 Select pizza
  - Pizza menu

Figure 14.5: Pizza 1, courtesy: Tino Procaccini

Figure 14.6: Pizza 2, courtesy: Tino Procaccini

Figure 14.7: Pizza 3, courtesy: Tino Procaccini

Figure 14.8: Pizza 4, courtesy: Tino Procaccini

- Pizza
▶ UT 1.2 Order pizza
  - Payment information
  - Delivery information
  - Order summary
  - Order confirmation
▶ UT 1.3 Monitor status
  - Delivery status
▶ UT 1.4 Tip driver
  - Tip options
  - Tip confirmation

Object attributes

Pizza menu   The pizza menu lists pizzas with attributes as shown in Table 14.2 on the facing page.

A pizza menu consists of single pizzas, each described with the following attributes:

▶ Name
▶ Image
▶ Price
▶ Diet

Example pizzas are listed below.

Pizza   Example content is shown in Table 14.2 on the next page.

Payment information   The payment information assumes the use of a credit card:

▶ Name on credit card: Heinrich Helmut Degen
▶ Credit card number: 8888 8888 8888 8888
▶ Expiration date: 12/99
▶ Zip code: 08536
▶ Security code: ***

Delivery information

▶ Street name: 123 Main Street
▶ Apartment: (empty)
▶ City: Plainsboro
▶ State: NJ
▶ Zip code: 08536

Pizza name	Price	Rating	Diet	Calories	Number of reviews
Margherita	$9.99	4.7	Vegetarian	1,120	13,798
Napolitana	$11.99	4.6	Vegetarian	1,240	2,509
Frutti di Mare	$12.99	4.2	Seafood	1,180	1,743
Prosciutto e Funghi	$11.99	4.7	Beef	1,320	5,873
Capricciosa	$9.99	4.9	Beef	1,360	2,034
Romana	$10.99	4.5	Vegetarian	1,140	3,870
Sicilia	$11.99	4.6	Seafood	1,280	2,937
Quattro Stagioni	$12.99	4.4	Beef	1,250	2,999
Quattro Formaggi	$12.99	4.8	Vegetarian	1,380	4,871
Tonno	$12.99	4.4	Seafood	1,220	2,739
Vegetariana	$10.99	4.3	Vegetarian	1,250	1,492
Calzone	$12.99	4.9	Vegetarian	1,450	3,826

Table 14.2: Content for pizza menu. The pizzas and prices are fictitious and not from Tino's restaurant.

Shopping cart

- ▶ Greeting: Hey Helmut, thanks for your interest in our delicious pizza.
- ▶ Pizza: 1 x Margherita: $9.99
- ▶ Subtotal: $9.99
- ▶ Sales tax: 7% ($0.70)
- ▶ Delivery fee: 10% of subtotal, minimum $7.00
- ▶ Total: $17.69
- ▶ Credit card on file: *8888.
- ▶ Delivery address: 123 Main Street, Plainsboro, NJ 08536
- ▶ Estimated time of delivery: 1:23 pm (in 40 min.)

Order summary

- ▶ Greeting: Hey Helmut, here is your order summary.
- ▶ Pizza: 1 x Margherita: $9.99
- ▶ Subtotal: $9.99
- ▶ Sales tax: 7% ($0.70)
- ▶ Delivery fee: 10% of subtotal, minimum $7.00
- ▶ Total: $17.69
- ▶ Credit card: *8888
- ▶ Delivery address: 123 Main Street, Plainsboro, NJ 08536
- ▶ Estimated time of delivery: 1:23 pm (in 40 min.)

Order confirmation

- ▶ Greeting: Hey Helmut, thanks for your order.
- ▶ Ordered: 1 x Margherita: $9.99
- ▶ Subtotal: $9.99
- ▶ Sales tax: 7% ($0.70)
- ▶ Delivery fee: 10% of subtotal, minimum $7.00
- ▶ Total: $17.69
- ▶ Order number: 2022888888
- ▶ Credit card: *8888
- ▶ Delivery address: 123 Main Street, Plainsboro, NJ 08536
- ▶ Estimated time of delivery: 1:23 pm (in 40 min.)

Delivery status

- ▶ Order number: 2022888888
- ▶ Status: On the road
- ▶ Delivery address: 123 Main Street, Plainsboro, NJ 08536
- ▶ Estimated time of delivery: 1:25 pm (in 15 min.)

Tip options

For the tip, the following information is useful:

- ▶ Greeting: Thanks for your order. Please select a tip for Joe.
- ▶ Subtotal: $9.99
- ▶ Tip options: 15%, 18%, 20%, 22%, 25% (of subtotal)
- ▶ Calculated tip: $1.50, $1.80, $2.00, $2.20, $2.50

Tip confirmation

- ▶ Greeting: Hey Helmut, thanks for the generous tip.
- ▶ Tip: $2.00
- ▶ Tax (0%): $0.00
- ▶ Total: $2.00
- ▶ Order number: 2022888889
- ▶ Credit card: *8888

General remark If a project is rather large with a lot of content, the use of a dedicated content repository is recommended to ensure that all project members work with the same sample content.

Content object relationships

Some content objects are related to each other. User involvement enables us to view or manipulate such content objects. In order to present their content, we need to understand their relationship. The technique proposed here is based on the Unified Modeling Language (UML) class diagram technique; however, it only shows each piece of content as an object, without displaying its attributes [214, 215]. It is important to emphasize that the modeled content object relationships do not describe a technical implementation, but rather the content relationships from the domain perspective.

Template Each object is represented as a rectangle. If two objects have a relationship, it is identified by a solid connecting line. Each line is annotated with cardinalities. A cardinality defines the numerical relationship between instances of objects. An object is a type (e.g., an order), and an instance is a specific order with an order number.

The most frequently used cardinalities are shown in Figure 14.9:

Object Relationship Cardinalities

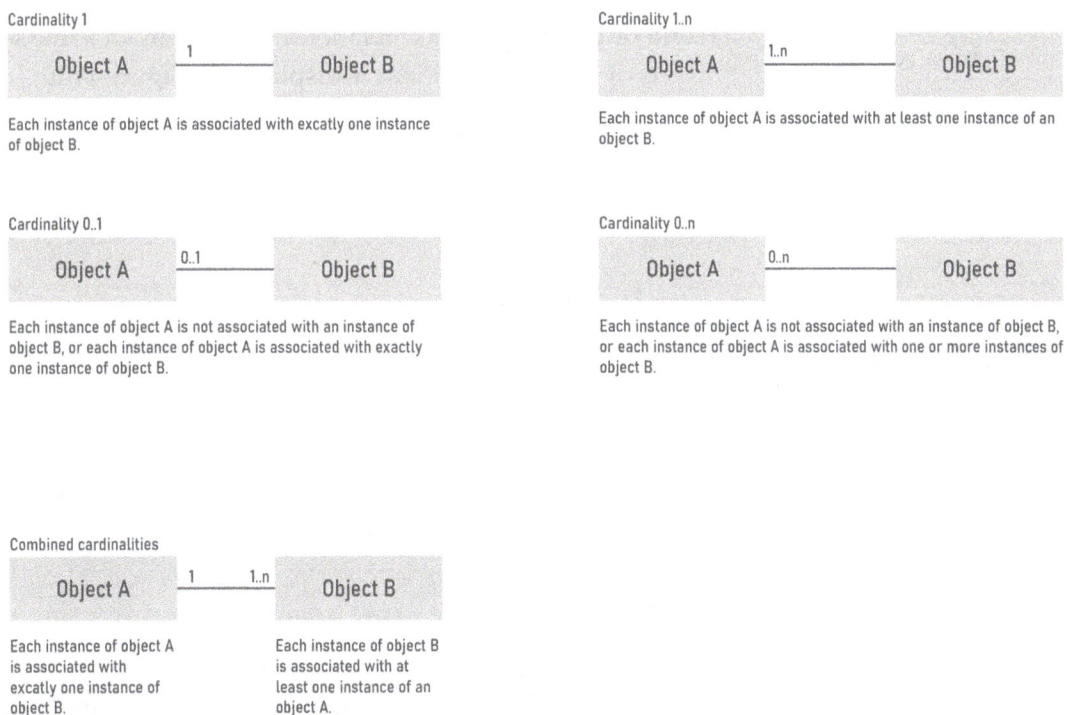

Cardinality 1

| Object A | —1— | Object B |

Each instance of object A is associated with excatly one instance of object B.

Cardinality 1..n

| Object A | —1..n— | Object B |

Each instance of object A is associated with at least one instance of an object B.

Cardinality 0..1

| Object A | —0.1— | Object B |

Each instance of object A is not associated with an instance of object B, or each instance of object A is associated with exactly one instance of object B.

Cardinality 0..n

| Object A | —0.n— | Object B |

Each instance of object A is not associated with an instance of object B, or each instance of object A is associated with one or more instances of object B.

Combined cardinalities

| Object A | —1——1..n— | Object B |

Each instance of object A is associated with excatly one instance of object B.

Each instance of object B is associated with at least one instance of an object A.

Figure 14.9: Object relationship template

▶ Cardinality 1: Each instance of object A is always associated with exactly one instance of object B. WoP example: A pizza order (object A) is always associated with exactly one user (object B) who submitted the order.

▶ Cardinality 0..1: Each instance of object A is not associated with an instance of object B, or each instance of object A is associated with exactly one instance of object B. WoP example: An order (object A) is not associated with a tip (object B) (meaning the patron did not tip the driver) or an order is associated with exactly one tip (object B) (meaning the patron tipped the driver).

▶ Cardinality 1..n: Each instance of object A is associated with at least one instance of an object B. WoP example: An order (object A) is associated with one or more pizzas (object B), assuming that only pizzas can be ordered.

▶ Cardinality 0..n: Each instance of object A is not associated with an instance of object B, or each instance of object A is associated with one or more instances of object B. WoP example: A user (object A) is not associated with an order (object B) (meaning a user has just registered and has not ordered a pizza yet), or a user (object A) is associated with one or more orders (object B) (meaning a user has submitted one or more orders).

World of Pizza   An object relationship diagram for some selected objects of the World of Pizza is displayed in Figure 14.10.

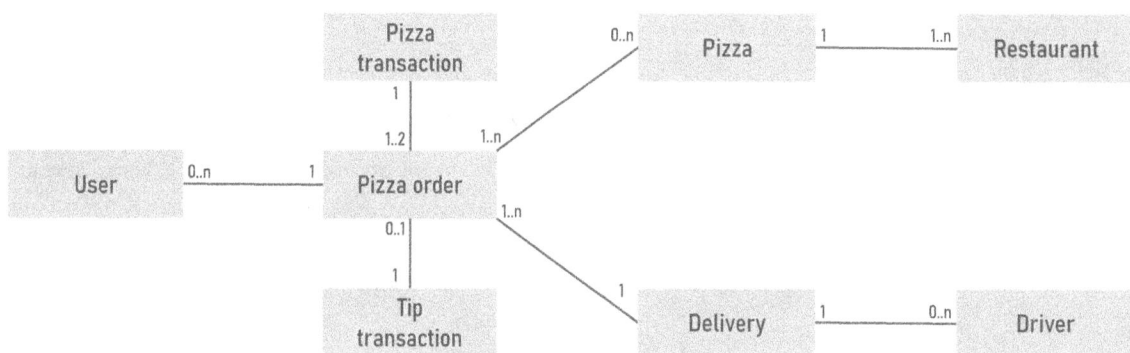

Figure 14.10: Object relationships for WoP

The individual relationships between the objects are briefly described below. The objects with their cardinalities are identified in the following way: "object A" (cardinality) → "object B".

▶ Delivery (1) → Driver: Each delivery is associated with exactly one driver.

▶ Delivery (1) → Pizza order: Each delivery is associated with exactly one pizza order. This relationship can become a bottleneck. It could be beneficial to combine several pizza orders with one delivery, for instance if the deliveries are in the same neighborhood.

▶ Driver (0..n) → Delivery: Each driver is associated with no or at least one delivery.

▶ Pizza (0..n) → Pizza order: Each pizza is associated with either no orders or at least one order. "0" means that a pizza has not been ordered (yet).

▶ Pizza (1) → Restaurant: Each pizza is associated with exactly one restaurant.

▶ Pizza order (1..n) → Delivery: Each pizza order is associated with at least one delivery. This means that if an order contains pizzas from different restaurants, different drivers will deliver them. It also means that the status information for several drivers should possible be considered in the order status.

▶ Pizza order (1..n) → Pizza: Each pizza order is associated with at least one pizza. This relationship ignores the fact that patrons can order a salad only and no pizza. If an order contains multiple pizzas and they are from different restaurants, the restaurants should probably be listed in the order summary and the order status.

▶ Pizza order (1..2) → Pizza transaction: Each pizza order is associated with one or two pizza transactions. In most cases, a pizza order will have one transaction only. The second transaction is needed only if the first is canceled.

▶ Pizza order (0..1) → Tip transaction: Each pizza order is associated with no tip transaction or one tip transaction. This means the patron has tipped the driver (=1) or has not (=0). The cardinality excludes the possibility of a patron tipping a driver a second time.

▶ Pizza order (1) → User: Each pizza order is associated with exactly one user.

▶ Pizza transaction (1) → Pizza order: Each pizza transaction is associated with exactly one pizza order.

▶ Restaurant (1..n) → Pizza: Each restaurant is associated with at least one pizza.

▶ Tip transaction (1) → Pizza order: Each tip transaction is associated with exactly one pizza order.

▶ User (0..n) → Pizza order: Each user is associated with either no pizza order (i.e., a user has registered but not ordered yet) or at least one pizza order (a user has submitted at least one order).

State transitions

Besides the relationships between content objects, it is worthwhile to look at relevant states and their changes of such objects. In our case, the state of the object "order" is relevant. We use a technique called a "state-transition diagram," also called a "finite state machine," to specify the states [216, 217].

Template   Figure 14.11 shows a simple example of a state-transition diagram. It contains states, represented as circles, and transitions, represented as arrows between the states. It also shows conditions that trigger a state change. What is special about a state-transition diagram is that it focuses on states and not so much on activities.

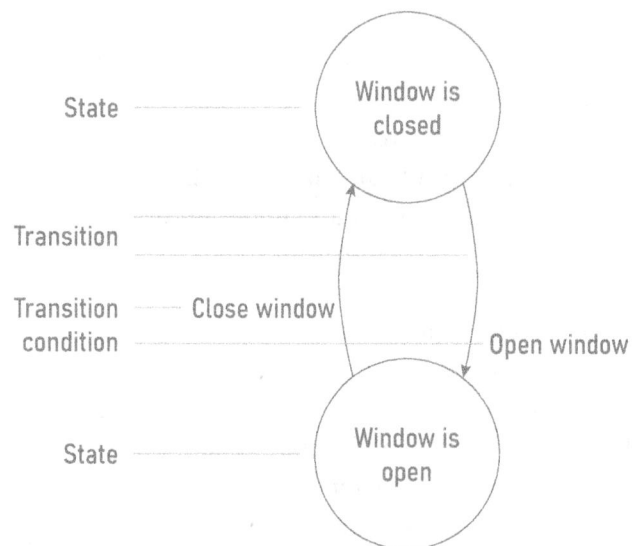

Figure 14.11: State-transition diagram – window example

The example represents the state of a window as the object of interest. The state-transition diagram considers two states: window is closed and window is open. One state can have one or more associated transitions. In the case of the window example, each state has only one associated transition. If the window is in the "closed" state and the condition "open window" becomes true, the state changes from "window is closed" to "window is open." If the state is "window is open" and the condition "close window" becomes true, the state changes from "window is open" to "window is closed."

Function triggering user actions often cause state changes. In experience design, it is often necessary to understand which objects can have which states, and which transitions are needed to change the states.

World of Pizza The state-transition diagram technique is used to model the different states of the content object "pizza order," including its transitions (see Figure 14.12).

All eight states in Figure 14.12 are visible to patrons. That's why they are shown here as an experience *design* artifact and not as an experience *architecture* artifact. For each state pair and its related state transition, it is specified which UIP triggers the transition.

UIP 1 is needed to support condition 0 (cancel order), condition 1 (add to cart), 3 (order now), and 5 (submit order). State 3 (ordered), state 4 (baking), state 5 (ready for pick-up), state 6 (delivering), and state 7 (delivered) are visible to the patron. The transitions to those states are supported by UIP 3 (baker), and UIP 4 (driver). According to this specification, a patron can cancel an order up to point of state 3 (ordered). When an order is in the baking process (state 4: baking), the patron can no longer cancel it.

When an order scheduling feature is implemented, condition 2 (initiate scheduled order) and condition 4 (confirm order) are realized by the TIP as a function.

The names of the states are not necessarily the same ones used for the user interface. State-transition diagrams sometimes show internal states that are not be visible to end users. Such states should not be in the diagram at all. When discussing state diagrams with technical professionals, internal states might be added, but if so, it is useful to mark such states as internal states to separate them from external, user visible states.

Functions

Another input is the functions we need to realize the state changes and other changes. It makes sense to distinguish between transformational functions (change of content) and view functions (change of canvas). Table 14.3 on page 407 shows functions per object and object list.

In the next step we will address which of the identified content objects and functions are used for which user tasks.

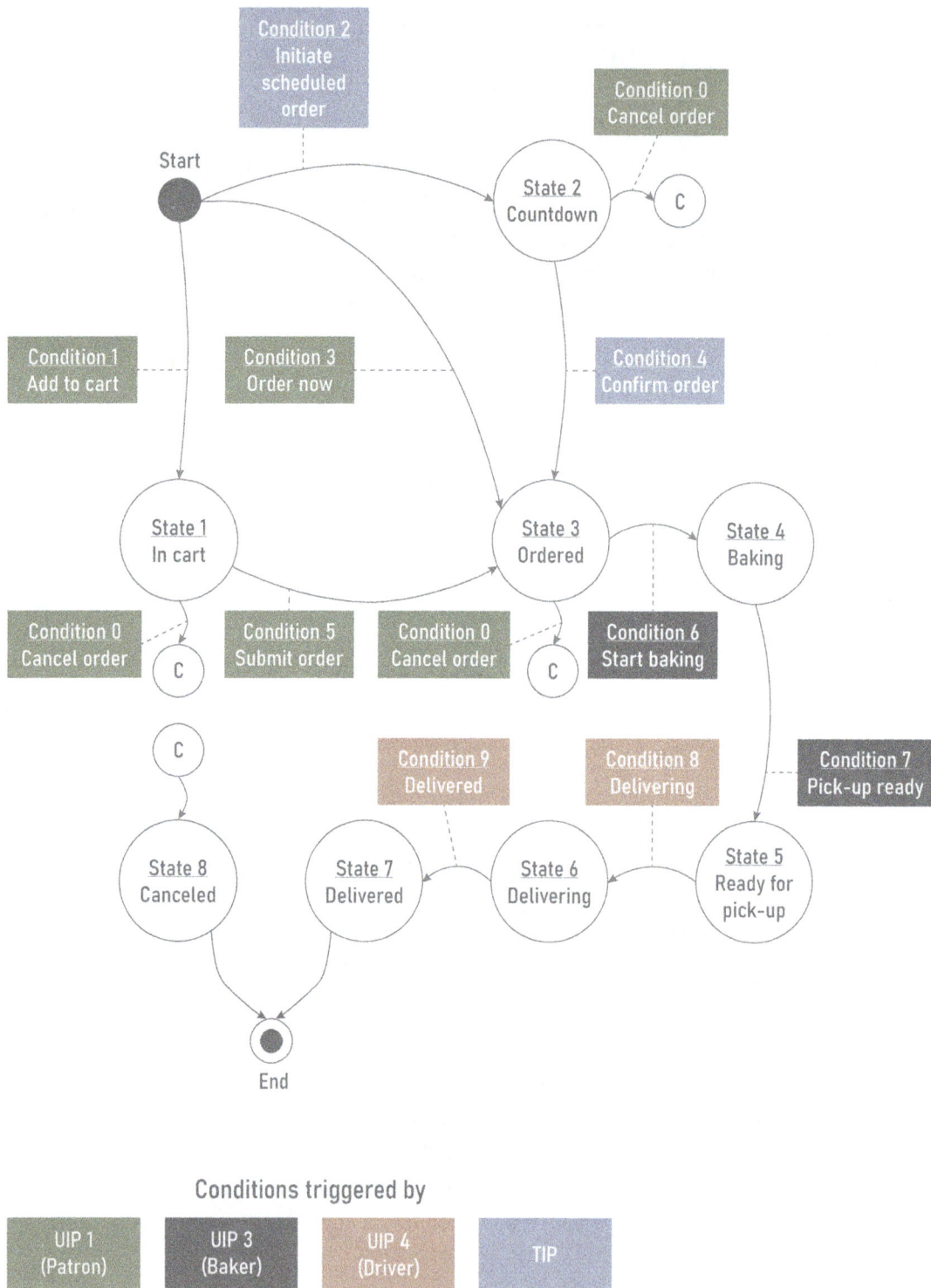

Figure 14.12: State-transition diagram: WoP (order status)

Table 14.3: Functions for objects and object lists

Object list / object	Content-changing functions	Canvas-changing functions
UT 1.1 Select pizza (Primary user task)		
Pizza list	n/a	View, close, sort, filter, change view type
Pizza	Add to cart, submit order, cancel order	View, close
UT 1.2 Order pizza		
Payment information	Modify	View, close
Delivery information	Modify	View, close
Order summary	Submit, cancel	View, close
Order confirmation	Cancel	View, close
UT 1.3 Monitor order		
Delivery status	Update	View, close
UT 1.4 Tip driver		
Tip options	Submit, cancel	View, close
Tip confirmation	Cancel	View, close

Select design elements

UT 1 **UT 2** **UT 3**

Canvas

Overlay canvas

Canvas control

Canvas function

Content

Alert

Content control

Content function

● User action

● System action

Interaction device

System function

Figure 14.13: Design elements

Technique

After we have clarified the content per user task, we can answer the task questions by identifying the needed content and the related design elements (see Figure 14.13).

If you are in doubt about whether or not a design element should be considered, *leave it out*! Here is why: It is relatively easy to add a design element later. It is difficult, I'd say almost impossible, to remove a design element later. This advice leads us to the next design principle:

If in doubt, leave it out

Start with the minimal number of design elements. If in doubt, leave a design element out – for now. Rather, encourage users to experiment with the concept and let *them* comment on design elements they feel are missing; they can be added later. This way, you keep the canvas clean and clutter-free.

World of Pizza

Table 14.4 shows which content and design elements have been selected to provide answers to the identified task questions:

Table 14.4: Mapping of design elements to task questions

Task questions	Selected design element
UT 1.1 Select pizza (primary user task)	
TQ 1.1 What is the price of the pizza?	DE 1 Price (content)
TQ 1.2 How does the pizza look?	DE 2 Pizza image (content)
TQ 1.3 Does the pizza confirm to my diet constraints?	DE 3 Diet information (content), DE 4 Diet filter (control)
TQ 1.4 How long does delivery take?	DE 5 Estimated time of delivery (content)
TQ 1.5 How good is the service?	DE 6 Restaurant rating (content), DE 7 Restaurant reviews (content)
UT 1.2 Order pizza	
TQ 2.1 What was ordered?	DE 8 Ordered items (content)
TQ 2.2 What is the order value?	DE 9 Order value (content)
TQ 2.3 When will it be delivered?	DE 5 Estimated time of delivery (content)
TQ 2.4 What amount was actually charged?	DE 10 Charged value (content)
UT 1.3 Monitor status	
TQ 3.1 What is the order status?	DE 11 Order status (content)
TQ 3.2 Where is the driver?	DE 12 Driver's location (content, control)
TQ 3.3 What is the updated ETD?	DE 5 Estimated time of delivery (content)
UT 1.4 Tip driver	
TQ 4.1 What is the order value?	DE 9 Order value (content)
TQ 4.2 What tip amounts are reasonable?	DE 13 Tip options (content)
TQ 4.3 What amount was actually charged?	DE 10 Charged value (content)

Some reflections

Before we move on and start the layout steps, I'd like to reflect a bit on what we have done and why it is important. We have assumed that we will be able to articulate task questions first, then identify the content, and then answer the task questions. This is often possible if the domain is somewhat familiar to us.

If a domain is rather foreign, or completely unknown, it is possible that an experience professional will not be able to formulate task questions. It has happened to me several times. In this situation, it is better to first identify the needed content, task driven or not task driven, and then derive the task questions from that content. Afterward, it should be possible to assign answers to the questions. Going back to our bridge metaphor, it simply means that the bridge can be built either from the involvement domain side or from the application domain side (see Figure 14.14).

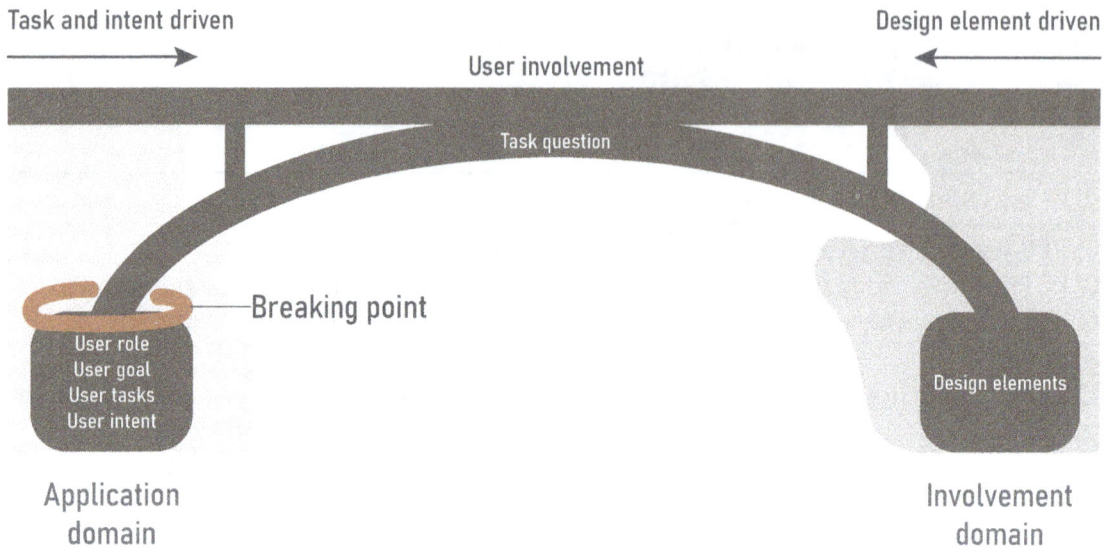

Figure 14.14: Different ways to build the Application – Involvement bridge

If possible, I prefer building the bridge from the application domain side. If the bridge is built from the involvement domain, it is important that the task questions are eventually rooted in and motivated by the user goal, user tasks, and user intent (i.e., the application domain), so the questions are an actual translation of the application domain into the involvement domain. It is also important that the selected design elements provide a sufficient answer to the task questions.

The breaking point of this bridge is the connection between the application domain and the task questions. What we try to avoid is that the re-engineering the questions to justify the identified or available design elements without their having a sound connection to the application domain. If this occurs, the bridge will be too weak and unstable to carry the load of the upcoming user involvement. It will crumble and break.

This is a typical situation when someone with a technical solution is searching for a real-world problem. If that happens, engineers and product managers often refer to such a situation with the metaphor of the hammer (the answer, or the technical solution) and the nail (the question, or the real-world problem). Many things seems to be perceived as nails (the question) that justify the technical solution as a hammer (the answer).

There are some indicators that a bridge might be too weak. One is if the task questions are self-answering (e.g., how do I select a filter element in a drop-down list?). Another indicator is if the task questions are not elicited from user representatives, or user representatives have not confirmed that the task questions represent their needs, goals, and intents. A third indicator is that the selected design elements (i.e., the answers) do not really answer the task questions.

Map canvases to user tasks

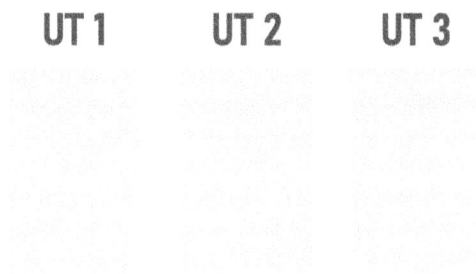

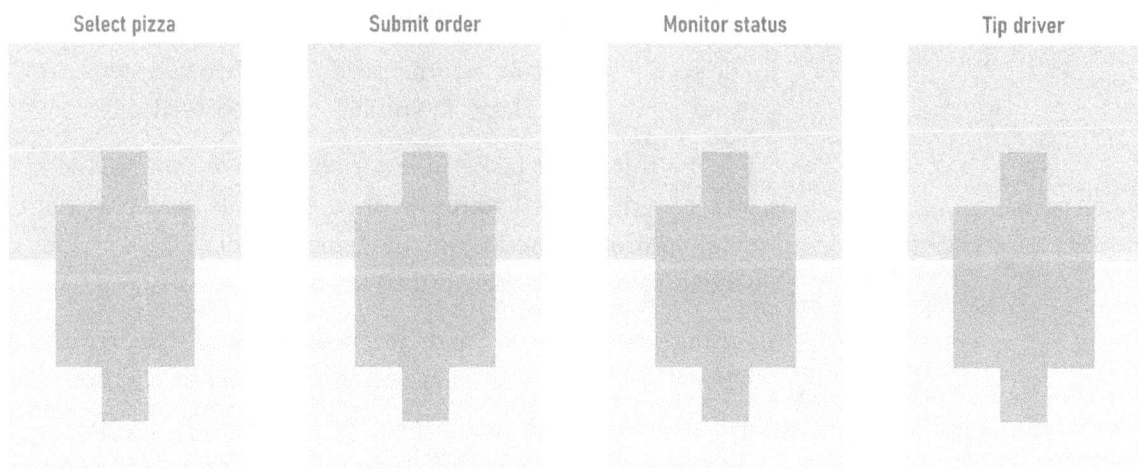

UT 1   UT 2   UT 3

Technique

The steps described so far have built the foundation for placing design elements on the canvas. Now we will start using canvases. The first step is to define the canvas flow. To do that, we map one or more canvases to one or more user tasks. For mobile applications, we often map one or more canvases to one user task. For desktop applications, one canvas is often assigned to more than one user task.

World of Pizza

In our WoP example, we have assigned one canvas to each user task. The canvas cast is shown in Figure 14.15.

Map canvases to tasks

| Select pizza | Submit order | Monitor status | Tip driver |

Figure 14.15: Canvases mapped to user tasks, using the introduced canvas template.

Identify step flow per canvas

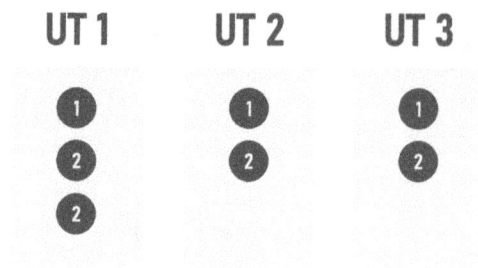

UT 1   **UT 2**   **UT 3**

(1)   (1)   (1)

(2)   (2)   (2)

(2)

Technique

We will now assign steps per user task to each user task-specific canvas. The steps have been identified before and will be placed on the canvas. When placing the steps on the canvas, the step flow is important for efficiency. We should avoid zig-zag patterns of the step flow that would reduce efficiency for the user. If possible, the step flow should be a straight line, either vertical or horizontal.

World of Pizza

For the WoP example, we will map the steps for each canvas (see Figure 14.16). The first user task "select pizza" is broken down into two steps: "view pizza" and "select pizza." Since we expect to see a list of pizzas, we keep these two steps together ("view pizza," "select pizza") and organize them horizontally. In an alternative seed concept, a pizza list could also be organized horizontally, so that the sequence would change.

The second user task, "submit order," also has two steps: "review order" and "order pizza." It will be organized vertically.

For the third user task, "monitor status," we can assume that a step called "request status" will be available, allowing the user some control over refreshing the screen to get a status update. The second step is to "review order status."

For the forth user task, "tip driver," we assume a list of precalculated tips will be displayed. The user needs to select a tip option (step 1) and then submit the tip (step 2). The two steps are organized vertically. The third step, "review order confirmation," is not considered here because it requires a different canvas.

Now that the steps are laid out, we can assign design elements to them. However, before we do that, we must first identify zones, which is described in the next step.

Identify step flow per canvas

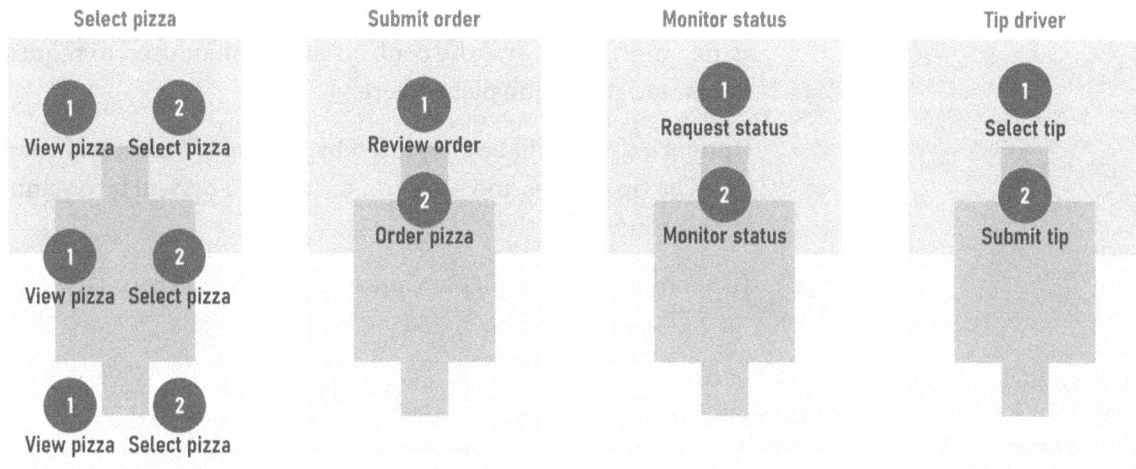

Figure 14.16: Map steps to the canvas

Mark zones

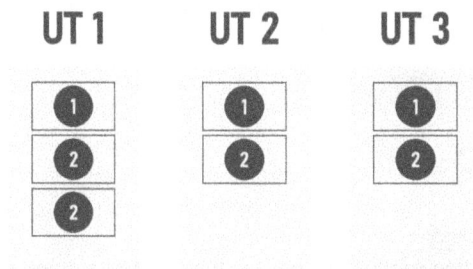

Technique

In this step, we mark zones that will define areas reserved for design elements. Each zone is marked with a zone name. A zone may contain one step or multiple steps.

World of Pizza

On the first canvas, "select pizza," both steps are grouped into one zone ("view pizza"). It would be expected that information about a pizza (to support the step "view pizza") and the ability to select a pizza would be in the same zone.

The second canvas has one zone for both steps, "review order" and "order pizza," since reviewing details about a pizza and ordering the pizza are so closely related.

One zone is identified for the third canvas, "monitor status." The status information and the controls and content used to request a status update will be placed here.

Tipping a driver will be supported by one zone, "select and submit tip." The tip options and a control to submit a tip will be organized in this zone.

The zoning of the steps per canvas is shown in Figure 14.17.

Mark zones

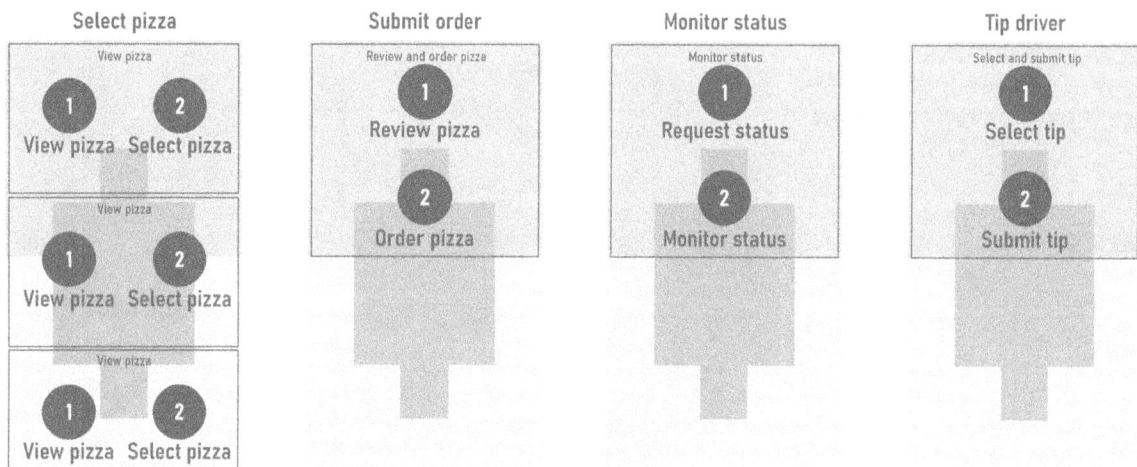

Figure 14.17: Mark zones

The next step is to place design elements into the identified zones.

Map design elements

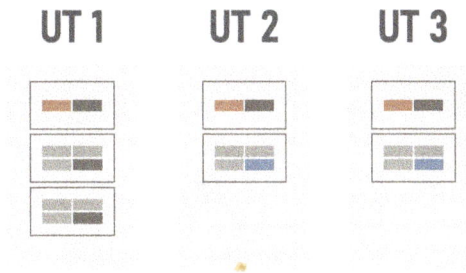

Technique

Now we can assign the already identified design elements to the zones. We simply map the design elements that were assigned to each task question per user task and assign them to the appropriate zones. We should only use the design elements that are answers to task questions.

If you want to be more radical, you may even leave out some of the identified design elements.

In this step, we do not create a layout. We just drop the elements into a zone.

World of Pizza

Now that we have identified the zones, we can map the design elements to them. The design elements have already been identified (see Table 14.4 on page 409). A sample result is depicted in Table 14.5.

Some of the design elements identified in Table 14.4 on page 409 are not used here. This is done to keep the design minimal. Remember: if in doubt, leave it out. If the user does not like something, you'll receive their feedback and you can add the element later. On the other hand, users typically do not mention or give feedback on design elements they don't need.

Figure 14.18 shows the design elements mapped to the canvases and zones.

The assignment of design elements to zones is a major step in concept creation. If done correctly, it establishes a foundation for the baseline concept.

Table 14.5: Mapping of design elements to canvases and zones

Canvas	Zone	Design elements
Select pizza	Select pizza	DE 1 Price (content) DE 2 Pizza image (content) DE 4 Diet filter (control)
Submit pizza	Review and order pizza	DE 2 Pizza image (content) DE 3 Diet information (content) DE 5 Estimated time of delivery (content)
Monitor status	Monitor status	DE 11 Order status (content) DE 12 Driver's location (content, control)
Tip driver	Select and submit tip	DE 9 Order value (content) DE 13 Tip options (content)

Map design elements to zones

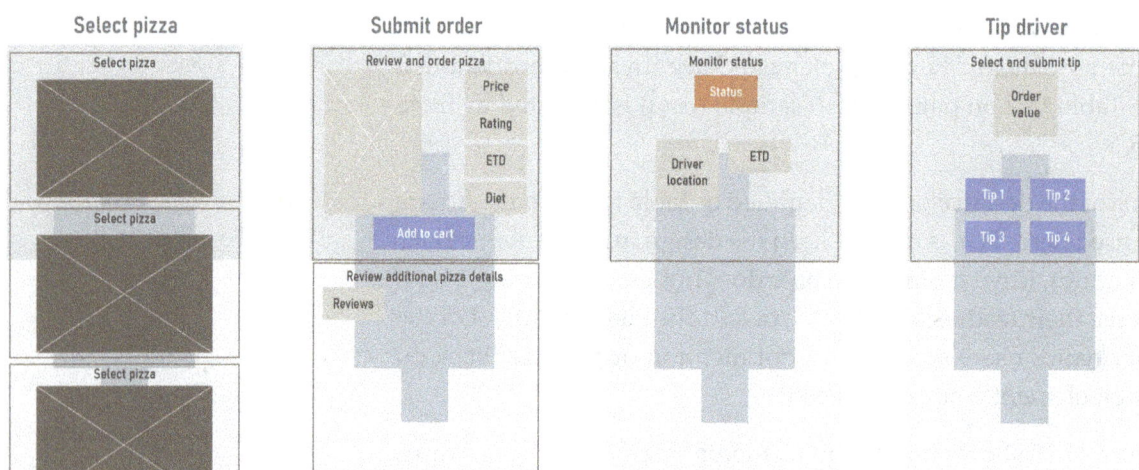

Figure 14.18: Map design elements to zones

Create the baseline concept

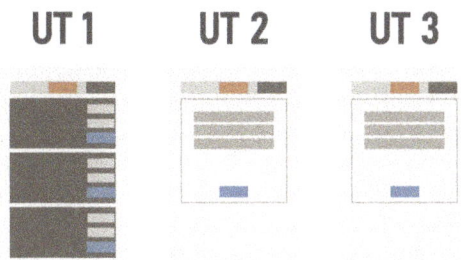

Technique

We can now create a layout for each canvas. The layout should follow typical design principles and may consider constraints, e.g., design constraints from an applicable design system. The resulting concept is called the *baseline concept*. It can be used as a reference for all future concepts and concept refinements.

Definition 27 (Baseline concept) *Ground truth concept.*

World of Pizza

The design elements are reorganized in size and position for each canvas. The result of this design act leads to an initial canvas cast (see Figure 14.20) and an initial canvas flow (see Figure 14.19).

The canvas flow is organized per user task. If canvases needed to complete a user task are missing, they will be added using the same approach. The target involvement steps (TAS) and the actual involvement steps (AAS) are displayed per flow.

Baseline concept - canvas cast

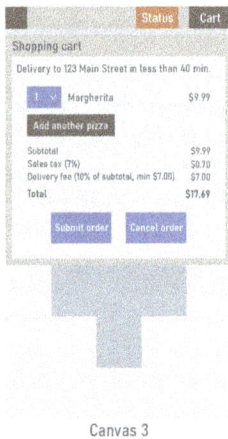

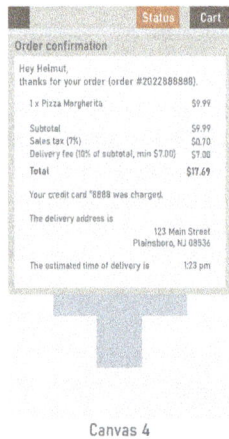

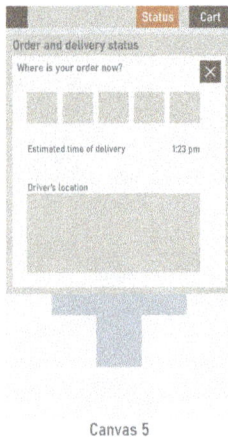

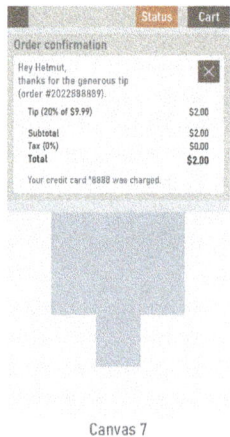

Canvas 1   Canvas 2

Canvas 3   Canvas 4

Canvas 5   Canvas 6   Canvas 7

Figure 14.19: Baseline concept - Canvas cast

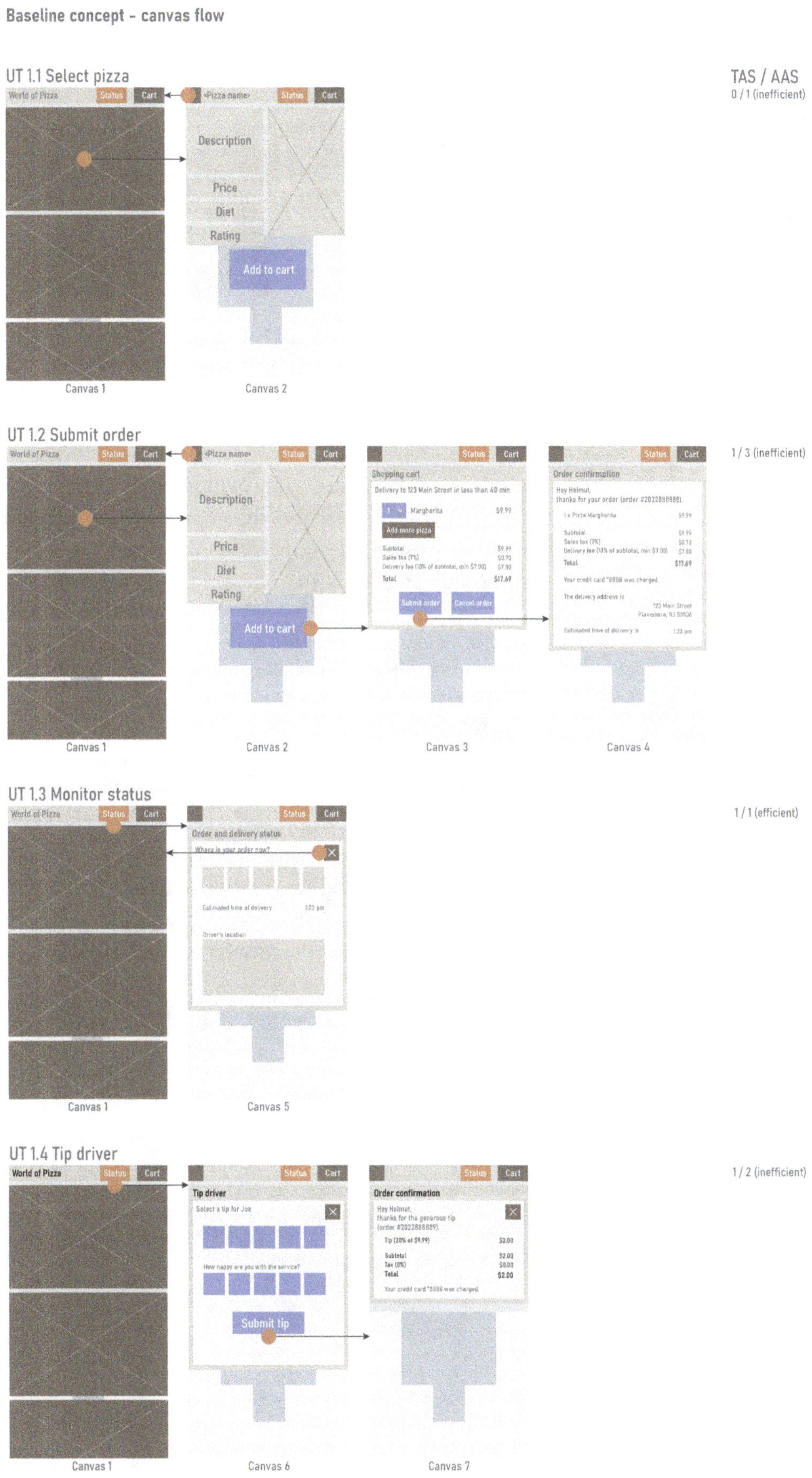

Baseline concept – canvas flow

Figure 14.20: Baseline concept - Canvas flow

Explore seed concepts

Technique

The aim of the last step is to explore seed concepts. This refers to the design universe and the attempt to find as many design options as possible that belong to the design space. In a project, you should come up with at least five different seed concepts. Ten would be even better.

This step is often called "design ideation." For many professionals, particularly for the less experienced [218], this is not easy. Those performing this step can benefit from structured guidance. For instance, Daly [219] proposes 77 design heuristics for industrial designs to stimulate the ideation process. Recker [220] suggests thinking in four styles and proposes 15 thinking patterns. Dam [221] offers 20 ideation techniques. There seems to be a correlation between personality type and the effectiveness of ideation methods [222], so the personality types of individuals participating in the ideation should be considered when selecting ideation methods.

Based on personal experience, here is a list of design ideation techniques (see also Figure 14.21):

Design Ideation Techniques

1-2-3

Canvas types

Start

Promotion

Orientation

Numbers

(A)symmetry

Gestalt

Shapes

Grouping

Helmut Degen (CC BY-NC-SA 4.0)

Figure 14.21: Design ideation techniques

▶ 1-2-3. Identify the top three most relevant design elements and rank them from most to least relevant and place them on the canvas according to their relevance. An alternative approach is to remove design elements, step by step, relative to their relevance. WoP example: Remove restaurant name, remove filter bar, remove attributes per pizza.

▶ Canvas type. Explore the different canvas types (see Section 13 (Path flows) on page 351).

▶ Start. Explore to start with content first (e.g., pizza Margherita), with tasks (e.g., select and order a pizza), or with functions (e.g., Add to shopping cart).

▶ Promotion. Make one item the prominent item, and organize the other items around it. WOP example 1: Promote a pizza of the week, with a larger canvas footage. The other pizza items are smaller. WoP example 2: The most recently ordered pizza is larger, and other pizzas have a smaller footage.

▶ Orientation. Apply vertical and horizontal navigation, or organize content vertically, horizontally, or as a grid.

▶ Numbers. Increase or decrease the number of items. WOP example: Experiment with how many pizzas are placed on a canvas. Place only one pizza on the canvas, then two pizzas, three pizzas etc.

▶ (A) symmetry. Change the organization, from a symmetric formation to an asymmetric formation or the other way around, or from landscape to portrait or the other way around. WoP example: Display a list of pizzas in portrait mode. Apply the pizza items of the portrait mode to the landscape mode and adjust when necessary. Display a list of pizzas in landscape mode. Apply the pizza items of the landscape mode to the portrait mode and adjust when necessary.

▶ Gestalt. Arrange design elements so they form a Gestalt. For instance, organize the pizza images to form a square, a circle etc. [223–225]

▶ Shapes. Alternate the shapes of design elements, e.g., use circles, triangles, rectangles with round corners etc.

▶ Grouping. Group design elements by different criteria. For WoP, the pizzas can be organized by different pizza categories.

Furthermore, you may find inspirations by looking at competitor products or by products that have won a design award [226].

You also may find inspiration by looking at designs that support the same user task and that are from different domains. Check how other vendors are doing it. For instance, if you want to design a pizza configurator, you can check out configurators for computers, cars, or hamburgers.

World of Pizza

The entry canvases of four explored seed concepts are shown in Figure 14.22.

If you look at the bottom of the poster (see Figure 14.2), you can recognize 27 different seed concepts.

The canvas cast and the canvas flow for seed concept A "Pizza-Gram" are shown in Figure 14.23 (cast) and in Figure 14.24 (flow). The canvas cast and the canvas flow for seed concept B "Four-at-a-glance" are shown in Figure 14.25 (cast) and in Figure 14.26 (flow). The canvas cast and the canvas flow for seed concept C "Menu" are shown in Figure 14.27 (cast) and in Figure 14.28 (flow). Finally, the canvas cast and the canvas flow for seed concept D "Lane" are shown in Figure 14.29 (cast) and in Figure 14.30 (flow).

Here are the main differences between the four seed concepts:

- ► Vertical versus horizontal grouping of pizzas per category (orientation)
- ► Number of visible pizza items per focus area (numbers)
- ► Pizza items grouped or not grouped in categories (grouping)

The next three chapters will refine, evaluate, and assess the seed concept A "Pizza-Gram." In the second-to-last chapter, the sprout concept will be selected.

Explored seed concepts

Concept A: Pizza-Gram

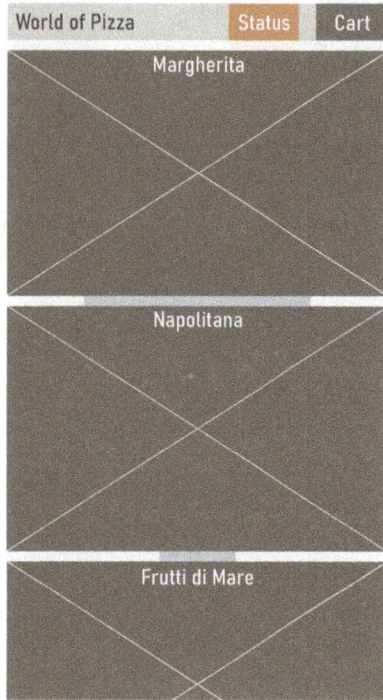

World of Pizza | Status | Cart

Margherita

Napolitana

Frutti di Mare

Concept B: Four-at-a-glance

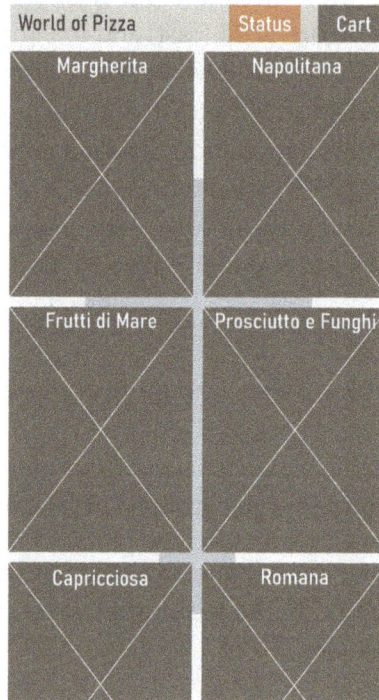

World of Pizza | Status | Cart

Margherita | Napolitana

Frutti di Mare | Prosciutto e Funghi

Capricciosa | Romana

Concept C: Menu

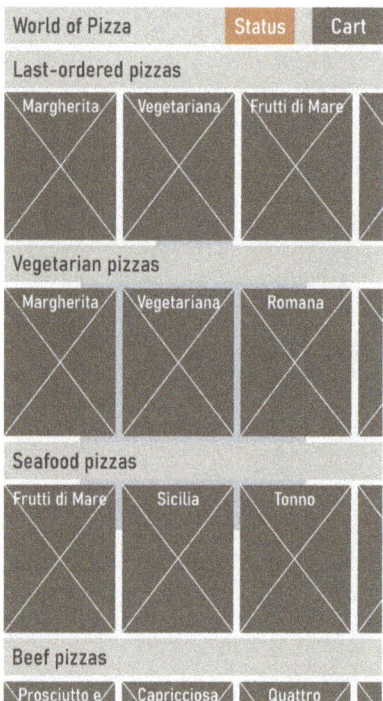

World of Pizza | Status | Cart

Last-ordered pizzas

Margherita | Vegetariana | Frutti di Mare

Vegetarian pizzas

Margherita | Vegetariana | Romana

Seafood pizzas

Frutti di Mare | Sicilia | Tonno

Beef pizzas

Prosciutto e | Capricciosa | Quattro

Concept D: Lane

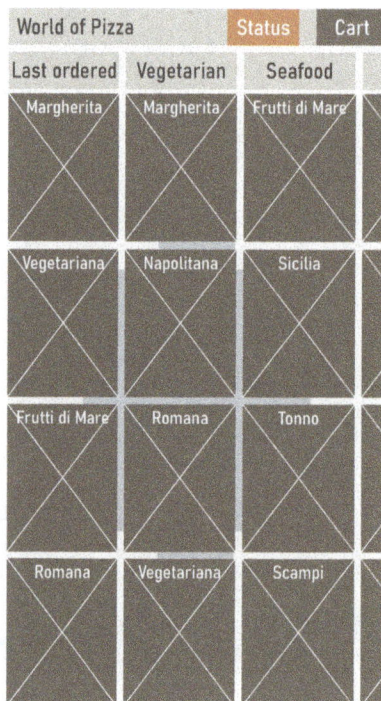

World of Pizza | Status | Cart

Last ordered | Vegetarian | Seafood

Margherita | Margherita | Frutti di Mare

Vegetariana | Napolitana | Sicilia

Frutti di Mare | Romana | Tonno

Romana | Vegetariana | Scampi

Figure 14.22: Explored seed concepts – Entry canvas per seed concept shown

Seed concept A: Pizza-Gram - Cast (iteration 1, step 1)

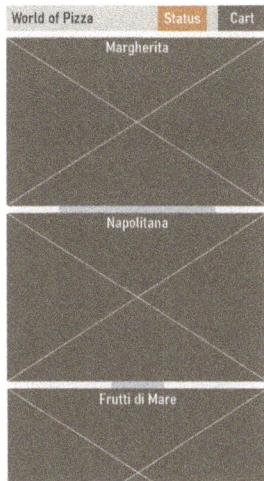

Canvas 1

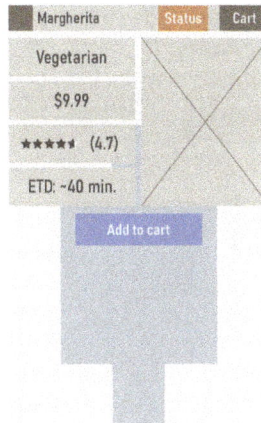

Canvas 2

Canvas 3

Canvas 4

Canvas 5

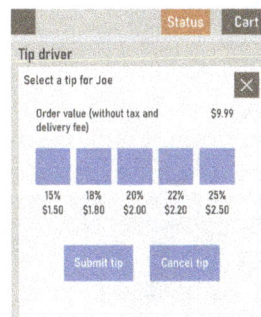

Canvas 6

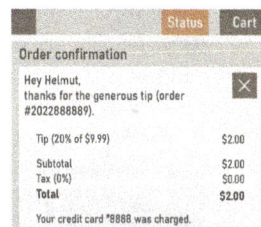

Canvas 7

Figure 14.23: Seed concept A: Pizza-Gram – Canvas cast (iteration 1, step 1)

Seed concept A: Pizza-Gram – Flow (iteration 1, step 1)

UT 1.1 Select pizza

TAS / AAS

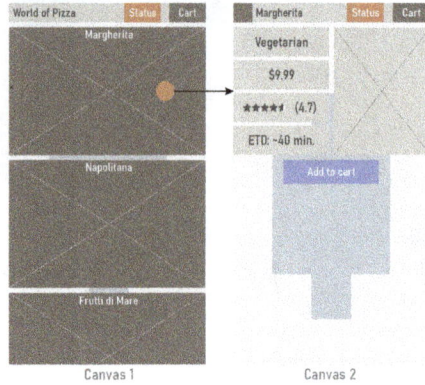

Canvas 1   Canvas 2

0 / 1
(inefficient)

UT 1.2 Order pizza

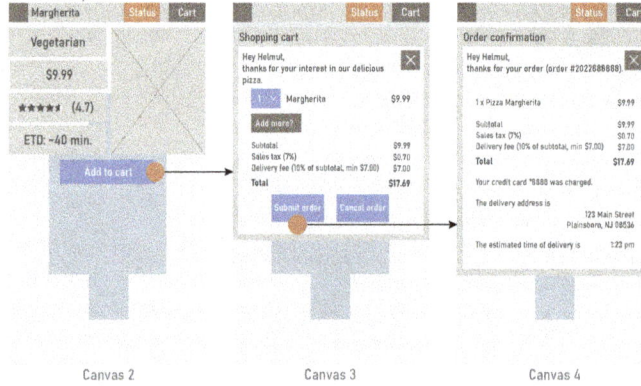

Canvas 2   Canvas 3   Canvas 4

1 / 2
(inefficient)

UT 1.3 Monitor status

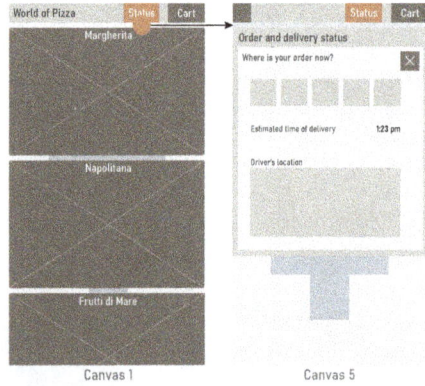

Canvas 1   Canvas 5

1 / 1
(efficient)

UT 1.4 Tip driver

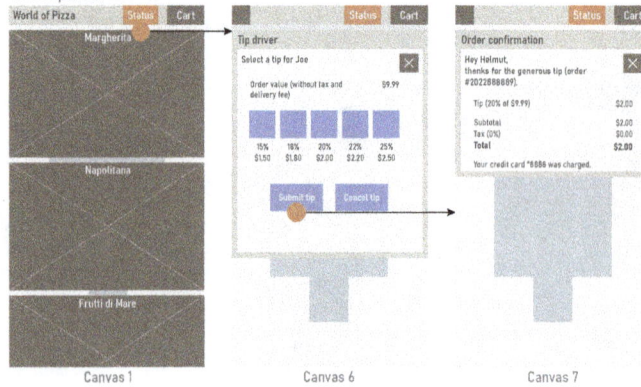

Canvas 1   Canvas 6   Canvas 7

1 / 2
(inefficient)

Figure 14.24: Seed concept A: Pizza-Gram – Canvas flow (iteration 1, step 1)

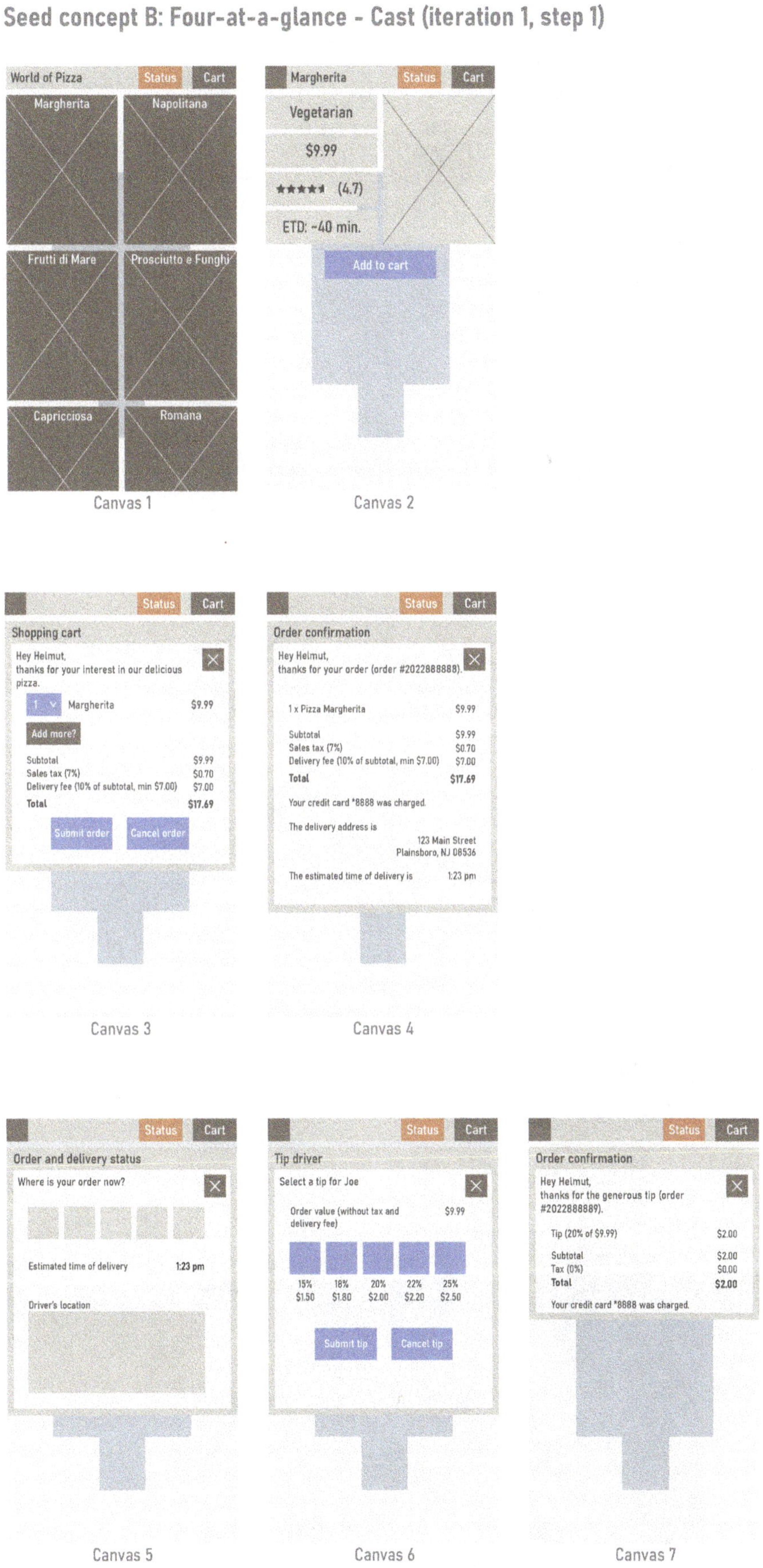

Seed concept B: Four-at-a-glance - Cast (iteration 1, step 1)

Figure 14.25: Seed concept B: Four-at-a-glance – Canvas cast (iteration 1, step 1)

Seed concept B: Four-at-a-glance - Flow (iteration 1, step 1)

UT 1.1 Select pizza

TAS / AAS

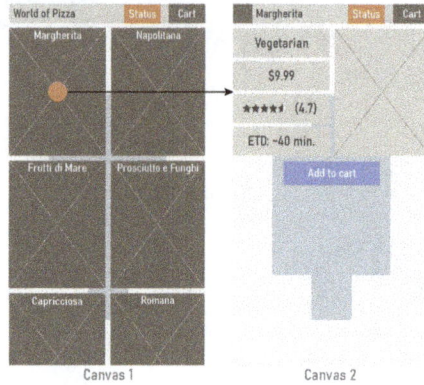

0 / 1
(inefficient)

UT 1.2 Order pizza

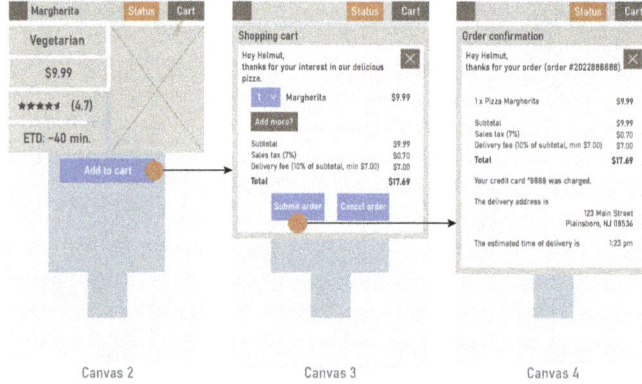

1 / 2
(inefficient)

UT 1.3 Monitor status

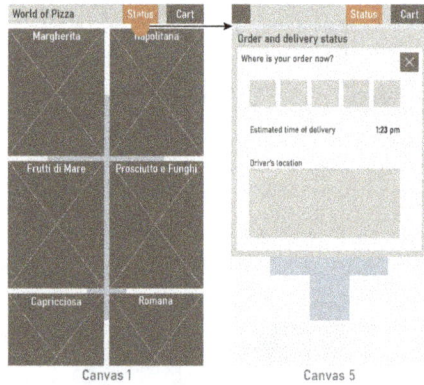

1 / 1
(efficient)

UT 1.4 Tip driver

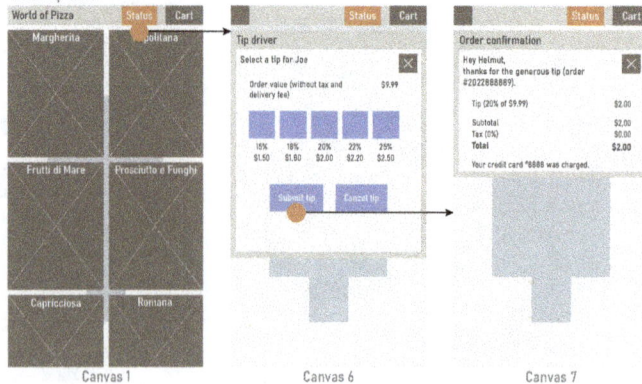

1 / 2
(inefficient)

Figure 14.26: Seed concept B: Four-at-a-glance – Canvas flow (iteration 1, step 1)

Seed concept C: Menu – Cast (iteration 1, step 1)

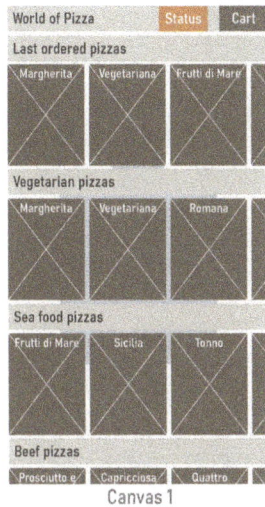

Canvas 1

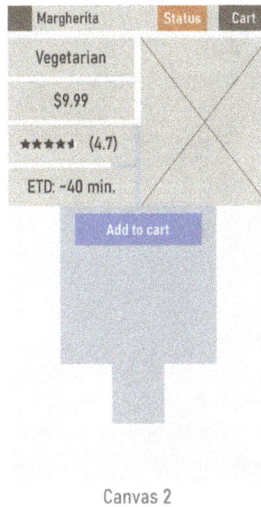

Canvas 2

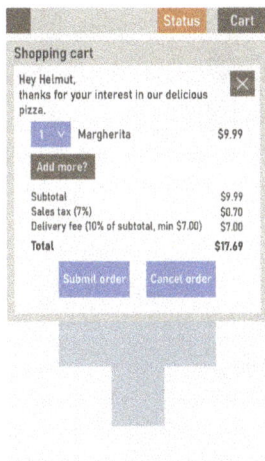

Canvas 3

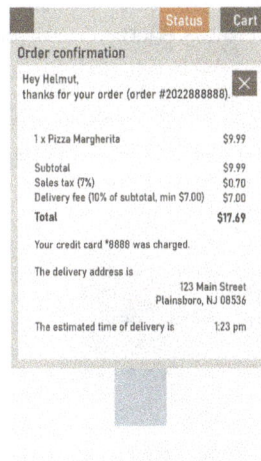

Canvas 4

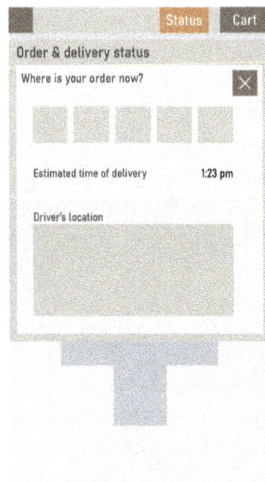

Canvas 5

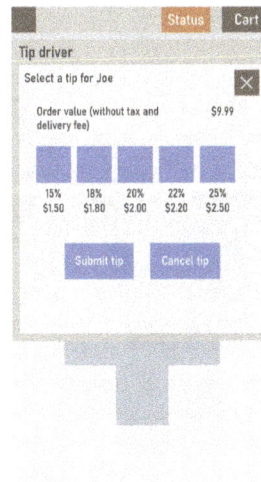

Canvas 6

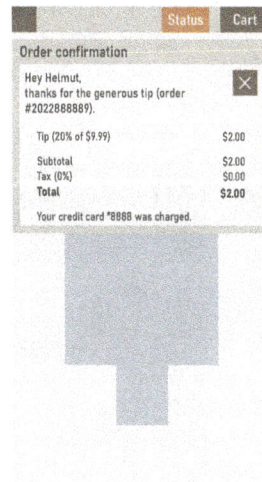

Canvas 7

Figure 14.27: Seed concept C: Menu – Canvas cast (iteration 1, step 1)

Seed concept C: Menu – Flow (iteration 1, step 1)

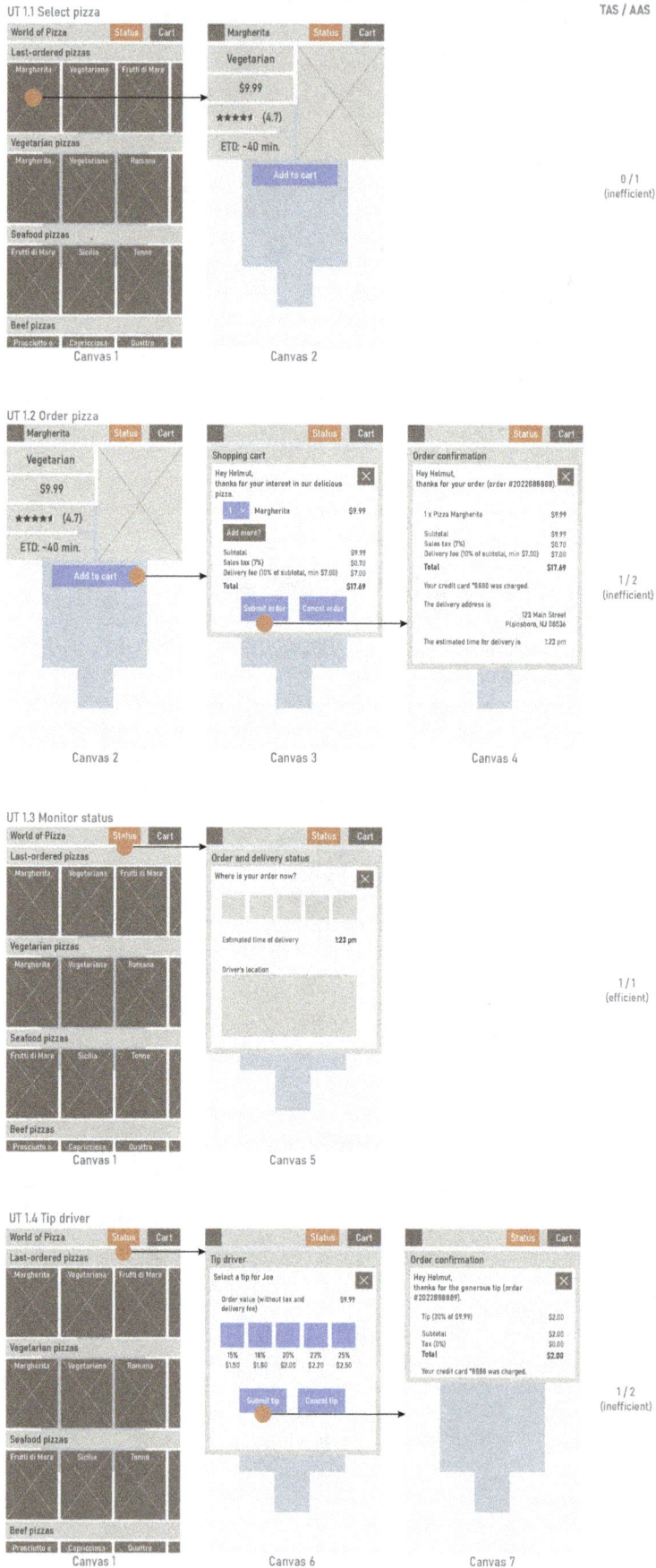

UT 1.1 Select pizza

TAS / AAS

0 / 1
(inefficient)

Canvas 1   Canvas 2

UT 1.2 Order pizza

1 / 2
(inefficient)

Canvas 2   Canvas 3   Canvas 4

UT 1.3 Monitor status

1 / 1
(efficient)

Canvas 1   Canvas 5

UT 1.4 Tip driver

1 / 2
(inefficient)

Canvas 1   Canvas 6   Canvas 7

Figure 14.28: Seed concept C: Menu – Canvas flow (iteration 1, step 1)

Seed concept D: Lane - Cast (iteration 1, step 1)

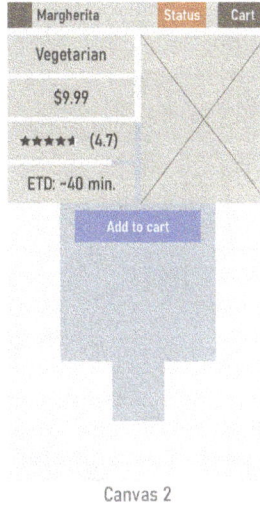

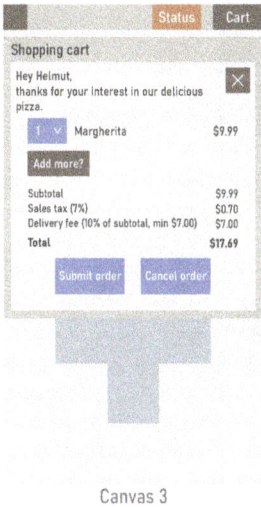

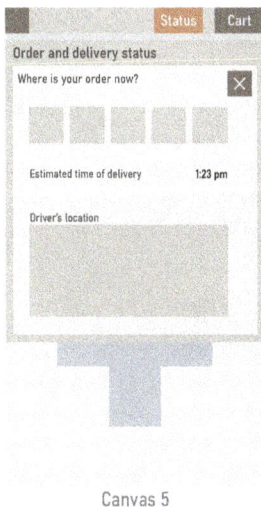

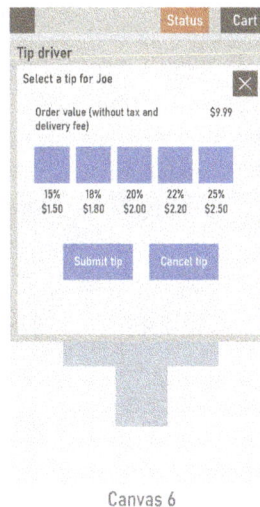

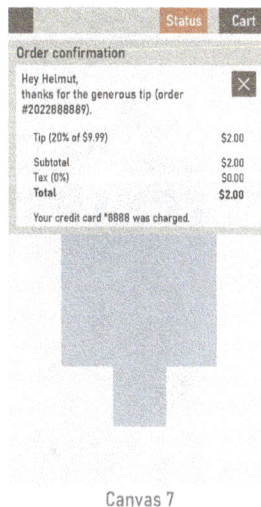

Figure 14.29: Seed concept D: Lane – Canvas cast (iteration 1, step 1)

Seed concept D: Lane – Flow (iteration 1, step 1)

TAS / AAS

UT 1.1 Select pizza

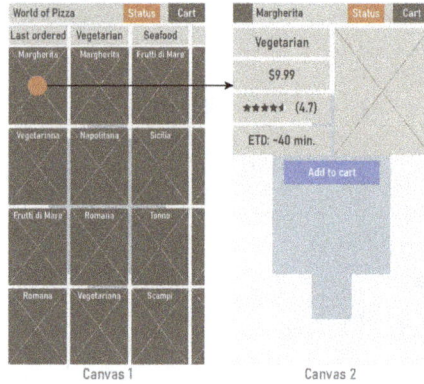

0 / 1
(inefficient)

UT 1.2 Order pizza

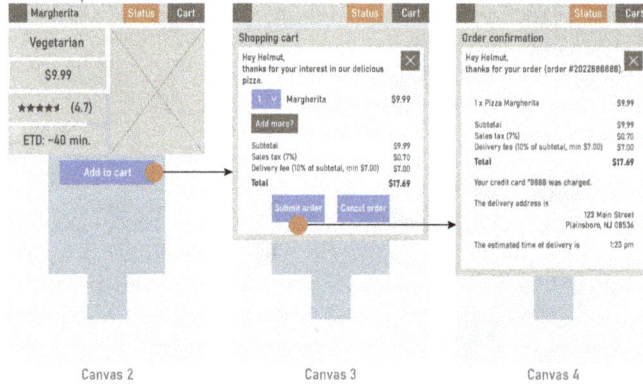

1 / 2
(inefficient)

UT 1.3 Monitor status

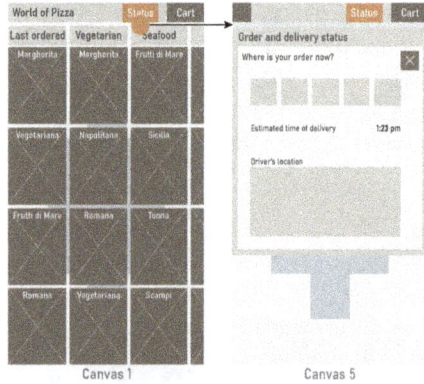

1 / 1
(efficient)

UT 1.4 Tip driver

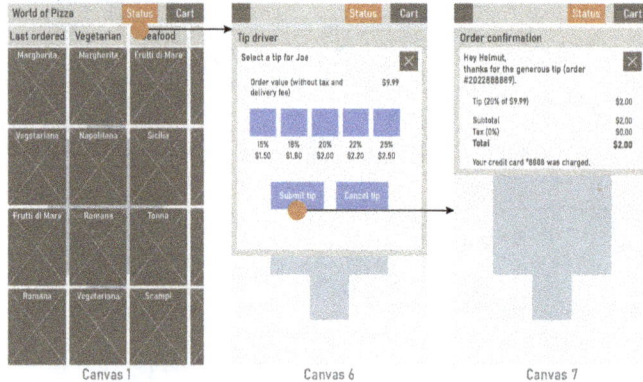

1 / 2
(inefficient)

Figure 14.30: Seed concept D: Lane – Canvas flow (iteration 1, step 1)

Summary

Step 1: Explore Concepts

▶ Move on to Step 2: Refine Concepts
◀ Go back to Define Involvement Goals

Seed concept A: Pizza-Gram – Flow (iteration 1, step 1)

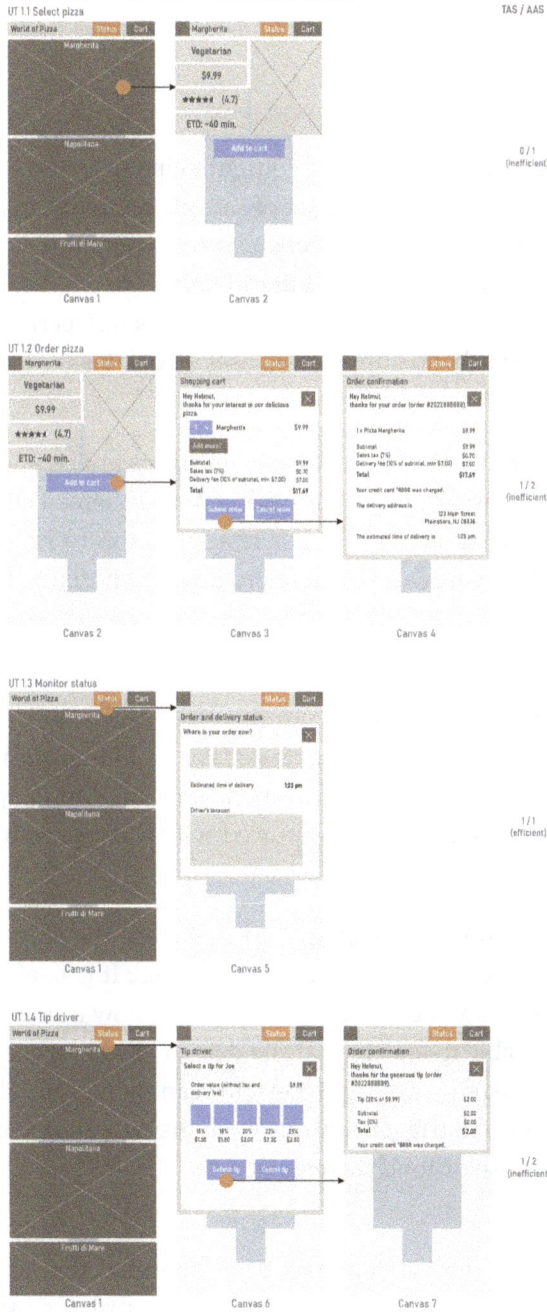

UT 1.1 Select pizza

TAS / AAS

0 / 1
(inefficient)

UT 1.2 Order pizza

1 / 2
(inefficient)

UT 1.3 Monitor status

1 / 1
(efficient)

UT 1.4 Tip driver

1 / 2
(inefficient)

Lessons learned

Refine user tasks   When refining the user questions, the user's intent is reduced from the scope of the user involvement point to the scope of the user task. The pre- and post-conditions define the boundaries of a user task. If the user task appears to be large in scope, it can be broken down into user steps. The steps are also needed later for identifying the zones.

Ask task questions   Asking the task questions is a technique to build a connection between the application domain and the involvement domain. The task questions should be formulated with user representatives.

Identify content   Identifying content helps us understand what needs to be considered. One set of sample content can be reused for many design artifacts and ensures consistency. If it is difficult to identify task questions, content can help to re-engineer the questions. However, we must confirm that the re-engineered questions are actually valid and support the user's goal, tasks, and intent.

Select design elements   The task questions are be answered by selecting and assigning design elements to them. There should be minimal design elements per task question to keep the user interfaces clutter-free and clean to provide for efficiency. If in doubt, leave it out.

Map canvases to user tasks   In this step, one or more canvases are mapped to one or more user tasks. For mobile applications, one canvas is often mapped to one user task. For desktop applications, multiple user tasks will be supported with a single canvas.

Identify step flow per canvas   In this step, the steps per user task are assigned to the canvas per user task. It is useful to order the steps in a sequence. The order should follow a straight line as much as possible to ensure that the design elements are placed in a way that makes it easy for the eye to scan them. This also makes it easy for users to trigger controls when using interaction devices, such as a mouse or touch screen.

Mark zones   After the steps have been identified, they are grouped into zones. The zones then mark the area for placing the design elements.

Map design elements to zones Based on the steps, the design elements that were identified in the "select design elements" step are placed in the zones. It is recommended that only the identified design elements be used, and maybe not all of them.

Create the baseline concept After the placement of the design elements, the initial layout can be created. The layout establishes the first seed concept. The initial layout is also called the "baseline concept." It functions as a reference for future seed concept explorations and refinements. The baseline concept is considered the "concept ground truth."

Explore seed concepts Additional seed concepts are explored. The benefit of exploration is not only having a larger set of concepts to refine and select from, but it also allows the experience professional to learn which design elements, or combination of design elements, help to achieve the involvement goals. Exploration is a learning experience for experience professionals.

Tips and tricks

The ten steps look very time intensive. With some practice, it will take just a few minutes per step to apply them. For me, they have become second nature. They provide safe-guards for the design. They allow me to check the design options to explain them to others. Applying the steps makes the design process predictable and the design decisions explainable.

I like to compare the approach here to traffic barriers that have the function of outlining the boundaries of a road. They keep the traffic in check. Many traffic barriers have retro-reflectors for guidance at night. The approach presented here is similar. It guides the experience professional to ask the right questions and to make the right decisions in the right order.

The task questions have saved many of my concept projects from going on a fishing tour. I use "fishing tour" as a metaphor for achieving an outcome mostly by chance. I personally don't like the chance-based approach. As a consultant, I need to deliver a certain design quality within a certain time frame, and chance is not the best compass. Instead of me finding the fish, I want the fish to find me. And this is what I can achieve with the described design approach. The most visible savings is the reduction of iterations with users. Due to the process, and mostly the task questions, the number of iterations was significantly reduced. Initially, I needed three to five iterations for a concept, and now I only need only one or two. This reduction not only saves time and resources for everyone involved, it also lets me appear to be an experience professional who seems to know what he is doing - which is not the worst reputation to have.

The object relationship diagram and the state-transition diagram provide a different, necessary view of the design task. They add a structure to the objects that allows the experience professional to talk to subject matter experts at eye level. This is necessary not only to be respected as an equal partner, but also to understand dependencies that need to be supported with the involvement concept. I highly recommend that you get familiar with such structures and apply them to everyday objects, such as elevators, heating systems, or coffee machines (for state-transition diagrams) and borrowing books or renting surf-boards (for object-relationship diagrams).

Mapping steps to zones, and then design elements to zones, avoids the problem of having to make significant changes later in the design process.

The approach presented in this chapter is not only applicable to entire applications, but it can be applied to the design of UI widgets too. I remember that I applied it to the design of a search feature for an engineering tool. It was satisfying to see how it guided me. The ten steps, in combination with GAIS, lead to a very efficient final design. I had no problem at all communicating the result and the rationale to my stakeholders. They enjoyed that process, too, because many of them still thought that design is based on opinions and gut feelings and not on objective rationales.

Exercise 3.2

Goal   Explore at least five seed concepts for your application.

Material   User involvement point, refined user tasks, task questions, identified content, object relationship diagram, state-transition diagram, content, functions, design elements, canvas, zones, baseline concept, seed concepts, canvas cast, canvas flows.

Completion criteria:

> ► For one selected user involvement point: all user tasks are refined and the refinement is documented.
> ► For all refined user tasks: Task questions are identified and documented.
> ► For all refined user tasks: Content is identified; an object relationship diagram and a state-transition diagram are created and documented.
> ► For all refined user tasks: The canvases are identified and assigned to user tasks.
> ► For all canvases: The steps and zones are marked.
> ► For all canvases: The design elements are mapped to zones
> ► The canvas cast and the canvas flow for the baseline concept is created and documented.
> ► For at least five seed concepts: The canvas cast and the canvas flow are created and documented. The differences between the seed concepts are documented.

Refine Concept | **15**

Time is free, but it's priceless
Harvey Mackay

Purpose

After seed concepts have been explored, they will be refined (see Figure 15.1).

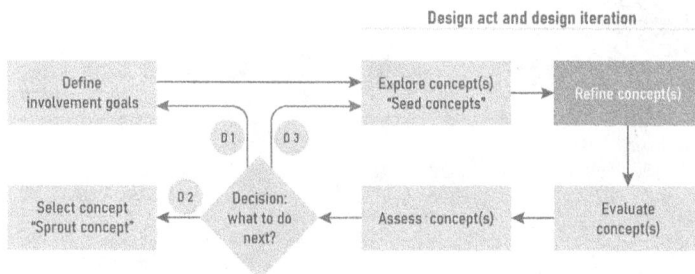

Figure 15.1: Refine concept

This section introduces twelve design efficiency techniques that help to optimize an involvement concept for efficiency (see Figure 15.2). Six of them are layout-oriented and six are function-oriented.

Design Efficiency Techniques

Apply batch usage

Aggregate content

Align content hierarchy

Concatenate functions

Streamline the gaze flow

Reuse the user's choices

Move up content

Schedule action

Move up control

Propose action

Fix positions

Execute action

www.designforefficiency.com
(CC BY-NC-SA 4.0).

Figure 15.2: Design Efficiency Techniques

The intent of each technique will be described, along with how it can be applied to the World of Pizza. The assumption is that the involvement concept under efficiency optimization was created by applying the ten steps used to create a seed concept (see Chapter 14 (Explore Concepts) on page 387).

Apply batch usage

Technique

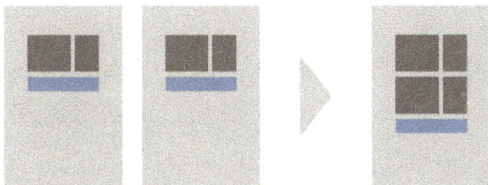

Checkpoints

- ▶ CP 1: Are all content elements identified that could benefit from batch usage?
- ▶ CP 2: Are sufficient filters available to select subsets of content objects?
- ▶ CP 3: Are functions available that can be applied to batches?

The first efficiency technique is a bit different from the other ones. It potentially requires the redesign of entire screens or concepts due to the lack of beneficial batch usage. This is the main reason it is listed first.

Many applications use multiple content objects of the same type that are part of a set of content objects. For example, in World of Pizza, pizzas are content objects that are part of a restaurant's pizza list (set of content objects). Creating and maintaining a list of pizzas involves dealing with each content object (e.g., pizza) and its attributes (e.g., name, price, calories). Relatively often, a user's task is applied to several content objects and their attributes.

Instead of applying a single task multiple times to multiple content objects, one by one, a task can be applied to multiple content objects (the batch) at once. In this book, we call this "batch usage." (see Figure 15.3). Batch usage increases the efficiency for users.

The ability to apply batch usage requires two things: (1) the ability to identify a set of content objects (the batch) and (2) the ability to apply a function to the group of content objects (the batch function).

Batch usage cannot be demonstrated well with UIP 1. Therefore, we will employ a user task from UIP 2 "Manager" to demonstrate the benefits of batch usage. The selected user task is "maintain pizza list." The described batch usage techniques are examples and most likely not complete.

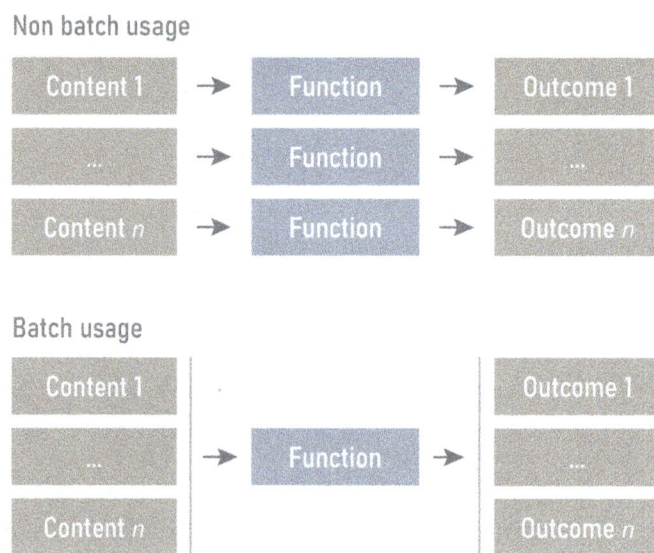

Non batch usage

Content 1	→	Function	→	Outcome 1
...	→	Function	→	...
Content n	→	Function	→	Outcome n

Batch usage

Content 1				Outcome 1
...	→	Function	→	...
Content n				Outcome n

Figure 15.3: Applying functions to batch groupings

WoP

Review content objects To be able to modify content objects and their attributes, the user first needs to be able to review the content objects and their attributes at a glance. A set of content objects including their attributes is often represented in a list, but sometimes in a grid or in other forms. It does not matter which visualization style is used, but it should be a style that allows the user to review and compare attributes at a glance across different content objects. For demonstration purposes, we use a list here (see Figure 15.4).

Clone content objects One example of batch usage is cloning content objects. Cloning refers to selecting one or more content objects and creating duplicates.

ID	Name	Price	Diet	Calories	State
1	Margherita	9.99	Veggie	1,120	Not published
2	Napolitana	11.99	Veggie	1,240	Not published
3	Frutti di Mare	12.99	Seafood	1,180	Not published
4	Prosciutto e Funghi	11.99	Beaf	1,320	Not published

Figure 15.4: Review objects

Figure 15.5 depicts the result we would get after cloning the first four content objects of our pizza list twice.

ID	Name	Price	Diet	Calories	State
1	Margherita	9.99	Veggie	1,120	Not published
2	Napolitana	11.99	Veggie	1,240	Not published
3	Frutti di Mare	12.99	Seafood	1,180	Not published
4	Prosciutto e Funghi	11.99	Beaf	1,320	Not published
5	Margherita	9.99	Veggie	1,120	Not published
6	Napolitana	11.99	Veggie	1,240	Not published
7	Frutti di Mare	12.99	Seafood	1,180	Not published
8	Prosciutto e Funghi	11.99	Beaf	1,320	Not published
9	Margherita	9.99	Veggie	1,120	Not published
10	Napolitana	11.99	Veggie	1,240	Not published
11	Frutti di Mare	12.99	Seafood	1,180	Not published
12	Prosciutto e Funghi	11.99	Beaf	1,320	Not published

Figure 15.5: Cloning objects. Objects 5 to 8 are added as a result of the first clone, and objects 9 to 12 are added as a result of the second clone.

Treat errors with tolerance   When cloning content objects, it is possible that errors will occur because sometimes rules or constraints are violated by the cloned objects. For example, some attribute must have a value within a defined range, some attributes have a value that must be unique, and sometimes only a certain number of values can occur in one set of content objects. If cloning leads to violations, the resulting errors should be handled with tolerance[1].

There are various techniques for dealing with violations. One method is addressing each violation before the cloned content object is accepted and appears in the list of content objects. This technique is effort-intensive for the user and should be avoided. Treating violations in this way often leads to the use of error-tolerant external applications (e.g., spread sheets) which is not an efficient task flow for the users.

Instead, the cloned content objects with their violations should be

1: Error tolerance is included in one of the interaction principles of ISO 9241-110, called "Use error robustness." The interaction principle is described as "The interactive system assists the user in avoiding errors and in case of identifiable errors treats them tolerantly and assists the user when recovering from errors" [227, clause 5.6]. Kirwan and Reason provide additional resources for human errors [228, 229] added to the list of content objects, and the violations should be indicated. The user then has the opportunity to fix them one by one.

In our example, each pizza name should be used only once (see Figure 15.6).

ID	Name	Price	Diet	Calories	State
▲ 1	Margherita	9.99	Veggie	1,120	Not published
▲ 2	Napolitana	11.99	Veggie	1,240	Not published
▲ 3	Frutti di Mare	12.99	Seafood	1,180	Not published
▲ 4	Prosciutto e Funghi	11.99	Beaf	1,320	Not published
▲ 5	Margherita	9.99	Veggie	1,120	Not published
▲ 6	Napolitana	11.99	Veggie	1,240	Not published
▲ 7	Frutti di Mare	12.99	Seafood	1,180	Not published
▲ 8	Prosciutto e Funghi	11.99	Beaf	1,320	Not published
▲ 9	Margherita	9.99	Veggie	1,120	Not published
▲ 10	Napolitana	11.99	Veggie	1,240	Not published
▲ 11	Frutti di Mare	12.99	Seafood	1,180	Not published
▲ 12	Prosciutto e Funghi	11.99	Beaf	1,320	Not published

Figure 15.6: Treat errors with tolerance; the triangle indicates that the related pizza name violates a rule or constraint.

Replace attributes manually It should be possible to replace attribute values. Even if it is not a batch function, being able to manually modify the attributes is important for the user (see Figure 15.7).

ID	Name	Price	Diet	Calories	State
1	Margherita	9.99	Veggie	1,120	Not published
2	Napolitana	11.99	Veggie	1,240	Not published
3	Frutti di Mare	12.99	Seafood	1,180	Not published
4	Prosciutto e Funghi	11.99	Beaf	1,320	Not published
5	Capricciosa	9.99	Beaf	1,360	Not published
6	Romana	10.99	Veggie	1,140	Not published
7	Sicilia	11.99	Seafood	1,280	Not published
8	Quattro Stagioni	12.99	Beaf	1,250	Not published
9	Quadro Formaggi	12.99	Veggie	1,380	Not published
10	Tonno	12.99	Seafood	1,220	Not published
11	Vegetariana	10.99	Veggie	1,250	Not published
12	Calzone	12.99	Veggie	1,450	Not published

Figure 15.7: Replace attributes manually

Search and replace attributes In addition to manual replacement, it should be possible to search and replace content automatically or semiautomatically. The automatic mode (replace all instances of "old content" with "new content") is one of the batch functions. The semiautomatic mode (replace all instances of "old content" by "new content" and each replacement is user-confirmed) is called here "semi-batch."

In our case, we want to correct the typo "Beaf," which means we want to replace "Beaf" with "Beef."

ID	Name	Price	Diet	Calories	State
Replace "Beaf" with "Beef"					
1	Margherita	9.99	Veggie	1,120	Not published
2	Napolitana	11.99	Veggie	1,240	Not published
3	Frutti di Mare	12.99	Seafood	1,180	Not published
4	Prosciutto e Funghi	11.99	Beef	1,320	Not published
5	Capricciosa	9.99	Beef	1,360	Not published
6	Romana	10.99	Veggie	1,140	Not published
7	Sicilia	11.99	Seafood	1,280	Not published
8	Quattro Stagioni	12.99	Beef	1,250	Not published
9	Quadro Formaggi	12.99	Veggie	1,380	Not published
10	Tonno	12.99	Seafood	1,220	Not published
11	Vegetariana	10.99	Veggie	1,250	Not published
12	Calzone	12.99	Veggie	1,450	Not published

Figure 15.8: Search and replace attributes

Filter by attribute Filters are useful for enabling focused batch usage. They allow you to apply a batch function to a defined subset of content objects. In our case, we want to use a filter to apply the search and replace batch function.

We decide that the dietary term "veggie" is too colloquial and should be replaced by "vegetarian." In this case, we filter the list first by applying the filter criterion "veggie" (see Figure 15.9). Then, we apply the replacement function "replace 'veggie' with 'vegetarian'" (see Figure 15.10).

ID	Name	Price	Diet	Calories	State
			Veggie ✕		
1	Margherita	9.99	Veggie	1,120	Not published
2	Napolitana	11.99	Veggie	1,240	Not published
6	Romana	10.99	Veggie	1,140	Not published
9	Quadro Formaggi	12.99	Veggie	1,380	Not published
11	Vegetariana	10.99	Veggie	1,250	Not published
12	Calzone	12.99	Veggie	1,450	Not published

Figure 15.9: Filter by attribute

ID	Name	Price	Diet	Calories	State
	Replace "Veggie" with "Vegetarian"		Veggie ✕		
1	Margherita	9.99	Vegetarian	1,120	Not published
2	Napolitana	11.99	Vegetarian	1,240	Not published
6	Romana	10.99	Vegetarian	1,140	Not published
9	Quadro Formaggi	12.99	Vegetarian	1,380	Not published
11	Vegetariana	10.99	Vegetarian	1,250	Not published
12	Calzone	12.99	Vegetarian	1,450	Not published

Figure 15.10: Apply a function to selected content objects

Apply a function to several objects When applying a batch function to a set of content objects, we need to select the set first. The set can be the entire set (as a default) or a subset.

If the batch consists of the entire set, we need to apply a control to the batch. Such an example for our pizza list is the "Publish all" control shown in Figure 15.11.

ID	Name	Price	Diet	Calories	State
1	Margherita	9.99	Vegetarian	1,120	Not published
2	Napolitana	11.99	Vegetarian	1,240	Not published
3	Frutti di Mare	12.99	Seafood	1,180	Not published
4	Prosciutto e Funghi	11.99	Beef	1,320	Not published
5	Capricciosa	9.99	Beef	1,360	Not published
6	Romana	10.99	Vegetarian	1,140	Not published
7	Sicilia	11.99	Seafood	1,280	Not published
8	Quattro Stagioni	12.99	Beef	1,250	Not published
9	Quadro Formaggi	12.99	Vegetarian	1,380	Not published
10	Tonno	12.99	Seafood	1,220	Not published
11	Vegetariana	10.99	Vegetarian	1,250	Not published
12	Calzone	12.99	Vegetarian	1,450	Not published

Publish all

Figure 15.11: Apply a batch function to all object items

If you frequently need to apply the batch function to a subset of content objects, the use of filters or selectors should be enabled. When selectors are used, it should be possible to select all displayed content objects at once (see the control "select all" at the top of the list in Figure 15.12).

	ID	Name	Price	Diet	Calories	State
☑		Select all				
☑	1	Margherita	9.99	Vegetarian	1,120	Not published
☑	2	Napolitana	11.99	Vegetarian	1,240	Not published
☑	3	Frutti di Mare	12.99	Seafood	1,180	Not published
☑	4	Prosciutto e Funghi	11.99	Beef	1,320	Not published
☑	5	Capricciosa	9.99	Beef	1,360	Not published
☑	6	Romana	10.99	Vegetarian	1,140	Not published
☑	7	Sicilia	11.99	Seafood	1,280	Not published
☑	8	Quattro Stagioni	12.99	Beef	1,250	Not published
☑	9	Quadro Formaggi	12.99	Vegetarian	1,380	Not published
☑	10	Tonno	12.99	Seafood	1,220	Not published
☑	11	Vegetariana	10.99	Vegetarian	1,250	Not published
☑	12	Calzone	12.99	Vegetarian	1,450	Not published

Publish selected

Figure 15.12: Select content objects

Align content hierarchy

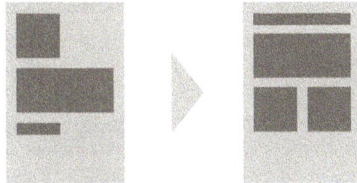

Technique

Checkpoints

▸ CP 1: Is the content that belongs to a hierarchy identified?
▸ CP 2: Is the content hierarchy defined?
▸ CP 3: Does the zone layout consider the content hierarchy?

In this technique, the zone layout for each seed concept is refined. The idea is to ensure that the zones are considered in the content hierarchy, something that was not necessarily done when creating the baseline concept, so the user can find the design elements more efficiently and more intuitively.

WoP

The pizzas are content elements that can be reasonably structured in a hierarchy, which can be broken down into the following levels:

▶ Level 0: All pizzas (unfiltered pizza list)
▶ Level 1: Pizza filter
▶ Level 2: List of (filtered) pizzas
▶ Level 3: Pizza details

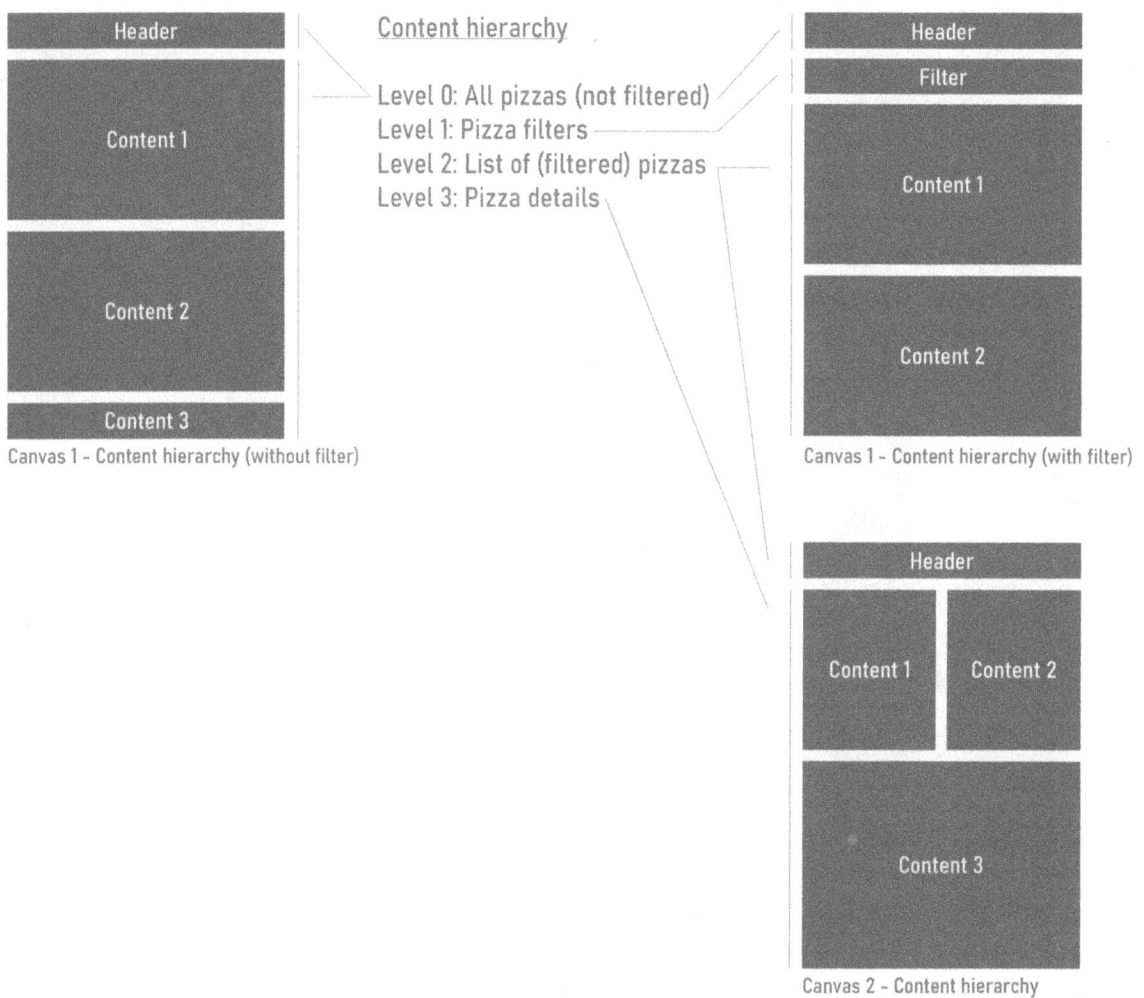

Figure 15.13: Align content hierarchy

"World of Pizza" is at the top level, here called the "root" or level 0. Beneath the top level, we have two content hierarchies: one about the pizza and one about the orders. The content hierarchy for pizzas should be included in the prime area because it is needed for the primary user task (UT 1.1 select pizza). For now, we will ignore the "orders" hierarchy and concentrate on the content hierarchy for pizzas (see Figure 15.13).

There is a deficiency in the seed concept regarding the hierarchy: it does not provide a zone for a filter and it does not provide a zone for a pizza description (see Figure 15.14).

Align hierarchy - before

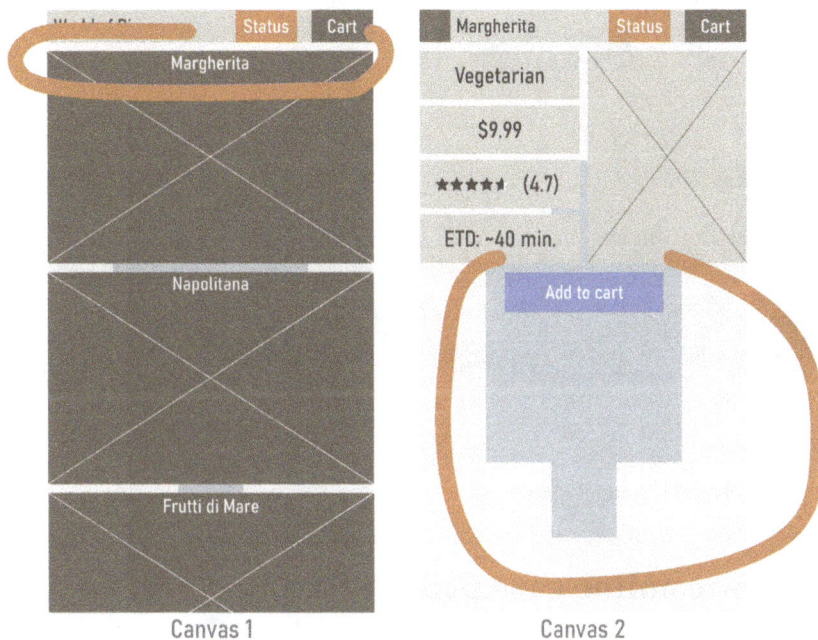

Figure 15.14: Align hierarchy: Before

The missing zones are added and the result of the hierarchy refinement is shown in Figure 15.15. For the remainder of this chapter, the filter zone will only be shown when used.

Align hierarchy - after

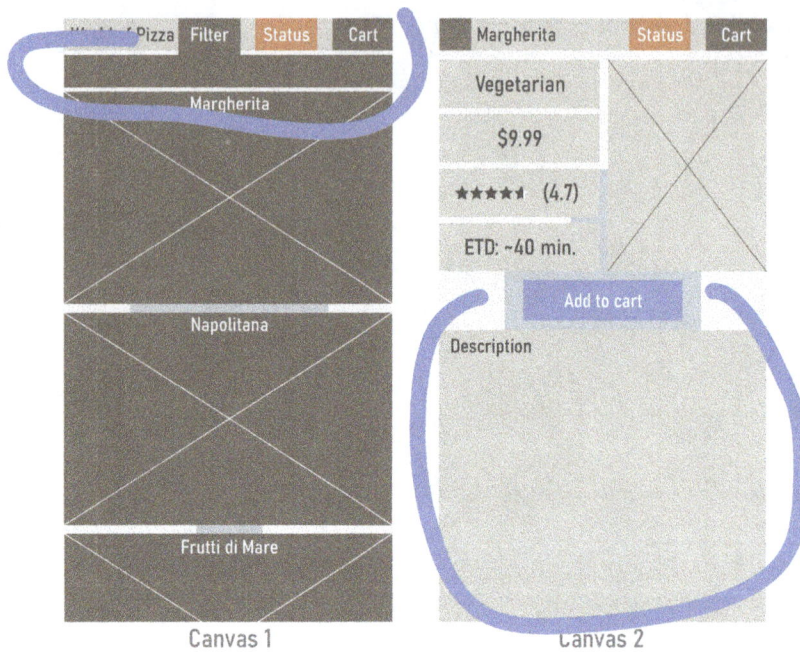

Figure 15.15: Align hierarchy: After

Streamline gaze path

Technique

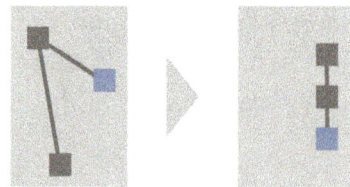

Checkpoint

- ▶ CP 1: Are design elements organized to support the (assumed) gaze path?
- ▶ CP 2: Is the gaze path efficient?

To support our intent of achieving high efficiency, we want the eye to be able to scan the canvas efficiently. Therefore, we are interested in a straight, simple gaze path[2] .

There are two major patterns for how humans seem to scan canvases: the F-pattern and the Z-pattern ([194, 231], see also Figure 15.16 and Figure 15.17). The gaze path principle for both patterns is similar: from left to right and from top to bottom.

2: "Fixations are eye movements that stabilize the retina over a stationary object of interest." [230, p. 44] The gaze path is understood here as the sequence of fixations.

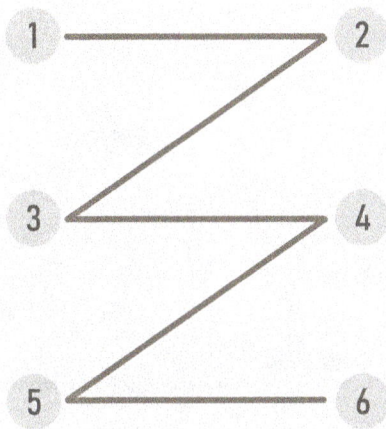

Figure 15.17: Z- or F-shape scanning pattern

We want to enable the user to scan content elements and control elements efficiently within a zone, without inefficient direction changes for the eye, the mouse pointer, or the finger. Figure 15.19 breaks down the gaze path to enable efficient scanning of zones, following the left-right and top-down principles of gaze patterns.

To support the experience professional in establishing efficient gaze paths, modular grid systems [232–235] can provide guidance to achieve consistency and scanning efficiency (see Figure 15.18).

Figure 15.16: Gaze path has a Z-shape or F-shape scanning pattern; source: Norman-Nielsen [231]

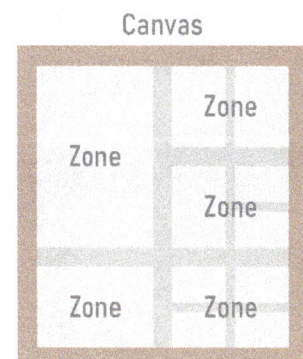

Figure 15.18: Modular grid system sample, applicable to canvases and zones

Gaze paths

Efficient paths*

Water path

L-shaped path

Double water path

Jump path

Typing path

*For users who used to read and
write from left to right and from top
to bottom.

Inefficient paths*

Salmon path

Dance path

Stitch path

Jump back path

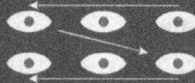

Carriage return path

Wild path

Figure 15.19: Gaze paths examples

WoP

Designing for an efficient gaze path requires an assumption about the sequence in which the user is going to scan the elements on the canvas. Eye-tracking studies [53] indicate that humans "scrutinize" [236] pictures on shopping site that are relevant to their goal. This includes pictures of real products [236].

To support an efficient user behavior and to allow users to easily scrutinize a product picture, we will enable the user to look at the pizza picture first. The following sequence of content was created based on self-observation, reflecting the intended gaze path. Our assumption about the preferred gaze path is as follows:

1. Pizza picture
2. Pizza name
3. Rating
4. Price
5. Diet
6. Estimated time of delivery (ETD)
7. Order

An efficient top-down and left-right scan is not supported in our current design (see Figure 15.23). To fix it, we will reorganize the elements to support the intended gaze flow (see Figure 15.24).

Figure 15.20: Salmon jumping a waterfall; source: Pixabay license. License: Pixabay

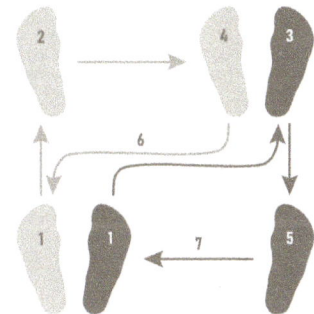

Figure 15.21: Dance steps. Which dance is illustrated here?

Figure 15.22: Typewriter. The carriage carries the paper. When the typist has reached the end of a line, the carriage is in the leftmost position. The typist moves the carriage manually back to the right ("carriage return"), to continue typing; source: Wikimedia; owner: Sommeregger. License: GNU Free Documentation License 1.2

Fixation path - before

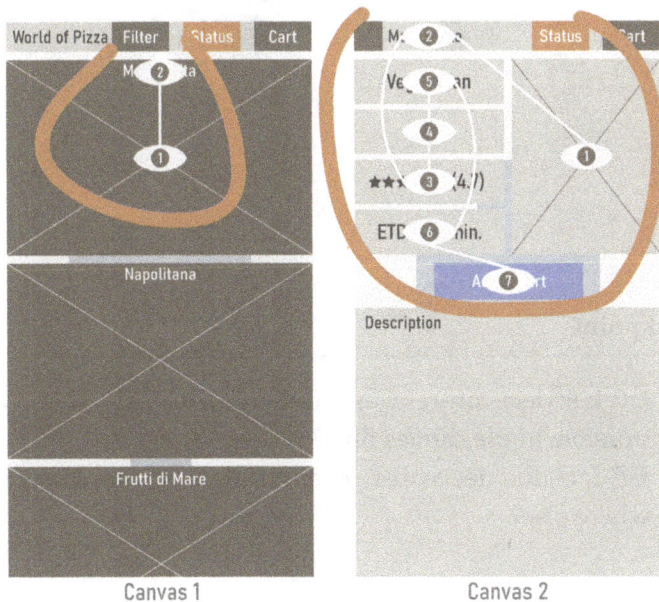

Canvas 1   Canvas 2

Figure 15.23: Gaze path: Before. Gaze path shows "salmon path" on the left-hand side and "dance path" on the right-hand side.

Fixation path – after

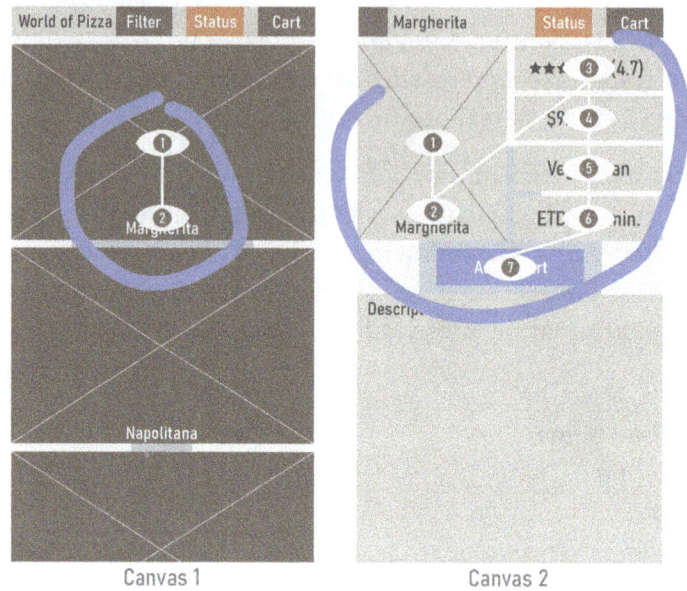

Canvas 1   Canvas 2

Figure 15.24: Gaze path: After. Improved gaze path shows "water path" on the left-hand side and "double water path" on the right-hand side.

Move up content

Checkpoint

▶ CP 1: Is decision-relevant content displayed as early as possible in the canvas flow?

▶ CP 2: Is non decision-relevant content displayed somewhere else?

One reason for inefficiency is that the content of interest is positioned late in the canvas flow. It means that the user involvement increases to find the content of interest.

The "move up content" technique addresses the issue of relocating the content early in the canvas flow to minimize involvement steps, so the user does not have to navigate to the content or, even worse, search for it. This applies especially to content needed for the execution of the primary user tasks. We sometimes have the tendency to organize content in hierarchical information architectures. The "move up content" technique provides shortcuts to content in a lower level of an information architecture by promoting it to the top level, e.g., to the prime area of the entry canvas.

Move up content - before

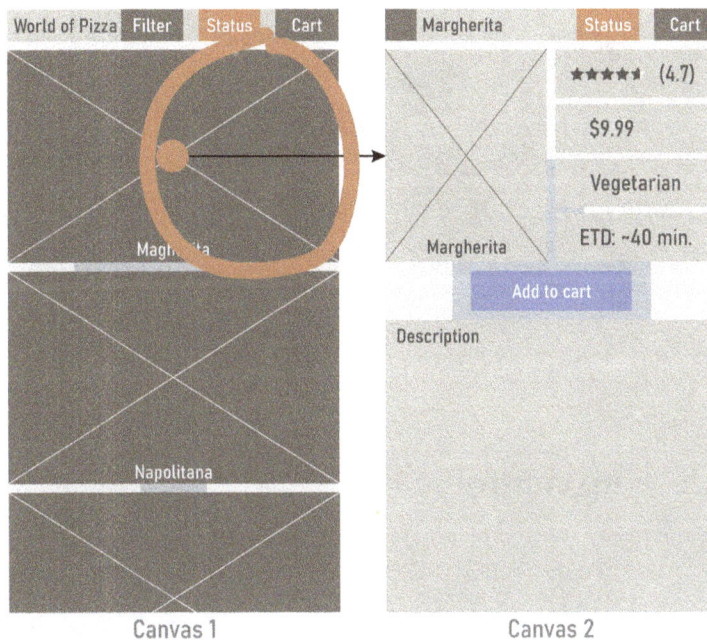

Figure 15.25: Move up content: Before

In our pizza example, we move the decision-relevant content about estimated time of delivery, rating, and price one canvas up, so that the user does not have to go to the details canvas and therefore saves two involvement steps (see Figure 15.28).

The "move up content" technique can be applied to many applications across industries. The risk of applying this technique is that you can end up with too much content in the entry or prime area. Therefore, only the decision-relevant content needed for the primary user task should be promoted. All other content can be pushed down.

Move up content - after

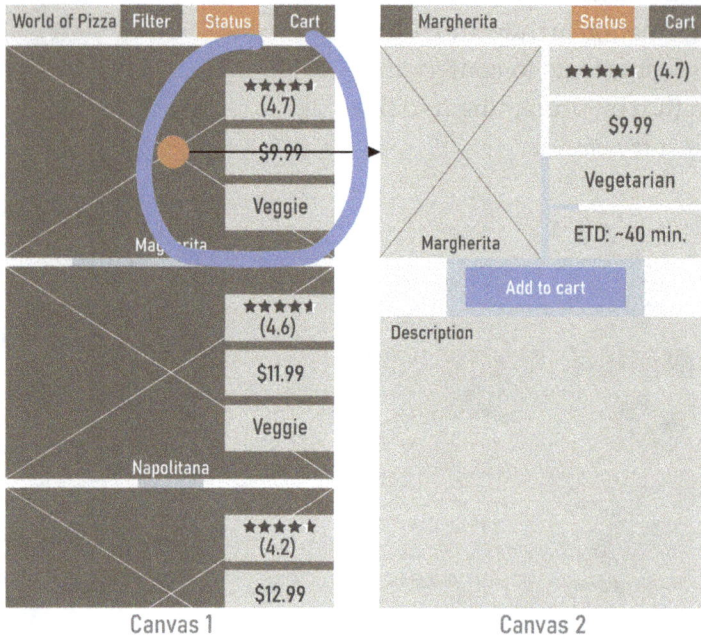

Figure 15.26: Move up content: After

Move up control

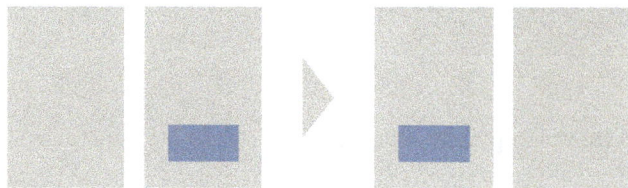

Checkpoint

▶ CP 1: Are decision-relevant controls displayed as early as possible in the canvas flow?
▶ CP 2: Are non decision-relevant controls displayed somewhere else?

This technique is similar to the previous one. However, here we move up a content control, hence the user saves several involvement steps to access the control.

In our pizza example, there is no order-related control on canvas 1 that could make the involvement more efficient (see Figure 15.27).

Move up control – before

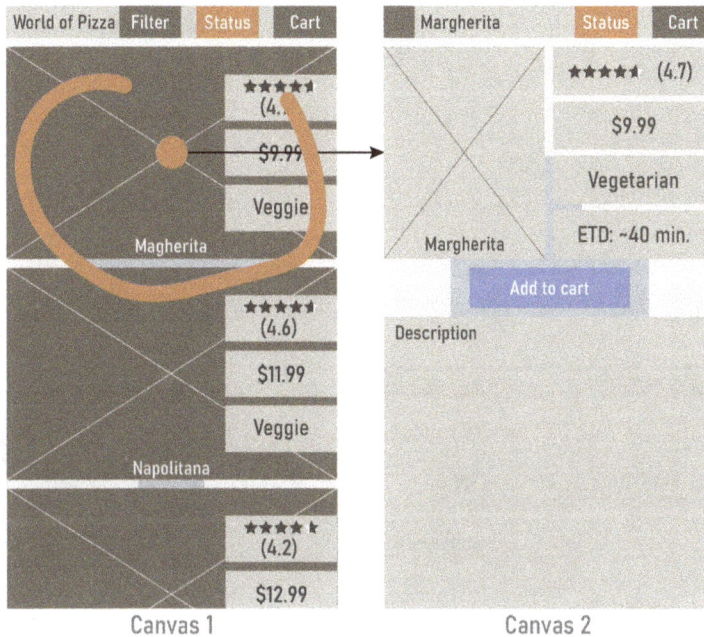

Figure 15.27: Move up control: Before

To fix this issue, we are going to move the control "add to cart" to each single pizza item on canvas 1. This allows the user to add a pizza to the cart with one involvement step (see Figure 15.28).

Move up control - after

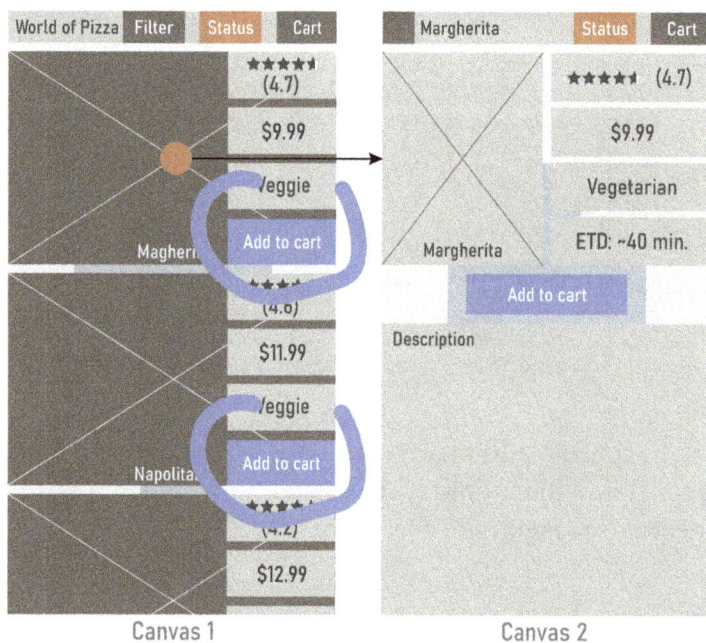

Figure 15.28: Move up control: After

Fix positions

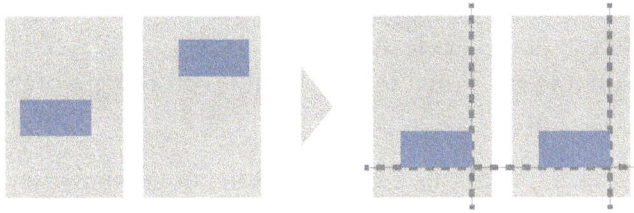

Checkpoint

▶ CP 1: Are key design elements in exactly the same x/y position across canvases?

Another design guideline is the use of fix positions for key design elements. Key design elements are those that help the user to move the user task forward. Canvas and content controls are strong candidates for fix positions, as well as some selected content elements needed to produce the outcome of value.

Let me clarify two variations of the idea of "fix positions." One is a logical fix position. It means that, for instance, a "Cancel" control is always to the right of an "OK" control, maybe within a 20-pixel distance.

The other is an x/y fix position. It means that a design element is always in a certain absolute position, identified by an x/y coordinate on the canvas, not by positions relative to other design elements. This second variation is the one that applies here. The reason is that the human user behaves not in a virtual environment but in a real environment with absolute positions, relative to their hands, their eyes, and their interaction devices. For that reason, fix positions are meant to be fix.

Keeping certain design elements in the same position makes it easier and faster for the user to perform the user tasks. It is very convenient for users to find the same key elements in the same position on each canvas. The user can then build a mental model of the different canvases and does not need to reposition the mouse or the finger.

A useful technique to achieve fix positions is the use of modular grid systems [232–235]. The candidates we are considering for fix positions are marked in Figure 15.29).

Canvas overlays are used here to place orders and to keep the user informed about order status (canvases three to seven). The "fix positions" step declutters the overlays and adds some layout structure to them. The greetings are in the same top area, the content of the canvases is in the central area, and the controls are in the bottom area. When reasonable, the controls are of the same height. All controls are in the control area.

As an interim result, the current canvas flow is shown in Figure 15.32 and the current canvas cast is shown in Figure 15.31.

Although this design efficiency technique is only about the layout, it is very difficult to achieve, particularly across a range of products and product releases. It requires a very good understanding of the application and involvement domain, as well as the design space. You won't find it very often realized in commercially available applications. This is easy to test: Mark the position of a key control on the screen and see where similar controls are positioned. Another way to test it is to keep the mouse pointer (for desktop applications) or a finger (for touch screens) in one position and observe how the controls are moving around it. If you find an application that has succeeded at this technique, it is a sign of high-quality design, a passion for detail, and the willingness to go the extra design mile.

This concludes the layout techniques. We now move on to the functional techniques.

Fix positions - before

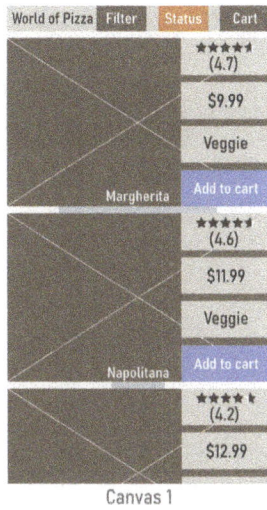

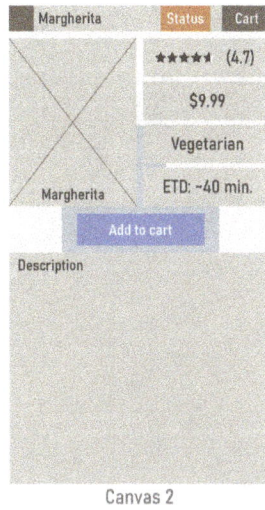

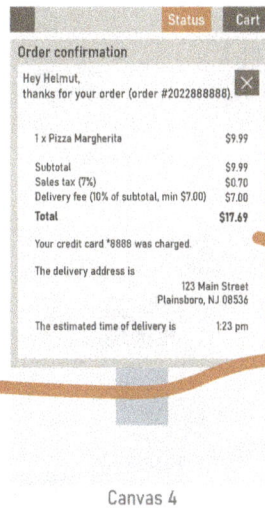

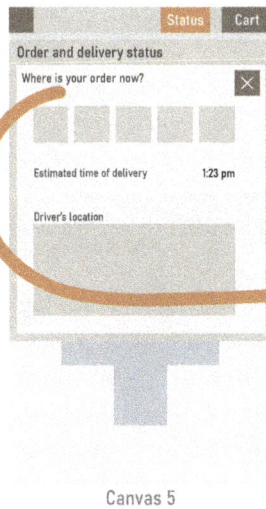

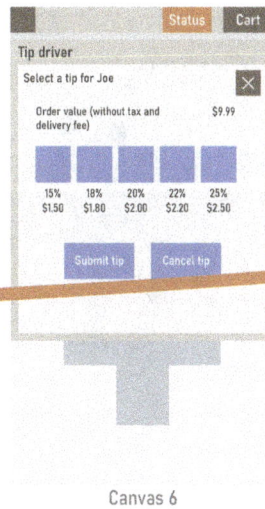

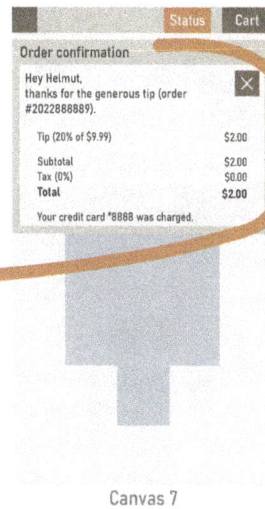

Figure 15.29: Fix positions: Before

Fix positions - after

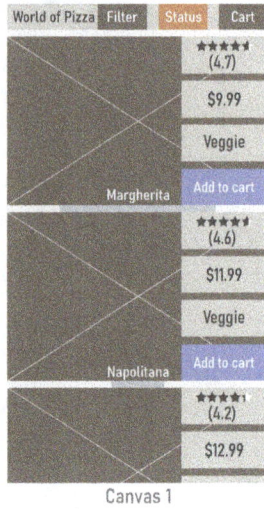

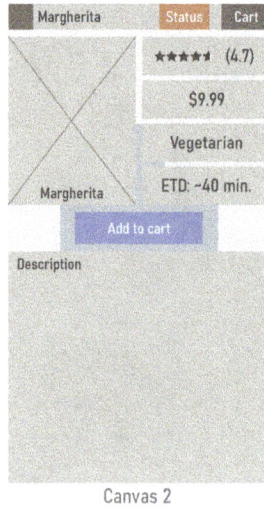

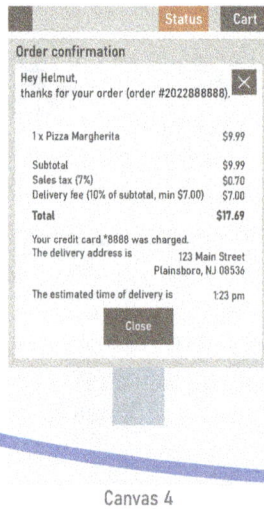

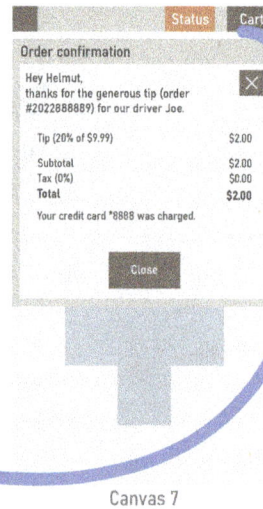

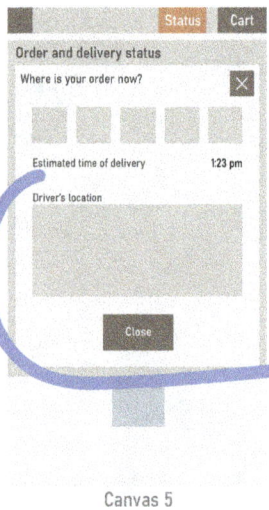

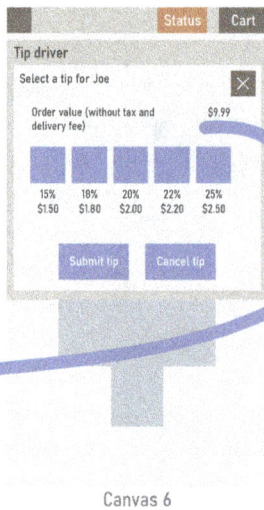

Figure 15.30: Fix positions: After

Seed concept A: Pizza-Gram - Cast (iteration 1, step 2, fix positions)

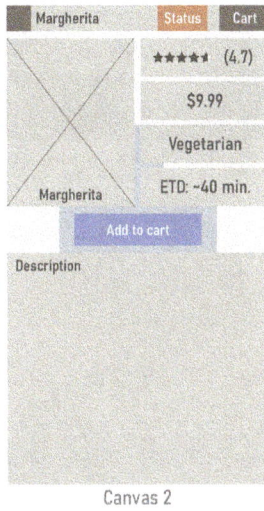

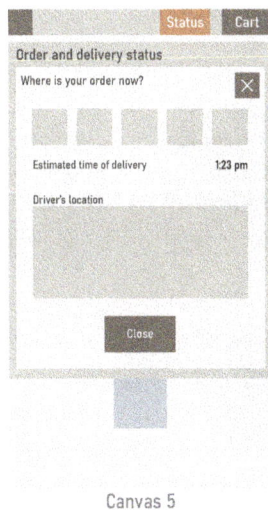

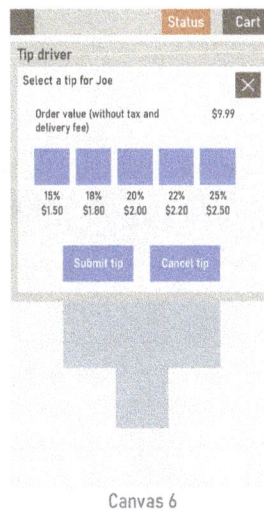

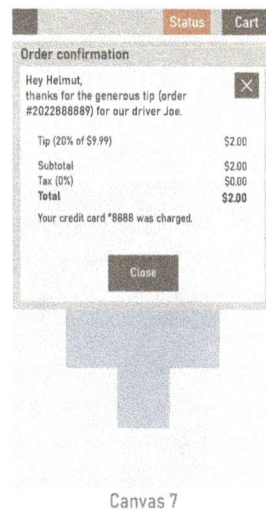

Figure 15.31: Seed concept A: Pizza-Gram – Canvas cast (Iteration 1, step 2, fix positions)

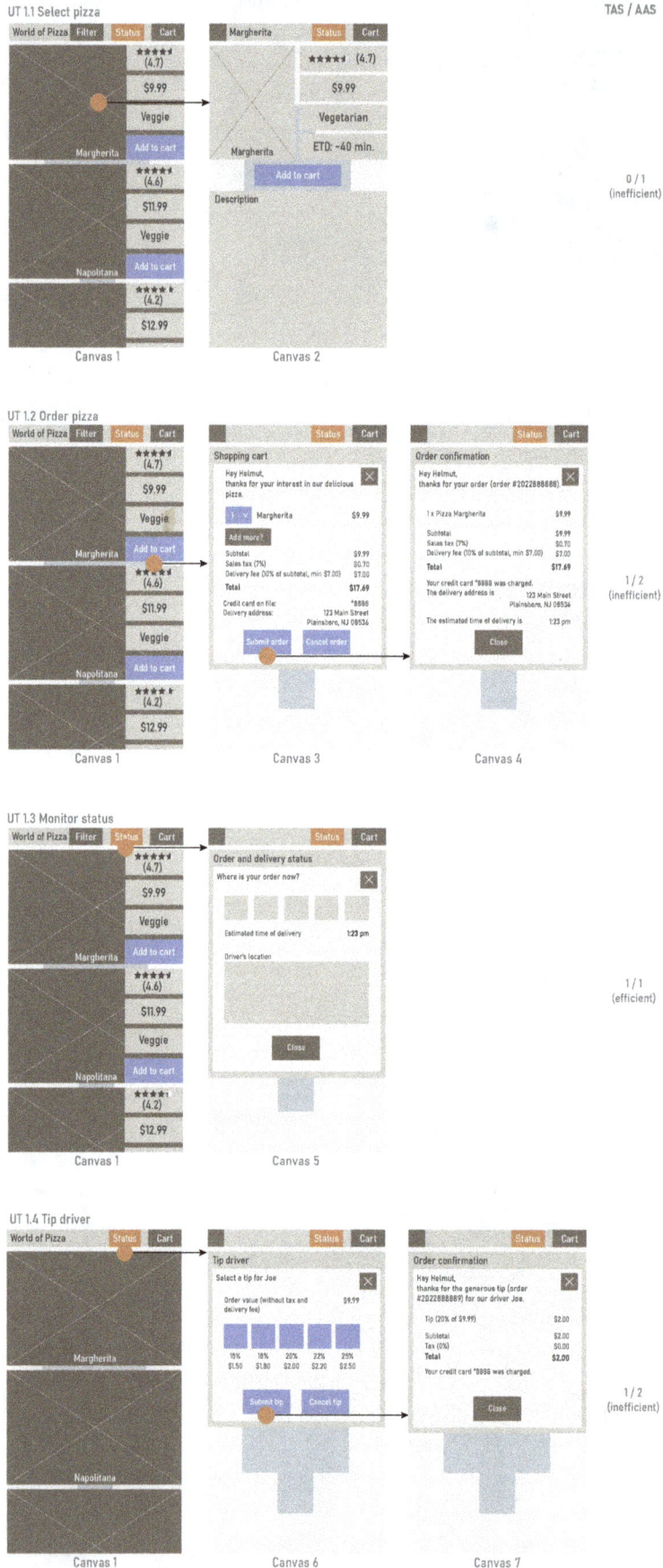

Figure 15.32: Seed concept A: Pizza-Gram – Canvas Flow (Iteration 1, step 2, fix positions)

Aggregate content

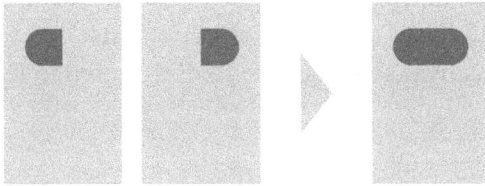

Checkpoint

- ▶ CP 1: What is the sequence of canvases from the start to the intended outcome (to achieve the user's goal)?
- ▶ CP 2: Which canvas in the sequence is closest to the intended outcome and still gives the user sufficient control?

You may wonder which of the twelve design efficiency techniques is the one with the biggest impact on efficiency. For my line of work, I'd pick this one. It is the one that brings users closest to their goals and intended outcomes and provides the user with sufficient control to make decisions.

Aggregating content means creating and combining content for the user that is close or is even identical to the intended outcome. The latter is desirable. This technique best reflects the application of the design hypotenuse, which was introduced in Section 12 (Reduce user involvement steps) on page 314.

To accelerate the application of this design efficiency technique, it is important to think backward, meaning starting from the end: what is the intended outcome? This leads us to the next design principle.

Backward is forward

To successfully address the user's need and achieve the user's goal, the designer needs to design backward, from the needs to the design elements. Thinking backward moves the design process forward.

Since we are often not good at thinking backward, we approach "backward" by working forward. It is advisable to outline a sequence of canvases, from an initial canvas to a canvas that reflects the outcome of value. Such a sequence reflects the involvement arc (see Section 12 (User involvement hypotenuse) on page 316). An example of a canvas sequence for WoP is shown in Figure 15.33.

Aggregate content: Entry canvas selection - Before

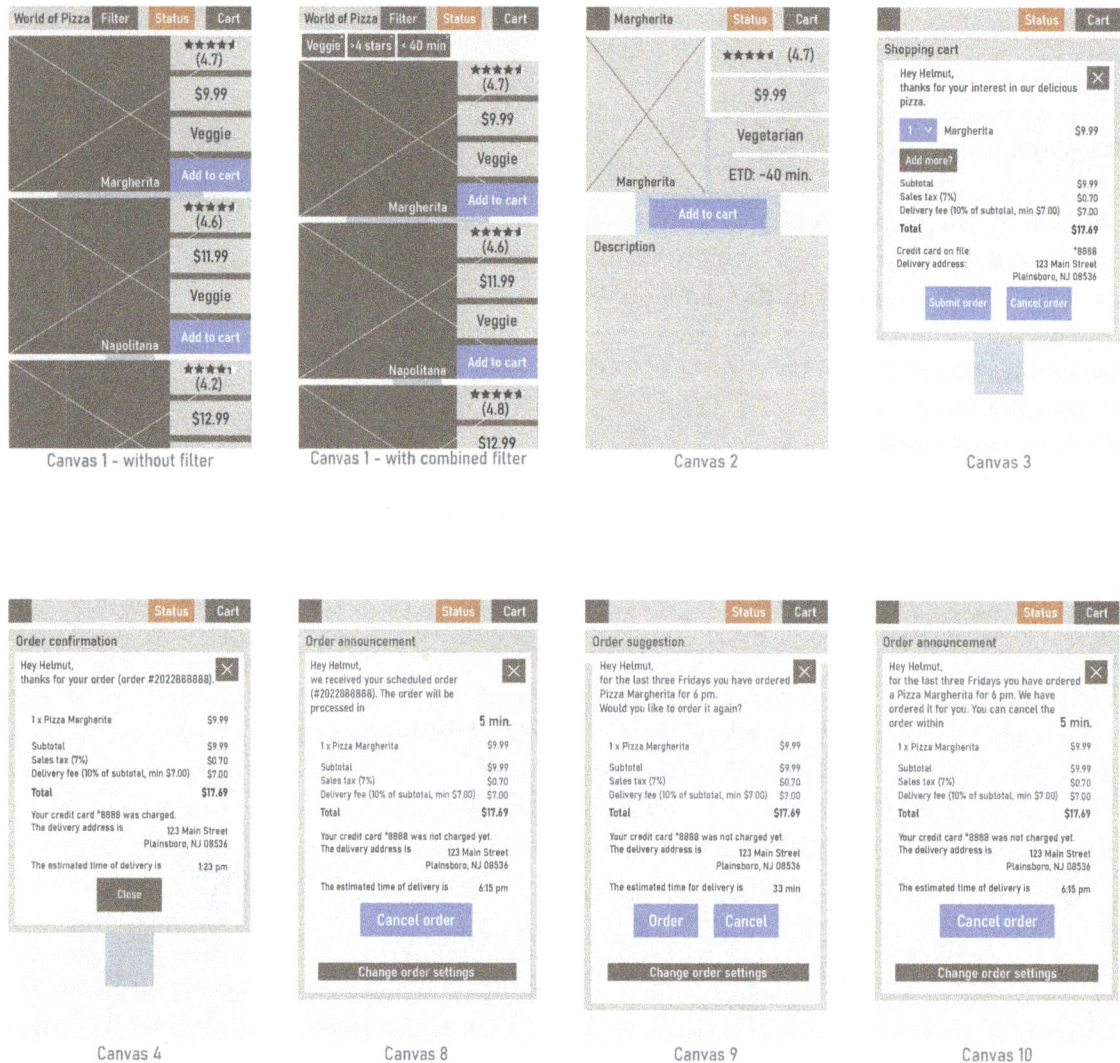

Figure 15.33: Aggregate Content: Entry canvas selection - Before

The first five canvases (canvases 1 to 4) look familiar. To ensure that the outcome of value is captured, three new canvases have been added. Canvas 8 assumes that an order is scheduled (we have a dedicated design efficiency technique for this). The scheduler triggers an order at a certain point in time. The user can still cancel it.

Canvas 9 suggests an order based on the user's past order. The user can accept the suggested order, and it will be placed.

Canvas 10 informs the user about an order that will be placed if they do not abort it within a certain amount of time.

The term "aggregate content" refers to the idea that the content for the entry canvas is not generated step-by-step and, driven by the user (for instance, going through the process from canvas 1 to canvas 4). Instead, the content for the entry canvas is aggregated automatically for the user without their involvement, which increases efficiency for the user. In this sense, aggregating content refers to a shortcut, which is the basic idea of the involvement hypotenuse (see Figure 15.34).

Pizzas displayed (not filtered)

Pizzas filtered

Last-ordered pizza selected

Selected pizza in shopping cart

Order for selected pizza proposed

Pizza automatically ordered

Figure 15.34: Involvement hypotenuse for WoP

Canvases 8, 9, and 10 are close to the intended outcome. If users are control freaks, they may perceive that the options go too far and that they do not have sufficient control. On the other hand, a more laid-back user might be happy that they do not need to submit the order, and they would be fine with canvas 8, 9, and 10. Delivering food without confirming each individual order is a known delivery model that many people find beneficial.

The user's selection of canvas 8, 9, and 10 would allow us to exceed the quantitative involvement goals regarding target involvement steps (see Table 12.3 on page 334).

The decision to be made here is which canvas will be used as the entry canvas which is the starting point for choosing and ordering a pizza. From an efficiency perspective, the entry canvas should be as close as possible to the outcome of value (ordered pizza) and provide sufficient control for the user.

The canvas that was ultimately selected is canvas 1 (with combined filters). It provides a good starting point without taking away the option of selecting a certain pizza (see Figure 15.35). It is assumed that the quantitative involvement goals can be met with canvas 1 (with combined filters). We will see later whether this assumption was correct.

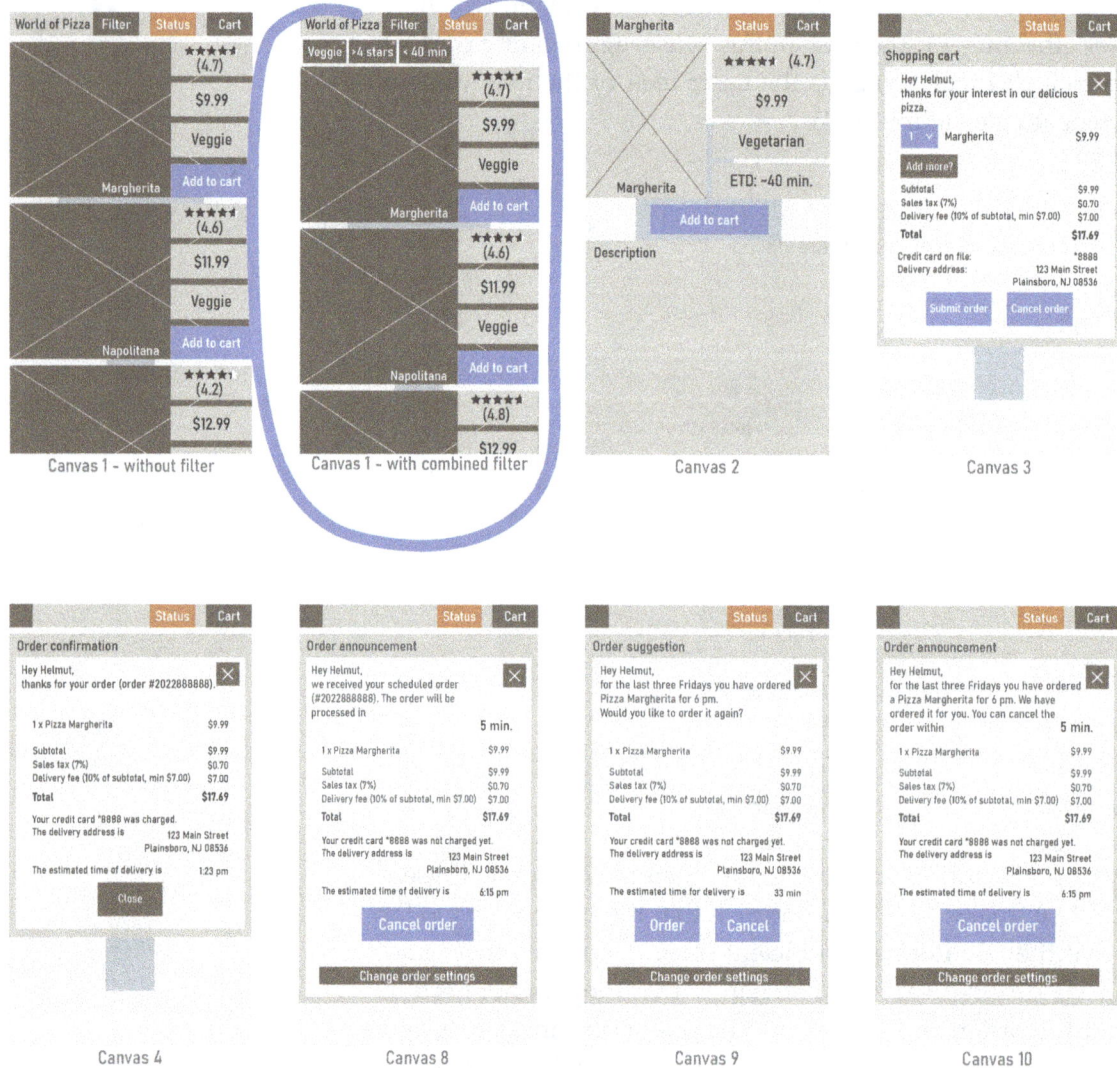

Figure 15.35: Aggregate content: Entry canvas selection - After

Concatenate functions

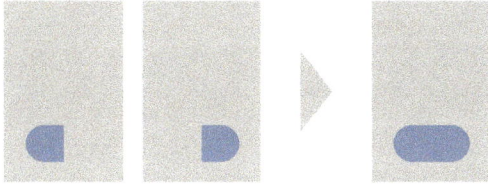

Checkpoint

► CP 1: Are the content functions concatenated that can be concatenated?

The next technique is to concatenate, or link, two or more functions into one. If two or more functions are concatenated, the user has to trigger the function only once, not several times (see Figure 15.36).

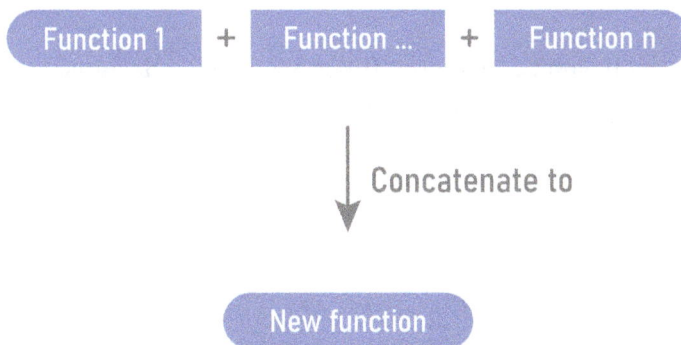

Figure 15.36: Concatenation example

In our pizza example, we have concatenated to "add to cart" and "submit order" into the (concatenated) function "order now." The user can order the pizza with only one involvement step (see Figure 15.37 and Figure 15.38), directly from the pizza list or from the pizza details. In the pizza detail view, the user can still add a pizza to the shopping cart and in fact can add more than one.

Functions are a non-perceivable and a great way to achieve higher efficiency. The fact that they are not user-perceivable does not mean that we designers have no say in what some functions should

Concatenate functions - before

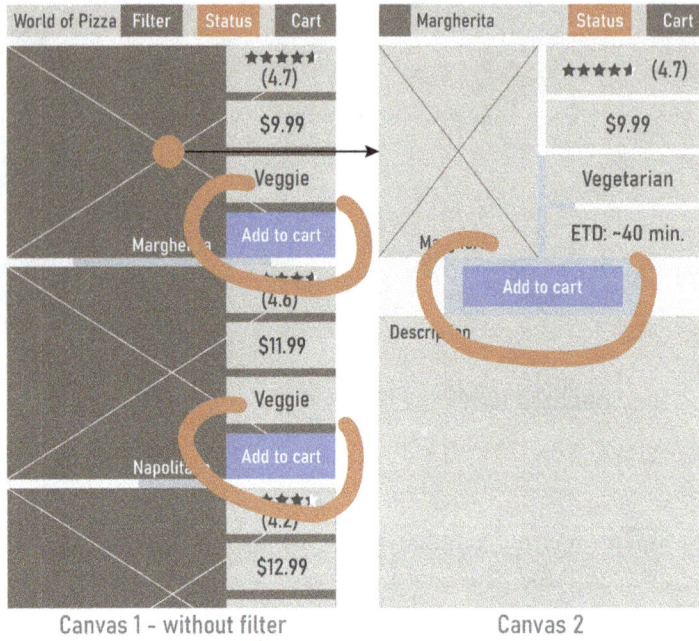

Figure 15.37: Concatenate function: Before

do. If you haven't considered functions in your designs, I highly encourage you to start doing so.

Concatenate functions - after

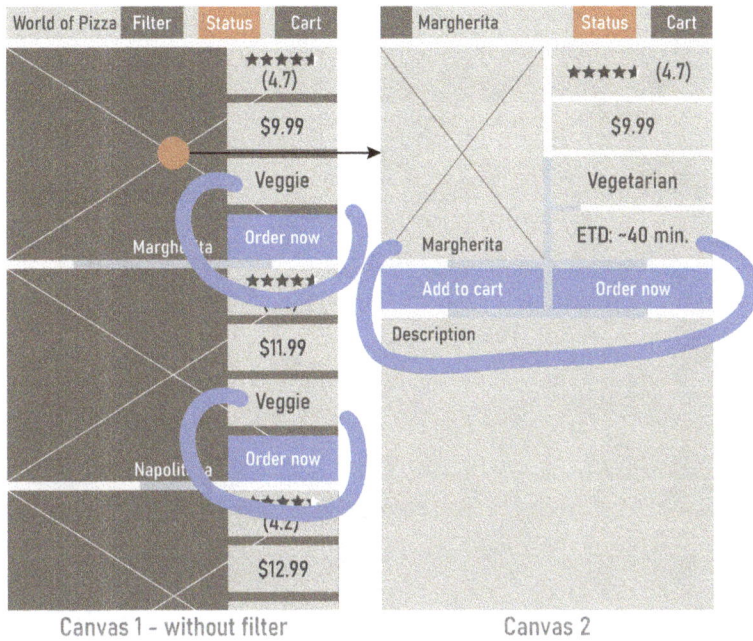

Figure 15.38: Concatenate function: After

Reuse the user's choices

Checkpoint

► CP 1: Are user's choices reused?

Many users have their own way of exploring content and making decisions. We know that, and we offer options so the user can make those choices (typically pertaining to views, filters, sorting, and content type). We can assume that the user has a reason for making certain choices, and we should be careful to respect the time they have spent exploring them. We can also assume that a user reapplies those choices. For that reason, it is good practice to apply a user's choices when they come back to the application. It is also good practice to offer a "default" control that resets the choices.

Reuse choice - before

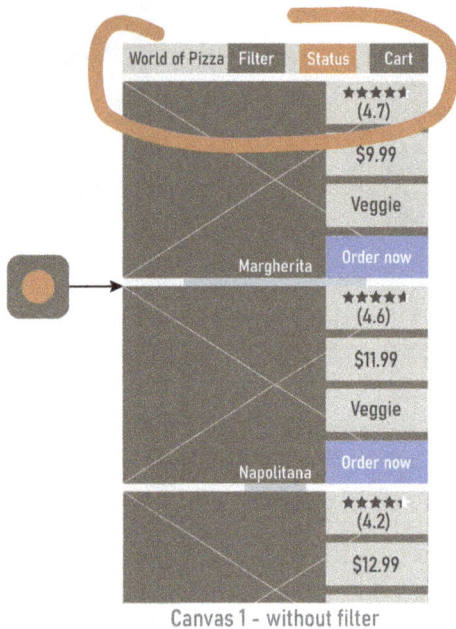

Canvas 1 - without filter

Figure 15.39: Reuse the user's choices: Before

In our pizza example, we assume that the user has made choices during the selection, such as filtering or sorting of pizza types. The underlying assumption is that the user's preferences won't change too often. Therefore, the choices are stored and automatically applied the next time the user opens the app (see Figure 15.40).

The idea of reusing user's choices can be extended to the content itself. Considering the WoP example, the app could display the recently ordered pizzas first. This makes sense under the assumption that users have pizza preferences and the likelihood is great that they will choose previously ordered pizzas.

In other applications, the efficiency improvements can be even greater. For instance, in design and engineering applications, users create design artifacts, such as artistic drawings, engineering models, etc. Such design artifacts can be automatically stored as templates for later reuse.

Let's take an example. If a user wants to create a drawing of a table. the parts of the table are needed. The parts are the legs and the tabletop. Each part is constructed of elements consisting

Reuse choice - after

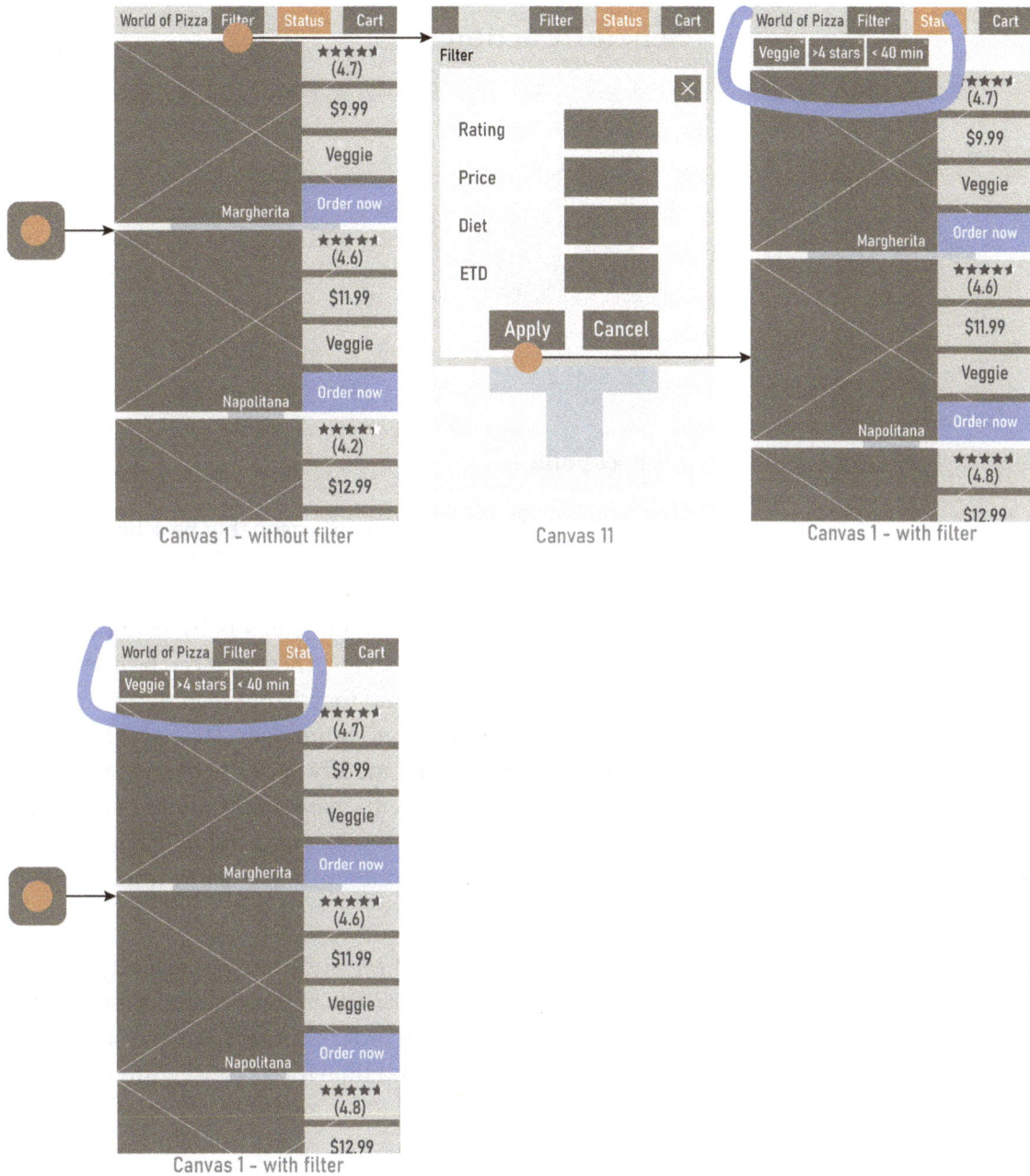

Figure 15.40: Reuse the user's choices: After

of lines and basic shapes. To increase efficiency for the user, the design artifact and each created part can be automatically stored as a template for later reuse (e.g., table legs, table top). In case the user needs to create another table the next time, the stored parts can be used and altered. The user decides whether it is more efficient to reuse stored templates or to create parts from scratch.

Unfortunately, the design and engineering application cannot be adequately depicted in the World of Pizza scenario.

Schedule action

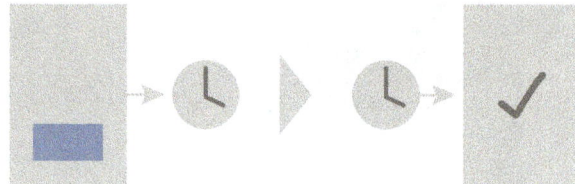

Checkpoint

▶ CP 1: Which actions can reasonably be scheduled?

One way to reduce involvement steps is by using a scheduler, which allows a user to schedule an action. It can be applied to user tasks that can be planned and that do not require user input. Good examples are order tasks and reminders. The user should be able to access set schedules and modify or delete them as needed. If the scheduler triggers a task with major implications (e.g., ordering a product), the user should be able to cancel the task before it gets fully executed. This checkpoint provides some level of control for the user.

In our pizza example, we have added an opportunity for the user to schedule frequent orders. When the system has scheduled the order, the user receives an order confirmation and should be able to cancel it within a defined time frame (see Figure 15.42).

Schedule action - before

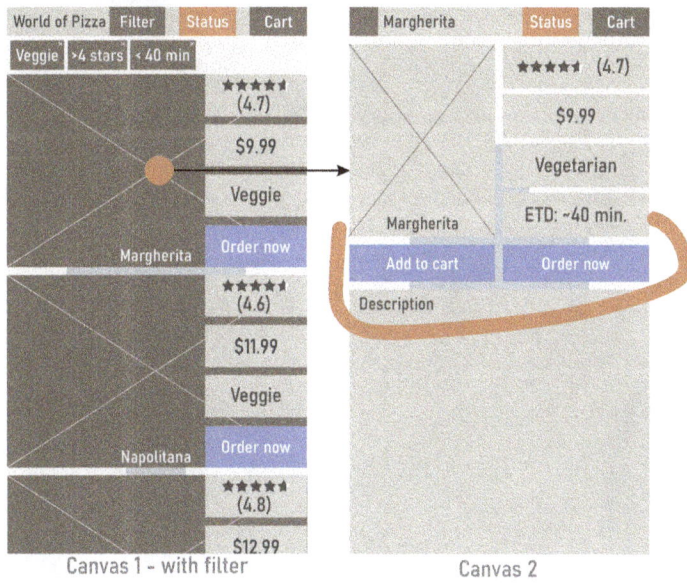

Figure 15.41: Schedule action: Before

Schedule action - after

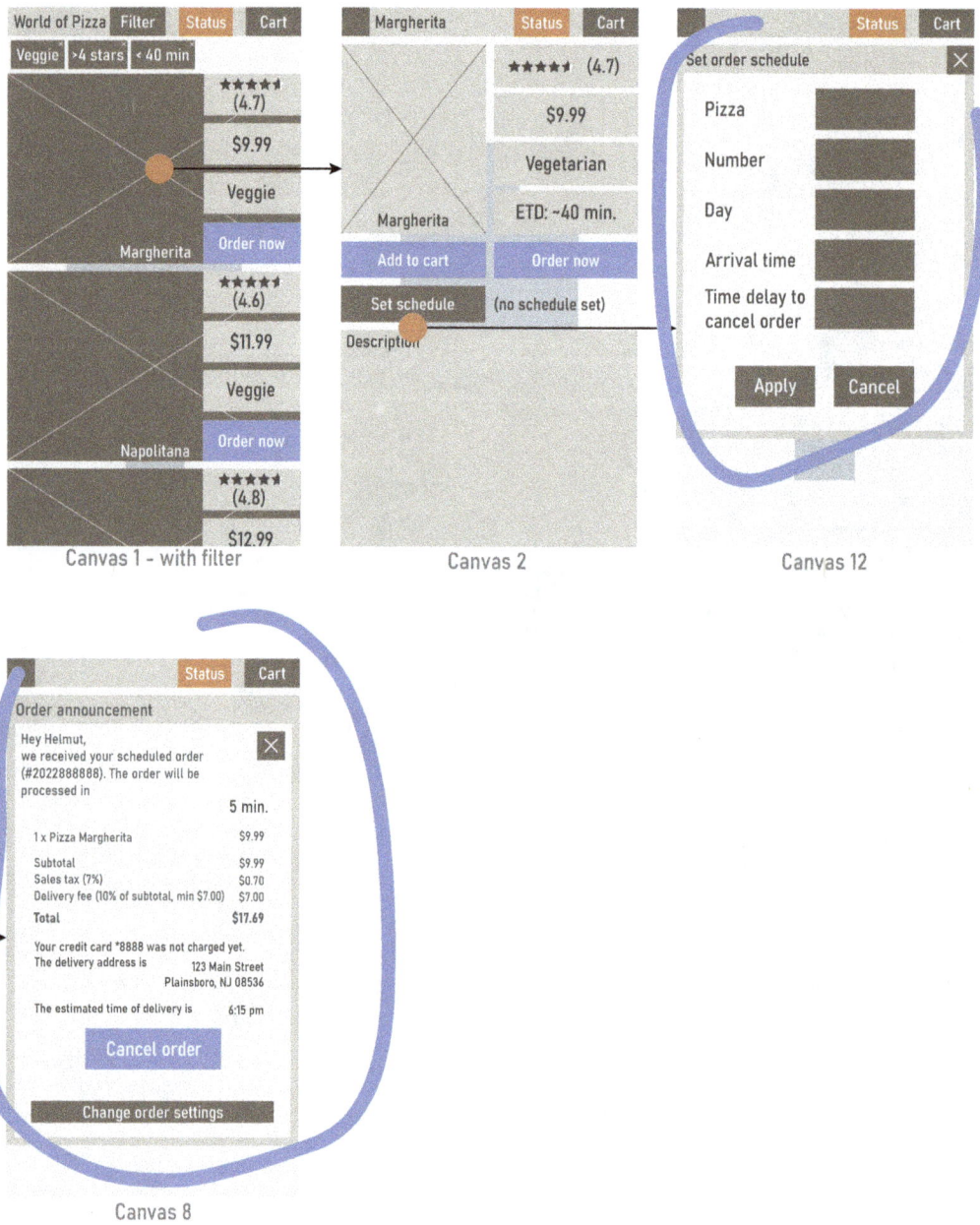

Figure 15.42: Schedule action: After

Propose action

Checkpoints

- ▶ CP 1: Are reasonable actions, based on a user's past behavior, proactively proposed?
- ▶ CP 2: Is a reason given for why the action is proposed?
- ▶ CP 3: Is the action properly described?
- ▶ CP 4: Can the user cancel the proposed action?
- ▶ CP 5: Can the user modify the trigger for proposing actions?

Another way to reduce user involvement is to observe how a user uses an app, learn the usage pattern, and then perform actions mimicking the user's behavior.

In our pizza example, the app may observe that a certain user typically orders a pizza when on their way home from work. The app could offer to order automatically, and all the user would have to do is accept the offer or decline it. The user would still be in control (see Figure 15.43).

Notes: This functionality requires that the app has acknowledged that it tracks the user's behavior and derives actions from it. In many countries, tracking of user's actions requires the user's explicit permission. It is also good practice to ask the user for permission to propose such actions. Otherwise, not being aware of the app's capabilities, the user might be startled to see such a personalized proposal and reject such an application completely.

Propose action - after

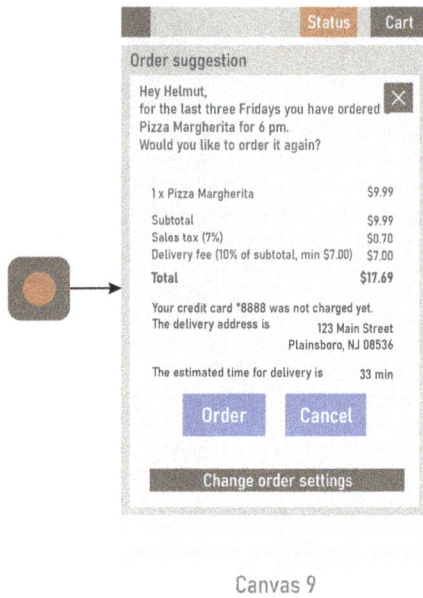

Canvas 9

Figure 15.43: Propose action: After

Execute action

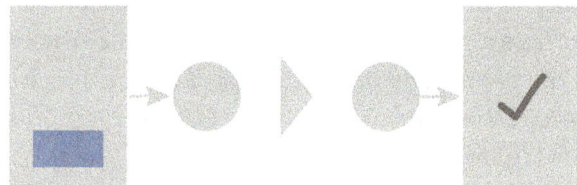

Checkpoints

▶ CP 1: Are reasonable actions, based on a user's past behavior, proactively executed?
▶ CP 2: Was the user made aware of such automatically executed actions?
▶ CP 3: Is the user able to undo the automatically executed actions?
▶ CP 4: Is a reason mentioned for executing an action?
▶ CP 5: Can the user modify the automation trigger?

A more extreme way to reduce user involvement is to observe

how the user uses an app, learn the usage pattern, and then automatically execute the action accordingly. The user still gets a confirmation for the executed action and can still abort it.

In our pizza example, the app may observe that the user orders a pizza every Friday after leaving the office. The app will order the pizza automatically and inform the user about the order. The user has a predefined amount of time to cancel the order, which means that they still have some control (see Figure 15.44).

Execute action - after

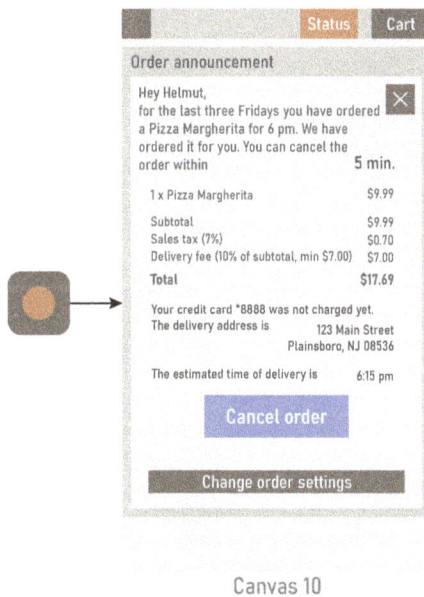

Canvas 10

Figure 15.44: Execute action: After

Note: This functionality requires the app to track the user's behavior and derive actions from it. In many countries, tracking of user's actions requires the user's explicit permission. It is also good practice to ask the user for permission to execute actions automatically. Otherwise, not being aware of the app's capabilities, the user might be startled to see such a personalized proposal and reject such an application completely. Automation offers the highest level of efficiency with the lowest level of control for the user.

Refined seed concepts

After the deficiencies of the different seed concepts were checked and partially repaired, we refined the initial seed concepts to achieve higher efficiency. Figure 15.45 shows the two canvases that were changed and Figure 15.46 shows the implication for the canvas flow and the effect on the actual involvement steps.

The other three seed concepts have been refined accordingly.

Seed concept A: Pizza-Gram - Cast (iteration 1, step 2)

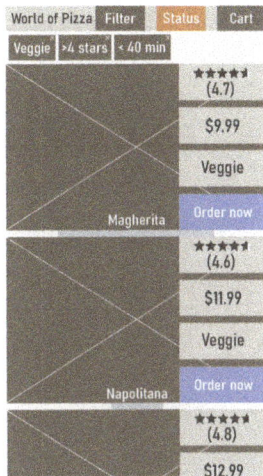

Canvas 1 - with filter

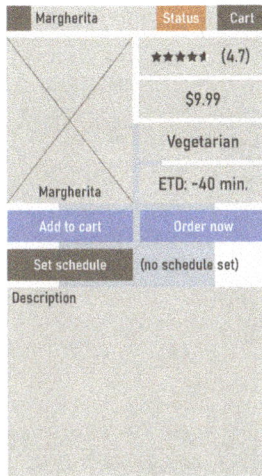

Canvas 2

Canvas 3

Canvas 4

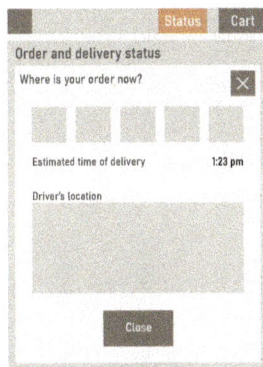

Canvas 5

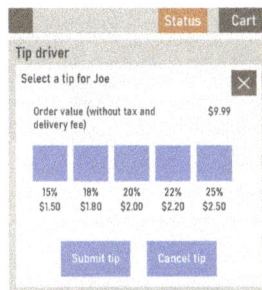

Canvas 6

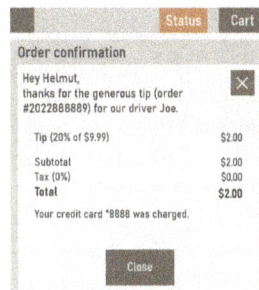

Canvas 7

Canvas 8

Canvas 9

Canvas 10

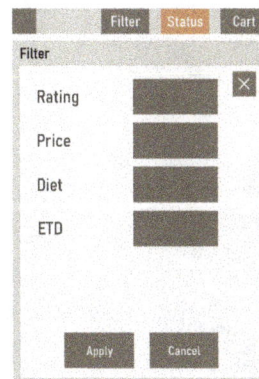

Canvas 11

Canvas 12

Figure 15.45: Seed concept A: Pizza-Gram – Canvas cast (iteration 1, step 2)

Seed concept A: Pizza-Gram - Flow (iteration 1, step 2)

UT 1.1 Select pizza

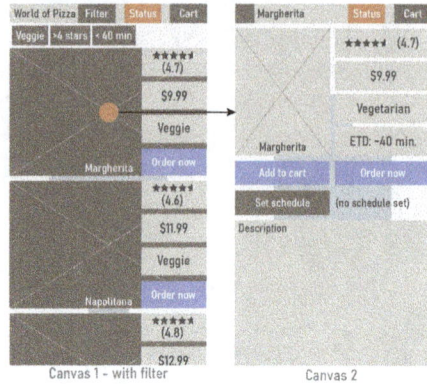

TAS / AAS

0 / 1
(inefficient)

UT 1.2 Order pizza

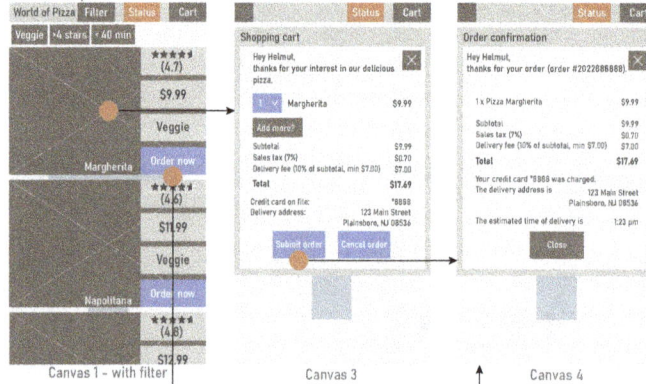

1 / 1
(efficient)

UT 1.3 Monitor status

1 / 1
(efficient)

UT 1.4 Tip driver

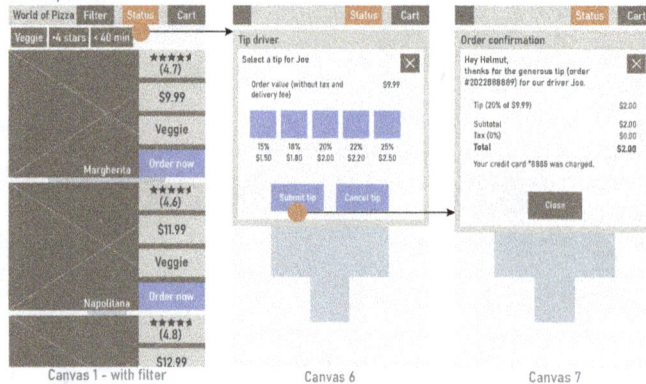

1 / 2
(inefficient)

Figure 15.46: Seed concept A: Pizza-Gram – Canvas flow (iteration 1, step 2)

Seed concept B: Four-at-a-glance - Cast (iteration 1, step 2)

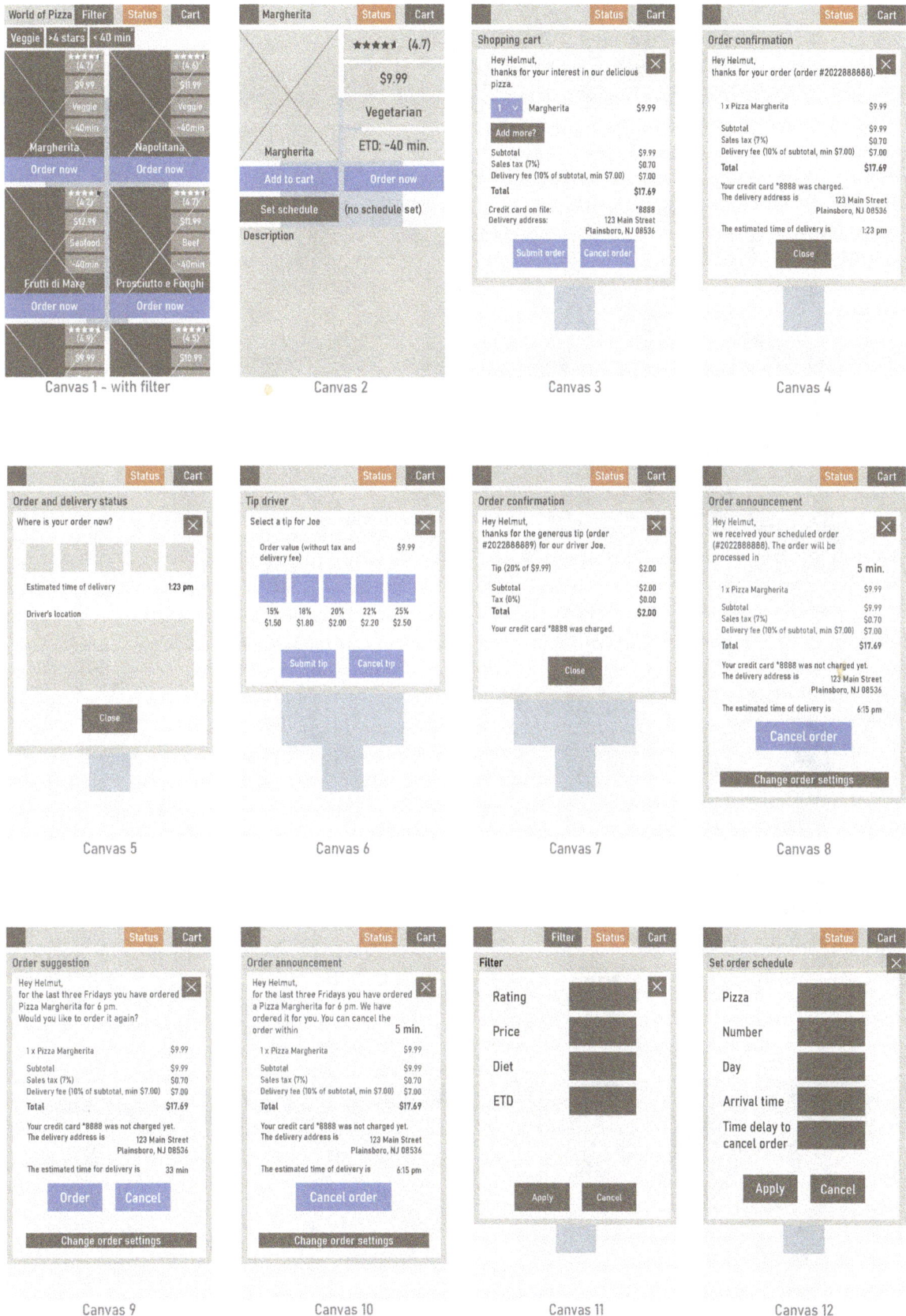

Figure 15.47: Seed concept B: Four-at-a-glance – Canvas cast (iteration 1, step 2)

Seed concept B: Four-at-a-glance - Flow (iteration 1, step 2)

Figure 15.48: Seed concept B: Four-at-a-glance – Canvas flow (iteration 1, step 2)

Seed concept C: Menu - Cast (iteration 1, step 2)

Canvas 1 - with filter

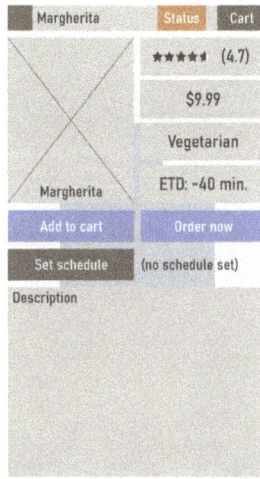

Canvas 2

Canvas 3

Canvas 4

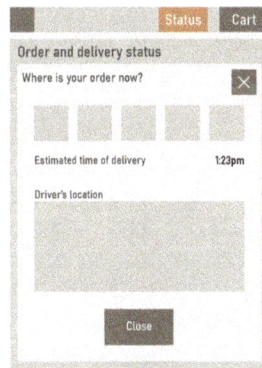

Canvas 5

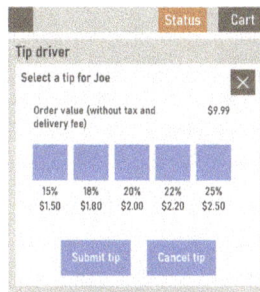

Canvas 6

Canvas 7

Canvas 8

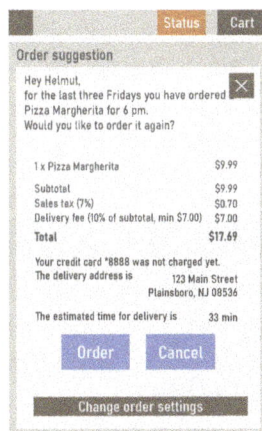

Canvas 9

Canvas 10

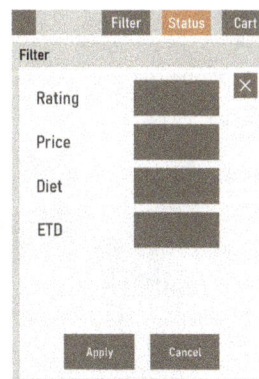

Canvas 11

Canvas 12

Figure 15.49: Seed concept C: Menu – Canvas cast (iteration 1, step 2)

Seed concept C: Menu – Flow (iteration 1, step 2)

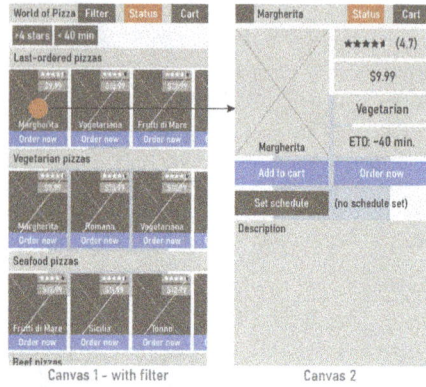

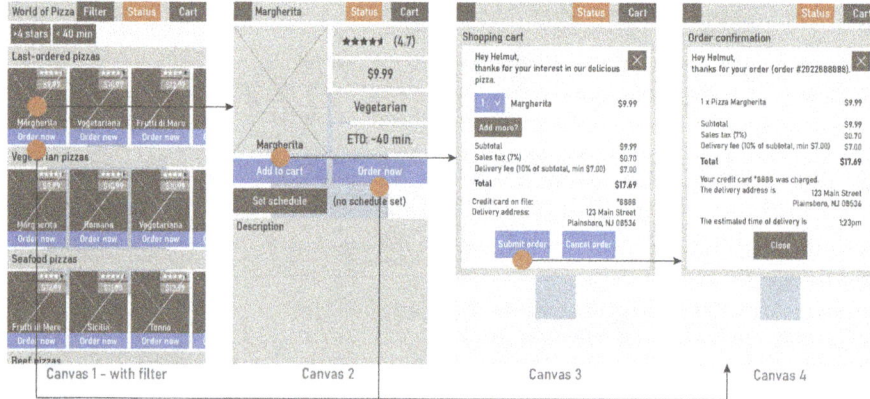

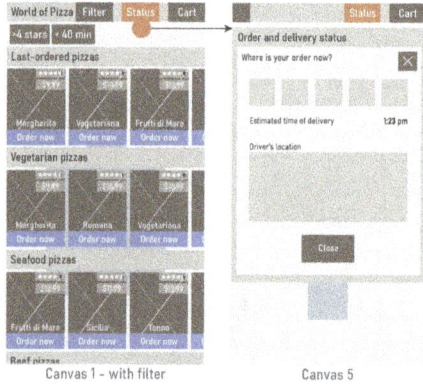

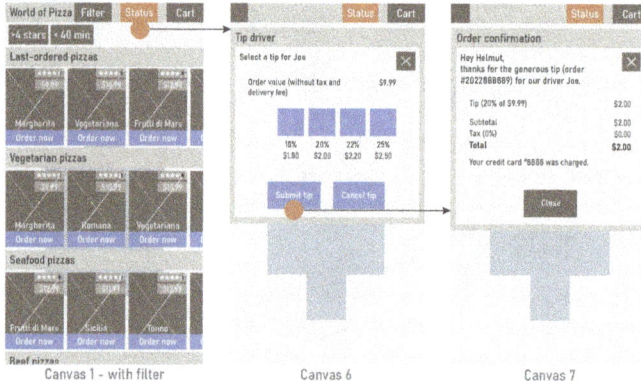

Figure 15.50: Seed concept C: Menu – Canvas flow (iteration 1, step 2)

Seed concept D: Lane - Cast (iteration 1, step 2)

Canvas 1 - with filter

Canvas 2

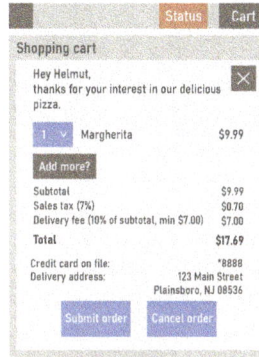

Canvas 3

Canvas 4

Canvas 5

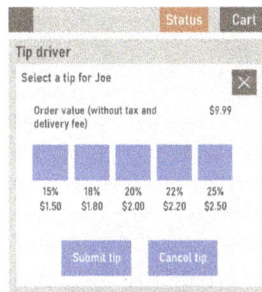

Canvas 6

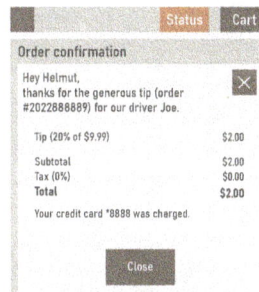

Canvas 7

Canvas 8

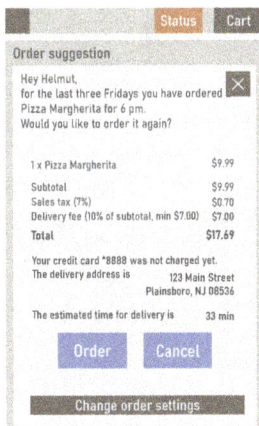

Canvas 9

Canvas 10

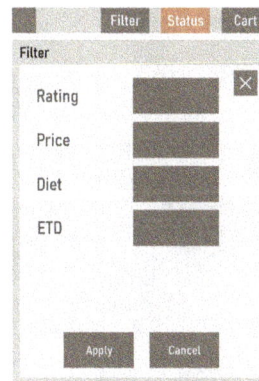

Canvas 11

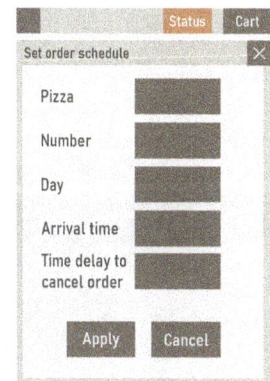

Canvas 12

Figure 15.51: Seed concept D: Lane – Canvas cast (iteration 1, step 2)

Seed concept D: Lane – Flow (iteration 1, step 2)

UT 1.1 Select pizza

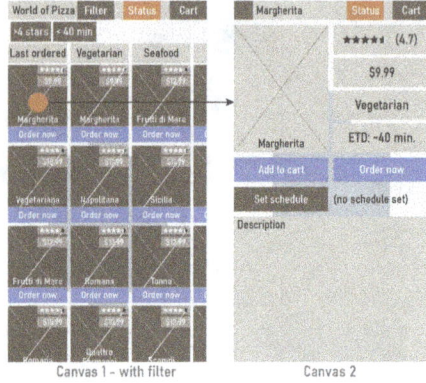

TAS / AAS

0 / 1
(inefficient)

Canvas 1 – with filter   Canvas 2

UT 1.2 Order pizza

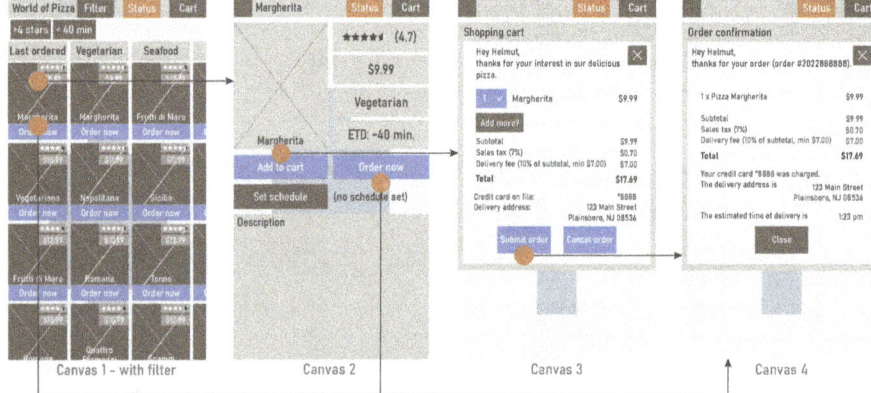

1 / 1
(efficient)

Canvas 1 – with filter   Canvas 2   Canvas 3   Canvas 4

UT 1.3 Monitor status

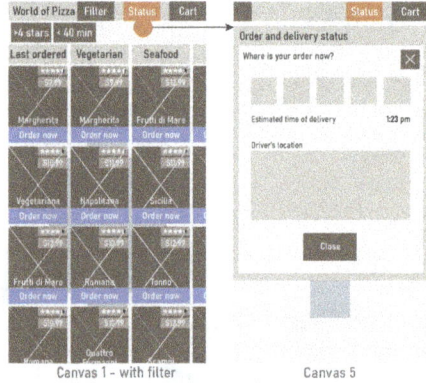

1 / 1
(efficient)

Canvas 1 – with filter   Canvas 5

UT 1.4 Tip driver

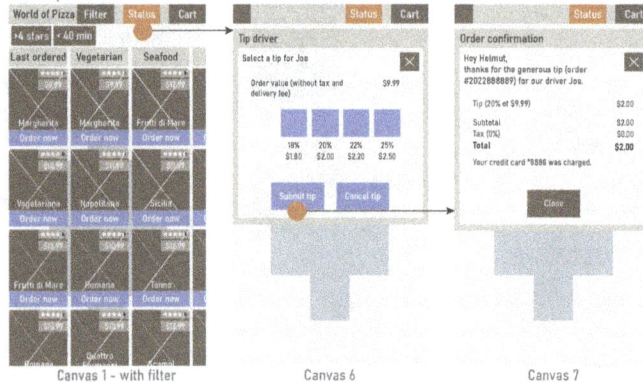

1 / 2
(inefficient)

Canvas 1 – with filter   Canvas 6   Canvas 7

Figure 15.52: Seed concept D: Lane – Canvas flow (iteration 1, step 2)

User involvement system as a campus metaphor

Figure 15.53: Seed concepts explored

Summary

Step 2: Refine Concepts

▶ Move on to Step 3: Evaluate Concept
◀ Go back to Step 1: Explore Concept

Seed concept A: Pizza-Gram – Flow (iteration 1, step 2)

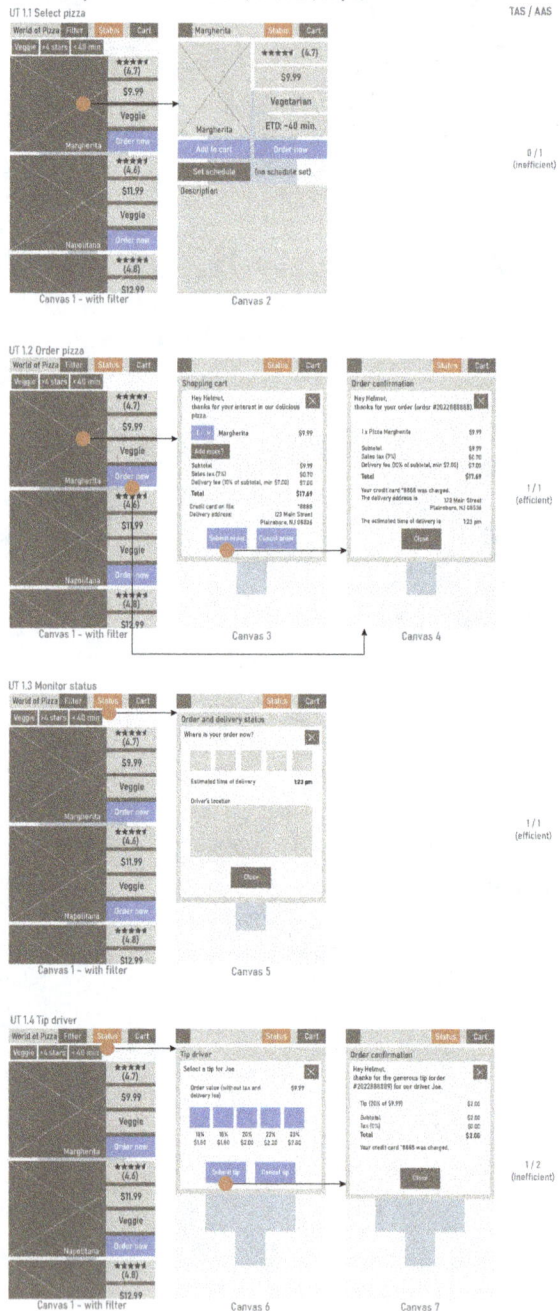

UT 1.1 Select pizza

TAS / AAS

0 / 1
(inefficient)

Canvas 1 – with filter   Canvas 2

UT 1.2 Order pizza

1 / 1
(efficient)

Canvas 1 – with filter   Canvas 3   Canvas 4

UT 1.3 Monitor status

1 / 1
(efficient)

Canvas 1 – with filter   Canvas 5

UT 1.4 Tip driver

1 / 2
(inefficient)

Canvas 1 – with filter   Canvas 6   Canvas 7

Lessons learned

We have seen that the design efficiency technique provides guidance for refining a seed concept so that it becomes more efficient. Not all techniques will be applicable to all applications and screens. Before applying the behavioral techniques, you should involve users by asking for their preferences and feedback. If you work on a website, you can do A/B testing and compare the effectiveness and acceptance of different options.

Tips and tricks

Well, in this chapter there are no more tips and tricks than those communicated through the design techniques themselves. When you have a seed concept, just apply the techniques, and see where the concept can benefit from changes, motivated by the design efficiency techniques.

Exercise 3.3

Goal   Refine the explored seed designs.

Material   Seed design, design efficiency techniques, users

Completion criteria:

- ► For each of your seed designs, all twelve design efficiency techniques have been applied. The result is documented for each design efficiency technique.
- ► The refined seed concepts are documented.
- ► The differences in the seed designs (before/after comparisons) are documented.

Evaluate Concepts | **16**

The wisest are the most annoyed at the loss of time.
Dante Alighieri

Purpose

The third step in creating an involvement concept is to evaluate
the refined seed concepts (see Figure 16.1).

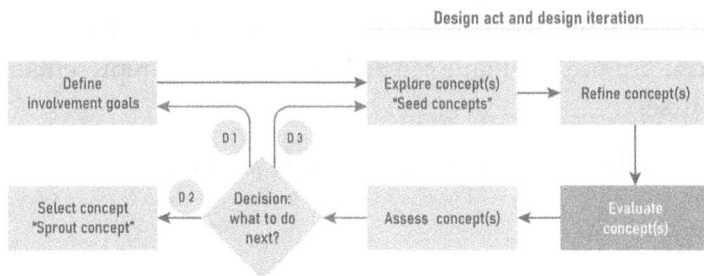

Figure 16.1: Evaluate concept

Three techniques are presented here that will help you to evaluate
the efficiency of a refined seed concept: use-use-use, the speed test,
and the big I notation.

Use, use, use

After the seed concepts have been refined, the best thing is to use
them repeatedly and often. The idea is not to perform a usability
test with user representatives but to practice using the concept as
an experience professional. There are several reasons why this is
necessary and beneficial.

One reason is that what we design is a time-based experience. We do not design static posters or images, but a canvas flow. A sequence of canvases enables a user involvement behavior, and it is very difficult for many humans, including experience professionals, to anticipate its dynamics. An effective way to understand a behavior's dynamics and how the design elements support it is by using the refined seed concepts and experiencing the flow *repeatedly and often*.

A second reason is that there are underlying, hidden dependencies. Such dependencies belong to selected, unnecessary design elements and very often to missing ones. Such design elements will emerge from the design ground through the use of the seed concept. Missing design elements will be added to a seed concept in another iteration and unnecessary design elements will be removed.

Therefore, it is a good idea to build a clickable mockup from the canvas flow and play with it, ten times, twenty times, thirty times, or even more. The learning gained during the experience of using the seed concepts will improve the final user experience.

If the experience professional is not happy with the flows of a seed concept, the target user groups most likely won't be happy with them, either. If the experience professional is satisfied with the flows, the target user groups might be satisfied as well. In most cases, they will have many comments that can help to improve it. The use-use-use technique can be extended to user representatives, of course.

This thought leads us to the next design principle:

Iterations build a solid foundation

To achieve a high-quality experience, designers and users need to experience the concepts so they can be systematically and continuously improved. Unnecessary design elements will be removed, poorly designed elements will be improved, missing elements will be added, and misplaced elements will be reallocated. This purification process takes place through iterations. Many iterations – and time – are key ingredients in building a solid foundation.

Speed test

Technique

The intent of the speed test is to measure how long it takes a user to perform a specified user task in order to understand how fast it can be done. Therefore, a user may perform the same user task several times, and we are interested in the fastest time per user task. Most speed tests have an element of competition. However, here we are not interested in measuring the capability and skills of the user, but the application under design in terms of efficiency of user involvement.

It is usually best to ask representatives of the user groups to perform speed testes for you. However, before you do that, I encourage you to apply the speed test to yourself, first.

What we try to do is to optimize a seed concept for speed, like a Formula 1 or NASCAR race car. When you try to perform the actions in high-speed mode, you'll recognize design elements that are in your way and need to be changed or removed. If you recognize such a design element, just make a note of it. In addition, write down the actual user involvement time (AAT) per user task. We want to monitor the time over the various iterations. This is essential for efficiency.

Figure 16.2: Ferrari with Michael Schumacher, 2004; source: Wikimedia; photographer: Rick Dikeman; license: CC BY-SA 3.0

WoP

An interactive mockup was created (see Figure 16.4 and Figure 16.5) to perform the speed test.

We measured the following mean Actual Involvement Times (see Table 16.1).

Figure 16.3: Ricky Rudd drives Ford Taurus No. 21; Daytona International Speedway - Practice run on Feb 11, 2004; source: Wikimedia; photographer: Larry McTighen; license: public domain

User task	Target Involvement Time (TAT)	Actual Involvement Time (AAT)
UT 1 Select pizza (EVOT)	30 seconds	5 seconds
UT 2 Order pizza (EVOT)	30 seconds	7 seconds
UT 3 Monitor status (EVOT)	30 seconds	6 seconds
UT 4 Tip driver (EVOT)	30 seconds	10 seconds

Table 16.1: Measured elapsed involvement time

The times are already pretty good. In step 4 of the iterative design process, we will assess whether or not the measured times meet the target involvement times.

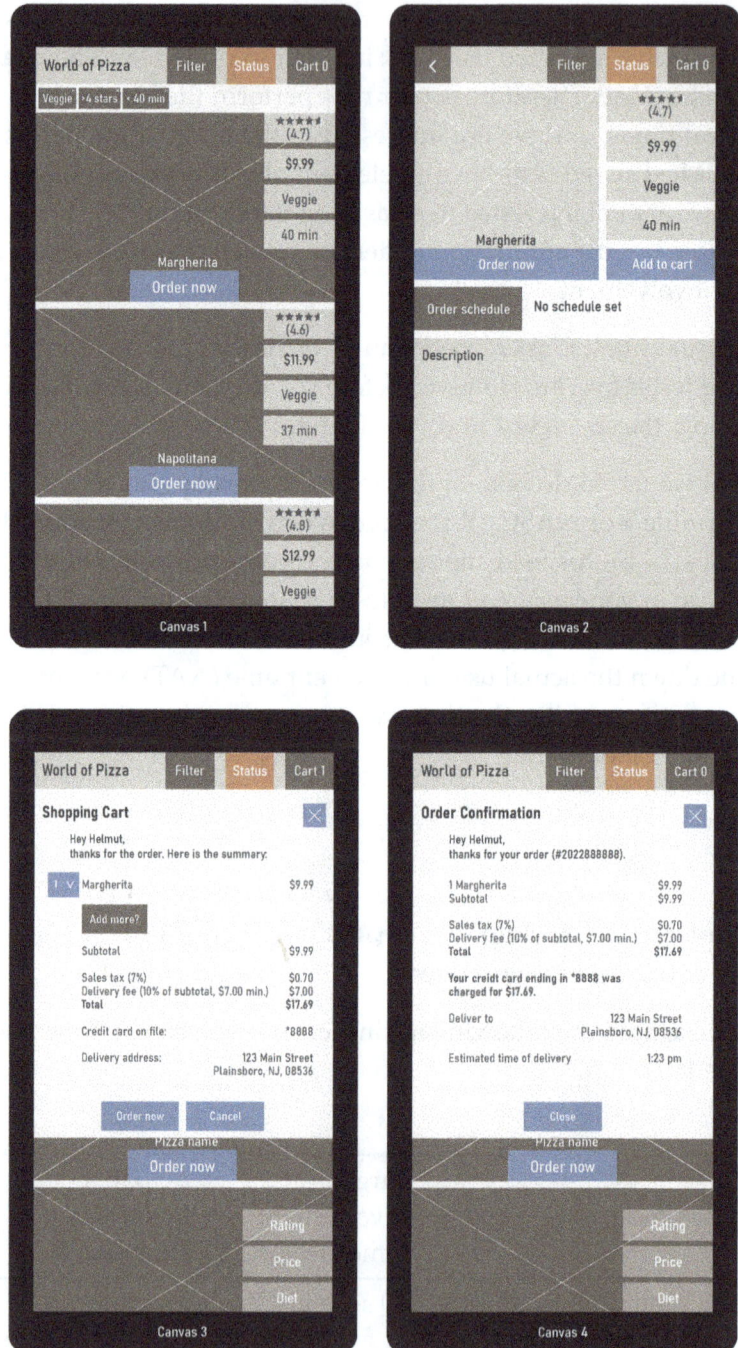

Figure 16.4: Interactive mockup, canvases 1 to 4

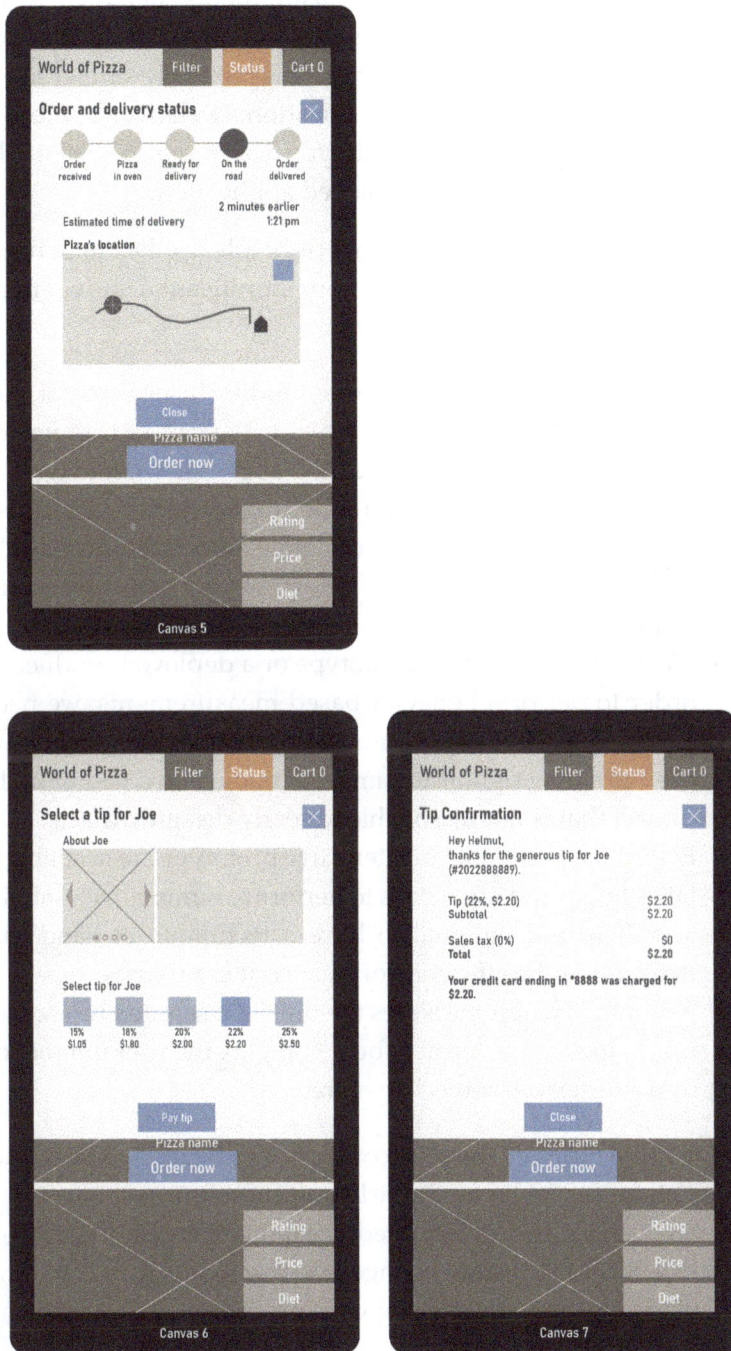

Figure 16.5: Interactive mockup, canvases 5 to 7

Interaction complexity

Motivation

There are a number of established techniques for measuring the experience or usability quality. The method of choice for efficiency is a speed test, summative usability test, or a field test. It measures the time it takes for a user to accomplish a test scenario.

Such testes are behavior-based measurements. Behavior-based measurements have many advantages; probably the most important ones is that the measured behavior is relatively similar to the actual behavior of a deployed application. "Relatively" refers to the fact that the quality of the prototype determines how close the application under test is to a deployed application.

Everything in life has a price. This principle applies to summative usability tests, too. There are four significant disadvantages inherent in summative usability tests:

- ► We need user representatives. Finding user reps for consumer applications is not difficult. We can find them "on the street." But for most industrial applications, finding user reps is a challenge. It requires recruitment effort, incentives beyond the price of a cup of coffee, and often non disclosure agreements. Recruiting industrial user reps, particularly from customer organizations, takes significant effort.
- ► We need an interactive prototype or a deployed product. In order to perform behavior-based measurements, we need a prototype that covers the test scenarios. This means we need to spend significant time and budget on a part of in the project that is not reasonable for early design artifacts.
- ► Even if user reps and an interactive prototype are available, it takes hours and often days to perform a summative usability test. It would be ideal to have a technique at hand that determines the efficiency of a concept in minutes.
- ► A summative test measures the time of a selected test scenarios. It does not determine how complex the user interaction or user intervention is in general.

The idea is to evaluate the seed concepts for efficiency deficiencies so that changes can be made early and therefore cost-effectively. The later changes are implemented, the more they cost. The change of a concept is the cheapest change possible (see Figure 16.6). This particularly true for efficiency, since many critical design elements enabling efficiency are not perceivable – they are functions. This last point is supported by data on committed costs versus spent cost: only about 8% of total life cycle costs are incurred in the concept phase, but about 70% of the life cycle costs are committed during that phase. We want to make sure that some of the committed costs support efficiency for user involvement.

It would therefore be beneficial to have a technique at hand that helps to determine how efficient an early design artifact is, e.g., a seed concept. It would be great if such a technique did not have the limitations mentioned above.

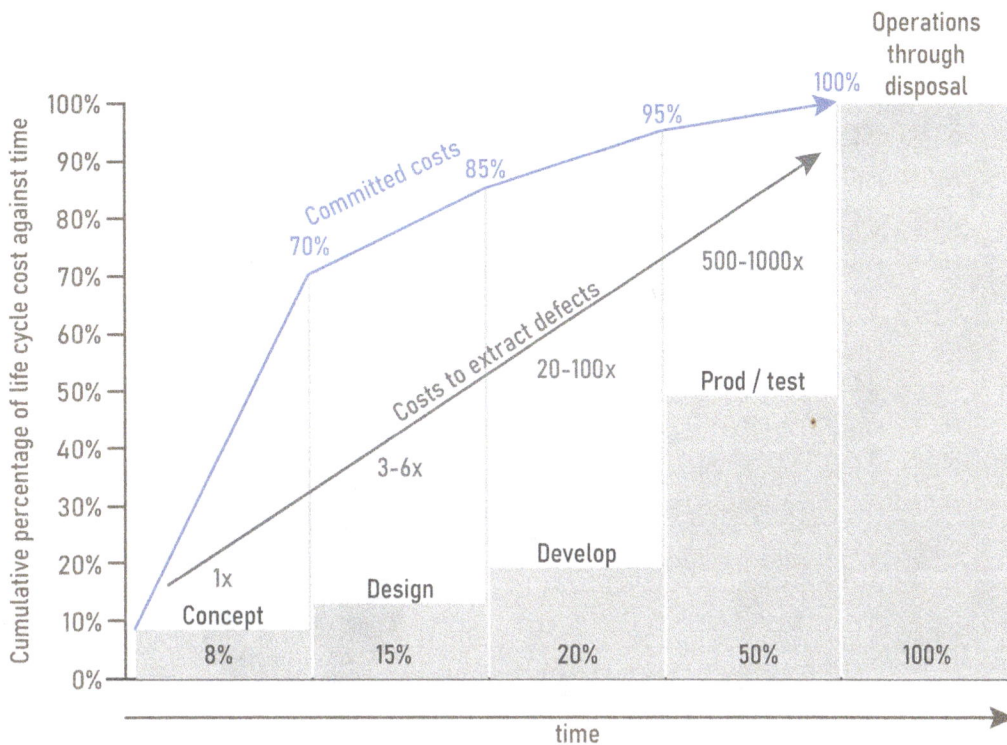

Figure 16.6: Lifecycle cost; source: based on [109, p. 14]

To better explain and to motivate the thought process, I'd like to introduce a simple real-life example: the design of a footpath. Let's assume someone is asked to design a footpath that connects point A with point B. How can the efficiency of a footpath be measured, and at which point in the project? In the involvement domain, the typical way is to run a summative usability test. This means the footpath has to be there, somehow, so that people can walk on it and the time can be measured. This is a common behavior-based measurement approach.

We can apply a different, analytical-based approach early in the project. We can simply make a scale drawing and use a tape measure to measure the length of the footpath. The tape measure can be used without the need to recruit walkers. Even more important, the tape measure can be applied during the concept phase. We do not need a real footpath to determine its efficiency. The common-sense assumption is that a footpath, connecting point A to point B, with a length of 20 meters (21.9 yards) has a higher efficiency for walkers than one connecting the same points of but having a length 40 meters (43.8 yards). Furthermore, the distance measure is more objective than the time measure. The measured time depends on the fitness of the walkers we may recruit for test walks (see Figure 16.7).

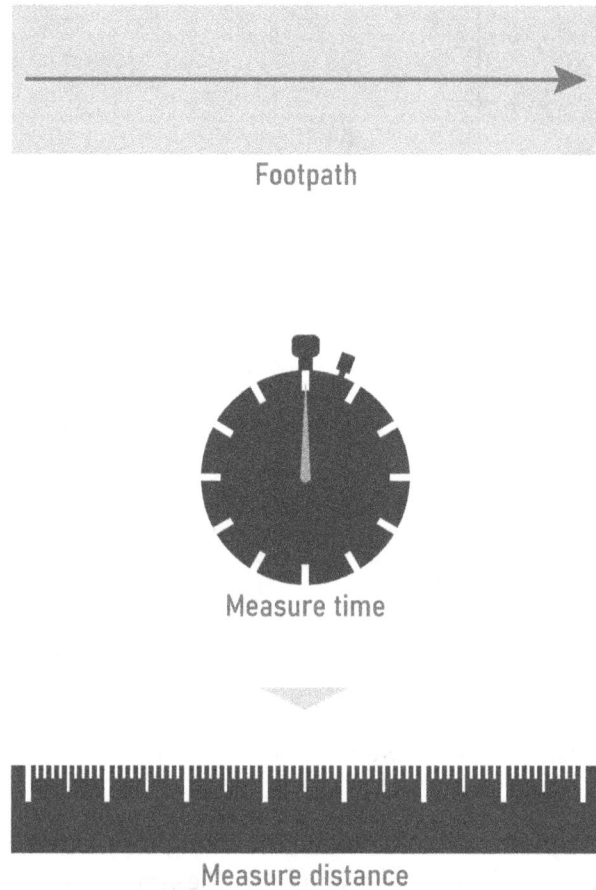

Footpath

Measure time

Measure distance

Figure 16.7: Determine the length of a footpath

This thought experiment can be transferred to the efficiency measurement of a seed concept. Distance is usually an easy way to measure physical objects. In the virtual world, distances often depend on the resolution and size of a screen. Since resolution and screen sizes vary a lot, distance is not a reliable metric. A metric for the virtual world that is more reliable is the number of steps. The number of steps needed to perform a user task is determined by the selected design elements and can be measured objectively and without a user representatives (see Figure 16.8).

In the remainder of this section, the big I notation is discussed. It is a cognitive task analysis technique that assists in determining the interaction complexity of a design artifact for a given user task, based on determining the number of interaction steps. To

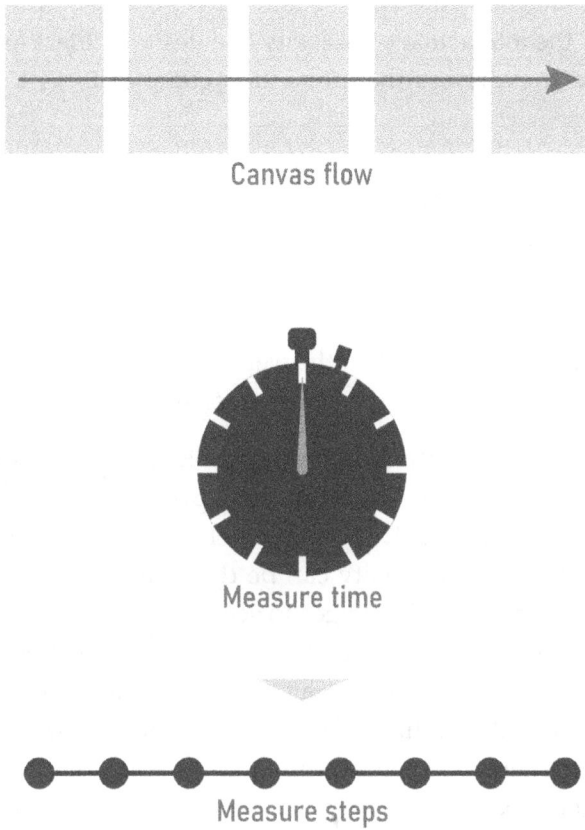

Figure 16.8: Determine the length of a canvas flow

demonstrate its use, it is applied to two examples.

Technique

The *big I notation* (the capital letter I represents "Interaction") estimates the interaction complexity of a design artifact for a given user task. It expresses the interaction complexity as a function [237].

> **Definition 28** (Interaction complexity) *A function that estimates the number user actions that must be performed for a given user task and for a given design artifact.*

The big I notation is based on the well-known *big O notation* that is used to calculate the complexity of algorithms [238–241].

The big I notation technique is applicable to all kinds of design artifacts, including baseline, seed, and sprout concepts as well as fully designed, specified, and implemented user interfaces. With big I, interaction complexity can be determined for the earliest design artifacts, so that changes to seed concepts can be applied early in the design process and therefore cost-effectively. Based on the interaction complexity, a baseline or seed concept can be selected, rejected, or refined. The big I notation can also be used to express an interaction complexity target that can be added to the involvement goal matrix.

The big I notation considers the following action types for estimation:

- ▶ T: User processes interaction elements cognitively ("Think")
- ▶ E: User enters content ("Enter"); entering content is modality agnostic.
- ▶ S: User triggers a canvas control ("Scroll" or "Swipe"); triggering a canvas control is modality agnostic
- ▶ C: User triggers a content control ("Click"); triggering a content is modality agnostic
- ▶ X: User performs a step via an external application ("eXternal")

When big I notation is applied, the following six steps need to be performed:

- ▶ Step 1 "Determine variables" (Result: Design-dependent and design-independent variables): The designer determines which variables have an influence on the number of interaction steps for the user task under estimation.
- ▶ Step 2 "Calculate interaction steps per user step" (Result: Interaction steps per user task): There are n user steps per user task. The results are n functions $f_i(\vec{m})$ $(1 \leq i \leq n)$, one

function per user step i; $\vec{m}$ is a vector of none, one, or multiple design-dependent and design-independent variables: $f_i(\vec{m}) = p_i(\vec{m})_T \cdot T + p_i(\vec{m})_E \cdot E + p_i(\vec{m})_S \cdot S + p_i(\vec{m})_C \cdot C + p_i(\vec{m})_X \cdot X$, and $p_i(\vec{m})$ are functions themselves ("calculated interaction steps per user step").

▶ Step 3 "Summate interaction steps" (Result: Interaction step baseline): The result is the sum of the interaction steps for n user steps: $f_s(\vec{m}) = \sum_{i=1}^{n} f_i(\vec{m})$ ("interaction step baseline per user task")

▶ Step 4 "Normalize interaction steps" (Result: Normalized interaction step baseline): The action types T, E, S, C, X are normalized by replacing each action type with a general interaction step IS. The result is $f_{IS}(\vec{m})$.

▶ Step 5 "Simplify interaction steps" (Result: Estimated interaction complexity, interaction complexity level): The previous step calculates the interaction steps for specific values, but it does not show the growth function. The growth function is calculated by applying the big I notation. The result is $I(g_{IS}(\vec{m}))$ ("estimated interaction complexity"). Based on the determined growth, the applicable interaction complexity level is selected ("estimated interaction complexity level").

▶ Step 6 "Instantiate interaction steps" (Result: Estimated interaction steps): For each variable, a number is selected and the total number of interaction steps is estimated. The result is $g_{IS}(\vec{m} = \vec{z}), z_i \in \mathbb{N}_0 \ (1 \leq i \leq n)$ ("estimated interaction steps"). The instantiation helps to quantify the interaction complexity differences between various design artifacts.

Comparison of initial seed concept A with refined seed concept A

Let's apply the big I notation technique to our pizza example, for the user task "select and order pizza." To show the benefits of the technique, we estimate the interaction complexity for the initial seed concept A (illustrated in Figure 16.9) for the refined seed concept A (in Figure 16.10).

Initial seed concept A

Step 1: Determine variables The first step is to identify the variables that influence the interaction complexity. Variables can be design-dependent or design-independent. In our WoP example, design-dependent variables is the number of pizzas that are displayed at a glance (e.g., two versus six or nine). An example of a design-independent variable is the number of pizzas in the list. The experience designer does not influence the number of pizzas.

In our case, we have one design-independent variable: the number of pizzas that the user reviews before selecting and ordering one.

▶ Number of pizzas reviewed: r (design-independent)
▶ Number of pizzas displayed at a glance: d (design-dependent)

Step 2: Calculate interaction steps

The interaction steps are expressed by adding up the aforementioned action types. For instance, if a user reviews a pizza and selects the pizza to look at more details, the function is expressed as $f = T + S$. "T" stands for a thinking step (looking at a pizza and processing the image and content cognitively) and "S" stands for a canvas control (clicking on an image that takes the user to a more detailed view).

If we want to express that a user views a pizza (T), clicks on it (S), and reviews the details (T), and then goes back to the list (S), the function is expressed as: $f = T + S + T + S$. If the user does this for r number of pizzas, the function is expressed as $f(r) = r \cdot (T + S + T + S)$.

Let's say, we want to express that a user reviews r - 1 pizzas without ordering any of them. Then the user reviews one more pizza, the rth pizza, adds it to the shopping cart, orders it, reviews the order summary, and closes the order summary. This is expressed as:

▶ Review r - 1 pizzas in pizza list: $f_1(r, d) = (r - 1) \cdot T$
▶ Select r - 1 pizzas in pizza list to look at the details: $f_2(r, d) = (r - 1) \cdot S$
▶ Review r - 1 detailed pizza descriptions: $f_3(r, d) = (r - 1) \cdot T$
▶ Go r - 1 times back to pizza list: $f_4(r, d) = (r - 1) \cdot S$
▶ Scroll down the pizza list: $f_5(r, d) = (\lceil \frac{r}{d} \rceil - 1) \cdot S$; Example 1: The canvas displays two pizzas at a glance ($d = 2$) and the user wants to review two pizzas ($r = 2$). This means the user does not need to scroll at all. $f_3(r = 2, d = 2) = (\lceil \frac{r=2}{d=2} \rceil - 1) \cdot S = (\lceil 1 \rceil - 1) \cdot S = (1 - 1) \cdot S = 0 \cdot S = 0$. Example 2: The canvas displays two pizzas at a glance ($d = 2$) and the user wants to review three pizzas ($r = 3$). In this case, the user needs to scroll once. $f_3(r = 3, d = 2) = (\lceil \frac{r=3}{d=2} \rceil - 1) \cdot S = (\lceil 1.5 \rceil - 1) \cdot S = (2 - 1) \cdot S = 1 \cdot S$. Example 3: The canvas shows two pizzas at a glance ($d = 2$) and the user wants to review four pizzas ($r = 4$). This means the user needs to scroll once: $f_3(r = 4, d = 2) = (\lceil \frac{r=4}{d=2} \rceil - 1) \cdot S = (\lceil 2 \rceil - 1) \cdot S = (2 - 1) \cdot S = 1 \cdot S$. Example 4: The canvas shows two pizzas at a glance ($d = 2$) and the user wants to review five pizzas ($r = 5$). The

user needs to scroll twice: $f_3(r = 5, d = 2) = (\lceil \frac{5}{2} \rceil - 1) \cdot S = (\lceil 2.5 \rceil - 1) \cdot S = (3 - 1) \cdot S = 2 \cdot S$.

- ▶ Review r^{th} pizza in pizza list: $f_6(r, d) = T$
- ▶ Select r^{th} pizza in pizza list: $f_7(r, d) = S$
- ▶ Review r^{th} detailed pizza description: $f_8(r, d) = T$
- ▶ Add pizza to shopping cart: $f_9(r, d) = C$
- ▶ Review order summary: $f_{10}(r, d) = T$
- ▶ Submit order: $f_{11}(r, d) = C$
- ▶ Review order confirmation: $f_{12}(r, d) = T$
- ▶ Close order confirmation page: $f_{13}(r, d) = S$

The individual interaction steps and their relationship to the seed concept are depicted in Figure 16.9

Initial seed concept A: Calculate interaction steps (step 2)

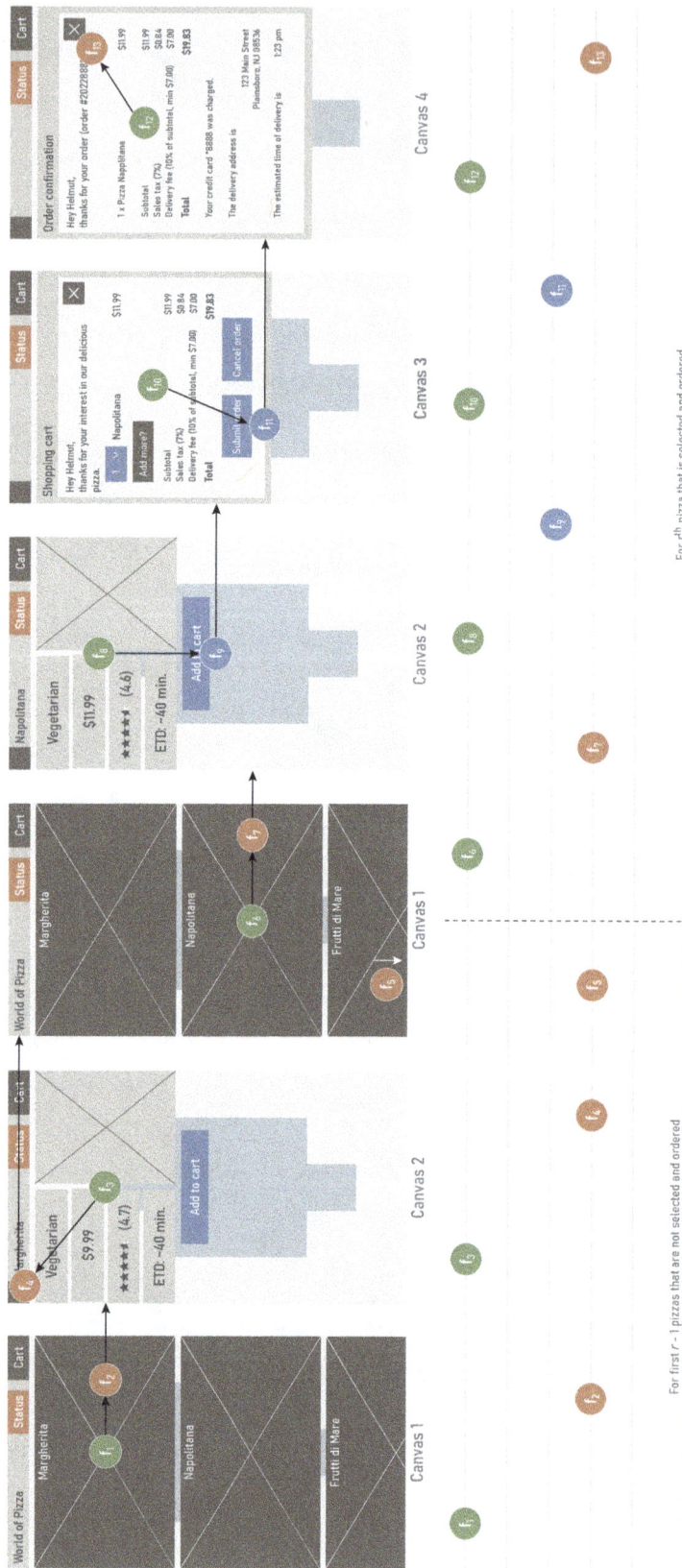

Canvas 1   Canvas 2   Canvas 1   Canvas 2   Canvas 3   Canvas 4

Interaction steps											
Think (T)											
Enter content (E)											
Trigger content control (C)											
Trigger canvas control (S)											
User external app (X)											

For first r − 1 pizzas that are not selected and ordered

Review (r−1) pizzas: $f_1(r,d) = (r-1) \cdot T$	Select (r−1) pizzas: $f_2(r,d) = (r-1) \cdot S$	Review (r−1) detailed pizza description: $f_3(r,d) = (r-1) \cdot T$	Go (r−1) times back to pizza list: $f_4(r,d) = (r-1) \cdot S$	Scroll down pizza list: $f_5(r,d) = \left(\left\lceil \frac{r}{d} \right\rceil - 1 \right) \cdot S$

For r^{th} pizza that is selected and ordered

Review r^{th} pizza list: $f_6(r,d) = T$	Select r^{th} pizza list: $f_7(r,d) = S$	Review r^{th} detailed description: $f_8(r,d) = T$	Add r^{th} pizza to shopping cart: $f_9(r,d) = C$	Review order summary: $f_{10}(r,d) = T$	Submit order: $f_{11}(r,d) = C$	Review order confirmation page: $f_{12}(r,d) = T$	Close order confirmation page: $f_{13}(r,d) = S$

Figure 16.9: Apply big I notation to initial seed concept A

Step 3: Summate interaction steps

The thirteen functions are summed up: $f_s(r,d) = \sum_{i=1}^{13} f_i(r,d) =$
$(r-1)\cdot T + (r-1)\cdot S + (r-1)\cdot T + (r-1)\cdot S + (\lceil\frac{r}{d}\rceil - 1)\cdot S + T + S + T + C + T + C + T + S$

The function is reorganized and grouped around each action type: T, E, S, C, and X (where applicable) – which gives us the interaction step baseline:

$f_s(r,d) = ((r-1) + (r-1) + 4)\cdot T + ((r-1) + \lceil\frac{r}{d}\rceil - 1 + (r-1) + 2)\cdot S + C + C =$
$(2r+2)\cdot T + (2r + \lceil\frac{r}{d}\rceil - 1)\cdot S + 2\cdot C$ (Interaction step baseline)

The interaction step baseline is a metric of interest for experience professionals. Here, we can see that the number of reviewed pizzas has an influence on how often a user thinks (process the content cognitively) and how much a user changes the canvas or the focus area.

Step 4: Normalize interaction steps

In this step, the different action types (T, E, S, C, X) are normalized, meaning they are replaced by a generic interaction step ("IS").

$f_{IS}(r,d) = (2r + 2 + 2r + \lceil\frac{r}{d}\rceil - 1 + 2)\cdot IS = (4r + \lceil\frac{r}{d}\rceil + 3)\cdot IS$
(Normalized interaction step baseline)

Often, the abbreviation "IS" is omitted for the sake of brevity.

Step 5: Simplify interaction steps

The big I notation is applied to determine the function growth, depending on the function variables. The highest-growing function per variable, along with its coefficient, is kept. All other functions are removed. Here are a few simplification examples:

- $2n + 1$ is replaced by ("→") $2n$; reason: $2n$ is the highest-growing function.
- $2n^2 + 2n + 1 \rightarrow 2n^2$; reason: $2n^2$ is the highest-growing function for the variable n.
- $2n^2 + 2n + 1 + m \rightarrow 2n^2 + m$; reason: $2n^2$ is the highest-growing function for the variable n; m is the highest growing function for the variable m.
- $m^3 + \pi\cdot m^2 + 55m + c \rightarrow m^3 + c$; reason: m^3 is the highest-growing function for the variable m; c is the highest growing function for the variable c.
- $n^m + 3n^2 + 5m^7 + p \rightarrow n^m + 5m^7 + p$; reason: n^m is the highest-growing function for the variable n; $5m^7$ is the highest-growing function for the variable m; p is the highest-growing function for the variable p.
- $2 \rightarrow 2$; reason: there is no variable. If the interaction complexity is expressed with a constant only, the constant remains.

The simplification is now applied to the normalized interaction step baseline.

$I(g_{IS}(r,d)) = I(4r + \lceil \frac{r}{d} \rceil + 3) = I((4 + \frac{1}{d}) \cdot r + 3) = I(\frac{4d+1}{d} \cdot r + 3) = I(\frac{4d+1}{d} \cdot r)$ (Estimated interaction complexity)

For brevity, the "estimated interaction complexity" can be called "interaction complexity," abbreviated IC.

In addition, the interaction complexity level is determined. It is a language characterization of the estimated interaction complexity. Here is a list of interaction complexity levels:

- $I(0)$ - Zero-step interaction complexity (or "no user involvement")
- $I(1)$ - One-step interaction complexity (or "constant interaction complexity")
- $I(2)$ - Two-step interaction complexity (or "constant interaction complexity")
- $I(3)$ - Three-step interaction complexity (or "constant interaction complexity")
- $I(4)$ - Four-step interaction complexity (or "constant interaction complexity")
- $I(a)$ - Multiple-step interaction complexity (or "constant interaction complexity"); a is a constant
- $I(n)$ - Linear interaction complexity; n is a variable
- $I(2 \cdot n)$ - Double linear interaction complexity; n is a variable
- $I(3 \cdot n)$ - Triple linear interaction complexity; n is a variable
- $I(4 \cdot n)$ - Quadruple linear interaction complexity; n is a variable
- $I(a \cdot n)$ - Multiple linear interaction complexity; a is a constant, n is a variable
- $I(log(n))$ - Logarithmic interaction complexity; n is a variable
- $I(2 \cdot log(n))$ - Double logarithmic interaction complexity; n is a variable
- $I(3 \cdot log(n))$ - Triple logarithmic interaction complexity; n is a variable
- $I(4 \cdot log(n))$ - Quadruple logarithmic interaction complexity; n is a variable
- $I(a \cdot log(n))$ - Multiple logarithmic interaction complexity; a is a constant, n is a variable
- $I(n^2)$ - Quadratic interaction complexity; n is a variable
- $I(2 \cdot n^2)$ - Double quadratic interaction complexity; n is a variable
- $I(3 \cdot n^2)$ - Triple quadratic interaction complexity; n is a variable
- $I(4 \cdot n^2)$ - Quadruple quadratic interaction complexity; n is a variable

- $I(a \cdot n^2)$ - Multiple quadratic interaction complexity; a is a constant, n is a variable
- $I(n^a)$ - Polynomial interaction complexity; a is a constant, n is a variable
- $I(a^n)$ - Exponential interaction complexity; a is a constant, n is a variable
- $I(n^p)$ - Super-polynomial interaction complexity; n and p are variables

If the estimated interaction complexity is between two levels, it is advisable to pick the one with the higher complexity. The initial seed concept A has an interaction complexity of $I(\frac{4d+1}{d} \cdot r)$, which is classified as "multiple linear" and not as "quadruple linear."

The interaction complexity level for the initial seed concept A is "multiple linear."

Step 6: Instantiate interaction steps

We assume that $r = 8$ and $d = 2$.

$g_{IS}(r = 8, d = 2) = \frac{4 \cdot 2 + 1}{2} \cdot 8 \cdot IS = 4.5 \cdot 8 \cdot IS = 36 \cdot IS$ (Estimated interaction steps).

Refined seed concept A

Step 1: Determine variables

- Number of pizzas reviewed: r (design-independent)
- Number of pizzas displayed at a glance: d (design-dependent)

Step 2: Calculate interaction steps
The user performs the following user steps:

- Review r - 1 pizzas in pizza list: $f_1(r, d) = (r - 1) \cdot T$
- Scroll down the pizza list: $f_2(r, d) = (\lceil \frac{r}{d} \rceil - 1) \cdot S$
- Review r^{th} pizza in pizza list: $f_3(r, d) = T$
- Order pizza: $f_4(r, d) = C$
- Review order confirmation: $f_5(r, d) = T$
- Close order confirmation: $f_6(r, d) = S$

The individual interaction steps and their relationship to the seed concept are depicted in Figure 16.10

Refined seed concept A: Calculate interaction steps (step 2)

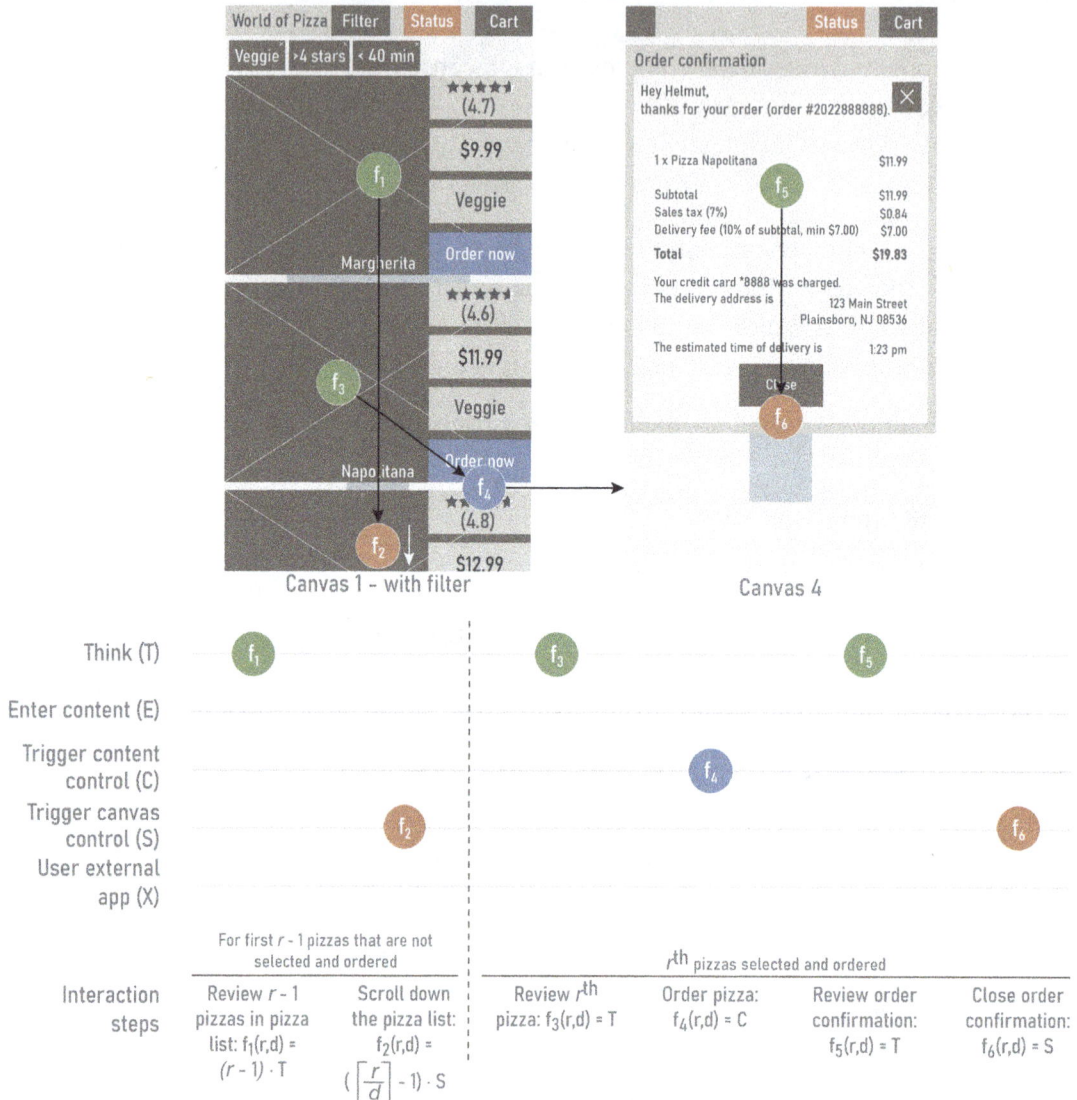

Figure 16.10: Apply big I notation to refined seed concept A

Step 3: Summate interaction steps

The functions for the user steps are summed up:

$$f_s(r,d) = \sum_{i=1}^{5} f_i(r,d) =$$
$$(r-1) \cdot T + (\lceil \tfrac{r}{d} \rceil - 1) \cdot S + T + C + T + S =$$
$$(r+1) \cdot T + \lceil \tfrac{r}{d} \rceil \cdot S + C \text{ (Interaction step baseline)}$$

Step 4: Normalize interaction steps

The different action types (T, E, S, C, X) are normalized with interaction steps (IS).

$$f_{IS}(r,d) = ((r+1) + \lceil \tfrac{r}{d} \rceil + 1) \cdot IS = (r + \lceil \tfrac{r}{d} \rceil + 2) \cdot IS \text{ (Normalized interaction step baseline)}$$

Step 5: Simplify interaction steps

The big I notation is applied to determine the growth, depending on the variables.

$I(g_{IS}(r,d)) = I(r + \lceil \frac{r}{d} \rceil + 2) = I(\frac{d+1}{d} \cdot r + 2) = I(\frac{d+1}{d} \cdot r)$ (Estimated interaction complexity)

The interaction complexity level for the refined seed concept A is "double linear."

Step 6: Instantiate interaction steps

We assume that $r = 8$ and $d = 2$.

$g_{IS}(r = 4, d = 2) = (\frac{2+1}{2} \cdot 8) \cdot IS = 1.5 \cdot 8 \cdot IS = 12 \cdot IS$ (Estimated interaction steps).

Comparison of estimated interaction complexity measurements

As we can see, the estimated interaction complexity for the initial seed concept A is $I((4 + \frac{1}{d}) \cdot r)$ and for the refined seed concept is $I(\frac{d+1}{d} \cdot r)$, where r is the number of reviewed pizzas. This is a reduction of about 66%. If we assume that a user reviews eight pizzas and orders the eighth one, the result is 36 estimated interaction steps for the initial seed concept A is twelve and for the refined seed concept A.

The estimated interaction steps and complexity levels for both concepts are displayed in Table 16.2.

Interaction complexity metrics	Initial seed concept A	Refined seed concept A
Interaction step baseline $f_s(r)$	$(2r+2)\cdot T+(2r+ \lceil \frac{r}{d} \rceil -1)\cdot S+2\cdot C$	$(r+1) \cdot T + \lceil \frac{r}{d} \rceil \cdot S + C$
Normalized interaction step baseline $f_{IS}(r)$	$(4r+\lceil \frac{r}{d} \rceil+3)\cdot IS$	$(r + \lceil \frac{r}{d} \rceil +2)\cdot IS$
Estimated interaction complexity $I(g_{IS}(r))$	$I(\frac{4d+1}{d} \cdot r)$	$I(\frac{d+1}{d} \cdot r)$
Estimated interaction complexity level	Multiple linear	Double linear
Estimated interaction steps $g_{IS}(r = 8, d = 2)$	$\frac{4\cdot2+1}{2} \cdot 8 = 4.5 \cdot 8 = 36$	$\frac{2+1}{2} \cdot 8 = 1.5 \cdot 8 = 12$

Table 16.2: Seed concepts A: Comparison of interaction complexity measurements

After the interaction complexity has been estimated for the refined concepts B,C, and D, we see that their interaction complexity level are identical to that of the refined concept A. The estimated interaction steps are different due to the different numbers of products displayed at a glance (see Table 16.3).

Table 16.3: Refined seed concepts A, B, C, and D: Comparison of interaction complexity measurements

Interaction complexity metrics	Refined seed concept A	Refined seed concept B	Refined seed concept C	Refined seed concept D
Interaction step baseline $f_s(r)$	$(r+1) \cdot T + \lceil \frac{r}{d} \rceil \cdot S + C$	$(r+1) \cdot T + \lceil \frac{r}{d} \rceil \cdot S + C$	$(r+1) \cdot T + \lceil \frac{r}{d} \rceil \cdot S + C$	$(r+1) \cdot T + \lceil \frac{r}{d} \rceil \cdot S + C$
Normalized interaction step baseline $f_{IS}(r)$	$(r + \lceil \frac{r}{d} \rceil + 2) \cdot IS$	$(r + \lceil \frac{r}{d} \rceil + 2) \cdot IS$	$(r + \lceil \frac{r}{d} \rceil + 2) \cdot IS$	$(r + \lceil \frac{r}{d} \rceil + 2) \cdot IS$
Estimated interaction complexity $I(g_{IS}(r))$	$I(\frac{d+1}{d} \cdot r)$	$I(\frac{d+1}{d} \cdot r)$	$I(\frac{d+1}{d} \cdot r)$	$I(\frac{d+1}{d} \cdot r)$
Estimated interaction complexity level	Double linear	Double linear	Double linear	Double linear
Estimated interaction steps $g_{IS}(r = 8, d)$, d=2 for concept A, d=4 for concept B, d=9 for concept C, d=12 for concept D	$\frac{2+1}{2} \cdot 8 =$ $1.5 \cdot 8 = 12$	$\frac{4+1}{4} \cdot 8 =$ $1.25 \cdot 8 = 10$	$\frac{9+1}{9} \cdot 8 =$ $1.1 \cdot 8 = 8.8$	$\frac{12+1}{12} \cdot 8 =$ $1.1 \cdot 8 = 8.8$

Find a flight

Let's apply the big I notation to a second example, which better reveals its strength. We'll switch the application domain from ordering a pizza to selecting a flight. The user wants to find the cheapest flight from among a combination of departure and arrival airports. We will assume that the user can departure from five different airports and can arrive at five different airports. The seed concepts are shown in Figure 16.11).

Seed concept A allows the user to enter a single departure airport and a single arrival airport only. Seed concept B allows the user to enter multiple departure airports and multiple arrival airports at the same time. Seed concept C allows the user to enter one departure airport and one arrival airport and then draw a circle on a map around each airport that defines which other departure and arrival airports should be considered. Seed concept D allows the user to enter one departure airport and one arrival airport and then specify a radius (such as 200 miles / 320 km) used to identify other airports that are located within the specified radius and considered for the search.

Which of the four seed concepts is most efficient? You may want to study them and select one for yourself. Later you can check whether the one you chose is the same as the one that was determined using the big I notation.

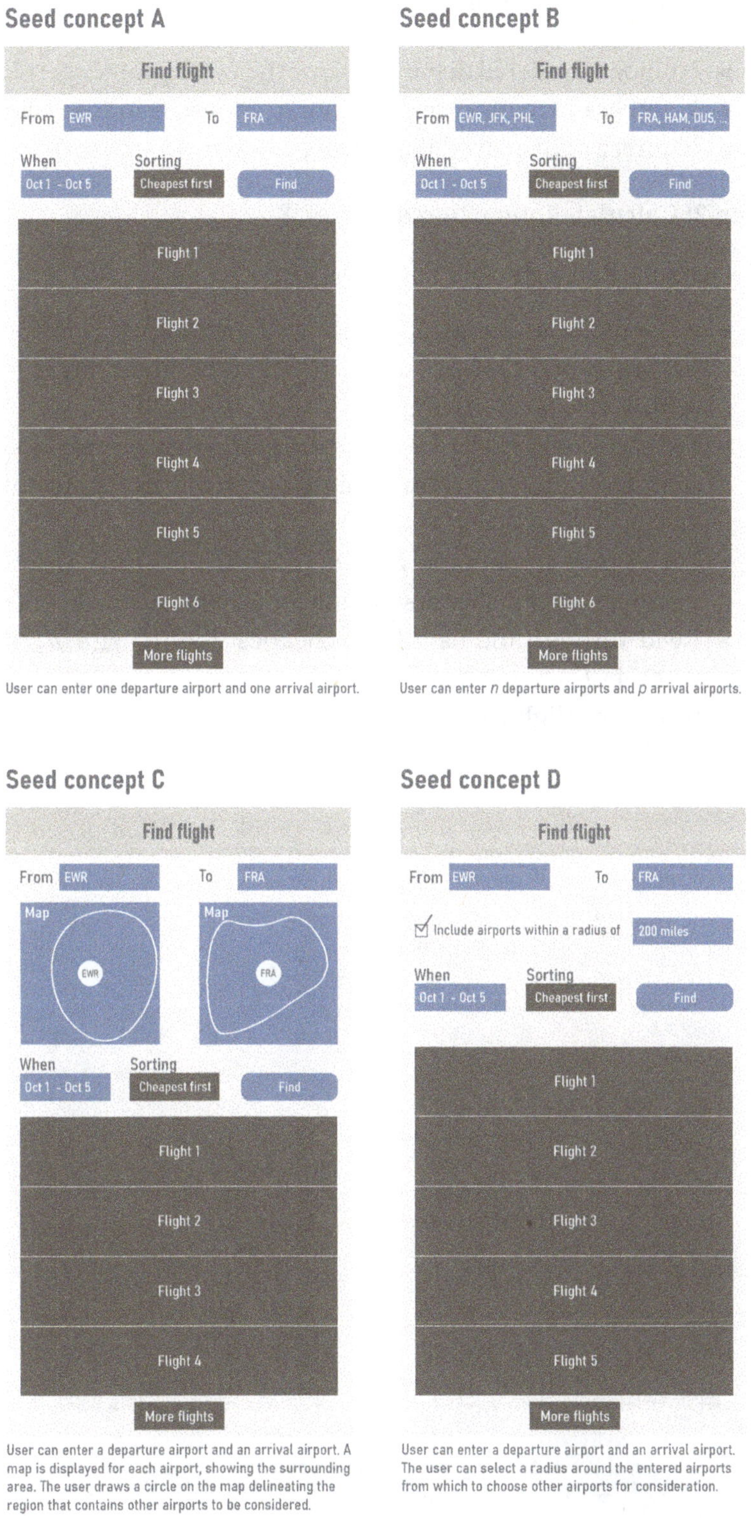

Seed concept A

Find flight	
From EWR	To FRA

When	Sorting	
Oct 1 – Oct 5	Cheapest first	Find

Flight 1

Flight 2

Flight 3

Flight 4

Flight 5

Flight 6

More flights

User can enter one departure airport and one arrival airport.

Seed concept B

Find flight	
From EWR, JFK, PHL	To FRA, HAM, DUS, …

When	Sorting	
Oct 1 – Oct 5	Cheapest first	Find

Flight 1

Flight 2

Flight 3

Flight 4

Flight 5

Flight 6

More flights

User can enter n departure airports and p arrival airports.

Seed concept C

Find flight	
From EWR	To FRA
Map (EWR)	Map (FRA)

When	Sorting	
Oct 1 – Oct 5	Cheapest first	Find

Flight 1

Flight 2

Flight 3

Flight 4

More flights

User can enter a departure airport and an arrival airport. A map is displayed for each airport, showing the surrounding area. The user draws a circle on the map delineating the region that contains other airports to be considered.

Seed concept D

Find flight	
From EWR	To FRA

☑ Include airports within a radius of 200 miles

When	Sorting	
Oct 1 – Oct 5	Cheapest first	Find

Flight 1

Flight 2

Flight 3

Flight 4

Flight 5

More flights

User can enter a departure airport and an arrival airport. The user can select a radius around the entered airports from which to choose other airports for consideration.

Figure 16.11: Seed concepts for selecting a flight

Seed concept A

Seed concept A allows the user to enter exactly one departure airport and exactly one arrival airport.

Step 1: Determine variables

▶ Number of entered departure airports: d (design-independent)
▶ Number of entered arrival airports: a (design-independent)
▶ Number of displayed list items: l (design-dependent)

Step 2: Calculate interaction steps

The user performs the following user steps:

▶ Enter multiple queries ($d \cdot a$), each with one departure airport (E), with one arrival airport (E), and then submit it (C): $f_1(d,a,l) = d \cdot a \cdot (E + E + C)$
▶ For each combination of departure and arrival airport ($d \cdot a$), read through the resulting flight list (top four flights only) ($4 \cdot T$): $f_2(d,a,l) = d \cdot a \cdot 4 \cdot T$
▶ Per airport combination ($d \cdot a$), make a note on a sheet of paper of the four cheapest flights ($4 \cdot X$): $f_3(d,a,l) = d \cdot a \cdot 4 \cdot X$
▶ Read through the list of the cheapest flights: $f_4(d,a,l) = d \cdot a \cdot 4 \cdot T$
▶ Select one flight: $f_5(d,a,l) = T$

Step 3: Summate interaction steps

The functions for the user steps are summed up:

$$f_s(d,a,l) = \sum_{i=1}^{5} f_i(d,a,l) =$$
$$(d \cdot a \cdot (E + E + C)) + (d \cdot a \cdot 4 \cdot T) + (d \cdot a \cdot 4 \cdot X) + (d \cdot a \cdot 4 \cdot T) + T$$

The function is restructured per action type:

$$f_s(d,a,l) = (8 \cdot d \cdot a + 1) \cdot T + 2 \cdot d \cdot a \cdot E + d \cdot a \cdot C + 4 \cdot d \cdot a \cdot X$$
(Interaction step baseline)

Step 4: Normalize interaction steps

The different action types (T, E, S, C, X) are normalized with interaction steps (IS).

$$f_{IS}(d,a,l) = (8 \cdot d \cdot a + 1) \cdot IS + 2 \cdot d \cdot a \cdot IS + d \cdot a \cdot IS + 4 \cdot d \cdot a \cdot IS =$$
$$(13 \cdot d \cdot a + 1) \cdot IS \text{ (Normalized interaction step baseline)}$$

Step 5: Simplify interaction steps

The big I notation is applied to determine the growth, depending on the variables.

$$I(g_{IS}(d,a,l)) = I(13 \cdot d \cdot a + 1) = I(13 \cdot d \cdot a) \text{ (Estimated interaction}$$
complexity)

The estimated interaction complexity level for seed concept A is "multiple quadratic."

Step 6: Instantiate interaction steps

It is assumed that the top four flights are considered for selection.

$$g_{IS}(d = 5, a = 5, l = 4) = 13 \cdot 5 \cdot 5 = 325 \cdot IS \text{ (Estimated interaction}$$
steps)

Seed concept B

Seed concept B allows the user to enter different departure airports and different arrival airports.

Step 1: Determine variables

▶ Number of entered departure airports: d (design-independent)
▶ Number of entered arrival airports: a (design-independent)
▶ Number of displayed list items: l (design-dependent)

Step 2: Calculate interaction steps

The user performs the following user steps:

- Enter a query for a departure locations and b arrival locations and submit it: $f_1(d,a,l) = d \cdot E + a \cdot E + C$
- Read the flight list (top four flights): $f_2(d,a,l) = 4 \cdot T$
- Select a flight: $f_3(d,a,l) = T$

Step 3: Summate interaction steps
The functions for the user steps are summed up:

$$f_s(d,a,l) = \sum_{i=1}^{3} f_i(d,a,l) =$$
$$d \cdot E + a \cdot E + C + 4 \cdot T + T$$

The function is restructured per action type:

$$f_s(d,a,l) = 5 \cdot T + (d + a) \cdot E + C \text{ (Estimated interaction step baseline)}$$

Step 4: Normalize interaction steps
The different action types (T, E, S, C, X) are normalized with interaction steps (IS).

$$f_{IS}(d,a,l) = 5 \cdot IS + (d + a) \cdot IS + IS =$$
$$(5 + d + a + 2) \cdot IS = (d + a + 7) \cdot IS \text{ (Normalized interaction step baseline)}$$

Step 5: Simplify interaction steps
The big I notation is applied to determine the growth, depending on the variables. $I(g_{IS}(d,a,l)) = I(d + a + 7) = I(d + a)$ (Estimated interaction complexity)

The estimated interaction complexity level for seed concept B is "linear."

Step 6: Instantiate interaction steps

It is assumed that the top four flights are considered for selection.

$g_{IS}(d = 5, a = 5, l = 4) = (5+5) \cdot IS = 10 \cdot IS$ (Estimated interaction steps)

Seed concept C

Seed concept C allows the user to enter one departure airport and one arrival airport. The user is then able to delineate a region on a map that identifies other airports to be included in the flight search.

Step 1: Determine variables

- Number of entered departure airports: d (design-independent)
- Number of entered arrival airports: a (design-independent)
- Number of displayed list items: l (design-dependent)

Step 2: Calculate interaction steps
The user performs the following user steps:

- Enter query for a departure locations and b arrival locations and submit it: $f_1(d, a, l) = E + E$
- Draw a circle on a map around the departure and arrival locations and submit it: $f_2(d, a, l) = E + E + C$
- Read the flight list (top four flights): $f_3(d, a, l) = 4 \cdot T$
- Select a flight: $f_4(d, a, l) = T$

Step 3: Summate interaction steps
The functions for the user steps are summed up:

$$f_s(d, a, l) = \sum_{i=1}^{4} f_i(d, a, l) =$$
$$(E + E) + (E + E + C) + (4 \cdot T) + T$$

The function is restructured per action type:

$f_s(d, a, l) = 5 \cdot T + 4 \cdot E + C$ (Estimated interaction step baseline)

Step 4: Normalize interaction steps
The different action types (T, E, S, C, X) are normalized with interaction steps (IS).

$f_{IS}(d, a, l) = 5 \cdot IS + 4 \cdot IS + IS = 10 \cdot IS$ (Normalized interaction step baseline)

Step 5: Simplify interaction steps
The big I notation is applied to determine the growth, depending on the variables. $I(g_{IS}(d, a, l)) = I(10)$ (Estimated interaction complexity)

The estimated interaction complexity level for seed concept C is "constant."

Step 6: Instantiate interaction steps

It is assumed that the top four flights are considered for selection.

$g_{IS}(d = 5, a = 5, l = 4) = 10 \cdot IS$ (Estimated interaction steps)

Seed concept D

Seed concept D allows the user to enter one departure airport and one arrival airport. The user can select a radius from which to automatically include other airports in the flight search.

Step 1: Determine variables

- Number of entered departure airports: d (design-independent)
- Number of entered arrival airports: a (design-independent)

▶ Number of displayed list items: l (design-dependent)

Step 2: Calculate interaction steps

The user performs the following user steps:

▶ Enter query for a departure locations and b arrival locations and submit it: $f_1(d, a, l) = E + E$
▶ Select a radius and submit it: $f_2(d, a, l) = E + C$
▶ Read the flight list (top four flights): $f_3(d, a, l) = 4 \cdot T$
▶ Select a flight: $f_4(d, a, l) = T$

Step 3: Summate interaction steps

The functions for the user steps are summed up:

$$f_s(d, a, l) = \sum_{i=1}^{4} f_i(d, a, l) =$$
$$(E + E) + (E + C) + 4 \cdot T + T$$

The function is restructured per action type:

$$f_s(d, a, l) = (4 + 1) \cdot T + 3 \cdot E + C = 5 \cdot T + 3 \cdot E + C \text{ (Estimated}$$
interaction step baseline)

Step 4: Normalize interaction steps

The different action types (T, E, S, C, X) are normalized with interaction steps (IS).

$$f_{IS}(d, a, l) = 5 \cdot IS + 3 \cdot IS + IS = 9 \cdot IS \text{ (Normalized interaction}$$
step baseline)

Step 5: Simplify interaction steps

The big I notation is applied to determine the growth, depending on the variables. $I(g_{IS}(d, a, l)) = I(9)$ (Estimated interaction complexity)

The estimated interaction complexity level for seed concept D is "constant."

Step 6: Instantiate interaction steps

It is assumed that the top four flights are considered for selection.

$g_{IS}(d = 5, a = 5, l = 4) = 9 \cdot IS$ (Estimated interaction steps)

Comparison of estimated interaction complexity measurements

The estimated interaction steps and complexity levels are displayed in table Table 16.4 on the facing page.

Because seed concepts B, C, and D require a similar number of interaction steps (10, 10, 9), one might infer that they have a similar interaction complexity. This conclusion would not be correct. Since

Table 16.4: Select flight: Comparison of interaction complexity measurements

Interaction complexity metrics	Seed concept A	Seed concept B	Seed concept C	Seed concept D
Estimated interaction step baseline $f_s(d,a,l)$	$(8 \cdot d \cdot a + 1) \cdot T + 4 \cdot d \cdot a \cdot E + d \cdot a \cdot C + 4 \cdot d \cdot a \cdot X$	$5 \cdot T + (d+a) \cdot E + C$	$5 \cdot T + 4 \cdot E + C$	$5 \cdot T + 3 \cdot E + C$
Normalized interaction step baseline $f_{IS}(d,a,l)$	$13 \cdot d \cdot a + 1$	$d + a + 7$	10	9
Estimated interaction complexity $I(g_{IS}(d,a,l))$	$I(13 \cdot d \cdot a)$	$I(d+a)$	$I(10)$	$I(9)$
Estimated interaction level	Multiple quadratic	Linear	Constant	Constant
Estimated interaction steps $g_{IS}(d=5, a=5, l=4)$	$13 \cdot 5 \cdot 5 = 325$	$5 + 5 = 10$	10	9

the big I notation determines a function, not a single value, we can see that the estimated interaction complexity level for seed concept B is *linear* and the estimated complexity levels for seed concepts C and D are *constant*.

The difference means that, for seed concept B, the number of interaction steps increases if the number of departure or arrival airports increases. This is because the user has to enter each departure and arrival airport.

Seed concepts C and D do not have that dependency. Even if the number of departure and arrival airports increases, the number of user involvement steps does not increase. The reason is that the design requires one user interaction step, namely, to mark an area (concept C) or to specify a radius (concept D), which can then identify multiple airports. The one user interaction step is independent from the number of departure and arrival airports included. The big I notation is capable of identifying and expressing such a significant difference.

From an efficiency perspective, concepts C and D are comparable, and preferred over concepts A and B. In making a selection about which to use, feasibility considerations can play a role as well as user feedback. In a project, it is probably worthwhile to evaluate both options with users and to check their feasibility and cost implications. If a project allows you to proceed with only one seed concept, a feasibility consideration is most likely influencing the decision, which would probably lead to the selection of seed concept D. If you are in doubt about which concept to choose, a speed test can identify additional actionable insights. Users may want to combine design elements from different concepts, such as using both C and D (defining a radius and showing it on a map). It would not increase the interaction complexity and would provide useful feedback to the user.

The short discussion here shows that the big I notation introduces a different way of thinking about design decisions. Furthermore, it introduces a new language that facilitates discussion of seed concepts and design decisions and enables you to make informed design decisions focusing on efficiency considerations. Furthermore, the big I notation helps to identify efficiency drivers. All of this is helpful for systematically achieving higher efficiency.

Twelve efficiency techniques

The twelve design efficiency techniques were introduced in Chapter 15 (Refine Concept) on page 439 with their claims to increase efficiency. With the big I notation, we can measure the interaction complexity savings of each design efficiency technique. The results are shown in Table 16.5 and in Table 16.6 on the next page.

Table 16.5: Interaction complexity measurements, applied to design efficiency techniques (before and after) (part 1)

Design efficiency technique	Main contributing action(s)	Interaction complexity measurements (before)	Interaction complexity measurements (after)
Apply batch usages	Influences S and C; n is number of content objects	$f_1(n) = n \cdot E$ (select n content objects); $f_2(n) = n \cdot C$ (apply content function to each content object); $f_s(n) = n \cdot E + n \cdot C$; $I(2n)$ (double linear)	$f_1(n) = E$ (Select all content objects with one input, e.g., filter); $f_2(n) = C$ (apply content function to all selected content objects); $f_s(n) = E + C$; $I(2)$ (two-steps)
Align content hierarchies	Influences T	(IC cannot be estimated without concept)	(IC cannot be estimated without concept)
Streamline gaze flow	Influences T	(IC cannot be estimated without concept)	(IC cannot be estimated without concept)
Move up content	Influences T, S; n expresses distance in canvas flow where content is placed	$f_1(n) = n \cdot T$ (review canvas); $f_2(n) = n \cdot S$ (select next canvas); $f_s(n) = n \cdot T + n \cdot S$; $I(2n)$ (double linear)	$f_1(n) = T$ (review canvas with content); $f_s(n) = T$; $I(1)$ (one-step)
Move up control	Influences T, S; n expresses distance in canvas flow where control is placed	$f_1(n) = n \cdot T$ (review canvas); $f_2(n) = n \cdot S$ (select next canvas); $f_3(n) = C$ (trigger control); $f_s(n) = n \cdot T + n \cdot S + C$; $I(2n)$ (double linear)	$f_1(n) = T$ (review canvas); $f_2(n) = C$ (select control); $f_s(n) = T + C$; $I(2)$ (two-steps)
Fix positions	Influences T	(IC cannot be estimated without concept)	(IC cannot be estimated without concept)

For those design efficiency techniques that could be estimated, the interaction complexity was reduced from double linear to constant.

Table 16.6: Interaction complexity measurements, applied to design efficiency techniques (before and after) (part 2)

Design efficiency technique	Main contributing action(s)	Interaction complexity measurements (before)	Interaction complexity measurements (after)
Aggregate content	Influences T, C; n expresses number of canvases on which content is distributed	$f_1(n) = n \cdot T$ (review canvas); $f_2(n) = n \cdot S$ (change to another canvas); $f_s(n) = n \cdot T + n \cdot S$; $I(2n)$ (double linear)	$f_1(n) = T$ (review canvas with aggregated content); $f_s(n) = T$; $I(1)$ (one-step)
Concatenate functions	Influences T, C; n expresses number of functions that are not concatenated	$f_1(n) = n \cdot T$ (review canvas); $f_2(n) = n \cdot C$ (trigger content function); $f_s(n) = n \cdot T + n \cdot S$; $I(2n)$ (double linear)	$f_1(n) = T$ (review canvas); $f_2(n) = C$ (trigger concatenated content function); $f_3(n) = T$ (review result of applied function); $f_s(n) = T + C + T$; $I(3)$ (three-steps)
Reuse the user's choice	Influences T, E; n expresses the number of user's choices	$f_1(n) = n \cdot T$ (review canvas); $f_2(n) = n \cdot E$ (select a choice); $I(n \cdot 2)$ (double linear)	$f_1(n) = T$ (check reused choices); $f_s(n) = T$; $I(1)$ (one-step)
Schedule action	Influences E, C; set schedule for one user task (UT), executed by the scheduler	$f_1(n) = UT$ (performs user task); $f_s(n) = UT$; $I(UT)$	$f_1(n) = E$ (select user task); $f_2(n) = E$ (set day); $f_3(n) = E$ (set time); $f_4(n) = E$ (set frequency); $f_5(n) = C$ (activate schedule); $f_s(n) = 4 \cdot E + C$; $I(5)$ (constant)
Propose action	Influences T, C; propose a user task to be executed	$f_1(n) = UT$ (performs user task manually); $f_s(n) = UT$; $I(UT)$	$f_1(n) = T$ (review proposed user task); $f_2(n) = C$ (confirm or reject proposed user task); $f_s(n) = T + C$; $I(2)$ (two-steps)
Execute action	Influences T, C; notifies about executed user task UT	$f_1(n) = UT$ (performs user task manually); $f_s(n) = UT$; $I(UT)$	$f_1(n) = T$ (review executed user task); $f_2(n) = C$ (do nothing or undo executed user task); $f_s(n) = T + C$; $I(2)$ (two-steps)

User involvement efficiency benchmarks

In the introduction of this book, we expressed that we want to increase efficiency by minimizing user involvement. This means reducing the user involvement steps to one or none where acceptable (see Figure 16.12).

One involvement step*

Step $\longrightarrow$ Outcome

No involvement step*

Outcome

*Works surprisingly often

Figure 16.12: User involvement efficiency goals

We consider the two goals here as the *user involvement efficiency benchmarks*. We can apply the big I notation to determine the estimated interaction complexity of the user involvement efficiency benchmarks.

One user involvement step

Step 1: Determine variables

▶ No variable

Step 2: Calculate interaction steps
The user performs the following user steps:

▶ Review canvas: $f_1 = T$
▶ Trigger content control: $f_2 = C$
▶ Review outcome: $f_3 = T$

Step 3: Summate interaction steps
The functions for the user steps are summed up: $f_s = \sum_{i=1}^{3} f_i =$
$T + C + T = 2 \cdot T + C$ (Interaction step baseline)

Step 4: Normalize interaction steps
The different action types (T, E, S, C, X) are normalized with interaction steps (IS).

$f_{IS} = (2 + 1) \cdot IS = 3 \cdot IS$ (Normalized interaction step baseline)

Evaluate Concepts

Step 5: Simplify interaction steps
The big I notation is applied to determine the growth, depending on the variables.

$I(g_{IS}(n)) = I(3)$ (Estimated interaction complexity)

The interaction complexity level is "three-step."

Step 6: Instantiate interaction steps The estimation does not use a variable.

$g_{IS} = 3 \cdot IS$ (Estimated interaction steps).

No user involvement step

When applying the big I notation to scenarios with no user involvement step, it is assumed that the user will still check the system outcome (one thinking step). The estimated interaction complexity is $I(1)$ (constant).

Step 1: Determine variables

▶ No variable

Step 2: Calculate interaction steps
The user performs the following user steps:

▶ Review outcome: $f_1 = T$

Step 3: Summate interaction steps
The functions for the user steps are summed up: $f_s = \sum_{i=1}^{1} f_i = T$ (Interaction step baseline)

Step 4: Normalize interaction steps
The different action types (T, E, S, C, X) are normalized with interaction steps (IS).

$f_{IS} = 1 \cdot IS$ (Normalized interaction step baseline)

Step 5: Simplify interaction steps
The big I notation is applied to determine the growth, depending on the variables.

$I(g_{IS}) = I(1)$ (Estimated interaction complexity)

The interaction complexity level is "one-step."

Step 6: Instantiate interaction steps The estimation does not use a variable.

$g_{IS} = 1 \cdot IS$ (Estimated interaction steps).

$I(1)$ and $I(3)$ are the estimated interaction complexities for the user involvement efficiency benchmarks.

The user involvement efficiency benchmarks can also be expressed with canvas flows, GAIS determined target involvement steps, and big I estimated interaction complexity (see Figure 16.13).

User involvement efficiency benchmarks

One involvement step

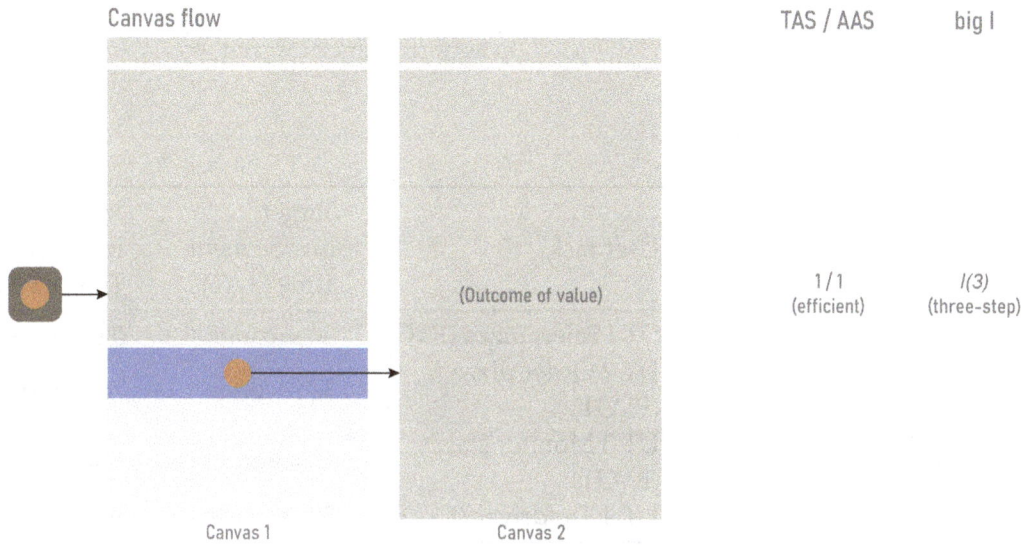

Canvas flow	TAS / AAS	big I

(Outcome of value)

1 / 1
(efficient)

I(3)
(three-step)

Canvas 1   Canvas 2

No involvement step

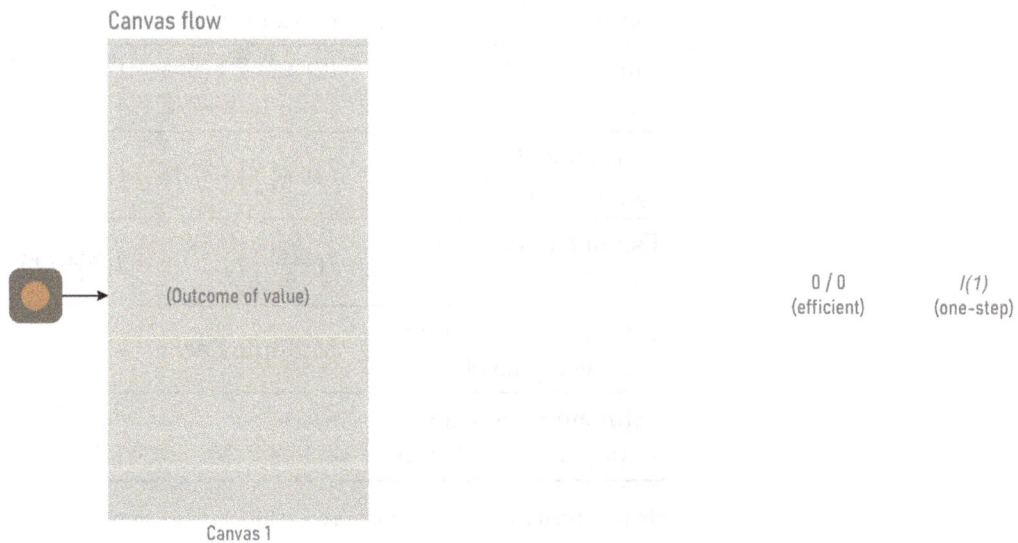

Canvas flow

(Outcome of value)

0 / 0
(efficient)

I(1)
(one-step)

Canvas 1

Figure 16.13: User involvement efficiency benchmarks

The reason why the numbers deviate between big I and GAIS is because big I estimates the complexity based on user *actions* while GAIS counts user involvement *steps*.

Summary

Step 3: Evaluate Concept

Seed concept A "Pizza-Gram" evaluated

▶ Move on to Step 4: Assess Concepts
◀ Go back to Step 2: Refine Concepts

User task	Target Involvement Time (TAT)	Actual Involvement Time (AAT)
UT 1 Select pizza (EVOT)	30 seconds	5 seconds
UT 2 Order pizza (EVOT)	30 seconds	7 seconds
UT 3 Monitor status (EVOT)	30 seconds	6 seconds
UT 4 Tip driver (EVOT)	30 seconds	10 seconds

Table 16.7: Measured elapsed involvement time

Interaction complexity metrics	Initial seed concept A	Refined seed concept A
Interaction step baseline $f_s(r)$	$(2r+2)\cdot T + (2r + \lceil\frac{r}{d}\rceil - 1)\cdot S + 2\cdot C$	$(r+1)\cdot T + \lceil\frac{r}{d}\rceil \cdot S + C$
Normalized interaction step baseline $f_{IS}(r)$	$(4r + \lceil\frac{r}{d}\rceil + 3)\cdot IS$	$(r + \lceil\frac{r}{d}\rceil + 2)\cdot IS$
Estimated interaction complexity $I(g_{IS}(r))$	$I(\frac{4d+1}{d}\cdot r)$	$I(\frac{d+1}{d}\cdot r)$
Estimated interaction complexity level	Multiple linear	Double linear
Estimated interaction steps $g_{IS}(r=8, d=2)$	$\frac{4\cdot2+1}{2}\cdot 8 = 4.5\cdot 8 = 36$	$\frac{2+1}{2}\cdot 8 = 1.5\cdot 8 = 12$

Table 16.8: Seed concept A: Comparison of interaction complexity measurements

Lessons learned

Use, use, use

Repeated use of the seed concepts with an interactive mockup will reveal behavioral issues that cannot be uncovered through analysis. If an experience designer has behavioral issues with a seed concept, the target user group will most likely have issues, too. If the experience designer does not have behavioral issues with a seed concept, the target user group will most likely find some.

Speed test

One of the best ways to evaluate an involvement concept is by using it. We are interested in efficiency, and a speed test can reveal design decisions that lead to inefficiencies.

It is helpful if the tool used for performing the speed test determines the user involvement times per user task and the user steps automatically.

Big I notation

A speed test provides times, but it does not reveal the interaction complexity of an involvement concept. This is where the big I notation assists. Comparison of the estimated interaction complexities of various seed concepts can help you to select one or show where further improvements can be mode to a concept.

The big I notation determines the action types that influence the interaction complexity per user task. Therefore, it not only estimates the interaction complexity, but it also helps to identify the action types that add significant and potentially avoidable complexity. Using big I notation helps the experience professional to think differently about design choices and their consequences.

In this sense, the big I notation follows the idea of the user involvement arc, the user involvement hypotenuse (see Figure 16.14) and GAIS to reduce user involvement as much as possible, but keep it at a level that is still acceptable for target users.

After applying the big I notation many times, there are some additional lessons learned what we can share here:

State transitions without user involvement hypotenuse

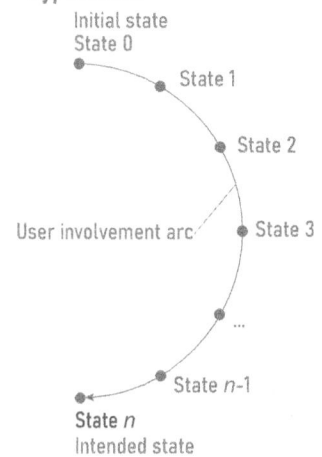

Initial state
State 0
State 1
State 2
User involvement arc   State 3
...
State *n*-1
State *n*
Intended state

n user involvement steps needed to achieve the intended state from the initial state

Transferred initial state with user involvement hypotenuse

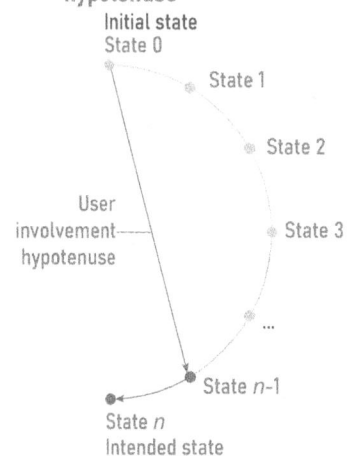

Initial state
State 0
State 1
State 2
User involvement hypotenuse   State 3
...
State *n*-1
State *n*
Intended state

One user involvement step needed to achieve the intended state from the new initial state

Figure 16.14: User involvement arc with user involvement hypotenuse

Use a small number of variables The number of variables should not be too large; otherwise, the calculations become too convoluted and difficult to follow. A good rule of thumb is to use less than five variables.

Use the same variables The design-independent variables should be derived from the task analysis (e.g., GAIS). Design-dependent variables are derived from the concepts. The same variables should be used across different interaction concepts.

Simplify the highest-growing functions The interaction step baseline is frequently used to analyze an seed concept by identifying the action types with the highest-growing function. It also helps to analyze the concepts and to simplify design choices contributing to the highest-growing function.

A large amount of time to estimate indicates lack of understanding In most cases, the estimation of the interaction complexity took about 15 minutes per user task. In a few cases, it actually took two to three hours. The reason was a difficulty in identifying the variables that drive the interaction complexity. This difficulty was due to an insufficient understanding of the application domain and the user tasks. After the knowledge gap was closed, the interaction complexity could be measured in about 15 minutes.

Choose letters that differentiate the names of objects or object attributes When choosing a letter to represent a variable, it is good practice to pick one that differentiates objects from others. For instance, let's say we need to choose a variable to express the frequency of the user step "Enter departure airport." The action "enter" is already mentioned in the action type E, so representing "enter" in the variable letter would not add value. The object "airport" would not add value because one user step is "enter departure airport" and another is "enter arrival airport." A word that *would* be useful in reflecting the variables are "departure." Therefore, to reflect the user step "enter departure airport," the letter "d" for "departure airport" would be appropriate.

Mathematical expressions as a design rationale Mathematical expressions are typically trusted. This principle applies to the big I notation, too. The estimated interaction complexity and level are used as design rationales. The measurements communicate a design quality that moves design discussions out of the opinion zone into an objective zone. And they help to put the focus on the design inputs with the greatest influence on the highest-growing function.

Complexity measurements for different target audiences The estimated complexity measurements (i.e., interaction step baseline, normalized interaction step baseline, estimated interaction complexity, interaction complexity level, estimated interaction steps) introduce different views on the interaction complexity for different target audiences. Executive management likes it simple, so the estimated interaction complexity with the interaction complexity level and the estimated interaction steps are useful and simple measures.

Designers and product managers typically like more details, so they often prefer to see the unfiltered measurements, expressed as the interaction step baseline. Thus design discussions become more focused and objective. Such focused discussions didn't take place prior to using the big I notation. The mathematical expression associated with the interaction concept introduces a language that is used by involved stakeholders across target audiences and disciplines. It also helps to change the perception of the experience discipline as a whole, by showing that many (but not all) design decisions are a matter of reaching a set involvement goals, and not just a matter of personal taste and style.

Exercise 3.4

Goal Determine the fastest performance of the defined user tasks for each seed concept. Identify misplaced or unnecessary design elements.

Material Speed test, big I notation, seed concepts

Completion criteria:

- ▶ For each seed concept: At least ten speed test runs have been performed for all user tasks. The actual involvement time (AAT) for each user task is documented.
- ▶ For each seed concept: The interaction complexity has been estimated, and design changes that can increase efficiency have been discussed.

Assess Concepts | 17

*There's only one thing more precious than our time
and that's who we spend it on*
Leo Christopher

Purpose

The purpose of this chapter is to demonstrate how the refined and
evaluated seed concepts are assessed against the involvement goals
(see Figure 17.1).

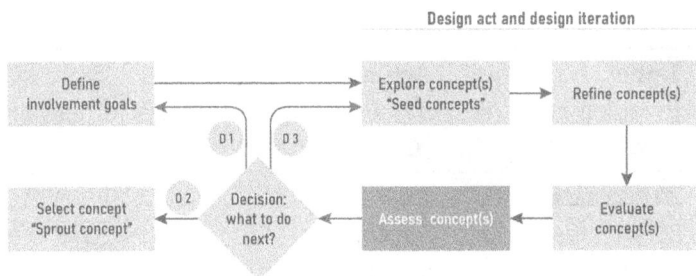

Figure 17.1: Assess concepts

In this chapter, the seed concept A, Pizza-Gram (see Figure 15.45
and Figure 15.46), is under assessment. We will look at each
involvement goal group separately. The result of the assessment
is documented in the involvement goal matrix (see Table 12.3 on
page 334).

Quantitative involvement goals

We have four involvement-step-related involvement goals. Based on the involvement step counting, as documented in Figure 15.46, we can discern how well the concept complies with the set involvement step goals (see Table 17.1).

Table 17.1: Quantitative involvement steps - Assessment results

Involvement goal	Target involvement steps (TAS)	Actual involvement steps (AAS)	Assessment result
QnG 1 Select pizza	0 Involvement step	1 Involvement step	No
QnG 2 Order pizza	1 Involvement step	1 Involvement step	Yes
QnG 3 Monitor status	1 Involvement step	1 Involvement step	Yes
QnG 4 Tip driver	1 Involvement step	2 Involvement steps	No

If an involvement goal is not met or not compliant, the respective assessment result will be marked as "No" and highlighted in orange.

Based on the speed test results (see Table 16.1 on page 495), the assessment results are documented in Table 17.2.

Table 17.2: Quantitative involvement time – Assessment results

Involvement goal	Target Involvement Time (TAT)	Actual Involvement Time (AAT)	Assessment result
QnG 5 Select pizza (EVOT)	30 seconds	5 seconds	Yes
QnG 6 Order pizza (EVOT)	30 seconds	7 seconds	Yes
QnG 7 Monitor status (EVOT)	30 seconds	6 seconds	Yes
QnG 8 Tip driver (EVOT)	30 seconds	10 seconds	Yes
QnG 9 Select, order, and receive pizza (EVOT)	33 minutes	TBD	TBD

The measurement for QnG 9 is not available yet. We need to have the entire ecosystem set up before we can measure how long the order and delivery process takes.

For reasons of simplicity, we use binary assessment values here: yes or no. Other approaches are possible. Pugh uses three values: "+," "-," and "same." The "+" value means that a concept under assessment is better than what's stated in the goal. "-" means that a concept under assessment is worse than what's stated in the goal, and "same" means that a concept under assessment is as good as what's stated in the goal [207, p. 77].

Qualitative involvement goals

We assessed the refined seed concept against the qualitative involvement goals (see Table 17.3). For each assessment result, a brief reason is documented.

Table 17.3: Qualitative involvement goals - Assessment results

Qualitative goal	Explanation	Assessment result
QIG 1 Enable finding pizzas by attribute (incl. diets)	Filters are supported (canvas 1)	Yes
QIG 2 Display pizza attributes (incl. calories, ingredients, image)	Attributes are displayed (canvas 1, canvas 2)	Yes
QIG 6 Support reuse of user-entered content and settings	Filter settings and payment / delivery content is reused	Yes
QIG 7 Provide access to previously ordered pizzas	Not supported	No
QIG 8 Support group orders	Not supported	No

Two of the qualitative involvement goals are not yet met.

Vendor involvement goals

We also assessed the refined concept against the vendor involvement goals. The result is displayed in Table 17.4).

Table 17.4: Vendor involvement goals - Assessment results

Vendor goal	Explanation	Assessment result
VG 1 Enable comparison of pizzas from different restaurants	Pizzas from different restaurants can be displayed	Yes
VG 2 Enable extension of the product list	More pizzas can be added	Yes
VG 3 Enable the display of at least nine products at a glance	Two pizzas can be displayed at the same time (canvas 1)	No

VG 3 is not met. Seed concept A is designed for a large images; the image size is a significant aspect of the design and thus makes VG 3 not compliant.

Assessment summary

Refined seed concept A

An overview of the involvement goals and their assessment results for seed concept A, "Pizza-Gram," is shown in Table 17.5.

Involvement goal	Assessment result
Quantitative goal	
QnG 1 Select pizza: 0 involvement step	No
QnG 2 Order pizza: 1 involvement step	Yes
QnG 3 Monitor status: 1 involvement step	Yes
QnG 4 Tip driver: 1 involvement step	No
QnG 5 Select pizza: 30 seconds (EVOT)	Yes
QnG 6 Order pizza: 30 seconds (EVOT)	Yes
QnG 7 Monitor status: 30 seconds (EVOT)	Yes
QnG 8 Tip driver: 30 seconds (EVOT)	Yes
QnG 9 Order and receive pizza: 33 minutes (EVOT)	TBD
Qualitative goal	
QlG 1 Enable finding pizzas by attribute (incl. diets)	Yes
QlG 2 Display pizza attributes (incl. calories, ingredients, image)	Yes
QlG 6 Support reuse of user-entered content and settings	Yes
QlG 7 Provide access to previously ordered pizzas	No
QlG 8 Support group orders	No
Vendor goal	
VG 1 Enable comparison of pizzas from different restaurants	Yes
VG 2 Enable extension of the product list	Yes
VG 3 Enable the display of at least nine products at a glance	No

Table 17.5: Involvement goal matrix - Assessment results for refined seed concept A "Pizza-Gram"

We can see that the refined seed concept A complies with many involvement goals, but not all.

Refined seed concepts A, B, C, D

In the previous section, we focused on seed concept A only to introduce how the assessment is performed and documented. In most projects, more than one seed concept is explored, refined, evaluated, and assessed. The assessment results for all four refined seed concepts is shown in Table 17.6.

Table 17.6: Refined seed concepts after iteration 1 – Involvement goal assessment result

Involvement goals	Refined seed concept A "Pizza-Gram"	Refined seed concept B "Four-at-a-glance"	Refined seed concept C "Menu"	Refined seed concept D "Lane"
Quantitative involvement goal				
QnG 1 Select pizza: 0 involvement step	No	No	No	No
QnG 2 Order pizza: 1 involvement step	Yes	Yes	Yes	Yes
QnG 3 Monitor status: 1 involvement step	Yes	Yes	Yes	Yes
QnG 4 Tip driver: 1 involvement step	No	No	No	No
QnG 5 Select pizza: 30 seconds (EVOT)	Yes	Yes	Yes	Yes
QnG 6 Order pizza: 30 seconds (EVOT)	Yes	Yes	Yes	Yes
QnG 7 Monitor status: 30 seconds (EVOT)	Yes	Yes	Yes	Yes
QnG 8 Tip driver: 30 seconds (EVOT)	Yes	Yes	Yes	Yes
QnG 9 Order and receive pizza: 33 minutes (EVOT)	TBD	TBD	TBD	TBD
Qualitative involvement goal				
QlG 1 Enable finding pizzas by attribute (incl. diets)	Yes	Yes	Yes	Yes
QlG 2 Display pizza attributes (incl. calories, ingredients, image)	Yes	Yes	Yes	Yes
QlG 6 Support reuse of user-entered content and settings	Yes	Yes	Yes	Yes
QlG 7 Provide access to previously ordered pizzas	No	No	Yes	Yes
QlG 8 Support group orders	No	No	No	No
Vendor involvement goal				
VG 1 Enable comparison of pizzas from different restaurants	Yes	Yes	Yes	Yes
VG 2 Enable extension of the product list	Yes	Yes	Yes	Yes
VG 3 Enable the display of at least nine products at a glance	No	No	Yes	Yes

In the next chapter, we will discuss the assessment results and decide how we should move forward.

Summary

Assess concept

► Move on to Step 5: Decide about Iteration
◄ Go back to Step 3: Evaluate Concept

Table 17.7: Refined seed concepts after iteration 1 – Involvement goal assessment result

Involvement goals	Refined seed concept A "Pizza-Gram"	Refined seed concept B "Four-at-a-glance"	Refined seed concept C "Menu"	Refined seed concept D "Lane"
Quantitative involvement goal				
QnG 1 Select pizza: 0 involvement step	No	No	No	No
QnG 2 Order pizza: 1 involvement step	Yes	Yes	Yes	Yes
QnG 3 Monitor status: 1 involvement step	Yes	Yes	Yes	Yes
QnG 4 Tip driver: 1 involvement step	No	No	No	No
QnG 5 Select pizza: 30 seconds (EVOT)	Yes	Yes	Yes	Yes
QnG 6 Order pizza: 30 seconds (EVOT)	Yes	Yes	Yes	Yes
QnG 7 Monitor status: 30 seconds (EVOT)	Yes	Yes	Yes	Yes
QnG 8 Tip driver: 30 seconds (EVOT)	Yes	Yes	Yes	Yes
QnG 9 Order and receive pizza: 33 minutes (EVOT)	TBD	TBD	TBD	TBD
Qualitative involvement goal				
QlG 1 Enable finding pizzas by attribute (incl. diets)	Yes	Yes	Yes	Yes
QlG 2 Display pizza attributes (incl. calories, ingredients, image)	Yes	Yes	Yes	Yes
QlG 6 Support reuse of user-entered content and settings	Yes	Yes	Yes	Yes
QlG 7 Provide access to previously ordered pizzas	No	No	Yes	Yes
QlG 8 Support group orders	No	No	No	No
Vendor involvement goal				
VG 1 Enable comparison of pizzas from different restaurants	Yes	Yes	Yes	Yes
VG 2 Enable expansion of the product list	Yes	Yes	Yes	Yes
VG 3 Enable the display of at least nine products at a glance	No	No	Yes	Yes

Lessons learned

The assessment of the seed concepts against the involvement goals identifies non-compliances. Such non-compliances require our attention when moving forward.

The assessment of the seed concepts against the quantitative goals is relatively straight forward. Since involvement steps are already counted as part of exploration and refinement, the numbers can simply be copied per user task.

Assessment of the qualitative goals and the vendor goals requires some interpretation. It is therefore useful to write down a brief reason, with a reference to a canvas or a design element that justifies the assessment result.

With the involvement goal matrix, the further refinement and selection of a concept becomes *explainable*. The involvement goals are the explanation for why a seed concept was explored, refined, evaluated, and assessed. The matrix also explains how compliant a seed concept is against the involvement goals.

Tips and tricks

Design bias   When assessing different concepts, there is a risk of design bias – I also call it the "love trap." It means that you love your design so much that you can't recognize any shortcomings or limitations it may have. As experience professionals, we should be critical of our own work all the time. We know that a seed concept is just a means to an end for a user, not the purpose (the purpose is the outcome of value and the user goal). Sometimes keeping a distance from our own work is a challenge.

To avoid design bias, or the love trap, it's a good idea to bring in a peer, to whom you explain your assessment results. In other words, you explain and defend your decisions. If your explanation is not convincing enough, you may be caught in the love trap. The peer will tell you that, and then you should revise your decisions (if the peer is not able to be honest with you, you have picked the wrong peer and need to look for someone else). The peer will help you to make your assessment results explainable and defensible.

Stakeholder buy-in   The use of an involvement goal matrix with its assessment results is an important step in the entire presented approach. In my project experience, it typically leads to buy-in from stakeholders and to their belief that the design decisions are not just opinion- or experience-based but that there is a methodology behind them. Most industrial stakeholders I meet and work with appreciate such a structured, relatively objective approach.

When stakeholders raise concerns about a seed concept, I always try to map the concern to one of the design inputs, such as workflow (to be), user roles, the user involvement system, a user involvement point, a primary user task, or involvement goals. Redirection of a concern to a design input keeps the conversation focused and fact-based. The design inputs justify the concept: therefore, rather than adjusting the concept as an immediate response to the critique, concerns should be directed to the relevant design input, which can be either confirmed or modified. A change of a design input will lead logically to a change of concept if necessary.

It happens frequently that the involvement goals do not reflect the expectations of internal project stakeholders. In such cases, the stakeholder expectations should be captured as one or more additional vendor goals. The project stakeholders should agree on the added vendor goals as a new involvement goal baseline. Most likely, the seed concepts will need to be modified afterward to comply with the such additional vendor goals.

If you plan to apply this approach, I recommend getting stakeholders' buy-in step-by-step for the following interim results:

- ▶ Workflow (as is) with summarized pain points
- ▶ User role profile
- ▶ Workflow (to be) with user involvement metrics and targets
- ▶ User involvement system with its scenarios
- ▶ User involvement points with their primary user task
- ▶ Involvement goal matrix with its involvement goals (quantitative, qualitative, vendor)
- ▶ Explored and refined seed concepts
- ▶ Later: Selection of the sprout concept from the compliant seed concept and the rationale for the selection

Each result is a baseline and foundation for the next result. For instance, the workflow (as is) is the foundation and baseline for the workflow (to be). The workflow (to be) is the foundation and baseline for the user involvement system, and so on.

When presenting a result, its foundation and baseline should be given first. For instance, before you present the explored and refined seed concepts, offer the involvement goals as their foundation and baseline. When presenting the seed concepts, show how the involvement goals have influenced the design decisions.

Exercise 3.5

Goal   Assess each seed concept against the involvement goals.

Material   Evaluated seed concepts, involvement goal matrix

Completion criteria:

- ► Each seed concept is assessed against the involvement goal. For each assessment result, a brief reason is documented.
- ► The involvement goal matrix with the assessment results is documented.

Decide about Iteration | 18

All we have to decide is what to do with the time that is given to us
J.R.R. Tolkien

Purpose

The purpose of this chapter is to demonstrate how to decide what to do next after the completion of a design iteration (see Figure 18.1).

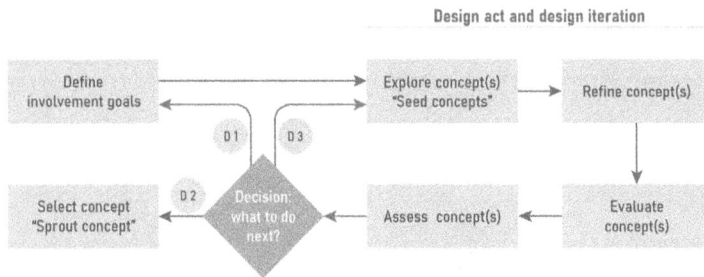

Figure 18.1: Iteration decision

The three decisions – D1, D2, and D3, indicated in Figure 18.1 – are explained in this chapter.

Decision flow

Technique

At the end of each design iteration, a decision needs to be made about how to proceed. The decision is guided by the following questions:

▶ Q 1 Are the involvement goals achievable (i.e., is the design space existent)?
▶ Q 2 Will we select a sprout concept from the seed concepts?
▶ Q 3.1 Which of the seed concepts will go through another design iteration?
▶ Q 3.2 Do we need to explore more seed concepts?

The questions are organized in a decision flow, depicted in Figure 18.2.

Decisions at the end of each design iteration

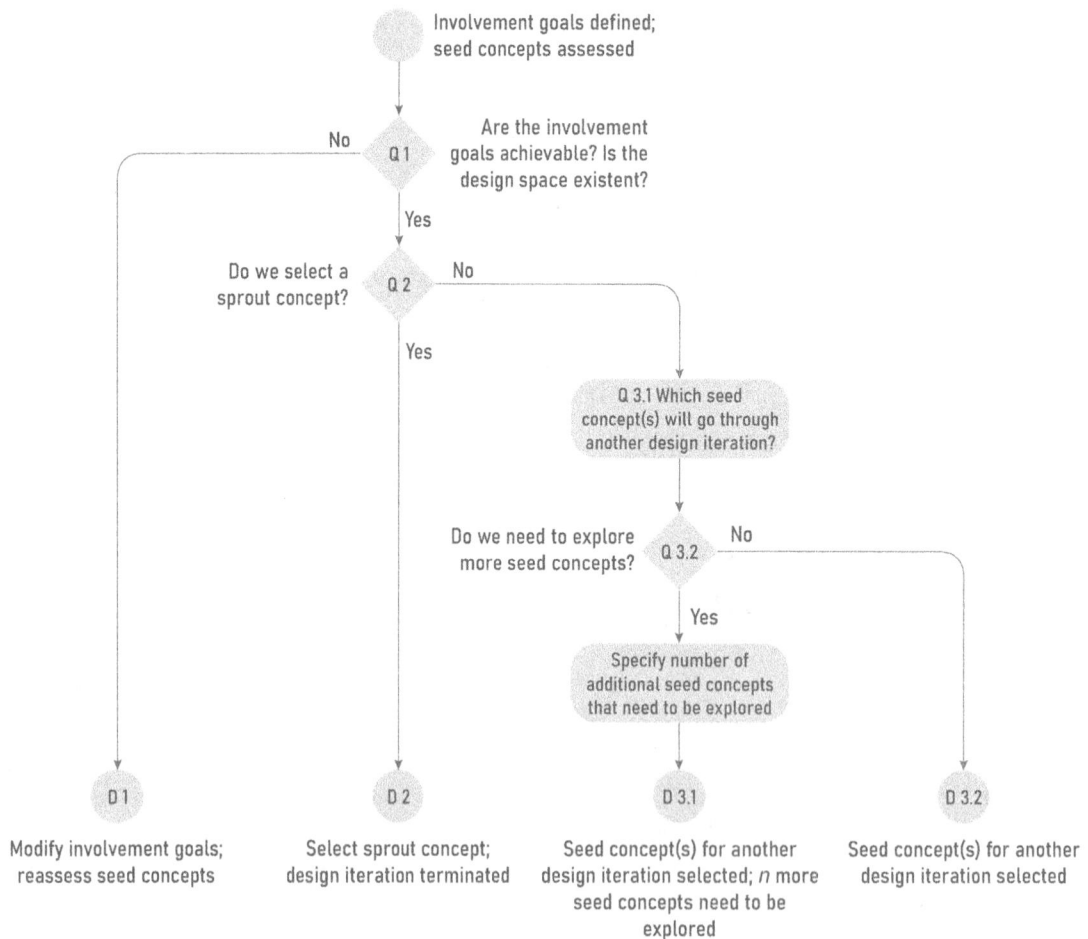

Figure 18.2: Decisions to be made at the end of each design iteration

Question Q 1 prompts us to reflect on the defined involvement goals. Setting goals is one thing; being able to meet them is another. Question Q 1 asks whether the involvement goals are achievable, and for instance, whether they conflict with each other. In other words, the question is asking whether the design space is existent or non-existent.[1] A strong indicator of achievable involvement goals is if the first design iteration has created at least one seed concept that is already compliant with most of the involvement goals. If there is not a single seed concept that meets at least a few involvement goals, some of the defined involvement goals might be unreasonable and require modification or removal. After the involvement goals are modified, the refined seed concepts need to be reassessed against the modified involvement goals.

Question Q 2 addresses the seed concepts that are fully or mostly compliant with the involvement goals. This question motivates a decision about whether the set of explored, refined, evaluated, and assessed seed concepts is mature enough so that one of them can be selected as the sprout concept. If the answer to this question is 'yes', the design iteration terminates and a sprout concept will be selected from one of the seed concepts. If the answer is 'no', at least one more design iteration is needed. This decision leads us to questions Q 3.1 and Q 3.2.

Asking questions Q 3.1 and Q 3.2 indicates that the decision was made that another design iteration is needed. This can mean that the explored, refined, evaluated, and assessed seed concepts are not compliant, or not compliant enough, with the involvement goals. It can also mean that the explored seed concepts are not broad enough and that the project would benefit from additional design options. Question Q 3.1 asks which of the existing seed concepts should be selected for another design iteration. The assumption here is that a seed concept might not be compliant with all the involvement goals but still have the potential to become compliant. Such seed concepts will be selected for another iteration ("seed concept is selected for another iteration"). If a seed concept, due to its structure and design decisions, cannot become compliant with involvement goals, it will be terminated at this stage ("seed concept is terminated").

After looking at the seed concepts that have been selected for another design iteration, the question to ask is whether the selected seed concepts are rich enough or whether more seed concepts should be explored. This is what question Q 3.2 asks. If this question is answered with a 'yes', it should be clarified how many more seed concepts should be explored. If the answer to question Q 3.2 is 'no', no more seed concepts will be explored.

The decisions D 1, D 2, and D 3 are also marked in Figure 18.1.

1: As a reminder: A design space is existent if there is at least one design option that complies with the defined involvement goals. A design space is non-existent if no design option exists that complies with the involvement goals. An existent design space can be empty; this simply means that a design option exists that complies with the involvement goals, but it has not yet been found. (The design universe and the design space were introduced in Section 1 (Design universe) on page 371).

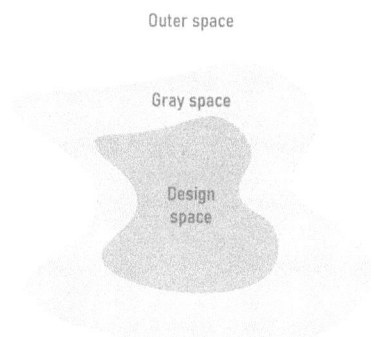

Figure 18.3: Design universe

What appears to be a rather mechanical and cumbersome process is, in reality, very fast and agile. Some conceptual ideas are selected for refinement, and others are rejected. In most of my projects, the number of design iterations range from about five to fifty. If the application is innovative, the number of iterations is closer to fifty than to five.

WoP after iteration 1

We will go through the three questions to determine how to proceed from this point.

Q 1 Are the involvement goals achievable (i.e., is the design space existent)?

According to the involvement goal matrix (see Table 17.6 on page 535), there is no seed concept that fully complies with all involvement goals. However, most of the involvement goals are already met after the first iteration. We can assume so far that haven't yet been met will be. So we answer this question is a 'yes'.

The first involvement goal, QnG 1, is not achievable as written. The original intent of the goal was to express that "UT 1.1 select pizza" and UT 1.2 order pizza" should both be performed with one involvement step. To better reflect this intent, we will replace QnG 1 with "QnG 1* select and order pizza." We will remove QnG 2 as an involvement goal.

Now that we have modified the involvement goals, all four seed concepts are compliant with the new QnG 1*.

Q 2 Will we select a sprout concept from the seed concepts?

In order to select a sprout concept, we should, ideally, have seed concepts that are compliant with all involvement goals. We are not there yet. For now, the answer to question Q 2 is 'no.'

Q 3.1 Which of the seed concepts will go through another design iteration?

To answer this question, we need to look at the involvement goals that are not met yet. For each of them, we need to ask a question pertaining to each seed concept: can we modify the seed concept so it becomes compliant? If the answer is yes, we will keep the concept and iterate it. If the answer is no for one of the involvement goals, we need to decide whether this non-compliance is acceptable. For the sake of demonstration, if the answer is no, the concept will be terminated.

QnG 4 Tip driver (1 involvement step) None of the concepts supports to tipping the driver with one involvement step. That is because the user has to trigger opening the tip area with one involvement step and then select the tip amount with another involvement step. To reduce the involvement steps, the tip area should appear automatically after the driver has finished the delivery; then the user could tip the driver with one involvement step.

QlG 7 Provide access to previously ordered pizzas Since many users reorder a previously ordered pizza, this goal is an efficiency booster. It requires that a seed concept provides a designated area to display previously ordered pizzas. Seed concepts A and B have only one list of pizzas, which is filtered and sorted by the previously selected filter and sort criteria. These two concepts are not able to meet this goal. Seed concepts C and D have categories of pizzas. One of those can be designated for previously ordered pizzas.

QlG 8 Support group orders None of the seed concepts has support right now for group orders, but group orders can be added as a feature to each of the seed concepts. Therefore, we will not terminate a seed concept based on this goal.

VG 3 Enable the display of at least nine products at a glance This goal was set by the project sponsor. It requires the display of at least nine pizzas at the same time. Seed concept A displays two pizzas and seed concept B displays four. Seed concepts C and D display nine pizzas at the same time. Based on this goal, seed concepts A and B will be terminated, and seed concepts C and D will be kept.

Decision The discussion has been reflected in an updated involvement goal matrix (see Table 18.1 on the following page). The seed concepts that do not comply with some of the involvement goals and that are not able to comply with them are marked in orange. The seed concepts that do not comply with some of the involvement goals but that are able to comply with them after some modifications, are marked in blue.

Because seed concepts A and B have non-achievable involvement goals, they are terminated. Seed concepts C and D will be iterated.

Table 18.1: Seed concepts after iteration 1 - Achievable goals are marked in green and not achievable goals are marked in red

Involvement goals	Refined seed concept A "Pizza-Gram"	Refined seed concept B "Four-at-a-glance"	Refined seed concept C "Menu"	Refined seed concept D "Lane"
Quantitative involvement goal				
QnG 1* Select and order pizza: 1 involvement step	Yes	Yes	Yes	Yes
QnG 3 Monitor status: 1 involvement step	Yes	Yes	Yes	Yes
QnG 4 Tip driver: 1 involvement step	No	No	No	No
QnG 5 Select pizza: 30 seconds (EVOT)	Yes	Yes	Yes	Yes
QnG 6 Order pizza: 30 seconds (EVOT)	Yes	Yes	Yes	Yes
QnG 7 Monitor status: 30 seconds (EVOT)	Yes	Yes	Yes	Yes
QnG 8 Tip driver: 30 seconds (EVOT)	Yes	Yes	Yes	Yes
QnG 9 Order and receive pizza: 33 minutes (EVOT)	TBD	TBD	TBD	TBD
Qualitative involvement goal				
QlG 1 Enable finding pizzas by attribute (incl. diets)	Yes	Yes	Yes	Yes
QlG 2 Display pizza attributes (incl. calories, ingredients, image)	Yes	Yes	Yes	Yes
QlG 6 Support reuse of user-entered content and settings	Yes	Yes	Yes	Yes
QlG 7 Provide access to previously ordered pizzas	No	No	Yes	Yes
QlG 8 Support group orders	No	No	No	No
Vendor involvement goal				
VG 1 Enable comparison of pizzas from different restaurants	Yes	Yes	Yes	Yes
VG 2 Enable extension of the product list	Yes	Yes	Yes	Yes
VG 3 Enable the display of at least nine products at a glance	No	No	Yes	Yes

Q 3.2 Do we need to explore more seed concepts?

For the sake of brevity, we will not explore more seed concepts. We have two promising seed concepts and will iterate them.

Refined concepts after iteration 2

Influenced by the assessment, seed concept C and seed concept D have been refined again (now iteration 2). The iteration result for seed concept C is shown in Figure 18.4 and Figure 18.5 . The iteration result for seed concept D is shown in Figure 18.6 and Figure 18.7. The changes are marked.

Seed concept C: Menu – Cast (iteration 2, step 2)

Canvas 1 - with filter

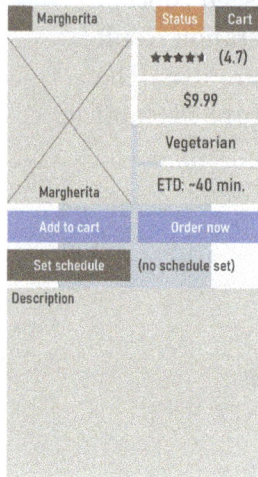

Canvas 2

Canvas 3

Canvas 4

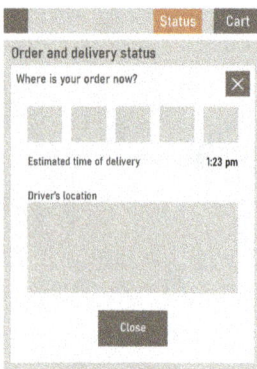

Canvas 5

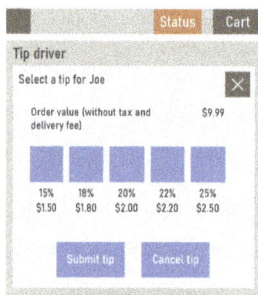

Canvas 6

Canvas 7

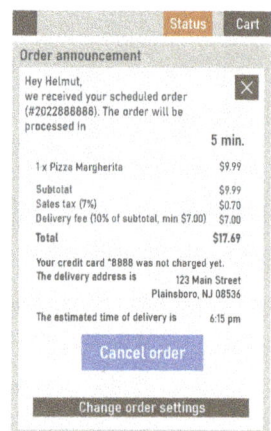

Canvas 8

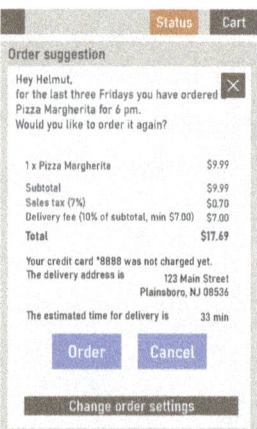

Canvas 9

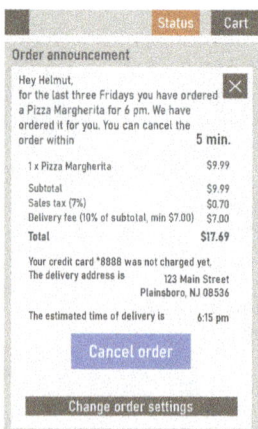

Canvas 10

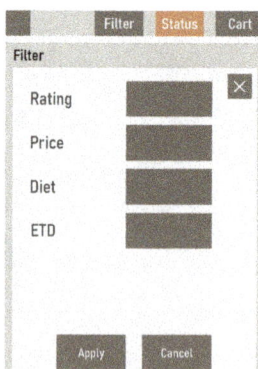

Canvas 11

Canvas 12

Figure 18.4: Seed concept C: Menu – Canvas cast (iteration 2, step 2)

Seed concept C: Menu – Flow (iteration 2, step 2)

UT 1.1* Select and order pizza

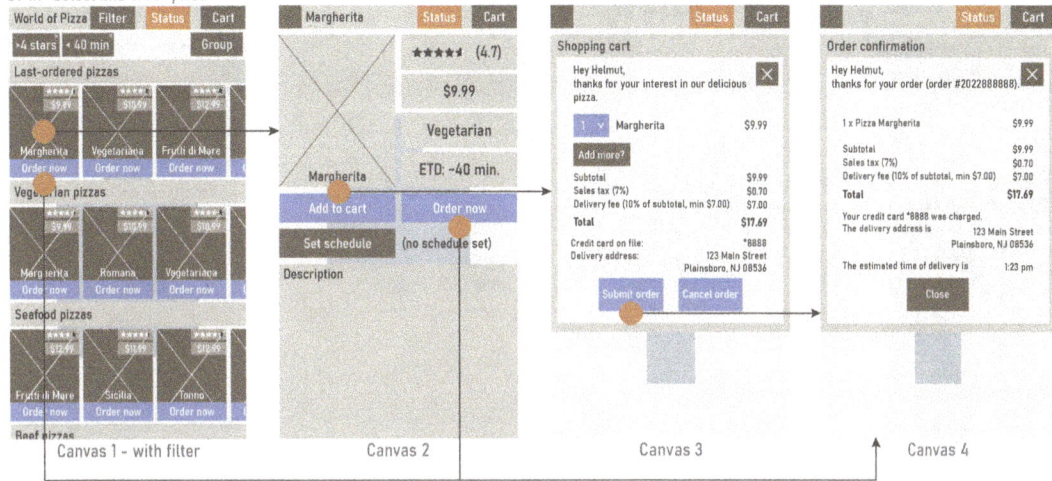

TAS / AAS

1 / 1 (efficient)

Canvas 1 - with filter   Canvas 2   Canvas 3   Canvas 4

UT 1.3 Monitor status

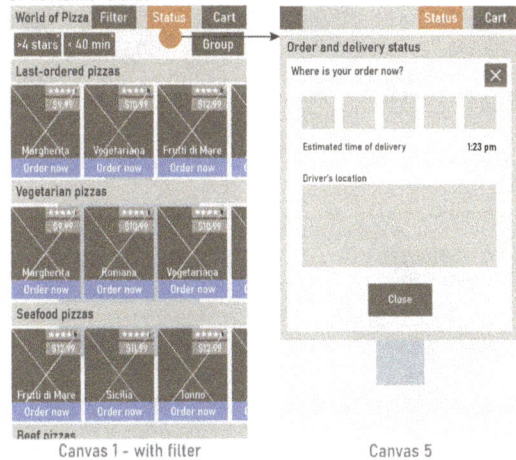

1 / 1 (efficient)

Canvas 1 - with filter   Canvas 5

UT 1.4 Tip driver

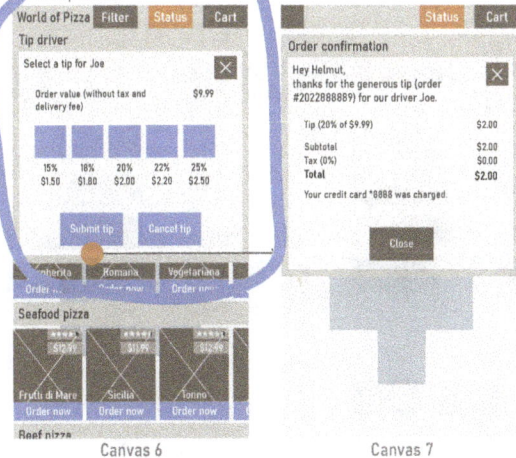

1 / 1 (efficient)

Canvas 6   Canvas 7

Figure 18.5: Seed concept C: Menu – Canvas flow (iteration 2, step 2)

Seed concept D: Lane - Cast (iteration 2, step 2)

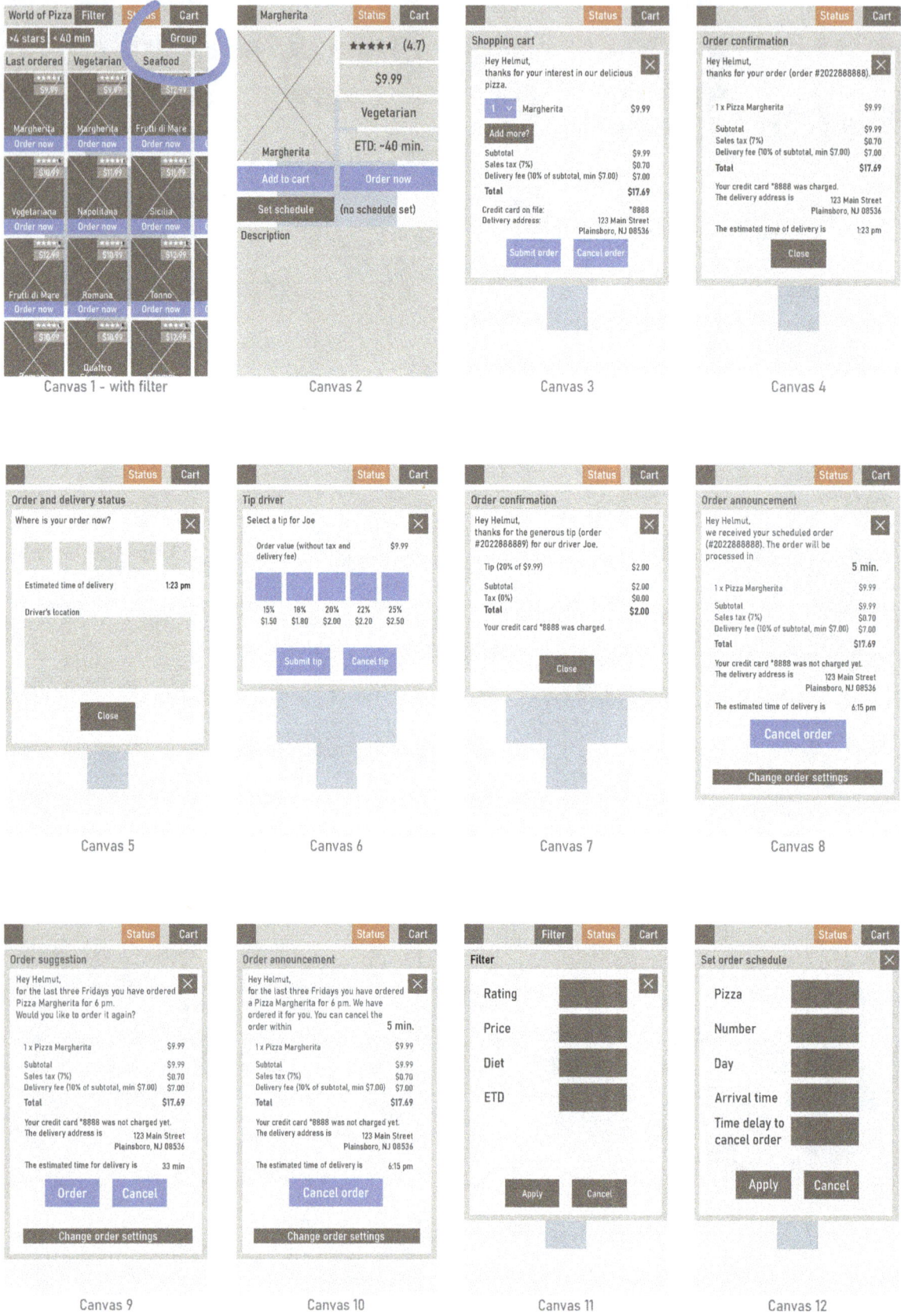

Figure 18.6: Seed concept D: Lane – Canvas cast (iteration 2, step 2)

Seed concept D: Lane - Flow (iteration 2, step 2)

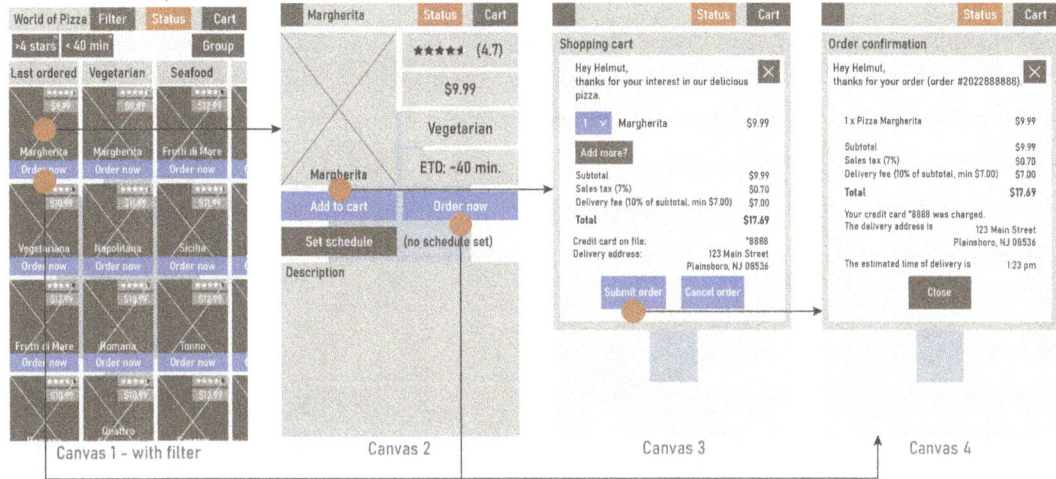

UT 1* Select and order pizza

TAS / AAS

1/1 (efficient)

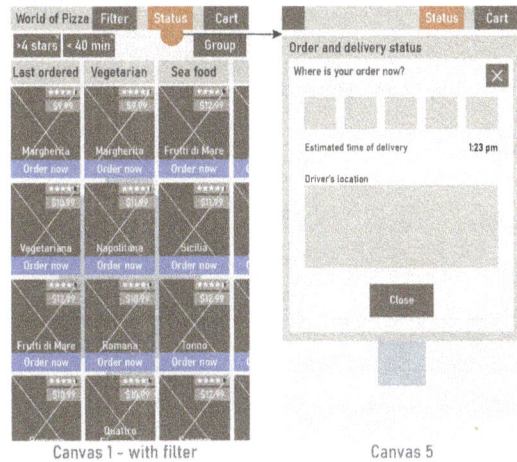

UT 3 Monitor status

1/1 (efficient)

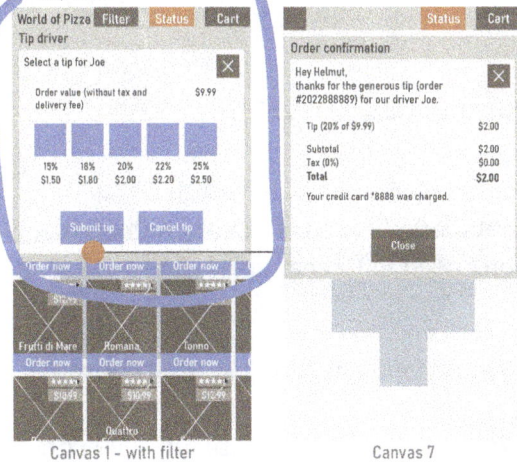

UT 4 Tip driver

1/1 (efficient)

Figure 18.7: Seed concept D: Lane – Canvas flow (iteration 2, step 2)

Assessment of the refined concepts after iteration 2

After the second iteration of refinement, evaluation, and assessment, we can update the involvement goal matrix (see Table 18.2).

Table 18.2: Seed concepts after iteration 2 - Involvement goal assessment

Involvement goals	Seed concept C "Menu"	Seed concept D "Lane"
Quantitative involvement goal		
QnG 1* Select and order pizza: 1 involvement step	Yes	Yes
QnG 3 Monitor status: 1 involvement step	Yes	Yes
QnG 4 Tip driver: 1 involvement step	Yes	Yes
QnG 5 Select pizza: 30 seconds (EVOT)	Yes	Yes
QnG 6 Order pizza: 30 seconds (EVOT)	Yes	Yes
QnG 7 Monitor status: 30 seconds (EVOT)	Yes	Yes
QnG 8 Tip driver: 30 seconds (EVOT)	Yes	Yes
QnG 9 Order and receive pizza: 33 minutes (EVOT)	TBD	TBD
Qualitative involvement goal		
QlG 1 Enable finding pizzas by attribute (incl. diets)	Yes	Yes
QlG 2 Display pizza attributes (incl. calories, ingredients, image)	Yes	Yes
QlG 6 Support reuse of user-entered content and settings	Yes	Yes
QlG 7 Provide access to previously ordered pizzas	Yes	Yes
QlG 8 Support group orders	Yes	Yes
Vendor involvement goal		
VG 1 Enable comparison of pizzas from different restaurants	Yes	Yes
VG 2 Enable extension of the product list	Yes	Yes
VG 3 Enable the display of at least nine products at a glance	Yes	Yes

Let's go through the decision iteration questions again.

Q 1 Are the involvement goals achievable (i.e., is the design space existent)?

Since both seed concepts comply with all involvement goals, they are achievable and don't need to be changed.

Q 2 Will we select a sprout concept from the seed concepts?

Since we are happy with the two fully compliant seed concepts, we will select one of them. The answer to question Q 2 is yes.

Therefore, we do not need to answer questions Q 3.1 and Q 3.2.

Summary

Step 5: Decide about Iteration

> ► Move on to Step 6: Select Concept
> ◄ Go back to Step 4: Assess Concepts

Table 18.3: Seed concepts after iteration 2 - Involvement goal assessment

Involvement goals	Seed concept C "Menu"	Seed concept D "Lane"
Quantitative involvement goal		
QnG 1* Select and order pizza: 1 involvement step	Yes	Yes
QnG 3 Monitor status: 1 involvement step	Yes	Yes
QnG 4 Tip driver: 1 involvement step	Yes	Yes
QnG 5 Select pizza: 30 seconds (EVOT)	Yes	Yes
QnG 6 Order pizza: 30 seconds (EVOT)	Yes	Yes
QnG 7 Monitor status: 30 seconds (EVOT)	Yes	Yes
QnG 8 Tip driver: 30 seconds (EVOT)	Yes	Yes
QnG 9 Order and receive pizza: 33 minutes (EVOT)	TBD	TBD
Qualitative involvement goal		
QlG 1 Enable finding pizzas by attribute (incl. diets)	Yes	Yes
QlG 2 Display pizza attributes (incl. calories, ingredients, image)	Yes	Yes
QlG 6 Support reuse of user-entered content and settings	Yes	Yes
QlG 7 Provide access to previously ordered pizzas	Yes	Yes
QlG 8 Support group orders	Yes	Yes
Vendor involvement goal		
VG 1 Enable comparison of pizzas from different restaurants	Yes	Yes
VG 2 Enable extension of the product list	Yes	Yes
VG 3 Enable the display of at least nine products at a glance	Yes	Yes

Decision: One of the two seed concepts will be selected as the sprout concept.

Lessons learned

After completing a design iteration, we need to make a decision about how to move forward. Four questions will help to make that decision:

- ▶ Q 1 Are the involvement goals achievable (i.e., is the design space existent)?
- ▶ Q 2 Will we select a sprout concept from the seed concepts?
- ▶ Q 3.1 Which of the seed concepts will go through another design iteration?
- ▶ Q 3.2 Do we need to explore more seed concepts?

Question Q 1 reflects on the involvement goals and how achievable they are. If some of them are not achievable, or are conflicting, they need to be modified. After the modification of involvement goals, the seed concepts need to be assessed against the modified involvement goals.

Question Q 2 checks whether the explored, refined, evaluated, and assessed seed concepts are mature enough that one of them can be selected as a sprout concept. A 'yes' answer terminates the design iterations.

If questions Q 3.1 and Q 3.2 are asked, it means that we are still in the middle of design iterations. These questions help us to select the seed concepts that should be iterated (Q 3.1) and to decide whether new seed concepts should be explored, and if so, how many (Q 3.2).

Tips and tricks

It is good practice to bring in a design peer to who you will explain the answers to the questions. This will help you to reduce design bias (the love trap).

The number of available iterations and the number of new seed concepts depends on the project constraints, particularly budget and time. It is normal that you may need to stop iterating after some time (e.g., days or weeks) and accept what you have achieved. If you have maintained the involvement goal matrix, you have documented which goals the best seed concept is compliant with and not compliant with, so an informed decision can be made by the project stakeholders.

Exercise 3.6

Goal   Decide how to proceed with the assessed seed concepts.

Material   Seed concepts, involvement goal matrix, design iteration questions

Completion criteria:

▶ All applicable questions are answered, and the answers are documented.

Select Concept | 19

The trouble is, you think you have time
Buddha

Purpose

The purpose of this chapter is to describe how to select a sprout concept from the remaining seed concepts (see Figure 19.1).

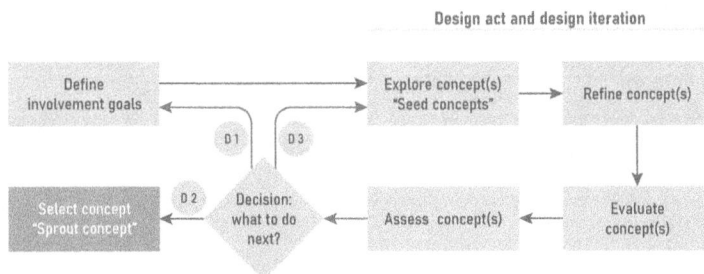

Figure 19.1: Select concept

Selection

Technique

The technique applies when a sprout concept can be selected from more than one seed concept. There are several approaches to how to select the sprout concept:

- ▶ Goal weights
- ▶ Cost and/or risks
- ▶ User feedback

▶ Qualitative criteria
▶ Combined approach

Goal weights If more than one seed concept complies with the involvement goals, or if they do not comply with all involvement goals, the goals can be weighted. Inspired by Pugh [207, p. 77], the idea is if a seed concept scores better than a certain goal, the number 2 can be assigned. If the concept does not meet the goal, the number 0 is assigned, and if it just meets the goal, the number 1 is assigned.

In addition to giving numbers for goal compliance, the goals themselves can have weights. For instance, the qualitative goals may have a weight of 3, the quantitative goals 2, and the vendor goals 1.

Table 19.1 on the facing page shows the numeric assessment results per goal and the goal weights. If goal weights were not used, seed concept 3 would be selected (it has the highest total 14). If goal weights were applied, seed concept 4 would be selected (total of 27).

Table 19.1: Selection of seed concept with goal weights

Seed concept	Seed concept 1	Seed concept 2	Seed concept 3	Seed concept 4
Quantitative involvement goals (goal weight: 3)				
QnG 1	1	1	1	1
QnG 2	2	1	1	1
QnG 3	1	1	1	2
Qualitative involvement goals (goal weight: 2)				
QlG 1	1	1	1	2
QlG 2	1	1	2	2
QlG 3	1	1	2	2
Vendor involvement goals (goal weight: 1)				
VG 1	1	2	2	1
VG 2	1	1	2	1
VG 3	1	2	2	1
Total (without goal weights)	$4 + 3 + 3 = 10$	$3 + 3 + 5 = 11$	$3 + 5 + 6 = 14$	$4 + 6 + 3 = 13$
Ranking (without goal weights)	4	3	1	2
Total (with goal weights)	$(3 \cdot 4) + (2 \cdot 3) + (1 \cdot 3) = 21$	$(3 \cdot 3) + (2 \cdot 3) + (1 \cdot 5) = 20$	$(3 \cdot 3) + (2 \cdot 5) + (1 \cdot 6) = 25$	$(3 \cdot 4) + (2 \cdot 6) + (1 \cdot 3) = 27$
Ranking (with goal weights)	3	4	2	1

Cost and/or risks   Another approach is the consideration of costs or risks. If several seed concepts are equally selectable from a goal compliance perspective, the balance can be tipped by using cost or risk considerations to provide additional information per seed concept. From all concept candidates, the one with the lowest cost or risk estimate can be selected.

User feedback   Users can be invited to experiment with the different concepts and share their preferences. It might even be possible to perform a usability test or even to run field tests to provide real life experience of the application under design.

Qualitative criteria   We can consider qualitative criteria. During concept exploration, refinement, evaluation, and assessment, it often happens that we learn something about the concepts that can become additional qualitative criteria. Such criteria are often not "promoted" through involvement goals; however, they become important inputs for design decisions. Such additional criteria can be used to assess the remaining seed concepts.

Combined approach   Any of the aforementioned individual approaches can be combined. The results per approach can be expressed numerically and summarized in a decision table (see Table 19.2). When using a decision table, it is advisable to use numbers for the various decision categories, which are added up to provide a total score. Doing this will help to make your decisions as objective and explainable as possible. Otherwise, you may end up in a battle of opinions.

When using numbers, it is advisable to keep it simple with just a few numbers, such as three. If a concept scores better than average for a certain category, the number 3 can be assigned. A concept that scores on the average is assigned a number 2, and one that scores less than average gets a 1. The sum of the numbers provides the score that can be used to select one of the concepts.

Table 19.2: Combined approach

Seed concept	Seed concept 1	Seed concept 2	Seed concept 3	Seed concept 4
Goal weight	3	3	3	3
Cost / risk	2	2	1	2
Additional criteria	1	2	2	3
User feedback	3	2	2	2
Total	9	9	8	10

In the case of the four sample concepts in Table 19.2 on the facing page, seed concept 4 scores the most points and would be selected.

World of Pizza

To select one of the two concepts, we need to look into the differences between them and discuss whether some of the differences constitute an advantage or a disadvantage. This means we look at "qualitative criteria."

Seed concept C (Menu) organizes the list of pizzas per category horizontally. Seed concept D (Lane) organizes the list of pizzas per category vertically (see Figure 19.2).

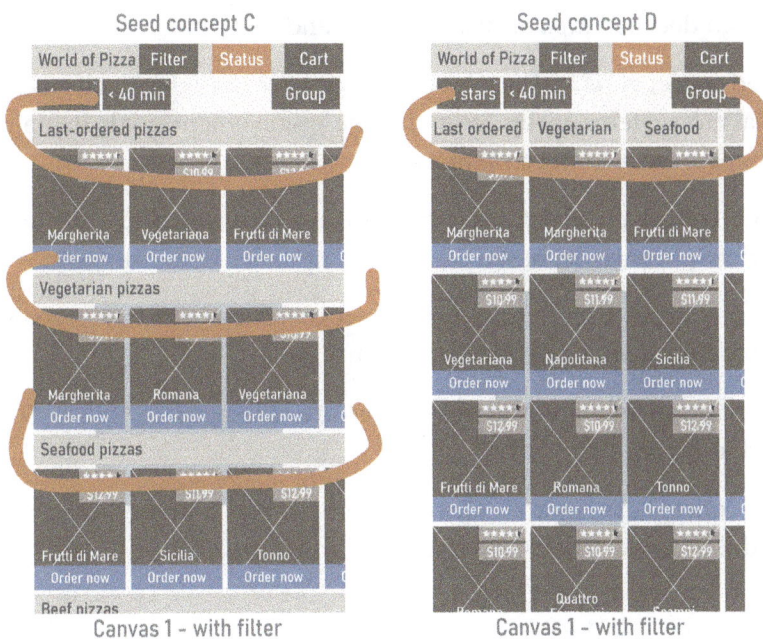

Figure 19.2: Comparison of concept C and concept D (canvas 1)

In concept C, the category area covers the entire width of the canvas. It can be used not only for long labels, but also, potentially, for additional controls. The category area in concept D only covers the width of one column and is therefore rather short. Additional design elements could not be placed there.

Another aspect of the category label is the footage it requires. In concept C, each category label requires a separate row, which takes up canvas footage. The category labels of concept D are in one row only. The advantages and disadvantages of the two concepts in regard to the category labels are shown in Table 19.3 on the next page.

Seed concept	Seed concept C	Seed concept D
Advantage	Category label has full screen width	All category labels are in one row
Disadvantage	Each category label requires its own row	Category label has limited column width

Table 19.3: Advantages and disadvantages of seed concepts C and D

The question is how to judge the advantages and disadvantages. Since both concepts comply with VG 3 (display at least nine products at a glance), and readability is important for users, concept C is selected as the sprout concept.

As you can see, the way we have selected concept C make the design decision *explainable*, *defensible*, and *efficient*.

Seed concept C is *explainable* because we have used the involvement goals to systematically refine it. The involvement goals explain what we were trying to achieve.

Seed concept C is *defensible* because we have selected it from a variety of concepts, based on their compliance with the goals.

Seed concept C is *efficient* because it meets our efficiency goals, expressed as quantitative involvement goals.

The canvas flow and the canvas cast are displayed in Figure 19.3 and in Figure 19.4

The concept explorations and exclusions for the four seed concepts and the two iterations are visualized in Figure 19.5.

Sprout concept: Menu - Cast

Canvas 1 - with filter

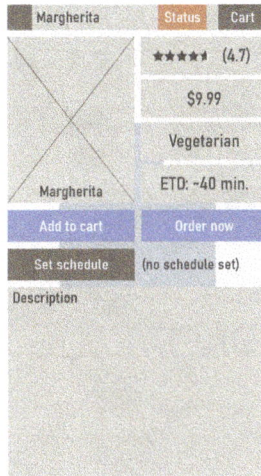

Canvas 2

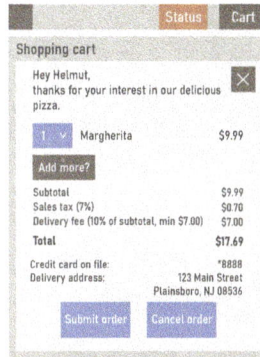

Canvas 3

Canvas 4

Canvas 5

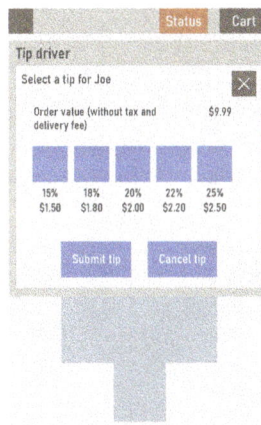

Canvas 6

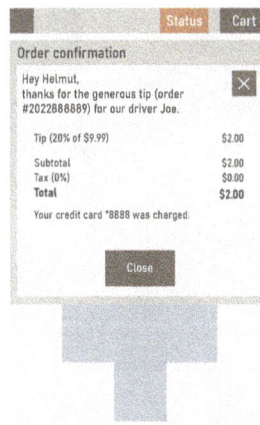

Canvas 7

Canvas 8

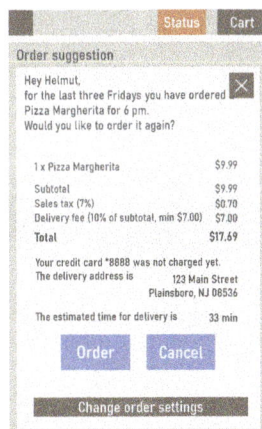

Canvas 9

Canvas 10

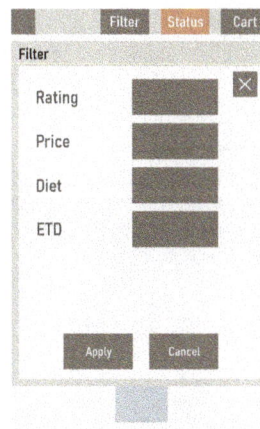

Canvas 11

Canvas 12

Figure 19.3: Sprout concept: Menu – Canvas cast

Sprout concept: Menu - Flow

UT 1.1* Select and order pizza

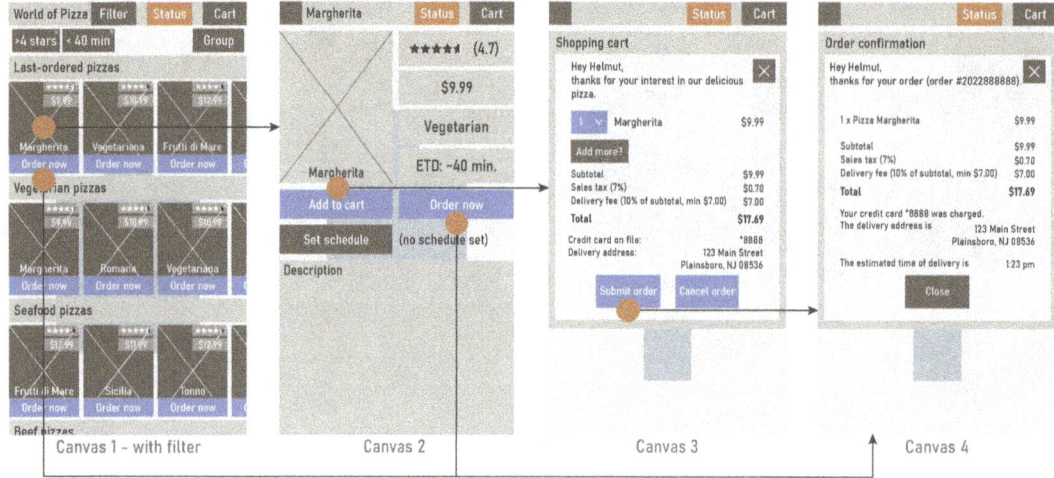

Canvas 1 – with filter   Canvas 2   Canvas 3   Canvas 4

TAS / AAS

1 / 1
(efficient)

UT 1.3 Monitor status

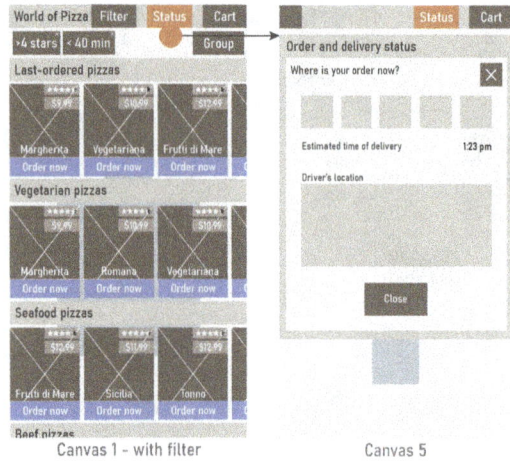

Canvas 1 – with filter   Canvas 5

1 / 1
(efficient)

UT 1.4 Tip driver

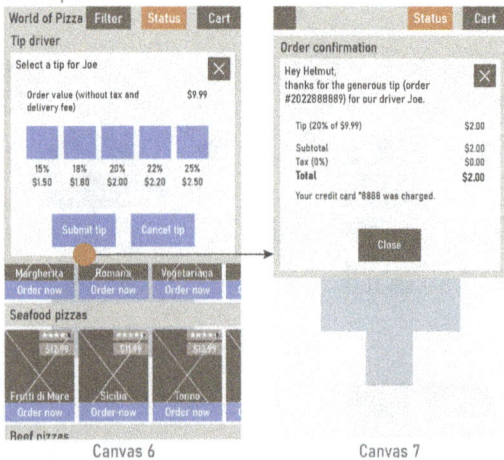

Canvas 6   Canvas 7

1 / 1
(efficient)

Figure 19.4: Sprout concept: Menu – Canvas flow

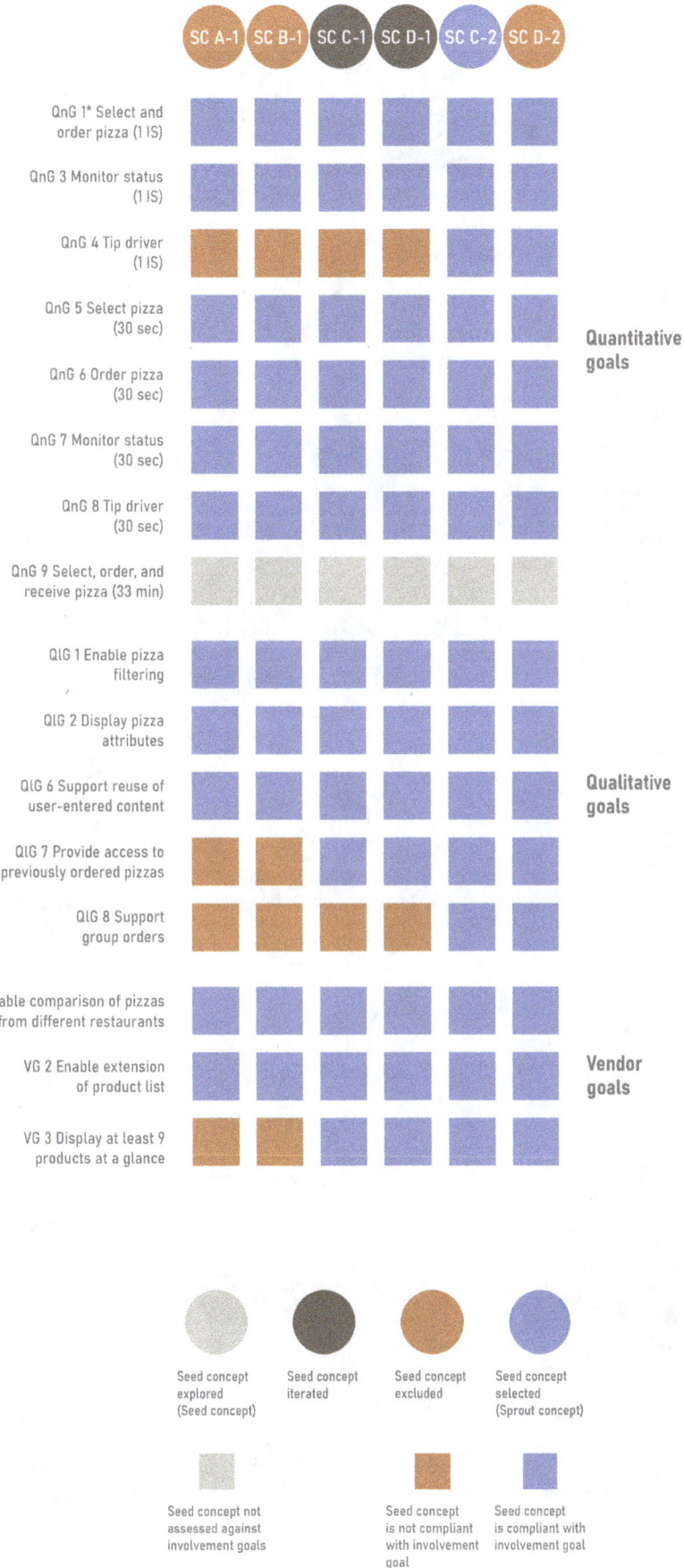

Figure 19.5: Seed concept exploration, exclusion, iteration, and selection

User involvement system as a campus metaphor

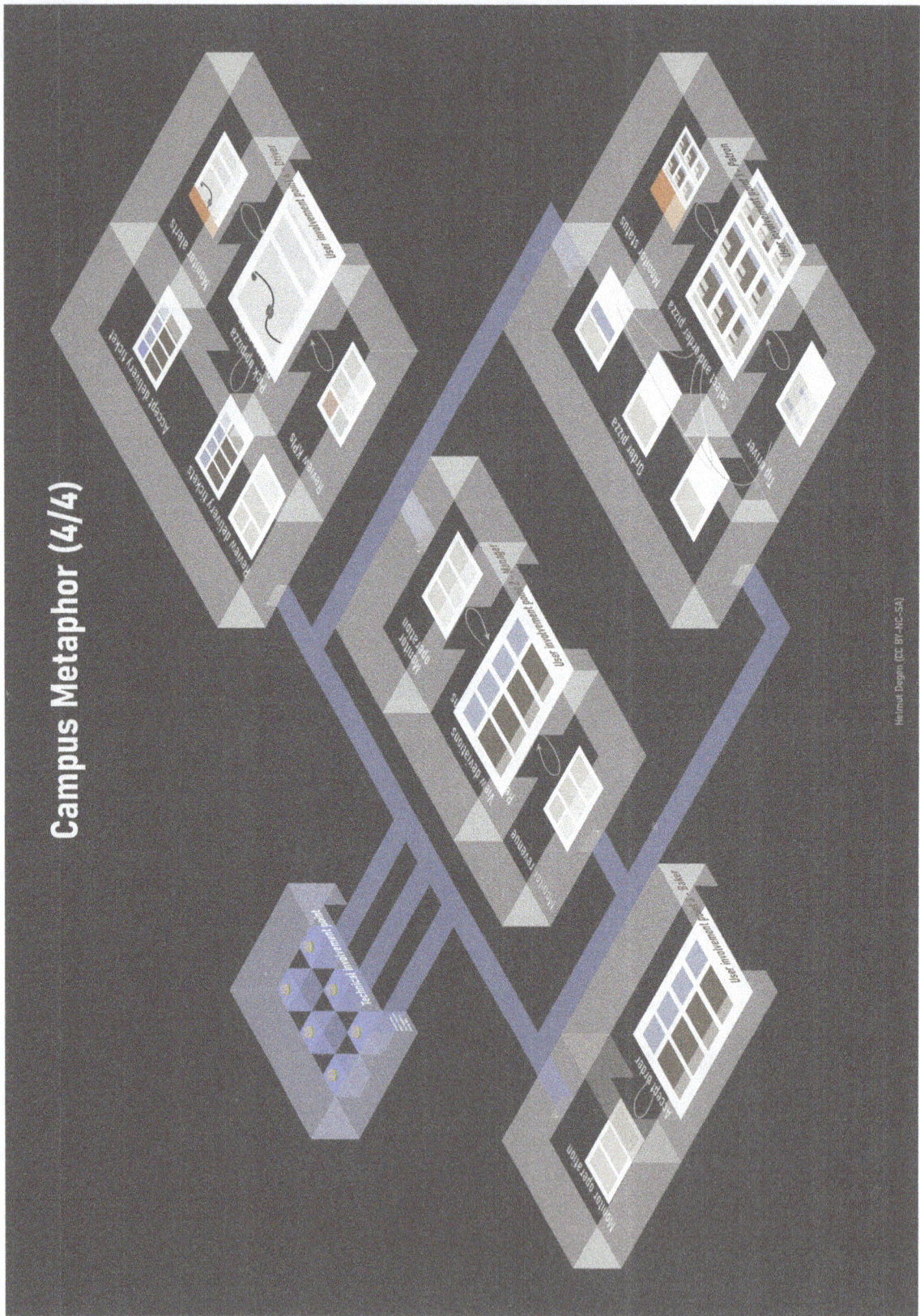

Figure 19.6: Sprout concept selected

Summary

Step 6: Select concept

◀ Go back to Step 5: Decide about Iteration

Sprout concept: Menu – Flow

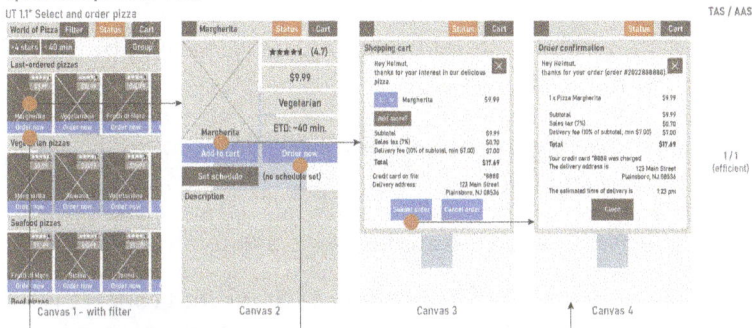

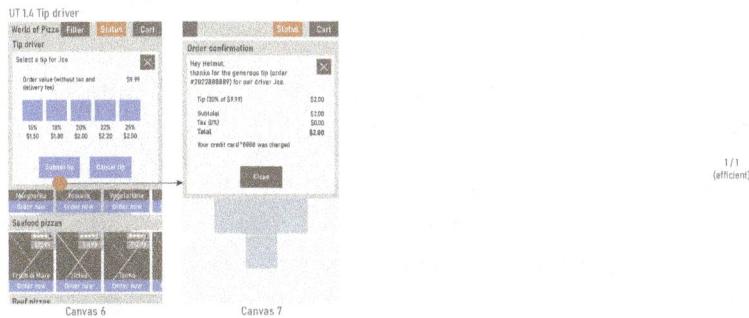

Lessons learned

If one seed concept complies with the involvement goals, it can be selected without additional analysis. If more than one seed concept complies with the involvement goals, one or more selection techniques can be applied.

The technique that allows a more qualitative comparison between seed concepts is the qualitative criteria technique. It allows you to compare differences in design choices and to weight their advantages and disadvantages.

The selection criteria should help you to select one of the seed concepts as the sprout concept.

With the proposed approach, the selected sprout concept is *explainable*, *defensible*, and *efficient*.

It is *explainable* because it complies with the involvement goals.

It is *defensible* because it was selected as the sprout concept from a number of seed concepts.

It is *efficient* because it complies with the quantitative involvement goals.

Tips and tricks

There is one last thought that is worthwhile to share here. The use of involvement goals provides an effective way to influence design choices and to select concepts. But involvement goals are an abstraction of what we are trying to achieve.

Such abstraction has its advantages and its disadvantages. The advantage is that it rationalizes design decisions.

There are two disadvantages of using involvement goals. The first is that they are not easy to extract. The abstraction requires some training and some "vision." It is not for everyone. Because of this disadvantage, sometimes involvement goals are not complete enough, and as a result they may set the design in an unintended direction, because the experience professional was not able to express a gut-feeling direction with an involvement goal. This is not unusual.

During the design iterations, we learn what is more and what is less important for a concept. If we see that the concept should take a direction that is not expressed through the existing involvement goals, we should correct that. The involvement goals, even if not directly influenced by user inputs, should be modified accordingly, so that they provide a foundation for an intended design direction.

It is at the discretion of the experience professional to push the design in a given direction. So don't be shy about using the involvement goals as a mechanism to steer the concepts into the intended direction. Keep the vendor and customer needs in mind. They still serve the purpose of a being documented rationale for design decisions, so that the selected sprout concept is still explainable, defensible, and efficient.

Exercise 3.7

Goal Select the sprout concept.

Material Seed concepts, involvement goal matrix, selection techniques

Completion criteria:

- ▶ If selection techniques were applied, document their application.
- ▶ Select the sprout concept and document the reason.

Next Steps 20

Time waits for no one
Folklore

What's next?

You've made it so far – congratulations!

In this book, we covered the first three phases of the human-centered design and development process (see Figure 20.1).

Based on my experience, what we have done so far is only about 30 percent of the entire experience effort. About 50 percent goes into the refinement and specification of the design (including visual design; all user interfaces; (interactive) mockup; visual, audio, and potentially other assets; requirements; UI specification; visual design specification) and about 20 percent goes into implementation guidance and quality assurance. Depending on the nature of the project and the application, the effort distribution can vary.

The evaluation of an application requires additional effort. It depends not necessarily on the size and complexity of a project, but on the evaluation's scope and goal, the evaluation method, the frequency of the evaluation, the selected user roles, the user tasks, the interaction devices, and the target regions.

There is more to do ...

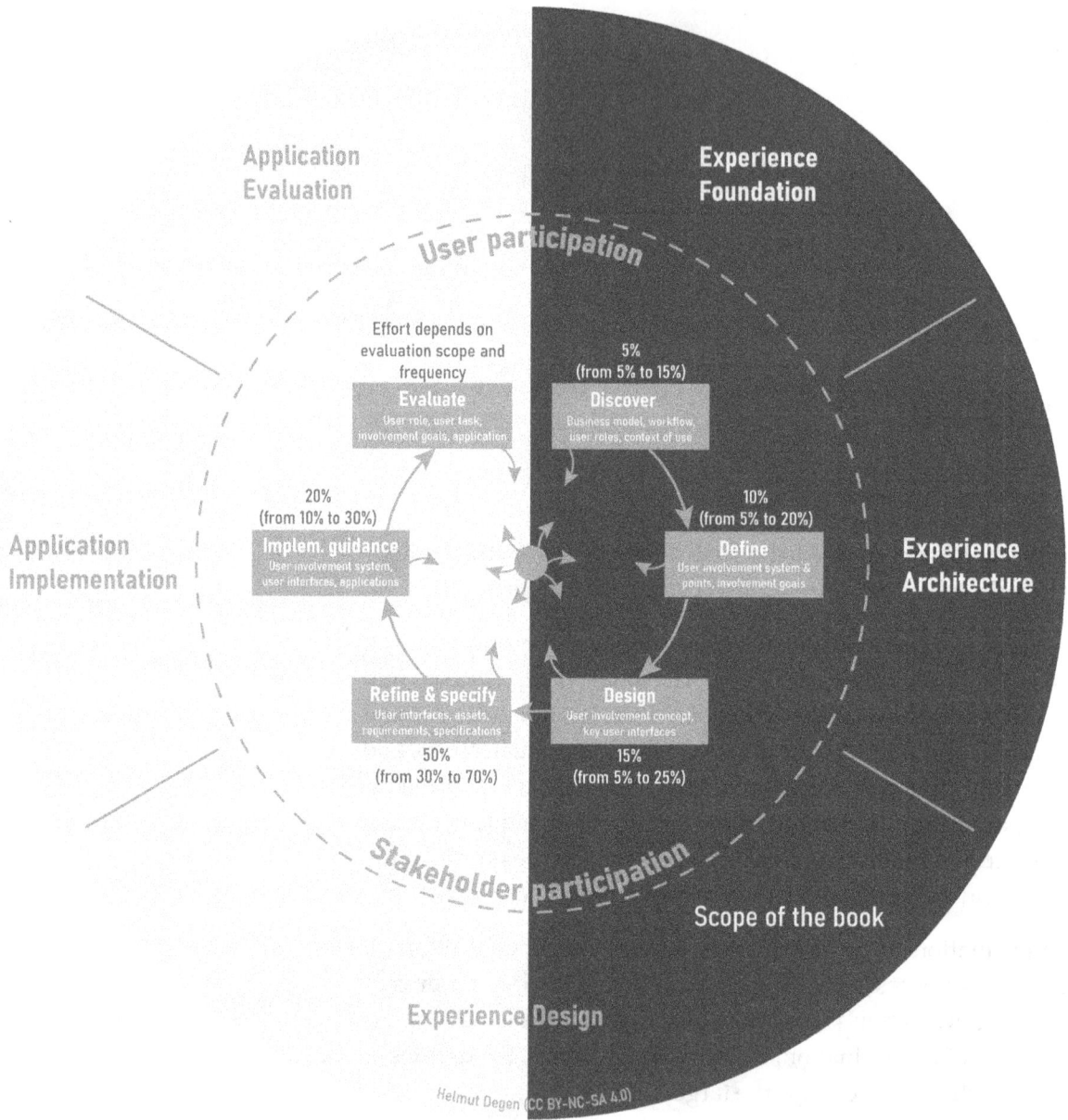

Figure 20.1: Human-centered design and development process

APPENDIX

Experience Architect | 21

Responsibilities

The responsibilities of an experience architect are to ...

- ▶ embrace the business model, so the involvement system supports or even strengthen it, to achieve *viability*. This responsibility includes letting the project sponsor know when a design contribution won't support the business model and they need to pull the plug.
- ▶ understand the domain, its terminology, processes, workflows, user roles, regulations, payment models, tools, objects, functions, and limitations, to create *value*.
- ▶ consider the long-term implications of involvement architecture and design decisions and the chosen technology, e.g., long-term use of energy, resources and maintainability, total cost of ownership, to achieve *sustainability*.
- ▶ understand the users with their mental models, preferences, behavioral patterns and limitations, to achieve *acceptability*, *effectiveness*, *memorability*, and *efficiency*.
- ▶ set the design direction and the involvement goals, to achieve effectiveness, efficiency and delight.
- ▶ define technical functions and have early discussions with the development team, to achieve *feasibility* and *efficiency*. This may include the selection of technology, the development of new technology and/or the customization of existing technology.
- ▶ guide and monitor the implementation, pixel by pixel, datum by datum, function by function, click by click, to achieve *compliance* with the involvement goals and the specification.
- ▶ talk to all project stakeholders all the time, to keep the project and its targets in balance and to manage expectations and scout for upcoming change requests.

Skills and experiences

The skill set of an experience architect should include expertise in ...

- ► using human-centered design and development processes
- ► the definition, design, and implementation of user involvement systems
- ► the definition, design, and implementation of user interfaces
- ► the definition, design, and use of design systems
- ► round-trip design (deriving design decisions from insights; explaining and defending design decisions against the design inputs)
- ► stakeholder management and expectation setting
- ► business models and value propositions
- ► business process modeling
- ► project management
- ► requirements engineering
- ► proficient in system thinking
- ► proficient in design thinking
- ► proficient in (cognitive) psychology

Design Principles | 22

A value decision is an experience decision

Which endeavor an experience architecture and design contributes to – or not – is the first decision: The "what" (application, user roles, user tasks), the "why" (needs and goals), and the "whom" (user roles) all determine the value of the experience contribution. This value decision is the first design decision.

A case needs a base

To demonstrate that a new design introduces improvements, we first need to determine a baseline of the current situation. Otherwise, we have no evidence that the new design will improve anything. For that reason, measuring the baseline is a necessity. Furthermore, the baseline provides useful guidance throughout the design process.

No design *is* design

The decision to involve the user also entails the decision not to involve the user. The decision to design something includes the decision not to design something. There isn't no design.

Goals impact the design act

Involvement goals inform the designer about desired properties of the envisioned involvement concept. They outline the border of the design space and keep the design act focused. The involvement goals make the design process itself efficient, they make design decisions explainable and defensible, and they support the creation of an efficient involvement concept.

If in doubt, leave it out

Start with the minimal number of design elements. If in doubt, leave a design element out – for now. Rather, encourage users to experiment with the concept and let *them* comment on design elements they feel are missing; they can be added later. This way, you keep the canvas clean and clutter-free.

Backward is forward

To successfully address the user's need and achieve the user's goal, the designer needs to design backward, from the needs to the design elements. Thinking backward moves the design process forward.

Iteration build a solid foundation

To achieve a high-quality experience, designers and users need to experience the concepts so they can be systematically and continuously improved. Unnecessary design elements will be removed, poorly designed elements will be improved, missing elements will be added, and misplaced elements will be reallocated. This purification process takes place through iterations. Many iterations – and time – are key ingredients in building a solid foundation.

User Involvement Metrics | 23

All metrics are composed of the user involvement metrics (UIMs) introduced in the UIM taxonomy (see Figure 23.1).

User involvement metric taxonomy

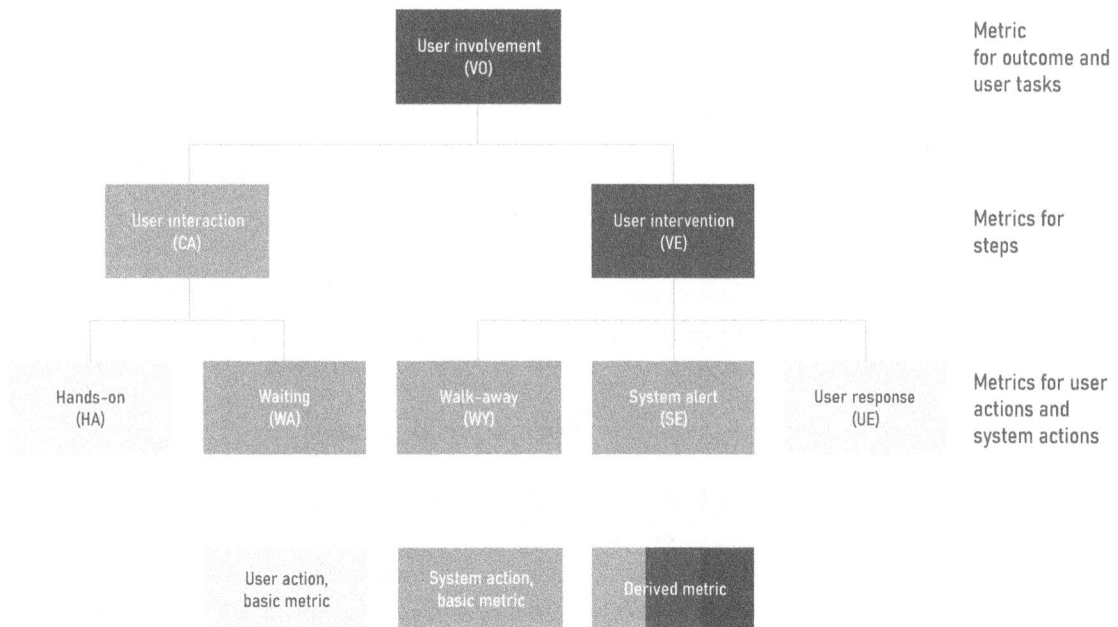

Figure 23.1: User involvement metric taxonomy

Metric syntax

The metric syntax is designed to be customizable and extendable and therefore is designed as a modular system. The metric syntax is shown in Figure 23.2.

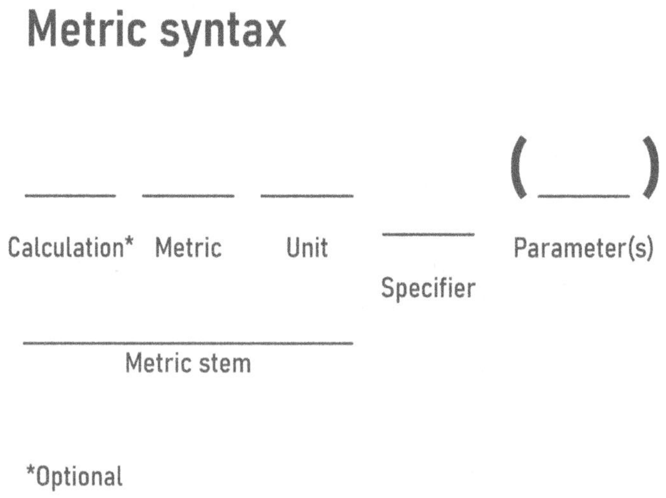

Metric syntax

Calculation* Metric Unit Specifier Parameter(s)

Metric stem

*Optional

Figure 23.2: Metric syntax

Computation

The computation element expresses the type of calculation employed. We differentiate between absolute and relative computations.

Examples of absolute computations:

- Elapsed (E): measures the time between the starting point and the completion point
- Total (T): measures the time for all user and system actions
- Net (N): measures the time for all dependent and independent user and system actions without walk-away times
- Minimum (Min): measures the minimum time of several considered times
- Mean (M): measures the mean time of several times
- Maximum (Max): measures the maximum time of several times

Examples of relative computations:

- Relative elapsed (RE): measures the relative elapsed time between two time metrics

- Relative total (RT): measures the relative total time between two time metrics
- Relative net (RN): measures the relative net time between two time metrics
- Relative minimum (RM): measures the relative minimum time between two time metrics

An example of productivity:

- Productivity (P): measures the outcome per time or frequency

Basic time and frequency metrics do not have a computational element.

Metric

The metric element reflects what involvement type is being measured. It uses the elements of the user involvement metric taxonomy.

- Hands-on (HA): Identifies a user-initiated hands-on action
- Waiting (WA): Identifies waiting, a system-initiated action
- Walk-away (WY): Identifies a walk-away, a system-initiated action
- System alert (SE): Identifies a system-alert action
- User response (UE): Identifies a user-response action
- User interaction (CA): Identifies an interaction step, consisting of one or more actions
- User intervention (VE): Identifies an intervention step, consisting of one or more actions
- User involvement (VO): Identifies one or more user tasks or a generated outcome of value
- System actions (SA): Identifies all system-initiated actions (i.e., waiting, walk-away, system alert)
- User actions (UA): Identifies all user-initiated actions (i.e., hands-on, user response)

Unit

The unit element reflects what is being measured:

- Time (T): Measures the time
- Frequency (F): Measures the frequency of an activity

Filter

The filter element identifies a subsystem of measurements considered for a calculation:

- ▶ <no filter element>: No filter
- ▶ Independent (I): Filters those actions that are not necessary to generate an outcome of value
- ▶ Dependent (D): Filters those actions that are necessary to generate an outcome of value

Activity

The parameter activity defines for which activity the time or frequency should be measured:

- ▶ Action (A): Measurement for one action or multiple actions
- ▶ Step (S): Measurement for one step or multiple steps
- ▶ Task (T): Measurement for one user task or multiple user tasks

Scope

Scope is a parameter that defines which activities are included in a user involvement measurement:

- ▶ Action (A): Measurement of one or more actions
- ▶ Step (S): Measurement of one or more steps
- ▶ Task (T): Measurement of one or more user tasks
- ▶ Outcome (O): Measurement of the generation of one or more outcomes

The typical scope value is "Outcome" (O).

The relationship between "activity" and "scope" can be illustrated with some examples. We can express that we want to know how many steps are needed (activity) to perform a certain user task (scope). Or we want to know how much time it will take for a user task (activity) to generate an outcome (scope).

Time metric examples

Here are a few time metrics examples:

- ▶ $EHAT(A, O)$: Measures the elapsed hands-on time for action A to generate an outcome of value O

- $EUET(A, O)$: Measures the elapsed user response time for action A to generate an outcome of value O
- $EVET_I(S, O)$: Measures the elapsed independent intervention time for step S to generate an outcome of value O
- $EVOT(UT_{1..n}, O)$: Measures the elapsed user involvement time for all user tasks U to generate an outcome of value O
- $EVOT(UT_{1..n}, 2 \times O)$: Measures the elapsed user involvement time for all user tasks to generate two outcomes of value O

Frequency metric examples

Here are a few frequency metrics examples:

- $HAF(A, O)$: Measures how often the hands-on action A is performed to generate the outcome of value O
- $WYF(UT_{1..n}, O)$: Measures how often a user could walk away for all user tasks to generate an outcome of value O
- $VEF_I(S_{1..n}, O)$: Measures how often all user involvement steps are performed to generate an outcome of value O
- $VOF(UT_{1..n}, O)$: Measures how often all user tasks are performed to generate an outcome of value O
- $VOF(UT_{1..n}, 2 \times O)$: Measures how often all user tasks are performed to generate two outcomes of value O

Relative time metric examples

Here are a few relative time metric examples:

- $REHAT(UT_{1..n}, O)$: Measures the relationship between the elapsed hands-on time for all user tasks U relative to the elapsed involvement time for all user tasks U to generate an outcome of value O
- $RESET(UT_{1..n}, O)$: Measures the relationship between the elapsed system response time for all user tasks U relative to the elapsed involvement time for all user tasks U to generate an outcome of value O
- $RECAT(UT_{1..n}, O)$: Measures the relationship between the elapsed interaction time for all user tasks U relative to the elapsed involvement time for all user tasks U to generate an outcome of value O
- $REVET(UT_{1..n}, O)$: Measures the relationship between the elapsed intervention time for all user tasks U relative to the elapsed involvement time for all user tasks U to generate an outcome of value O

Productivity metric examples

Here are a few productivity metric examples:

- $PEVOT(O)$: Measures the number of outcomes per elapsed involvement time for all user tasks
- $PNVOT(O)$: Measure the number of outcomes per net involvement time for all user tasks
- $PTVOT(O)$: Measure the number of outcomes per total involvement time for all user tasks
- $PVOF(O)$: Measure the number of outcomes per user involvement frequencies

Selected absolute time metrics

Basic metrics

$$HAT(A_i, O) \qquad \text{(Hands-on time of action i per outcome)}$$

$$EHAT(A,O) = \sum_{i=1}^{HAF(A,O)} HAT(A_i, O)$$
$$\text{(Elapsed hands-on time per outcome)}$$

$$WAT(A_i, O) \qquad \text{(Waiting time of action i per outcome)}$$

$$EWAT(A,O) = \sum_{i=1}^{WAF(A,O)} WAT(A_i, O)$$
$$\text{(Elapsed waiting time per outcome)}$$

$$WYT(A_i, O) \qquad \text{(Walk-away time of action i per outcome)}$$

$$EWYT(A,O) = \sum_{i=1}^{WYF(A,O)} WYT(A_i, O)$$
$$\text{(Elapsed walk-away time per outcome)}$$

$$SET(A_i, O) \qquad \text{(System alert time of action i per outcome)}$$

$$ESET(A, O) = \sum_{i=1}^{SEF(A,O)} SET(A_i, O)$$

(Elapsed system alert time per outcome)

$$UET(A_i, O) \qquad \text{(User response time of action i per outcome)}$$

$$EUET(A, O) = \sum_{i=1}^{UEF(A,O)} UET(A_i, O)$$

(Elapsed user response time per outcome)

Derived metrics

$$ECAT(S, O) = EHAT(A, O) + EWAT(A, O)$$

(Elapsed user interaction time for action per outcome)

$$ECAT_D(S, O) = EHAT_D(A, O) + EWAT_D(A, O)$$

(Elapsed user intervention time for dependent actions per outcome)

$$ECAT_I(S, O) = EHAT_I(A, O) + EWAT_I(A, O)$$

(Elapsed user intervention time for independent actions per outcome)

$$EVET(S, O) = EWYT(A, O) + ESET(A, O) + EUET(A, O)$$

(Elapsed user intervention time for action per outcome)

$$EVET_D(S, O) = EHAT_D(A, O) + EWAT_D(A, O)$$

(Elapsed user intervention time for dependent actions per outcome)

$$EVET_I(S, O) = EHAT_I(A, O) + EWAT_I(A, O)$$

(Elapsed user intervention time for independent actions per outcome)

$$TVOT(U, O) = ECAT(S, O) + EVET(S, O)$$
(Total user involvement time for action per outcome)

$$EVOT(U, O) = ECAT(S, O) + EVET_D(S, O)$$
(Elapsed user involvement time for action per outcome)

$$NVOT(U, O) = ECAT(S, O) + EVET_D(S, O) + EVET_I(S, O) - EWYT(A, O)$$
(Net user involvement time for action per outcome)

$$MVOT(A, O) = ECAT(S, O) + EUET_D(A, 0)$$
(Minimal user involvement time for action per outcome)

Aggregated metrics

$$EUAT(A, O) = EHAT(A, O) + EUET(A, O)$$
(Elapsed user action time for action per outcome)

$$EUAT_D(A, O) = EHAT_D(A, O) + EUET_D(A, O)$$
(Elapsed user action time for dependent actions per outcome)

$$EUAT_I(A, O) = EHAT_I(A, O) + EUET_I(A, O)$$
(Elapsed user action time for independent actions per outcome)

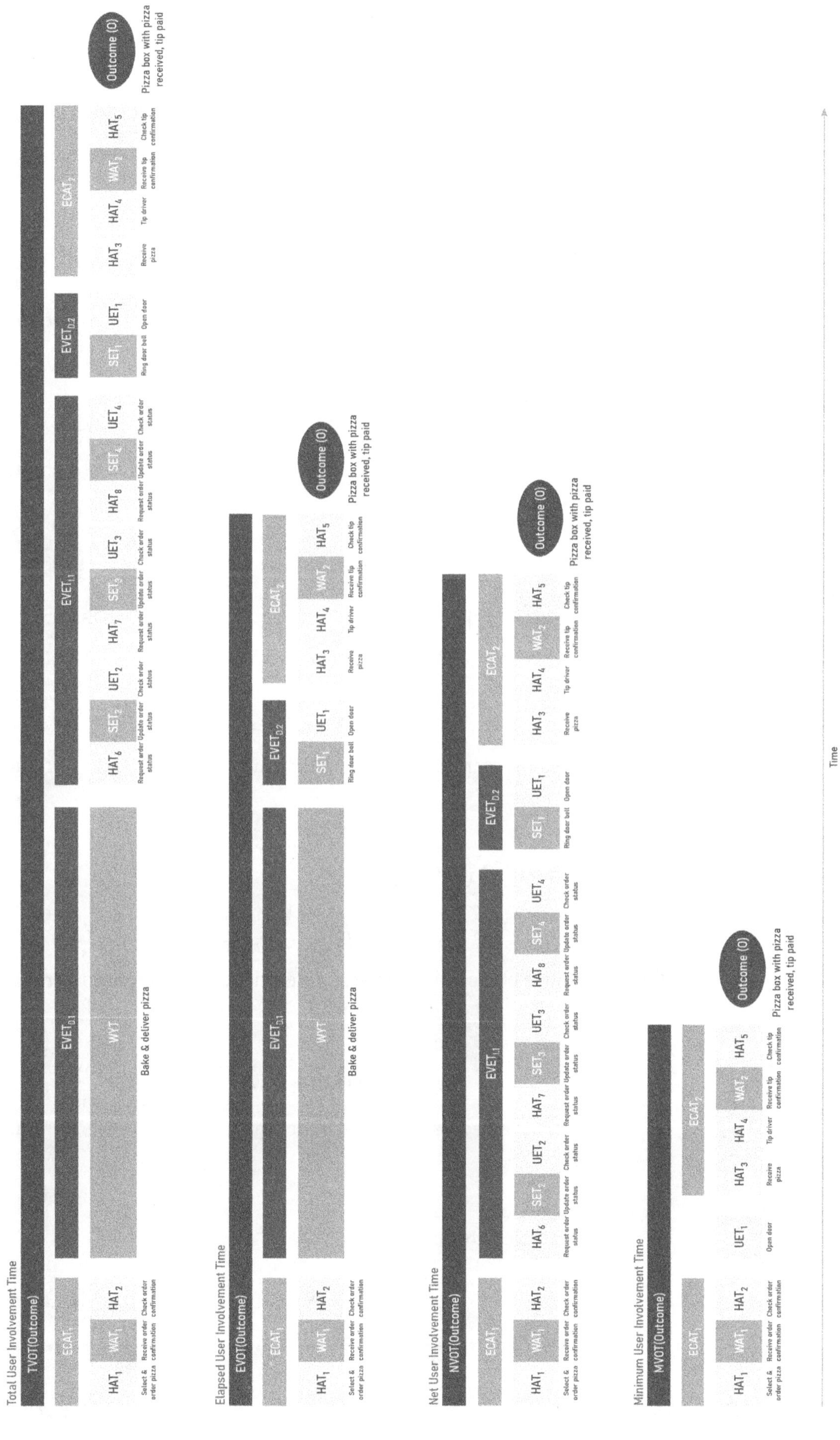

Figure 23.3: Derived time metric samples

Selected relative time metrics

Basic metrics

$$REHAT(UT_{1..n}, O) = \frac{EHAT(UT_{1..n}, O)}{EVOT(UT_{1..n}, O)}$$
(Relative elapsed hands-on time for all user tasks per outcome)

$$REWAT(UT_{1..n}, O) = \frac{EWAT(UT_{1..n}, O)}{EVOT(UT_{1..n}, O)}$$
(Relative elapsed waiting time for all user tasks per outcome)

$$REWYT(UT_{1..n}, O) = \frac{EWYT(UT_{1..n}, O)}{EVOT(UT_{1..n}, O)}$$
(Relative elapsed walk-away time for all user tasks per outcome)

$$RESET(UT_{1..n}, O) = \frac{ESET(UT_{1..n}, O)}{EVOT(UT_{1..n}, O)}$$
(Relative elapsed system alert time for all user tasks per outcome)

$$REUET(A, O) = \frac{EUET(A, O)}{EVOT(A, O)}$$
(Relative elapsed user response time for all user tasks per outcome)

Derived metrics

$$RECAT(UT_{1..n}, O) = \frac{ECAT(UT_{1..n}, O)}{EVOT(UT_{1..n}, O)}$$
(Relative elapsed user interaction time for all user tasks per outcome)

$$REVET(UT_{1..n}, O) = \frac{EVET(UT_{1..n}, O)}{EVOT(UT_{1..n}, O)}$$
(Relative elapsed user intervention time for all user tasks per outcome)

Aggregated metrics

$$REUAT(UT_{1..n}, O) = \frac{EUAT(UT_{1..n}, O)}{EVOT(UT_{1..n}, O)}$$
(Relative elapsed user action time for all user tasks per outcome)

$$RESAT(UT_{1..n}, O) = \frac{ESAT(UT_{1..n}, O)}{EVOT(UT_{1..n}, O)}$$

(Relative elapsed system action time for all user tasks per outcome)

Selected absolute frequency metrics

Basic metrics

$HAF(A, O)$ (Hands-on frequency for action per outcome)

$HAF_D(A, O)$

(Hands-on frequency for dependent actions per outcome)

$HAF_I(A, O)$

(Hands-on frequency for independent actions per outcome)

$WAF(A, O)$ (Waiting frequency for action per outcome)

$WAF_D(A, O)$

(Waiting frequency for dependent actions per outcome)

$WAF_I(A, O)$

(Waiting frequency for independent actions per outcome)

$WYF(A, O)$ (Walk-away frequency for action per outcome)

$WYF_D(A, O)$

(Walk-away frequency for dependent actions per outcome)

$$WYF_I(A, O)$$
(Walk-away frequency for independent actions per outcome)

$$SEF(A, O) \quad \text{(System alert frequency for action per outcome)}$$

$$SEF_D(A, O)$$
(System alert frequency for dependent actions per outcome)

$$SEF_I(A, O)$$
(System alert frequency for independent actions per outcome)

$$UEF(A, O) \quad \text{(User response frequency for action per outcome)}$$

$$UEF_D(A, O)$$
(User response frequency for dependent actions per outcome)

$$UEF_I(A, O)$$
(User response frequency for independent actions per outcome)

Derived metrics

$$CAF(A, O) = HAF(A, O) + WAF(A, O)$$
(User interaction frequency for action per outcome)

$$CAF_D(A, O) = HAF_D(A, O) + WAF_D(A, O)$$
(User interaction frequency for dependent actions per outcome)

$$CAF_I(S, O) = HAF_I(S, O) + WAF_I(S, O)$$
(User interaction frequency for independent actions per outcome)

$$VEF(A, O) = WYF(A, O) + SEF(A, O) + UEF(A, O)$$
(User intervention frequency for action per outcome)

Aggregated metrics

$$UAF(A, O) = HAF(A, O) + UEF(A, O)$$
(User action frequency for action per outcome)

$$UAF_D(A, O) = HAF_D(A, O) + UEF_D(A, O)$$
(User action frequency for dependent actions per outcome)

$$UAF_I(A, O) = HAF_I(A, O) + UEF_I(A, O)$$
(User action frequency for independent actions per outcome)

$$SAF(A, O) = WAF(A, O) + WYF(A, O) + SEF(A, O)$$
(System action frequency for action per outcome)

$$SAF_D(A, O) = WAF_D(A, O) + WYF_D(A, O) + SEF_D(A, O)$$
(System action frequency for dependent actions per outcome)

$$SAF_I(A, O) = WAF_I(A, O) + WYF_I(A, O) + SEF(_I A, O)$$
(System action frequency for independent actions per outcome)

Selected relative frequency metrics

Basic metrics for actions

$$RHAF(A, O) = \frac{HAF(A, O)}{VOF(A, O)}$$
(Elapsed relative hands-on frequency for action per outcome)

$$RHAF_D(A, O) = \frac{HAF_D(A, O)}{VOF(A, O)}$$

(Elapsed relative hands-on frequency for dependent actions per outcome)

$$RHAF_I(A, O) = \frac{HAF_I(A, O)}{VOF(A, O)}$$

(Elapsed relative hands-on frequency for independent actions per outcome)

$$RWAF(A, O) = \frac{WAF(A, O)}{VOF(A, O)}$$

(Elapsed relative waiting frequency for action per outcome)

$$RWAF_D(A, O) = \frac{WAF_D(A, O)}{VOF(A, O)}$$

(Elapsed relative waiting frequency for dependent actions per outcome)

$$RWAF_I(A, O) = \frac{WAF_I(A, O)}{VOF(A, O)}$$

(Elapsed relative waiting frequency for independent actions per outcome)

$$RWYF(A, O) = \frac{WYF(A, O)}{VOF(A, O)}$$

(Elapsed relative walk-away frequency for action per outcome)

$$RWYF_D(A, O) = \frac{WYF_D(A, O)}{VOF(A, O)}$$

(Elapsed relative walk-away frequency for dependent actions per outcome)

$$RWYF_I(A, O) = \frac{WYF_I(A, O)}{VOF(A, O)}$$

(Elapsed relative walk-away frequency for independent actions per outcome)

$$RSEF(A, O) = \frac{SEF(A, O)}{VOF(A, O)}$$

(Elapsed relative system alert frequency for action per outcome)

$$RSEF_D(A,O) = \frac{SEF_D(A,O)}{VOF(A,O)}$$

(Elapsed relative system alert frequency for dependent actions per outcome)

$$RSEF_I(A,O) = \frac{SEF_I(A,O)}{VOF(A,O)}$$

(Elapsed relative system alert frequency for independent actions per outcome)

$$RUEF(A,O) = \frac{UEF(A,O)}{VOF(A,O)}$$

(Elapsed relative user response frequency for action per outcome)

$$RUEF_D(A,O) = \frac{UEF_D(A,O)}{VOF(A,O)}$$

(Elapsed relative system alert frequency for dependent actions per outcome)

$$RUEF_I(A,O) = \frac{UEF_I(A,O)}{VOF(A,O)}$$

(Elapsed relative system alert frequency for independent actions per outcome)

Derived metrics for steps

$$RCAF(S,O) = \frac{CAF(S,O)}{VOF(S,O)}$$

(Elapsed relative user interaction frequency for steps per outcome)

$$RCAF_D(S,O) = \frac{CAF_D(S,O)}{VOF(S,O)}$$

(Elapsed relative user interaction frequency for dependent steps per outcome)

$$RCAF_I(S,O) = \frac{CAF_I(S,O)}{VOF(S,O)}$$

(Elapsed relative user interaction frequency for independent steps per outcome)

$$RVEF(S,O) = \frac{VEF(S,O)}{VOF(S,O)}$$

(Elapsed relative user intervention frequency for steps per outcome)

$$RVEF_D(S,O) = \frac{VEF_D(S,O)}{VOF(S,O)}$$

(Elapsed relative user intervention frequency for dependent steps per outcome)

$$RVEF_I(S,O) = \frac{VEF_I(S,O)}{VOF(S,O)}$$

(Elapsed relative user intervention frequency for independent steps per outcome)

Derived metrics for user tasks

$$RCAF(UT_{1..n},O) = \frac{CAF(UT_{1..n},O)}{VOF(UT_{1..n},O)}$$

(Elapsed relative user interaction frequency for all user tasks per outcome)

$$RVEF(UT_{1..n},O) = \frac{VEF(UT_{1..n},O)}{VOF(UT_{1..n},O)}$$

(Elapsed relative user intervention frequency for all user tasks per outcome)

Aggregated metrics for actions

$$RUAF(A,O) = \frac{UAF(A,O)}{VOF(A,O)}$$

(Elapsed relative user action frequency for actions per outcome)

$$RSAF(A,O) = \frac{SAF(A,O)}{VOF(A,O)}$$

(Elapsed relative system action frequency for actions per outcome)

$$RSAF_D(A,O) = \frac{SAF_D(A,O)}{VOF(A,O)}$$

(Elapsed relative system action frequency for dependent actions per outcome)

$$RSAF_I(A,O) = \frac{SAF_I(A,O)}{VOF(A,O)}$$

(Elapsed relative system action frequency for independent actions per outcome)

Selected productivity metrics

Derived productivity - time metrics for all user tasks

$$PEVOT(UT_{1..n}, O) = \frac{O}{EVOT(UT1..n, O)}$$
(Number of outcomes per elapsed user involvement time)

$$PTVOT(UT_{1..n}, O) = \frac{O}{TVOT(UT_{1..n}, O)}$$
(Number of outcomes per total user involvement time)

$$PNVOT(UT_{1..n}, O) = \frac{O}{NVOT(UT_{1..n}, O)}$$
(Number of outcomes per net user involvement time)

Derived productivity - frequency metrics

$$PVOF(A_{1..n}, O) = \frac{O}{VOF(A_{1..n}, O)}$$
(Number of outcomes per action frequency)

$$PVOF(S_{1..n}, O) = \frac{O}{VOF(S_{1..n}, O)}$$
(Number of outcomes per step frequency)

$$PVOF(UT_{1..n}, O) = \frac{O}{VOF(UT_{1..n}, O)}$$
(Number of outcomes per user task frequency)

Selected savings metrics

Derived estimated times savings

$$EATS(UT_{1..n}, O) = AAT(UT_{1..n}, O) - AAT(UT_{1..n}, O)$$
(Absolute time saving)

$$ERTS(UT_{1..n}, O) = \frac{AAT(UT_{1..n}, O) - AAT(UT_{1..n}, O)}{AAT(UT_{1..n}, O)}$$

(Relative time saving)

Derived estimated frequency savings

$$EAFS(UT_{1..n}, O) = AAF(UT_{1..n}, O) - AAF(UT_{1..n}, O)$$

(Absolute frequency saving)

$$ERFS(UT_{1..n}, O) = \frac{AAF(UT_{1..n}, O) - AAF(UT_{1..n}, O)}{AAF(UT_{1..n}, O)}$$

(Relative frequency saving)

Bibliography

Here are the references in citation order.

[1] Wikipedia. *Digital Ecosystem*. accessed 8. Feb. 2020. URL: https://en.wikipedia.org/wiki/Digital_ecosystem (cited on page 2).

[2] Wikipedia. *Critical Path Method*. accessed 22. Jan 2022. URL: https://en.wikipedia.org/wiki/Critical_path_method (cited on page 2).

[3] Larry LeRoy Constantine and Lucy A. D. Lockwood. *Software for Use: A Practical Guide to the Models and Methods of Usage-Centered Design*. Pearson Education, 1999 (cited on pages 2, 285).

[4] Alan Cooper et al. *About Face: The Essential of Interaction Design*. 4th ed. John Wiley and Sons, Ltd, Apr. 2014 (cited on page 2).

[5] Donald A. Norman and Stephen W. Draper. *User Centered System Design: New Perspectives on Human-Computer Interaction*. Hillsdale, NJ, USA: Taylor & Francis, 1986 (cited on pages 2, 204).

[6] Donald A. Norman. *The Design of Everyday Things*. Revised and expanded. New York City, NY, USA: Basic Books, 2013 (cited on pages 2, 152).

[7] Jakob Nielsen. *Usability Engineering*. San Francisco, CA, USA: Morgan Kaufmann Publishers Inc., 1994 (cited on page 2).

[8] Ben Shneiderman et al. *Designing the User Interface: Strategies for Effective Human-Computer Interaction*. 6th ed. Pearson, 2016 (cited on page 2).

[9] Louis Rosenfeld, Peter Morville, and Jorge Arango. *Information Architecture: For the Web and Beyond*. 4th ed. O'Reilly Media, Inc., 2015 (cited on page 2).

[10] Edward Rolf Tufte. *Envisioning Information*. 1st ed. Cheshire, CT, USA: Graphics Press, May 1990 (cited on page 7).

[11] Edward Rolf Tufte. *Visual Explanations*. 2nd ed. Cheshire, CT, USA: Graphics Press, 2001 (cited on page 7).

[12] Edward Rolf Tufte. *The Visual Display of Quantitative Information*. 2nd ed. Cheshire, CT, USA: Graphics Press, 2001 (cited on page 7).

[13] Robert Glatter. *Good Design Is Good Business*. accessed 8. Feb. 2020. 2012. URL: https://www.ibm.com/ibm/history/ibm100/us/en/icons/gooddesign/ (cited on page 11).

[14] Benedict Sheppard et al. *The business value of design*. Tech. rep. accessed 29. Jan. 2020. McKinsey & Company, Oct. 2018 (cited on pages 11, 12).

[15] Randolph G. Bias and Deborah J. Mayhew. *Cost-Justifying Usability: An Update for the Internet Age*. 2nd ed. San Francisco, CA, USA: Morgan Kaufmann Publishers Inc., 2005 (cited on pages 12, 15).

[16] InVision. *The new design frontier. The widest ranging report to date examining design's impact on business*. Tech. rep. accessed 9. Feb. 2020. Apr. 2019 (cited on pages 12–14).

[17] Jakob Nielsen. *Corporate UX Maturity: Stages 1-4*. accessed 12. Feb. 2020. Apr. 2006. URL: https://www.nngroup.com/articles/ux-maturity-stages-1-4/ (cited on page 14).

[18] Jakob Nielsen. *Corporate UX Maturity: Stages 5-8*. accessed 12. Feb. 2020. Apr. 2006. URL: https://www.nngroup.com/articles/ux-maturity-stages-5-8/ (cited on page 14).

[19] Clare-Marie Karat. 'Cost-benefit analysis of iterative usability testing'. In: *Proceedings of the IFIP TC13 Third Interational Conference on Human-Computer Interaction*. North-Holland Publishing Co. 1990, pp. 351–356 (cited on page 15).

[20] J. Black. 'Usability is next to profitability'. In: *Business week online* (Dec. 2002) (cited on page 15).

[21] Frog Design. *General Electrics: Supporting an Industrial Giant*. Couldn't find the original source. 2014. URL: https://www.frogdesign.com/work/ge-digital-transformation (cited on page 15).

[22] William J. Baumol, Edward N. Wolff, and Sue Ann Batey Blackman. *Productivity and American Leadership: The Long View*. Cambridge, MA, USA: MIT Press, Oct. 1991 (cited on page 15).

[23] ISO 9241-11:2018(E). *Ergonomics – Ergonomic requirements for office work with visual display terminals (VDTs) – Part 11: Usability: Definitions and concepts*. Standard. Geneva, CH: International Organization for Standardization, Mar. 2018 (cited on pages 15, 190, 288, 615, 616).

[24] Steven C. Seow. *Designing and Engineering Time: The Psychology of Time Perception in Software*. 1st ed. Addison-Wesley Professional, 2008 (cited on page 16).

[25] Rina A. Doherty and Paul Sorenson. 'Keeping Users in the Flow: Mapping System Responsiveness with User Experience'. In: *Procedia Manufacturing* 3 (2015). 6th International Conference on Applied Human Factors and Ergonomics (AHFE 2015) and the Affiliated Conferences, AHFE 2015, pp. 4384–4391. DOI: https://doi.org/10.1016/j.promfg.2015.07.436 (cited on page 17).

[26] Mihaly Csikszentmihalyi. *Flow*. New York City, NY, USA: Harper Collins, 2008 (cited on pages 17, 18).

[27] Jim Dabrowski and Ethan V. Munson. '40 years of searching for the best computer system response time'. In: *Interacting with Computers* 23.5 (June 2011), pp. 555–564. DOI: 10.1016/j.intcom.2011.05.008 (cited on page 17).

[28] Jonathan Deber et al. 'How Much Faster is Fast Enough? User Perception of Latency & Latency Improvements in Direct and Indirect Touch'. In: *Proceedings of the 33rd Annual ACM Conference on Human Factors in Computing Systems*. CHI'15. Seoul, Republic of Korea: Association for Computing Machinery, 2015, pp. 1827–1836. DOI: 10.1145/2702123.2702300 (cited on page 18).

[29] A. J. Thadhani. 'Factors Affecting Programmer Productivity during Application Development'. In: *IBM Syst. J.* 23.1 (Mar. 1984), pp. 19–35. DOI: 10.1147/sj.231.0019 (cited on page 18).

[30] T. Goodman and R. Spence. 'The Effect of System Response Time on Interactive Computer Aided Problem Solving'. In: *SIGGRAPH Comput. Graph.* 12.3 (Aug. 1978), pp. 100–104. DOI: 10.1145/965139.807378 (cited on page 18).

[31] Raymond E. Barber and Henry C. Lucas. 'System Response Time Operator Productivity, and Job Satisfaction'. In: *Commun. ACM* 26.11 (Nov. 1983), pp. 972–986. DOI: 10.1145/182.358464 (cited on page 18).

[32] Jan L. Guynes. 'Impact of System Response Time on State Anxiety'. In: *Commun. ACM* 31.3 (Mar. 1988), pp. 342–347. DOI: 10.1145/42392.42402 (cited on page 18).

[33] Michael Trimmel, Monika Meixner-Pendleton, and Sandra Haring. 'Stress Response Caused by System Response Time when Searching for Information on the Internet'. In: *Human Factors* 45.4 (Dec. 2003). PMID: 15055458, pp. 615–622. DOI: 10.1518/hfes.45.4.615.27084 (cited on page 18).

[34] Glen Anderson, Rina Doherty, and Eric Baugh. 'Diminishing Returns? Revisiting Perception of Computing Performance'. In: *Proceedings of the SIGCHI Conference on Human Factors in Computing Systems*. CHI'11. Vancouver, BC, Canada: Association for Computing Machinery, 2011, pp. 2703–2706. DOI: 10.1145/1978942.1979338 (cited on page 18).

[35] Bojan Pavic, Chris Anstey, and Jeremy Wagner. *Why does speed matter?* Accessed 2. Jan. 2022. July 2020. URL: https://developers.google.com/web/fundamentals/performance/why-performance-matters (cited on page 18).

[36] Sam Ratnam et al. 'Workflow and Maintenance Characteristics of Five Automated Laboratory Instruments for the Diagnosis of Sexually Transmitted Infections'. In: *Journal of Clinical Microbiology* 52.7 (July 2014), pp. 2299–2304. DOI: 10.1128/JCM.03549-13 (cited on pages 19, 80, 100).

[37] Insook Cho et al. 'Comparing usability testing outcomes and functions of six electronic nursing record systems'. In: *International Journal of Medical Informatics* 88 (Apr. 2016), pp. 78–85 (cited on page 19).

[38] Peter Ramsey. *Opening twelve bank accounts*. accessed 8. Jun. 2020. June 2020. URL: https://builtformars.com/case-studies/opening-12-bank-accounts (cited on page 19).

[39] Erietta Sapounakis. *Efficiency. Customer efficiency directly correlates to satisfaction and advocacy, and is the most accurate indicator of future behavior.* accessed 2. Feb. 2020. Aug. 2011. URL: https://uxmag.com/articles/efficiency (cited on pages 19, 151).

[40] Matthew Dixon, Karen Freeman, and Nicholas Toman. 'Stop Trying to Delight Your Customers'. In: *Harvard Business Review* (July 2010). Accessed 28. Jun. 2020 (cited on page 20).

[41] Zaha Hadid. *Beijing Daxing International Airport*. accessed 16. Jan. 2020. Sept. 2019. URL: https://www.zaha-hadid.com/architecture/beijing-new-airport-terminal-building/ (cited on page 22).

[42] Wikipedia. *Moore's Law*. accessed 22. Jan. 2022. URL: https://en.wikipedia.org/wiki/Moores_law (cited on page 24).

[43] Gordon E. Moore. 'Cramming more components onto integrated circuits, ' in: *Electronics. Reprinted from Electronics* 38.8 (Apr. 1965), pp. 114–117. DOI: 10.1109/N-SSC.2006.4785860 (cited on page 24).

[44] Vikas Kumar and Gabriel Ogunmola. 'Web Analytics for Knowledge Creation: A Systematic Review of Tools, Techniques, and Practices'. In: *International Journal of Cyber Behavior, Psychology and Learning* 10 (1 Dec. 2019), pp. 1–14. DOI: 10.4018/IJCBPL.2020010101 (cited on page 25).

[45] Ivan Bekavac and Daniela Garbin Praničević. 'Web analytics tools and web metrics tools: An overview and comparative analysis'. In: *Croatian Operational Research Review* 6 (2 Oct. 2015), pp. 373–386. DOI: 10.17535/crorr.2015.0029 (cited on page 25).

[46] Nivia Cruz Quental et al. 'Automating GUI Response Time Measurements in Mobile and Web Applications'. In: *Proceedings of the 14th International Workshop on Automation of Software Test*. AST'19. Montreal, Quebec, Canada: IEEE Press, 2019, pp. 35–41. DOI: 10.1109/AST.2019.00011 (cited on page 25).

[47] Zhen Ming Jiang and Ahmed E. Hassan. 'A Survey on Load Testing of Large-Scale Software Systems'. In: *IEEE Transactions on Software Engineering* 41.11 (2015), pp. 1091–1118. DOI: 10.1109/TSE.2015.2445340 (cited on page 25).

[48] Ian Gorton. *Essential Software Architecture*. 2nd ed. Springer Publishing Company, Incorporated, 2011 (cited on page 25).

[49] HTTP Archive. *Loading Speed*. accessed 5. May 2022. May 2022. URL: https://httparchive.org/reports/loading-speed (cited on page 25).

[50] Jeffrey Rubin and Dana Chisnell. *Handbook of Usability Testing: How to Plan, Design, and Conduct Effective Tests*. 2nd ed. Indianapolis, IN, USA: John Wiley and Sons, Ltd, May 2008 (cited on pages 25, 76).

[51] William Craig Tomlin. *The Principles of Scientific Management. Combining Behavioral UX and Usability Testing Data to Optimize Websites*. 1st ed. New York City, NY, USA: Apress Media, LLC, 2018 (cited on page 25).

[52] ISO/IEC 25062:2006(E). *Software engineering – Software product Quality Requirements and Evaluation (SQuaRE) – Common Industry Format (CIF) for usability test reports*. Standard. Geneva, CH: International Organization for Standardization, Apr. 2006 (cited on pages 25, 76).

[53] Aga Bojko. *Eye Tracking the User Experience: A Practical Guide to Research*. 1st ed. Brooklyn, NY, USA: Rosenfeld Media Inc., Dec. 2013 (cited on pages 25, 453).

[54] Stuart K. Card, Allen Newell, and Thomas P. Moran. *The Psychology of Human-Computer Interaction*. 1st ed. Mahwah, NJ, USA: L. Erlbaum Associates Inc., 1983 (cited on pages 25, 76, 152).

[55] Albrecht Schmidt and Thomas Herrmann. 'Intervention User Interfaces: A New Interaction Paradigm for Automated Systems'. In: *Interactions* 24.5 (Aug. 2017), pp. 40–45. DOI: 10.1145/3121357 (cited on pages 26, 27, 206, 617).

[56] Thomas Herrmann, Christopher Lentzsch, and Martin Degeling. 'Intervention and EUD'. In: *End-User Development*. Ed. by Alessio Malizia et al. Cham: Springer International Publishing, 2019, pp. 67–82. DOI: 10.1007/978-3-030-24781-2_5 (cited on pages 26, 206).

[57] Wikipedia. *Interaction*. accessed 6. Nov. 2021. URL: https://en.wikipedia.org/wiki/Interaction (cited on pages 26, 616).

[58] Philip N. Johnson-Laird. *Mental Models: Towards a Cognitive Science of Language, Inference, and Consciousness*. USA: Harvard University Press, 1986 (cited on pages 27, 152).

[59] Jörn Hurtienne. 'How Cognitive Linguistics Inspires HCI: Image Schemas and Image-Schematic Metaphors'. In: *International Journal of Human-Computer Interaction* 33.1 (2017), pp. 1–20. DOI: 10.1080/10447318.2016.1232227 (cited on page 27).

[60] Andy Dearden, Michael Harrison, and Peter Wright. 'Allocation of function: scenarios, context and the economics of effort'. In: *International Journal of Computer-Human Studies* 52.2 (Feb. 2000), pp. 289–318. DOI: 10.1006/ijhc.1999.0290 (cited on pages 34, 320).

[61] Mica R. Endsley and Esin O. Kiris. 'The Out-of-the-Loop Performance Problem and Level of Control in Automation'. In: *Human Factors* 37.2 (Feb. 1995), pp. 381–394. DOI: 10.1518/001872095779064555 (cited on page 34).

[62] Mica R. Endsley and David B. Kaber. 'Level of automation effects on performance, situation awareness and workload in a dynamic control task'. In: *Ergonomics* 42.3 (1999). PMID: 10048306, pp. 462–492. DOI: 10.1080/001401399185595 (cited on page 34).

[63] Christian P. Janssen et al. 'History and future of human-automation interaction'. In: *International Journal of Human-Computer Studies* 131.November 2019 (Nov. 2019). 50 years of the International Journal of Human-Computer Studies. Reflections on the past, present and future of human-centred technologies, pp. 99–107. DOI: https://doi.org/10.1016/j.ijhcs.2019.05.006 (cited on pages 34, 320).

[64] Linda Onnasch et al. 'Human Performance Consequences of Stages and Levels of Automation: An Integrated Meta-Analysis'. In: *Human Factors* 56.3 (2014). PMID: 24930170, pp. 476–488. DOI: 10.1177/0018720813501549 (cited on page 34).

[65] Raja Parasuraman, Thomas B. Sheridan, and Christopher D. Wickens. 'A model for types and levels of human interaction with automation'. In: *IEEE Transactions on Systems, Man, and Cybernetics - Part A: Systems and Humans* 30.3 (May 2000), pp. 286–297. DOI: 10.1109/3468.844354 (cited on page 34).

[66] Thomas B. Sheridan and Raja Parasuraman. 'Human-Automation Interaction'. In: *Reviews of Human Factors and Ergonomics* 1.1 (2005), pp. 89–129. DOI: 10.1518/155723405783703082 (cited on page 34).

[67] Christopher D. Wickens Wickens. 'Situation Awareness and Workload in Aviation'. In: *Current Directions in Psychological Science* 11.4 (2002), pp. 128–133. DOI: 10.1111/1467-8721.00184 (cited on page 34).

[68] Stavroula Ntoa et al. 'User Experience Evaluation in Intelligent Environments: A Comprehensive Framework'. In: *Technologies* 9.2 (2021). DOI: 10.3390/technologies9020041 (cited on page 34).

[69] Matt Turek. *Explainable Artificial Intelligence (XAI)*. Accessed 3. Mar 2020. Aug. 2016. URL: https://www.darpa.mil/program/explainable-artificial-intelligence (cited on page 34).

[70] Amina Adadi and Mohammed Berrada. 'Peeking Inside the Black-Box: A Survey on Explainable Artificial Intelligence (XAI)'. In: *IEEE Access* 6 (2018), pp. 52138–52160. DOI: 10.1109/ACCESS.2018.2870052 (cited on pages 34, 209).

[71] Juan M. Ferreira et al. 'Impact of usability mechanisms: An experiment on efficiency, effectiveness and user satisfaction'. In: *Information and Software Technology* 117 (2020), p. 106195. DOI: https://doi.org/10.1016/j.infsof.2019.106195 (cited on pages 34, 209).

[72] Riccardo Guidotti et al. 'A Survey of Methods for Explaining Black Box Models'. In: *ACM Comput. Surv.* 51.5 (Aug. 2018), pp. 1–42. DOI: 10.1145/3236009 (cited on pages 34, 209).

[73] Tim Miller. 'Explanation in Artificial Intelligence: Insights from the Social Sciences'. In: *Artif. Intell.* 267 (2019), pp. 1–38 (cited on pages 34, 209).

[74] Alejandro Barredo Arrieta et al. 'Explainable Artificial Intelligence (XAI): Concepts, taxonomies, opportunities and challenges toward responsible AI'. In: *Information Fusion* 58 (2020), pp. 82–115. DOI: https://doi.org/10.1016/j.inffus.2019.12.012 (cited on pages 34, 209).

[75] Donghee Shin. 'The effects of explainability and causability on perception, trust, and acceptance: Implications for explainable AI'. In: *International Journal of Human-Computer Studies* 146 (2021), p. 102551. DOI: https://doi.org/10.1016/j.ijhcs.2020.102551 (cited on pages 34, 209).

[76] Erico Tjoa and Cuntai Guan. 'A Survey on Explainable Artificial Intelligence (XAI): Toward Medical XAI'. In: *IEEE Transactions on Neural Networks and Learning Systems* PP (Sept. 2020). DOI: 10.1109/TNNLS.2020.3027314 (cited on pages 34, 209).

[77] Sina Mohseni, Niloofar Zarei, and Eric D. Ragan. *A Multidisciplinary Survey and Framework for Design and Evaluation of Explainable AI Systems.* 2020. URL: https://arxiv.org/abs/1811.11839 (cited on pages 34, 209).

[78] Roberto Confalonieri et al. 'A historical perspective of explainable Artificial Intelligence'. In: *WIREs Data Mining and Knowledge Discovery* 11.1 (2021), e1391. DOI: https://doi.org/10.1002/widm.1391 (cited on pages 34, 209).

[79] Helmut Degen and Lauren Reinerman-Jones, eds. *Artificial Intelligence in HCI - First International Conference, AI-HCI 2020, Held as Part of the 22nd HCI International Conference, HCII 2020, Copenhagen, Denmark, July 19-24, 2020, Proceedings.* Vol. 12217. Lecture Notes in Computer Science. Springer, 2020. DOI: 10.1007/978-3-030-50334-5 (cited on pages 34, 209).

[80] Helmut Degen and Stavroula Ntoa, eds. *Artificial Intelligence in HCI - Second International Conference, AI-HCI 2021, Held as Part of the 23rd HCI International Conference, HCII 2021, Virtual Event, July 24-29, 2021, Proceedings.* Vol. 12797. Lecture Notes in Computer Science. Springer, 2021. DOI: 10.1007/978-3-030-77772-2 (cited on pages 34, 209).

[81] Constantine Stephanidis et al., eds. *HCI International 2020 - Late Breaking Papers: Multimodality and Intelligence - 22nd HCI International Conference, HCII 2020, Copenhagen, Denmark, July 19-24, 2020, Proceedings.* Vol. 12424. Lecture Notes in Computer Science. Springer, 2020. DOI: 10.1007/978-3-030-60117-1 (cited on pages 34, 209).

[82] Helmut Degen et al. 'How to Explain it to Facility Managers? A Qualitative, Industrial User Research Study for Explainability'. In: *HCI International 2021 - Late Breaking Papers: Multimodality, eXtended Reality, and Artificial Intelligence. 23rd HCI International Conference, HCII 2021, Virtual Event, July 24-29, 2021, Proceedings.* Ed. by Constantine Stephanidis et al. Cham, Switzerland: Springer Nature Switzerland AG, 2021, pp. 401–422 (cited on pages 34, 209).

[83] Helmut Degen and Stavroula Ntoa. 'From a Workshop to a Framework for Human-Centered Artificial Intelligence'. In: *Artificial Intelligence in HCI - Second International Conference, AI-HCI 2021, Held as Part of the 23rd HCI International Conference, HCII 2021, Virtual Event, July 24-29, 2021, Proceedings.* Ed. by Helmut Degen and Stavroula Ntoa. Vol. 12797. Lecture Notes in Computer Science. Springer, 2021, pp. 166–184. DOI: 10.1007/978-3-030-77772-2_11 (cited on pages 34, 209).

[84] Constantine Stephanidis et al., eds. *HCI International 2021 - Late Breaking Papers: Multimodality, eXtended Reality, and Artificial Intelligence - 23rd HCI International Conference, HCII 2021, Virtual Event, July 24-29, 2021, Proceedings.* Vol. 13095. Lecture Notes in Computer Science. Springer, 2021. DOI: 10.1007/978-3-030-90963-5_31 (cited on pages 34, 209).

[85] Google. *Advancing AI for Everyone.* accessed 22. Apr. 2020. URL: https://ai.google/ (cited on page 34).

[86] ISO 9241-210:2019(E). *Ergonomics of human-system interaction – Part 210: Human-centred design for interactive systems.* Standard. Geneva, CH: International Organization for Standardization, July 2019 (cited on pages 36, 204).

[87] Wikipedia. *Business Model.* accessed 6. May 2020. URL: https://en.wikipedia.org/wiki/Business_model (cited on pages 49, 615).

[88] Alexander Osterwalder and Yves Pigneur. *Business Model Generation: A Handbook for Visionaries, Game Changers, and Challengers.* 1st ed. Hoboken, NJ, USA: John Wiley and Sons, Ltd, July 2010 (cited on page 49).

[89] Dan Olsen. *The Lean Product Playbook.* John Wiley and Sons, Ltd, May 2015 (cited on page 49).

[90] Jaime Levy. *UX Strategy: Product Strategy Techniques for Devising Innovative Digital Solutions.* O'Reilly Media, Incorporated, 2021 (cited on pages 49, 57).

[91] Monica Guillen-Royo. 'Human Needs'. In: *Encyclopedia of Quality of Life and Well-Being Research.* Ed. by Alex C. Michalos. Dordrecht, Netherlands: Springer Netherlands, 2014, pp. 3027–3030. DOI: 10.1007/978-94-007-0753-5_1345 (cited on pages 53, 616).

[92] ISO/IEC 25064:2013(E). *Systems and software engineering – Software product Quality Requirements and Evaluation (SQuaRE) – Common Industry Format (CIF) for usability: User needs report.* Standard. Geneva, CH: International Organization for Standardization, Sept. 2013 (cited on page 54).

[93] Abraham H. Maslow. 'A Theory of Human Motivation'. In: *Psychological Review* 50.4 (1943) (cited on page 55).

[94] Wikipedia. *Abraham Maslow.* accessed 19. Sep. 2019. URL: https://en.wikipedia.org/wiki/Abraham_Maslow (cited on page 55).

[95] Matthew Harrison and Cathering Firth. *Introducing the Business-To-Business Hierarchy of Needs.* accessed 30. Nov. 2019. URL: https://www.b2binternational.com/ (cited on page 56).

[96] Wikipedia. *Value Proposition.* accessed 23. Jan. 2022. URL: https://en.wikipedia.org/wiki/Value_proposition (cited on pages 58, 617).

[97] Carsten Hirschberg et al. *The changing market for food delivery.* Tech. rep. accessed 29. Jan.2020. McKinsey & Company, Nov. 2016 (cited on page 58).

[98] George A. Miller. 'The Magical Number Seven, Plus or Minus Two: Some Limits on our Capacity for Processing Information'. In: *Psychological Review* 63.2 (1956), pp. 81–97. DOI: https://doi.org/10.1037/h0043158 (cited on page 61).

[99] Wikipedia. *Total addressable market.* accessed 13. Jan. 2021. URL: https://en.wikipedia.org/wiki/Total_addressable_market (cited on page 62).

[100] Gassmann, Oliver and Frankenberger, Karolin. *Business Model Navigator.* accessed 4. Jun. 2022. St. Gallen, Switzerland. URL: https://businessmodelnavigator.com/ (cited on page 66).

[101] Wikipedia. *Hindu-Arabic numeral system.* accessed 6. Feb. 2021. URL: https://en.wikipedia.org/wiki/Hindu%E2%80%93Arabic_numeral_system (cited on page 75).

[102] Rebecca Klemm and Rachel Wallace. 'Exploring Universality: Does the World Really Use the Same Numbers?' In: *Childhood Education* 93.6 (2017), pp. 500–506. DOI: 10.1080/00094056.2017.1398563 (cited on page 75).

[103] Dengfeng Yan and Jorge Pena-Marin. 'Round Off the Bargaining: The Effects of Offer Roundness on Willingness to Accept'. In: *Journal of Consumer Research* 44.2 (Feb. 2017), pp. 381–395. DOI: 10.1093/jcr/ucx046 (cited on page 75).

[104] Helmut Degen, Gustavo Guillen, and Holger Schmidt. 'Effectiveness and Cost-Benefit Ratio of Weekly User Group Sessions'. In: *Design, User Experience, and Usability. Design Philosophy and Theory - 8th International Conference, DUXU 2019, Held as Part of the 21st HCI International Conference, HCII 2019, Orlando, FL, USA, July 26-31, 2019, Proceedings, Part I.* 2019, pp. 208–221. DOI: 10.1007/978-3-030-23570-3_16 (cited on pages 76, 156).

[105] Helmut Degen. 'Workshop: Design- and specification methods for efficient user involvement'. In: *Wirtschaftsinformatik 2022 Proceedings. Nuremberg, Germany.* Feb. 2022 (cited on page 77).

[106] Parinitha Naragaja and Helmut Degen. 'A user involvement measurement technique for user involvement metric'. In: *Wirtschaftsinformatik 2022 Proceedings. Nuremberg, Germany.* Feb. 2022 (cited on page 77).

[107] Silvester Stallone. *Rocky. Movie script.* Jan. 1976. URL: https://www.scriptslug.com/assets/scripts/rocky-1976.pdf (cited on page 150).

[108] ISO/IEC/IEEE 15288:2015(E). *Systems and software engineering – System life cycle processes.* Standard. Geneva, CH: International Organization for Standardization, May 2015 (cited on pages 150, 272, 341, 343, 616).

[109] David D. Walden et al., eds. *INCOSE Systems Engineering Handbook: A Guide for System Life Cycle Processes and Activities.* 4th ed. Vol. 1. Hoboken, NJ, USA: John Wiley and Sons, Ltd, June 2015 (cited on pages 151, 272, 499).

[110] Peter Checkland. *Systems, Thinking, System Practice. Includes a 30-year Retrospective.* Chichester, West Sussex, England, UK: John Wiley and Sons, Ltd, 1999 (cited on page 151).

[111] Claus Emmeche, Simo Køppe, and Frederik Stjernfelt. 'Explaining emergence: Towards an ontology of levels'. In: *Journal for General Philosophy of Science* 28.1 (Jan. 1997), pp. 83–117. DOI: 10.1023/A:1008216127933 (cited on page 151).

[112] Brian Whitworth and Aldo de Moor, eds. *Handbook of Research on Socio-Technical Design and Social Networking Systems.* Hershey, PA, USA: Information Science Reference, 2009 (cited on page 152).

[113] Gordon Baxter and Ian Sommerville. 'Socio-technical systems: From design methods to systems engineering'. In: *Interacting with Computers* 23.1 (Aug. 2010), pp. 4–17. DOI: 10.1016/j.intcom.2010.07.003 (cited on page 152).

[114] Thomas Herrmann, Isa Jahnke, and Alexander Nolte. 'A problem-based approach to the advancement of heuristics for socio-technical evaluation'. In: *Behaviour & Information Technology* (Sept. 2021), pp. 1–23. DOI: 10.1080/0144929X.2021.1972157 (cited on page 152).

[115] Robert Wayne Atkins. *Work Measurement and Ergonomics.* 1st ed. Grandpappy, Inc., 1992 (cited on page 152).

[116] Katrin E. Kroemer, Henrike B. Kroemer, and Anne D. Kroemer Hoffman. *Ergonomics. How to design for ease and efficiency.* 3rd ed. Academic Press, 2018 (cited on page 152).

[117] Chris Forsythe et al. *Cognitive Neuroscience of Human Systems: Work and Everyday Life.* Viking Adult, Jan. 2014 (cited on page 152).

[118] Stephen J. Guastello. *Human Factors Engineering and Ergonomics. A Systems Approach.* 2nd ed. Boca Raton, FL, 33487, USA: CRC Press, 2014 (cited on page 152).

[119]   Kjell B. Zandin, ed. *Maynard's Industrial Engineering Handbook*. 5th ed. McGraw-Hill standard handbooks. New York City, NY, USA: McGraw-Hill Education, 2001 (cited on pages 152, 196).

[120]   Gavriel Salvendy and Waldemar Karwowski, eds. *Handbook of Human Factors and Ergonomics*. 5th ed. John Wiley and Sons, Ltd, Aug. 2021 (cited on page 152).

[121]   Barry Tillman et al. *Human Factors and Ergonomics Design Handbook*. 3rd ed. New York, Chicago, San Francisco, Athens, London, Madrid, Mexico City, Milan, New Delhi, Singapore, Sydney, Toronto: McGraw-Hill Education, 2016 (cited on page 152).

[122]   Wikipedia. *Clock rate*. accessed 11. Dec 2021. URL: https://en.wikipedia.org/wiki/Clock_rate (cited on page 152).

[123]   Robert A. Whelan. 'Effective Analysis of Reaction Time Data'. In: *The Psychological Record* 58 (June 2008), pp. 475–482. DOI: 10.1007/BF03395630 (cited on page 152).

[124]   Kenneth J. W. Craik. *The Nature of Explanation*. Philosophy: science CAM. Cambridge University Press, 1943 (cited on page 152).

[125]   David Kieras and Susan Bovair. *The Role of a Mental Model in Learning to Operate a Device*. Technical Report No. 13 (UARZ/DP/TR-83/ONR-13). University of Arizona, AZ, USA: University of Arizona, AZ, USA, Mar. 1983 (cited on page 152).

[126]   JoAnn T. Hackos and Janice C. Redish. *User and Task Analysis for Interface Design*. Vol. 1. New York City, NY, USA: John Wiley and Sons, Ltd, 1998 (cited on pages 157, 189).

[127]   Karen Holtzblatt and Hugh Beyer. *Contextual Design, Second Edition: Design for Life*. 2nd ed. San Francisco, CA, USA: Morgan Kaufmann Publishers Inc., 2016 (cited on pages 157, 189).

[128]   Paul S. Bellet and Michael J. Maloney. 'The Importance of Empathy as an Interviewing Skill in Medicine'. In: *JAMA* 266.13 (Oct. 1991), pp. 1831–1832. DOI: 10.1001/jama.1991.03470130111039 (cited on page 157).

[129]   Joni Salminen, Soon-Gyo Jung, and Bernard J. Jansen. 'Detecting Demographic Bias in Automatically Generated Personas'. In: *Extended Abstracts of the 2019 CHI Conference on Human Factors in Computing Systems*. CHI EA'19. Glasgow, Scotland Uk: Association for Computing Machinery, 2019, pp. 1–6. DOI: 10.1145/3290607.3313034 (cited on page 158).

[130]   Emily Sheng et al. 'Revealing Persona Biases in Dialogue Systems'. In: *CoRR* abs/2104.08728 (2021) (cited on page 158).

[131]   ISO/IEC 25010:2010(E). *Systems and software engineering – Systems and software Quality Requirements and Evaluation (SQuaRE) – System and software quality models*. Standard. Geneva, CH: International Organization for Standardization, Mar. 2011 (cited on page 158).

[132]   A. Dickinson, J. Arnott, and S. Prior. 'Methods for human – computer interaction research with older people'. In: *Behaviour & Information Technology* 26.4 (2007), pp. 343–352. DOI: 10.1080/01449290601176948 (cited on page 163).

[133]   Alan Newell et al. 'Methodologies for Involving Older Adults in the Design Process'. In: *Universal Acess in Human Computer Interaction. Coping with Diversity*. Ed. by Constantine Stephanidis. Berlin, Heidelberg, Germany: Springer Berlin Heidelberg, 2007, pp. 982–989 (cited on page 163).

[134] Constantine Stephanidis and Margherita Antona, eds. *Universal Access in Human-Computer Interaction: Aging and Assistive Environments: 8th International Conference, UAHCI 2014, Held as Part of HCI International 2014, Heraklion, Crete, Greece, June 22-27, 2014, Proceedings, Part III.* Vol. 8515. Lecture Notes in Computer Science. Cham, Heidelberg, Germany: Springer, 2014. DOI: 10.1007/978-3-319-07446-7 (cited on page 163).

[135] Michael Bernard, Chia Hui Liao, and Melissa Mills. 'The Effects of Font Type and Size on the Legibility and Reading Time of Online Text by Older Adults'. In: *CHI'01 Extended Abstracts on Human Factors in Computing Systems.* CHI EA '01. Seattle, Washington: Association for Computing Machinery, 2001, pp. 175–176. DOI: 10.1145/634067.634173 (cited on page 163).

[136] Iain Darroch et al. 'The effect of age and font size on reading text on handheld computers'. In: *In Human-Computer Interaction - INTERACT 2005.* 2005, pp. 253–266 (cited on page 163).

[137] Tami Katzir, Shirley Hershko, and Vered Halamish. 'The Effect of Font Size on Reading Comprehension on Second and Fifth Grade Children: Bigger Is Not Always Better'. In: *PLoS ONE* 8.9 (Sept. 2013). DOI: 10.1371/journal.pone.0074061 (cited on page 163).

[138] Peiyi Ko et al. 'Effects of Font Size and Reflective Glare on Text-Based Task Performance and Postural Change Behavior of Presbyopic and Nonpresbyopic Computer Users'. In: *Proceedings of the Human Factors and Ergonomics Society Annual Meeting* 56.1 (2012), pp. 2378–2382. DOI: 10.1177/1071181312561514 (cited on page 163).

[139] German Federation of the Blind and Partially Sighted. *Fontsize calculator.* URL: https://www.leserlich.info/werkzeuge/schriftgroessenrechner/index-en.php (cited on pages 163, 191).

[140] World Health Organization. *Disabilities.* accessed 12. Mar. 2020. URL: https://www.who.int/topics/disabilities/en/ (cited on page 165).

[141] ISO/IEC 30071-1:2019(E). *Information technology – Development of user interface accessibility – Part 1: Code of practice for creating accessible ICT products and services.* Standard. Geneva, CH: International Organization for Standardization, May 2019 (cited on page 165).

[142] Constantine Stephanidis. *The Universal Access Handbook.* 1st. USA: CRC Press, Inc., 2009 (cited on page 165).

[143] Elizabeth Goodman, Mike Kuniavsky, and Andrea Moed. *Observing the User Experience, Second Edition: A Practitioner's Guide to User Research.* 2nd ed. San Francisco, CA, USA: Morgan Kaufmann Publishers Inc., 2012 (cited on page 189).

[144] Martin Maguire. 'Context of Use within usability activities'. In: *International Journal of Human-Computer Studies* 55.4 (2001), pp. 453–483. DOI: 10.1006/ijhc.2001.0486 (cited on page 189).

[145] ISO/IEC 25063:2014(E). *Systems and software engineering – Systems and software product Quality Requirements and Evaluation (SQuaRE) – Common Industry Format (CIF) for usability: Context of use description.* Standard. Geneva, CH: International Organization for Standardization, Mar. 2014 (cited on page 190).

[146] Ralph M. Barnes. *Motion And Time Study Design And Measurement Of Work.* 7th ed. New York City, NY, USA: Wiley India Pvt. Limited, 2009 (cited on page 196).

[147] Frederick Winslow Taylor. *The Principles of Scientific Management.* New York, London: Harper & Brothers Publishers, 1919 (cited on page 196).

[148] Frank B. Gilbret. *Motion Study. A method for increasing the efficiency of the workman.* New York City, NY, USA: D. von Nostrand Company, 1911 (cited on page 196).

[149]   Apple. *Apple Introduces Macintosh Advanced Personal Computer*. accessed 18. Dec. 2021. Jan. 1984. URL: https://web.stanford.edu/dept/SUL/sites/mac/primary/docs/pr1.html (cited on page 203).

[150]   Tim Berners-Lee. *World Wide Web*. accessed 18. Dec. 2021. Dec. 1990. URL: http://info.cern.ch/hypertext/WWW/TheProject.html (cited on page 203).

[151]   V. V. Arutyunov. 'Cloud computing: Its history of development, modern state, and future considerations'. In: *Scientific and Technical Information Processing* 39 (3 July 2012), pp. 173–178. DOI: 10.3103/S0147688212030082 (cited on page 203).

[152]   Tom Farley. 'Mobile telephone history'. In: *Telektronikk* 101.3/4 (Feb. 2005), pp. 22–34 (cited on page 203).

[153]   ETSI. *5G*. Standard. Sophia-Antipolis, France: European Telecommunications Standards Institute (cited on page 203).

[154]   Naur, Peter and Randell, Brian. *Software Engineering. Report on a conference sponsored by the NATO SCIENCE COMMITTEE. Garmisch, Germany, 7th to 11th October 1968*. Report. Jan. 1969 (cited on page 204).

[155]   Edsger W. Dijkstra. 'The Humble Programmer'. In: *Commun. ACM* 15.10 (Oct. 1972), pp. 859–866. DOI: 10.1145/355604.361591 (cited on page 204).

[156]   ISO 13407:1999(E). *Human-centred design processes for interactive systems*. Standard. Geneva, CH: International Organization for Standardization, June 1999 (cited on page 204).

[157]   Kent Beck et al. *Manifesto for Agile Software Development*. 2001. URL: https://agilemanifesto.org/ (cited on page 204).

[158]   Geoffrey Makstutis. *Design Process in Architecture: From Concept to Completion*. Laurence King Publishing, 2018 (cited on page 204).

[159]   Dieter Rams. *Less, but better*. 7th ed. Hamburg, Germany: Gestalten, 2014 (cited on page 204).

[160]   Frederik Brudy et al. 'Cross-Device Taxonomy: Survey, Opportunities and Challenges of Interactions Spanning Across Multiple Devices'. In: *Proceedings of the 2019 CHI Conference on Human Factors in Computing Systems*. New York, NY, USA: Association for Computing Machinery, 2019, pp. 1–28 (cited on page 205).

[161]   George D. Montañez, Ryen W. White, and Xiao Huang. 'Cross-Device Search'. In: *Proceedings of the 23rd ACM International Conference on Conference on Information and Knowledge Management*. CIKM '14. Shanghai, China: Association for Computing Machinery, 2014, pp. 1669–1678. DOI: 10.1145/2661829.2661910 (cited on page 205).

[162]   Wikionary. *Architekton*. accessed 23. Oct. 2020. URL: https://en.wiktionary.org/wiki/architecton (cited on page 211).

[163]   Terry Winograd. 'From Computing Machinery to Interaction Design'. In: *Beyond Calculation: The Next Fifty Years of Computing*. Ed. by Peter J. Denning and Robert M. Metcalfe. Heidelberg, Germany: Springer Nature, 1997, pp. 149–162 (cited on page 211).

[164]   Terry Winograd. 'Interaction Spaces for 21st Century Computing'. In: *Human-computer Interaction in the New Millennium*. Ed. by John M. Carroll. ACM Press Series. ACM Press, 2002, pp. 603–625 (cited on page 211).

[165]   Wikipedia. *Planning Poker*. accessed 19. Sep. 2019. URL: https://en.wikipedia.org/wiki/Planning_poker (cited on page 239).

[166]   Yoren Gaffary and Anatole Lécuyer. 'The Use of Haptic and Tactile Information in the Car to Improve Driving Safety: A Review of Current Technologies'. In: *Frontiers in ICT* 5 (Mar. 2018). DOI: 10.3389/fict.2018.00005 (cited on page 269).

[167]   Udara E. Manawadu et al. 'A haptic feedback driver-vehicle interface for controlling lateral and longitudinal motions of autonomous vehicles'. In: *2016 IEEE International Conference on Advanced Intelligent Mechatronics (AIM)*. 2016, pp. 119–124. DOI: 10.1109/AIM.2016.7576753 (cited on page 269).

[168]   Atilla Wohllebe. 'Consumer Acceptance of App Push Notifications: Systematic Review on the Influence of Frequency'. In: *International Journal of Interactive Mobile Technologies (iJIM)* 14 (Aug. 2020), pp. 36–47. DOI: 10.3991/ijim.v14i13.14563 (cited on page 269).

[169]   Abhinav Mehrotra and Mirco Musolesi. 'Intelligent Notification Systems: A Survey of the State of the Art and Research Challenges'. In: *CoRR* abs/1711.10171 (2017) (cited on page 269).

[170]   Shamsi T. Iqbal and Eric Horvitz. 'Notifications and Awareness: A Field Study of Alert Usage and Preferences'. In: *Proceedings of the 2010 ACM Conference on Computer Supported Cooperative Work*. CSCW'10. Savannah, Georgia, USA: Association for Computing Machinery, 2010, pp. 27–30. DOI: 10.1145/1718918.1718926 (cited on page 269).

[171]   Tadashi Okoshi et al. 'Attention and engagement-awareness in the wild: A large-scale study with adaptive notifications'. In: *2017 IEEE International Conference on Pervasive Computing and Communications (PerCom)*. 2017, pp. 100–110. DOI: 10.1109/PERCOM.2017.7917856 (cited on page 269).

[172]   Niranjan Bidargaddi et al. 'Predicting which type of push notification content motivates users to engage in a self-monitoring app'. In: *Preventive Medicine Reports* 11 (2018), pp. 267–273. DOI: https://doi.org/10.1016/j.pmedr.2018.07.004 (cited on page 269).

[173]   Leanne G. Morrison et al. 'The Effect of Timing and Frequency of Push Notifications on Usage of a Smartphone-Based Stress Management Intervention: An Exploratory Trial'. In: *PLOS ONE* 12.1 (Jan. 2017), pp. 1–15. DOI: 10.1371/journal.pone.0169162 (cited on page 269).

[174]   SEBoK Editorial Board. *Guide to the Systems Engineering Body of Knowledge (SEBoK), version 2.2*. Ed. by R. J. Cloutier (Editor in Chief). 2.2. Hoboken, NJ, USA: The Trustees of the Stevens Institute of Technology, May 2020 (cited on page 272).

[175]   Alistair Cockburn. *Writing Effective Use Cases*. Crystal collection for software professionals. Addison-Wesley, 2001 (cited on page 284).

[176]   Larry L. Constantine and Lucy A. D. Lockwood. 'Structure and Style in Use Cases for User Interface Design'. In: *Object Modeling and User Interface Design: Designing Interactive Systems*. USA: Addison-Wesley Longman Publishing Co., Inc., 2001, pp. 245–279 (cited on page 285).

[177]   IEC 62366-1:2015. *Medical devices – Part 1: Application of usability engineering to medical devices*. Standard. Geneva, CH: International Electrotechnical Commission, Feb. 2015 (cited on pages 294, 371).

[178]   Christopher Alexander et al. *A Pattern Language: Towns, Buildings, Construction*. Center for Environmental Structure Berkeley, Calif: Center for Environmental Structure series. New York City, NY, USA: Oxford University Press, 1977 (cited on page 299).

[179]   Christopher Alexander. *The Timeless Way of Building*. Center for Environmental Structure Berkeley, Calif: Center for Environmental Structure series. New York City, NY, USA: Oxford University Press, 1979 (cited on page 299).

[180] Jenifer Tidwell, Charles Brewer, and Aynne Valencia. *Designing Interfaces: Patterns for Effective Interaction Design*. 3rd ed. Sebastopol, CA, USA: O'Reilly Media, Jan. 2020 (cited on page 299).

[181] Theresa Neil. *Mobile Design Pattern Gallery: UI Patterns for Smartphone Apps*. O'Reilly Media, Inc., 2014 (cited on page 299).

[182] Helmut Degen. 'Goals - Assumption - Interaction Steps (GAIS): Practical Method to Determine a Quantitative Efficiency Benchmark for UX Interaction Design Concepts'. In: *Engineering Psychology and Cognitive Ergonomics - 16th International Conference, EPCE 2019, Held as Part of the 21st HCI International Conference, HCII 2019, Orlando, FL, USA, July 26-31, 2019, Proceedings*. 2019, pp. 3–19. DOI: 10.1007/978-3-030-22507-0_1 (cited on page 319).

[183] Paul M. Fitts et al. *A report prepared for the Air Navigation Development Board by the Ohio State University Research Foundation under the auspices of the NRC Committee on Aviation Psychology*. Ed. by Paul M. Fitts. Washington, D.C., USA: National Research Council. Division of Anthropology and Psychology. Committee on Aviation Psychology, Mar. 1951 (cited on page 320).

[184] Erik Hollnagel and Andreas Bye. 'Principles for modelling function allocation'. In: *SIGACT News* 52.2 (Feb. 2000), pp. 18–24. DOI: 10.1006/ijhc.1999.0288 (cited on page 320).

[185] David B. Kaber and Mica R. Endsley. 'The effects of level of automation and adaptive automation on human performance, situation awareness and workload in a dynamic control task'. In: *Theoretical Issues in Ergonomics Science* 5.2 (2004), pp. 113–153. DOI: 10.1080/1463922021000054335 (cited on page 320).

[186] John Lee and Neville Moray. 'Trust, control strategies and allocation of function in human-machine systems'. In: *Ergonomics* 35.10 (1992), pp. 1243–1270 (cited on page 320).

[187] Colin Corbridge and Catherine A. Cook. 'Future Challenges for Function Allocation'. In: *Proceedings of the Human Factors and Ergonomics Society Annual Meeting* 43.19 (1999), pp. 1027–1031. DOI: 10.1177/154193129904301903 (cited on page 320).

[188] Paul Clements and Len Bass. *Relating Business Goals to Architecturally Significant Requirements for Software Systems*. Tech. rep. CMU/SEI-2010-TN-018. Pittsburgh, PA, USA: Software Engineering Institute, Carnegie Mellon University, May 2010 (cited on page 328).

[189] Lianping Chen, Muhammad Ali Babar, and Bashar Nuseibeh. 'Characterizing Architecturally Significant Requirements'. In: *IEEE Software* 30.2 (2013), pp. 38–45. DOI: 10.1109/MS.2012.174 (cited on page 328).

[190] Lewis Carroll. *Alice's Adventures in Wonderland & Through the Looking-Glass and What Alice Found There*. 1st ed. London, UK: Pan MacMillan, 2011 (cited on page 342).

[191] Wikipedia. *Landing Page*. accessed 5. Feb. 2022. URL: https://en.wikipedia.org/wiki/Landing_page (cited on page 347).

[192] Jakob Nielsen. *F-Shaped Pattern For Reading Web Content (original study)*. accessed 27. Mar. 2020. Apr. 2006. URL: https://www.nngroup.com/articles/f-shaped-pattern-reading-web-content-discovered/ (cited on page 360).

[193] Kara Pernice. *F-Shaped Pattern of Reading on the Web: Misunderstood, But Still Relevant (Even on Mobile)*. accessed 27. Mar. 2020. Nov. 2017. URL: https://www.nngroup.com/articles/f-shaped-pattern-reading-web-content/ (cited on page 360).

[194] Kara Pernice. *Text Scanning Patterns: Eyetracking Evidence*. accessed 27. Mar. 2020. Aug. 2019. URL: https://www.nngroup.com/articles/text-scanning-patterns-eyetracking/ (cited on pages 360, 451).

[195] Pekka Parhi, Amy K. Karlson, and Benjamin B. Bederson. 'Target Size Study for One-Handed Thumb Use on Small Touchscreen Devices'. In: *Proceedings of the 8th Conference on Human-Computer Interaction with Mobile Devices and Services*. MobileHCI'06. Helsinki, Finland: Association for Computing Machinery, 2006, pp. 203–210. DOI: 10.1145/1152215.1152260 (cited on page 363).

[196] Yong S. Park and Sung H. Han. 'Touch key design for one-handed thumb interaction with a mobile phone: Effects of touch key size and touch key location'. In: *International Journal of Industrial Ergonomics* 40.1 (2010), pp. 68–76. DOI: https://doi.org/10.1016/j.ergon.2009.08.002 (cited on page 363).

[197] Jinghong Xiong and Satoshi Muraki. 'Effects of age, thumb length and screen size on thumb movement coverage on smartphone touchscreens'. In: *International Journal of Industrial Ergonomics* 53 (2016), pp. 140–148. DOI: https://doi.org/10.1016/j.ergon.2015.11.004 (cited on page 363).

[198] Yu Zhang et al. 'Touch Behavior Analysis for Large Screen Smartphones'. In: *Proceedings of the Human Factors and Ergonomics Society Annual Meeting*. Vol. 59. 1. 2015, pp. 1433–1437. DOI: 10.1177/1541931215591311 (cited on page 363).

[199] Food and Drug Administration (FDA). *Part 820 Quality System Regulation*. Title 21 – Food and Drugs; Chapter I–Food and Drug Administration; Department of Health and Human Services, Subchapter H – Medical Devices, Part 820, Quality Syste Regulation. Silver Spring, MD , USA: Food and Drug Administration, July 2020 (cited on page 371).

[200] ISO 13485:2016(E). *Medical devices - Quality management systems - Requirements for regulatory purposes*. Standard. Geneva, CH: International Organization for Standardization, Mar. 2016 (cited on page 371).

[201] Michael E. Wiklund, Jonathan Kendler, and Allison Y. Strochlic, eds. *Usability Testing of Medical Devices*. 2nd ed. Boca Raton, FL, USA: CRC Press, Jan. 2016 (cited on page 371).

[202] EN 50126:2017. *Railway Applications - The Specification and Demonstration of Reliability, Availability, Maintainability and Safety (RAMS) - Part 1: Generic RAMS Process*. Standard. Brussels, Belgium: European Committee for Standardization, Oct. 2017 (cited on page 371).

[203] EN 50126:2017. *Railway Applications - The Specification and Demonstration of Reliability, Availability, Maintainability and Safety (RAMS) - Part 2: Systems Approach to Safety*. Standard. Brussels, Belgium: European Committee for Standardization, Oct. 2017 (cited on page 371).

[204] EN 50128: 2011. *Railway applications - Communications, signalling and processing systems - Software for railway control and protection systems*. Standard. Brussels, Belgium: European Committee for Standardization, June 2011 (cited on page 371).

[205] EN 50129:2018. *Railway applications - Communication, signalling and processing systems - Safety related electronic systems for signalling / Applies in conjunction with EN 50126-1 (2017-10), EN 50126-2 (2017-10), EN 50128 (2011-06)*. Standard. Brussels, Belgium: European Committee for Standardization, Nov. 2018 (cited on page 371).

[206] ISO/IEC/IEEE 29148:2018(E). *Systems and software engineering – Life cycle processes – Requirements engineering*. Standard. Geneva, CH: International Organization for Standardization, Nov. 2018 (cited on page 374).

[207] Stuart Pugh. *Total Design: Integrated Methods for Successful Product Engineering*. Wokingham, England, UK: Addison-Wesley, 1991 (cited on pages 375, 533, 558).

[208] Daniel D. Frey et al. 'The Pugh Controlled Convergence method: model-based evaluation and implications for design theory'. In: *Research in Engineering Design* 20.6 (Sept. 2009), pp. 41–58. DOI: 10.1007/s00163-010-0087-0 (cited on page 375).

[209] Wikipedia. *Design Space Exploration.* accessed 20. Feb 2020. URL: https://en.wikipedia.org/wiki/Design_space_exploration (cited on page 375).

[210] Luigi Nardi, David Koeplinger, and Kunle Olukotun. 'Practical Design Space Exploration'. In: *2019 IEEE 27th International Symposium on Modeling, Analysis, and Simulation of Computer and Telecommunication Systems (MASCOTS).* 2019, pp. 347–358. DOI: 10.1109/MASCOTS.2019.00045 (cited on page 375).

[211] Torsten Kempf, Gerd Ascheid, and Rainer Leupers. 'Principles of Design Space Exploration'. In: *Multiprocessor Systems on Chip: Design Space Exploration.* New York, NY, USA: Springer New York, 2011, pp. 23–47. DOI: 10.1007/978-1-4419-8153-0_3 (cited on page 375).

[212] Kurtis Danyluk et al. 'A Design Space Exploration of Worlds in Miniature'. In: *Proceedings of the 2021 CHI Conference on Human Factors in Computing Systems.* CHI '21. Yokohama, Japan: Association for Computing Machinery, 2021. DOI: 10.1145/3411764.3445098 (cited on page 375).

[213] João Manuel Paiva Cardoso, José Gabriel de Figueiredo Coutinho, and Pedro C. Diniz. *Embedded Computing for High Performance: Efficient Mapping of Computations Using Customization, Code Transformations and Compilation.* 1st ed. San Francisco, CA, USA: Morgan Kaufmann Publishers Inc., 2017 (cited on page 375).

[214] Object Management Group (OMG). *UML Website.* Accessed 23. Oct 2021. URL: https://www.uml.org/ (cited on page 401).

[215] Grady Booch, James Rumbaugh, and Ivar Jacobson. *The Unified Modeling Language User Guide.* USA: Addison Wesley Longman Publishing Co., Inc., 1999 (cited on page 401).

[216] Wikipedia. *Finite-state machine.* accessed 17. Apr. 2020. URL: https://en.wikipedia.org/wiki/Finite-state_machine (cited on page 404).

[217] Harold Thimbleby. 'Action Graphs and User Performance Analysis'. In: *International Journal of Human-Computer Studies* 71.3 (Mar. 2013), pp. 276–302. DOI: 10.1016/j.ijhcs.2012.10.014 (cited on page 404).

[218] Saeema Ahmed, Ken M. Wallace, and Luciënne Blessing. 'Understanding the differences between how novice and experienced designers approach design tasks'. In: *Research in Engineering Design* 14 (2003), pp. 1–11. DOI: 10.1007/S00163-002-0023-Z (cited on page 420).

[219] Shanna R. Daly et al. 'Teaching Design Ideation'. In: *2011 ASEE Annual Conference & Exposition.* Vancouver, BC, Canada: ASEE Conferences, June 2011. DOI: 10.18260/1-2--18507 (cited on page 420).

[220] Jan Recker and Michael Rosemann. 'Systemic ideation: A playbook for creating innovative ideas more consciously'. In: *360° - the Business Transformation Jounal* 13 (July 2015). DOI: https://eprints.qut.edu.au/85884/ (cited on page 420).

[221] Rikke Friis Dam and Teo Yu Siang. *Introduction to the Essential Ideation Techniques which are the Heart of Design Thinking.* accessed 20. Feb. 2020. Jan. 2021. URL: https://www.interaction-design.org/literature/article/introduction-to-the-essential-ideation-techniques-which-are-the-heart-of-design-thinking (cited on page 420).

[222] *Ideation Methods: A First Study on Measured Outcomes With Personality Type.* Vol. Volume 7: 2nd Biennial International Conference on Dynamics for Design; 26th International Conference on Design Theory and Methodology. International Design Engineering Technical Conferences and Computers and Information in Engineering Conference. V007T07A019. Aug. 2014. DOI: 10.1115/DETC2014-34954 (cited on page 420).

[223] Max Wertheimer. 'Experimentelle Studien über das Sehen von Bewegung'. In: *Zeitschrift für Psychologie und Physiologie der Sinnesorgane* 61.1 (Apr. 1912), pp. 161–265 (cited on page 422).

[224] Kurt Koffka. 'Perception: an introduction to the Gestalt-Theorie'. In: *Psychological Bulletin* 19.10 (Oct. 1922), pp. 531–585. DOI: 10.1037/H0072422 (cited on page 422).

[225] Wolfgang Köhler. *Gestalt Psychology.* 1st ed. New York City, NY, USA: H. Liveright, 1929 (cited on page 422).

[226] Wikipedia. *Design Awards.* accessed 25. Apr. 2020. URL: https://en.wikipedia.org/wiki/List_of_design_awards (cited on page 422).

[227] ISO 9241-110:2020(E). *Ergonomics of human-system interaction – Part 110: Dialogue principles.* Standard. Geneva, CH: International Organization for Standardization, May 2020 (cited on page 443).

[228] Barry Kirwan. *A Guide To Practical Human Reliability Assessment.* Boca Raton, FL, USA: Taylor & Francis, 1994 (cited on page 443).

[229] James Reason. *Human Error.* Cambridge, UK: Cambridge University Press, 1990 (cited on page 443).

[230] Andrew T Duchowski. *Eye tracking methodology: Theory and practice.* 3rd ed. Cham, Switzerland: Springer Nature, 2017 (cited on page 451).

[231] Kara Pernice. *The Layer-Cake Pattern of Scanning Content on the Web.* accessed 27. Mar. 2020. Aug. 2019. URL: https://www.nngroup.com/articles/layer-cake-pattern-scanning/ (cited on page 451).

[232] Josef Müller-Brockmann. *Grid Systems in Graphic Design: A Visual Communication Manual for Graphic Designers, Typographers and Three Dimensional Designers.* Bilingual. Salenstein, Switzerland: Niggli Verlag, Oct. 1996 (cited on pages 451, 459).

[233] Kimberley Elam. *Grid Systems: Principles of Organizing Type.* Design brief. Principles of organizing type. New York, NY, USA: Princeton Architectural Press, Aug. 2004 (cited on pages 451, 459).

[234] Timothy Samara. *Making and Breaking the Grid, Second Edition, Updated and Expanded: A Graphic Design Layout Workshop.* 2nd ed. Rockport Publishers, July 2017 (cited on pages 451, 459).

[235] Mads Soegaard. *The Grid System: Building a Solid Design Layout.* accessed 15. May 2022. 2021. URL: https://www.interaction-design.org/literature/article/the-grid-system-building-a-solid-design-layout (cited on pages 451, 459).

[236] Jakob Nielsen. *Photos as Web Content.* accessed 5. May 2022. Oct. 2010. URL: https://www.nngroup.com/articles/photos-as-web-content/ (cited on page 453).

[237] Helmut Degen. 'Big *I* Notation to estimate the interaction complexity of interaction concepts'. In: *International Journal of Human-Computer Interaction* (Jan. 2022), pp. 1–25. DOI: 10.1080/10447318.2021.2004699 (cited on page 502).

[238] Paul Bachmann. *Zahlentheorie. Versuch einer Gesamtdarstellung dieser Wissenschaft in ihren Hauptteilen. Zweiter Teil: Die analytische Zahlentheorie.* Vol. 2. Leipzig, Germany: B. G. Teubner, 1894 (cited on page 502).

[239] Edmund Landauer. *Handbuch der Lehre von der Verteilung der Primzahlen.* Leipzig, Berlin, Germany: BG Teubner, 1909 (cited on page 502).

[240] Donald E. Knuth. 'Big Omicron and Big Omega and Big Theta'. In: *SIGACT News* 8.2 (Apr. 1976), pp. 18–24. DOI: 10.1145/1008328.1008329 (cited on page 502).

[241] Wikipedia. *Big O Notation.* accessed 7. Apr. 2020. URL: https://en.wikipedia.org/wiki/Big_O_notation (cited on page 502).

Terms

A

Acceptable efficiency maximum Highest level of efficiency that is still acceptable for users. 34

AEMax see acceptable efficiency maximum. 34

Application domain Aspects of the field in which an application is used. These aspects provide an answer to the application related "what" question. 54

Application goal Intended state within the application domain. An application goal addresses a need. 57

B

Baseline concept Ground truth concept. 417

Business model Rationale of how an organization creates, delivers, and captures value [87]. 49

C

Canvas Virtual region for placing and organizing design elements. 345, 346

Critical efficiency path Sequence of user actions or system actions determining the minimum elapsed user involvement time and minimum number of user involvement steps to generate an outcome of value. 2

D

Design element A building block enabling user involvement. 345

Design maturity Degree to which an organization formalizes, integrates, and optimizes design processes continuously to support business strategies and objectives. 12

Design system Set of interconnected components with a consistent form factor (e.g., colors, typeface, dimensions, texture, material, style) establishing a coherent visual, interaction, and/or involvement language for one or more modalities and channels. 385

E

Effectiveness Accuracy and completeness with which user achieve specified goals [23, clause 3.1.12]. 15

Efficiency Resources used in relation to the results achieved [23, clause 3.1.13]. 15

Experience architect Role responsible for the definition and specification of the experience architecture for an ecosystem. 210

Experience architecture Organization principle of a user involvement system. 26, 210, 211

Experience design A creative act specifying user involvement, aiming to achieve stated goals within given constraints. 341

H

Human-centered design Approach to system design and development that aims to make interactive systems more usable by focusing on the use of the system; applying human factors, ergonomics and usability knowledge and techniques [23, clause 3.2.6]. 36

Human-technical system System consisting of one or more users and a technical application working together to achieve one or more stated purpose. 150, 151

I

Interaction Action that occurs between one or more people and one or more technical systems that have an effect upon one another (based on [57]. 26

Interaction complexity Function that estimates the number of performed user actions for a given user task and for a given design artifact. 502

Involvement domain Aspects of involvement between a user and an application. These aspects provide an answer to the application related "how" question. 54

Involvement goal Desired property of a user involvement concept. 313

Involvement goal matrix List of all significant involvement goals, used to explore and exclude involvement concepts. 332

Involvement hypotenuse Transfer of the initial state on the user involvement arc from state 0 to another state. 316

N

Need Drivers of peoples' actions [91]. 53, 58

Need domain Aspects that motivate users to use an application. These aspects provide an answer to the application related "why" question. 53

O

Outcome of value Intended result of user involvement. An outcome of value is the result of performing one or more user tasks. 151

P

Primary user task The user task for which the involvement concept will be optimized. 290

Productivity Outcome per used resources. 15

S

Satisfaction extent to which the user's physical, cognitive and emotional responses that result from the use of a system, product or service meet the user's needs and expectations [23, clause 3.1.14]. 15

System Combination of interacting elements organized to achieve one or more stated purposes [108, clause 4.1.46]. 150

System element Member of a set of elements that constitute a system [108, clause 4.1.47]. Examples: Hardware, software, data, humans, processes (e.g., processes for providing service to users), procedures (e.g., operator instructions), facilities, materials, and naturally occurring entities or any combination. 150

T

Target involvement time Planned maximum time for performing a user task. 298

Technical application see interactive system. 149

Technical involvement point (technical) system element of a user involvement system. 250

Technical system A system that does not need users to achieve the stated purpose. 150

Technology-centered design Design and development process in which designers and developers focus on the technology in each phase of the design and development process. 154

U

Usability Extent to which a system, product or service can be used by specified users to achieve specified goals with effectiveness, efficiency and satisfaction in a specified context of use [23, clause 3.1.1]. 15

User experience User's perceptions and responses that result from the use and/or anticipated use of a system, product or service [23, clause 3.2.3]. 156

Alphabetical Index

About the Author

Helmut Degen is a senior experience architect for software-intensive products and a researcher in human-computer interaction (HCI). He has worked all of his career in product definition, most of the time in complex industrial domains. For a few years, he designed mobile phone applications for consumers. Helmut is driven by the challenge of simplifying applications and making them valuable, understandable, trustworthy, actionable, and efficient for humans. He sometimes calls himself a professional simplifier.

He developed many of the techniques presented in this book for his industrial projects. He believes that a well-defined process guides the experience architecture and design work and provides sufficient space and time for creativity and exploration. He also believes that good architecture and design decisions should include the non-perceivable underlying structure and functions, not only the perceivable surface. Helmut's priorities are as follows:

- ► Value (addressing business and user needs)
- ► Efficiency (minimizing execution and waiting time as well as cognitive load)
- ► Memorability (offering a unique and emotionally appealing design language)

Helmut is co-chair of the "AI in HCI" Conference (Artificial Intelligence in Human-Computer Interaction, affiliated with the HCI International Conference) that brings together researchers from industry and academia to share advances in the research area of AI in HCI. He won a Red Dot Award in 2019.

Helmut received a PhD (Dr. phil.) from the Freie Universität Berlin and a master's in Computer Science (Diplom-Informatiker) from the Karlsruhe Institute of Technology (both in Germany).

In his spare time, he writes stories for kids.